the West in the Life of the Nation

the West in the Life of the Nation

ARRELL MORGAN GIBSON
University of Oklahoma, Norman

D. C. HEATH AND COMPANY
Lexington, Massachusetts   Toronto   London

For
Lorene Davis Gibson
Mother and Mentor

Preface

    The West in the Life of the Nation narrates and interprets the saga of Western America from prehistoric times to 1976. It depicts the 350-year contest waged by Spain, France, Great Britain, Russia, and, belatedly, the United States to control the territory and rich natural bounty of the West. The long struggle culminated in the American absorption of this vast region and, ultimately, its emergence as an equal—if not pre-eminent—voice in the affairs of the American nation. Considerable attention is given to the plight of the aboriginal Americans who were caught up in this imperial struggle for territorial domination.

    I have extended the concept of Western America in time and space. With few exceptions, writers on Western America have concluded their work with 1890—the year, they believed, that frontier processes in the West came to an end. Recent scholarship has shown that setting the termination of the frontier at 1890 was premature and peremptory; the momentum of inherently frontier forces has continued in Western America well into the twentieth century. This work, therefore, undertakes to trace the evolution of the American West to 1976. It also extends the American West's geographic concept beyond the continental limits to include Alaska and Hawaii, where the same Americanization processes that bound the contiguous West into the national life were active. In the context of this work, the American West as we think of it in the twentieth century extends from the western border of Missouri into the Pacific Basin.

    My purpose in writing *The West in the Life of the Nation* was sixfold. Overall, I have sought to combine into new conceptual models selected portions of the traditional history of this region and information derived from recent scholarship. This effort includes (1) reshaping the geographical regions of Western America; (2) countering the ethnocentric view of Western America's conquest under the Anglo-American aegis by applying a pluralistic approach, thus giving well-deserved weight to non–Anglo-American streams of imperial occupation, exploitation, and cultural impress; (3) humanizing Western America's epic by providing more than passing notice to the role of Indians, Mexican-Americans, various Oriental peoples, and Blacks in the metamorphosis of Western America from wilderness to coequal region in the American community; (4) enriching Western America's chronicle by intermixing with the traditional political, military, and economic aspects the region's important social, cultural, and intellectual dimensions; (5) tempering some of the absolutes of Western historiography (especially the Turner thesis); and (6) composing the whole within the framework of a thesis in which the West is seen as the principal source of national strength and nationalizing currents are understood as the chief determinant of Western development.

In 1893, Frederick Jackson Turner introduced his frontier thesis. It deflected attention from the European origins of Anglo-American civilization to America's interior, the West. The Turner thesis, a multi-faceted analytical scheme for interpreting the American heritage, cast the nation's history into a Western context. It concluded that the pioneering experience was the principal determinant of American institutions, culture, values, and national character and that Western America was the seedbed of democracy.

Turner's thesis remained the overpowering force in American interpretive history until the 1920s, when it came under professional attack as a naive oversimplification of complex processes. Within a decade, Turner's influence and that of his thesis in American historiography had waned. The study of Western history became a casualty of the controversy, as professional Brahmins intimidated timorous researchers and writers with an interest in Western history and diverted them into other fields of historical inquiry.

During the 1970s, a flush of neo-Turnerian interest is apparent. The new wave is a result of the determined application of researchers, writers, and students to engaging and productive Western themes such as Indian history and studies in economic, institutional, urban, social, cultural, and intellectual history as these relate to the frontier and the West. Similarly, the appropriation of Turner methodology and interpretation in comparative frontiers by geographers and anthropologists—often in league with historians—augurs a genuine resurgence of interest in the frontier thesis.

This work attempts to place Turner's provocative and controversial insight in the historiographic perspective where it properly belongs, not as an absolute but a relative and very useful concept for studying frontiers and the American West. Although it acknowledges Turner's very creative role as a pioneer breaking new conceptual ground, *The West in the Life of the Nation* does not accept the Turner view that the pioneering experience was the ultimate force in creating distinctly American culture, institutions, values, and national character. Likewise, by discerning persuasive evidence that frontier processes survive well into the twentieth century, it denies that the frontier as a pioneer social, cultural, economic, and political entity expired in 1890. Lastly, it takes issue with the ethnocentric Turnerian view that the continental conquest was a predominantly Anglo-American effort.

Nonetheless, there is much in the Turner thesis that is instructive and useful, particularly his cyclical-frontiers concept for explaining the occupation of successive segments of Western territory. In the progression of American dominion from the Appalachians to the Pacific shore, Turner identified the fur-trade frontier, mining frontier, stockraising frontier, and the agricultural frontier as the vanguard groups for Americanizing the West. In *The West in the Life of the Nation*, this concept is refined by identifying frontiers as essential expansion entities; moreover, the group is expanded to include the overland-trader frontier, the maritime-trader frontier, the missionary frontier, and the civilized-Indian frontier. (The latter frontier was made up of Indians from the East, particularly the Southern tribes that were forcibly colonized in the New West by the federal government.)

The magnificent spectacle of the emergent American nation breaching the Appalachian barrier and, like a human floodtide, surging with incredible velocity and irrepressible force westward across the continent into the Pacific Basin, ranks with the grandest epics of human history. This is the essence of *The West in the Life of the Nation*. It is composed around the thesis that the West has been the prime determinant of national economic direction and development and the principal source of national wealth and strength. At the same time, it denies that Western pioneering experiences were the principal determinants of a distinctly American character or of our peculiar political and cultural institutions. While acknowledging that frontier vicissitudes often altered well-established patterns, it shows that the West was not the generation zone for American democracy. Nonetheless, Westerners did refine and expand the democratic processes transplanted from the seaboard, and they did contribute in important ways to the fulfillment of a cumulative stream begun in early Colonial times.

The geographical format constructed for *The West in the Life of the Nation* includes a shift in the division of Western America. Most writers plot the progress of the American frontier by dividing Western America into the trans-Appalachian or transmontane West and the trans-Mississippi West. This dichotomy forces awkward and overlapping treatment of frontier processes occurring in that region comprised of the first tier of states west of the Mississippi River. A more realistic division was between two broad regions designated the Old West and the New West. Thus the trans-Appalachian West, which becomes the Old West, is expanded to include the first tier of states west of the Mississippi River. The Old West consists of three provinces—the Old Northwest, the Old Southwest, and the Mississippi Valley. This is a more manageable arrangement because the same cultural, economic, demographic, and political processes at work in the Old Northwest and Old Southwest—processes that bound these provinces into the national life—were contemporaneously at work in the Mississippi Valley.

The New West, therefore, embraces all American territory between the western border of Missouri and the Pacific shore, plus the Pacific Basin states of Hawaii and Alaska. The New West survives as the modern West, a region that only in the twentieth century has emerged as a viable political, economic, and social force.

Part One sets forth the concepts "Western," "frontiers," and "nationalizing currents." It assesses the influence of pioneering in forging national character, the West's impact on national life and development, and the American West in the twentieth century. There follows the basis for a pluralistic interpretation of Western development—describing the imperialist struggle among European nations for control of its territory and natural bounty, as well as the late emergence of the United States as a contestant for the region.

Part Two, The Old West, analyzes Anglo-American expansion processes and how they were first applied, tested, and refined in preparation for the continuing thrust across the continent and into the Pacific Basin. This section includes an appraisal of pioneer society and the determinative role of the Old West in the national life.

Part Three, The New West, traces the Americanization of the region extending from the western border of Missouri into the Pacific Basin, changing public images of the New West, the role of the mining frontier in the demographic and political development of the region, the Civil War in the West (stressing the comprehensive militarization of the region that this struggle precipitated), the American Indian as a casualty of this military buildup, the special role of technology in the Bonanza Age of postwar Western development, and the reluctant but eventual acceptance of the New West into the national life.

Part Four, The West in the Twentieth Century, narrates the economic, social, and political maturation of the territory extending from the western border of Missouri to the Pacific Basin states of Alaska and Hawaii. It demonstrates how the West, since 1900, has become a coequal region in the American community, regularly contesting its Eastern mentor for preeminence in national affairs.

Throughout the text, the term "frontier" has been used freely, variously referring to a geographic situation, an expansion entity, and a state of mind. I have attempted to show the metaphysical impact of the frontier and the West on national culture and on the American mind. The daring participated directly in the frontier experience; the timid, and those with personal limitations or responsibilities, shared vicariously in the drama of the Westward movement. Frontier as a state of mind has traditionally conjured up for the American public the idea of opportunity, a fresh start, and perhaps an escape from the encapsulating restraints of an increasingly complex Eastern lifestyle.

Arrell Morgan Gibson
Norman, Oklahoma

Contents

Part One

THE AMERICAN WEST: INTRODUCTION

1 The West in the Life of the Nation   3
2 The Natural Setting   19
3 European Exploration and Early Settlement in Western America   35
4 The European Contest for Western America, 1700–1763   45

Part Two

THE OLD WEST

5 Western America Divided: Spain and Great Britain, 1763–1776   65
6 The New Challenge in Western America   83
7 American Beginnings in the West, 1783–1800   97
8 The Old West   115
9 The Old Northwest   133
10 The Old Southwest   149
11 The Mississippi Valley   169
12 Pioneer Society in the Old West   189
13 The Old West in the Life of the Nation   211

Part Three

THE NEW WEST

14 Emergent American Dominion: Military Reconnaissance
   and Occupation   225
15 New West Pioneer Enterprises: The Fur Trade   243
16 New West Pioneer Enterprises: Commerce by Land and Sea   271
17 The New West as an Indian Colonization Zone   287

18 American Expansion in the New West: Texas   307
19 American Expansion in the New West: Oregon   323
20 American Expansion in the New West: New Mexico,
     California, and the Great Basin   339
21 The New West's Economic Development to 1861   361
22 The New West's Political Evolution to 1861   385
23 The Civil War in the New West   405
24 Pacification and Consolidation of the Western Tribes   427
25 Technological Conquest of the New West: The Railroad   455
26 Plundering the New West's Natural Bounty   473
27 State-Making in the New West   497
28 The Pacific Territories: Hawaii and Alaska   519
29 Pioneer Society in the New West   537
30 The New West in the Life of the Nation   561

Part Four
THE WEST IN THE TWENTIETH CENTURY

31 Western Economic Maturation   571
32 Western Society in the Twentieth Century   585
33 Politics in the Twentieth-Century West   597

Maps
Western America   7
Physiographic Provinces of the West   22
Aboriginal Peoples of the United States, 1820–1840   30
The Old West, 1763–1783   71
The Old West, 1800   117
Western America, 1820   170
American Western Explorations, 1804–1846   233
The New West, 1850   351
Stage, Mail, Freight, and Immigrant Routes in the New West   380
New West Indian Reservations, 1890   449
Transcontinental Railroad Routes, 1900   461
The New West Mining Frontier, 1849–1900   486

Index   617

PART ONE *the American West: Introduction*

Chimney Rock in the Cumberland Gap, Tennessee
National Park Service Photograph

Pioneer Woman Statue, Ponca City, Oklahoma

1

The West in the Life of the Nation

THE westward progression of the American nation from the upper Ohio Valley to the Pacific basin during the nineteenth century is one of the most intriguing phenomena of recent history. The Anglo-American civilization planted at Jamestown in 1607 required over 150 years to reach the stage of maturity and strength required to sustain itself in the Western wilderness. Then, with incredible velocity and sustained momentum, the American nation swept from its seaboard nursery, over the Appalachian barrier, and into the continental interior. By the 1840s it had reached the Pacific and soon occupied lands in between. This rapid occupation, organization, and exploitation of territory produced countless personal economic successes and a concomitant increase in national strength.

INTRODUCTION

The saga of American Western expansion has generated a substantial literary chronicle—rich in tales of bold private and public action—as well as a body of conflicting interpretation. The present account of the West in the life of the nation is constructed around the theme that the development of the resources of the West has been the prime determinant of national direction and the principal source of national economic strength and hegemony. We will show that the United States evolved from a weak, struggling nation, born of secession in the late eighteenth century, into a twentieth-century international power in direct proportion to the success of its citizens in occupying and developing the trans-Appalachian region and integrating it into the national life. This nationbuilding process was

3

the result of bold, pragmatic action by American frontiersmen who were consistently supported by nationalizing currents in their government in the form of supportive laws, aggressive diplomacy, and military action.

On the other hand, this work denies that Western pioneering experiences were the principal determinants of distinctively American social and political character and cultural institutions. It is true that conditions on the frontier often produced interesting variations on well-established patterns. Yet geographic separation from Europe and *laissez faire* imperial management of the seaboard community by the British government for a century and a half had earlier provided the principal genesis for the emerging differences between Americans and Europeans. Americans were already well inured to democratic processes before their entry into the West; the Watauga and Transylvania constitutions of Kentucky and Tennessee in the 1770s were but continuations of a deep-rooted democratic heritage transplanted from the seaboard cultural nursery. (*See* Chapter 5.) Westerners refined and expanded, but did not originate, democratic processes; they contributed to the fulfillment of a stream begun in early colonial times.

Another facet of this work emphasizes the pluralistic view of Western development. Thus it challenges the monistic approach that depicts the Anglo-American frontiersmen's struggle with a pristine wilderness and relegates to passing notice the substantive role of Spain, France, Great Britain, and Russia. These mercantilist-oriented nations valued Western America as a rich imperial prize; and for nearly two hundred years before the advent of the Anglo-Americans, Spain and France, and later Great Britain and Russia, contested for its bounty.

From a vantage point in the lower Mississippi Valley during the seventeenth and eighteenth centuries one could have beheld the drama of European forces converging on the resource-rich trans-Appalachian region. First the Spanish, from bases in the Caribbean and Mexico, established a rim of settlements from St. Augustine, around the Gulf shore to Pensacola, and into Texas, New Mexico, Arizona, and California. The French entered North America via the St. Lawrence River and, from Canadian stations, established themselves in the Old Northwest and drove south and west into the Mississippi Valley. And in the eighteenth century Russians, crossing from Siberia along the Aleutian chain, prepared to advance down the Pacific coast to the approaches of San Francisco Bay.

On the Atlantic seaboard English and Dutch settlements became bases for penetrating America's interior. New Amsterdam supported Dutch traders in their move up the Hudson to Fort Orange where, through Iroquois minions, they thrust trade tentacles into the fur-rich territory of the Old Northwest. And, finally, the English colonies, which nourished Anglo-American civilization for over 150 years, were a beachhead from which the British built strength sufficient to support their ultimate extension into the trans-Appalachian region late in the eighteenth century.

So it was that Anglo-Americans were latecomers to the West. One writer observed that "in truth, the Anglo frontiersman only occasionally met a virgin or unprepared wilderness as he pushed westward from the crest of the Appalachian highlands. . . . There were white men's frontiers antedating the Anglo-American, some of them decades and others even centuries old. Further, these pre-Anglo frontiers in many instances prepared for and made possible much of the phenomenal success of Anglo-American enterprises of the late eighteenth and the nineteenth centuries in the 'West.'" Anglo frontiers often were second frontiers. The Northwest, Southwest, and Mississippi Valley had been exploited by the French and Spanish before the Anglo-American entry. "When the Anglos pushed out to the farther edge of the Mid-Continent and beyond, they found the groundwork already laid in a good half of the area. The Spaniards had been in New Mexico almost ten years before there was a Jamestown. . . . Thus, much of the continent had been seen and charted and even 'fron-tierized' before the first Anglos appeared."[1]

Nonetheless, acknowledging that Anglo-American frontiersmen were latecomers to the West does not tarnish their efforts, but rather places their spectacular continental conquest in more precise perspective. If Anglo-Americans were not the first to enter the trans-Appalachian region, they offset this tardiness by the vigor of their drive across the West, by their sustained, comprehensive occupation and development of America's interior, by succeeding where others had faltered. By recognizing the presence and contribution of European precursors in American continental expansion, we enrich our awareness of the interaction and inevitable conflict of cultures—European, Indian, and Anglo-American—that marked the contest for pre-eminence in Western America. Pluralistic considerations suffuse a flavor to Western history that is lacking in the ethnocentric emphasis on Anglo-American frontiersmen.

THE GEOGRAPHY OF THE FRONTIER

Perspective and viewpoint on the American West are also enhanced by correcting certain stereotyped geographic conceptualizations. The *American West* is a strictly Anglo-American concept. Spanish orientation to the vast region between the Appalachians and the Pacific was north from Mexico. The French viewed America's interior as south from Canada. Even in the British context the view was frequently south from Canada or north from West Florida. But intensive efforts by Atlantic seaboard-based Anglo-Americans to settle and exploit the trans-Appalachian territory provided the enduring viewpoint *Western*. Their rapid occupation of the region following the American Revolution revealed the dynamic nature of the concept *West*.

[1] John F. Bannon, ed., *Bolton and the Spanish Borderlands* (Norman, Okla., 1964), pp. 4–5.

In 1783, the upper Ohio Valley was momentarily the West, but it quickly became a bridge for the march of American settlements toward the Mississippi Valley and, eventually, to the Pacific.

Concurrent with the progress of Western expansion was the overflow of cultural forces from the seaboard that quickly metamorphosed the nearer frontier territory into an extension of the eastern United States. This had the effect of dividing the Western entity and requires the application of the terms *Old West* and *New West* as more precise geographical and cultural designations. The seaboard's early absorption of the immediate transmontane portion of the Old West created the modern-day Midwest, which served as geographic connective tissue linking the East and the New West. Indeed, in the twentieth-century mind, the West as a geographic and cultural entity is limited to the region extending from the western border of Missouri to the Pacific shore, plus Alaska and Hawaii.

Commonly, the American frontier is plotted by dividing Western America into the Transmontane West and the Trans-Mississippi West. This separation forces awkward and overlapping treatment of frontier processes in the region comprising the first tier of states west of the Mississippi River—Louisiana, Arkansas, Missouri, Iowa, and Minnesota. A more realistic division therefore, and the one followed in this work, is to separate the American West into two broad regions designated Old West and New West. The Transmontane West becomes the Old West and is extended to include the first tier of states west of the Mississippi River. Thus the Old West consists of three provinces—the Old Northwest, the Old Southwest, and the Mississippi Valley. The same cultural, economic, demographic, and political processes that were binding the Old Northwest and Old Southwest into the national life were contemporaneously at work in the Mississippi Valley province. In fact, Louisiana—the southernmost state in the Mississippi Valley province—was admitted to the Union in 1812, several years *before* statehood was accorded the Old Northwest territories of Indiana and Illinois or the Old Southwest territories of Mississippi and Alabama.

The New West, now a more manageable unit, therefore consists of all American territory between the western border of Missouri and the Pacific shore, as well as the Pacific basin states of Hawaii and Alaska. The New West thus survives as today's American West, a region that only in the twentieth century has emerged as "an assertive" political, economic, and social force in the life of the nation.

AMERICAN PATTERNS OF EXPANSION

Other nations had made a beginning in Western America, faltered and retired. The Anglo-Americans persevered and succeeded. Their success is attributable largely to geographic propinquity, management of the Western territory based on equality between the national government and the settlers, and efficient expansion technique.

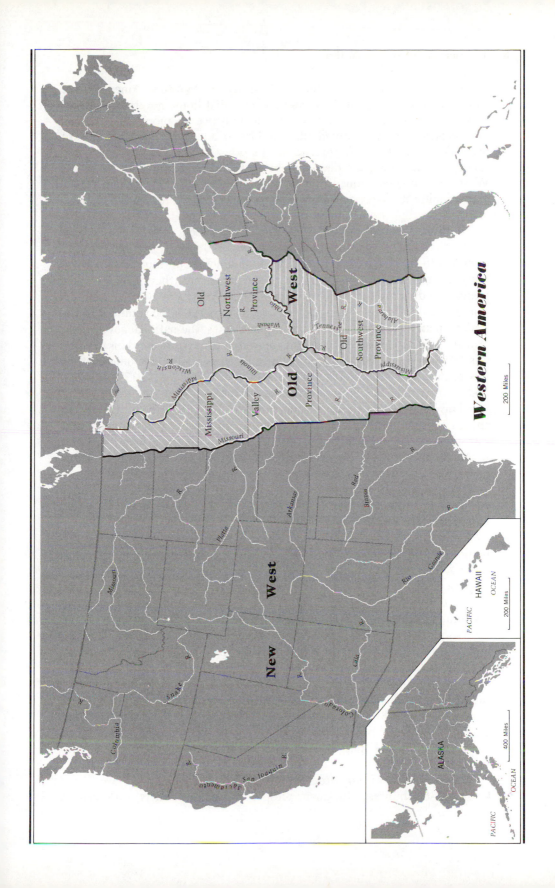

Western America

200 Miles

Old Northwest Province

Old West

Old Southwest Province

Tennessee R

Alabama

Mississippi

Ohio R

Wabash R

Illinois R

Wisconsin R

Mississippi

Old Province

Mississippi Valley

Missouri

Missouri R

Arkansas

Red

Brazos

R

R

R

Platte

Rio Grande

New West

Missouri R

Snake R

Columbia R

R

Gila R

Colorado R

San Joaquin R

Sacramento

HAWAII

PACIFIC OCEAN

200 Miles

ALASKA

PACIFIC OCEAN

400 Miles

The European nations holding territory in Western America were handicapped by the great distances that separated home governments from these lands. Slow communications and dependence on monolithic colonial bureaucracies severely limited their ability to adequately manage distant possessions. The U.S. government, on the other hand, as the constitutional agency for managing the development of United States' territories in the West, was situated immediately adjacent to its trans-Appalachian estate. This simple yet strategic advantage permitted far more responsive management.

Early in the national life, American leaders eschewed the temptation to designate the West an unorganized imperial reserve, its people and resources to be managed and exploited by a colonial bureaucracy solely for the benefit of the thirteen proprietary states. Rather, they made the very productive decision that the trans-Appalachian West was to be settled, developed, and organized into states; and each state was to be admitted to the Union on an equal footing with the original states, the national government providing guidance and direction for the state-making process. This decision was first made in 1781 at the acceptance of the Articles of Confederation, was reaffirmed by the Northwest Ordinance of 1787, and in 1791 was embodied in Article IV, Section III of the Constitution.

This decision was decisively and successfully applied to the Old West; and its consummation provided the pattern and precedent for equality that was subsequently applied to American territory in the New West, and later to Alaska and Hawaii. The results of this decision are immeasurable. One effect was to endow the American frontiersman with a sense of being a local part of a greater democratic process and of having a private and public stake in the future of the region; by the exercise of personal sovereignty through the ballot, he could play a directive role in that process.

American expansion technique evolved from private and public pragmatic methods of adjustment to the Western milieu and crystallized into more-or-less established patterns for national integration used from the Appalachians into the Pacific basin. The Old West served as a stage where the drama of American expansion was first enacted and the processes for consummating emergent national goals were tested.

Also in the Old West there occurred the dynamic interplay of Eastern and Western cultural forces. The more genteel Eastern forces leavened the Old West's crude, impulsive, earthy qualities and gradually triumphed, forcing the frontier to retreat toward the Pacific. This metamorphosis is illustrated by Ohio, which increased in population during the decade between 1800 and 1810 from 45,000 to 231,000; this led one writer to report that it "already resembled an eastern state, boasting several important cities, a passable road and transportation system, and millions of acres of cultivated land."

In the drama of American expansion the principal figures were frontiersmen—fur hunters, stockmen, prospector-miners, soldiers, missionaries, civilized Indians, itinerant merchants, and pioneer settlers. Each successive group created an identifiable frontier or community in which its members established increasingly the American presence.

The fur hunters moved well ahead of the line of agricultural settlement, taking the wild animal pelts in which the wilderness abounded or trading with Indian hunters for them. Their enterprise was intensive, highly destructive, and restlessly mobile. As the harvest of pelts faded in a given hunting zone, the fur hunters moved on to virgin territory. Their migrations opened new fur frontiers and marked paths in the wilderness that became highways for later groups.

Often pressing close behind the fur hunters were stockmen, who grazed their herds of cattle and horses on the public lands of the United States. Stockmen too progressed ahead of the line of agricultural settlement. Their open-range enterprise required no investment of labor and capital in enclosures, and the natural mobility of their livestock made marketing simple. In the New West, Anglo-American stockmen blended their stockraising culture with the already well established Spanish-American methods.

The mining frontier coursed across the Western wilderness as the prospector-miner restlessly searched for crude but essential minerals such as lead and the more romantic gold and silver. His discoveries led to stampedes or rushes, demographic bursts that created urban pockets in the Western wilderness and accelerated the progress toward cultural integration.

The military frontier occupied another vanguard position in the American advance. The soldier generally established American presence in the wilderness ahead of the line of permanent agricultural settlement. He constructed forts at strategic locations in the forests, on the prairies and plains, and in the mountains. These tiny military enclaves often served as the first urban nucleus in the wilds of the Old West and later the New West. The soldier hewed roads across the frontier, established the first communications systems, fought the Indians, and drove them from lands coveted by the settlers. He explored and mapped the remote portions of Western America and provided the first law and order for the region.

Another frontiersman in the vanguard of American expansion was the missionary. He worked among the Eastern Indian tribes, attempting to shape aboriginal communities to be receptive to the American advance. He also resettled tribes ahead of the Anglo-American settlement line, ostensibly to protect the Indians from the corrupting influences of the American settlements; nonetheless he served the national purpose, removing Indians without the use of military force and eviction. The missionary was also in the vanguard of the American presence in Hawaii and the Pacific Northwest.

The frontiersman community also included what were known as "civilized Indians." Long before the national government began its formal program of forcing the Eastern tribes to abandon their homelands and move to the New West, bands of Kickapoos, Shawnees, Delawares, and Cherokees had pulled away from the parent Indian communities and roamed the middle border—a region flanked on the east by the Mississippi River and on the west by the Great Plains. These Indian pioneers moved on a north-south concourse, from the Arkansas River deep into Spanish Texas. They served as carriers of Anglo-American culture, particularly technology, through the weapons, tools, and textiles they traded to the Comanches, Kiowas, and other southwest tribes. Later the Choctaws, Cherokees, Creeks, Seminoles, and Chickasaws, forcibly removed by the national government from the Old Southwest to the New West, planted constitutional government, slaveholding, public schools, and other civilization items in the wilderness just as their Anglo-American counterparts did in Arkansas, Missouri, and Texas.

The mercantile frontier was yet another prime carrier of Anglo-American culture. From depots at Westport and Fort Smith—the heads of navigation on the Missouri and Arkansas rivers for most of the year—the wilderness merchant moved his goods in heavy-wheeled freight wagons drawn by great gangs of oxen and mules south to the goods-starved Spanish American settlements on the Rio Grande and into Chihuahua. The economic interests the trader built up in foreign territory were zealously protected by the national government; whenever they were threatened by the host government, it became a matter of deep diplomatic concern and sometimes cause for military intervention by his government, corroborating the ancient maxim that "the flag follows the commerce."

The pioneer-settler frontier has as its classic hero the frontiersman, usually the first Anglo-American agriculturist. Opening clearings in the forests and along the alluvial bottoms, he then sold out to the latecomers—the permanent farmers, planters, and town builders—and moved on to develop new speculative holdings. The pioneer-farmer frontiersman was less often the noble, daring, picturesque individualist he has been portrayed than a crude, ill-mannered rogue. His avaricious desolations of the advanced Indian settlements along the Cherokee and Creek frontier during the removal period of the 1830s are infamous. And on the southwestern frontier around Fort Smith this opportunist demanded that the national government use the army to clear the wilderness of settlement hazards. Then through the years he lived there supported by the federal establishment. When the government wanted to close the fort as an economy move, the frontiersman's objections were similar to those raised today when federal officials attempt to close a military station or other public facility.

A strategic entity for establishing American presence in the remote portions of the New West was the sea trader's frontier. Before 1800, New England merchantmen were rounding the Horn and trafficking at ports of Spanish California. They established commerce with the Indians living along the Pacific Northwest coast and sailed north to Alaska; their trade yielded great quantities of highly esteemed sea otter pelts and other valuable skins.

By early in the nineteenth century the maritime trader had developed a pattern of commercial contact and exchange that approximated a vast triangle. The first stops in the California ports, to take on hides and tallow, were followed by calls at trading stations in the Pacific Northwest and Alaska for sea otter pelts. Then, sailing across 2,500 miles of open ocean, they reached the second point in the triangular pattern—the Sandwich Islands (Hawaii). There in the sparkling Pacific archipelago, crews restored their land legs, frolicked with the exquisite island women, took on cargoes of sandalwood, and lifted anchor for the rich markets on the China coast— the third point. The maritime trader's frontier established American interest in the Pacific basin region, seeded an American presence there, and thereby reserved this water hemisphere with its strategic land points—the Pacific Coast, Alaska, and Hawaii—as the nation's last frontier.

Except for the maritime trader's frontier, there was no particular order to the progression of these frontiers from the Old West across the New West, although most often the fur hunter's frontier and the military frontier preceded the others. On occasion, fortuitous mineral strikes caused the mining frontier to become the vanguard group.

THE SPECIAL ROLE OF THE WEST

If, as we have seen, westward expansion was made up of so many different frontiers, the oft-repeated thesis that the "pioneering experience was a principal determinant of American character and culture" would seem to be an oversimplification of a very complex process. Evidence shows that pioneering was traumatic, and people submitted to the ordeal only because it provided them opportunities for economic improvement. As soon as they succeeded in mining, stockraising, or farming, they either returned to the East or imported Eastern fashions in homes, furnishings, clothing, and cuisine to the West. Eastern goods, capital, management, and culture generally—as well as the nationalizing currents of government and politics— coursed into every Western settlement, shaping institutions, casting the West in the Eastern image, and driving away the frontier environment and mentality. The West was obsessively imitative, rarely innovative.

But, if the pioneering experience only flavored, but by no means served as a principal determinant of American character and culture, must the American West as the environment in which the pioneering experience was consummated also rate a secondary role? We think not, for the West *can* persuasively claim special status as a major force in determining national direction. After 1800, the impact of the West and its resources on the life of the nation steadily increased. As a Midas-rich producer of food and raw materials it supported the nation's industrial thrust. Production of vast quantities of Western gold and silver during the nineteenth century increased the nation's specie wealth and provided a stabilizing capital base to meet the needs of its growing industrial establishment. In addition to supporting economic growth, the West's broad spectrum of natural resources encouraged diversification of the national economy. By the mid-twentieth century, according to every measure of national strength—territory, resources, and population—the nation had grown in strength and achieved status as a world leader largely in proportion to the development of the American West.

What evolved during the nineteenth century was a symbiotic, mutually reciprocal relationship between the East and the West. The national government served as patron, the frontiersman as the agent, in generating the essential nationalizing currents that bound the West to the nation as a whole. In the period 1800 to 1828, these currents were refined and regularized. The national government nourished the West, responding to its needs by acquiring new territory, reducing the Indian menace, and adopting laws tailored to Western needs—including statutes providing for purchase of public land on credit. As citizens of new territories and states in the federal system, Westerners voiced their needs through the ballot, through the representatives they selected to represent them in Congress, and occasionally, by petitions to leaders of the national government.

Technology

Besides propinquity, shared management, and efficient expansion techniques, the American nation's Western conquest was substantively abetted by improving technology. Needs arising from expansion and development were frequently met by the seemingly fortuitous appearance of innovative processes and inventions. The most important early technological development was the application of steam power to river and ocean craft, to mining equipment for extracting and processing minerals, and to machines for grinding grain and sawing timber. The steam-powered locomotive—its first transcontinental line completed in 1869—began the process of integrating remote sections of the continental New West into the life of the nation.

Technological advances in American industry following the Civil War contributed additional items that accelerated the Western conquest and development process; these included weapons, barbed wire for enclosures, and well-drilling and pumping equipment. In the late nineteenth century, the application of steam power to tractors and reapers, followed in the twentieth century by the gasoline engine and irrigation, revolutionized agriculture and completed the conquest of the West's last agrarian frontier —the Great American Desert.

American technological progress in the twentieth century has had immense effect on the West, striking its remoteness and binding it ever more closely into the national life. No device has had greater integrative effect than the automobile and the highway system. Mid-century developments in air travel and communications have completed the spatial conquest of the New West, making it possible to absorb the remote Pacific basin states of Alaska and Hawaii into the national life.

Population

Population, along with territorial and economic factors, has been an important measure of national strength. The nation's population increase—from about 3 million at its birth as an independent republic to over 200 million at the mid-twentieth century—is a demographic marvel. This phenomenal human increase is due to many factors, including a flow of migrants from Europe, Asia, and Africa. But the internal natural increase has also been spectacular, the West far exceeding the East as a fertility zone and confirming the demographer's belief that vacant land and opportunity for economic improvement accelerate population growth.

The West proved to be an optimum fertility milieu; the procreative performance of the "fecund frontiersman" increased the population throughout the nineteenth century at a rate of about 40 percent each decade—twice the national average! Pioneer America was largely rural and agrarian, and frontier values stressed large families to provide labor for the farms. The laws of Western states and territories encouraged early marriages by setting the age of marital majority at sixteen for males and fourteen for females; they protected the family unit by making divorce little short of impossible. As national leaders came to understand and appreciate the strategic effect of the "American multiplication table" on territorial expansion, they relied upon it to extend American dominion by populating the wilderness and establishing vital American presence. One congressman in explaining this phenomenon commented: "Go to the West and see a young man and his mate of eighteen; after a lapse of thirty years, visit them again, and instead of two you will find twenty-two." [2]

Politics

Almost from the beginning, the West exercised some influence on national affairs, a trend that has continued and perhaps accelerated. During the nineteenth century the West determined the stream of major national legislation, as well as Indian and military policy. Similarly, the nation's diplomacy often had Western roots, largely because through much of the nineteenth century the United States shared the region between the Appalachians and the Pacific with several foreign nations. The nation's intense and prolonged preoccupation with its continental development produced strong, enduring attitudes of insularity; and that vast, protective territory reaching all the way to the Pacific bred international provincialism.

[2] *Congressional Globe*, 29 Cong., 1 Sess., p. 180.

Certainly American foreign policy was steeped in isolationism from the earliest days of the republic. The Monroe Doctrine was in many respects a defensive manifestation of national commitment to concerns on the American continent.

Early in its life as a political region, the West contributed leadership to the nation. Several congressmen and senators from the Old West maintained a directive influence in the Congress until the middle of the nineteenth century. As the dominant voice in Congress for nearly four decades, Henry Clay of Kentucky maintained an uneasy sectional peace over issues generated by Western expansion. And Missouri Senator Thomas Hart Benton's concept of "Road to India" provided the foundations for the rhetoric of Manifest Destiny. By 1840, the Old West had supplied the nation with two presidents, Generals Andrew Jackson and William Henry Harrison. In this regard, the West fed the ironic American propensity for military leadership; the martial image as a primary consideration for political preferment continued in American politics through the 1950s. The West also influenced national politics by coloring political campaigns with homespun allusions and the simplistic, folksy appeal to the electorate. The West regularly generated strong nationalistic currents, which precipitated martial outbursts such as the War of 1812 and the Mexican War. And during the nineteenth century, the West forced the periodic realignment of national political parties around the Western issues of public land distribution, national expansion, the extension of slavery, and the national monetary system.

With regard to national unity, the West has played a contradictory role. On the one hand it produced centripetal, integrating forces. Following the Revolutionary War, it provided the issue—the Western public domain —that bound the nation into a more stable political community. During the War of 1812, Western nationalism tempered New England sectionalism, turned back that region's threat of secession, and unified the nation in perhaps its darkest hour before 1861. On the other hand, the West, by its very presence in the national community, between 1820 and 1850 also produced centrifugal, disintegrating forces that threatened national unity. Western-based issues were among the principal causes for Southern secession in 1861.

Perhaps the greatest political legacy from the West was its role in suffusing democracy into the bastions of privilege, oligarchy, and limited franchise. By popularizing the franchise, the West forced extension of democracy and produced the shift from Jeffersonian to Jacksonian democracy, from rule by leaders from the elite and selected by limited suffrage, to rule by leaders drawn from the community of the common man, selected by manhood suffrage.

In the early nineteenth century, the West provided a means to achieve a "national identity apart from Europe." The engaging drama of Western expansion and development provided citizens a "common identity which could give them a claim to nationhood." [3] Even those Easterners who did not go pioneering participated vicariously in the nationalistic strivings of continental conquest, which contributed materially to sundering the European umbilical cord and forming the American national myth.

Of the two regions in the American West, the Old West, during the nineteenth century, exercised more directive influence on national development than the New West. For most of its life, the New West was managed as a colonial territory, and exploited politically and economically by Eastern politicians and capitalists. Only a few nineteenth-century leaders anticipated the New West's promise and, perhaps, its threat to the Eastern establishment. Illinois Senator Stephen A. Douglas, while commenting on New West prospects in 1853, presciently declared that "there is a power in this nation greater than either the North or the South—a growing, increasing, swelling power, that will be able to speak the law to this nation, and to execute the law as spoken. That power is the country known as the Great West. . . . There, sir, is the hope of this nation—the resting place of the power that is not only to control, but to save the nation." [4] In the twentieth century, the New West may be fulfilling the promise of Senator Douglas' prophecy.

What we now know as the American West—the region between the Missouri border and the Pacific shore, including the Pacific basin states of Alaska and Hawaii—retains much of its frontier heritage and its Western style. At the same time it is an integral part of the national life. And because of its spectacular demographic expansion, its concomitant increase in political power, and its economic maturation, the West is becoming the dominant region of the American community.

SELECTED SOURCES

The writings of Frederick Jackson Turner contain the seminal concepts and analyses of American expansion, the frontier, and national development. Especially important are *The Frontier in American History* (New York, 1920) and *The Significance of Sections in American History* (New York, 1932). Supporting works of merit include Ray A. Billington, *Frederick Jackson Turner: Historian, Scholar, Teacher* (New York, 1973), and, by the same author, *America's Frontier Heritage* (New York, 1966); the latter places Turner's frontier conceptualizations in the context of social science methodology. Other provocative works on the place of the West and the frontier in the folk

* Available in paperback.

[3] Henry E. Fritz, "Nationalistic Response to Frontier Expansion," *Mid America: An Historical Review* 51 (Oct. 1969): 228.

[4] Quoted in E. Douglas Branch, *Westward: The Romance of the American Frontier* (New York, 1930), p. 448.

life of America are *Henry Nash Smith, Virgin Land: The American West As Symbol and Myth (Cambridge, 1950), and Henry E. Fritz, "Nationalistic Response to Frontier Expansion," Mid America: An Historical Review 51 (Oct. 1969): 227–43.

The pluralistic viewpoint on Western development is supplied by *Charles Gibson, Spain in America (New York, 1966); *W. J. Eccles, The Canadian Frontier (New York, 1969); George M. Wrong, The Rise and Fall of New France (New York, 1953); and John F. Bannon, ed., Bolton and the Spanish Borderlands (Norman, Okla., 1964).

There are numerous useful survey and reference studies on the West, the frontier, and American expansion. Among the best are LeRoy R. Hafen, W. Eugene Hollon, and Carl G. Rister, Western America: The Exploration, Settlement and Development of the Region Beyond the Mississippi (Englewood Cliffs, N.J., 1970); Ray A. Billington, Westward Expansion: A History of the American Frontier (4th ed., New York, 1974); Frederic L. Paxson, History of the American Frontier, 1763–1893 (Boston, 1924); Robert E. Riegel and Robert G. Athearn, America Moves West (New York, 1971); Kent Ladd Steckmesser, The Westward Movement: A Short History (New York, 1969); Thomas D. Clark, Frontier America: The Story of the Westward Movement (New York, 1959); and *Gerald D. Nash, The American West in the Twentieth Century: A Short History of an Urban Oasis (Englewood Cliffs, N.J., 1973).

Photo by Harold M. Lambert

Grand Canyon, Arizona

Alpine Meadow in Mt. Rainier National Park, Washington

2

The Natural Setting

ON the eve of discovery by European navigators, the American West was a pristine wilderness of spreading forests, sweeping grassland, towering mountains, forbidding deserts, and ocean-washed headlands. It was a land rich in natural bounty—varied minerals, dense stands of timber, and productive soils. It was home to all manner of wild creatures, from small fur-bearing creatures—such as beaver, mink, and otter—to large game animals—bear, elk, deer, and bison. Migratory waterfowl and birds flourished in the Western wilderness, and its sparkling streams teemed with fish. This primeval milieu was sparsely populated by aboriginal peoples who pursued simple lifestyles, sustaining themselves by hunting, fishing, gathering, agriculture, and intertribal trade. After 1500, the wilderness became the stage for an unfolding drama —an international struggle for control of this resource-rich territory.

GEOGRAPHY

The physical landscape of the American West extends from the Appalachian Mountains to the Pacific islands, and from Canada to Mexico, with a jump north to Alaska; it embraces all states of the Union except the Atlantic coastal plain. Seven distinctive geographic provinces are discernible in the American West: the Appalachian Highlands, the Gulf Coastal Plains, Interior Plains, Interior Highlands, Rocky Mountains, Intermontane Basins and Plateaus, and the Pacific Basin (which includes the Pacific Mountains and Valleys, the Arctic Plains and Highlands of Alaska, and the Pacific Islands of Hawaii).

Appalachian Highlands Province

This mountain system forms the region's eastern perimeter and extends from the St. Lawrence River in the north, southward through western New York and Pennsylvania, eastern Ohio, Kentucky, and Tennessee; it grades into the Coastal Plain in Georgia and Alabama. The Appalachians maintain an average height of 3,000 feet above sea level, with some peaks approaching 7,000 feet.

Several important Western rivers, including the Allegheny and Monongahela, which unite to form the Ohio, originate in the Appalachians' maze of alternating ranges, twisted ridges, narrow valleys, and sweeping plateaus. Dense mixed conifer and hardwood forests combined with tangled liana-type growth enshrouded the Appalachian chain until the middle of the eighteenth century. The mountains' tumbled relief and near-impenetrable floral shield contained the Anglo-American civilization evolving on the Atlantic coast for 150 years.

By the middle of the eighteenth century, seaboard-based agents and surveyors employed by speculator land companies and traders had found circuitous routes through the trans-Appalachian barrier. They crossed the drainage divide and followed the valleys formed by the Allegheny, Monongahela, Watauga, Clinch, Holston, and other transmontane rivers into the West. In 1750, Thomas Walker made a spectacular discovery when he chanced onto the Cumberland Gap, a depression in the highland chain that provided easy passage from the Virginia and North Carolina settlements to Kentucky.

Gulf Costal Plains Province

These lowlands rim the West along the Gulf shore from Florida to the Rio Grande in Texas. Alabama, Mississippi, Louisiana, and eastern Texas are situated in this geographic province. An irregular tongue of Gulf Coastal Plains environment extends up the Mississippi Valley to the Ohio River and covers western Tennessee and Kentucky, southeastern Missouri, and eastern Arkansas.

Coastal Plains characteristics include low elevation—rarely exceeding 500 feet above sea level—generally flat land, numerous swamps and marshes, prairie grassland, and mixed oak, pine, and cypress forests. The streams draining the Coastal Plains are slow-moving and navigable and include the Chattahoochee, Mobile, Pearl, Mississippi, Arkansas, Red and Sabine rivers. Alluvial deltas on the lower reaches of these rivers contain some of the nation's richest soil. In the early eighteenth century European colonizers established fortified settlements on strategic estuaries of these rivers to control access to the interior of the West.

Coastal Plains climate is subtropical, warm and humid, except near the Rio Grande, where declining rainfall produces a steppe-type climate. The region generally has long summers and mild winters.

Interior Plains Province

This vast region embraces the great heartland of the American West, extending from the Appalachians to the Rocky Mountains. It is characterized by flat to rolling country that varies from about 500 feet above sea level in the east to nearly 5,000 feet at the base of the Rocky Mountains. It is conspicuously divided along the 100th meridian by a climatic fault—abruptly diminishing rainfall—which produces substantive environmental differences. East of this line humid conditions prevail; west of it arid conditions are usual. The western section of the Interior Plains is called the Great Plains.

Interior Plains vegetation varies by section. East of the 100th meridian, forests and prairie-type grasslands predominate. Coniferous softwood forests flourish in the north, while mixed hardwood stands are found in the central and southern sections. By contrast, most of the Great Plains segment is a sweeping, rolling grassland, although trees are by no means absent. Deep-rooted, thick-sodded buffalo, grama, bluestem, and mesquite grasses comprise the principal vegetative cover. Creeks and rivers are marked by ribbons of cottonwood and willow stands. Cedars flourish on the uplands, patches of scrub oak and shinnery are found in the Central Plains, and mesquite trees dot the Southern Plains. Interior Plains Province soils vary in color and fertility, determined by parent rock material and humus content. Eastern soils with substantial amounts of limestone and humus are gray to black and generally are the more fertile. Western soils vary in color from brown to red. Interior Plain soils are well suited to the production of grains.

At least two environmental anomalies contradict the stereotypical image of the monotonous Great Plains grassland. One is the Llano Estacado, the Staked Plains, a 20,000-square mile arid wasteland astride eastern New Mexico and the western Texas Panhandle; it is covered by sparse bunch grass, sand dunes, and cacti. The second is a dense belt of forest called the Cross Timbers, which marks the eastern margin of the Southern Plains; it extends northeast of Fort Worth, Texas to the Canadian River in central Oklahoma. There white oak, black jack, and hickory stands laced with green briar and brambles barred easy passage across the Southern Plains.

Interior Plains climate ranges broadly from humid continental (30–35 inches of rainfall annually) in the East to arid conditions (15 or less inches of rainfall annually) in the West. The eastern segment has a humid climate with three distinct belts: (1) the northern tier—comprised of Michigan, Wisconsin, and Minnesota—is humid continental with short summers; (2) the central area—Ohio, Indiana, Illinois, Missouri, eastern Kansas, and Iowa—is humid continental with long summers; (3) to the south—Kentucky, Tennessee, Arkansas, eastern Oklahoma—a humid, subtropical climate predominates. Throughout the eastern area the evaporation rate is low and the humidity level is high, as a rule.

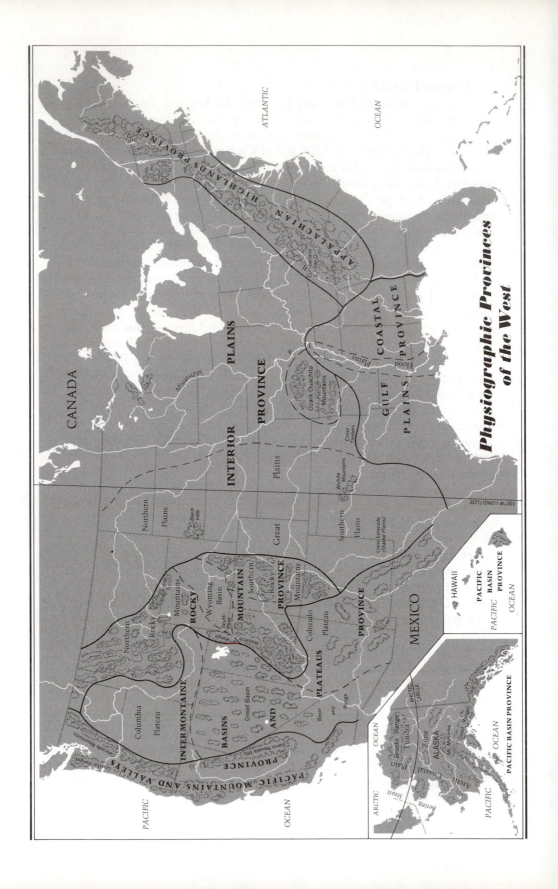

Physiographic Provinces of the West

The Great Plains or western segment of the Interior Plains geographic province has an arid steppe-type climate, and intense continental influences produce unpredictable meteorological conditions. Thus rainfall varies greatly from year to year, averaging fifteen to twenty inches annually. One reason for the variation in precipitation is that eastward-moving winds are milked of their moisture as they rise to cross the Rocky Mountains. The region's conspicuous daily and seasonal variations in temperature—intense summer heat and occasional bitter winter cold—are accompanied by low relative humidity, a high evaporation rate, dry air, much sunshine, and steady winds, generally blowing from south to north.

Periodically, warm and cold air masses collide over the Great Plains to produce abrupt weather changes—a sudden rise or fall in temperature, northers carrying destructive blizzards, and violent thunderstorms dispensing hail, lightning, and heavy rainfall. Throughout the year, but especially during the late spring and early summer, these fronts spawn funnel-shaped, death-dealing tornadoes.

The Mississippi River system drains both the eastern and western segments of the Interior Plains province. Its principal tributaries flowing from the east are the Wisconsin, Illinois, Ohio, and Yazoo rivers. The Missouri, Arkansas, and Red rivers drain most of the western segment.

Interior Highlands Province

Within the Interior Plains are scattered the remnants of ancient and eroded mountain systems. West and south of Lake Superior the Canadian or Laurentian Shield, an area of low rounded hills, is surrounded by prairies. During the Great Ice Age glaciers gouged out depressions in which numerous lakes and swamps formed. In primeval times thick conifer and mixed hardwood forests covered this highland region. Further south, rising from the rolling prairies of southern Missouri, western Arkansas, and eastern Oklahoma are the Ozark-Ouachita Mountains, a collection of flattened peaks—occasionally reaching 2,000 feet—broad plateaus, flaring ridges, and narrow valleys that are covered with mixed hardwood and coniferous forests. The Great Plains section of the Interior Plains is also dotted with highlands. These include the Black Hills in South Dakota and the Wichita Mountains in southwestern Oklahoma.

Rocky Mountain Province

Dramatically succeeding the Interior Plains region in the American West's landscape, this rugged, lofty cordillera flares irregularly across northwestern Washington, northern and eastern Idaho, western Montana, western Wyoming, northeastern Utah, and central Colorado into northern New Mexico. The chain is divided into the northern and southern Rockies by a dip in the cordillera in western Wyoming known as the Wyoming Basin; 250 miles wide, the basin provides relatively easy access from the Interior Plains to the Intermontane Basins and Plateaus province beyond. Early nineteenth century fur trappers discovered this crossing, which came to be known as South Pass. Serving as the continental divide, the Rockies separate the nation's drainage and generate east-flowing streams, including the Missouri and Arkansas, and west-flowing streams, including the Snake—which joins the Columbia—and the Green—which joins the Colorado.

Through most of its length, the Rocky Mountain chain is forested at lower elevations with sage and other arid region plants, succeeded by thick stands of conifers and aspens at higher levels, and grass patches in the alpine meadows. Rocky Mountain province climate is vertical; that is, climatic changes coincide with varying elevations. Arid, semi-desert conditions prevail in the lowlands, and increases in elevation produce milder temperatures and higher humidity. The towering peaks deflect moisture-bearing winds, causing them to precipitate as rain showers in summer and frequent heavy snows in winter.

Intermontane Basins and Plateaus Province

This province is the geographic interval between the Rocky Mountain and Pacific Coast cordilleras. Although less lofty than the flanking ranges, the region contains extensive plateaus and mountains that usually rise at least 3,000 feet above sea level. Its relief is tumbled, rugged, and difficult of human access, and the rivers have cut deep gorges—principally the Columbia, draining the north, and the Colorado, draining the south. The Intermontane Basins and Plateaus province has enough local variation to justify three descriptive subdivisions: the Columbian Plateau, the Colorado Plateau, and the Basin and Range Country.

The *Columbian Plateau*, a high, semi-arid tableland, covers eastern Washington and Oregon and southern and western Idaho. Its lava-derived soil sustains sagebrush and sparse forest growth. The *Colorado Plateau* extends across portions of Colorado, Utah, Arizona, and New Mexico. Its characteristics include rolling uplands, plateaus, some mountains, and deep canyons; the principal one, Grand Canyon, was carved by the Colorado River drainage.

The most extensive subregion of the Intermontane Basins and Plateaus province is the *Basin and Range Country*, which stretches from southern Oregon through portions of Idaho, Colorado, Utah, Arizona, eastern California, New Mexico, Texas, and most of Nevada. Many of the low-lying areas in this subregion are separated by highland dykes and have no external drainage. Between the Wasatch Mountains of Utah and the Sierra Nevadas of California is an extensive depression called the Great Basin. The Basin and Range Country has very low rainfall, generally less than ten inches a year. Its vegetation consists of bunch grass, sagebrush, and some timber on the higher slopes. The areas of the subregion in California, Nevada, Arizona, southern New Mexico, and southern Texas contain true desert.

Pacific Basin Province

The American West's landscape contains three additional geographic components—Pacific Mountains and Valleys, Arctic Plains and Highlands, and Pacific Islands—that may be considered as a single environmental unit, the Pacific Basin. The Pacific Mountains and Valleys and the Arctic Plains and Highlands are linked by a common cordillera; and both these regions and the Pacific island section are washed by the Pacific and form a sort of forward basin for this vast water hemisphere. In addition, the geographic components comprising the Pacific Basin province share a common cultural heritage as the last frontier of the American West.

The *Pacific Mountains and Valleys region* lies to the west of the Intermontane Basins and Plateaus province. Fronting the ocean from the Gulf of California to the Arctic Circle is the province's major component, the Coast Range. It extends along the California coast, continues through Oregon and Washington, and bends into Alaska. Coast Range elevation varies from about 5,000 feet—with an occasional 10,000-foot summit—in southern California, to nearly 10,000 feet in Oregon and Washington. The Coast Range is called the Cascades in Oregon and Washington, where its peaks include the spectacular Mount Rainier, 14,410 feet, and Mount Hood, 11,245 feet. On the Alaskan shore, the Coast Range juts abruptly out into the sea, its fjordlike peaks often exceeding 10,000 feet. North of the Alaskan Panhandle, glaciers descend the Coast Range and extend out into the Pacific Ocean.

Like connective tissues, the Klamath Mountains of northern California and other interesting highland systems link the Coast Range with the inland ranges. Besides linking the Coastal Range and the Sierra Nevadas, the Klamath range marks the beginning of the Cascades cordillera and, like a giant highland dyke, separates the Central Valley of California from the Willamette Valley of Oregon. In the southern interior is the high and rugged Sierra Nevada range; one of its peaks, Mount Whitney, rises to nearly 15,000 feet. In California the Coast Range and the Sierra Nevadas separate to form the Central Valley. This world-famous agricultural region, 50 miles wide and 500 miles long, is drained by the Sacramento and San Joaquin rivers, which empty into San Francisco Bay.

Climatic conditions vary among the different sections of the Pacific Mountains and Valleys region and produce varied flora schemes. In the arid south, succulents, thorny shrubs, and dwarf trees—chaparral-type growth—prevail in the lowlands, while non-deciduous forests cover the highlands. Advancing up the Pacific shore, aridity gives way to marine West Coast climatic influences. Cool summers, mild winters, and abundant rainfall nourish lush and varied vegetative cover. Thick coniferous softwood forests carpet the mountains, and rank grasses grow in the valleys. One of the world's botanical wonders, the giant, ancient redwood forests, grow in the highlands of northern California.

Alaska, the nation's forty-ninth state, shares the *Arctic Plains and*

Highlands region with Canada. The largest American state, it has a variety of natural features. The Coast Range, a strip often 100 miles deep, rims the Alaskan littoral as far north as the Bering Straits; it includes Mount Mc-Kinley, North America's highest mountain at 20,320 feet. The Bering Strait area is a mix of mountains and glaciers, some of the glaciers exceeding in size the nation's smallest state.

Alaska's vast interior consists of plains, intermontane basins, and plateaus and is drained by the Yukon River. The Brooks Range, an extension of the Rocky Mountain system, flanks the Alaskan interior on the north. This cordillera is about eighty miles wide, with peaks varying in elevation from 3,000 feet in the Bering Straits area to over 9,000 feet near the Canadian border on the east. Farthest north of the Alaskan geographic zones is the crescent-shaped Arctic coastal plain. Much of interior Alaska is covered with tundra-vegetation—mosses, lichens, sedges, hardy grasses, and low-growing shrubs. Dense coniferous forests cover the lowland interior and the Coast Range, except on the Aleutian Islands, which are nearly devoid of trees but abound in grasses and shrubs.

The only portion of Alaska with a mild climate is the southern coast, where marine West Coast influences apply. Much of Alaska's interior is in the tundra belt; this area, which averages from one to four months of above-freezing temperatures a year, is characterized by permanently frozen subsoil. No month of the year has an average temperature above fifty degrees. South of the tundra zone is a belt of subarctic climate, with long cold winters and brief cool summers.

Finally, situated 2,100 nautical miles west of San Francisco, is the outermost section of the Pacific Basin province, the *Pacific Islands region* or the Hawaiian archipelago, known in history as the Sandwich Islands. The nation's fiftieth state encompasses 6,424 square miles on eight volcanic and coral islands that rise from oceanic depths of nearly 20,000 feet. Hawaii, Oahu, Kauai, Niihau, Maui, Molokai, and Lanai are the principal islands of the archipelago, with the Big Island—Hawaii—containing 62 percent of the land area. The topography is primarily rugged upland. Most of the islands boast peaks of 3,000 to 5,000 feet, snow-capped Mauna Kea on the island of Hawaii rising to 13,784 feet. Slender valleys and narrow coastal plains make up the habitable areas of each island's geography. Volcanic eruptions, earthquakes, and *tsunamis*—great waves resulting from geological disturbances—occasionally occur in the islands. The islands are situated astride the trade winds that wash the windward slopes of the archipelago with abundant rains throughout the year. The exotic island flora includes luxuriant flowering plants, shrubs and trees, ferns, lichens, and thick tropical forests.

THE ABORIGINAL INHABITANTS OF THE WEST

The American West's natural milieu, continental and maritime (including Hawaii and Alaska), was populated in prediscovery times by three different aboriginal groups. They were the American Indians, the Polynesians, and the meso-Indians designated as Aleuts and Eskimos, that is, the Alaskan peoples.

American Indians

On the eve of the European intrusion, North American Indians numbered perhaps 1,500,000 and were grouped into over 200 tribes. No tribe had a system of writing, although several used pictographic line drawings and manual sign language for intertribal communication. Delawares and other Algonkian-speaking tribes used belts and strings of wampum—tiny colored shells—to communicate war, peace, and other tribal intentions. Scholars have identified over fifty different language families among the North American tribes.

Although the tribes of North America varied in culture, they had some common practices. Most had a religious system that included a concept of life after death and required elaborate mortuary rites in which weapons, tools, personal effects, and food were buried with the deceased. They shared a common creator and a number of lesser deities, and attempted to placate with rituals and specific kinds of behavior the variety of spirits, good and bad, that populated the natural universe. Indians used their religion to explain lightning, thunder, and other natural phenomena. Many tribes, notably the Natchez, Chickasaw, and Cherokee, supported an elite class of priests. These *hopoye*, or holy men, presided at religious rites and served as healers; because sickness was regarded as due to infiltration of the body by spirits from the natural world, the *hopoye* acted as exorcists.

Related to tribal religion were certain annual rites and festivals, ranging from the green corn festival, or busk, of the southeastern tribes, the water spirit fête of the Pacific Northwest tribes, to the sun dance of the Plains tribes. The purpose of the various annual rites was symbolic cleansing, personal purification, and tribal renewal. They required several days of fasting; in some cases the "black drink" was taken to induce vomiting and thus achieve internal cleansing. Dancing, then feasting followed the ritual purification. In the case of the sun dance, worshipers fasted for several days, danced, and endured self-torture in order to reach a trance state in which the communicant was believed to receive guidance for the future. The Natchez, Pawnee, and certain other tribes also practiced human sacrifice to propitiate a wrathful deity.

The social organization of the tribes was patriarchal although a combination matrilineal and patrilineal descent system, with the maternal line dominant, was prevalent. Most tribes consisted of a collection of clans, which were in turn composed of a cluster of families. The clan provided education, local government, identity for the individual, and regulation of marriage. Most tribes were exogamous, that is, they required that marital partners be from outside the clan. Marriage customs varied; most tribes permitted polygamy although monogamy was the rule. Tribal council members and leaders of the tribe were drawn from the prominent clans.

Mobility and status within the clan and the tribe were determined by talent in some art or craft, wisdom, or valor in battle.

Each tribe had a system of law based on custom to regulate behavior of tribal members, protect life and personal property, and safeguard clan and tribal integrity and honor. Clan elders served as a judicial body to pass judgment on offenses against the laws of the tribe; punishment, however, was often privately handled, particularly in cases of homicide.

One of the most unusual customs of the North American tribes was the "potlatch" practiced by the Pacific Northwest Indians. Tribal members gained the ultimate in prestige and stature by competitive giving. He who gave the most received the greatest glory. Often the "potlatch" occurred during a marriage feast or the naming ceremony for a son; the host, to gain honor, extended himself to give to guests the greater part of his personal property.

Each family in the tribe was a self-sufficient economic unit. Indians supported themselves by hunting, fishing, food gathering, agriculture, and intertribal trade. As every American school child learns, corn was the principal crop of the agricultural tribes occupying the territory from the Atlantic seaboard to the Mississippi Valley. It is less well known that many agricultural Indian communities of the desert Southwest produced corn by using irrigation. Other food crops included squash, melons, beans, and pumpkins. Some Great Lakes tribes also gathered wild rice.

The buffalo was the focus of the economy of the Kiowas, Comanches, Cheyennes, Arapahoes, and other tribes of the Great Plains. The animal's flesh provided food, and its thick hide was used for shelter—the cover for the mobile tipi—clothing, and footwear. Indian women fashioned implements from the bones; they also cleaned sections of the intestines, tied the ends, and used them as water containers.

California Indians subsisted largely on the acorn. Women and children gathered this fruit of the oak tree, and cleaned, leached, and crushed it into flour. The Northwest Coast tribes depended on fish, mostly salmon, sturgeon, and eels, which were trapped in weirs and preserved by smoking over slow-burning fires.

The simple technology of the North American Indians yielded a wide range of articles essential to and adequate for life in the natural state. They had no wheeled vehicles and no domesticated animals except the dog. From nature they drew herbs, leaves, and roots from which they compounded surprisingly effective cures for many ailments. Indian artisans contrived textiles, mats, baskets, covers and other household items from grasses, reeds, vegetable fibers, hickory withes, cattails, and other natural materials. Stone was sculptured into figures for worship, pipes, tools, and weapons. Clay was fashioned into bricks for buildings and into ceramic vases, pots, and other household utensils. Metalsmiths used gold, silver, and copper to fabricate exquisite ceremonial pieces and articles of adornment.

For the most part, the North American Indians were town dwellers.

Their shelters varied from the crude brush wickiups of California Indians to earth-covered lodges of the Pawnees of the Plains. The Algonkian-speaking tribes who lived on the Atlantic coast and north of the Ohio River constructed wigwams that were dome-shaped, framed with bent poles, and covered with woven mats of bark and cattails. Most of the buffalo hunting tribes of the Great Plains—the Kiowas, Comanches, Cheyennes, and Arapahoes—used the conical tipi, made of a pole-frame covered with hides. Many tribes of the desert Southwest constructed pueblos, multi-family dwellings of stone and sundried brick.

The wonders of North American aboriginal advance were the Indians of the Iroquois Confederation—the Seneca, Cayuga, Oneida, Mohawk, and Onandaga of the northern Appalachians. The Iroquois Confederation, under which the five nations resided in large towns in a planned urban arrangement, was functioning at the time of the European intrusion into the upper Hudson-Mohawk Valley. Each town was enclosed by a log pallisade. Iroquois society centered around the mother and her children; each family unit was known as a fireside. Collective firesides comprised clans. Women as mothers dominated the confederacy, for they headed the fireside groups or clans and named the male council members and other officials; the men thus held office at the pleasure of the matriarchy. Iroquois law, cohesiveness, and pride in the confederation made it the most awesome and successful Indian community in North America before the Anglo-American advance took over its territory.

Polynesians

The natives of Hawaii were bronze-skinned island dwellers of Polynesian stock. At the peak of their cultural development there were an estimated 200,000 Hawaiians on the islands. In some respects they were more advanced culturally than the North American Indians. The Hawaiian economy was based on fishing, agriculture, and interisland trade. The principal crops were sugar cane, a starchy root called taro, yams, bananas, and breadfruit. Island farmers intensively cultivated the narrow coastal strips of arable land through the construction of terraces and irrigation. The island milieu encouraged development of navigational skills; Hawaiian sailors coursed the Pacific waters in large twin-hulled outrigger sailing craft fitted with oars, guided by their mastery of celestial navigation and knowledge of prevailing winds and currents in the waters adjacent to their islands.

Hawaiian craftsmen had no metals but creatively used local woods, woven fibers, shell, bone, and stone for utensils, building, and for arts and crafts. Religious images were shaped from stone, bone, and wood. Because of the mild climate, dwellings and most public buildings were simple wood-framed structures with thatch roofs and woven mat walls. Stone was used to construct temples. A widely used cloth called kapa (tapa elsewhere in Polynesia) was made from the inner bark of the paper mulberry plant, but

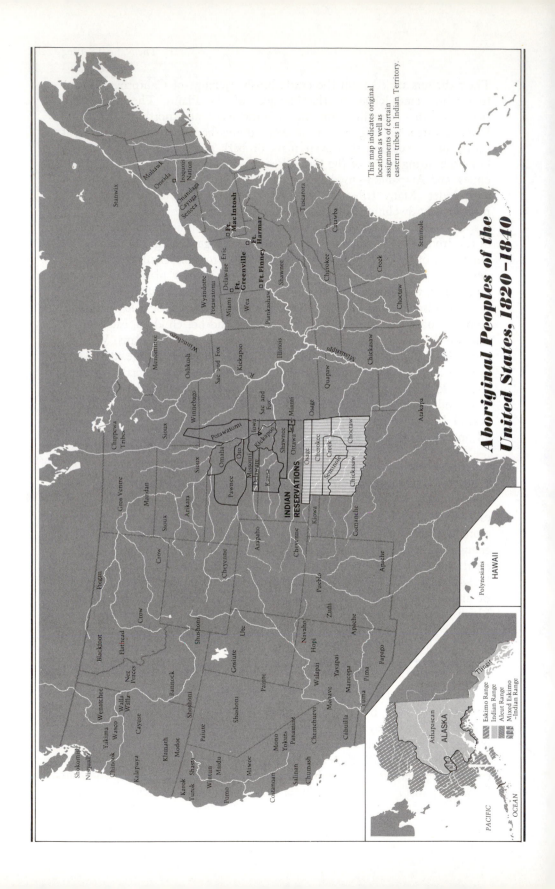

Aboriginal Peoples of the United States, 1820–1840

This map indicates original locations as well as assignments of certain eastern tribes in Indian Territory.

INDIAN RESERVATIONS

PACIFIC OCEAN

HAWAII

Polynesians

ALASKA

Athapascan

Tlingit

Eskimo Range
Indian Range
Aleut Range
Mixed Eskimo–Indian Range

the most decorative Hawaiian garments were exquisite featherwork cloaks or headgear fashioned from bird's plumage.

Hawaiians generally followed the matrilineal mode of descent and had a hierarchical social organization. By the time of discovery, island clans had rigidified into castes, and tribal organization on each island approached a form of primitive monarchy, with the tribal chiefs assuming the role of hereditary kings. In the prediscovery period, natives practiced plural marriage—both polygyny (more than one wife) and polyandry (more than one husband)—and among the *alii* (ruling caste), brother-sister marriage was not uncommon.

The basic unit of Hawaiian society was the family, and several families in a clustered residence area comprised a village. Each village was governed by male elders who served as law givers, enforcers, teachers of the young, and guardians of tradition. The Hawaiians had no system of writing, so instruction and tradition were transmitted orally by the village elders to the young.

Hawaiian government was an extension of the social caste system. Tribal chiefs became hereditary rulers, basing their right to rule on the claim of descent from the gods for themselves and their heirs. The island kings were supreme and exercised total power over their subjects. As an earthly agent of the gods, even the land belonged to them; the use of it was a privilege bestowed upon the people by the benevolent monarch.

Below the royal family in the Hawaiian social structure were the priests, or *kahunas*, who presided over the religious system. The priests' principal functions were to placate the island deities and to foretell the future through divination. The placating process often included human sacrifice. The Hawaiian religious system was polytheistic and animistic. The principal deities were Kane, Ku, Lono, and Kanaloa. Kane was the greatest force in the Hawaiian universe for he was the deity of light, in a sense the sun god. The Hawaiian myth of creation included the concept of the sky as the father and the earth the mother. The religious system included use of idols representing deities of the spiritual universe; these were placed in stone temples (*marae*), households, and used as fetishes to ward off evil spirits.

A class below the priests were the civil agents of island kings, courtiers, and leaders of the warrior army. Next in the Hawaiian social strata were the commoners—farmers, fishermen, artisans, and traders.

Alaskan Peoples

The aboriginal peoples of Alaska are both meso-Indians and Indians. The meso-Indian community is comprised of two groups, Aleuts and Eskimos; the principal difference between them is habitat. While the Aleuts occupy the Aleutian Island chain extending west from the Alaskan mainland, Eskimos reside mostly in the Arctic region of Alaska.

Aleuts and Eskimos are similar physically, exhibiting the characteristics of their Asian kinsmen and speaking a virtually common language.

In prediscovery times, these two meso-Indian communities subsisted by hunting the seal, walrus, sea lion, whale, and caribou, by fishing, and by gathering berries and roots. Their principal crafts consisted of weaving useful and attractive baskets from local plant materials and carving figures from bone and sea mammal ivory. Both Aleuts and Eskimos used the kayak and other water craft.

Harsh environment in the northland region required a simple social organization consisting of small family groups that migrated seasonally in quest of food. Just as simple was their polytheistic religion, which centered on a sea goddess. Annual festivals included dancing and singing, the participants wearing masks representing deities of their primal pantheon.

The Indian segment of the Alaskan aboriginal community included the Haidas, Tlingits, and Tinnehs or Denes. These tribes, consisting of scattered hunting families, occupied coastal islands and the Alaskan mainland between the Eskimo range of the north and the Aleut island domain in the west. They subsisted on salmon fishing, hunting, and gathering berries. The Tlingit particularly developed sophisticated skills in wood carving and fashioning long rounded timbers—totem poles—into animal and fish figures. For transportation, the Alaskan Indians used bark-covered canoes in summer and in winter sleds pulled by dogs over the ice and snow.

The differing physical environments of the various provinces of the West each required special adjustment and, at times, substantive alteration in attitudes and patterns of exploitation before effective human use, in the modern imperial context, could proceed. Although the native peoples preceded whites by many hundreds of years, it is the European and Anglo-American contest for dominion over this resource-rich territory that comprises the substance of Western history. In Chapter 3 we begin our discussion of the contributions of the earliest European explorers of the West—the Spanish and French.

SELECTED SOURCES

Western America's geographic setting is discussed by physical regions and provinces in Ralph H. Brown, *Historical Geography of the United States* (New York, 1948); Wallace W. Atwood, *The Physiographic Provinces of North America* (Boston, 1940); N. M. Fenneman, *Physiography of the Western United States* (New York, 1931); and C. Langdon White and Edwin J. Foscue, *Regional Geography of North America* (New York, 1943). *Walter P. Webb's *The Great Plains* (Boston, 1931) analyzes the impact of the natural environment on culture and technology.

A vast literature is available on the aboriginal peoples of Western America. On the subject of the American Indians examine Frederick W. Hodge, ed.,

* Available in paperback.

Handbook of American Indians North of Mexico (New York, 1910, 1959), 2 vols., for synoptic articles on each of the tribes. Surveys of Indian culture include *Harold E. Driver, *Indians of North America* (Chicago, 1961), and *Alvin Josephy, *The Indian Heritage of America* (New York, 1968). A superb study of cultural contact and conflict is *Edward W. Spicer, *Cycles of Conquest: The Impact of Spain, Mexico and the United States on the Indians of the Southwest, 1533–1960* (Tucson, 1962).

Readable descriptive accounts of Hawaii's aboriginal people include Edward Joesting, *Hawaii: An Uncommon History* (New York, 1972), and *Gavan Daws, *Shoal of Time: A History of the Hawaiian Islands* (New York, 1968). Alaska's native people are described in Stuart R. Tompkins, *Alaska: Promyshlennikik and Sourdough* (Norman, Okla., 1945), and H. W. Clark, *Alaska: The Last Frontier* (New York, 1939).

The Spanish Mission at Carmel, California

3

European Exploration and Early Settlement in Western America

SEEN from the vantage point of the Mississippi Valley in the sixteenth century the raw wilderness beauty of the American West stretched from the Appalachians to the Pacific. The drama of its discovery by Europeans was about to begin. The Spanish, the first to arrive, thrust north from their bases in Mexico (New Spain) and the Caribbean. *Conquistadores* explored the rim of Western America, from Florida's Gulf shore to the California-Oregon littoral. The early peregrinations of these adventurers, by land and sea, provided a strong basis for Spain's claim to much of Western America.

Spain's first important challenge for pre-eminence in Western America came from France. Thwarted in attempts to enter Spanish America from the lower Atlantic seaboard and the Caribbean in the seventeenth century, the French obliquely insinuated their way into Western America by way of the Canadian passage, moving from Quebec across the Great Lakes, threading the northern rivers flowing into the Mississippi, and following that stream to the Gulf of Mexico, thus cutting directly across Spanish territory in Western America.

Two later intruders were the British and the Russians, who arrived in the eighteenth century. The British challenge to Spanish and French dominion in Western America came from well established settlements on the Atlantic seaboard. The Russian intrusion followed the route probably used centuries earlier by the ancestors of the aboriginal Americans—from Siberia across the Aleutian chain into Alaska. In the late eighteenth century Russian traders established settlements in Alaska and ranged south along the Pacific shore to northern California in search of furs.

SPANIARDS IN WESTERN AMERICA

The Spanish, who were already established in the Caribbean by 1513, were the first Europeans to discover and develop Western America, and its early history must be told from their viewpoint. In the early days of Spanish presence in the Western Hemisphere, conquistadors ranged across Western America in search of fabled centers of wealth—the Seven Cities of Cibola, Cale, Apalache, and Gran Quivira. They also sought an east-west passage through the continent by water, the mythical Strait of Annian.

The Narváez Expedition

In 1528, an expedition commanded by Pánfilo de Narváez was exploring the Gulf shore of Florida in search of a landing close to Apalache, rumored to be an Indian community of high civilization and great wealth. Storms wrecked the two ships and scattered survivors on the beaches. In their search for Apalache the members of the Narváez expedition found no gold, only hostile Indians and a primeval wilderness of dark forests, impenetrable thickets, swamps, and death for most of those who had survived the shipwreck. In roughly made boats the survivors sailed west around the Gulf of Mexico, to land at Galveston Bay. Their numbers were further decimated by injury and disease, and one small party, consisting of Álvar Núñez Cabeza de Vaca, two Spaniards, and a black named Estevanico, roamed the Southwest for six years. Finally in 1536 they reached Culiacán, the most northerly Spanish settlement on the west coast of Mexico. Cabeza de Vaca's arrival in Mexico provoked much interest among Spanish officials, and his report of the lands to the north generated several new expeditions.

The De Soto Expedition

During the spring of 1539, an expedition consisting of 600 soldiers and commanded by Hernando de Soto landed at Tampa Bay. They too sought Apalache, a second native kingdom—Cale—reported to abound in pearls, and the Strait of Annian. De Soto led his men across the southern United States, striking the Mississippi River near Memphis. Crossing into Arkansas, they explored west perhaps as far as Little Rock, then returned to the Mississippi by way of the Arkansas River. At this point, De Soto died and the command fell to Luis de Moscoso. By this time the expedition had despaired of finding Cale or the water strait; their only hope was to discover a route through the wilderness of Western America to the Spanish settlements in Mexico. Moscoso struck a southwesterly course from the Mississippi River across Louisiana and into Texas; but he then turned eastward to return again to the Mississippi. There the ragged, dispirited survivors of the proud De Soto expedition constructed crude boats and drifted into the Gulf current; they arrived at Panuco, a Spanish settlement on the Mexican Gulf shore, in 1543.

The Coronado Expedition

In response to the interest generated by Cabeza de Vaca's report on the lands to the north, Viceroy Antonio de Mendoza directed Estevanico to reconnoiter the frontier of Spanish Mexico, preliminary to a planned large scale exploration. Accompanied by Friar Marcos—a Franciscan missionary—and several Indian guides, Estevanico set out from Culiacán in March 1539. After several weeks' march, the party arrived at the Zuñi pueblos, an extensive Indian settlement on the margins of western New Mexico, which Estevanico identified with the fabled Seven Cities of Cíbola. Indian guards killed Estevanico, but Marcos escaped and rushed back to the Spanish settlements to report their discovery. The Spanish embroidered Brother Marcos' account of the Zuñi pueblos: the large Indian settlement was transformed into a sparkling city in the wilderness, perhaps greater in size than Seville; its outer walls were constructed of gold, and its doors were covered with turquoise and were green like a forest!

Viceroy Mendoza gave the exploration assignment to Francisco Vásquez de Coronado, governor of the Mexican province of Nueva Galicia. Coronado's force, consisting of nearly 300 Spaniards and 1,000 Indians, set out from Compostela in northwestern Mexico in late February 1540. During the summer Coronado reached the Seven Cities of Cíbola, but the Zuñi people refused to receive the intruders. Thereupon the Spaniards stormed the city walls and occupied the settlement. To their great disappointment they found no gold, only food.

Establishing a base at Zuñi, Coronado dispatched exploring parties to check out Indian reports of other towns. One group found the Colorado River and the Grand Canyon. Despairing of finding wealth in that sector, Coronado led his men to Tiguex, a pueblo cluster near Albuquerque on the Rio Grande. At Tiguex he learned that far to the East lay a land called the Gran Quivira, where gold was so plentiful it was used to construct common utensils. The prospects of finding wealth stirred the Spaniards to resume their march. Coronado's column crossed the flat grassy plains of eastern New Mexico and Texas, turned north in western Oklahoma and, in July 1541, arrived at Quivira—a community of dome-shaped grass dwellings on the Arkansas River in central Kansas, inhabited by Wichita Indians. These sedentary people, conspicuous for their tattooed bodies, sustained themselves by agriculture, producing corn, beans, squash, and pumpkins, and by hunting the buffalo. A disappointed Coronado wrote his king, "What I am sure of is that there is not any gold nor any other metal in all that country."

Before departing for Tiguex and returning to Mexico Coronado met in council with the tribal leaders of Quivira. Later he wrote his king that the chiefs had taken an oath of fealty pledging their "obedience to Your Majesty and placing themselves under your Royal Lordship." By virtue of his council on the Arkansas, Coronado brought the western half of the Mississippi valley under Spanish dominion.

During the journey to Quivira and the return to Tiguex, Coronado observed other tribes, notably the Plains Apaches. These daring hunters roamed the grasslands, preying on the buffalo herds. He noted that unlike the tribes along the Rio Grande and Arkansas, the Apaches planted no crops, but sustained themselves on what he called hump-backed cows. The Apaches were reported to use dogs hitched to travois poles for transporting their buffalo-hide shelters and other camp equipment. Coronado also told his king that away from the gullies and rivers, wood was scarce on the Plains, and his men had to cook their rations of buffalo meat over buffalo dung fires.

Pacific Coast Explorations

By 1540, Spanish explorers had been probing the bays and inlets of Pacific waters north of Mexico for some time. Francisco de Ulloa, leading three vessels north in 1539, lost one ship but reached the head of the Gulf of California, proving that the ribbon of land forming the gulf was a peninsula and not an island as had been speculated. He also reconnoitered the outer coast of the peninsula. To support Coronado's reconnaissance of the northern frontier, Viceroy Mendoza had ordered an expedition by sea. Hernando de Alarcón commanded the sea-born support arm of the expedition, which consisted of two ships. Sailing from Acapulco, Alarcón reached the head of the Gulf of California and proceeded up the Colorado River for an estimated eighty-five leagues.

Spanish exploration of the Pacific coast continued, the primary goal still being to find the hoped-for water strait through the hemisphere. In 1542 Juan Rodríguez Cabrillo sailed from Navidad. He found San Diego Bay and several other anchorages, including Drake's Bay and the Santa Barbara channel, where he died. His pilot, Manuel Ferrelo, sailed north in 1543 and explored the Oregon Coast. These explorations had somehow failed to reveal Monterey and San Francisco bays.

This land and sea reconnaissance of Western America's rimland was disappointing to the Spaniards, for their bold efforts had yielded no centers of wealth. However, they did produce more exact knowledge of the land and people north of Mexico. Also Spain's discovery and exploration of the vast territory from Florida to the Pacific provided the legal basis for its claim to exclusive dominion over the entire northland.

Another result of this early Spanish incursion into Western America was the introduction to the Indian of European ways and things. The horse had a particularly drastic impact on the lifestyle of the Plains Indian. Animals escaping from the Spanish *remuda* (a sort of portable corral), added to by later expeditions, seeded the coastal areas of Western America with horses. At first Indians hunted and ate these animals. But as they gradually learned to manage and ride them, the men became more effective buffalo hunters and more deadly warriors. Horses also greatly increased the tribes' mobility, as horses were substituted for dogs to pull travois poles laden with household impedimenta.

Spanish Settlements in New Mexico

Near the middle of the sixteenth century, prospectors found rich gold and silver deposits north of Mexico City. For a time developing the mines so absorbed the Spaniards that they neglected their northern territory. But intrusions by the French and English, and later the Russians, into Western America led the Spanish to consider their northern territory as a defensive buffer to insulate the rich mines in Mexico from the threat of foreign attack. Thus for the next 250 years, Spanish settlement in the northern territory was for the most part in response to foreign threats. It became a challenge and response situation. The principal motivation for establishing Spanish presence and power by settlement—from the Florida Gulf shore, around the lower Mississippi Valley, and into Texas, New Mexico, and the California coast—was to checkmate intruding foreign powers.

The English were among the early intruders in Spanish territory. Their predatory thrusts aroused the Spaniards and precipitated what was to become the inevitable Spanish response. The intrepid Elizabethan, Sir Francis Drake, sailed his *Golden Hind* into Pacific waters during the 1570s. He plundered several Spanish towns on the Pacific shore and, in 1579, explored Drake's Bay, north of San Francisco, naming the area New Albion. Then in 1586 Thomas Cavendish coursed along Drake's Pacific route. In California coastal waters he captured, plundered, and burned the Manila Galleon, the Spanish supply ship plying between the Philippine Islands and the Pacific ports of New Spain.

Spanish officials were determined to establish bases in their northern territory to protect the Manila Galleon, to ward off the threat of English settlement on the Pacific coast, and to determine by additional exploration whether, as some feared, Drake and other English mariners had found the water strait. Two extensions of the Spanish presence—one by sea, the other by land into the north—occurred at the beginning of the seventeenth century. The former was undertaken by Sebastián Vizcaíno. Sailing out of Acapulco with three ships in 1602, he explored the coast north of San Diego Bay. Among his discoveries was Monterey Bay, which was designated as an intermediate port for the Manila Galleon.

The extension of Spanish presence by land was undertaken in 1598. The settlement line of New Spain had reached Santa Barbara in northern Mexico, and Spaniards were moving down the Conchos River to the Rio Grande. In 1581 a party of nine soldiers, missionaries, and traders, led by Fray Augustin Rodríguez, a Franciscan, ascended the Rio Grande and visited the pueblos. They then marched east to the plains, thence west to Zuñi, and returned to Santa Barbara. Two friars remained in the north. The following year another group, led by Antonio de Espejo, returned to

New Mexico, explored near Zuñi, and continued westward into Arizona where, Espejo claimed, he found silver deposits. Several Spanish explorers roamed the northland during the 1590s searching for Annian and Quivira; they included Gutierrez de Humana, who explored western Kansas and Nebraska.

In 1598 the viceroy of New Spain commissioned Juan de Oñate captain-general and directed him to colonize the upper Rio Grande region. Oñate's column included 130 soldiers, several families, Franciscan missionaries, and, reportedly, 7,000 head of livestock. He led his followers north to El Paso and proceeded up the Rio Grande where he established San Juan on the Chama River. Oñate sent out several expeditions from San Juan in search of the Strait of Annian and the Gran Quivira; in 1601 he personally led a party of seventy Spaniards across the Plains into western Oklahoma and Kansas in a fruitless quest for Quivira. In 1608 he was replaced by a royal governor, and the following year Santa Fe was founded. It became the capital for the Spanish settlements on the upper Rio Grande.

In sum total, the Spanish response to the English threat had led to only a moderate extension into Western America. Spain had established a limited control over the California coast as far north as Monterey Bay, and had extended settlements up the Rio Grande into the southern Rocky Mountains. Later, Spain would face a renewed threat of English intrusion into its northern territory; but it would come from the East by way of the English colonies on the Atlantic seaboard and in the Caribbean. Meanwhile, French colonial extensions in the New World were a more immediate threat to Spanish dominion in Western America.

THE FRENCH IN WESTERN AMERICA

Several attempts by French Protestants to establish settlements in the Carolinas and Florida around the middle of the sixteenth century caused the Spanish to found St. Augustine in 1565 as a base for expelling intruders. Spanish defensive coastal stations thus extended from St. Augustine around the Florida peninsula and along the Gulf. Missionaries and settlers from the shore stations moved into the interior; one of the farthest outposts was situated on the headwaters of the Chattahoochee River in northern Georgia. Meanwhile the French, searching for a foothold in the New World, thwarted by the Spanish in the South Atlantic and Gulf, and blocked along the Atlantic seaboard by emerging English and Dutch colonies, penetrated the continent from the far north by way of the St. Lawrence River.

The Western Fur Trade

From Quebec, French Jesuit missionaries and traders pressed west along the Great Lakes in the sixteenth and seventeenth centuries, establishing mission stations among the Huron, Algonquin, and Ottawa tribes. For a time in the 1640s and 50s French attempts to extend trading and mission activity to the Miamis, Illinois, Sac, Fox, Kickapoo, Potawatomi, and other tribes residing between the Great Lakes and the Ohio River were throttled by the intruding Iroquois Confederation.

The Mohawk, Oneida, Onondaga, Cayuga, and Seneca tribes, who resided in the Lake Champlain country, were fierce in war and singular in politics, and they were integrated into a powerful association known as the Iroquois Confederation. Dutch traders from New Amsterdam, eager to gain control of the rich fur-trading territory between the Great Lakes and the Ohio River, supplied these Iroquois warriors with arms and sent them into the West to expel the French-oriented tribes. The contest for control of this area, known as the Iroquois Wars, lasted from 1642 to 1653, when the aggressor tribes at last withdrew to their Eastern homeland.

Cessation of the Iroquois menace led to a rapid extension of French missions and trading in the Northwest, and the momentum of French development there eventually carried them across the Mississippi River into Minnesota in quest of new pelt areas. The French tide also flowed south, penetrating to the heartland of Spanish America.

Reconnaissance of the Mississippi River

In 1673, Louis Joliet and Jacques Marquette voyaged from Green Bay, by way of the Fox and Wisconsin rivers, to the Mississippi River, then followed that stream to the mouth of the Arkansas River before returning to the northland. They speculated that the Mississippi emptied into the Gulf of Mexico. If this were true, they realized, they had found a water strait through the continent—not the mythical east-west passage, but a north-south concourse via the St. Lawrence River, Great Lakes, and Mississippi River to the Gulf of Mexico. This prospect provoked great excitement among the French in Canada.

Robert Cavalier, Sieur de la Salle, who had expanded the French fur trade into the Ohio Valley after the Iroquois Wars, saw in the Joliet-Marquette discovery the means to drive a wedge through the heart of Spanish territory in Western America. In late 1681 and early 1682 he organized an expedition of twenty-three men to explore the Mississippi all the way to the Gulf. On the basis of that expedition, he claimed for France the vast Mississippi Valley, naming it Louisiana. Moreover, he devised a plan for occupying and exploiting the rich resources of Louisiana, including founding a fortified settlement at the mouth of the Mississippi River. Guarding the strategic Mississippi Valley from foreign attack, it would provide a base from which to settle the territory between French posts in the Northwest and the Gulf of Mexico, and—situated in a milder climate than the northern French settlements—it would give French traders a year-round export depot. Finally, the military station would place France in an advantageous position to control Gulf shipping and serve as a military base for invading mineral-rich New Spain.

La Salle journeyed to France, received royal approbation for his scheme, and during the summer of 1684 returned to the New World with four ships and an estimated 400 settlers. But, arriving in the Gulf, he failed to locate the mouth of the Mississippi, and during November he landed on the Texas coast at Matagorda Bay.

It had been arranged that Henry de Tonty, who had been associated with La Salle in the fur trade in the Northwest, would lead a French party down the Mississippi to the Gulf and join the expedition from France. Tonty searched for La Salle during 1685 but was unable to contact his leader. Nonetheless, while in the lower Mississippi Valley, Tonty established a post on the Arkansas River near the mouth.

At Matagorda Bay the colonists endured great hardship. La Salle, who led several unsuccessful exploring parties around the Gulf in search of the mouth of the Mississippi, was slain by his disenchanted followers in 1686. Survivors of the ill-fated expedition suffered various fates: many perished from disease and hunger; others were killed by Texas Indians. In 1687, three years after they had set out from France, a small party made its way to the Mississippi and followed it to the French settlements in the Northwest.

French Gulf Settlement

Although La Salle had failed in his attempt to breach the Spanish dominions in Western America, his Louisiana plan continued to intrigue French officials. In 1699, Pierre Lemoyne d'Iberville established fortified settlements on the Gulf, at Biloxi—Fort Maurepas—and at the mouth of the Mobile River—Fort Biloxi.

French activity in the Gulf of Mexico caused Spain to show fresh interest in that portion of its northern frontier; soon reports of French plans to colonize the area around the mouth of the Mississippi River filtered into Madrid. The intelligence was relayed to the viceroy of New Spain who, in 1698, sent Andres de Arriola to establish a military station at Pensacola to guard against the expected foreign intrusion.

Thus, by 1700, the setting for a diplomatic and military contest for control of Western America was nearly completed. Spanish claim to the territory north of Mexico had been successfully challenged by France, whose strength in the Mississippi Valley was increasing each year. French settlements in the country between the Great Lakes and the Ohio River were firmly established. French fur traders had even crossed the Mississippi and were ranging west across Minnesota to the upper Missouri River.

From their settlements in the West Indies and on the Atlantic seaboard, the English too were preparing to enter Western America to challenge both Spanish and French control. And, from the far Northwest, Russian traders soon would sweep across Siberia, thread the Aleutian chain, attach the Alaskan littoral, and probe southward into Spanish California. Since Spain's principal concern was to protect the rich mines of Mexico,

Spanish officials responded to these various foreign intrusions by seeding military and mission settlements around the rim of Western America from the Florida Gulf shore into Texas, and northwesterly into Arizona and California.

SELECTED SOURCES

General studies of Spanish and French exploration and colonization in North America include *Carl O. Sauer, *Sixteenth Century North America: The Land and the People As Seen by Europeans* (Berkeley, Calif., 1971), and Herbert E. Bolton and Thomas M. Marshall, *The Colonization of North America* (New York, 1935).

The beginnings of the Spanish empire in North America are discussed in *F. A. Kirkpatrick, *The Spanish Conquistadors* (New York, 1949); Herbert E. Bolton, *Coronado: *Knight of the Pueblos and Plains* (New York, 1949) and *The Spanish Borderlands* (New Haven, 1921); and *Charles Gibson, *Spain in America* (New York, 1966).

Works on the beginnings of the French empire in North America include George M. Wrong, *The Rise and Fall of New France* (New York, 1928), 2 vols.; Morris Bishop, *Champlain, the Life of Fortitude* (New York, 1948); Francis Parkmam, *Pioneers of France in the New World* (Boston, 1865) and *La Salle and the Discovery of the Great West* (Boston, 1889); Francis B. Steck, *The Joliet-Marquette Expedition, 1673* (Washington, 1928); W. B. Munro, *Crusaders of New France* (New Haven, 1918); N. W. Caldwell, *The French in the Mississippi Valley, 1740–1750* (Urbana, Ill., 1941); and *W. J. Eccles, *The Canadian Frontier, 1534–1760* (New York, 1969).

* Available in paperback.

HISTOIRE
DE
LAMERIQUE SEPTENTRIONALE

I.B. Scotin Sculp.

French Traders in North America

4

The European Contest for Western America, 1700-1763

Dᴜʀɪɴɢ the period between 1700 and 1763 Western America was the scene of expansion and conflict. The principals were Spain, France, Great Britain, and the aboriginal allies of each. The French continued to found trading and agricultural settlements along the Mississippi River and its tributaries. They ranged east to the Appalachians and west to the Rocky Mountains, vigorously incorporating the Indian tribes and their commerce into the French orbit. Although Spain responded forcefully by strengthening and extending its military stations on the northern frontier of New Spain, the French assault on Spanish dominion appeared triumphant until the British, from their seaboard colonies, attempted to break through the Appalachian barrier and share in the rich commerce of Western America. This breach threatened France's eastern flank, and the French were forced to divert more and more of their strength to check the British advance.

The challenge, pressure, and increasing propinquity of Spanish, French, and British settlements in Western America generated a series of bloody wars—some minor, others major—for control of this vast geographic prize. At the end of a major contest in 1763, France was ejected from Western America, leaving only the British and the Spanish to compete for all the territory between the Appalachians and the Pacific. Russia, on the fringe of Western America far to the north in Alaska, was not at this time regarded as a serious threat.

THE SPANISH COLONIAL ESTABLISHMENT

The Northern frontier of New Spain was developed by missionaries, soldiers, and civilian settlers. But it was generally the missionary who was the vanguard of Spanish civilization, and representatives of the Jesuit, Franciscan, and Dominican orders pioneered in establishing Spanish presence in Western America under sometimes appalling conditions. The typical missionary settled in an area populated by an Indian tribe and worked at converting the aborigines to Christianity. His mission station included a church, residences, and buildings for instructing Indian children and storing grain and other supplies. If the Indians were sedentary and mostly dependent upon agriculture for subsistence, the missionary simply sought to improve local practices. If the tribesmen were hunters, he attempted to persuade them to settle at the mission station and take up agriculture.

Besides Christian teachings, clerics at the mission stations gave instruction in vocational arts, agriculture, and animal husbandry. The Spanish missions were among the first European urban centers in Western America, and there native peoples were first exposed to European culture and technology. An important collateral benefit to Spain was that the mission often established dominion over a territory and people without the necessity of military conquest.

Another type of Spanish settlement in Western America was the presidio, a fortification with mixed military and civilian settlers that was established to guard some strategic point threatened by a foreign power or by recalcitrant Indians. A third type of settlement was the lay colony, populated by civilians following in the wake of the mission and presidio extension. These Iberian settlers opened farms and ranches in the northland, prospected and mined gold and silver, and traded with the Indian tribes.

Rio Grande Settlements

For several years the most substantial Spanish extension into Western America occurred along the upper Rio Grande in New Mexico near Santa Fe. Franciscan missionaries had established several missions among the Indian communities on the Rio Grande and its tributaries, and by 1620 these clerical pioneers had converted nearly 15,000 Indians. Missionaries introduced stockraising and a more diversified agriculture. Grain, cotton, and fruit flourished in mission fields, orchards, and vineyards. Franciscan teachers imparted rudiments of learning and vocational skills to Indian youth. The Indians of New Mexico, although primarily under the jurisdiction of the missionaries, had some political responsibilities as Spanish subjects. Among other obligations they were required to render annual grain and labor tribute to government officials at Santa Fe.

Santa Fe, New Mexico's capital, was the principal Spanish town in the northern frontier. By 1660, over 2,500 Europeans lived on the upper Rio Grande, from Taos and Santa Fe on the north along the Rio Grande to El Paso on the south. The Iberian settlers farmed, raised livestock, prospected and mined limited quantities of gold and silver, and engaged in the fur trade. Traders roamed the Southern Rockies in quest of pelts. They explored the Great Basin and opened trade with tribes living on the western slope of the Rocky Mountains. Each year Spanish settlers in New Mexico transported thousands of bales of furs by pack train south to Vera Cruz for export to Spain.

But in 1680 Indians on the upper Rio Grande revolted against Spanish rule. Popé, an Indian medicine man of the San Juan Pueblos, led the successful insurrection. Popé claimed that the Indians were mercilessly exploited by the Spaniards for labor, that they objected to the annual grain tribute and resented the missionaries who had overthrown their tribal gods. Over 400 Spaniards died in the outbreak, and approximately 2,000 survivors fled south to El Paso.

Gradually the Spanish reconquered the territory along the Rio Grande north of El Paso, and finally, in 1692, Diego de Vargas, governor of the Spanish settlements on the Rio Grande, undertook the complete reconquest of the area evacuated twelve years earlier. The fury of his invading army drove the Pueblo Indians from their strongholds and forced their leaders to capitulate. De Vargas completely restored Spanish rule on the upper Rio Grande when he stormed the Santa Fe government buildings, which had been used as a fortress by Indian defenders. Counter-resistance by Indian recalcitrants continued as late as 1696, but each outbreak was summarily crushed.

After the Iberian return to New Mexico, missionaries from stations on the Rio Grande searched in all directions for new areas in which to spread the Gospel. Squads of soldiers explored, mapped, and prepared reports on the Plains to the east, the mountains to the north and the rough highland-desert country to the west. Stockraising, farming, and mining expanded among the lay settlements of New Mexico, producing a substantial increase in population and number of towns. Albuquerque was founded in 1706. By 1760 nearly 8,000 Spaniards resided in fourteen towns on the upper Rio Grande, and an estimated 4,000 Spaniards populated the settlements in the El Paso district of Texas.

The expansion of the settlement zone in New Mexico put pressure on several Indian tribes roaming the perimeter of the Rio Grande pueblo region. These included Navajoes to the west, Utes to the north, Apaches to the southeast, and Comanches eastward on the Great Plains. Mounted bands of warriors from these tribes, mobile and deadly, regularly raided Spanish settlements and missions, plundering goods, taking captives, and stealing horses and mules. The relations of the Spaniards with these tribes alternated between peace and war. During periods of peace, Comanches, Utes, and other tribesmen came to the annual trading fair at Taos to exchange pelts, buffalo hides, and captives for horses, mules, and trinkets. In periods of war, the tribes were the quarry of wide-ranging Spanish columns on punitive expeditions.

Gulf Settlements

Spanish presence around the Gulf shore from the Florida peninsula to the mouth of the Mississippi had been thinly maintained since the

1560s by missionaries, traders, and an occasional amphibious landing of troops to investigate reports of foreign intrusion. The principal tribes contacted by Spanish missionaries and traders during this time were the Appalachees and Creeks, and, occasionally, the Cherokees. When officials in New Spain heard of French plans to build a military station near the mouth of the Mississippi, they directed the founding of Pensacola in 1698. This base soon became the focus of Spanish defensive activities in the western Gulf of Mexico. It also served as the assignment point of missionaries and a supply depot for traders trafficking among the southeastern and south central interior tribes.

Texas Settlements

The continuing French threat also led Spain to develop a defensive system in Texas. In 1689 a Spanish patrol on reconnaissance of the Texas Gulf coast found the remains of the abandoned LaSalle colony at Matagorda Bay. The next year Spanish missionaries founded two stations among the Asinai Indians on the Nucces River. Texas was established as a province of New Spain in 1691, and Domingo de Terán was named governor. He explored eastern Texas as far as the Red River, looking for sites for defensive outposts. When, in 1702, the Asinai Indians rose against the missionaries, they withdrew and Spain abandoned for a time serious attempts to establish a defensive colony in southeastern Texas. However, missionaries persisted in their attempts to convert the tribes of south Texas, regularly crossing the Rio Grande on missionary reconnaissances.

In 1715, further reports of French expansion up the Red River from the Gulf led Spain to reoccupy Texas. Domingo Ramón was placed in charge of an expedition of Franciscan missionaries, soldiers, and settlers, which in 1716 founded defensive works, pioneer settlements, and missions on the Angelina and Neches rivers among the Asinai Indians. Settlers, soldiers, and missionaries continued to enter Texas, and the following year additional mission stations and settlements were established on the eastern border of Texas across from the French base at Natchitoches, Louisiana. In 1718, Martin de Alarcón, new Spanish governor of Texas, founded San Antonio, which became the military, commercial, and ecclesiastical center for Spanish Texas. Los Adaes on the Louisiana-Texas border served for a time as the administrative capital of the Texas province. By 1750, 2,000 Spaniards resided in Texas.

Spanish officials found that in order for Texas to be an effective barrier to the French advance from Louisiana the internal threat posed by several Indian tribes, including the Tonkawas, Apaches, and Comanches, had to be reduced. Around 1750 the establishment of three stations and a presidio on the San Gabriel River among the Tonkawas pacified that tribe. In the early years of Spanish extension into Texas the Apaches too had challenged European control of the country northwest of San Antonio; but the invasion of their territory by the fierce Comanches caused the Apaches to appeal to the Spanish for protection. The Spaniards responded in the early 1750s by establishing a mission and presidio among the Apaches on the San Saba River.

Pimería Alta Settlements

A fourth area in Western America receiving Spanish attention during this period was situated northwest of the Mexican settlements and called Pimería Alta; it encompassed what is now northern Sonora, Mexico, and southern Arizona. In the early years, Pimería Alta was designated a Jesuit missionary province, and Father Eusebio Kino was the missionary-pioneer. From his base at Mission Dolores in the upper Sonora Valley, he labored for twenty-five years among the Pimería Alta tribes—particularly the Pimas. He converted an estimated 5,000 Indians. Kino first entered Arizona in 1691 on a missionary reconnaissance of the Santa Cruz and San Pedro river valleys. In 1700 he founded San Xavier del Bac Mission, which served as a base for Kino and his successors to extend Spanish settlement to the Colorado River.

In 1767, the Jesuits were expelled from New Spain, and Franciscan missionaries took their place in Pimería Alta. Soon after 1750 settlers entered the mission region of Arizona; where water was available for irrigation, they established farms and ranches and developed silver mines.

THE FRENCH COLONIAL ESTABLISHMENT

Spain's principal adversary for control of Western America in the early eighteenth century was France. The French challenge initially came on a north-south concourse, linking their Canadian and Gulf settlements with the Mississippi River. Once firmly established in this strategic zone, they surged west to challenge the Spaniards on the Rio Grande and east to consolidate control of territory abutting the Appalachians.

Northwest Settlements

From their Canadian towns French traders swept across the Great Lakes into the Northwest, developing a flourishing fur trade as far south as the Ohio River. On the narrows connecting Lake Huron and Lake Erie they founded Detroit in 1701. In 1699 and 1700 traders and missionaries established Cahokia and Kaskaskia in the Illinois country near the Mississippi River. Another French settlement grew up at Fort Miami, to guard the strategic portage between the Maumee and the Wabash rivers. Vincennes became a thriving post on the Wabash, and Fort de Chartres, established in 1720, protected French shipping on the upper Mississippi River.

Mississippi Valley Settlements

France's first overt challenge to Spain's northern frontier was the establishment, in 1699, of Biloxi at the mouth of the Mississippi. From this fledgling station French settlement fingered north, eventually linking up with the towns of the Northwest. In 1714 French pioneers erected Fort Toulouse on the Alabama River to serve as a depot for commerce with the Creeks. From there traders floated bales of furs downriver to Mobile. New Orleans was established in 1718 and four years later replaced Biloxi as the capital of French Louisiana.

A royal patent, issued in 1717, gave the Company of the Indies the monopoly for developing the resources of Louisiana. Capitalized at 100,000,000 livres, this enterprise, headed for a time by the fabulous Scotsman John Law, had complete economic and political authority over Louisiana. Under company direction the fur trade with the Indian tribes continued, but agriculture and mining were also encouraged. A steady stream of French emigrants flowed to Louisiana, and agricultural settlements grew up along the Yazoo and other tributaries of the Mississippi River.

By the mid-1720s, the European population in Louisiana exceeded 5,000. French planters imported several thousand black slaves during this period, and it is estimated that 500 blacks were imported from Santo Domingo to labor in the lead mines near the Maramec River in Missouri. The Company of the Indies also recruited 200 French miners for the lead fields. Regular shipments of furs and cargoes of grain, lead, and salt coursed down the Mississippi valley to New Orleans and Biloxi for export to France. John Law's grandiose scheme for tapping the rich resources of Louisiana— the Mississippi Bubble—faltered and burst in 1720; but the development of Louisiana and the extension of French dominion, east and west, continued.

Louisiana Fur Trade

Like their Spanish counterparts, French missions—managed by Jesuits, Carmelites, and Capuchins—were often the first settlements on the expanding French frontier. Also in the vanguard was the trader. During the early eighteenth century he probed the margins of Spanish America from French settlements around the Great Lakes, French towns in the Illinois country, and the westward-moving settlements in Louisiana.

In 1713 Louis de St. Denis established a settlement at Natchitoches on the Red River to service trading expeditions into Texas. His energetic enterprises and brazen trespass of Spanish territory aroused officials in New Spain and stirred them to direct the permanent occupation of Texas. But the region west of Natchitoches was vast, the Spanish defensive line was pathetically thin, and French traders found it easy to elude Spanish military patrols to traffic with the Texas tribes. From their base at Natchitoches the French could trade and explore west to the Rio Grande River.

In 1719 Bernard de la Harpe made a commercial reconnaissance from New Orleans up the Red River and thence across the Kiamichi highlands to the Arkansas River near the mouth of the Canadian River. The same year saw the colonization of the Arkansas Post at the head of the Arkansas.

La Harpe found the area teeming with the settlements of an agricultural people called Taovayas, who resided in domed dwellings covered with woven grass mats. He and his party were well received. The Taovayas showered gracious hospitality and benevolence on the French visitors. La Harpe's gifts from tribal leaders included thirty fine buffalo robes and an eight-year-old Apache captive. La Harpe commented in his journal that the Taovaya captors "had eaten a finger from each hand," of the boy "a mark that one was destined to serve one day as food to these cannibals." La Harpe added that a Taovaya spokesman "told me that he was sorry to have only one slave to present to me, that if I had arrived sooner he would have given me the seventeen that they had eaten in a public feast. I thanked him for his good will, regretting that I had not arrived in time to save the lives of these poor unfortunates."

La Harpe regarded this heavily populated middle border area—encompassing parts of present-day Texas, Oklahoma, and Kansas—as of strategic importance for advancing French commercial interests west to the Rio Grande. He stated in his journal that "there is not in the whole colony of Louisiana an establishment more useful to make than on the branch of this river not only because of the mild climate, the fertility of the land, the richness of the minerals, but also because of the possibility of trade that one might introduce with Spain and New Mexico. If one could control the trade which the Spanish carry on with the (Comanches). . . . one could become master of this region." [1]

In response to La Harpe's recommendation, French traders established posts on the Arkansas, Canadian, and Red rivers; Taovayas collected around the French settlements and became hunters of hides and furs and middlemen for carrying French goods to the Comanches on the Plains. Of all the French *entradas* into Spain's western domain, the Arkansas-Canadian-Red focus was the most productive. Each year, traders exported bales of beaver, otter, mink, and muskrat furs, tanned buffalo hides, and delicately soft buffalo robes from Ferdinandina, Twin Villages, and other settlements in the middle border country. The fur and hide cargoes moved to New Orleans by flatboats and pirogues via Arkansas Post or Natchitoches. Traders in remote regions used pack trains of horses and mules to reach the river landings on the Arkansas and Red rivers. Each season French traders returned with a new supply of knives, beads, axes, hatchets, hoes, cloth, blankets, mirrors, guns, paint, and other trade goods for their Taovaya middlemen to carry to the Comanches.

La Harpe's design for occupying this middle border region was intended principally to benefit commercial interests at New Orleans, but Frenchmen from the Illinois country also entered this zone from the north. In 1719 Claude de Tisne conducted a pack train of goods from the

---

[1] Quoted in Anna Lewis, "La Harpe's First Expedition in Oklahoma," *Chronicles of Oklahoma* 2 (Dec. 1924): 344, 347.

Missouri River southwesterly to the Arkansas River and traded with scattered Taovaya bands. Three years later Etienne Veniard de Bourgmond set out from Kaskaskia to open trade with the border tribes and to attempt to reach the Spanish settlements in New Mexico. Above the mouth of Grand River in Missouri he established Fort Orleans, which became a center for trade with the Otoes, Iowas, Pawnees, Missouris, and Osages. Through these tribes he began commercial contact with the Comanches and other tribes who ranged the Central Plains. His efforts netted a growing harvest of furs, hides, some gold and silver, and horses and mules.

Thus French trading interests in both Louisiana and the Illinois country prospered as a result of the commerce drawn through the middle border contacts. But, it seems, the traders were never satisfied, and the lure of the Spanish towns on the Rio Grande was compelling—reaching Santa Fe became a Gallic obsession. A number of daring Frenchmen did cross the Plains to Santa Fe during the early years of the eighteenth century, but most of them were arrested. Spanish officials confiscated their trade goods, and they were frequently convicted as intruders and held in local jails or even sent to the provincial prison at Chihuahua, Mexico.

One expedition of note did make it through, and its members were permitted to remain in Santa Fe for nearly a year. In 1739 Pierre and Paul Mallet organized a trading expedition in the Illinois settlements, stowed a varied cargo of trade goods on pack animals, and crossed the Plains, entering Colorado via the valley of the Platte, then proceeding south into New Mexico. For several months they pleaded with local Spanish officials to suspend the strict rule forbidding trade with foreigners, but to no avail. Disappointed, the Mallets returned to the Mississippi Valley by way of the Canadian and Arkansas rivers. In 1741, as a follow-up to the Mallet expedition, Louisiana Governor Bienville sent a survey party headed by Fabry de la Bruyère to attempt to open a trade route to New Mexico along the Canadian River. Bruyere failed to reach the Rio Grande.

French fur hunters also were active in the far north. Pierre de la Verendrye trafficked among the tribes northwest of Lake Superior. In 1738 in search of new trading territory, he reached the Minataree villages at the Great Bend of the Missouri. In less than five years, men in his employ had explored into the Rocky Mountains as far south as Wyoming. Verendrye's commercial reconnaissance stimulated an intensive exploitation of the trapping and trading resources of the area from Minnesota west to the Dakotas and south of the Missouri River into the Rocky Mountains. French goods were introduced among the Sioux, Cheyennes, Blackfeet, Snakes, and other tribes of the northern Plains and Rockies.

Indian Recalcitrance

As a general rule the French succeeded well in relations with the Indian tribes resident in their flaring territory in Western America's heartland. From the Choctaws on the Gulf to the Algonquins in the Great Lakes country tribesmen for the most part accepted French missionaries and traders, served French economic purpose in the fur and hide commerce, and fought for the French cause in the contest for Western America. Three notable exceptions were the Fox and their Sac allies, the Natchez, and the Chickasaws. These tribes refused to submit to French rule. After five years of bloody combat in the 1720s the Sac and Fox capitulated. The Natchez refused to bow to French will and were annihilated by superior French arms. The Chickasaws were never conquered by the French.

During the 1720s French officials attempted to resettle the Fox Indians near Detroit where they could be watched. The aborigines refused, and it required nearly a decade of campaigning by French troops and Indian allies in the Northwest before the Fox and their Sac allies submitted to French purpose. During this time, Fox war parties blocked trade west of Lake Michigan and threatened several times to close the upper Mississippi to French shipping.

The Natchez of the lower Mississippi Valley had attained a high state of advancement before the Europeans invaded their domain. When disputes with traders led to the killing of four Frenchmen by the Natchez, a French army from Mobile retaliated in 1716, and troops constructed Fort Rosalie on the bluffs at Natchez. The French military presence encouraged settlers to move upriver from the Gulf settlements, and they established farms on the rich Natchez lands.

Natchez leaders resented this appropriation of their territory, and in 1722 attempted to expel the French settlers. Troops suppressed the outbreak, and the Natchez remained quiet until 1729 when they struck back with great fury. Their warriors destroyed several military posts and settlements in their territory and massacred the garrisons, killing 250 Frenchmen and taking nearly 300 women and children hostage. Eventually the French army and Choctaw mercenaries avenged the massacre several times over and recovered most of the hostages. French and Choctaw troops captured over 400 Natchez and sent them to the West Indies as slaves. Several Natchez survivors fled northeast and settled among the Chickasaws, Creeks, and Cherokees. By 1731 France had entirely erased the Natchez nation.

The Chickasaws resided in northeastern Mississippi remote from the Mississippi River. Thus they were neglected by the French in the early years of European entry into the Gulf region. But around 1700 British agents entered their villages via the trader paths from Carolina. The first Chickasaw War, caused by the refusal of the Chickasaws to banish English traders from their towns, began in 1720. The French sent Choctaw mercenaries to raid Chickasaw settlements, and the Chickasaws retaliated by attacking Choctaw towns and by raiding French shipping on the Mississippi—the lifeline that connected Illinois and Louisiana. This tactic closed the river to French use for nearly four years, until French officers formed companies of Choctaws and led them against the Chickasaws; they paid a bounty of a gun, one pound of powder, and two pounds of bullets for each Chickasaw scalp. Nonetheless, by 1725 the Chickasaws remained unconquered, and commerce in Louisiana was at a standstill. French officials decided to call back their Choctaw raiders and make peace. A deceptive calm settled over the lower Mississippi Valley. Once again French boats navigated the Mississippi, and hunters and traders roamed the prairies and forests unmolested.

The second Chickasaw War, which began in 1732, had its roots in the tribe's refusal to meet renewed French demands to expel the growing community of British traders from their territory and to turn over all Natchez survivors who had taken refuge there. Again French officials sent their Choctaw mercenaries against the Chickasaws; in addition, they turned their Indians in the Illinois country against them. The Chickasaws responded with a fury of retaliatory attacks against the Choctaws and Illinois. Again they struck at French commerce on the Mississippi, and, when by 1734 they had virtually closed it to the French shipping, Governor Bienville declared to the French Colonial Office: "the entire destruction of this hostile nation . . . becomes every day more necessary to our interests, and I am going to exert all diligence to accomplish it." [2]

In 1736 Bienville planned a two-pronged attack on the Chickasaws. One column of 400 French and Indians from the Northwest, commanded by Major Pierre d'Artaguette, was to descend the Mississippi, land at Chickasaw Bluffs, and march east on the Chickasaw settlements. A second column of 600 French regulars and nearly 1,000 Choctaws, commanded by Bienville himself, was to march north on the Tombigbee River for an assault on the Chickasaw towns. Poor timing caused d'Artaguette to arrive first. The Chickasaws cut his column to pieces, captured the baggage train —which included 450 pounds of powder and 12,000 bullets—and burned d'Artaguette and several other captives at the stake. On May 26, 1736, Bienville's column reached the Chickasaw towns in northeastern Mississippi. Throughout the day Chickasaw sharpshooters cut down wave after wave of attacking French regulars, and the French failed to breach Indian defenses. Finally Bienville halted the carnage and marched the survivors back to the Gulf via the Tombigbee River.

Three years later Bienville made a third attempt to crush the Chickasaws. He mustered a regular army of 1,500 men from stations on the Gulf and 1,500 troops and Indians from the north. Heavy rains held up the French advance at Chickasaw Bluffs, and Bienville finally had to abandon the campaign and withdraw. In 1752 the French made one final attempt to annihilate the Chickasaw nation. A French army marched up the Tombigbee to the Chickasaw's fortified towns, was unable to dislodge the Chickasaws, and withdrew for the last time.

[2] Quoted in Arrell M. Gibson, The Chickasaws (Norman, 1971), p. 50.

THE FRENCH-SPANISH CONTEST

The Spanish and French early recognized how essential it was to control the Indian tribes in their territories as they contested with each other for control of Western America. The tribes were basic to the strategy and needs of each in several ways. First, they were regarded as subjects and were expected to render fealty to the crown through the monarch's representative in Western America. Second, peace with the tribes was essential to the economic exploitation of Western America, particularly the fur trade. Third, recalcitrant tribes could become a source of strength for the enemy in the contest for territory. Fourth and finally, with the sparse European population of Western America, warriors of the subject tribes were needed as troops to defend the interests of the colonial power.

Gulf Warfare

As Spain and France extended their respective jurisdictions in Western America, the simple rule of propinquity inevitably came into play, and their competitive struggle for the region intensified. One of the early Spanish-French wars resulting from the contest between these powers erupted in 1718. Spanish squadrons challenged the French for maritime control of the Gulf by preying on French supply ships. Spanish agents also disturbed prospering French trade with the Indian tribes of the lower Mississippi Valley. French officials retaliated by sending an expedition from Mobile against Pensacola. French troops captured and held this Spanish bastion for two years.

Conflict on the Plains

At about the same time a French force from Natchitoches drove the Spaniards out of east Texas and momentarily occupied Spanish settlements there. During 1720 Spanish officials at Santa Fe feared that a French force from the Northwest settlements would strike overland at the towns on the upper Rio Grande. To guard against this they sent Pedro de Villazur and a force of 110 Spanish regulars and Indian troops to reconnoiter the northeastern approaches to Santa Fe. Villazur marched across eastern Colorado searching for sign of the enemy. Finding none he turned back toward the Rio Grande. On the South Platte River his troops marched into an ambush, carried out by eastern tribesmen armed with French weapons. Only thirteen Spaniards escaped the slaughter.

Through the early years of the eighteenth century several additional engagements were fought between Spanish and French forces, each side braced with Indian allies. One of the most notable battles between these contestants occurred in 1759 at a settlement of Taovaya Indians and French traders on the Red River. Known as Twin Villages, this stockaded compound was one of the most lucrative trade depots on Louisiana's western margins. The Taovayas, as middlemen for the French, traded with the

Comanches on the Plains, exchanging guns, shot, powder, and blankets for buffalo robes, horses and mules plundered from the Spanish, and Indian slaves.

The particular quarry of Comanche slave-hunting expeditions were the Apaches of Texas. When the Apaches appealed to the Spaniards for protection, the Spanish responded by establishing a mission and a presidio—San Luis de Las Amarillas—near the Apache settlement on the San Saba River. In 1758 Comanche raiders destroyed the San Saba mission. Diego Ortíz Parilla, commander of the nearby presidio, organized an expedition of 300 men from the Spanish settlements to punish the Norteños, as the Taovayas and their Comanche allies were called. During 1759 he marched his column north to Twin Villages on the Red River. As he neared the enemy's position, he observed that the compound was enclosed by palisade walls, complete with a tall pole flying the French flag. Parilla's troops attacked the Taovaya battlements time and again, but each assault was repulsed by the French and Indian defenders. Moreover, counterattacking horsemen struck the Spanish flanks and captured Parilla's artillery. Reluctantly the Spanish commander gathered the surviving remnants of his army and retreated south. The battle of Twin Villages was the largest military engagement to take place in the New West in the eighteenth century.

BRITISH ENTRY INTO WESTERN AMERICA

Ironically, less than four years after Parilla's dismal defeat, Spain received from France all of Louisiana, not by force of arms but by the diplomatic settlement that concluded the French and Indian War. The principals in this epochal struggle—known in Europe as the Seven Years' War—were France and Great Britain, with Spain a reluctant ally of France. The war germinated in the growing struggle between France and Great Britain for control of that portion of Western America between the Appalachians and the Mississippi River.

Pioneer British Traders

The British, as we have said, entered the international contest for Western territory belatedly. They found the southern entry to Western America by sea blocked by Spanish and French Gulf settlements. The uncharted Appalachians discouraged penetration by land, and even beyond the mountains, human barriers confronted them. The region north of the Ohio River swarmed with French traders and their aboriginal minions. Fierce Shawnees controlled the upper Ohio Valley. South of the Ohio Spanish and French traders attached to the Creeks, Cherokees, and other populous Indian communities acted as checks to British expansion into the Southwest.

Energetically and tenaciously the British turned to the task of removing these obstacles to Western expansion. During the seventeenth century British traders probed the Appalachians for passages to the West. From the colony of Virginia in 1673 James Needham and Gabriel Arthur found a mountain crossing and proceeded to the Cherokee towns on the upper Tennessee River. Several renegade French traders familiar with the trans-Appalachian region had taken up residence in the British settlements, and they guided Englishmen through the mountains over trader paths. In 1692 Arnout Viele led a party of Englishmen, from New Jersey, across Pennsylvania to the Allegheny River, and down that stream to the Ohio, and thence to the Wabash.

The Chickasaw Nation Enclave

On these early reconnaissances of the trans-Appalachian region, British traders found the northern passage from Albany via the Mohawk Valley to the Great Lakes blocked by French-Indian presence. Shawnees controlled the upper Ohio Valley. The area most vulnerable to British exploitation thus lay west of Charleston, South Carolina. By 1700 British traders were moving over a well-marked trader path from Charleston to the Chickasaw towns near the Mississippi. They took up residence there and permanently attached the Chickasaw nation to British interests. Thus Great Britain was provided with a strategic enclave on the Mississippi River, shielded by the impressive fighting might of the Chickasaws.

Early British extension into Western America was economic, centering on the fur trade. In the routine conduct of his private business the trader played a variety of roles. As a frontier merchant he exchanged with Indian hunters his trade goods for furs and hides. His collateral roles included that of diplomat sans portfolio, confirming the maxim that the flag follows the commerce; for his negotiations with the Indian tribes in his own interests inevitably served those of his sovereign as well. And the British trader in particular was the vanguard of a more permanent type of settlement. Hard on his heels came the land speculator and the agriculturalist.

Trading interests in Charleston prospered substantially from the commerce derived from the Chickasaw establishment. Englishmen not only monopolized the Chickasaw trade but, from their strategic forward base in that western Indian nation, they drew substantial amounts of Choctaw and Creek trade away from the Spanish and French. And, through Chickasaw intermediaries, they traded with tribes on the west bank of the Mississippi River. In the north, New York trading interests, thwarted by the concentrated French-Indian presence along the Mohawk Valley west to the Great Lakes, used the Iroquois as middlemen to carry their goods to the tribes of the French Northwest.

Penetrating the Ohio Valley

A trader named George Croghan established the British presence on the Ohio River. In 1741 Croghan took a pack train of goods from his depot near Harrisburg through the mountains and founded trade stations on the Allegheny River—five miles above the forks of the Ohio—and at Logstown —eighteen miles below the forks. Croghan's employees ranged west to the Wabash and northwest to Lake Erie's south shore. Their principal clients were the Shawnees, Miamis, and Wyandots. Soon the quality of Croghan's goods and the fairness of his dealings softened Shawnee belligerence, and in 1748 he negotiated the Treaty of Logstown, in which the Shawnees committed their allegiance to the British. The Delawares and Wyandots also signed the treaty.

THE DECISIVE CONTEST

The growing British presence in the trans-Appalachian region understandably concerned the French. Officials in New France and Louisiana were informed that British traders were resident in most Indian villages along the Ohio River and that they were venturing up the Wabash. French Indian hunters were defecting to the British traders who, it was claimed, carried higher quality goods at lower prices than the French. Guns, lead, powder, flints, paints (particularly vermillion), rum, hatchets, knives, wampum, and cloth products (including strouds—coarse blanket material—calicoes, lace, ribbons, and thread) were standard items of trade. In their southern enclave in the Chickasaw nation, British trade depots were attracting increasing numbers of Choctaws and other French Indians. This base was a particular threat because of its location near the Mississippi and because Chickasaw fighting prowess had thrice defeated French attempts to gain control of the area.

Origins of Franco-British Conflict

The decisive precipitant for the French and Indian War, which settled finally the question of supremacy in that portion of the West between the Appalachians and the Mississippi, was the British attempt to establish a colony on the Ohio River. The British justified this step by the Treaty of Lancaster of 1744—whereby the Iroquois had surrendered to the British their claim to the Ohio Valley—and the Treaty of Logstown of 1748—in which the Shawnees authorized British occupation of the Ohio Valley. They also based their expansion on crown land grants which extended the territories of Virginia and other seaboard colonies west of the Appalachian Mountains.

In 1749 the British crown granted to the Ohio Company of Virginia— a group of British and colonial businessmen—a 200,000-acre tract south of the forks of the Ohio. The company was required to fortify the area and colonize at least 200 families on the tract within a seven-year period. Company officials sent Christopher Gist, a frontier surveyor, to make a reconnaissance of the area. Indian informants brought French officials in the Northwest tidings of Gist's visit to the Forks. In response, the governor of

New France sent an expedition commanded by Celeron de Blainville to strengthen France's claim to that region. De Blainville planted a number of lead plates, inscribed with the French declaration of title, at likely settlement points in the area. In addition, French agents led parties of Indians in raids on British trade settlements along the Ohio.

These actions failed to intimidate the Ohio Company, and plans continued apace to establish the trans-Appalachian colony. French officials in Canada countered by ordering the construction of a line of posts from Lake Erie to the forks of the Ohio, including Fort Venango on the Allegheny River. Colonial officials in Virginia sent a note protesting French trespass on English territory and demanding evacuation. It was carried by Major George Washington of the Virginia militia, then aged twenty-one. In December 1753 Gist guided him to Fort Venango, where the French flatly rejected the British claim to territory in the Ohio country.

In the spring of 1754 Virginia officials sent out a work crew to construct a fort at the forks of the Ohio to guard the colonists expected momentarily. Colonial troops marched up the Monongahela Valley to guard the workmen. Washington commanded one column of 400 militia. But before the Virginia troops reached the Forks, a French force arrived, drove off the workmen, destroyed their fortification, and erected a more substantial post, which was named Fort Duquesne. Hearing of the incident, Washington halted his troops at Great Meadows on the approaches to Fort Duquesne and ordered the erection of a stockade named Fort Necessity. A French and Indian army attacked his position on July 3, 1754. Faced with a superior attacking force, Washington capitulated on condition that he be permitted to withdraw his small army to Virginia.

The French and Indian War

The battle at Great Meadows opened the French and Indian War, a vicious, bloody contest that settled, for a time, the question of pre-eminence in Western America. It became a world-wide contest when the French and British governments declared war on each other in 1756. Both nations then sent regular troops to Western America, the former to check the British challenge to French supremacy in the trans-Appalachian region and the latter to drive the French from this prize territory.

British strategy aimed at striking the French at three points: (1) through the lower Mississippi Valley where, from their powerful position in the Chickasaw nation, they planned to use warriors from that Indian community to close the Mississippi, thus separating Louisiana and the Gulf from the French Northwest and Canada; (2) through the tongue of trade territory developed by Croghan in the upper Ohio Valley; and (3) through the St. Lawrence into New France's vitals, striking at the principal settlements of Quebec and Montreal.

British agents and Chickasaw warriors successfully drove a wedge between Louisiana and the Northwest by gaining control of both banks of the Mississippi River near Chickasaw Bluffs, thus cutting this vital French lifeline. Next, they prepared to conquer the territory around the forks of the Ohio. General Edward Braddock, British commander in America, mustered an army of regulars and Virginia militia numbering slightly more than 2,000 men and marched up the Potomac River to Fort Cumberland, thence down the Monongahela Valley toward Fort Duquesne. Woodsmen slashed a passage through the dense forests to permit passage of Braddock's supply wagons and artillery. On July 9, 1755, French and Indian troops engaged Braddock's column ten miles from Fort Duquesne. The ensuing battle resulted in a humiliating defeat for the British; casualties were heavy, and General Braddock was among those slain. Only about 500 survived to make the rushing retreat up the Monongahela toward the safety of Fort Cumberland.

Yet Braddock's defeat only increased British determination to drive the French from the Ohio Valley, and in the summer of 1758 General John Forbes led an army west from the Pennsylvania settlements over a freshly cut road to Fort Duquesne. French forces evacuated the fort ahead of the British advance. Forbes renamed it Fort Pitt.

The Diplomatic Settlement

Victorious in the Ohio Valley and successful in separating French Gulf settlements from the Northwest, the British next turned to Canada, capturing Quebec in 1759 and Montreal the following year. France signed a surrender agreement on September 8, 1760. By the terms of the Treaty of Paris, signed on February 10, 1763, France ceded to Great Britain all territory, except New Orleans, in the trans-Appalachian region west to the Mississippi River, and Canada. Spain, which had belatedly entered the war as an ally of France, lost Florida to the victorious British.

To assuage Spain's loss of Florida, in 1762 France ceded New Orleans and Louisiana to Spain by the Treaty of Fontainebleau. Thus one power—France—had been ejected from Western America. Great Britain's share in Western America now extended from the Appalachian Mountains to the Mississippi River and from the Great Lakes to the Gulf, and Spain's territorial position was enhanced by its undisputed title to Louisiana.

SELECTED SOURCES

There is an abundant literature on the Spanish colonial establishment in Western America. The following works depict its evolution: Hubert H. Bancroft, *History of the North Mexican States and Texas,* (San Francisco, 1884); W. F. McCaleb, *Spanish Missions of Texas* (San Antonio, 1954); John F. Bannon, **The Spanish Borderlands Frontiers, 1531–1821* (New York, 1970)

* Available in paperback.

and *Bolton and the Spanish Borderlands* (Norman, Okla., 1964); Herbert E. Bolton, ed., *Spanish Exploration in the Southwest, 1542–1706* (New York, 1916), *Rim of Christendom* (New York, 1936), and *Athanase de Mezieres— The Louisiana–Texas Frontier: 1768–1780* (Cleveland, 1914), 2 vols; and George P. Hammond and Agapito Rey, eds., *The Rediscovery of New Mexico, 1580–1594* (Albuquerque, 1966).

The expanding French colonial establishment in Western America is detailed in H. A. Ennis, *The Fur Trade in Canada* (New Haven, 1930); Clarence Vandiveer, *The Fur-Trade and Early Western Exploration* (Cleveland, 1929); Paul C. Phillips and J. W. Smurr, *The Fur Trade* (Norman, 1961), 2 vols.; William T. Hagan, *The Sac and Fox Indians* (Norman, 1958); Francis Parkman, *Count Frontenac and New France Under Louis XIV* (Boston, 1902); John G. Shea, *History of the Catholic Missions Among the Indian Tribes of the United States, 1529–1854* (New York, 1881); Emma H. Blair, ed., *The Indian Tribes of the Upper Mississippi Valley and Region of the Great Lakes* (Cleveland, 1911), 2 vols.; Arrell M. Gibson, *The Chickasaws (Norman, 1971), and *The Kickapoos: Lords of the Middle Border* (Norman, 1963); Norman W. Caldwell, *The French in the Mississippi Valley 1740–1750-*(Urbana, Ill., 1941); and P.F.X. de Charlevoix, *History and General Description of New France* (Chicago, 1962), 6 vols.

Sources on British penetration of the American West include Verner W. Crane, *The Southern Frontier, 1670–1732* (Philadelphia, 1929); James Adair, *The History of the American Indians* (Johnson City, Tenn., 1930); John R. Alden, *John Stuart and the Southern Colonial Frontier* (Ann Arbor, 1944); and Wilbur R. Jacobs, *Diplomacy and Indian Gifts* (Stanford, 1950) and ed., *Appalachian Indian Frontier: The Edmond Atkin Report and Plan of 1755* (originally, *Indians of the Southern Colonial Frontier*) (repr. ed., Albuquerque, 1967).

The imperial conflict for control of Western America, culminating in the French and Indian War, is traced in Theodore Calvin Pease, ed., *Illinois on the Eve of the Seven Years' War, 1747–1755* (Springfield, Ill., 1940); Max Savelle, *The Origins of American Diplomacy: The International History of Anglo-America, 1492–1763* (New York, 1968); *Francis Parkman, *A Half-Century of Conflict* (Boston, 1898; repr. ed., New York, 1962), 2 vols.; Henri Folmer, *Franco-Spanish Rivalry in North America, 1524–1763* (Glendale, Calif., 1953); and *Howard H. Peckham, *The Colonial Wars, 1689–1762* (Chicago, 1964).

PART TWO *the Old West*

The Central Great Plains
Nebraska Department of Agriculture

The Eighteenth-Century Indian Trade

5

Western America Divided: Spain and Great Britain, 1763–1776

WHILE European statesmen at Fontainebleau and Paris were still negotiating the diplomatic settlement that concluded the Seven Years' War (French and Indian War), Spanish and British officials prepared to formally take possession of the territory in Western America ceded by France. The British moved more swiftly than the Spanish to occupy their new territory.

BRITISH MANAGEMENT OF WESTERN AMERICA

Anticipating the collapse of French resistance in Canada, during 1760 British officials detached from the Canadian invasion army a force of 200 Royal Rangers under Major Robert Rogers and directed him to occupy all French posts around the Great Lakes. Rogers marched into Detroit during late 1760; by the close of the following year, British troops were garrisoned in all military stations from Niagara to Green Bay. British plans to occupy the Ohio River Valley and take over the new territory south to the Gulf were delayed by an extensive and bloody upsurge of resistance among the Northwest tribes.

Pontiac's Revolt

The Ottawas, Miamis, and many other tribes of the Northwest were desolated by the departure of their long-time French patrons, for they found their new masters arrogant and detached. General Jeffrey Amherst, commander of British troops in America, applied rigid military law to the conquered territory and required his troops to maintain a stern, disciplined attitude toward the Indians. He forbade the customary distribution of presents to tribal leaders. Indian discontent and alarm mounted as

65

traders, land speculators, and settlers from the seaboard swarmed with impunity over tribal lands, protected in their trespass by the British army of occupation. French traders residing among these tribesmen exploited the Indians' anxiety, promising that France soon would send an army to drive out the British.

Near Detroit was an Ottawa village headed by a strong, intelligent chieftain named Pontiac. He was particularly incensed at the growing number of British traders, speculators, and settlers who were moving into Detroit, and he was antagonized by Amherst's Indian policy. On May 7, 1763, he struck Detroit with a strong force. The Ottawa warriors stormed the fort and slashed and burned the settlement near the post, killing nearly 200 civilians. Failing to breach the garrison, Pontiac set up a determined siege.

News of his revolt spread across the Northwest and stirred other tribes to strike at the new British rulers. No English trader or settler was safe, as French-influenced Indians struck them down wherever they could. Troops on patrol were driven into the safety of stockaded forts, several of which were captured by furious tribal assaults. Potawatomi warriors invading Fort St. Joseph and Chippewa warriors at Fort Michilimackinac captured and butchered the garrison defenders. On the eastern edge of the Northwest, Seneca, Shawnee, and Delaware bands swept through the settlements in western New York and Pennsylvania, forcing the British to retreat toward the seaboard. Fort Pitt and Fort Niagara were under close siege.

British action was prompt and devastating. During the summer a relief column commanded by Captain James Dalyell carried supplies and ammunition through the Ottawa siege ring to succor the garrison at Fort Detroit. On August 5, 1763, Colonel Henry Bouquet smashed a Shawnee-Delaware force at the Battle of Bushy Run and lifted the siege of Fort Pitt. The failure of the promised French aid to materialize and the inability of his Ottawa fighters to break through the determined British resistance at Detroit caused Pontiac to withdraw south to the Illinois country during October 1763. British troops maintained constant pressure on the Indian rebels in the East. The Delaware will to fight was finally smashed during 1764 by Bouquet's army on the Muskingum River in the Ohio country.

In the territory south of Lake Erie, Colonel John Bradstreet's campaign destroyed the ability of the Shawnees and associated tribes to resist British reoccupation of the Northwest. Intimidated by successive British victories and disillusioned with the French, leaders of most of the insurgent tribes capitulated at a general council held at Fort Niagara during the summer of 1764.

British Occupation of the Northwest

Having pacified the areas around Fort Pitt and the south shore of the Great Lakes, the British prepared to move down the Ohio River and occupy the Illinois country. General Thomas Gage, successor to General Amherst as commander of British troops in America, ordered the mission. George Croghan, the Ohio River frontier trader, was placed in charge. He left Fort Pitt during the spring of 1765 at the head of a small convoy of river boats laden with gifts for tribal leaders. Pontiac, now resident in the Illinois country, still wielded a wide and powerful influence among the tribes of the lower Ohio Valley, and Croghan's special assignment was to find the Ottawa chief and win him to the British cause. Securing Pontiac's friendship would assure success with the tribes tributary to his influence.

Near the mouth of the Wabash, a Kickapoo raiding party ambushed Croghan's convoy, plundered the cargo, and carried Croghan to their towns and held him captive. Croghan was known and trusted by many of the Wabash tribes from his trading expeditions before the French and Indian War. Leaders of these tribes interceded with the Kickapoos and in a short time gained his release and restoration of his goods. He proceeded to Fort Quiatanon, found Pontiac, and won his assent to a general peace council. The treaty with the Wabash tribes negotiated by Croghan provided for peace and acceptance of British suzerainty.

Following Croghan's successful mission to the Wabash, a British army from Fort Pitt moved down the Ohio River to occupy the remaining French posts and settlements in the Northwest. The last French station, Fort de Chartres, situated on the Mississippi River between Kaskaskia and Cahokia, was garrisoned by British troops in early October 1765.

British Occupation of the Southwest

The Indian attempt to prevent British occupation of the Northwest had failed, but the territory south of the Ohio River was yet to be occupied. The British already had an island of strength in this region through the Chickasaw nation and the large resident English trader population. During August 1763, British troops landed at Pensacola and Mobile. French and Spanish troops—and most of the French and Spanish traders and settlers in the Florida Gulf area—moved to New Orleans.

British troops quickly garrisoned Fort Charlotte at Mobile, Fort Bute at Manchac on the Gulf, and Fort Panmure at Natchez on the Mississippi River. The principal tribes of the Southwest—Cherokees, Creeks, Choctaws and Chickasaws—did not resist the British takeover of the Southwest. They were received into British dominion by officials of the crown at the Augusta council of 1763 and the Mobile council of 1765.

British Western Administration

The governance of the British portion of Western America was a maze of ambivalent aims and shifting processes, for three parties, each presuming to possess special privilege and interest in the trans-Appalachian region, vied one with the other for pre-eminence in its development. First, was the government of Great Britain, asserting its right as the primary proprietor and director of administration and development for this portion of its vast overseas empire. Second were certain colonies in America, particularly Virginia and North Carolina, which somewhat presumptuously claimed territory in the trans-Appalachian region. Such claims were derived from founding charters that contained sea-to-sea land grants and thereby the right to develop Western lands. Third were individual entrepreneurs—traders, speculators, settlers—selfishly determined to pursue their own particular interests in exploiting the rich Western resources.

Properly, the crown spoke first in announcing a system for governing and developing the new territory. The British government followed an evolutionary policy that, in essence, began with the Proclamation of 1763. The crown's first concern was peace and order in the West. The government believed that the Indian tribes, already in a state of insurrection, had to be assured that their new European masters would protect them from exploitation by unpoliced traders and invasion by speculators and settlers. The so-called Proclamation of 1763, issued on October 7 of that year, divided the British lands north of Florida at the drainage divide of the Appalachian Mountains. Settlement west of that line was forbidden, and persons already in residence there were required to evacuate. The area west of the Proclamation Line was, for the time being, to be a vast Indian reservation, in which military law was to prevail. Troops stationed at the Western posts were to enforce the regulations and expel intruders. Only licensed traders were permitted west of the Proclamation Line.

Administratively the area was divided into two huge reservation zones. The territory and tribes north of the Ohio River were assigned to William Johnson, whose title was Indian superintendent. The territory and tribes from the Ohio River south to Florida were assigned to Indian Superintendent John Stuart. Each of the two districts was divided into smaller jurisdictions that were to approximate the farming, village, and hunting lands of each tribe. Each tribe was assigned an agent (called a commissary), an interpreter, and a blacksmith. To assure fair dealing for Indian hunters, all trade was to be carried out at the local tribal agency under the supervision of the commissary. This intricate system for regulating commerce and Indian relations in British Western America proved cumbersome and susceptible to evasion. The Indian reservation zone covered so much territory that limited Indian superintendency staffs and military garrisons were unable to administer the region effectively. Its very vastness made surveillance of outlaw traders virtually impossible, and colonial governments continued to license traders in defiance of the royal monopoly. Moreover, renegade traders, both French and British, prospered in the Western wilderness, finding a ready market for their contraband pelts at New Orleans.

Indian superintendents Johnson and Stuart were much more attentive to their negotiations with Indian leaders than in carrying out their basic commissions to protect the Indians from commercial exploitation, prevent trespass west of the line set by the Proclamation of 1763, and maintain order. The goals of Johnson's and Stuart's diplomacy were treaties ceding tribal title to lands on the eastern margins of the trans-Appalachian West in order to open new tracts for the speculator, the land company, and the settler. In Johnson's case cupidity was definitely involved for he was a principal stockholder in one of the land-speculating companies that benefitted from his negotiations.

In 1768 the British government simplified its administrative system, drastically reducing the number of military garrisons in the Old West. By 1771 only Forts Niagara, Mackinac, Detroit, Charlotte, Bute, and Panmure were garrisoned. The Indian superintendents were to serve primarily as royal representatives in the Indian country to oversee treaties with the tribes, especially those providing for land cessions. The authority to regulate trade with the tribes, including licensing traders, was returned to the seaboard colonies.

Before 1776, one additional substantive change was made in the governance of the trans-Appalachian West. Residing in the Northwest were several thousand Frenchmen and people of mixed French and Indian background who were Roman Catholics. Since the beginning of the British occupation they had been subject to military law, but in the 1770s they sought civil government, recognition as legal residents, and protection of their religion. In 1774 the British government adopted the Quebec Act, which answered the complaints of French Catholics at Kaskaskia, Vincennes, and other settlements in the Northwest. The boundary of the province of Quebec was extended to the Ohio River so as to encompass the old French Northwest, and civil law and religious toleration were guaranteed to all citizens of the area.

Tribal Cessions

The compelling force at work in the trans-Appalachian region before the American Revolution was expansion of the area of settlement. Elaborate negotiations were carried out with Indian tribes; the results were further land cessions, formation of speculation companies by British and colonial businessmen, increased flow of settlement into the ceded areas, and, inevitably, wars in which the tribes desperately resisted expansion of white settlement.

That the Proclamation Line of 1763 was only a temporary expedient was manifested by a series of treaties negotiated between 1768 and 1770. Business and political leaders in England and the American colonies founded companies to obtain Western land grants and to speculate in their value by promoting settlement. An obstacle to fruition of their ventures were the claims of various Indian tribes to lands just west of the 1763 boundary. Pressured by land-company stockholders, some of whom were highly placed government officials, during 1768 the crown directed Johnson and Stuart to begin negotiations that would extinguish tribal title to the desired tracts.

Several colonies, including Virginia, continued to claim Western lands under their charters and negotiated with several tribes on behalf of certain colonial interests. A cloud over both crown and colonial efforts were individuals who negotiated with the Indian tribes for tracts of land and formed land development companies independent of both crown and colonial franchise.

In 1766 at Fort Stanwix in the colony of New York, Johnson convened delegations from most of the northern tribes, dominated by the Iroquois Confederation, to begin the cession negotiations. Representatives of land companies expecting to benefit from the negotiations were also present. Johnson's Fort Stanwix Treaty contained provision for a cession of lands extending from Oswego in New York, along the Allegheny River to the Ohio River, and west on that stream to the mouth of the Tennessee River. The signatory tribesmen received goods valued at over £10,000 for consenting to this grant. The treaty opened for settlement southwestern New York, western Pennsylvania, and territory along the Ohio River, including much of Kentucky.

Adjacent territory south of the Ohio was cleared of tribal encumbrance by Stuart's negotiations with the Cherokees. By the treaty of 1768, concluded at the Cherokee village of Hard Labor, he obtained a cession extending west and north from the Proclamation Line—at Chiswell's Mine and Tryon Mountain (North Carolina) in the Cherokee nation—to the mouth of the Great Kanawha on the Ohio River. A second cession agreement with the Cherokees, Stuart's Treaty of Lochaber of 1770, enlarged the grant on the west. This treaty was negotiated to accommodate Virginia land companies that had pressed him to obtain additional territory. The colony of Virginia paid the Cherokees £2,500 worth of goods for the extended cession. The next year John Donelson committed a deliberate error in surveying the boundary of the Lochaber cession, and the line was set still further west, to the Kentucky River.

Thus the Treaty of Fort Stanwix, the Treaty of Hard Labor, the Treaty of Lochaber, and Donelson's survey error produced an irregular westward pointing triangular bulge in the line set by the Proclamation of 1763. The exaggerated triangle had its point on the Ohio River; its upper line bent northeasterly from the mouth of the Tennessee River to Oswego in New York; and its southern line tended southeasterly from the mouth of the Kentucky River to Tryon Mountain in the Cherokee nation. (*See* Map 4.)

Western Land Companies

By 1775 the territorial triangle ceded by the 1760s treaties, complicated by overlapping assignments and grants extending beyond the treaty line, was a maze of patented lands; speculator companies with royal or colonial patents and individual speculators holding land grants derived from private

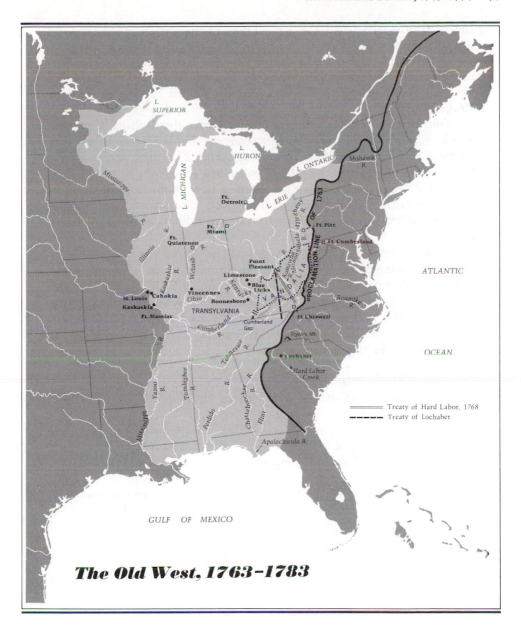

The Old West, 1763–1783

Indian treaties chequered the area. These companies included the Mississippi Company of Virginia, the Illinois Company, the Indiana Company, the Loyal Land Company, and the Grand Ohio Company. Founding members of the companies included George Washington, Benjamin Franklin, George Croghan, William Johnson, Patrick Henry, and Thomas Walpole.

One of the largest of these companies was the Indiana Company, which, through negotiations with several smaller land companies, consolidated into a vast syndicate controlling nearly 25 million acres near the Forks of the Ohio River. Its officers petitioned the crown to permit it, as the Grand Ohio Land Company, to form a new proprietary colony to be called Vandalia. The crown favorably received the proposal, and probably only the outbreak of the Revolution prevented fulfillment of the Vandalia plan.

Richard Henderson of North Carolina epitomized the individual speculator. He formed the Transylvania Company and in 1775 negotiated privately with certain Cherokee leaders at Sycamore Shoals on the Watauga River for the purchase of a vast tract between the Kentucky and Cumberland rivers. The land was paid for by goods valued at £10,000. Henderson planned to colonize his tract and profit from the venture by leasing land to tenants and collecting annual quitrents.

West Florida Settlements

While land companies were preparing to colonize the trans-Appalachian West under the aegis of their patents and charters, pioneers were already entering the region and establishing settlements on their own initiative. Four areas of settlement had emerged by 1775. The first to develop was West Florida. The Appalachicola River was the dividing line between East and West Florida. The colonial government of West Florida consisted of an appointed royal governor, a council, and an elective assembly. The first royal governor was George Johnstone. Pensacola became the capital, while Mobile, where most of the trading houses were situated, became West Florida's commercial center. The firms of Swanson and McGillivray and Panton and Leslie dominated the interior trade with the Choctaws, Chickasaws, Cherokees, and Creeks. Agents of the two trading companies also intruded into Spanish territory west of the Mississippi River to trade with the Quapaws, Osages, and other tribes situated on the eastern edge of the Plains.

Settlement in West Florida was permitted even though it was west of the Proclamation Line. Soon after the British takeover, a heavy migration from England, the seaboard colonies, and the West Indies flowed into the Gulf settlements and the area around the mouth of the Mississippi. West Florida lands were so esteemed that in 1764 the crown expanded the settlement zone by moving the northern boundary from 31° to a line east from Natchez on the Mississippi River, at 32° 28′.

Transmontane Settlements

Settlers from the seaboard also crossed the Appalachians into the West. Well-worn trails had been blazed by traders, hunters, and curious adventurers who simply had to see the other side of the mountains. George Croghan had planted two trading stations in the Ohio country during the 1740s. Thomas Walker, on a reconnaissance of a tract granted to the Loyal Land Company, explored eastern Kentucky in 1750. Ascending the Appalachians' Blue Ridge eminences in company with a small party, he found a depression in the highlands, which he named the Cumberland Gap. The Walker Party also explored the country drained by the Cumberland and Kentucky rivers. In 1752 Pennsylvanian John Finley had explored along the Ohio River and up the Kentucky River, trading with the Shawnees. Several wide-ranging hunters explored eastern Tennessee before the French and Indian War. In 1746 Stephen Holston wandered over the region, giving his name to one of the principal feeders of the Tennessee River. Christopher Gist and Thomas Cresap, through their excursions to the Forks of the Ohio around 1750, added to the knowledge of the region already provided by Croghan. Besides information about new areas, which they shared with the Eastern settlements, and the trails they blazed across the mountain fastnesses, traders and hunters also served as guides for surveyors, land-company officials, and settlers bound for the trans-Appalachian West.

The extension of the British military frontier had also opened pathways into the West. General Braddock's wilderness road coursed over Gist's route up the Potomac to the Fort Cumberland settlement, thence to the Monongahela and the Forks of the Ohio. General Forbes' mountain passage provided a route from Philadelphia to Fort Pitt. Before the end of the French and Indian War settlements had developed to sustain the westward-bound homeseekers who began drifting over these roads.

Pioneers defied the Proclamation of 1763 to settle western Pennsylvania along the Allegheny and Monongahela rivers. By 1763 a settlement of over 300 families had grown up around Fort Pitt, which came to be called Pittsburgh. Troops from Fort Pitt drove thousands of settlers east of the Proclamation Line and discouraged their return by burning cabins and destroying improvements. The Indian outbreak stirred by Pontiac also forced the evacuation of a number of transmontane settlements. After the Fort Stanwix Treaty, however, settlers flooded the region around Pittsburgh, and by 1770 an estimated 10,000 families had settled in the river valleys north and south of Pittsburgh.

By 1766 a second stream of settlement flowed from Virginia and North Carolina into the Holston, Watauga, and Nolichucky valleys of eastern Tennessee. The Nolichucky Valley pioneer settlement was west of the Lochaber Treaty line within Cherokee territory. To resolve this problem pioneer Tennesseans selected two commissioners, James Robertson and James Bean, to negotiate a Cherokee cession of the already-settled territory. The Cherokees assented upon payment of a substantial quantity of goods advanced by North Carolina speculators. Collectively these Tennessee wilderness communities were called the Watauga settlements, and there was some question whether they were a part of Virginia or of North Carolina. The issue was settled momentarily by the Wataugans themselves in 1770. Representatives elected from the scattered settlements met, adopted a compact of government, and formed the Watauga Association. By the terms of the compact, a committee of five elected members was to serve as the governing body for Watauga, functioning as an executive committee and tribunal and vested with the power to organize a militia for frontier defense. The Watauga Association existed until 1778, when the settlements were attached to North Carolina.

The transmontane region of Kentucky was also the scene of early settlement. Daniel Boone was a pioneer explorer of Kentucky. Born in Pennsylvania and reared in North Carolina, Boone became a hunter at an early age; by 1767 he was ranging over the Blue Ridge Mountains into Kentucky. In 1769 he and John Finley guided the first party of colonial speculators through the Cumberland Gap on a reconnaissance of Kentucky. Thereafter, Boone spent nearly a decade hunting in Kentucky and leading land seekers into this attractive settlement zone.

During the early 1770s surveyors from Virginia—including George Washington, who was employed by land companies—swarmed over Kentucky. Small bands of settlers also drifted through the Cumberland Gap into eastern Kentucky. But the region teemed with wild game and was a prime hunting ground for the Shawnees, Cherokees, and other tribes, and they were determined to hold back the settlements. Their wars for control of this rich game area caused Kentucky to be called the "Dark and Bloody Ground." The fate of James Harrod, the founder of the Harrodsburg settlement, was typical. In 1774 his colony was forced to evacuate to the safety of Eastern towns because of Indian resistance to their trespass. Boone too made several attempts to found colonies in Kentucky; his efforts met the same fate.

Clearly, before permanent settlement could take place, a bloody Indian war would have to be fought. In the Upper Ohio Valley as well, the Shawnees were being pressured by the British settlements thrusting out from Pittsburgh. Shawnee relations with Virginia officials became increasingly tense as the colonials attempted to dominate trans-Appalachian development. In 1774 Shawnee war parties struck at the settlements in the Ohio Valley. Lord Dunmore, royal governor of Virginia, mustered an army and marched against the Shawnees. Near the mouth of the Kanawha River at Point Pleasant one of Dunmore's columns defeated the Shawnees under Chief Cornstalk. As spoils of their victory, the Virginians accepted Shawnee capitulation and tribal assent to the white settlement of Kentucky.

After Lord Dunmore's War and the Shawnee surrender, settlers flocked into Kentucky. Harrodsburg was re-established in 1775. Other settlements sprang up. The most substantial colonizing effort in Kentucky was undertaken by Richard Henderson of North Carolina, who, as we noted earlier, had purchased from the Cherokees a vast tract between the Kentucky and Cumberland rivers. Henderson developed his enterprise through the Transylvania Company and named his proposed colony Transylvania. He employed Daniel Boone and a crew of workmen to mark a passage from the North Carolina settlements to the bluegrass region of Kentucky. The settlers' trail, completed by Boone during the spring of 1775 and called the Wilderness Road, coursed through dense forests and over rough highlands to the Kentucky River by way of the Cumberland Gap. As Henderson's advance agent, Boone founded the settlement of Boonesborough. Henderson planned to organize Transylvania as a proprietary colony.

During the spring of 1775 delegates from the Kentucky settlements sponsored by Henderson, as well as representatives from Harrodsburg and other independent communities, met and drafted a plan of self-government that resembled the compact adopted by the Watauga Association. Henderson's attempts to manage his vast estate as a proprietary colony, particularly his plan to collect quitrents, were defied by the Kentucky settlers. He also failed to obtain the approval by the British government—and subsequently of the revolutionary Continental Congress—for his Transylvania colony plan. Kentucky settlers thwarted Henderson by petitioning Virginia for incorporation, and in 1777, the government of Virginia officially recognized Kentucky as a county of that now revolutionary state.

In the years following the French and Indian War British colonial managers moved with dispatch to establish dominion over their new Western territories. The ultimate intent of royal administrators was to develop the trans-Appalachian region under the aegis of favored proprietary land companies. But this plan was thwarted by waves of pioneers from the seaboard who occupied on their own the lands intended for the proprietary companies. Growing insurgency on the part of the seaboard colonies also played a role as control shifted to the colonial governments.

SPANISH MANAGEMENT OF WESTERN AMERICA

In the period after 1763, Spain's management of its vast estate in Western America—which extended from the Mississippi River to the Pacific shore—included reform of colonial administration, occupation of Louisiana, and continued exploration and settlement of the northwestern frontiers of New Spain. The Spanish king, Charles III, directed the improvement of administration in Western America so that it could more effectively serve its purpose as a defensive buffer to insulate New Spain from invasion by a foreign power. He encouraged immigration to the territory north of Mexico, urged the development of resources in this region and expansion of its commerce, and directed the reform of its administration. His special representative in the New World to implement the royal policies for Western America was José de Gálvez, who carried the title of Visatador General.

Colonial Reforms

One of the first tangible manifestations of administrative reform of Spanish imperial management in Western America occurred in 1767 when a royal order directed the expulsion of the Jesuit order from the mission frontier of Spanish Western America. The Jesuits' area of activity had been Baja California and the Pimería Alta settlements near the head of the Gulf of California. Their mission property and ecclesiastical function were taken over by the Franciscans and Dominicans.

Visitador General Gálvez acted swiftly to fulfill his royal commission, sending agents to inspect Spanish settlements and defenses along the rimland of Western America. During 1766 the Marquis de Rubí made a reconnaissance of Spanish stations from Sonora to Louisiana. His recommendations led to a shift and consolidation of Spanish military strength to the northern border as a check to threats posed by Comanche and Apache raiders. The result was a chain of military posts extending from near the Colorado River in Arizona to La Bahía in eastern Texas.

In 1768 Gálvez visited Sonora and Baja California, where he supervised the extension of presidios, missions, and lay settlements. Indian resistance to expanding Spanish settlements led to a bloody and destructive frontier war. Gálvez personally mustered and led a Spanish army recruited from the border settlements against the hostile tribesmen. The Gálvez campaign pacified portions of Pimería Alta and made the peaceful extension of Spanish settlements in southern Arizona possible. Intelligence of growing Russian and English activity along the Pacific coast also led Gálvez to direct the extension of Spanish settlements north into Alta California.

His direct knowledge of much of Spanish Western America and his agents' reports on the state of affairs in the northern frontier led Galvez to devise a plan for reorganizing the administration of all territory on the northern frontier except Louisiana. The Gálvez plan, put into effect in 1776, integrated California, Arizona, New Mexico, and Texas into an administrative jurisdiction called the Provincias Internas. The government was centralized and controlled by the military, virtually free of oversight by the viceroy of New Spain in Mexico City. It was headed by an official called the Comandante General, who was responsible directly to the Spanish king. The city of Chihuahua was designated the capital for the Provincias Internas. The first Comandante General to administer this portion of Western America for Spain was Teodoro de Croix.

Spanish Occupation of Louisiana

The Spanish acquisition of Louisiana had substantive ramifications for Spanish use of Texas. In the imperial scheme to guard New Spain against invasion by land from the northeast, Texas had been primary. But with

Louisiana as a forward buffer to protect the interior of New Spain, Spanish officials could drastically reduce their military and settlement efforts in Texas. In the 1760s defenses, missions, and lay settlements in east Texas that had been established to thwart the French in lower Louisiana were evacuated to San Antonio. This town became the administrative center for Texas. During the mid-1770s Spanish settlers were permitted to return to the area, and several new settlements—including Nacogdoches, established in 1779—grew up on the Texas-Louisiana border.

The tightening of Spanish authority in Western America included the development of a communications grid linking settlements in the Mississippi Valley with centers in Texas, New Mexico, Arizona, and California. Roads and trails, many of them established by an engineer-surveyor named Pedro Vial, tied Santa Fe on the Rio Grande to San Antonio, Natchitoches, Nacogdoches, and St. Louis. Roads and trails west of the Rocky Mountains connected Santa Fe to Chihuahua, the Arizona settlements (including Tubac), and areas west to the Colorado River and into the California coastal towns and missions.

While these administrative and defense reforms and communications extensions were being developed, Spanish officials also occupied Louisiana, ceded by France in 1763. Until this time, the expanding Spanish territories in Western America had been populated by Indians, and the Spanish technique of establishing dominion was largely based on the mission and the presidio. Occupying Louisiana, however, was different, for while the new territory contained several thousand Indians, it was also populated by Blacks and Europeans, mostly French. Moreover, Spanish occupation up to this time had been principally in coastal regions. The only permanent continental extension by Spain had been that tongue of settlement that thrust up the Rio Grande to the southern edge of the Sangre de Cristo Mountains in northern New Mexico and west into southern Arizona.

At the time of the Spanish takeover of Louisiana there was a sprinkling of small French trading and agricultural settlements on the lower Missouri River and along the Red and Arkansas rivers. The densest concentration, estimated at about 7,000 people—more than half of them blacks—was near the Gulf of Mexico, in and around New Orleans. Other French towns in Louisiana included St. Charles on the Missouri River, Ste. Genevieve, Cavagnolle near the mouth of the Kansas River, Ferdinandina and Arkansas Post on the Arkansas, and Twin Villages and Natchitoches on the Red River. Several new settlements were formed in Louisiana after France ceded the Northwest to Great Britain in 1763. Many French moved across the Mississippi River and established towns along the lower Missouri River. The principal new settlement was St. Louis. French plantations on the lower Mississippi Valley produced rice, indigo, tobacco, grain, and livestock. Lead mining in eastern Missouri and the fur trade comprised the principal industries of upper Louisiana.

Spain formally took possession of Louisiana during March 1766 when

Governor Don Antonio de Ulloa reached New Orleans. The French in lower Louisiana strongly opposed Ulloa, for he ignored the Gallic opposition and set to work establishing Spanish dominion over the new province. He sent squads of Spanish troops to the French settlements as far north as the Missouri River, and he issued regulations for the conduct of citizens and the fur trade. Sustained French opposition to Spanish rule and Governor Ulloa generated a number of minor insurrections in the New Orleans area. In 1769 General Alexandro O'Reilly replaced Ulloa, entering Louisiana with 4,500 troops to restore order and assure submission to Spanish rule. His officers arrested the leaders of the French opposition, executed five, and imprisoned many others. O'Reilly vigorously extended Spanish law, power, and dominion to all settlements in Louisiana.

Following O'Reilly's pacification of Louisiana, Luis de Unzaga y Amezaga was appointed civil governor of the province. Louisiana was never under the jurisdiction of New Spain or the succeeding Provincias Internas, as was the rest of Spanish Western America. For most of its existence as a Spanish province its officials were appointed, and their authority was derived from the Council of the Indies. Louisiana's population increased substantially under Spanish rule, due to immigration and natural increase. By 1800 the non-Indian population of Louisiana amounted to about 50,000.

To manage and control the Indian tribes of Louisiana, Spain used experienced French traders, commerce in pelts, and annual gifts rather than missions. St. Louis, Arkansas Post, and Natchitoches became the principal fur trade centers for Spanish Louisiana. Chiefs came to these towns each year to council with Spanish officials and to receive gifts and medals. Many French traders from east of the Mississippi moved west and became a part of the Spanish frontier commerce system. In several cases these traders brought bands of Northwest Indians with them. The new tribes established villages along the Missouri, Arkansas, and Red rivers and their tributaries, hunting across the trans-Mississippi region for pelts to trade with their French sponsors. These immigrant Indians included bands of Kickapoos, Sac, Fox, Delawares, and Shawnees. Thus a voluntary migration of portions of Eastern tribes was underway years before the United States government inflicted its forced removal program on the Eastern tribes.

Spanish Occupation of California

In the period after 1763 Spain also extended its dominion up the Pacific shore in response to the threat of Russian and English intrusion on territory claimed by Spain. Beginning in 1728 Vitus Bering explored for Russia the straits connecting Siberia and Alaska—the eastern and western hemispheres—seeking a northern water passage from the Pacific to the Atlantic. On an expedition in 1741 Bering surveyed the coast of Alaska and returned to Russia with seal and sea otter pelts. Russian traders soon established a line of trading settlements on the Aleutian chain and the islands along the Alaskan coast, and coastal trading vessels ranged as far south as the Columbia River in the quest for trade in pelts.

The Spanish response was to extend settlement and exploration further north and to claim territorial jurisdiction on that basis. In 1768 Gálvez had directed the occupation of Alta California to counter the Russian coastal threat. The California colony consisting of Franciscan missionaries, soldiers, and settlers from the towns of Baja California was divided into two parties: one group set out for Alta California aboard two ships. A second group went by land. Gaspar Portolá, governor of Baja California, was in charge of the military and settler component of the California colony. Father Junípero Serra was in charge of the Franciscan missionaries. The sea and land parties converged at San Diego Bay, where in 1769 they founded a mission, presidio, and lay settlement. Portolá and an exploring party marched north along the California coast in search of Monterey Bay. They found it but passed by, considering it too shallow to be the long-sought anchorage. They continued north, discovered San Francisco Bay, and returned to San Diego. A second expedition traveled to Monterey, and in 1770 the Spaniards founded a mission and presidio there.

Distance from the southward coast settlements and the uncertainty of communication and supply by sea led officials to establish a land route from the Arizona settlements to California. Preliminary exploration for a route had been undertaken in 1771 by Father Francisco Garcés, a Franciscan missionary in charge of the mission at San Xavier del Bac. He explored along the Gila River to the Colorado River, then went west across the Yuma Desert to the eastern approaches to the Sierras. Three years later he guided a Spanish military column from the Arizona settlements— twenty men commanded by Captain Juan Bautista de Anza—along this route, thence over the Sierras to the coast, and into Monterey.

The next year Anza formed a colony of 150 persons from settlers, soldiers, and missionaries in the Pimería Alta region and, with a herd of cattle and horses, marched over the Garcés Trail to Monterey; from there they went north to San Francisco Bay, arriving in mid–1776. The settlement of San Francisco dates from that year. The lands between San Diego and San Francisco were gradually filled with towns, missions, and presidios. San Jose, in the Santa Clara Valley near the head of San Francisco Bay, was founded as a lay settlement in 1777; near Mission San Gabriel Spanish settlers founded Los Angeles in 1781.

By 1782 the Spanish establishment in Alta California consisted of presidios at San Francisco, Santa Barbara, Monterey, and San Diego. San Jose and Los Angeles were pueblos or lay towns. And there were nine missions between San Francisco and San Diego. Father Junípero Serra, who died in 1784, has been credited with founding this far-flung ecclesiastical establishment in California and converting over 4,000 Indians. In 1777, Monterey became the capital of Spanish California.

Renewed Land and Sea Reconnaissance

Spanish explorers continued to find alternative land routes to California and to extend Spanish dominion up the Pacific shore by claiming the rights of discovery. Several attempts were made to trace a land route from Santa Fe on the Rio Grande to California. A major effort occurred in 1776 when Fathers Silvestre Escalante and Francisco Domínguez explored portions of Colorado, Utah, the Great Basin, and the Green River country, then returning south to the Colorado River. They did not, however, succeed in crossing the Sierras before returning to Santa Fe, although reports of their travels led to additional reconnaissances of the territory west of Santa Fe.

Spanish ships also explored the Pacific coast north of San Francisco in search of foreign intruders and sites for forward stations to thwart the threatened English and Russian trespasses. In 1774 officials sent Juan Pérez north to take possession of the country as far as to 60° north latitude. He sailed to 55°, exploring Nootka Sound en route. The next year two Spanish vessels commanded by Bruno de Heceta and Tomas Bodega y Cuadra attempted to reach a point on the Pacific shore at 60°, regarded as the most northerly point for an east-west passage. Heceta sailed as far as 45° and discovered the mouth of the Columbia River. Bodega proceeded farther to 58° north and discovered the anchorage that came to be called Bodega Bay. The final Spanish seagoing reconnaissance of the Northwest Pacific shore occurred in 1779, when Juan Arteaga and Tomas Bodega, again in two vessels, attempted to reach 60° north. This time Arteaga succeeded.

The diplomatic settlement of 1763, which divided Western America between Spain and Great Britain lasted less than twenty years. Secessionist activity in the British seaboard colonies during 1775–1776 burgeoned into a surprisingly successful war of independence and produced a new nation. As successor to British territory in Western America, the United States was a new, young antagonist facing Spain in the Mississippi Valley.

SELECTED SOURCES

Great Britain and Spain maintained conspicuously contrasting systems of imperial management over their vast territories in Western America. The British system is discussed in Clarence W. Alvord, *The Mississippi Valley in British Politics* (Cleveland, 1916), 2 vols.; Thomas P. Abernethy, *Western Lands and the American Revolution* (New York, 1937); Howard H. Peckham, *Pontiac and the Indian Uprising* (Princeton, 1947); Albert T. Volwiler, *George Croghan and the Westward Movement, 1741–1782* (Cleveland, 1929); Nicholas B. Wainwright, *George Croghan, Wilderness Diplomat* (Chapel Hill, N.C., 1959); Jack M. Sosin, *Whitehall and the Wilderness: The Middle West in British Colonial Policy, 1760–1775* (Lincoln, Neb.,

1961) and *The Revolutionary Frontier, 1763–1783 (New York, 1967);
*Francis S. Philbrick, The Rise of the West 1754–1830 (New York, 1965);
*Wilbur R. Jacobs, ed., Appalachian Indian Frontier: The Edmond Atkin
Report and Plan of 1755 (Albuquerque, 1967); and John R. Alden, John Stuart
and the Southern Colonial Frontier (Ann Arbor, 1944).

Spanish imperial administration, reform, and expansion are subjects treated
in Herbert E. Bolton, Outpost of Empire (New York, 1930) and *Texas in
the Middle of the Eighteenth Century (Berkeley, Calif., 1915); F. A. Golder,
Russian Expansion on the Pacific, 1641–1850 (Cleveland, 1941); *Abraham P.
Nasatir and Noel M. Loomis, Pedro Vial and the Roads to Santa Fe (Norman,
Okla., 1967); Raymond H. Fisher, The Russian Fur Trader, 1550–1770 (Berkeley, Calif., 1943); Charles Gayarre, History of Louisiana (New Orleans, 1932),
4 vols.; Charles E. Chapman, The Founding of Spanish California, 1687–1783
(New York, 1916) and A History of California: The Spanish Period (New
York, 1921); and Louis Houck, ed., The Spanish Regime in Missouri (Chicago,
1909), 2 vols.

* Available in paperback.

The Fort at Boonesborough, Kentucky

6

The New Challenge in Western America

IN 1775 Spain and Great Britain shared the great continental mass of Western America. Russia had extended its dominion over the Aleutian Islands and the coast of Alaska through the expanding activity of trading companies and fur hunters. The Lexington and Concord incident in the colony of Massachusetts on April 19, 1775, set in motion a war of secession between Great Britain and Colonial America. British troops were unable to snuff out this insurrection, and it evolved into a bloody international war involving several European nations—including France and Spain—and culminated in an independent United States. By the terms of the Treaty of Paris, the diplomatic settlement that ended the war in 1783, the United States fell heir to British holdings in Western America.

THE ENEMY IN THE WEST

At the outbreak of hostilities in 1775, most of the British troops in America were concentrated in the seaboard colonies. The only British posts garrisoned in the trans-Appalachian West were Mackinac, Detroit, and Niagara. Small detachments of British regulars were also stationed in the Northwest towns of Vincennes on the Wabash River and Kaskaskia and Cahokia near the Mississippi. Most of the British regulars at the West Florida posts had been reassigned to trouble spots on the Atlantic. West Florida officials organized militia companies among the settlers and assigned them to the forts of Natchez, Manchac, Mobile, and Pensacola.

British Western Strategy

Despite the paucity of regular troops in the trans-Appalachian region, British officials succeeded in organizing a deadly, destructive strike force in the West, maintained a sustained military pressure on the American settlements, and nearly triumphed in that sector. The manpower for British Western operations was derived from the Indian tribes (supplied and led by British agents at Detroit and Pensacola), cadres of British regulars assigned to the Indian expeditionary forces, and Tories.

British Indian Allies

In the early stages of the war, the principal agents for mustering tribal warrior power for strikes against the American settlements were the two Indian superintendents. John Johnson, son of the late William Johnson, was in charge of the territory west of the Appalachians and north of the Ohio River. John Stuart was still in charge of the territory south of the Ohio. Johnson counciled with the leaders of the old Iroquois Confederacy (Senecas, Oneidas, Mohawks, Onandagas, and Cayugas), as well as the Delawares, Shawnees, and Ottawas. He warned the tribes of what would happen to their hunting grounds if the expansive, land-hungry rebels triumphed in this war; he supplied them with presents and arms for their warriors and sent them against the frontier settlements. Stuart followed much the same practice in his councils with tribes south of the Ohio River —the Cherokees, Creeks, Choctaws, and Chickasaws.

In the later stages of the war, the most notorious and successful agent for managing the British cause in the West was Henry Hamilton, lieutenant-governor of Canada. From his Detroit headquarters, Hamilton supplied Indian armies with guns, ammunition, knives, hatchets, blankets, and provisions; he fired them to fury pitch with warnings of the Indian's grim future if the greedy rebels won the war and launched them on devastating campaigns against settlements on the Allegheny and Monongahela rivers and across the Ohio River into Kentucky. The trans-Appalachian Americans called Hamilton "the hair-buyer" from the claim that he paid his aboriginal minions a bounty for each rebel scalp—man, woman, or child—that they delivered to Detroit.

AMERICAN WESTERN ACTION

The revolutionary body that directed the affairs of the new American nation in its early years, the Continental Congress, attempted to check the British plan to loose the Western tribes on the trans-Appalachian settlements. In July 1775, the Continental Congress created three Indian departments to have jurisdiction over the tribes of the Northwest, the Southwest, and the Indian communities in the Fort Pitt area. Each department was headed by a commissioner, who was charged with maintaining regular contact with the Western tribes and countering British influence over them.

American Western Strategy

The commissioner at Fort Pitt was Colonel George Morgan. In October 1775, Morgan convened the commissioners in council with the leaders of the Shawnees, Delawares, and other tribes residing in the upper Ohio Valley. From these sessions came a pact between the commissioners and the Indian leaders that committed the tribes to neutrality. Each party agreed to abstain from attacks on the other.

American Limitations

But British blandishments prevailed, for American commissioners were handicapped by the poverty of their new nation in conducting relations with the Western tribes. They lacked the resources in gifts and other considerations that the aboriginal leaders and their warriors had come to expect as a part of the apparatus for maintaining a cooperative relationship. British agents were able to provide gifts and other expected considerations in abundance, and their warnings of rebel expansion onto Indian hunting grounds were confirmed by the extension of American settlements in the trans-Appalachian region while the war was still in progress.

THE WAR IN THE WEST

From 1776 to 1783 the trans-Appalachian West was bloodied time and again by campaigns against the American settlements, led by British agents and Tories, and manned by Indian troops. Counter slashes against Western Indian and British settlements were carried out by vengeance-driven frontier militia.

British-Cherokee Raids

Among the first to do the British bidding were the Cherokees. Warrior bands from this populous Indian nation struck hard at the Watauga settlements in July 1776. James Robertson and John Sevier rallied the harried settlers, collecting them at Sycamore Shoals on the Watauga and at Eaton's Station on Long Island in the Holston River; they supervised construction of a strong log fort at each location. The Cherokee raiders, led by an esteemed warrior chieftain, Dragging Canoe, maintained a tight siege on the Watauga forts for nearly three weeks. Finally Robertson and Sevier led the cooped-up settler militia in a counterattack that broke the siege and forced the Cherokees to withdraw.

Cherokee raids on the American settlements extended from the Watauga-Holston frontier in the trans-Appalachian region eastward into Virginia, North Carolina, South Carolina, and Georgia. During the late summer of 1776 militia columns from each of these new American states joined with a Western army mustered from the Watauga and Nolichucky settlements to carry out a retaliatory campaign against the Cherokees. The American armies desolated the Cherokee country in western North and South Carolina and eastern Tennessee, burning villages and destroying crops. These operations crushed Cherokee martial power; thereafter only on isolated occasions were raiding parties from this tribe able to strike at the intruding American settlements.

During 1777 the conquering Americans extracted from reluctant Cherokee leaders two agreements—the Treaty of DeWitt's Corner and the Treaty of Long Island—obligating the Cherokees to cede all tribal territory in western South Carolina and the part of their range east of the Blue Ridge Mountain divide in North Carolina and reiterating their cession of the Watauga and Nolichucky settlement zone in eastern Tennessee.

Beleaguered Kentucky

Kentucky was in a continual state of siege from 1776 to 1782. During this travail the people lived in forts. The scattered communities were evacuated, and the pioneers took up residence in three principal fortified settlements—Boonesborough, Harrodsburg, and Logan's Station.

The community fortification was constructed of heavy logs. The upper ends of the logs were fashioned into a sharp point and placed vertically in the ground like fence posts; they formed a solid palisade wall ten to twelve feet high. Portholes in the walls and inner walkways enabled riflemen to fire on attackers from varied positions. The palisade walls formed a rectangle enclosing cabins and stables. A projecting blockhouse on each corner of the stockade provided a vantage point for directing crossfire against enemy attempts to breach the walls. Children herded livestock outside the stockade during lulls in the fighting but drove them inside to safety when the alarm sounded. The stockade was erected around a spring or well to provide fresh water for the defenders and the livestock. Rather constant pressure on the Kentucky frontier from 1776 to 1782 kept most frontier families bottled up in these forts. Unable to raise crops of corn and other foodstuffs, they subsisted principally on fresh meat brought in by hunters and greens gathered in season near the stockade.

American Counter Action

Both the Continental Congress and the government of Virginia attempted to succor the Kentucky settlements, but both were hard pressed to maintain even a limited military effort against the British on the seaboard. Occasionally General George Washingon, commander of the Continental Army, dispatched parties of American regulars to Fort Pitt in an attempt to bolster sagging American fortunes around Pittsburgh. During 1777, he sent General Edward Hand to rehabilitate the defenses of that old post and to galvanize the local militia forces. In early 1778 General Hand led an expedition from Fort Pitt into the Northwest, campaigning as far

north as the Shawnee and Delaware settlements at Sandusky and destroying several villages and corn fields. The Indians faded ahead of his advance,
and at no time was he able to force them to battle.

The new state of Virginia shared as it could men and supplies to defend
its western county of Kentucky. Virginia still claimed the territory north
of the Ohio River from its colonial charter and sought to confirm this claim
by military defense. Men from Virginia at times helped garrison Fort Pitt
and constructed Fort Kittanning on the Allegheny above Fort Pitt, Fort
Henry on the Ohio River below Fort Pitt—which became the town of
Wheeling—and Fort Randolph at the mouth of the Great Kanawha. This
was a fringe-type of defense, and mobile British-Indian raiding columns
based at Detroit simply flanked the defenses and swept into Kentucky. The
raids during 1776 were of a reconnaissance, feeling-out type, but in 1777
they became sustained, destructive, extended campaigns of terror and death
for Kentuckians.

Virginia Governor Patrick Henry appointed George Rogers Clark a
major of the Kentucky militia and directed him to mount the defense of
his military jurisdiction. Clark in his turn appointed three captains—
Daniel Boone at Boonesborough, James Harrod in charge at Harrodsburg,
and James Logan at Logan's Station. Each was in command at his community fort. Clark and his captains kept their troops supplied with powder
and shot by evading enemy patrols and threading the dangerous path
linking Kentucky and the Virginia arsenal.

Northwest Conquest

Clark wearied of the containment imposed on his command area by
the ubiquitous British and Indian invaders. He determined to lift the siege
of Kentucky by breaking out, taking the offensive, and ultimately reaching
Detroit, the command center for the torment inflicted on the settlers south
of the Ohio River. Henry authorized Clark to raise an army of 350 men and
pledged to support the expedition as much as the limited resources of
Virginia would permit. Clark sent out his call for troops to gather at Fort
Pitt, but only 175 men responded. Clark moved his motley- armed and
attired frontier battalion from Fort Pitt on flatboats in June 1778. He
halted for a short time at the falls of the Ohio River, then proceeded to
near the mouth of the Cumberland River. There the American army
beached their transports and marched to the Mississippi River towns of
Kaskaskia and Cahokia, 120 miles away.

The principal reason for Clark's oblique movement was the establishment of a base on the Mississippi River near the Spanish town of St.
Louis. Far removed from his source of supply in Virginia, he had to rely
on the Spaniards for shot, powder, and provisions. The principal American
agent at New Orleans was Oliver Pollock, who had obtained supplies from
the Spanish to sustain the Western war effort against the British since
1776. Clark expected Pollock to arrange for essential supplies from Spanish

depots at New Orleans and St. Louis to support his campaign against Detroit. During the march to Kaskaskia, Clark received the heartening news of the recently negotiated American-French alliance.

On July 4, 1778, Clark's army reached Kaskaskia. This town of 500 people, mostly French, capitulated without the firing of a single shot. The small British garrison, stunned by the sudden appearance of the Americans, surrendered quietly. The French population favored the Americans, especially after Clark informed them of the American-French alliance. Cahokia, St. Phillippe, and Prairie du Rocher also quickly accepted American dominion. Vincennes, situated on the Wabash River 180 miles northeast of Kaskaskia, joined the American cause through the efforts of French traders from Kaskaskia.

When Detroit's Governor Hamilton learned of Clark's daring thrust to the Mississippi and into the British Northwest, he collected an army of 500 British and Indians and personally led this force south to expel the rebel army. Hamilton reoccupied Vincennes in December 1778. Clark reacted by moving his army out of Kaskaskia on February 6, 1779, toward Vincennes. The Americans suffered every conceivable hardship on this 180-mile march: winter's bitter cold, snow, rain, sleet, and frozen ground mingled with thaw and impassable mud. Heavy rains had flooded the approaches to Vincennes; for the last twenty miles of their agonizing march, the Americans waded through water that was sometimes neck deep.

Clark's army reached Vincennes on February 24 and set up a siege. The scathing, deadly fire of Clark's sharpshooters—who were armed with long rifles—cut down the British defenders. Hamilton's supplies ran low; no relief from Detroit could reach him because of the floods; and he surrendered. Clark sent him to Virginia in irons as a prisoner of war.

Clark was eager to follow up his victory at Vincennes with an attack on Detroit. He appealed to Virginia officials for 500 reinforcements, but when only 30 fresh troops reached Vincennes, Clark resigned himself to a holding action in the Northwest. He erected Fort Nelson at the falls of the Ohio River as a middle station and dispersed his men around the rim of the Northwest, from Kaskaskia to the new post. American squads patrolled the Ohio River in crude gunboats and guarded the crossings in an attempt to check British, Tory, and Indian raids into Kentucky. Isolated nearly 600 miles from supply sources in Virginia, Clark had to rely on the Spanish at St. Louis and New Orleans for powder, shot, and provisions.

The Spanish Alliance

Spain entered the war on the side of the United States in 1779, and Clark found himself in the curious position of having, in a sense, to protect the Spanish and thus his own life line. During early 1780 a British-Tory-Indian force of 750 men from Canada collected at Mackinac and moved on St. Louis via the Mississippi River; their double purpose was to hit at Britain's new enemy and at the same time capture the American source of supply for the Northwest. Clark gathered his troops in the Kaskaskia-Cahokia area and, cooperating with a Spanish force from St. Louis, smashed the British invasion and drove it back to Canada. Warnings that a second British attempt to capture St. Louis would be mounted in 1781 led Spanish officials at St. Louis—braced by a contingent of Clark's troops—to strike at the British post of St. Joseph. Situated on the southern tip of Lake Michigan, the fort had been the British supply center for the St. Louis attack. The American-Spanish force captured the post and destroyed the supplies stored there.

The need to protect the New Orleans-St. Louis life line was also crucial in the lower Mississippi Valley, where a continuing source of British power was the fierce Chickasaw nation, whose territory extended across western Kentucky and Tennessee into middle Mississippi. There was the real danger that the Chickasaws would close the Mississippi River to Spanish shipping, as they had repeatedly done to the French in colonial times, and thus cut off Clark's source of supply at St. Louis. To guard against this possibility the American commander in the West took steps to establish American presence south of the Ohio. Attempts already had been made to strengthen the American position in the lower Mississippi Valley. In 1778 James Willing of Natchez, who had become an active American agent when the Revolution broke out, led 100 volunteers, crammed into two small boats, from Pittsburgh down the Ohio to the British settlements in the lower Mississippi Valley. Willing's raiders destroyed plantations between Natchez and Walnut Hills, then proceeded to New Orleans.

The Fort Jefferson Disaster

In 1780 Clark's men constructed a post below the mouth of the Ohio, inside Chickasaw territory. Named Fort Jefferson, the new station was garrisoned by 100 troops. Settlers collected around the fort and started farms. Chicasaw scouts discovered the American outpost and reported it to Superintendent Stuart. Before the end of 1780 a Chickasaw-Tory army swept into the settlement, drove the settlers inside the post, burned their cabins, and set up a siege. The Chickasaws sealed the routes supplying Fort Jefferson, killed or captured stragglers from the garrison, and at one time subjected the post to such a close and protracted siege that only the timely arrival of reinforcements saved it from destruction. In desperation, Clark's besieged detachment and the settlers fought their way out of Fort Jefferson in June 1781, abandoning it to the Chickasaws and Tories.

Renewed Cherokee Raids

After the Cherokee defeat in 1777, most of the military action against the trans-Appalachian settlements was carried out by slashing British-Tory-Indian raider corps based in Detroit. However, a dissident Cherokee faction, the Chickamaugas—headed by Dragging Canoe and Bloody Fellow—longed for vengeance on the American intruders. During 1778 the British delivered guns, powder, and shot from their arsenal at Pensacola to the Chicka-mauga towns. Dragging Canoe and his followers moved against the Amer-ican settlements, closing the Wilderness Road—the principal link between Virginia and Kentucky—and driving the Watauga and Holston river set-tlers into forts.

In retaliation Colonel Evan Shelby collected a frontier army of 600, invaded Chickamauga territory in the Tennessee River Valley, and wreaked such a destructive fury on the Indian settlements that this recalcitrant fac-tion of the Cherokee nation sued for peace. Occasionally thereafter war-riors from certain sections of the Cherokee nation, feeling the pressure of expanding American settlements in their territory, rose in fury at the trespass and attempted to expel the intruders. However, they resorted to military action only to defend their homeland and not as British merce-naries or allies. Nonetheless, during late 1780 Watauga militiamen deso-lated Cherokee towns on the upper French Broad River on the pretext of avenging Cherokee raids on the Americans. They forced the vanquished Cherokees to cede additional territory into which their settlements could expand. After Dragging Canoe's second defeat in 1779, Cherokees for the most part remained subdued and quiet.

After Spain's declaration of war against Great Britain in 1779, Bernardo de Gálvez, governor at New Orleans, moved against the principal British towns and fortifications of West Florida. By 1781 Spanish naval and land forces had captured Natchez, Baton Rouge, Mobile, and Pensacola. This conquest closed off the British source of armaments for the Cherokees.

Battle of King's Mountain

One additional southern military engagement should be noted before we return to consideration of the focus of combat in the trans-Appalachian West—Kentucky. Known as the Battle of King's Mountain, this bloody encounter took place on October 7, 1780, near the northern border of South Carolina's interior. A detached British column of 1,100 under Major Patrick Ferguson marched north as part of the general British movement commanded by Lord Cornwallis. Ferguson's operations in the back country of the Carolinas galvanized the frontier. A nondescript army of 1,500 militia from the Watauga-Holston settlements and western Virginia, led by Isaac Shelby, William Campbell, and John Sevier, moved to intercept Ferguson. Their point of contact was in the rough, tumbled terrain called King's Mountain. The frontier riflemen, fighting a fluid, defensive style of war-fare using trees and rocks for cover, cut down the advancing British col-umns that were marching in tight charge formation with fixed bayonets.

The victory at King's Mountain, which was fought mostly by settlers from the trans-Appalachian regions, was one of several key triumphs over the formidable British land force moving from Savannah to Virginia. The attrition effect of the King's Mountain defeat, along with other reverses, seriously reduced Lord Cornwallis' manpower advantage over Washington's

Continental Army and contributed substantially to his capitulation at Yorktown on October 18, 1781. For all intents and purposes Yorktown ended hostilities between the United States and Great Britain.

The Western Stalemate

The war continued in the West with unabated fury long after Cornwallis' capitulation, but Clark's goal of conquering Detroit was never realized. The momentum of his offensive peaked with the conquest of Vincennes in 1779 and was lost due to the failure of Virginia and Kentucky to provide manpower and supplies to rehabilitate his tiny, bedraggled army. Thereafter Clark's Western army, dispersed in squads along the Ohio River to intercept invaders, served only a defensive function.

American commanders at Fort Pitt too had attempted to penetrate the Indian country at the southern approaches to Detroit. During October 16, 1778, Commandant Lachlan McIntosh marched nearly 1,000 troops from Fort Pitt on a campaign intended to terminate in the conquest of Detroit. His column halted on Big Beaver Creek, only fifty miles northeast of Pittsburgh on the north bank of the Ohio River, to erect Fort McIntosh as a forward base. North of Fort McIntosh, the Americans located and destroyed several Indian villages, but at no time were they able to make contact with the enemy—British or Indian. The cold of winter forced McIntosh to call in his troops and return to Fort Pitt.

Clark's capture of Detroit's Lieutenant-Governor Hamilton, the "hair buyer," at the Battle of Vincennes was hailed throughout the trans-Appalachian West as a grand coup, but it had little effect on British resolve to drive the expansionist Americans east of the mountains. Nor was there any abatement of fury and barbarity of the war in the West. In fact, after 1780, perhaps because the contest was in its waning stages, there was a noticeable acceleration of local military action; the Western adversaries lashed at one another, each desperately attempting to win one decisive victory.

Detroit continued to be the base for British Western operations. Hamilton was succeeded by an awesome trio: Colonel Alexander McKee, a particular favorite with the Northwest tribes; Captain Henry Bird, McKee's aide and an inventive strategist; and Simon Girty, leader of the Western Tories and indisputably the most notorious, bloodthirsty raider in the trans-Appalachian region. Several times between 1780 and 1782, McKee, Bird, and Girty led British-Tory-Indian armies out of Detroit and into Kentucky. The enemy columns slipped past Clark's thin Ohio River defenses to burn, plunder, and desolate the irrepressible Kentucky settlements. The Americans, barricaded behind their heavy-timbered stockades, successfully repulsed the enemy's attempts to storm their battlements, but they suffered untold terror and want from the protracted sieges. After numerous repulses, Captain Bird had his armory at Detroit contrive a mobile artillery unit, and thereafter each raiding column carried cannon.

During June 1780, a British-Tory-Indian attack force of 1,000 swarmed into the Kentucky settlement of Rundle's Station. After several charges against the stockade walls had been driven back with heavy losses, Bird's gunners moved up the cannon and shelled the palisade. The projectiles splintered the picket walls, and the defenders surrendered. One report claimed that nearly 200 men, women, and children were slain by the raiders after the capitulation. Clark, informed of the Rundle Station massacre at his Kaskaskia headquarters, returned to Kentucky, mustered an army, and marched north of the Ohio River. There the Americans cut a retributive swath of death and destruction among the Shawnee and Delaware settlements at Chillicothe and Piqua. A Tory-Indian army led by Simon Girty moved up to intercept the Kentuckians at Piqua and was annihilated by the Americans, who attempted to collect from the corpses of the slain, scalps equal to those taken at the Rundle Station massacre.

British raids and retaliatory American strikes by 1781 had made a wasteland of the Ohio Valley. And during the following year, even while negotiations between American and European representatives at Paris were progressing toward a diplomatic conclusion of the American Revolution, conflict in its most debased form continued in the trans-Appalachian region. Two incidents occurring in 1782 illustrate the depravity of the adversaries— British, Tory, Indian, and American. During 1781 Seneca war parties from the North and Delaware-Shawnee raiders from the West had smeared the settlements of western Pennsylvania with the blood of American settlers. Early in the spring of the following year a 300-man militia collected from the survivors, debauched by vengeance, campaigned west of the Allegheny River into the Ohio country. Their line of march took them to Gnadenhutten, a missionary outpost established by the Moravians among the Delawares. Ninety Indian converts were at this station. The Pennsylvania militiamen killed every one of them—men, women, and children.

Later in the same year, Colonel William Crawford led an army from Fort Pitt into the Ohio country to search out and destroy Indian settlements suspected of providing manpower for heavy raiding in the settlements around Fort Pitt and into eastern Kentucky. A British-Tory-Indian army trapped Crawford's column, scattered it, and captured several Americans—including the commander. Crawford and the other captives were turned over to the Delawares, who tortured and mutilated the Americans, then burned them at the stake.

THE WEST AND AMERICAN INDEPENDENCE

The diplomatic settlement that ended the American Revolution was concluded at Paris on September 3, 1783. John Jay, John Adams, and Benjamin Franklin were the American commissioners. Richard Oswald was spokesman for the British government, and Charles de Vergennes represented the French government.

The Diplomatic Settlement

The Treaty of Paris acknowledged American independence and shifted suzerainty in the American West. The United States would share dominion over the vast trans-Appalachian region with Spain, for Great Britain ceded to it all the territory bounded on the north by the Great Lakes, by the Mississippi River on the west, and south to 31° north. Also of interest to settlers in the West were treaty provisions giving Americans the right of navigation on the Mississippi and dictating British evacuation of Detroit and other posts in the Northwest. A proviso guaranteed Tories restitution or indemnity for property confiscated by American authorities during the war. Because of its entry into the war in 1779 and its conquests of Mobile, Pensacola, and other British settlements in West Florida, Spain was granted title to the territory situated between 31° and the Gulf of Mexico.

Western Legacy of the War

The legacy of the War in the West was multi-dimensional. Recovery of the strategic strip of territory in West Florida meant that Spain could control the rivers flowing into the Gulf. Coupled with its ownership of Louisiana and the mouth of the Mississippi this acquisition gave Spain the opportunity to throttle American economic development in the West. This opportunity and the American propensity for expansion soon pitted Spain and the United States in a military-diplomatic contest for control of the Gulf and lower Mississippi Valley.

Moreover, the reluctance of Americans to fulfill the Treaty of Paris clause providing for the restitution of Tory property caused the British to retain control of Detroit and other Northwest posts on American soil. Their presence in the Northwest had a continuing influence over the local Indian tribes and thwarted American settler advance in that part of the new territory. The problem was not finally settled until a second war was fought with Great Britain, in 1812.

British use of Indian armies in their campaigns against the Western settlements resulted in a drastic depopulation of the once great and powerful tribes that lived between the seaboard and the trans-Appalachian West. The Iroquois Confederacy of western Massachusetts, New York, and Pennsylvania was reduced to shambles by American armies, never again to muster its awesome power of colonial times. Remnants of this once grand martial community drifted into the Ohio Valley to escape the settlement pressure of their new American masters. Other tribes, including the Cherokees, had campaigned against the American settlements as British mercenaries. They now resided on territory claimed by the United States. In the eyes of the victors their actions were tainted with treason, and retaliatory campaigns against them by Western militia armies consistently ended in defeat for the aborigines. Such campaigns were generally concluded with treaties calling for cessions of land to the Americans, self-righteously extracted as reparations for making war on their new masters. This became a common method for opening new Western lands to settlement.

The brutal, dehumanizing campaigns against American settlements in the trans-Appalachian West carried out by British-Tory-Indian armies had a lasting effect. Frontier militia matched the enemy in wanton destruction and general barbarity in their retaliatory strikes. At the close of hostilities, the British and Tories withdrew, but the Indians remained in the land, now the territory of the United States. The Indian image of a deadly, skulking, bloodthirsty savage emerged in colonial times and came to full flower in the vicious contest for the West. The pejorative image survived for at least a century in the minds of most Americans.

One last legacy was that Westerners, by sacrifice, daring, suffering, and hard labor, had planted American settlements in the trans-Appalachian region. Their occupation of this region had two substantive effects on the outcome of the war. First, by diffusing the American community beyond the seaboard, they had compounded logistical and strategic problems for the British and thus reduced the efficacy of the British military effort. Second, American presence in the trans-Appalachian region and the sustained effort of its people to defend it against British attempts at reconquest had added substantially to the territorial domain of the new nation. Westerners claimed, along with the seaboard patriots, a share in the purchase of American freedom; they exulted in pride and considered it their right to be included in the councils of the new nation. Eventual acknowledgement of this right by the parent seaboard community provided frontiersmen with compelling incentives for occupying, developing, and integrating the trans-Appalachian territory into the American Union.

SELECTED SOURCES

General studies which place the American West in the broader context of the struggle for American Independence include *Marshall Smelser, *The Winning of Independence* (Chicago, 1972); *Jack M. Sosin, *The Revolutionary Frontier, 1763–1783* (New York, 1967); Donald Higginbotham, *The War of American Independence: Military Attitudes, Policies, and Practice, 1763–1789* (New York, 1971); John R. Alden, *The American Revolution, 1775–1783* (New York, 1954); Thomas P. Abernethy, *Western Lands and the American Revolution* (New York, 1937); and Paul C. Phillips, *The West in the Diplomacy of the Revolution* (Urbana, Ill., 1913).

The American Revolution in the Northwest is described in Milo Quaife, *The Capture of Old Vincennes* (Indianapolis, 1927); Temple Bodley, *George Rogers Clark* (Chicago, 1928); August Derleth, *Vincennes: Portal to the West* (Englewood Cliffs, N.J., 1969); and Patricia Jahns, *The Violent Years: Simon Kenton and the Ohio-Kentucky Frontier* (New York, 1962).

Sources depicting the war in the Southwest include Robert S. Cotterill,

* Available in paperback.

History of Pioneer Kentucky (Cincinnati, 1917); John Bakeless, *Daniel Boone* (New York, 1939); John W. Caughey, *Bernardo de Galvez in Louisiana, 1776–1783* (Berkeley, 1934); Samuel C. Williams, *Tennessee During the Revolutionary War* (Nashville, 1944); John Alden, *The South in the Revolution* (Baton Rouge, La., 1957); and James A. James, *Oliver Pollock: The Life and Times of an Unknown Patriot* (New York, 1937).

Emigrants Descending the Ohio River

7

American Beginnings in the West, 1783–1800

At the close of the American Revolution, the American segment of the trans-Appalachian region was thinly populated; 50,000 non-Indian inhabitants were distributed in settlements around the rim. The most substantial settlement zone was near Pittsburgh —north along the Allegheny River and south along the Monongahela. Other communities were scattered across the eastern half of Kentucky and south into Tennessee. On the Great Lakes perimeter to the north mixed French and English fur trading settlements existed at Detroit, Mackinac, Sault Ste. Marie, and Green Bay; and on the western margins were the Mississippi River towns of Cahokia and Kaskaskia, populated by French, mixed French-Indian, and a few English people. The most important European settlement in the Northwest's interior was the old French town of Vincennes on the Wabash River. Scattered throughout the West's interior were scores of aboriginal communities. In the Northwest the principal tribes were the Miami, Ottawa, Kickapoo, Potawatomi, Delaware, Shawnee, Wyandot, and remnants of the once great Iroquois Confederation, notably the Senecas. The principal tribes occupying the interior of the Southwest were the Cherokee, Creek, Choctaw, and Chickasaw.

WESTERN WAR-TIME SETTLEMENT

New Kentucky Settlements

During the war, American Western settlement had continued, but at a reduced rate, the flow of pioneers being conditioned by the vicissitudes of war. As George Rogers Clark moved his army down the Ohio River to conquer the Northwest from the British, settler families followed in his wake. They dogged his steps throughout the region, a few stopping at the falls of the Ohio to found Louisville in 1778. Some of the more daring followed Clark as far as the Illinois country and opened farms near the Mississippi River towns of Cahokia and Kaskaskia. When Clark founded Fort Jefferson on the south bank of the Ohio River in far western Kentucky, several score of settler families squatted near the fort and established frontier farms.

New Tennessee Settlements

Another war-time stream of settlement moved into central Tennessee. During 1779, James Robertson, agent for Richard Henderson of North Carolina, explored the central Tennessee region and selected a site for a colony at French Lick at the great bend in the Cumberland River. Later that year Robertson led a party of colonists through the Cumberland Gap across Kentucky into the new settlement zone. During the winter of 1779–1780 he established Nashborough. At Henderson's behest, Captain John Donelson transported a second party of about 200 settlers to Nashborough by way of the Cumberland in river boats. In May 1780, the settlers adopted the Nashborough Compact, a frontier constitution that established local government for the French Lick region. The compact provided for land sales, the support of widows and orphans, and the organization of a militia for the common defense. The community was governed by twelve elected judges representing several scattered settlements. Robertson was elected the first chairman of the governing body.

THE WESTERN LANDS ISSUE

Most of the problems facing the new nation were Western-derived and centered around the proprietorship and management of the vast estate west of the mountains. People on the frontier felt little affinity for the far-off centers of administration in Virginia or North Carolina on whose lands they were developing farms and towns. Their detachment from Eastern state governments and their very real immediate need for local governmental apparatus to deal promptly with land survey and title problems, civil and criminal jurisdictional questions, and protection from Indian attacks led them to seek local solutions by attempting to organize state governments or by seceding and forming small independent nations.

Western Lands and the Articles of Confederation

The impact of the West on the young nation was felt early during debate on the Articles of Confederation. Six American states had no Western lands; seven states claimed Western lands. Spokesmen from the landless states, led by New Jersey and Maryland, stressed that since independence and Western territory had been dearly purchased by common sacrifice and struggle, the transmontane region should be a national estate, its benefits shared by all, and its lands a source of revenue for the new government.

Casting a cloud over the New Jersey–Maryland argument was the knowledge that a group of businessmen from these landless states led by Robert Morris had, in 1780, founded the Illinois-Wabash Company, a holding firm for component land companies that had purchased land in the Northwest from Indian tribes. Only if states holding lands in that area —notably Virginia and Connecticut—were to cede their tracts to the national government could the Illinois-Wabash grant become effective. The issue of cession of Western lands was the principal reason for delay in ratifying the Articles of Confederation. New York moved first in 1780, ceding state claims based on the Fort Stanwix Treaty of 1764 and New York's conquest of the Iroquois Confederation during the Revolution. By 1781 all land-holding states had agreed to cede their Western territories to the national government, and the Articles of Confederation, the nation's first constitution, went into effect.

Nationalization of Western Lands

However, most of the land-holding states fulfilled their pledges with utmost slowness. In 1781 Virginia ceded its Western lands in the Northwest with the exception of two tracts for state soldiers' bounties—the Virginia Military Reserve between Little Miami and Scioto rivers and a 150,000-acre tract across from Louisville, reserved for George Rogers Clark and his men. Virginia further stipulated that land-company purchases from Indian tribes in the area be declared null and void. This proviso wiped out the Illinois-Wabash Company. Connecticut in 1786 ceded its Western lands, retaining three and a half million acres along Lake Erie as the Western Reserve, for the benefit of "sufferers" of the war. North Carolina ceded its Western lands in 1784 but followed an ambiguous policy, from time to time reasserting control over its transmontane territory. Georgia did not finally cede its Western lands until 1802. Several Southern states with heavy war debts attempted to liquidate their obligations through sales of Western lands before they surrendered title. For much of the territory south of the Ohio River, therefore, about all the national government received from the transfer was jurisdiction.

The Northwest Ordinances

The national government took several steps to establish its dominion over the transmontane territory. In 1785 troops erected Fort Harmar at the mouth of the Muskingum River, on the Ohio River. Patrols from this frontier post were to guard the upper Ohio Valley, eject intruders from Kentucky, and keep peace with the Indian tribes. Congress also adopted three ordinances for the government and management of the territory north of the Ohio River.

The Ordinance of 1784 provided vaguely for the political organization of the Northwest, allowing the formation of new states from that region, each of which was to enter the union as an equal to the older states. A portion of the Northwest qualified for statehood when its population equalled that of the smallest state in the Union. Congress could then admit it by a two-thirds majority vote. The law contained no guidance nor set forth any procedures for organizing a state; and it made no provision for preliminary government before the state was ready for admission. By the Ordinance of 1784 ten states could be erected from the Northwest.

In 1785 Congress passed a second law for the Northwest Territory, in response to several needs. One was the necessity to produce some order out of the general chaos of land titles and surveys. All along the frontier, claims overlapped, and there was a complete lack of uniformity in surveys and land titles and in the method for recording claims. Two systems—one northern, one southern—functioned on the frontier. The northern mode developed from the New England scheme whereby settlement took place in an orderly fashion: precise surveys were made prior to settlement, and titles were filed and deeds recorded. On the southern frontier the settler usually acted independently, selecting his own tracts for purchase, defining the "meanderings of his boundary with as much accuracy as he could, and then procuring title from the province and record of his deeds at the county courthouse." This may, as some have claimed, "harmonized with the strong individuality of the frontier farmer and his uneasiness under restraint. But it produced conflicts of claims and interminable litigation over titles, much of which was not susceptible of precise adjudication." Overlapping claims were common "in the rapid settlement of Kentucky and Tennessee, where the southern system prevailed, the frontier lawyer sharpened his wits and filled his purse for years from the proceeds of boundary suits." [1]

It was to avoid the vagaries of the latter that most aspects of the New England system were made into law. According to the Ordinance of 1785, the public domain was to be surveyed into townships, each six miles square. Each township was divided by survey into sections of 640 acres each. Section sixteen in each township was reserved for the support of public schools. Half of the townships would be sold as a whole, the remainder by section; the minimum price was set at a dollar an acre. Officials planned to sell the land at public auctions in New York City.

The third and most important law passed by the Confederation Congress for the management of the Western estate was the Ordinance of 1787. It made more precise provisions for government in the region northwest of the Ohio River and created the Northwest Territory, from which three to five states could be created. Three stages were set for creating a state. In the first stage, a governor, secretary, and three judges, all ap-

[1] Frederic L. Paxson, *History of the American Frontier, 1763–1893* (New York, 1924), p. 59.

pointed by Congress, administered the territory. When the population of the territory reached 5,000 adult males, the settlers could elect a general assembly and a non-voting delegate to Congress. When the territory reached a population of 60,000, its citizens could write a constitution and apply for statehood.

The 1787 ordinance contained a bill of rights guaranteeing such freedoms as that of religion, and it prohibited slavery north of the Ohio River. It set a property qualification of 50 acres for voting and 200 acres for sitting in the assembly. By establishing the procedures for statehood the Ordinance of 1787 protected the West from permanent colonial status and served as the basic law for statemaking throughout the West, except for Texas and California.

Western Land Surveys

In 1785, Thomas Hutchins, the official geographer of the United States, began the systematic survey of the national domain north of the Ohio River. He started in the area of the "Seven Ranges" in southeastern Ohio. His field crews, harassed by Indians and slowed by dense timber and rough country, were able to survey only two ranges in two years. As the surveys proceeded, steps were taken to market the national estate. The Ordinance of 1785, which established the mode of selling large tracts, was tailor made for speculators, and in both the North and the South Western lands were subject to intense speculation. We will begin our view of the activities of the speculators south of the Ohio River.

The Yazoo Enterprise

The most extravagant, self-serving land deal in Western history was the Yazoo Enterprise. In 1789 the Georgia legislature adopted legislation that initiated the sale of over 25 million acres of Western land to the Tennessee Yazoo Company. Negotiations continued until 1795 when the obliging Georgia legislature increased the grant to over 30 million acres, to be conveyed to the three Yazoo companies for about one and a half cents an acre. Many prominent citizens were involved as stockholders in the three Yazoo land companies, including all but one member of the Georgia legislature. However, in 1796, a newly elected legislature annulled the Yazoo Company grants. The action had various and extended ramifications. One was the establishment of the Mississippi Territory by Congress in 1798 so as to provide some government for settlers moving into the disputed area. Congress also authorized the president to appoint three commissioners to negotiate with the state of Georgia for a final settlement of that state's Western lands. The result was the Georgia Compact, whereby Georgia ceded its remaining Western lands to the United States on condition that it receive $1,500,000 from the proceeds and that the United States extinguish title to all Indian lands in the state. The implications of these provisions for the West were far-reaching and will be dis-

cussed further in Chapter 10. The compact also provided that the ceded
territory was to be admitted as a slave state when its population reached
60,000, and that 5 million acres of the ceded territory was to be set aside
to satisfy the Yazoo claimants.

The issue of Western lands and legacy of the Yazoo enterprise nagged
at the national government for some time and led to a split in the Jeffersonian Republican Party. John Randolph led the "Quids," who claimed
that Jefferson had abandoned his states' rights stand of 1798 and was really
a Federalist because his support of the Yazoo Company interests protected
New England investors in Yazoo Company bonds. In 1810, in a landmark
decision, the United States Supreme Court in *Fletcher v. Peck* held that
Georgia had no right to nullify its contract with the Yazoo companies;
and in 1814 Congress appropriated $8 million to settle the Yazoo claims.

Western Land Companies

The members of the Confederation Congress were no less susceptible
to the attractions of speculation than the Georgia legislators. It was perhaps inevitable that high government officials would be involved in land-
company dealings in the Northwest, for the method of selling Northwest
land established by the Ordinance of 1785 favored the speculator. Land
was to be dispensed in large tracts, making it too expensive for the individual settler. Holding the public auction in New York City made it even
more difficult for the general public to benefit from the offering. When,
under the terms of the Ordinance of 1785, seven ranges beginning at the
western border of Pennsylvania were put on the market in 1788, sales were
disappointing to the revenue-hungry government. The large minimum
quantity of land and the relatively high cost of each transaction placed
the land out of reach for most purchasers. Settlers preferred to enter the
area as settlers rather than travel to New York to buy land.

At that point a horde of speculators stepped forward, offering to market the public domain. Congress signed contracts with three land companies: the Ohio Company of Associates, the Scioto Company, and the
John Cleves Symmes Company. The Ohio Company was formed in Massachusetts by Revolutionary War officers Samuel Parsons, Rufus Putnam,
and Benjamin Tupper; and their interest was represented in the Confederation Congress by Manasseh Cutler. The Ohio Company agreement provided for a grant of one and a half million acres at the rate of about eight
cents an acre on the instalment plan. The Ohio Company was to pay for
the land in depreciated currency issued during the war. A second land
jobber group, the Scioto Company, negotiated with Congress for five million acres of northwest land, also purchased on the instalment plan. Several
government officials, including William Duer, the Secretary of the Treasury
—the government agency in charge of land sales—were principal officers in
the Scioto Company. The third speculator combine, consisting of New
Jersey business interests headed by John Cleves Symmes, negotiated for a

million acres between the Little and Great Miami rivers. All three companies planned to profit by selling shares to Eastern and European investors.

The three speculator companies soon folded, defaulted on their payments for the land, and thereby annulled their contracts. But each company produced some settlement in the Northwest. In 1788 Rufus Putnam of the Ohio Company colonized nearly fifty families from New England and founded the town of Marietta near the mouth of the Muskingum River near Fort Harmar. The Scioto Company promoted its shares and recruited settlers in Europe. Joel Barlow, an American poet, and an Englishman, William Playfair, served as the company's agents. In Paris their promotion netted five hundred French colonists who reached the Ohio country and founded the town of Gallipolis. The hardships of the wilderness drove many of the French immigrants to the seaboard, but nearly 100 remained in Ohio. The Symmes Company in its short life attracted wide public notice to the Ohio country. Besides its promotion of farmland, the company was responsible for founding the town of Cincinnati.

WESTERN PACIFICATION

Before the national government could effectively administer the West as an integral part of the national domain and before settlers could assume permanent occupancy, the Indian problem had to be settled. The United States government continued to use the British approach in their relations with the tribes—that is, they recognized each tribe as a sovereign entity and dealt with them separately. As autonomous communities, the tribes governed and conducted internal affairs by traditional tribal methods. Anytime a change in relations between the tribe and the United States was required—such as making peace, altering trading privileges, or more importantly, ceding tribal lands—a treaty was negotiated by the president through his agents and ratified by the Senate, much like pacts with foreign powers.

Western Tribes and Foreign Intrigue

The Indian problem, both Northwest and Southwest, was complicated by foreign influences. Great Britain continued to occupy posts in the Northwest. Spain occupied an L-shaped perimeter boxing in the Americans in the Southwest; the Spanish settlements extended from Florida along the Gulf to the mouth of the Mississippi, then turned north of the 31° line at the east bank of the river. Spanish troops also occupied Natchez and a military post on the present site of Memphis at Chickasaw Bluffs.

British agents working among the Northwest tribes, particularly the Ottawas, Shawnees, Miamis, Delawares, and Kickapoos, provided warriors with guns, blankets, provisions, and gifts as inducements to raid the American settlements. Spanish agents attempted to forge the Indians of the

Southwest into a powerful defensive cordon to stem the American advance in that sector. Creek, Cherokee, and Choctaw leaders, and spokesmen for a small anti-American faction in the Chickasaw nation regularly met with Spanish representatives at Pensacola, Mobile, and New Orleans for direction. The Southern Indians in the Spanish defensive community were led by Alexander McGillivray, a mixed Scot-Creek chief, who was passionately attached to the land of his Indian forebears. Except for the small anti-American faction, the Chickasaw nation refused to join the Spanish cause. The Chickasaws, a staunch British ally in the long, bloody struggle for supremacy in the Mississippi Valley during colonial times, were largely responsible for driving the French from that region. For the most part they accepted the Americans after the war, and their stand against the Spanish and the Spanish-led Indians was a material factor in thwarting Spain's design for holding the Southwest against the American advance.

The new United States government began its relations with the Western tribes in the mid-1780s. By nationalizing Indian policy it took the initiative and prerogative from the states, which, as colonies, had each managed its Indian relations. Thus, instead of thirteen policies, there evolved a single uniform policy. In 1786 the Confederation Congress provided for the administration of Indian affairs through the creation of two departments, each in charge of a superintendent or commissioner. As in the old British system, the Ohio River was the dividing line. Congress also took steps to extend American dominion over the Western tribes through a series of councils presided over by American commissioners and attended by leaders of both Northern and Southern tribes.

The Northwest tribes first met with American commissioners at Fort Stanwix in 1784. There the remnants of the Iroquois Confederation tribes accepted American suzerainty and surrendered their claims to territory in the Northwest. A second session with the Northwest tribes was held at McIntosh in the Ohio country during 1785. Ottawa, Delaware, Chippewa, and Wyandot leaders acknowledged American dominion and ceded certain tribal lands in the Northwest. The third council session with the Northwest tribes was held at Fort Finney, Kentucky in 1786; Delaware, Wyandot, and Shawnee leaders acknowledged American dominion and assented to settlement in the Ohio country. In these treaties the American government agreed to keep settlers off Indian lands, and the Muskingum River was set as the boundary for settlement. To thwart American trespass west of the river, General Joseph Harmar constructed Fort Harmar at the mouth of the Muskingum.

South of the Ohio River were the Cherokees, who inhabited portions of Tennessee, northwestern Georgia, and northeastern Alabama; the Creeks, with a huge domain extending from western Georgia into Alabama; the Choctaws in southern Mississippi; and the Chickasaws in northern Mississippi and western Tennessee. The leaders of the Cherokee, Choctaw, and Chickasaw nations met with American commissioners at Hopewell in South Carolina in 1785–1786 to sign the Treaties of Hopewell, in which they accepted American suzerainty. The Creek nation did not accede until 1790, when they signed the Treaty of New York.

Pacification of the Northwest

Reaction among the Northwest tribes to the treaties, surveys, and expanding American settlements was prompt and devastating. Encouraged by British agents at Detroit and braced with arms, blankets, provisions, and gifts, warriors of the Wyandot, Shawnee, Delaware, Miami, Ottawa, Chippewa, Potawatomi, and Kickapoo tribes, and remnants of the Iroquois Confederation tribes prepared to ravage the intruding American settlements in southern Ohio. During 1787 Joseph Brant, the mixed Iroquois war leader, formed a confederacy among the Northwest tribes. The leaders pledged to cede no more land to the United States and repudiated the treaties of Fort Stanwix, Fort McIntosh, and Fort Finney. Spokesmen for the aboriginal confederacy met with American officials at Fort Harmar during January 1789, but Arthur St. Clair, governor of the Northwest Territory, would agree to nothing short of the conditions set forth in the earlier three treaties.

As settlements in the Ohio country increased, British-armed warriors cut a bloody swath from Chillicothe to the gates of Fort Harmar, and frontier militia companies retaliated with vengeance against the Indian towns on the Maumee. One estimate claims that 1,500 Ohio country settlers perished in British-directed Indian raids between 1783 and 1790. In 1790 President Washington called on Kentucky, Virginia, and Pennsylvania to send militia forces to the Northwest to pacify the frontier. During the summer of 1790, General Josiah Harmar mustered nearly 1,500 troops, motley and undisciplined, and marched toward the Maumee. Enroute his army destroyed several Indian villages. Miami, Shawnee, and Kickapoo war parties nagged at Harmar's flanks in the dark forests south of the Maumee. On September 19 a large Indian force struck from ambush, killing nearly 200 militiamen and sending the survivors in dreadful rout southward toward the safety of the Ohio River settlements.

The next year President Washington ordered Governor St. Clair to personally lead an army against the Northwest Indians. St. Clair's army consisted of six-month enlistees, most of them from the Eastern cities, and numbered about 3,000. The troops marched into the wilderness during the autumn of 1791 and constructed a line of support bases—Fort Hamilton, Fort St. Clair, and Fort Jefferson—along the line of march. On November 3, near the Maumee, St. Clair's army was struck by a surprise attack mounted by massed warriors; it provoked a confused, bloody retreat even worse than the preceding year's. Over 630 Americans died in battle, and nearly 300 were wounded. The survivors fled to Fort Jefferson, while the Indians followed up their smashing triumph over the American army with furious attacks on the Ohio settlements, forcing their evacuation to the Ohio River towns.

Once again, President Washington determined to end for all time the

Indian barrier to the American advance in the Northwest. To accomplish this he assigned General Anthony ("Mad Anthony") Wayne to command the new army of conquest. Wayne's men collected at Pittsburgh. There the Revolutionary War hero subjected them to intense training, stressing elementary discipline and the techniques of frontier warfare. During the autumn of 1793 Wayne's army entered the Northwest, occupied territory above old Fort Jefferson, and constructed Fort Greenville. The men wintered there and were given more drill and training in preparation for combat. The British countered Wayne's construction of Fort Greenville by erecting Fort Miami on the Maumee River to protect the approaches to Detroit. Over 2,000 warriors from the Northwest tribes collected at the new fort to meet the expected American spring offensive. Wayne's men constructed a post on the site of St. Clair's defeat; the commander expectantly named it Fort Recovery.

During June 1794, Wayne's well disciplined army was attacked by a large Indian force. Rather than breaking and fleeing in disorder toward the Ohio, the Americans, to the surprise of the aboriginal attackers, stood their ground, turned the assault, and won a victory. Again in August Wayne met the enemy in force at Fallen Timbers near Fort Miami. There the Americans won a second victory. To the consternation of the Indians on the battlefield, the British at nearby Fort Miami offered no aid and refused to open the post to the tribes during their retreat.

The Americans constructed Fort Wayne at the head of the Maumee, then, during 1795, collected the Northwest tribal leaders at Greenville. There they signed the Treaty of Greenville whereby the Indians conceded most of Ohio to the United States. In return the United States distributed $20,000 worth of goods to the signatory tribes and pledged an annuity of $10,000 to be shared by the subdued tribes, including the Delawares, Potawatomis, Wyandots, Shawnees, Miamis, Chippewas, Ottawas, and Kickapoos.

The smashing of Indian power in the Northwest just preceded and perhaps made possible an important diplomatic event. During November 1794, three months after Wayne's victory at Fallen Timbers, John Jay, American commissioner to Great Britain, negotiated the Jay Treaty, by which England pledged finally to surrender the Northwest posts no later than June 1, 1796. Thus, for a brief interval, both the British presence and Indian resistance to American expansion in the Northwest was ended.

Pacification of the Southwest

The Spanish-Indian link in the Southwest was an even more formidable barrier to American expansion. The Spanish used both diplomacy and Indian force to throttle the Americans. Because of their control of the Gulf and the mouth of the Mississippi River, the Spanish stranglehold was complete. Spanish officials regularly closed New Orleans and other ports to Americans who were attempting to export products from the Ohio Valley and the Southwest. In 1786, John Jay and Don Diego de Gardoqui negotiated the Jay-Gardoqui Treaty, which granted American shippers trading privileges in Spanish ports in return for the American abandonment of the right to navigate on the Mississippi River for twenty-five years. The treaty was not ratified by the Confederation Congress, but this obvious favor to Eastern seaboard mercantile interests at the expense of transmontane rights aroused great anxiety and fury in the West.

Spain also used military power to throttle Americans by occupying two military posts on the east bank of the Mississippi River—both on American soil, at Natchez and Chickasaw Bluffs—and by operating a fleet of heavily armed gunboats on the river. Spain's greatest strength in the Southwest, however, was derived from its success in consolidating the Choctaws, Creeks, and Cherokees into a defensive cordon. Spanish agents supplied them with arms and at times sent them against American settlements in Tennessee. The Creek Alexander McGillivray was the center of intertribal leadership for Spain's cause in the Southwest. The Spanish also conspired for American defection, attempting to persuade leaders and settlers in Kentucky and Tennessee to secede from the United States and join the Spanish empire. In 1789 Spanish policy even encouraged Americans to move to Florida and Louisiana, where, they were promised, they would enjoy religious toleration, equal commercial privileges, and free land.

The Spanish anti-American scheme in the Southwest collapsed during the 1790s, principally because of counter-diplomacy by the United States to win the loyalty of Alexander McGillivray, leader of the Spanish-Indian confederation. McGillivray visited the nation's capital, then at New York City, in 1790 by invitation of President Washington. There he was feted by federal officials and awarded the rank of brigadier-general, United States Army, with an annual salary of $1,200. McGillivray continued as Spanish agent but with considerably less vigor. He died in 1793, terminating the most important link the Spanish had with the Southern Indians.

Another cause of the Spanish collapse was the successful Cherokee pacification. A growing segment of that populous nation had come to accept peace and American presence in their territory. The die-hard group, the Chickamaugas, perhaps seeing the inevitability of the American advance, began during the 1790s to drift west of the Mississippi River into Spanish territory and to settle permanently along the Arkansas and St. Francis rivers.

A third factor that thwarted Spanish purpose in the Southwest was the pro-American stand taken by the Chickasaw nation. Long attached to the British, the Chickasaws accepted the Americans after the Treaty of Hopewell, and, except for a small anti-American faction, they consistently refused to join McGillivray's Indian confederation. Creek war parties regularly invaded the Chickasaw domain in attempts to intimidate the Chickasaws into joining the Spanish-Indian confederation against the Americans. When, soon after 1790, Piomingo, the Mountain Leader, appealed to James Robertson of the Tennessee settlements for aid, Robertson generously supplied it in the form of powder and shot. Piomingo held firm. His American-armed warriors defeated the Creek invaders and destroyed all hope of forcing them into the alliance. Their towns also served as strategic centers for American agents in the Southwest.

Pressure by the United States government on Spain for evacuation of American Territory came to a climax in 1795, when Thomas Pinckney, the American commissioner, concluded the Treaty of San Lorenzo. By its terms Spain agreed to withdraw from territory on the east bank of the Mississippi River north of 31°, American rights to navigate the Mississippi were acknowledged, and they were granted "right of deposit" of export goods for three years at New Orleans. Spanish withdrawal from the territory north of 31° was not, in fact, completed until 1798.

WESTERN PARTICULARISM

Having settled for the time being trans-Appalachian West Indian and diplomatic problems, the national government turned to other problems generated by this vast region, principally the lack of effective political administration. For years the Western border had not received from the national government the prompt attention its people expected, and impatient Westerners became adept at organizing local government. The Watauga Association Compact and the Nashborough Compact established governmental structures sufficient for local needs. But these became inadequate as settlement expanded, population increased, and local needs impinged on regional and even national needs. Westerners were restive because they had no voice to speak for their interests in the national government. They became especially suspicious of the seaboard-dominated national government after the Jay-Gardoqui treaty negotiations, for, if ratified, the treaty would have sacrificed their vital life line on the Mississippi River for the benefit of Eastern mercantile interests.

The Western response to what they perceived as neglect by the national government took various forms, including conspiracies with French and Spanish officials, serious consideration of secession from the United States, and locally initiated attempts at integrating the scattered settlements into states or even a Western nation. The Western propensity for conspiracy and secession was fed by the ambitions of Western leaders, for this region had attracted strong, daring, ambitious men, anxious for wealth and power. Their schemes of private and public empire-building and their personal popularity among Westerners caused the national government constant concern and rather regular difficulty.

Western Cabals

One of the most extraordinary schemes for Western involvement began with the arrival at Charleston in 1793 of Edmond Charles Genêt, agent for the revolutionary government of France. His mission was to restore New Orleans and Louisiana to France, and to do so he planned to recruit a Western army from the transmontane American and French settlements. Genêt's representative in the West was André Michaux, the French naturalist. Michaux contacted the ever-willing George Rogers Clark, who accepted appointment as "Major General of the Independent and Revolutionary Legion of the Mississippi." Clark sent forth a call for troops for the Revolutionary Legion, promising recruits monthly pay of $30 and 1,000 acres of land for each year of service. President Washington halted Genêt's scheme by issuing a neutrality declaration and forbidding enlistment of troops in the legion.

During this period of neglect by the national government virtually every prominent Western figure consorted with Spanish officials. John Sevier and James Robertson, land speculators and founders of Tennessee settlements, were in communication with Esteban Miró, the Spanish governor at New Orleans, seeking his intercession with the Creeks raiding their settlements. They openly proposed alliances between Spain and the southwestern American settlements. George Rogers Clark regularly urged Spanish officials to permit him to found colonies in Spanish territory, and Clark's brother-in-law, James O'Fallon, proposed that Spain support Clark in founding a colony in the Yazoo valley on American territory. He would then create a new state and ally it to Spain. James White, a Tennessee adventurer, had a plan which he shared with Spanish officials calling for the American West to declare its independence and be taken under Spanish suzerainty.

But the most egregious rascal of all western adventurers was James Wilkinson of Maryland. At the age of twenty he rose to the rank of brigadier-general in the Continental Army. In the 1780s Wilkinson traveled to Kentucky and engaged in land speculation, trading, and other enterprises. He became acquainted with Spanish officials through his trading ventures in New Orleans, and was an open advocate of Western secession and attachment to Spain. He became an esteemed informant for the Spanish government; in 1791 Spanish officials placed him on the payroll as a secret agent, granted him special trading concessions at New Orleans, and assigned him the special mission of promoting secession of the West and attachment to Spain. When General Wayne died in 1796, Wilkinson succeeded him as commanding general of the American army in the West. According to one estimate, by the time of his appointment he had already received $30,000 as a Spanish agent. Through Wilkinson, Spanish officials were kept well informed of official American political and military plans for the West.

Another Southwesterner who mixed public duty and private ambition was William Blount. When Congress created the Southwestern Territory in 1790 he was appointed its first governor. The territory was admitted to the Union in 1796 as the state of Tennessee, and Blount was elected United States senator. He subsequently became involved in a conspiracy to raise a Southwestern army and, with support from the British fleet, conquer Spanish Florida and Louisiana for the benefit of Great Britain. Informants aborted Blount's conquest plan; he was exposed and in 1797 was expelled from the United States Senate.

One of the most mystifying incidents occurring in the West was the so-called Burr Conspiracy. Inevitably it involved the ubiquitous General James Wilkinson. Aaron Burr, vice-president of the United States (1801–1805), an outcast from the Jeffersonian Republican party because of his stance in the presidential election of 1800, was scorned in the East for killing Alexander Hamilton in a duel. He turned to the West and discussed Western schemes and empire-building with both British and Spanish officials. In Western towns he talked with local leaders, who stated that he announced plans for carving a Southwestern empire and of becoming emperor of Mexico. He corresponded with Wilkinson in code and also visited him. In 1806, Burr collected men and supplies in the Ohio Valley preparatory, many authorities believed, to making a thrust into the Spanish Southwest. Wilkinson informed President Jefferson of the Burr plot, which, he said, was bound for Vera Cruz. Eventually Burr was arrested, tried for treason in federal court at Richmond, and acquitted.

Western Secession

Activities such as these by ambitious, self-willed men kept the West in an uproar. The closest thing to a successful political entity formed as a response to the Western ferment was the state of Franklin. In 1784, North Carolina ceded its Western lands to the United States; it rescinded the action later the same year, but not before frontier politicians had formed the state of Franklin. At the Jonesboro convention the Tennessee settlements coalesced into a state—which they named Franklin in honor of Benjamin Franklin—and claimed attributes of both a state and a nation. The delegates drafted a constitution, declared independence, and elected John Sevier governor. The state sought recognition from other nations and certain American states; it also negotiated treaties with Indian tribes. Soon anti-Franklin forces in western North Carolina, mostly competing land speculators headed by John Tipton, organized a rival government for the region. Leaders of the two governments waged verbal warfare and on one occasion, overt, bloody combat. Both governments collapsed in 1788, and the following year North Carolina again ceded its Western lands to the United States.

WESTERN INTEGRATION

In the meantime, steps were being taken to construct a more effective instrument of government for the new nation, one with broader powers to enable it to act more effectively and promptly in managing the transmontane territory. The new constitution went into effect in 1789. Under it the federal government acted to solve the Western problem by providing guidance for establishing government for the region and by adopting land laws that made it easier for the individual settler to establish claims on the public domain.

Land Reform

The land problem was closely related to the problem of political organization, for there was no voice to sound the real needs of the West. Until the people of the Northwest Territory received this political voice through the congressional delegate, the settlers could only appeal to Congress by letter and memorial for more realistic land legislation. In 1796 Congress adopted a land act that provided credit for Westerners by permitting payments for land to be extended over twelve months. The act also directed the opening of land offices more convenient to Westerners, at Pittsburgh and Cincinnati, and increased the minimum price per acre from one to two dollars.

By 1799 the Ohio country had a high enough population to merit organization at the second level of territorial government, which included electing a territorial delegate to Congress. William Henry Harrison was elected to this office. He obtained congressional approval of the Land Law of 1800, which increased the number of land offices to four—Cincinnati, Marietta, Chillicothe, and Steubenville—each staffed with a registrar for drawing up deeds and a receiver to handle proceeds from public land sales. The act provided that east of the Muskingum River land was to be sold at auction in tracts of a section each; west of the river in tracts of 320 acres each. The minimum price of two dollars per acre was retained, with the purchaser required to pay the cost of survey. Any land unsold after auction was open to private entry at the minimum price. Credit was further extended by the requirement that only one-fourth of the purchase price was due at the time of sale, the balance falling due in instalments over the next four years. The Land Law of 1804 reduced the minimum purchase to 160 acres and, finally, the Land Law of 1817 set it at 80 acres.

Western State-Making

The Northwest Ordinance of 1787 was applied to the territory north of the Ohio River. South of the Ohio the national estate was encumbered by expanding settlements and conflicting state jurisdictions. Finally in 1790, Congress passed an act creating the Southwest Territory, which gave some direction to the organization of the clusters of settlements that were subsequently integrated into the state of Tennessee. In the 1780s and 90s Kentucky was a huge Western county of Virginia, and Kentuckians were restive. They particularly objected to the virtual inaccessibility of the courts. Residents of the county held a number of statehood conventions, and on three occasions Virginia approved statehood for the region, but each time the question of admission of Kentucky to the Union was stalled in the slow-moving Confederation Congress. Finally, in 1792, a more responsive

Congress, functioning under the system created by the new federal Constitution, admitted Kentucky to the Union. It was the first state created from the transmontane West. In 1796, Congress admitted Tennessee.

Slowly but with eventual certainty, nationalizing currents throbbed through the American West; their momentum developed during the 1790s and noticeably accelerated after 1800. Even though it never matched the speed of expansion by its people, by 1828 the national government had integrated the Northwest, the Southwest, and the Mississippi Valley into the American Union.

SELECTED SOURCES

The important early American concerns in the West were land policy, diplomacy, Indian relations, transmontane particularism, and state-making. Prime sources for exploring the topic of early land policy in the West include *Roy M. Robbins, Our Landed Heritage (Princeton, N.J., 1942); *Benjamin H. Hibbard, A History of Public Land Policies (New York, 1924); Payson J. Treat, The National Land System, 1785–1820 (New York, 1920); Marshall Harris, Origin of the Land Tenure System in the United States (Ames, Iowa, 1953); Merrill Jensen, "The Creation of the National Domain, 1781–1784," Mississippi Valley Historical Review 13 (December 1939); C. Peter McGrath, Yazoo: Law and Politics in the New Republic (Providence, R.I., 1966); and Paul W. Gates and Robert W. Swenson, History of Public Land Law Development (Washington, D.C., 1969).

The American diplomacy that moderated Spanish and British pressures on the American West is chronicled in Samuel F. Bemis, *Jay's Treaty (New York, 1924) and Pinckney's Treaty (Baltimore, 1926); E. Wilson Lyon, Louisiana in French Diplomacy, 1795–1804 (Norman, 1934); and *Arthur P. Whitaker, The Spanish-American Frontier, 1783–1795 (Boston, 1927).

Early national relations with Western Indian tribes are described in Harry E. Wildes, Anthony Wayne (New York, 1941); John W. Caughey, McGillivray of the Creeks (Norman, 1938); *Reginald Horsman, The Frontier in the Formative Years, 1783–1815 (New York, 1970); Walter H. Mohr, Federal Indian Relations, 1773–1788 (Philadelphia, 1933); and Francis P. Prucha, The Sword of the Republic: The United States Army on the Frontier, 1783–1846 (New York, 1969).

Manifestations of Western particularism are traced in Samuel C. Williams, History of the Lost State of Franklin (Johnson City, Tenn., 1924); Carl S. Driver, John Sevier (Chapel Hill, N.C., 1932); and James R. Jacobs, Tarnished Warrior: Major-General James Wilkinson (New York, 1938).

Early Western state-making can be traced in Thomas D. Clark, A History of Kentucky (New York, 1937); Robert S. Cotterill, History of Pioneer Kentucky (Cincinnati, 1917); Thomas P. Abernethy, From Frontier to Plantation in Tennessee (Chapel Hill, N.C., 1932) and The South in the New Nation, 1789–1819 (Baton Rouge, La., 1961).

* Available in paperback.

Tecumseh's Defeat at the Battle of the Thames, 1813.

The Battle of New Orleans, 1815

8

The Old West

AMERICAN expansion after 1800 developed an irrepressible momentum that successively absorbed great chunks of the trans-Mississippi West and, through its vanguard elements, threatened to engulf the adjoining territory all the way to the Pacific. The fruits of this sustained, aggressively expansive thrust—a substantial increase in American territory—produced a dichotomy in the identity of the trans-Appalachian region. The territory between the Appalachian Mountains and the first tier of emergent states west of the Mississippi River became the Old West. The region beyond that first tier became the New West. In the period between 1800 and 1828, the Old West crystallized into an identifiable geographic and cultural entity, consisting of three subregions or provinces—the Old Northwest and the Old Southwest, separated from each other by the Ohio River, and the Mississippi Valley.

AMERICAN BEGINNINGS IN THE OLD NORTHWEST

We have seen in Chapter 7 that the national government in the 1790s had provided for the governance of the territory north of the Ohio River and, by military force and diplomacy, had for the time removed the foreign and Indian obstacles to settlement. General Wayne's campaign had crushed the Northwest tribes and forced them to cede their claims to most of Ohio and a portion of Indiana. By the terms of the Jay Treaty the British had finally evacuated Detroit and other British-held settlements on American soil. Thirteen years after the end of the Revolution—on July 11, 1796—American troops occupied Detroit.

The Ohio Settlement

The line of military posts from Fort McIntosh at the mouth of Big River in western Pennsylvania, south and west through the Ohio country to Fort Washington (guarding Cincinnati), provided some order and security in the wilds of the Northwest. Settlers streamed into the Ohio country from three directions. Many moved out from Pittsburgh on flatboats and coasted the north bank of the Ohio in search of homesites. Others traversed Kentucky and Tennessee, then crossed the Ohio River to found settlements in the interior of the Northwest. Marietta and Cincinnati were the leading towns in the southern Ohio country.

By 1797, nine counties had been organized in the Ohio country. In that year the pioneers applied to the national government through Governor St. Clair for authority to proceed with the organization of a territorial government, as provided by the Northwest Ordinance. St. Clair designated Cincinnati the capital for the emergent territory. The following year Ohio voters elected their first territorial legislature and their congressional delegate, William Henry Harrison.

Ohio Statehood

The Ohio Territory swiftly met the congressionally designated conditions for statehood, and in 1802 Congress adopted the Ohio Enabling Act, which authorized the residents of the territory to select representatives to meet in convention to draft a state constitution. The delegates met at Chillicothe during November 1802, and composed the state's organic law, which vested the supreme power in a bicameral legislature. Eligible voters were defined as all white males, 21 years of age and over. This same group was also designated as the state militia; and officers in the militia through the rank of brigadier-general were to be elected by men in the ranks. The executive power of the new state was vested in a governor selected by popular election every two years. His authority was severely limited, and he lacked the power to veto legislation. The Ohio judiciary was also reduced to secondary status, in that judges were elected by the legislature to seven-year terms.

The fact that the Ohio constitution placed the supreme power in the legislature—the voice of the people—created a weak executive branch with no veto, and made the judiciary dependent on the legislature, has been taken by some as a manifestation of a new kind of frontier democracy. According to this idea, the Western influence altered American political institutions. However, from the perspective of the state-making as it took place all across the American West, these deviations appear to be due less to the influence of the frontier environment and more to local reaction to certain nationalizing currents. The Northwest Ordinance provided that, in a new territory, the president would appoint the governor and certain other officials, including the judiciary. Under territorial government, therefore, local citizens could elect only their municipal and county officials,

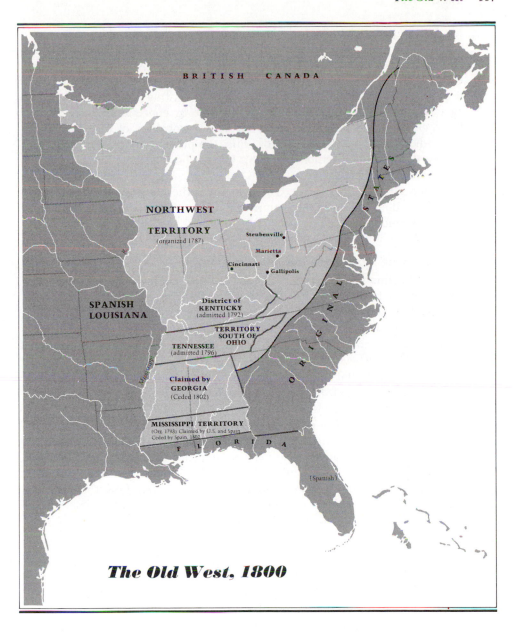

BRITISH   CANADA

NORTHWEST

TERRITORY
(organized 1787)

Steubenville

Marietta

Cincinnati

Gallipolis

SPANISH
LOUISIANA

District of
KENTUCKY
(admitted 1792)

TERRITORY
SOUTH OF
OHIO

TENNESSEE
(admitted 1796)

Claimed by
GEORGIA
(Ceded 1802)

MISSISSIPPI TERRITORY
(Org. 1793) Claimed by U.S. and Spain
Ceded by Spain, 1802

FLORIDA

[Spanish]

ORIGINAL STATES

The Old West, 1800

legislative representatives, and the congressional delegate. The governor and judges were thus independent of the popular will. Usually these officials were outsiders, and the people of the territories scorned "carpetbag rule." From the Ohio Territory to New Mexico, Arizona, and Oklahoma, regularly, the popular response at constitution-writing time was to react against territorial despotism and carpetbag rule by concentrating power in the legislature and reducing the power and prerogatives of the executive and judicial branches. In the case of Ohio, the public reaction was directed specifically against Governor Arthur St. Clair, who was very unpopular and denounced as a tyrant.

Ohio was admitted to the Union in 1803, the first state formed from the public domain; it set the pattern for most of the states to be created from the American West.

The New Territories: Indiana and Illinois

While Ohio was being readied for statehood, the national government was preparing the remainder of the Northwest Territory for settlement and statehood. In 1800, Ohio congressional delegate William Henry Harrison obtained approval of a law creating the Indiana Territory; originally Indiana embraced all of the United States domain in the Northwest outside of Ohio. Harrison, who was appointed first governor of the new territory, established the capital of the territory at Vincennes. The settler flow into Indiana exceeded 5,000 by 1805, and in that year Congress detached the northern portion of the Indiana Territory and created the Michigan Territory. Also in 1805, the citizens of Indiana elected their first territorial legislature. By the eve of the War of 1812, the Indiana Territory had a population of more than 25,000. Congress detached the western half of the Indiana Territory in 1809 and established the Illinois Territory; Ninian Edwards of Kentucky was appointed its first governor. Less than three years after its formation, the Illinois Territory had already attracted a population of 13,000 and had a territorial legislature.

AMERICAN BEGINNINGS IN THE OLD SOUTHWEST

Nationalizing currents were also flowing through that portion of the Western United States south of the Ohio River. There too diplomacy with foreign nations and Indian tribes had erased security threats and opened new lands to settlement. Congress had provided guidelines for the organization of territories and admission of states. Spain had agreed, through the Treaty of San Lorenzo (1795), to evacuate all American territory on the Mississippi River north of the international boundary, 31° north. Of great benefit to all Westerners were the provisions of the treaty acknowledging free navigation of the Mississippi River and the right of deposit—without payment of customs duties—at the Spanish port of New Orleans.

Mississippi Territory

In 1790, Congress had organized the federal domain south of the Ohio River into the Southwestern Territory, with headquarters at Nashville. William Blount was its first governor. Kentucky and Tennessee, formerly huge Western counties of Virginia and North Carolina, were admitted to the Union in 1792 and 1796.

The land between Tennessee's southern border and Spanish West Florida was claimed by Georgia. In 1785 Georgia organized Bourbon County in the Natchez district on the Mississippi River to accommodate the notorious Yazoo Land Company. Congress countered in 1798 by creating the Mississippi Territory; it was to include all land between Tennessee's southern border and 31° and extend west from the Chattahoochee-Apalachicola River to the Mississippi. At that time, the Mississippi Territory embraced all of the present states of Alabama and Mississippi north of 31°. Winthrop Sargent was appointed territorial governor. In 1802, by the Georgia Compact, the state finally acknowledged United States title to the Mississippi Territory.

Growth of Old Southwest Settlements

Under the aegis of the federal government—especially extension of the military frontier—the Old Southwest matched and in some respects exceeded the demographic and cultural development of the Old Northwest. Kentucky's population on the eve of statehood in 1790 was 73,700. By 1800, it had increased to 221,000. During the same period Tennessee's population increased from 35,700 to nearly 106,000. The Mississippi Territory in 1800, two years after its creation, had attracted nearly 10,000 settlers; and its population quadrupled by the end of the decade.

AMERICAN BEGINNINGS IN THE MISSISSIPPI VALLEY

The geographic perimeter of the Old West was completed soon after 1800 when the Mississippi Valley was integrated into the American community. The expansion virus that accomplished this extension—with the frontiersman serving as agent and the national government as patron—infected succeeding generations of Americans. Early expansion in the Old West served as the model for recurring territorial appropriation to the Pacific. Expansion had become a part of the national ethos.

Acquisition of the Mississippi Valley

American acquisition of the Mississippi Valley portion of the Old West was accomplished by a three-step process. Step one established American presence in the province. Americans moved into Spanish Florida and Louisiana in response to a royal Spanish decree issued in 1788. The decree promised American settlers grants of land and religious toleration in exchange for an oath of allegiance to Spain. By 1803, over 10,000 Americans had taken up residence near St. Louis, Cape Girardeau, New Madrid, Ste. Genevieve, and St. Charles in upper Louisiana. The immigrants included Daniel Boone of Kentucky, who developed agricultural settlements west of St. Louis, and Moses Austin, a Virginian who opened several lead mines in eastern Missouri. In lower Louisiana, immigrants established settlements along the Arkansas, Red, and Ouachita rivers. Another popular settlement zone for Americans was in West Florida near Baton Rouge and Mobile. The unexpectedly heavy American response to the offer of free land in West Florida and Louisiana caused Spanish officials to terminate the land grant decree in 1802.

Step two involved diplomacy. In 1800, by the Treaty of San Ildefonso, Spain returned Louisiana to France. News of the transfer of this strategic province provoked great concern in the United States, particularly in the West. Fears were confirmed in 1802 when both the right of deposit for American shippers at New Orleans and American immigration were revoked. Although Spanish officials continued to administer Louisiana, these anti-American measures were blamed on the French government, which was headed by Napoleon Bonaparte. Western legislatures sent memorials to the national government strongly urging retaliatory action.

President Thomas Jefferson feigned a military build-up—ostensibly preparatory to invading Louisiana—and made friendly gestures toward Great Britain, France's most committed antagonist in the bloody Napoleonic wars. Jefferson also developed a plan to break the shipping blockade by purchasing from France a parcel of Gulf frontage, including the port of New Orleans. In 1803 Jefferson sent special envoy James Monroe to join Robert Livingston, American minister at Paris, in presenting the plan to the French government. To the surprise of both Americans, Minister of Foreign Affairs Talleyrand responded by offering to sell to the United States all of Louisiana. The Louisiana Purchase agreement, negotiated on April 30, 1803, provided that France cede the entire province of Louisiana for the sum of $15 million—one-fourth of which was to be paid to Americans who had claims against France for maritime damages. On November 30, 1803, at New Orleans, then a city of 8,000 people, Spanish officials transferred Louisiana to representatives from France. The following December 20, in a public ceremony in the same city, French officials tendered Louisiana to American commissioners William C. C. Claiborne and James Wilkinson.

Step three involved the naked appropriation of Spanish territory by the American citizens. The Spanish land grant decree that had attracted a heavy flow of American settlers into Louisiana had a similar effect on West Florida. After 1803 American ownership of Louisiana created a threatening enclave in the Gulf, separating Spanish Florida from Spanish Texas and its contiguous territories. American settlers continued to press into West Florida, not only from the adjacent Mississippi Territory but, after 1803, from American Louisiana as well. By 1809 it was estimated that

90 percent of the population in the portion of West Florida west of the Pearl River were American immigrants.

In September 1810, an armed band of American settlers marched on Baton Rouge, captured the Spanish governor, and urged the United States government to annex West Florida. On October 27, President James Madison declared that West Florida was properly a part of Louisiana and directed Governor Claiborne to take possession of the strip of territory between 31° north and the Gulf, east of the Perdido River. At the time, however, American dominion was established only as far east as the Pearl River, leaving the territory around Mobile and Pensacola for later acquisition.

NATIONAL SUPPORT
OF OLD WEST DEVELOPMENT

We have seen how the national government, in the period between 1795 and 1812, contributed materially to the Anglo-American occupation of the Old West, conquering recalcitrant tribes and using the national diplomatic machinery to mitigate British and Spanish threats to Western settlements. Louisiana was acquired through negotiations, adding the vast Mississippi Valley province to American territory, and part of Spanish West Florida was annexed by American-settler occupation and presidential approval.

Land Law Reform

Additional steps taken by the national government to assure the sustained development of the trans-Appalachian Territory included adoption of laws that liberalized disposal of public lands. The Harrison Land Law of 1800 reduced the minimum acreage required for purchase from 640 acres to 320 acres, at a minimum price of two dollars per acre. This statute also extended to settlers much needed credit by permitting instalment buying: $160 as initial payment, the balance due in four years. In 1804, Congress lowered the minimum acreage to 160.

Western Road System

The national government also assisted Western states and territories in developing a system of public roads. In the late eighteenth century, Eastern states and private interests had constructed communication links across the mountains to the edge of the trans-Appalachian wilderness. Many of these roads followed old colonial military tracks; the oldest and most heavily traveled were Braddock's Road, which connected the upper Potomac settlements with Pittsburgh, and Forbes' Road, linking Philadelphia and Pittsburgh. The states of Maryland and Pennsylvania had improved Braddock's and Forbes' roads so that they could accommodate wagon traffic from the seaboard towns.

Eastern state governments and businessmen also financed new turnpikes (toll roads) suitable to wagon traffic to connect the seaboard with Pittsburgh and other trans-Appalachian entrepôts. The Lancaster Pike, constructed in part from a $100,000 subsidy provided by the state of Pennsylvania, terminated at Pittsburgh. Business interests from several New England and New York towns also organized turnpike companies and financed road building from the Eastern towns of their region to the settlements on the western border. The Mohawk Turnpike and the Catskill Turnpike were the two principal arteries carrying West-bound immigrants from the Northeast. The Great Genessee Road was connected to the Mohawk Turnpike at Utica and ran to the eastern shore of Lake Erie.

Another significant early road to the interior of Ohio was Zane's Trace, opened in 1796 by Ebenezer Zane. This thoroughfare ran from Wheeling on the upper Ohio River, through the Ohio settlements of Zanesville and Chillicothe, and angled southwesterly to the Ohio River across from the Kentucky settlement of Limestone.

Southern feeders into the West included the Great Valley Road and the Richmond Road in Virginia, which met in the mountains at Fort Chissell to form a single wagon road to the Cumberland Gap; there they joined the Wilderness Road across Kentucky to Louisville. The Jonesboro Road tied the North Carolina towns with the Tennessee settlements; it crossed the mountains to fuse with Knoxville, Nashville, and Walton roads.

The National Road

The national government's contribution to Western road building included the labor of soldiers who hacked roads through the trans-Appalachian wilds to connect the string of military fortifications and establish essential supply routes. These military roads were also used extensively by pioneers entering the new country. In addition, the government negotiated treaties with Indian tribes to obtain right-of-way for strategic arteries. One of the most important was an 1801 treaty with the Chickasaws whereby tribal leaders permitted the building of a public road through their nation between Nashville and Natchez on the Mississippi.

The statute that admitted Ohio to the Union in 1803 contained a clause providing that a portion of the proceeds from the sale of public lands in Ohio would be used for road building. A proposal for Western road building under direct national auspices was made during the Jefferson administration. Albert Gallatin, secretary of the treasury, conceived a plan for the construction of a public highway to be named the National Road; commencing at Cumberland, Maryland, it was to extend to Wheeling on the Ohio River. The surface of the National Road was crushed stone and stone bridges were built over creeks and rivers. Construction began in 1811; the Wheeling section was completed in 1818; and in 1833 an extension of the National Road reached Columbus, Ohio.

THE WAR OF 1812

During the period 1809 to 1815, the consummation of American purpose in the Old West was once more abruptly checked by an intruding European-aboriginal barrier, and another destructive, bloody war had to be fought before the vital frontier processes and nationalizing currents could resume their progress across the trans-Appalachian West.

Expansion as a Cause of Conflict

In both the Old Northwest and the Old Southwest an essential preliminary to settler advance was the erasure of Indian title to the land. Federal commissioners achieved spectacular success in reducing the domain of certain tribes in both the Northwest and the Southwest in order to keep an ample supply of land available for the oncoming settlers.

A consummate negotiator was William Henry Harrison, governor of the Indiana Territory. By 1809 he had completed fifteen treaties calling for substantial cessions of territory by the Piankeshaws, Weas, Delawares, Potawatomis, Miamis, Kickapoos, Ottawas, and other Northwest tribes. In 1809 at Fort Wayne he concluded a treaty with Delaware and Potawatomi leaders ceding 3 million acres of tribal land in Indiana to the United States in exchange for $7,000 and an annuity of $1,750. The Fort Wayne Treaty marked the high point of Harrison's treatymaking success.

Tecumseh and Indian Nationalism

Out of the crucible of Indian cultural deterioration came an integrating force that fused the scattered, confused, intimidated tribes of the Northwest into an awesome union. The brothers Tecumseh and Elskwatawa, known as the Prophet, were endowed by their Shawnee-Creek parentage with a rare combination of personality, perception, and rich eloquence. In the second decade of the century they combined their remarkable talents to forge a common brotherhood among the tribes of the Northwest.

In 1808 Tecumseh and the Prophet moved from a small Shawnee settlement near Greenville, Ohio, to the ruins of Kithtippecanoe, an old Indian town of Tippecanoe Creek. The settlement came to be called Prophetstown and was a center for the various tribes of the Northwest. Beginning with 140 followers, the Prophet and Tecumseh initiated an evangelistic crusade that inspired the periodic migration of thousands of Indian families to the council grounds on the edge of Prophetstown. There the listeners were entranced with the oratorical brilliance of Tecumseh and the mystical aberrations of the Prophet, each focusing his special talents on the theme of Indian nationalism. The popular teachings of the Prophet and Tecumseh described and interpreted the woes of the Indian: both pointed to rampant drunkenness and degeneracy, the reduction of tribal hunting grounds, internal divisions, and the abandonment of certain old customs that had been sources of Indian strength. The debauchery and poverty of the tribes, in fact every torment of the moment, were attributed to the American advance in the Northwest.

Elskwatawa was more of a zealot than Tecumseh, sometimes using mystical seizures to render messages from the Great Spirit. Through the Prophet, the Great Spirit promised that soon they would have the means to destroy every American. The Prophet assured his audiences that he had been endowed with the power to cure all disease, confound enemies, and stay the arm of death in sickness or on the battlefield. The Great Spirit, he claimed, had ordained a new way of life for his children, and all must purify themselves and adopt it. No follower was to have any dealings with Americans. The English were to be considered the friends of the Indians; the Americans, the enemies.

The stability of Tecumseh complemented his volatile brother. Avoiding the emotional dramatic technique of the Prophet, Tecumseh maintained a rational approach to the Indians' problems. His legalism was persuasive. He claimed no special access to the Great Spirit, but taught with directness: drunkenness and vice were condemned; the white man's ways were to be shunned; each warrior must return to certain old customs. As a symbol of Indian rejection of white culture, textile clothing should be abolished and the Indian should wear skins as of old. Each warrior was to reform his personal conduct in order to reconstruct his physical, moral, and spiritual strength.

Since most of the Indian-American friction grew out of the issue of land tenure, Tecumseh directed his attention, first, to retaining what was left of Indian lands, and, second, to recovering lands in the possession of the Americans. The basis for Tecumseh's argument was that in the beginning the Great Spirit had provided the land for the use of all his children. No single tribe was intended to be the sole proprietor of a given area; all land was ordained to be held in common. Therefore, no tribe or faction of a tribe could presume to transfer title of land to the United States without the common consent of all the Indians.

Most of the Indian communicants returned to their home villages to ponder the teachings of Tecumseh and the Prophet and to relate them to their fellow tribesmen. They returned from time to time to receive an interpretation of the most recent revelation by the mystical Elskwatawa or an exposition from the eloquent Tecumseh. Many, however, accepted Indian nationalism so completely that they separated from their tribes, built lodges for their families at Prophetstown, and settled there permanently. By 1811 the community could boast nearly 1,000 warriors from the various tribes.

After the Fort Wayne Treaty negotiations, Tecumseh personally confronted Governor Harrison and repudiated the treaty "on the ground that all the land belonged to all the Indians, and that not even the whole membership of a single tribe could alienate the property of the race."

Harrison was warned to keep surveyors and settlers out of the tract ceded by the Treaty of Fort Wayne. There ensued a two-year impasse. It was apparent to Harrison that if Tecumseh's will prevailed, a permanent Indian barrier would stretch across the northwestern corner of Indiana and would "exclude the United States from further expansion."

During 1811, Tecumseh, accompanied by a Kickapoo escort, visited the Indian tribes south of the Ohio River and urged them to join him in his cause to check the expansive Americans. At councils with the Choctaws, Chickasaws, Creeks, and Cherokees, he pointed to the menace of the on-rushing white horde. His orations usually included this galvanizing denunciation: "The white race is a wicked race. Since the day when the white race first came in contact with the red men, there has been a continual series of aggressions. The hunting grounds are fast disappearing, and they are driving the red man farther and farther to the west. Such has been the fate of the Shawnees, and surely will be the fate of all tribes if the power of the whites is not forever crushed. The mere presence of the white man is a source of evil to the red man. His whiskey destroys the bravery of our warriors, and his lust corrupts the virtue of our women. The only hope for the red man is a war of extermination against the paleface. Will not the warriors of the southern tribes unite with the warriors of the Lakes?" [1] Of all the Southern tribes, Tecumseh's doctrine appealed to only one faction in the Creek nation, the Red Sticks.

Battle of Tippecanoe

While Tecumseh was in the South, Governor Harrison determined to break the impasse and march on the pan-Indian settlement of Prophetstown. Mustering an army of 1,000 regulars and militia from Indiana and Kentucky, he moved on the intertribal town on Tippecanoe Creek, arriving on November 6, 1811. At dawn next day he deployed his troops in battle formation. Four hundred warriors began a series of suicidal assaults on Harrison's lines. The Americans fell back, finally rallied, and turned the charge, causing the attackers to retreat. The Prophet's medicine had failed them; they did not have the power to turn the enemy's bullets or stay the arm of death, for 38 of their fellow warriors lay dead on the battlefield. Their retreat was complete; they even abandoned the village. Harrison's army collected its 138 dead and countless wounded, burned Prophetstown, and returned to Vincennes, claiming victory.

After Harrison's army dispersed the confederated Indian community at Prophetstown, the aroused Indians fell upon the American settlements in the Northwest with great fury, forcing the pioneers to flee to the safety of Vincennes and other fortified towns. American officials, including Governor Harrison, charged that the Indians were supplied with arms, blankets, and provisions and incited to wage war on the American settlements by

---

[1] Quoted in Arrell M. Gibson, *The Chickasaws* (Norman, 1971), p. 96.

British agents at Fort Malden—a post erected on the Canadian side of the Detroit River after the British evacuation of Detroit.

Western-Southern War Sentiment

Americans in the Northwest reacted to the destructive Indian raids on their settlements by pleas to the national government for relief and protection. Other groups with grievances against Great Britain joined the settlers in their demand for national retaliation. American trappers and traders especially resented continuing British-Canadian competition in the Western fur trade, for the Jay Treaty allowed British subjects to continue to trap and trade in the American Northwest. They maintained trading posts at Green Bay, Prairie du Chien, and other points strategic to contact with the Indian tribes. American fur interests charged that Canadian trappers used their posts to arm and incite the Indians against American traders and settlers.

Southern planters joined Westerners in the rising cry for action against Great Britain. The European market for cotton had been drastically curtailed by the extended military contest between Great Britain and France. British naval supremacy enabled that nation to enforce peremptory maritime practices, including blockades, disregard of neutral rights, and harassment of American ships on the high seas. The drastic diminution of European markets produced an extended depression in the United States, particularly among the agricultural interests of the country. Western farmers producing grain, tobacco, and hemp for export suffered no less than the Southern planters. Their collective plight was blamed on Great Britain.

The War Hawks

Intense anti-British sentiment surfaced in Congress during 1811; it was articulated by a group of newly elected representatives and senators from the West and South. This group, popularly called the "War Hawks," included Henry Clay of Kentucky, John C. Calhoun from the Western border of South Carolina, and John Sevier and Felix Grundy of Tennessee. Through vigorous, assertive action, the War Hawks succeeded in electing Clay Speaker of the House. Their consuming goal was a retaliatory war on Great Britain. The fruits of the war they sought would include restoration of national honor, abatement of the Western Indian menace, and conquest of the remainder of Spanish Florida and British Canada. The virus of Western expansion had infected the war goals of the United States.

Southwestern pioneers and Southern planters coveted the remainder of Spanish Florida, particularly the port of Mobile, which blocked egress to the Gulf from the great valley drained by the Mobile River and its tributaries. A war declaration against Great Britain would legitimatize the seizure of Florida, for Spain was an ally of Great Britain in the European war. Americans in the Northwest were infatuated with the prospects of gaining control of Canada. According to their rhetoric, only after Canada became an American province could Northwest development proceed in a peaceful and orderly fashion. The War Hawks triumphed on June 18, 1812, when Congress voted to declare war on Great Britain. A combination of Western and Southern congressmen provided the essential margin in a vote of 19 to 13 in the Senate and 79 to 49 in the House.

But in spite of the vigor of the young War Hawks, the second American contest with Great Britain, the War of 1812, nearly destroyed the young nation. Externally, it was the awesome military power of Great Britain that threatened to disintegrate the nation. Internally, the low quality of political leadership, sectional divisions, and a general lack of commitment to the war posed a threat to national existence equally as serious as British military prowess.

It was a war of extremes. Militiamen from the Northeastern states refused to follow their commanders into Canada and generally brought shame and defeat to the American cause. The New England states virtually boycotted the war, thereby depriving the nation of the region's rich financial resources, manpower, and naval strength. American military fortunes plunged to the nadir when a British army captured and burned the nation's capital. But American naval forces on the high seas and the Great Lakes and Western armies in the Northwest snatched national honor from the jaws of defeat and provided, with their heroic actions, the nation a galvanizing pride which put down incipient sectionalism, preserved the Union, and rehabilitated nationalizing currents, causing them to resume their integrating flow.

Northwest Disasters

During the summer of 1812, the War Department named General William Hull commander of the Western army. His mission was to capture Fort Malden and bring that portion of Canada under American control. Hull, with his 2,000-man army, made a slow, hesitant thrust toward Malden. General Isaac Brock, British commander in this Canadian sector, cut off Hull's supply line, causing the timid American to fall back toward Detroit. On August 16, Brock marched into Detroit with his British and Indian army, and Hull surrendered. The fall of Detroit, coupled with the British and Indian conquest of Fort Dearborn at the southern tip of Lake Michigan, appeared to spell doom for the American cause in the Northwest.

Reconquest of the Northwest

Combined British and Indian armies began to probe south to the approaches to Fort Wayne and Fort Harrison in Indiana. The national government, in hopes of mitigating the effects of Hull's demoralizing surrender, assigned Governor Harrison of Indiana Territory the task of blunting the British invasion of the Northwest and driving the enemy back into Canada. For the remainder of 1812, Harrison directed his attention to strengthening the interior line of Northwest defenses. During the winter of 1812–13, an army of regulars and volunteers from Indiana and Kentucky prepared to move on Fort Malden. At Frenchtown on the Raison River near Malden, a column of 1,000 American troops was surprised by a British-Indian ambush and fell back in rout. The Raison River defeat cost the Americans 500 prisoners and 200 men slain.

Still, Harrison tenaciously hung to his task. In the early spring of 1813 he began a slow advance on Detroit and Malden, bracing his movement with a line of new fortifications, including Fort Meigs—situated on the Maumee River west of Lake Erie—and Fort Stephenson and Fort Seneca —in the Sandusky Valley south of Fort Meigs. During April 1813, Colonel Henry Proctor, successor to General Brock at Fort Malden, led a British-Indian army of 1,000 men on Harrison's new frontier defense line. But Harrison's engineers had done their work well, and Brock's artillery could not penetrate the earthworks and heavy log walls at Fort Meigs and the other posts. Brock's siege of Harrison's line of defense posts continued until May 7, when counterattacks caused the enemy to abandon the cause and return to Canada.

The thwarting of the British invasion at Fort Meigs, Fort Seneca, and Fort Sandusky marked the turning point in the war in the Northwest. The next step in the American reconquest was to gain control of Lake Erie, which bristled with British guns mounted on the lake flotilla. Lake Erie's long east-to-west shore provided the British lake fleet with an easy water highway from which to watch for and turn away any American invasion attempt on Canada from the Northwest. Nonetheless, the youthful American naval lieutenant Oliver Hazard Perry constructed a fleet of gunboats at Presque Island on the eastern edge of Lake Erie and moved them into battle formation against the British lake armada. On September 10, 1813, in a bloody three-hour battle, Perry's gunners swept the British from Lake Erie.

The naval threat removed, Perry transported General Harrison's army of 5,000 men, mostly Kentuckians, to the Canadian shore. The American troops overtook the retreating British and Indian army on the Thames River on October 5, 1813, and inflicted a smashing defeat, during which Tecumseh was slain. The Battle of the Thames was epochal for the American Northwest in that it ended for all time British-Indian power in that region. For the remainder of the war the major portion of the Northwest remained under American control. During 1813 an army of 1,500 Illinois and Missouri militiamen under General Benjamin Howard moved on British-supported Indian settlements in Illinois. On the fringe of the Northwest, the British held Prairie du Chien in Wisconsin until late in 1814 when American military pressure forced its abandonment. Only Mackinac and a few other remote Northwest posts remained in British hands at the conclusion of the war. When, during 1814, a huge British army of 15,000 was poised for an invasion of the United States from Canadian bases across Lake Champlain, Captain Thomas Macdonough's gunboats on the lake destroyed the British guardian flotilla and forced abandonment of the invasion.

Southwest Operations

General Andrew Jackson accomplished in the Old Southwest what General Harrison achieved in the Old Northwest. One American war goal was fulfilled during 1813 when troops under General Wilkinson occupied Mobile and the remainder of West Florida. The two most important military engagements of the War of 1812 in the Old Southwest were the Battle of Horseshoe Bend in 1814 and the Battle of New Orleans in 1815.

The only Indians south of the Ohio River to take the anti-American teachings of Tecumseh seriously were members of the Red Stick faction of the Creeks. Led by war chief Billy Weatherford, a worthy successor to the earlier Creek antagonist Alexander McGillivray, the Red Sticks ravaged the frontier settlements of western Georgia and Alabama during 1813–1814. Red Stick power reached its climax at the invasion of Fort Mims, a post on the lower Alabama River. Over 500 persons died in the attack. General Andrew Jackson, commander of military forces south of the Ohio River, mustered an army of 5,000 militia from Tennessee and Kentucky—augmented with regiments of loyal Creeks, Cherokees, Choctaws, and Chickasaws—and campaigned through the Creek country to avenge the Fort Mims massacre. The Red Stick Creeks concentrated at Tohopeka, a fortified town at the Horseshoe Bend of the Tallapoosa River in central Alabama. On March 27, 1814, Jackson's army surrounded the town. While cannon fire swept the battlements, loyal Creek, Choctaw, Cherokee, and Chickasaw fighters maneuvered around the flank down river. The offensive vice tightened, and over 800 Creeks were slain at the Battle of Horseshoe Bend.

General Jackson convened the leaders of the Creek nation at Fort Jackson on August 9, 1814. He made it clear that he held the entire Creek nation responsible for the Red Stick outbreak and took from the Creeks by the Treaty of Fort Jackson—as a sort of reparations of war—22 million acres of land in southern Georgia and central Alabama.

Later in 1814 the British fleet made movements toward Pensacola and Mobile. General Jackson placed his troops at key spots in West Florida and drove them off at Mobile. Next the British prepared to invade the Mississippi Valley by way of New Orleans. A transport armada carrying 10,000 troops commanded by Sir Edward Pakenham departed Jamaica for New Orleans late in 1814. General Jackson rushed his frontier army of Tennessee volunteers, regulars, and several companies of Southern Indians to New Orleans; on December 1, 1814, the Americans began preparations to receive the British invaders. The army built small forts and artillery placements along the principal accesses to New Orleans and felled trees to block roads and trails into the city. The British movement to New Orleans occurred on January 8, 1815, and produced one of the bloodiest battles ever fought on American soil. Well-placed artillery barrages of grapeshot poured into the British flank, causing the close-order columns to falter. Over 700 British regulars perished on the approaches to New Orleans; 500 were taken prisoner. Among the dead was the British commander, General Pakenham. American losses in the defense of New Orleans were incredibly small—eight killed and thirteen wounded.

The Diplomatic Settlement

While General Jackson was preparing to thwart the British invasion of the Mississippi Valley, American and British commissioners were concluding negotiations at Ghent, Belgium. The Treaty of Ghent, signed on December 24, 1814, provided for a mutual restoration of territory and for joint American-British commissions to study and resolve controversial questions, including the boundary separating Canada and the United States. Since the treaty was to become effective only after it had been ratified and proclaimed by both parties—which occurred after the Battle of New Orleans—General Jackson's victory over the British army on January 8, 1815, did in fact take place within the context of wartime operations and was not, as many have portrayed it, an after-the-fact incident.

Legacy of the War of 1812

The effects of the war on the West and the nation as a whole were many. An intensive nationalism had been generated in the West during the war's prelude; this nationalism produced not only the declaration of war but also a sense of involvement that affected the entire nation. It survived the war and provided the substance for the nationalistic "Era of Good Feeling." Most of the land victories against Great Britain took place in the West and were accomplished chiefly by Western troops and Western commanders. These victories were a source for national pride and intense patriotic spirit. Western commanders who managed these victories became national heroes and fastened on the American public the tradition for military leadership as a *sine qua non* for national political leadership, particularly the presidency. The war produced two future presidents— Jackson and Harrison. In a real sense, the War of 1812 also ended, from a military standpoint, the Indian problem in the Old Northwest and the Old Southwest. Western military successes shamed New England particularism into silence and, through the intense national spirit produced, quieted sectionalism for a time. And last, the Western propensity to resort to military force as a solution to problems with other nations became a national trait.

The War of 1812 removed those barriers in the trans-Appalachian territory that had arrested the region's development. Following the Treaty of Ghent, all sectors of the Old West—The Northwest, Southwest and Mississippi Valley—were the scene of accelerated settlement.

SELECTED SOURCES

The rapid integration of the Old West into the national life is a phenomenon of recent history. Quite early the identity of the Old West subregions—Old Northwest, Old Southwest, and Mississippi Valley—was evident. The following literature traces the rise of the Old Northwest: R. C. Downes, *Frontier Ohio, 1785–1803* (Columbus, 1935); Frederick A. Ogg, *The Old Northwest* (New Haven, 1920); Charles E. Slocum, *The Ohio Country Between the Years 1785 and 1815* (New York, 1910); Beverley Bond, *The Foundations of Ohio* (Columbus, 1941); *Charles R. Ritcheson, *Aftermath of the Revolution: British Policy toward the United States, 1783–1795* (Dallas, 1965); and R. C. Buley, *The Old Northwest* (Bloomington, Ind., 1951), 2 vols.

The American struggle for pre-eminence in the Old Southwest is chronicled in Arthur P. Whitaker, *Spanish–American Frontiers and the Mississippi Question* (New York, 1934); Archibald Henderson, *Conquest of the Old Southwest* (New York, 1920); Robert S. Cotterill, *The Old South* (Glendale, 1939), *Paul A. Varg, *Foreign Policies of the Founding Fathers* (East Lansing, 1963); J. Leitch Wright, Jr., *Anglo-Spanish Rivalry in North America* (Athens, 1971); and Isaac J. Cox, *The West Florida Controversy: 1798–1813* (Baltimore, 1918).

American expansion into the Mississippi Valley is the subject of J. K. Hosmer, *The Louisiana Purchase* (New York, 1902); Charles E. Gayarre, *History of Louisiana* (New Orleans, 1903), 4 vols.; E. Wilson Lyon, *The Man Who Sold Louisiana* (Norman, 1942) and *Louisiana in French Diplomacy, 1759–1804* (Norman, 1934); Merrill D. Peterson, *Thomas Jefferson and the New Nation: A Biography* (New York, 1970); and John G. Clark, *New Orleans, 1718–1812: An Economic History* (Baton Rouge, 1970).

The War of 1812 resolved a number of Western problems and marked the beginning of substantial Old West influence on the national life. The military history is detailed in Glenn Tucker, *Tecumseh, Vision of Glory* (Indianapolis, 1936); Francis F. Beirne, *The War of 1812* (New York, 1949); Freeman Cleaves, *Old Tippecanoe: William Henry Harrison and His Times* (New York; 1939); Marquis James, *Andrew Jackson, The Border Captain* (Indianapolis, 1933); *Robert V. Remini, *Andrew Jackson* (New York, 1966); *John W. Ward, *Andrew Jackson; Symbol of An Age* (New York, 1954); Bernard Mayo, *Henry Clay, Spokesman of the New West* (New York, 1937); Julius Pratt, *Expansionists of 1812* (New York, 1926); Frank A. Upchurch, *The Diplomacy of the War of 1812* (Baltimore, 1915); and Fred L. Engleman, *The Peace of Christmas Eve* (New York, 1953).

* Available in paperback.

The Bad Axe Massacre of 1832: The End of the Black Hawk War

9

The Old Northwest

I_N 1801 Gouverneur Morris perceptively observed on the promise of the youthful United States: "As yet we can only crawl along the outer part we inhabit in soil, in climate, in everything. The proudest empire in Europe is but a bauble compared to what America will be, must be, in the course of two centuries, perhaps in one." [1] The burst of individual and institutional energy applied to America's interior at the close of the War of 1812 augured well to fulfill Morris' prophecy. In the period between 1815 and 1828 the Old West was the focus of the nation's creative energy, with the result that its components— the Old Northwest, the Old Southwest, and the Mississippi Valley—were freed of barriers to development and were integrated into the nation's social, economic, and political life.

INDIAN REMOVALS

In the Old Northwest, where some political and economic development had taken place before the War of 1812, American expansion took the form of an extension of the military frontier. This vital nationalizing current established American presence in the far reaches of the territory. Although the British had, again, been evicted, their Indian allies remained. Extending its line of fortifications into the Indian country at a time when the defeated tribes were confused, divided, and uncertain was a strategic move on the part of the War Department. It also had the effect of pro-

---

[1] Quoted in Robert F. Riegel and Robert G. Athearn, *America Moves West* (New York, 1971), p. 63.

viding the vast Northwest interior with the essential beginnings of law and order.

Military Frontier Extension

In 1816 War Department officials directed that old Fort Wayne and Fort Harrison in the Indiana Territory be rehabilitated. In the far north, the Michigan Territory was strengthened by a line of posts on its eastern border that included Fort Shelby, Fort Gratiot, Fort Saginaw, and Fort Mackinac. In Illinois, Fort Dearborn, Fort Johnson, and Fort Clark were refurbished to protect the expanding settlements there. In western Illinois and Wisconsin, Fort Armstrong on Rock Island, Fort Crawford at Prairie du Chien, and Fort Howard near the mouth of Fox River were key United States locations in relation to tribal sites. These frontier stations were later augmented by Fort Winnebago on the Wisconsin River and Fort Atkinson on Lake Koshkonong.

West of the new state of Ohio, American settlements in the Northwest were concentrated on the Ohio River, the east bank of the Mississippi River, and along the Great Lakes' fringe, as well as in a tongue of settlement that ran up the Wabash River to Vincennes in the Indiana Territory. The vast heartland of the Northwest was still occupied by subdued but potentially powerful Indian communities, erstwhile minions of the British. The extension of the military frontier into the interior established American presence and power among these defeated peoples.

Evolution of Removal Policy

Preliminary to incorporating these lands into the public domain—before surveying, mapping by township, and dispensing them from local land offices—tribal titles had to be extinguished. Until 1815 the national government had usually negotiated with the tribes and taken portions of the tribal domain; the signatory tribes then retreated to a diminished territory adjacent to the ceded tracts. But by 1816 the national government was ready to change its policy drastically. First of all, from the American viewpoint, the Indians of the Northwest were in a most unfavorable position; as members of tribal communities under United States dominion, they had actively supported the British in the War of 1812, which could be regarded as treasonable conduct. As vanquished peoples they could expect to suffer some penalty, in the form of land reparations, for making war on the United States.

In addition, their potential collective power, which peaked under Tecumseh in 1811, had been destroyed by American victories in the Northwest. Government awareness of this very important fact was articulated by William Clark, superintendent of Indian affairs at St. Louis: "The relative condition of the United States on the one side, and the Indian tribes on the other" had drastically changed. Before the War of 1812, "the tribes nearest our settlements were a formidable and terrible enemy; since then, their power has been broken, their warlike spirit subdued, and themselves sunk into objects of pity and commiseration. While strong and hostile, it has been our obvious policy to weaken them; now that they are weak and harmless, and most of their lands fallen into our hands, justice and humanity require us to cherish and befriend them." Clark recommended that the tribes of the Old West be taught by government agents to "live in houses, to raise grain and stock, to plant orchards ... to establish laws for their government, to get the rudiments of common learning, such as reading, writing and ciphering ... the first steps toward improving their condition." Clark continued that to accomplish this, "the tribes now within the limits of the States and Territories should be removed to a country beyond" the Mississippi River "where they could rest in peace." [2] Thus it was that colonizing the tribes from the Old Northwest into the trans-Mississippi territory early became a certain and continuing policy of the national government, a solution to the problem of clearing the path for American expansion.

The Removal Treaties

Of course, the removal of the Old Northwest tribes did not occur in a single year; it was a gradual process, whose rate was largely determined by the press of the settlement line. As late as the 1840s tribal remnants were still being relocated in the trans-Mississippi West. Also, some Indian communities withdrew to lands so unattractive to settlers that they completely escaped removal to the West; even late in the twentieth century residual communities of Potawatomis, Menominees, and certain other tribes remain in isolated portions of the Old Northwest.

The first step in the process of liquidating tribal estates in the Old Northwest and removing resident tribes to the trans-Mississippi territory occurred duing 1815. This was, in a sense, a resumption of the work of former Governor Harrison of the Indiana Territory, whose progress in erasing title to tribal lands had been arrested by Tecumseh's powerful protest of the Treaty of Fort Wayne in 1809. American victories in the Northwest during the War of 1812 had settled the issues raised by Tecumseh's confrontation with Governor Harrison.

During the summer of 1815, leaders of the Northwest tribes met with United States commissioners William Clark, Ninian Edwards, and Auguste Chouteau at Portage des Sioux in Illinois Territory. The treaties that resulted from this council provided officially for resumption of American dominion over the tribes. All parties agreed that every injury or act of hostility by either party towards the other was "forgiven and forgotten," and each party pledged "perpetual peace and friendship." The next step was for American commissioners to negotiate cession treaties. Federal officials were particularly anxious to secure a strategic tract of over two million acres between the Illinois and Mississippi rivers. During the War of 1812, Congress had reserved this land for war bounties, and holders of land war-

---

[2] Arrell Gibson, *The Chickasaws* (Norman, 1971), pp. 160–61.

rants were demanding an opportunity for redemption. Between 1816 and 1818, government commissioners obtained cessions to portions of this tract from the Peorias, Kaskaskias, and several smaller tribes.

A considerable portion of the bounty lands, however, was held by the Kickapoos. This powerful pro-British tribe also controlled enclaves of territory on the Wabash River in the Indiana Territory and the rich Illinois and Sangamon river country in north central Illinois. Benjamin Parke, Auguste Chouteau, and Benjamin Stephenson were the negotiators assigned to deal with the Kickapoos. After much delay by tribal leaders and a good deal of pressure by the commissioners, in 1819 the Kickapoos finally agreed to exchange their Illinois and Wabash lands for a domain in the trans-Mississippi territory. By the treaties of Edwardsville and Fort Harrison, both negotiated in 1819, the tribe accepted a new home on the Osage River in the Missouri Territory. Nearly 2,000 Kickapoos moved west of the Mississippi River during 1819; but two renegade bands repudiated the cession treaties in 1819, refused to consider removal, and remained in Illinois.

One band, numbering about 250 and led by Mecina, was particularly incensed by the Treaty of Edwardsville. Mecina adamantly refused to acknowledge that the Kickapoo homeland had been surrendered to the United States. With frantic vigor, he regularly stated to Superintendent Clark the doctrine of Tecumseh, denying that his tribe or any other could unilaterally sign away tribal lands and "the resting places of the bones of their ancestors." Mecina's Kickapoo band preyed on the edge of the advancing line of American settlement in Illinois, looting isolated farmhouses, stealing horses, and shooting cattle and hogs. During 1824, a settlers' association in Fulton County, Illinois, stated in a petition to Congress that the continuing Kickapoo presence was a serious threat to life and property. They informed congressional leaders that the "inhabitants of this country have for a long time been . . . oppressed by the various tribes." Another petition of protest in 1825 from settlers along the Sangamon River complained that "a band of Kickapoo Indians . . . are infesting their neighborhood, killing their hogs before their eyes, and in defiance of the settlers, declaring the land is theirs and that the whites are intruders upon it; and that they will fight before they will leave it." [3] Federal troops and Illinois militia units responded to the settler appeals, and close and constant military surveillance finally caused Mecina to reluctantly lead his Kickapoo band west of the Mississippi.

Another recalcitrant Kickapoo band of about 250 members resided on the Vermillion River. Their leader was Kennekuk, a self-styled prophet. He taught his followers to lead a simple, peaceful life of meditation and to disregard the swirling pressure of the American settlements. Each of Kennekuk's disciples was required to endure a strict regimen of fasting

[3] Arrell M. Gibson, *The Kickapoos: Lords of the Middle Border* (Norman, 1963), p. 83.

and general rejection of materialism and to return to the ancient aboriginal lifestyle in which the communicant lived close to nature. Kennekuk promised his followers that by seeking "simple virtue" each would have as his reward eternal life in a holy place free of torment and American settlers. By means of passive resistance, Kennekuk defied the removal requirements of the 1819 treaties. His quiet determination and captivating rhetoric caused William Clark and other officials charged with the duty of clearing Indians from the Northwest to indulge the Kickapoo Prophet and his people. Endowed with abundant native ability, Kennekuk was exceedingly skilled in the art of delay; each time Clark pressed to take his followers west of the Mississippi, Kennekuk assured Clark that it was his wish to comply with the "demands of the Great Father in Washington that they leave Illinois," but, because the corn "was yet in the milk" or because of illness in his band, or, more often than not, because the Great Spirit had advised that this was not the time to move, the prophet remained in Illinois. Not until the spring of 1834 did Kennekuk lead his Kickapoo band from their Vermillion River homeland toward the West.

The Kickapoo cessions, accomplished by the treaties of 1819, cleared the lands most directly in the path of expanding American settlements. The next tribes to feel the pressure for surrender of Northwest lands were the Sac and Fox—who occupied western Illinois and Wisconsin—the Chippewas—who held the territory along the south shore of Lake Superior—certain Sioux communities west of the Great Lakes, Potawatomi bands populating the area south of Lake Michigan, Winnebagos on the Wisconsin River, and Menominees—who ranged over a domain from Lake Michigan to the Milwaukee River. Superintendent Clark and Lewis Cass, governor of the Michigan Territory, met in council with leaders of these tribes at Prairie du Chien, Wisconsin, during 1825. The resulting treaties provided for continuing peace between the tribes and the United States, a confirmation of tribal territories in the Northwest, and a commitment to future reduction of tribal estates.

The Prairie du Chien treaties were timely from the viewpoint of American expansion. The completion of the Erie Canal and the extension of mining and agricultural settlements in western Illinois and Wisconsin during 1825 accelerated the Americanization of the vast empty tracts in the Old Northwest. Within ten years after the signing of the Prairie du Chien treaties, virtually all Indians had been cleared from this component of the Old West. The Sac and Fox, Winnebago, Sioux, and most Potawatomi bands had been colonized west of the Mississippi River. The Chippewas had retreated far into northern Wisconsin, and the Menominees had been pushed beyond the Green Bay area.

Resistance to Removal

Two incidents marred the evacuation of Indian tribes from the Northwest. Discovery of rich lead deposits on the western border of Illinois and Wisconsin during the 1820s caused a rush of miners and farmers into the new bonanza territory. It was not long before mining camps and farms were intruding on lands claimed by the Winnebago, Sac, and Fox Indians. Red Bird, a patriot leader of the Winnebagos, prepared his people to resist this miner-settler intrusion. During 1827 he led several raids on the mining settlements, but was thwarted on each occasion by spirited local defense. Regular army units joined militia forces to destroy this threat to the Illinois-Wisconsin mining settlements. Red Bird and his Winnebago warriors fell back into the interior and finally were trapped between two American columns on the upper Wisconsin River. Red Bird's capitulation ended the Winnebago threat for all time.

The second incident centered on a massacre of Sac and Fox Indians, euphemistically called the Black Hawk War. Under pressure from miners and farmers a band of Sac and Fox Indians led by Black Hawk ranged the country between the Illinois and Wisconsin rivers. During the summer of 1831 the line of American settlements extended into their territory, and Black Hawk collected his people—numbering almost 1,000 men, women and children—and settled them near the old tribal grounds at Rock Island. Federal officials urged Black Hawk to move across the Mississippi River into Iowa; and when the Sac and Fox leader refused, troops marched into the village and forced the Indians to cross the river. But during the spring of 1832, Black Hawk and his band returned to their land in Illinois, bringing not only warriors but women and children as well. Settlers regarded the move as an invasion and in great panic demanded that state and federal officials protect them. Illinois militia units marched against Black Hawk's band and engaged the Indians in several minor brushes but were unable to turn them. Finally, federal troops from the Illinois posts and Jefferson Barracks in Missouri moved in. Black Hawk led his people north into the wilds of Wisconsin and was hotly pursued by regular army units and militia. Cornered on the Bad Axe River and exhausted and hungry from their long march, the Indians made a last stand. The carnage that followed, precipitated largely by the militia components of the converging host, left over 300 Indians dead. Black Hawk himself capitulated and was taken prisoner-of-war.

On August 7, 1832, General Winfield Scott met with Sac and Fox leaders at Fort Crawford. Their deliberations produced a treaty providing for the cession by the Sac and Fox of a strip of territory fifty miles wide on the west bank of the Mississippi River; this strip, the Black Hawk Purchase, was to serve as a buffer to restrain the Sac and Fox from returning to Illinois.

STATE-MAKING IN THE OLD NORTHWEST

The Indian removals were one manifestation that the flow of nationalizing currents into the Old Northwest resumed in full force after the War of 1812. Federal action in this regard transferred tribal estates to the public domain of the United States so that the lands could be surveyed, mapped by township, and dispensed to settlers on relatively easy credit terms. Another manifestation of the creative impact of nationalizing currents on the Old Northwest was the continuation of the state-making process.

Ohio

The Old Northwest's first public domain state, Ohio, had been admitted to the Union on March 1, 1803, with its capital at Chillicothe. Edward Tiffin was the state's first elected governor. In the immediate postwar era Ohio was politically dominated by the Jeffersonian Republicans. The state's development, arrested momentarily by the War of 1812, resumed with a surge in 1815. The National Road and its arteries as well as an expanding system of local roads and canals accelerated the settlement and development of the rich agricultural interior. In 1825, political and business leaders supported the construction of a north-south canal connecting Cleveland on Lake Erie with Portsmouth on the Ohio River. Other waterways within Ohio included the Miami and Erie Canal, which linked Cincinnati and Toledo. An expanding grid of surface and water routes opened the most remote portions of the young state to export accommodations via the Great Lakes and the Ohio-Mississippi route to Gulf markets.

Indiana

As we noted in Chapter 8, Congress had created the Indiana Territory in 1800. William Henry Harrison, congressional delegate from Ohio Territory, was appointed governor of the new territory, and the capital was situated at Vincennes on the Wabash River. Governor Harrison's vigorous action in clearing Indian title to lands in his jurisdiction was a principal cause of the War of 1812 in the Old Northwest. Long before the war a steady increase in population enabled Indiana to ascend to that level in territorial government in which its citizens were permitted to elect a legislature. The Indiana Territory's first general assembly met at Vincennes in 1805.

During the War of 1812 Harrison was appointed a major general in the United States army and was assigned the task of expelling the British and Indian invaders from the Northwest. In 1813 Corydon replaced Vincennes as the territorial capital. Three years later the territorial legislature petitioned Congress for an enabling act; Congress responded favorably, and the citizens of the territory elected delegates to a constitutional convention.

The Indiana constitutional convention met at Corydon during June 1816, the delegates completing their work in only nineteen days. The constitution for the proposed state was closely modeled after the constitution of Kentucky and included a bill of rights and a provision calling for a secret ballot in elections (as a substitute for the customary *vive voce* method of voting). Indiana was admitted to the Union in 1816, and in

1825 Indianapolis became the capital for the new state. During territorial times as well as in the early years of statehood, the Jeffersonian Republican Party dominated Indiana. Like its neighbor Ohio, Indiana was the scene of extensive internal improvements in transportation in the 1820s.

Illinois

In 1809, Congress detached the western portion of the Indiana Territory and created the Illinois Territory, with jurisdiction extending north to Canada and including most of present-day Wisconsin, a portion of Michigan, and a segment of Minnesota east of the Mississippi River. However, the presence of powerful Indian tribes, in Illinois' heartland, particularly the Kickapoos, thwarted development of the new territory except along the southern border on the Ohio and the western border on the Mississippi. Even so, sufficient settlement and development occurred in this rimland area to justify Congress's elevation of Illinois to the next level of territorial government; in 1812 the citizens were permitted to elect a legislative assembly and a congressional delegate. Ninian Edwards of Kentucky served as governor, and the territorial capital was situated at Kaskaskia. As in the Old Northwest generally, Illinois' development was arrested by the War of 1812. But after the war, treaties negotiated by federal commissioners with the defeated tribes, particularly the Kickapoo treaty of 1819, opened up the heartland. The period following the conclusion of the War of 1812 was a time of rapid settlement and development in the Illinois Territory.

In 1815 local leaders began to urge national officials to support statehood for Illinois, and in 1818 Congress responded by adopting the Illinois Enabling Act. An elected constitutional convention met at Kaskaskia and in twenty-two days produced a draft similar to the Ohio and Indiana constitutions. At that time the Illinois territory was about 2,000 short of the prescribed minimum for statehood of 60,000 residents; Congress nonetheless acted favorably on the work of the convention, and Illinois was admitted to the Union in 1818.

Michigan

In the process of state construction in the Old Northwest, Michigan and Wisconsin evolved more slowly than the states along the Ohio River. Statehood did not come to either of them until the frontier period had passed and the Old Northwest had largely lost its Western attributes.

In 1803 the wide tongue of land flanked by Lake Michigan and Lake Huron was incorporated into the Indiana Territory and was administered from Vincennes by Governor Harrison. Two years later Congress organized the Michigan Territory, designating Detroit the territorial capital. Its proximity to Canada and the continuing British threat from that quarter, as well as the presence of large and potentially powerful Indian communities, discouraged settlement and development of this northern territory. Moreover, gazetteers and immigrant guides for prospective Western settlers published in the East described Michigan as a vast, inhospitable swamp. The principal settlement and development zone in the territory before the War of 1812 was around Detroit.

In 1813 Lewis Cass was appointed governor of the Michigan Territory, and he continued in this position until 1831. Cass was a capable and energetic chief executive who did much to improve the image of the Michigan Territory as an area for settlement. In 1819, when the population was estimated at 8,100, Congress authorized local citizens to elect a territorial assembly and a congressional delegate. After 1815 transportation advances did much to accelerate settlement and development. Beginning in 1818, steamboats provided access to Detroit and other lakeside centers. And the opening of the Erie Canal—which ran from Albany to Buffalo, N.Y.—in 1825 contributed substantially to the population flow and settlement of the territory. Statehood was accorded the Michigan Territory in 1837.

Wisconsin

Long after the close of the War of 1812 Wisconsin remained a thinly populated frontier on the upper margins of the Old Northwest. Hunting and trapping continued to flourish there, and the settlements consisted of scattered fur-trade centers. The extension of the military frontier into Wisconsin after 1815 established essential American presence and provided greater security for agricultural settlers. Wisconsin was administered as a part of the Indiana Territory form 1800 to 1809, was shifted to the Illinois Territory in 1809, and remained under that jurisdiction until 1818, when it was attached to the Michigan Territory. Governor Cass organized several counties in the Wisconsin portion of Michigan Territory, and in 1824 this western portion was represented in the territorial assembly at Detroit.

Extinguishment of tribal title to much of Wisconsin and the discovery of lead mines on the Mississippi River in the 1820s led to settlement and development in western Wisconsin. In 1836, Wisconsin became a separate territory; for the first two years of its territorial status its western boundary extended into the trans-Mississippi territory as far as the Missouri River, including parts of present-day Minnesota and the Dakotas. Wisconsin was admitted to the American Union in 1848.

THE GREAT MIGRATION

The remarkably rapid political organization of the Old Northwest was due in part to a spectacular human surge into the trans-Appalachian West following the War of 1812. It is called the Great Migration, and resulted in a doubling of the Old West's population in the decade ending in 1820. By that year the states and territories of the Old West contained a population of about 2,250,000, approximately one-fourth the population of the entire nation. The Old Northwest and the Old Southwest components of the Old West nearly matched one another in pace of growth; the Mississippi Valley, the westernmost component, also increased in population, although at a slower rate than the Old Northwest and the Old Southwest.

National Prosperity and Migration

The Great Migration was abetted in part by a change in the national economy. An extended depression ended in 1815, and the nation entered a period of relatively prosperous conditions that lasted until about 1821. Western migration generally decreased during times of depression and increased in prosperous periods, for moving West required credit and some capital, both of which were more readily available in good times.

The Great Migration was also encouraged by increasingly attractive living conditions in the West. North of the Ohio River there was greater security for life and property than there had been before the war, for the threat from the British in Canada and their local Indian allies had been eliminated. Besides being safer, the Old Northwest offered an abundance of land for pioneering as a result of the national government's extensive program of liquidating tribal title to the land. Moreover, the Northwest Indian tribes were being removed to the trans-Mississippi West, thus eliminating them as competitors for land.

Transportation Advances

Pioneers composing the waves of the Great Migration found it easier to enter the West after 1815. As noted in Chapter 8, improved roads over the mountains—some of them toll roads financed by Eastern capitalists and state governments—eased the problem of moving people and goods into the Old Northwest. A growing federal road system that included the National Road and an expanding grid of state and territorial wagon roads was subsidized by the government from the proceeds of Western land sales and was an added inducement to settlement. An important auxiliary highway system was provided by the network of military roads linking the Northwest posts; these roads were for the most part constructed by federal troops.

During the 1820s Western transportation resources were materially enhanced by the excavation of canals connecting strategic east-west and north-south terminals. The Erie Canal, completed in 1825, provided a rapid and easy means for people and goods to enter the West via the Hudson and Mohawk valleys. Canal systems in Ohio and Indiana, coupled with the growing road system in these young states, opened the most remote interior portions to settlement and provided outlets to markets. River transportation was also important as a carrier of settlers into the West, and of the products of their farms and primary industries to Gulf markets. On the Ohio and Mississippi rivers, flatboats and keelboats were joined in 1811 by the first steamboats.

Public Land and Migration

Besides greater safety to life and property, the presence of organized and functioning governments, and improved transportation facilities, settlers also found the West attractive because of liberal land policies. We have mentioned that the Land Act of 1800 had provided for the dispersal of land offices throughout the territories and lowered the minimum acreage to 320 acres. After a tract had been surveyed and plotted, it was offered for sale at public auction for three weeks. Thereafter private entry and purchase was permitted at two dollars per acre. The purchaser was required to pay the survey cost of six dollars per section and make a deposit of ten cents an acre on the land reserved for purchase. The settler was permitted to make a small down payment, with additional payments spread over a four-year period. In 1804, Congress reduced the minimum acreage purchaseable to 160 acres, retaining the auction and credit features of the 1800 statute. The land law in 1820 abolished the credit system, reduced the minimum acreage to 80 acres and the cost per acre to one dollar and twenty-five cents, and retained the auction system.

Public lands were dispensed through local federal land offices situated in recently surveyed areas; there the settlers filed and negotiated their entries. Even after states were admitted to the Union, the national government retained control over the public lands situated therein, except for tracts granted to states for schools and other public purposes. A bureau of the Treasury Department supervised the sale of public domain lands until 1812, when Congress created the General Land Office, headed by a commissioner. This agency remained part of the Treasury Department until 1849 when Congress established the Department of the Interior and assigned the Land Office to it.

Western immigrants had several choices in obtaining land. Besides purchasing tracts from the public domain of the United States, they could settle on military bounty lands. An act of Congress during 1811 provided that every enlisted man and non-commissioned officer in the regular army, upon discharge, was to receive a warrant entitling him to 160 acres from the public domain. Subsequent legislation increased the military bounty to 320 acres and coverage was expanded to include some volunteer troops. The military bounty tracts were scattered throughout the West, the largest one being situated in western Illinois Territory. The War Department issued nearly 30,000 such warrants, and, since the warrants were negotiable, settlers and speculators were able to purchase them from veterans of the War of 1812. Settlers could also buy or lease land from the new Western states themselves, from the acreages granted them by Congress for support of schools and other public purposes. In addition, many pioneers simply moved ahead of the survey line and "squatted" on unorganized tracts; by improving it, they developed a right to the land, which they sought to have protected by act of Congress. "Squatter rights" were finally formally legalized by the Preemption Act of 1841.

Settler response to these varied opportunities for becoming land-owners was little short of phenomenal. After the War of 1812, land sales served as an accurate barometer of population flow and intensive settlement rate in the trans-Appalachian region. In 1814, land sales in the Old West amounted to slightly over 1,000,000 acres. Transactions increased steadily each year thereafter until in 1819 Western land offices reported settler entry for the year at 5,100,000 acres. Nearly 3,000,000 acres of this land was taken up in the Old Northwest.

Sources of the Great Migration

The Great Migration populated a great portion of the Old Northwest interior. Pioneers came from all sections of the Eastern United States. New England and the Middle Atlantic states contributed substantial flows to the Great Migration, but the South, particularly Virginia, was the heaviest feeder of the Northwest pioneering stream. Kentucky served as a highway for this regional population flow, the immigrants crossing its long northern border fronting the Ohio River and continuing to various points in Ohio, Indiana, and Illinois. Between 1810 and 1820—the last eight years of the decade corresponding to the time of the Great Migration—the population of the Old Northwest doubled. By 1820, Ohio's population approximated 600,000, Indiana accommodated about 160,000, and the Illinois population neared 60,000.

Urbanization of the Old Northwest

Most settlers populating the Old Northwest were farmers who took up claims under the federal and state land dispensing system and under military warrants. Thus the character of the Old Northwest was largely rural. But pioneers also came to populate existing towns and to develop new towns, so the urbanizing process was also at work, and it is possible to speak of the urban frontier in the Old Northwest.

The military frontier in the Old Northwest was responsible for the evolution of several towns. Pittsburgh (Fort Pitt), Fort Wayne, and Chicago (Fort Dearborn) were among the emergent urban centers that received their initial impetus from the vitalizing presence of adjacent military posts. Residuals of the fading fur frontier, former trading centers—including Vincennes, Kaskaskia, and Cahokia—metamorphosed into important agricultural frontier towns. Some Northwest towns grew up from more recent speculator and settler development—Cincinnati, Columbus, and Cleveland in Ohio; Lafayette, Richmond, Indianapolis, and Crawfordsville in Indiana; and Vandalia, Albion, and Alton in Illinois. Other recent towns originated because of fortuitous situations on the right-of-way of principal roads and canals in the Old Northwest; examples of such towns are Portsmouth and Toledo in Ohio.

The mining boomtown, which was to be more characteristic of the

New West, contributed to the evolution of the urban frontier in the Old Northwest during 1822; with the discovery of rich lead ore deposits on the western border of Illinois and Wisconsin, the population rush resulted in the rise of several mining camps in the vicinity of Galena, Illinois.

An expanding urban frontier also provided the Old Northwest with trade centers, slaughter and meat-processing facilities, mills for grinding grain (particularly meal for export), distilleries, tanneries, primitive factories for the manufacture of glass and rope, metal-working enterprises (largely blacksmithing), boatbuilding on the lakes and principal rivers, and distribution centers for dry goods and farm equipment. Pittsburgh, on the eastern border of the trans-Appalachian region, was the most important manufacturing center in the Old West; its growing enterprises provided paper, rope, glass, hats, iron products, and other essentials for Western pioneering. By creating important new markets, the demographic surge into the Old Northwest, aided and abetted by the resumption of the flow of nationalizing currents through the region, had a substantive impact on the development of the nation as a whole. Concomitant economic growth in the Old Northwest itself contributed to national strength and added to the growing diversification of the American economy.

This impact of the Great Migration on the urban frontier was more than the development of towns as trade and marketing centers. These pioneer communities also became social and cultural centers, nurseries where Eastern ideas, things, and ways were nourished and propagated throughout the hinterland. Thus it was largely the towns of the Old Northwest that produced the metamorphosis from wilderness to an increasingly sophisticated extension of the Eastern United States, purged the more primitive frontier attributes, and forced the West to retreat toward the Pacific.

Political Impact of the Great Migration

This demographic surge also had three pervasive and compelling effects on regional development and national politics. First, the new states called for increased representation in the Congress, and the Old Northwest thus gained a growing voice in the management of the federal government. The region's increasing electoral vote strength meant that it also exerted greater influence over national political parties and the presidential selection process. Second, the growing political power of the Old Northwest caused perceptive Eastern politicians, particularly those from New England, to feel threatened by the emerging shift in federal power. This concern led them to make several calculated attempts to check Western development; and their defensive reactions nourished incipient sectionalism. Third, by forbidding slavery north of the Ohio River, the Northwest Ordinance had in a sense predetermined the settlement and institutional development of the region. The heavy migration from the South contained some elements who favored extension of slavery into the new land; their representatives voiced this advocacy in the Indiana and Illinois constitutional conventions and in the deliberations of early state legislatures. The Old Northwest thus became an arena for the beginning of the national debate over the extension of slavery.

In the Old Northwest's companion province south of the Ohio comprehensive economic, social, and political developments were occurring contemporaneously. A principal difference for the Anglo-American pioneer in the Old Southwest was the Indian "problem." Whereas in the Old Northwest the aboriginal barrier to Anglo-American occupation and development was rather quickly resolved after 1815, in the Old Southwest the tribes held tenaciously to their lands and determinedly resisted removal. Most of the Southern tribes finally submitted to relocation in the West at the very end of the pioneering period in the Old Southwest.

SELECTED SOURCES

Removing the Indian tribes was an essential preliminary to the complete Anglo-American occupation of the Old Northwest. The policy and process of removal are described in Grant Foreman, *Last Trek of the Indians* (Chicago, 1946) and *Indian Removal* (Norman, 1942, 1972); William T. Hagan, *The Sac and Fox Indians* (Norman, 1958); Arrell M. Gibson, *The Kickapoos: Lords of the Middle Border* (Norman, 1963); and *Francis P. Prucha, American Indian Policy in the Formative Years* (Cambridge, 1962).

State-making in the Old Northwest can be traced in Beverley W. Bond, Jr., *The Civilization of the Old Northwest* (New York, 1934); A. B. Hinsdale, *The Old Northwest* (New York, 1931); R. C. Downes, *Frontier Ohio, 1788– 1803* (Columbus, 1935); R. C. Buley, *The Old Northwest* (Bloomington, 1951), 2 vols.; F. A. Ogg, *The Old Northwest* (New Haven, 1921); William E. Wilson, *Indiana: A History* (Bloomington, 1966); Theodore C. Pease, *The Story of Illinois* (Chicago, 1965); F. Clever Bald, *Michigan in Four Centuries* (New York, 1954); and William F. Raney, *Wisconsin: A Story of Progress* (New York, 1940).

The Great Migration, transportation development, and urbanization in the Old Northwest are subjects treated in Richard C. Wade, *The Urban Frontier* (Cambridge, 1959); Walter Havighurst, *Wilderness for Sale: The Story of the First Western Land Rush* (New York, 1956); John A. Caruso, *The Great Lakes Frontier* (Indianapolis, 1961); Daniel J. Elazar, *Cities of the Prairie: The Metropolitan Frontier and American Politics* (New York, 1970); and Philip D. Jordan, *The National Road* (New York, 1948).

* Available in paperback.

OLD FORT DEARBORN,
ERECTED AT THE MOUTH OF CHICAGO RIVER FOR DEFENCE AGAINST THE INDIANS.

The Trail of Tears, A 20th-Century View by Oklahoma Artist Richard West

10

The Old Southwest

THE Old Southwest province of the
Old West extended from the Appalachian Mountains to the Mississippi
River. Flanked on the north by the Ohio River and on the south by the
Gulf of Mexico, it embraced the present states of Kentucky, Tennessee,
Mississippi, Alabama, and a ribbon of the Florida Gulf shore. Like the
Old Northwest, the Old Southwest was the scene of comprehensive development during the period between 1815 and 1828. This growth included
some extension of the military frontier, the opening of wilderness areas
by an expanding grid of roads, a population growth that matched its companion region north of the Ohio River, rapid economic evolution, urbanization, the completion of its political format by the creation of additional
states, Indian removal, and a general resumption of nationalizing currents.

OCCUPYING THE SOUTHWESTERN WILDERNESS

In the Old Southwest two states had already been created and admitted to
the Union before the War of 1812: Kentucky (1792) and Tennessee
(1796). Both served as models for state-making in the region, particularly
for the writing of constitutions. They also served as feeders of population
into the new Southwestern territories, as highways for the movement of
population from the seaboard states into the wilderness areas, and as the
source of some capital and other essentials for developing the new land.

The Military Frontier

The resumption of the flow of nationalizing currents into the Old
Southwest at the end of the War of 1812 included some extension of the

military frontier. However, the rate of buildup was considerably lower than what occurred in the wilderness regions of the Old Northwest. Two circumstances made such an intensive military system unnecessary. First, there was no strong foreign power adjacent to this region, whereas the Old Northwest was contiguous to Canada, domain of the recent enemy. In the Old Southwest, United States territory extended to the Gulf and across the Mississippi River into Louisiana. It is true that Spain held Florida, but at this time it was a weak nation on the retreat in the western hemisphere. Second, the Indian tribes of the Old Southwest were generally peaceful. The Choctaws, Chickasaws, Cherokees, and most of the Creeks had remained loyal to the United States during the War of 1812; regiments of warriors from these tribes had in fact fought with General Jackson in his campaigns against the Red Stick Creeks and the British. For these reasons, the military frontier of the Old Southwest consisted for the most part of shore stations manned by artillery and infantry and stretching in a defensive line from Mobile to New Orleans. In fact, during the period 1815 to 1828, the War Department moved most of the troops in the Old Southwest to forts in the Northwest or across the Mississippi River to new posts in the New West.

Immigrant Concourses

The burst of humanity that populated most of the Old Northwest as a part of the Great Migration had a similar effect in the Old Southwest. This surge of pioneers into the land south of the Ohio River was encouraged by a number of regional improvements, including expansion of the national, state, and local road systems. There was no prime highway construction in the Old Southwest similar to the National Road, with its crushed-stone roadbed and masonry bridges. Federal, state and local roads in the Southwest were mostly trails hewed through the wilderness; stumps marked the roadbed, which was dusty in dry weather and a muddy bog full of deep ruts during the wet season. Crossings of rivers and creeks were accomplished by ferries or by fording the shallows. But in 1806 Congress authorized the building of a federal road to run from Athens, Georgia, via the settlements on the Tombigbee River, to New Orleans. In 1812 federal funds supported construction of another road, from the Ocmulgee-River-crossing in western Georgia to St. Stephens on the Tombigbee River. That same year the Natchez Trace, a major route connecting Nashville in central Tennessee with Natchez on the Mississippi River, was improved.

After the War of 1812, federal support for roadbuilding resumed. One highway began on the Chattahoochee River—at the junction of the Fall Line and Upper Road—to form the federal road across the Mississippi Territory to St. Stephens, where it truncated—one branch extending to Mobile, the other to Natchez. Another federal road, opened in 1815, connected the Great Valley of the Appalachians with Knoxville, dividing there into several branches—including one to Nashville and another to Huntsville in the Mississippi Territory. In 1820 General Andrew Jackson directed troops under his command—the Division of the South—to open a military road between Florence in the Mississippi Territory and Lake Pontchartrain in Louisiana.

Public Lands

Settlers moving into the Old Southwest found a less well ordered land system than in the Old Northwest. North of the Ohio, settlers could buy either land in the public domain of the United States or military bounty lands. They could also negotiate for lease or sale of lands held by the states. In the Old Southwest there was greater diversity in land liquidation. Some lands in the region were still held under old Spanish, French, and English grants. There were no federal public domain lands in Kentucky and Tennessee, as most of the land had been dispensed by the parent states of Virginia and North Carolina through grants to speculators. When Kentucky and Tennessee entered the Union they received title to the unsold tracts, and settlers had to purchase these lands from the state governments.

The residual claims of Georgia to Western territory further complicated the land question. In 1795 Georgia had sold a vast tract to the Yazoo Land Company, and title to this land was clouded until 1810 when the United States Supreme Court settled the question in Fletcher *v.* Peck. (*See* Chapter 7.) In addition, the Cherokees, Choctaws, Creeks, and Chickasaws claimed substantial portions of the Old Southwest as tribal domains. And, after the United States acquired Florida in 1821, the Seminole lands also became involved in the contest for occupancy rights. Federal officials had to extinguish tribal title to all these Indian domains before they could be surveyed, plotted, and sold to settlers under the federal land laws.

SOUTHWESTERN STATE-MAKING

Well before the national government concluded its negotiations with the Southeastern Indians for cessions of tribal estates, pioneers had established pockets of settlement in the areas that were open to entry. In 1790 Congress integrated these dispersed communities by creating the Southwestern Territory; it included the land between the southern border of Kentucky and 31° north, the boundary separating American and Spanish territory. When Tennessee was admitted to the union in 1796, all that remained of the Southwestern Territory was a strip of land extending from the southern border of Tennessee to 31°. Two years later, when the Southwestern Territory had a population of about 5,000, Congress changed its name to the Mississippi Territory and provided for a transitional territorial government. Winthrop Sargent was appointed the first governor of Mississippi Territory, and the capital was located first at Natchez, then in 1802 at the tiny settlement of Washington.

Mississippi

The Mississippi Territory, in terms of land area and effective jurisdiction, grew in a piecemeal fashion. In 1802, by the terms of the Georgia Compact, Georgia gave up its claim to all Western lands as far as the Mississippi River. The Georgia cession of 1802 and the Fletcher *v.* Peck decision of 1810 cleared away several substantive questions that had clouded the jurisdiction and the geographical extent of the Mississippi Territory. After the annexation in 1810 of a portion of West Florida, the region between the Pearl and Perdido rivers on the Gulf south of 31° north was also attached to the territory. Internally as well vast tracts were being opened to settlement as the result of negotiations between leaders of the resident tribes and federal commissioners. One of the most important cessions was that accomplished by the Treaty of Fort Jackson, which provided for the surrender of 22 million acres of Creek domain in the heart of present-day Alabama.

When its piecemeal growth had been completed, the Mississippi Territory consisted of a vast region of about 100,000 square miles. It extended from the Western border of Georgia to the Mississippi River, and from the southern border of Tennessee to the Gulf of Mexico. By the census of 1810, this emergent segment of the Old Southwest—comprising the future states of Alabama and Mississippi—had an American settler population of about 41,000.

In response to statehood petitions from the residents, in 1817 Congress divided the Mississippi Territory into two almost equal pieces. The western half was designated the Mississippi Territory, and its citizens were permitted by the enabling act to elect a constitutional convention and take the other preliminary steps to admission. The eastern half of Mississippi Territory was designated the Alabama Territory.

The Mississippi constitutional convention convened at Washington, the territorial capital, and the delegates worked for about six weeks on the draft of the state constitution. Like other Western constitutions, the Mississippi draft followed rather closely the Kentucky constitution. The organic law included a bill of rights, provision for the secret ballot, and no property qualification for voting. Continuing the Western tradition for restricting executive prerogative and vesting maximum powers in the voice of the people—the legislature—the Mississippi constitution made the law-making body supreme. The legislature could override the executive veto with a simple majority vote and to it was delegated the function of appointing most of the state officials, including judges. Mississippi was admitted to the American Union in 1817.

Alabama

The Alabama Territory was created by act of Congress in 1817 and was located between Georgia and Mississippi. William W. Bibb was named first governor of the new territory, whose capital was situated at

St. Stephens. The Alabama Territory underwent a phenomenal expansion of settler population. In 1810, while a part of Mississippi Territory, Alabama contained about 10,000 Americans. Only nine years later, at statehood, Alabama numbered 145,000—a fourteen-fold increase. Already it had nearly double the population of its territorial parent, Mississippi, which in 1820 contained an American settler population of about 75,000.

The rapid settlement and development of Alabama Territory led to immediate demands for statehood; in 1818 Congress passed the Alabama enabling act. The convention promptly completed its work, modeling the state's constitution after that of Mississippi, and Alabama was admitted to the American Union in 1819.

The Florida Question

Completion of the political format of the Old Southwest was accomplished while two burning diplomatic questions, strategically relevant to the region's continued development, were still unresolved. One concerned territorial cannibalizing by the United States in Spanish West Florida and Spain's reactions to the annexation actions by the United States. The other was the status of the populous Indian communities—Cherokees, Creeks, Choctaws, and Chickasaws—that were now incapsulated within the boundaries of the new states. The Indian problem was made even more difficult by the settlement of the Florida question, for the transfer of Florida to the United States brought the Seminoles too under American dominion. The Seminoles, with the other four tribes, were involved in the contest between Indian and settler for control of the land, and played a part of the tragic drama of removal to the New West.

After the War of 1812, the Gulf segment of Spanish Florida continued in a disordered state. Aboriginal patriots from the Red Stick faction of the Creek Nation, smarting from the defeat at Horse Shoe Bend and the resultant Treaty of Fort Jackson, took refuge in Florida and made menacing gestures toward American settlements on the Southwestern border. Seminole raider parties, armed by European traders (mostly British), swept from their Florida sanctuary to burn and plunder plantations in southwestern Georgia and southern Alabama. Runaway slaves found ready refuge in Florida.

General Jackson determined to end these border disorders by striking at the source. During March 1818, he marched at the head of a swift-moving column of regular and volunteer troops into Spanish Florida. His troops captured the principal Spanish settlements, including Pensacola and St. Marks. In the process they also destroyed a number of Indian settlements and hung two British traders. Protests by British and Spanish officials led to negotiations between the American representative John Quincy Adams and Spanish Minister Luis de Onis and culminated during 1819 in the Adams-Onis Treaty.

The pact provided for the cession of Florida to the United States in return for American payment of claims to its own citizens against Spain to the amount of $5 million. The Adams-Onis Treaty also provided for a settlement of the western boundary of the Louisiana Purchase separating American and Spanish territory. According to the treaty, the boundary was to begin at the mouth of the Sabine River and run up that stream to 32° north; thence it would turn north to the Red River and proceed up that stream to the 100th meridian; it would run along the meridian to the Arkansas River and up that stream to its source, then north to 42°, and west to the Pacific. The Adams-Onís Treaty was ratified in 1821, and General Jackson served as the first governor af Florida Territory.

The Florida question and its settlement by the Adams-Onis Treaty had at least five fundamental effects on the American West. First, it brought the Seminoles under United States jurisdiction. Their relocation to the Indian Territory in the trans-Mississippi West proved to be the most difficult, costly, and bloody of all Indian removals. Second, by assenting to the treaty, Spain legalized the sustained American cannibalizing of West Florida. In the division of the spoils after the War of 1812, long before the Adams-Onís Treaty, that portion of West Florida east to the Pearl River had been added to Louisiana at statehood. The strip of Gulf shore between the Pearl and Perdido rivers was attached to the Mississippi Territory. Thus, third, by conquest and diplomatic settlement, that fragmentary portion of Florida west of the trans-Appalachian line was added to the American dominion. Fourth, the United States, by accepting the Sabine River as the boundary separating Louisiana and Texas, had thereby surrendered its claim to Texas as a part of the Louisiana Purchase; this claim had been based primarily on LaSalle's colonizing attempts on the Texas Gulf shore. And fifth, Spain, by accepting the Adams-Onís Treaty boundary, surrendered its claim to all territory in the New West north of 42°.

INDIAN REMOVAL

The states of the Old Southwest pressed the national government to remove the populous Indian tribes from within their borders. By 1821 the Cherokee nation numbered about 20,000 people, the Choctaw nation about 22,000, the Seminole nation about 4,000, the Creek nation about 22,000, and the Chickasaw nation about 5,000. The Indians occupied valuable lands and, according to business and political leaders, held up settlement and development in each of the states. Each of the Indian nations also maintained a tribal government that had jurisdiction over members and, by treaty with the United States, the tribal citizens and tribal governments were exempt from state laws. To state leaders these tribal governments challenged state sovereignty and comprised, in a sense, states within a state; in some cases there was more than one nation within the borders of a single

Southwest state, and each one exercised complete sovereignty within its own tribal area.

By the 1820s successive land cessions negotiated by federal commissioners and tribal leaders had substantially reduced the tribal domains in the Old Southwest, with the result that the Cherokees were concentrated in eastern Tennessee, northwestern Georgia, and eastern Alabama; the Creeks in western Georgia and Alabama; the Choctaws in southern Mississippi and southwestern Alabama; the Chickasaws in northern Mississippi and northwestern Alabama; and the Seminoles in Florida.

A few national leaders were sensitive to the destructive effect on the tribes of being constantly pushed across the frontier by successive waves of settlement. For some time they had considered the possibility of establishing a permanent Indian colonization zone in the West beyond the line of settlement; there, they thought, the tribes need never be bothered again. President Jefferson hoped to make use of the westernmost margins of the Louisiana Purchase lands to develop such a permanent Indian relocation area beyond the pressure and influence of the American settlements.

Cherokee Relocation

The Cherokees were the first of the Southern tribes to succumb to pressure from national officials and to accept a Western domain. Georgia officials had consistently urged federal officials to fulfill that portion of the Georgia Compact whereby, in return for ceding its Western lands to the United States, the federal government was to extinguish tribal title to Indian lands in the state. In 1817 at the Cherokee Agency in Tennessee, Cherokee leaders George Lowry, Charles Hicks, and Going Snake met with federal commissioners Andrew Jackson, Joseph McMinn, and David Meriwether; they negotiated a treaty providing for the surrender of one-third of the Cherokee Eastern lands in exchange for a tract of equal size in northwest Arkansas between the White and Arkansas rivers. Emigration was voluntary, and by 1835, about 6,000 Cherokees had moved west.

Through the succeeding years federal officials encouraged the Eastern Cherokees to join their kinsmen in the West, but since they had made phenomenal progress in adopting the arts of Anglo-American civilization, most of them were prosperous, and they generally ignored appeals to cede their Eastern lands and move west. Many Eastern Cherokees had emulated their white neighbors, and a great number were prominent and wealthy as slaveowners and operators of grain and lumber mills, plantations, stock farms, and other businesses within the Cherokee nation. A Northern visitor during the 1820s observed that many Cherokees lived "in comfort and abundance, in good houses of brick, stone, and wood. We saw several houses built of hewn stone, superior to any we had ever seen before. The people seemed to have more money than the whites in our own settlements; they were better clothed. The women were weaving, the men cultivating corn, and raising beef and pork in abundance; butter and milk everywhere. We were at an election for delegates among the Cherokees to form a constitution. They were orderly, and well behaved." [1]

Schools, most of them operated by Moravian and Presbyterian missionaries, instructed Cherokee children in the rudiments of learning. Sequoyah, the Cherokee genius, had invented his syllabary, an 86-symbol alphabet that reduced the Cherokee language to written form. A tribal newspaper, the *Cherokee Phoenix*, edited by Elias Boudinot, who was part Cherokee, appeared for the first time in 1828; its columns were printed both in Sequoyah's syllabary and in English. The Cherokee nation abolished its tribal government in 1827 and formed a constitutional republic. Pathkiller, the last of the pure Cherokee hereditary tribal chiefs, was replaced by Charles Hicks, a brilliant man of mixed parentage who was the chief author of the constitution.

When the Cherokees organized their constitutional republic, the Georgia government attacked the change as subversive, claiming it constituted a state within a state. During 1828 and 1829 the Georgia legislature passed a special code of laws abolishing the Cherokee government, declaring all Cherokees subject to state law, forbidding the tribal officials to carry out their duties, and making it unlawful for the Cherokee Council to meet except to discuss removal to the West. By these laws, Indians could not be accepted as competent witnesses in Georgia courts, and all white persons residing in the Cherokee nation were required to obtain permits from state authorities. This latter provision was aimed at the missionaries, who were suspected by state officials of encouraging the Indians to oppose removal.

Cherokee troubles mounted. During 1829 gold was discovered in the mountains of northern Georgia, within the Cherokee nation. The state legislature passed a law forbidding Cherokees to prospect or mine gold on their own lands. The gold discovery set off a mad stampede. Over 3,000 whites stormed across the Cherokee domain, wrecking fences, violating households, and creating general ruin and anarchy. When the Indians brought charges against the intruders for trespass, stock theft, or violation of person, the Georgia courts refused to acknowledge their petitions on the grounds that their testimony was incompetent and inadmissible.

In 1831, eleven missionaries were arrested for failure to obtain state permits authorizing them to teach and preach in the nation. Georgia courts gave the accused the choice of following the requirements of the law or going to prison for four years. Nine missionaries bowed to the state requirement; only Samuel A. Worcester and Elizar Butler refused. In 1832 Chief Justice John Marshall issued the famous Worcester v. Georgia decision, in which he declared the state laws under which the two mission-

[1] Quoted in Arrell Gibson, *Oklahoma: A History of Five Centuries* (Norman, 1965), p. 111.

aries were imprisoned null and void and ordered the prisoners released. President Andrew Jackson, however, refused to carry out the order, and Worcester and Butler remained in Georgia state prison.

During 1834, the Georgia legislature authorized the survey of Cherokee lands and the disposal of most of the choice parcels in the nation by a state lottery. The estates of leading Cherokees, including Principal Chief John Ross, were confiscated and taken over by white planters. Spring Place Mission, long a center of learning and culture in Cherokee history, was included in the lottery. The person who drew this ticket was a bartender; he converted the mission into a saloon! In the year of the land lottery, the Georgia militia marched to the Cherokee capital at New Echota, seized the printing press and type of the *Cherokee Phoenix*, smashed some of the equipment, and threw it into the river. Suppression of the *Phoenix* was excused on the grounds that it had advocated resistance to removal.

This harassment provoked Cherokee indignation, and there developed in the nation a group who saw removal to the West as the lesser of two evils. The leader of this faction was Major Ridge, one of the wealthiest slaveowners in the Cherokee nation and speaker of the Cherokee National Council. His prominent followers were his son, John Ridge, Elias Boudinot, and the latter's younger brother, Stand Watie. Ridge's group came to be called the Treaty Party and it consisted mostly of men of mixed racial background. The group opposing removal, and the more numerous, were full-blooded Cherokees; because their leader was Chief John Ross, their faction was called the Ross Party.

Federal commissioners continued to offer the Cherokees various and ever-more favorable removal treaty terms. During 1835, when Chief Ross refused the national government's offer, American agents headed by John Schermerhorn turned to leaders of the Treaty Party; at New Echota on December 29 he negotiated a treaty of removal. The Ross Party members warned the Ridge Party followers that if they affixed their names to the Treaty of New Echota, they would in effect sign their own death warrants. They signed, nonetheless, and, by the terms of the Treaty of New Echota, the Cherokees sold their Eastern lands—a domain consisting of over 8 million acres—for $5 million. They were confirmed in joint ownership with the Western Cherokees of their lands in Indian Territory and were obligated to move within two years after ratification. The federal government was to pay the cost of removal and promised to support the immigrants for one year after their arrival in the West. The Ross Party refused to recognize the treaty and declared that its members were not bound by it because it had been negotiated by a minority of the nation. Only 2,000 Cherokees, most of them members of the Ridge Party, migrated peacefully under the terms of the Treaty of New Echota. When 1838 arrived and it was clear that the Ross Party Cherokees were determined not to migrate, United States troops were ordered to the Cherokee nation to round up the Indians and forcibly relocate them in Indian Territory. The Georgia militia assisted the federal troops.

The story of the Cherokee Trail of Tears is an epic of misery and death. "The troops were disposed at various points throughout the Cherokee country, where stockade forts were erected for gathering in and holding the Indians preparatory to removal. From these, squads of troops were sent to search out with rifle and bayonet every small cabin hidden away in the coves or by the sides of mountain streams, to seize and bring in as prisoners all the occupants. . . . Families at dinner were startled by the sudden gleam of bayonets in the doorway and rose up to be driven with blows and oaths along the weary miles of trail that led to the stockade. Men were seized in their fields or going along the road, women were taken from their wheels and children from their play. In many cases, on turning for one last look as they crossed the ridge, they saw their homes in flames, fired by the lawless rabble that followed on the heels of the soldiers to loot and pillage." [2]

After about 5,000 Cherokees had been ruthlessly uprooted and marched to Indian Territory, Chief Ross appealed to American officials to permit him and other Cherokee leaders to supervise the removal. With the army's permission, the Cherokees were organized into travel parties of 1,000 persons each, and the removal proceeded in a more orderly and humane fashion. Even so, their march to the West was marked by the gravestones of the perishing; the tribal population was reduced by 25 percent during the ordeal.

The Cherokee Treaty of 1817 was the first agreement with a Southern tribe to contain a provision for Indian migration to the West. Although many treaties had been negotiated with the Cherokees, Creeks, Choctaws, and Chickasaws before 1817, each of them providing for cession of territory to the United States, until then the cessions had amounted to a diminution of the tribal estate; the Indians remained in residence on their reduced domain. And, since only a portion of the Cherokee nation migrated under the terms of the 1817 treaty, additional negotiations were required to clear all the Cherokees from the eastern United States. But tribal migration did begin with the 1817 treaty, and it was to serve as a model for negotiations with the other Southwestern tribes.

Choctaw Relocation

The Choctaws were the next tribe to commit themselves to vacating their eastern lands and migrating to the West. Two treaties—the first negotiated in 1820—were required to accomplish their removal. Chief Pushmataha and other Choctaw leaders met with an American commission headed by General Jackson at Doak's Stand on the Natchez Trace. The agree-

[2] Quoted in Gibson, *Oklahoma*, p. 117.

ment issuing from the council provided that, in return for surrendering to the United States about a third of their Eastern domain, the Choctaws were to receive a vast tract of territory west of the Mississippi. The treaty pledged the United States government to supply to each emigrating Choctaw warrior a rifle, bullet mold, camp kettle, blanket, ammunition sufficient for hunting and defense for one year, and payment for any improvements he left in his ancestral home. Pushmataha insisted on the inclusion of a clause providing for 54 sections of Choctaw land to be surveyed and sold at auction, the proceeds to go into a special fund to support schools for Choctaw youth in the new country.

While government officials were hopeful that the Choctaws would remove at once and tribal leaders full well knew that total removal was inevitable, the treaty had made removal voluntary. Therefore, only about a fourth of the tribe moved west under its terms. Most members remained in Mississippi; since the Choctaws had surrendered only about a third of their Eastern lands, they still possessed a sizable domain in Mississippi.

During the 1820s the states of Mississippi and Alabama followed the Georgia pattern of applying negative persuasion in their attempt to force the Choctaws and other tribes to vacate their lands and migrate. Both the Alabama and Mississippi legislatures adopted laws abolishing tribal governments; chiefs who exercised their tribal duties were to serve a prison term. The Indians were also made subject to state law. When tribal leaders appealed to federal officials for protection from state action, as guaranteed by treaties with the United States, they were told that the national government was powerless to protect them. White settlers did their bit to make life miserable for the Creeks, Choctaws, and Chickasaws: they squatted on tribal lands, daring the Indians to evict them; they stole and killed Indian livestock and carried away other property with impunity. Law enforcement officers and the courts intervened only when white predators had to be protected from Indian wrath.

Reluctant as they were to leave the lands of their ancestors, Choctaw leaders saw the futility of attempting to thwart such a powerful combination of private citizens and state officials. High federal officials, including the president had made it clear that the Indians could expect no protection from the federal government. Therefore in 1830 Choctaw leaders met with federal commissioners at the Dancing Rabbit Creek council ground and signed a definitive removal treaty. By the terms of this treaty the Choctaw nation ceded to the United States all tribal lands in Mississippi. In return, the government bound itself to pay the cost of the Choctaw relocation, provide a payment to the tribe of $20,000 annually for a period of twenty years, finance the education of forty Choctaw youths each year, and pay to the Choctaw nation the sum of $50,000 to establish new schools in the West.

A few Choctaws were permitted to remain in Mississippi and receive allotments varying from 320 to 640 acres each. The Choctaw allottees were required to separate from the Choctaw nation and become subject to the laws of the state. About 4,500 Choctaws became allottees.

The Choctaw removal was less traumatic than the Cherokee removal, but intense suffering seemed the common lot of all immigrating parties, mostly because of poor planning by supervisory government agents. Most of the immigrants were caught on the trail in midwinter; temperatures regularly fell to zero, and several parties of Choctaws had to march through six inches of snow. Cholera, smallpox, malnutrition, and other maladies devastated the columns on their westward march.

Creek Relocation

The Creek nation had a similar removal ordeal. This tribe had two great divisions: the Lower Creeks, people of mixed white and Creek parentage who were led by the McIntosh family; and the Upper Creeks, who were of pure Creek background—their chief spokesman was Opothle-yaholo. Because their domain had been reduced by regular cessions of tribal land in 1814, 1818, and 1821, the Creek National Council in 1823 adopted a law prescribing the death penalty for any citizen who signed away Creek lands without approval of the council.

Nonetheless, increasing settler depredations and incessant pressure from federal officials caused Chief William McIntosh to meet with an American commission at the Indian Springs, Georgia, council grounds in 1825. There he signed the Treaty of Indian Springs, providing for additional cessions of tribal territory in exchange for a new Creek domain west of the Mississippi. McIntosh's justification was that the Creek nation had to migrate and had to do so soon. At present the government was willing to pay for the Creeks' Eastern lands, but before long the Americans "will take them and the little band of our people, poor and despised, will be left to wander without homes and be beaten like dogs. We will go to a new home and . . . till the earth, grow cattle and depend on these for food and life . . . and we shall grow and again become a great nation." [3]

Upper Creek chiefs led by Opothleyaholo refused to approve the Treaty of Indian Springs. The National Council ordered McIntosh's execution, and the order was carried out in a summary fashion. A hundred Creek warriors surrounded McIntosh's home, set fire to the dwelling, and, when heat and flames flushed McIntosh into the dooryard, they shot him to death.

The Senate ratified the Treaty of Indian Springs, but before President John Quincy Adams could put the agreement into effect he learned of the circumstances surrounding the negotiations. At his invitation a Creek delegation headed by Opothleyaholo journeyed to Washington. This delega-tion was authorized by the National Council to negotiate with the presi-

[3] Quoted in Gibson, Oklahoma, p. 88.

dent the question of ceding tribal lands; its members were therefore exempt from the treatment McIntosh had received. The willingness of the Creek government to proceed with an action that was unacceptable only a few months before was undoubtedly the result of the threat of civil war within the nation. The Lower Creeks were threatening to avenge McIntosh's death, and Opothleyaholo believed it would be better to allow the dissidents to migrate. He therefore negotiated the Treaty of Washington in 1826, whereby the Creeks exchanged a portion of their remaining Eastern lands for a new domain in the West. Most of the Lower Creeks migrated under the terms of this treaty.

Federal commissioners persisted in pressuring the Creeks to agree to a definitive treaty of land cession and removal, and land-hungry settlers assisted them by carrying on a merciless campaign of harassment. Squatting on Creek lands, stealing Indian livestock, and tormenting the Creeks until they fought back, they created incidents that were characterized as savage Indian reprisals. Like Georgia, the Alabama legislature abolished the Creek tribal government and made all Indians subject to state law. This peculiar system of law did not protect Indians from white aggression, but it did protect the whites from Indian retaliation.

By 1832 the Creek chiefs were finally persuaded of the futility of attempting to live in the land of their ancestors, and Opothleyaholo headed a tribal delegation to Washington to negotiate a final removal agreement. By the terms of the second Treaty of Washington, the Creek nation in Alabama was dissolved. Tribal members had the option of joining their kinsmen in the West at once—in which case the government would pay the removal expense—or they could remain in Alabama and receive allotments, which varied in size from 320 to 640 acres each. The United States government pledged to expel white intruders and insure that the Indian allottee could reside on and use his land. In exchange for title to its tribal estate in the East, the Creek nation was to receive an annuity of $12,000 for five years, followed by a $10,000 grant for the next fifteen years.

The Creeks accepting allotments were granted a five-year period in which to try living as individual citizens in Alabama. Since only 630 Indians prepared to emigrate to Indian Territory, most of the Creeks elected to try this new way of living; and it was new to them, for like other tribes, the Creeks had always held their lands in common. Few of the Creeks understood the intricacies of private land ownership, and the whites callously exploited their ignorance. There were widespread land frauds and attachments for false debt; dispossession was frequently ordered by courts friendly to white land seekers. And the federal government utterly failed to insure the Creek allottees the peaceful use of their lands. Settlers continued to harass the Indians; and when individual Creeks attempted to defend their homes and drive off their oppressors, they were arrested by state officers for assault and disorderly conduct. Finally, in 1836, a unified defense developed around a Creek chief named Eneah

Emothla. The encroaching settlers became alarmed, appealed for protection, and United States troops came to Alabama to put down the so-called Creek rebellion.

The Creek war was used as a justification for the wholesale removal of the nation from Alabama. Squads of soldiers swarmed over the countryside rounding up Indians and collecting them in heavily-guarded concentration camps until a party of 1,000 or so had accumulated. Then they were marched overland under military guard to Indian Territory. Torn from their homes, forced to abandon improvements, and most of their personal belongings, the Creek immigrants suffered more than any other tribe on their Trail of Tears. The army captured nearly 2,500 chiefs and warriors who were classed as hostiles and were therefore considered dangerous. During the bitterly cold winter of 1836–1837 many of this group were bound in shackles and driven to Fort Gibson in the West. One party of 300 Creeks was taken down the Alabama River to the Gulf, transported to the Mississippi, and placed on a river boat that had been condemned as unsafe. Upriver the rotting craft sank, and all passengers were lost. By the spring of 1837, 15,000 Creeks had reached the West. Over 3,500 died in the winter cold on the way west. The severe weather, lack of food, and general suffering killed virtually all infants as well as many small children and old people.

Chickasaw Relocation

Like the other Southern tribes, the Chickasaws were surrounded by American settlements, and government officials sought to persuade tribal leaders to sign a removal treaty. Successive cession agreements with the United States had already drastically reduced Chickasaw territory when an 1818 treaty cut off their range in western Kentucky and Tennessee and restricted them to northern Mississippi and northwestern Alabama. Through the years government commissioners encouraged the chiefs to cede this last vestige of their once vast domain. Like the other tribes, the Chickasaws suffered harassment, and, in the usual pattern, the Mississippi legislature erased the tribal government and made all Chickasaws subject to state law. The chiefs were aware that removal was inevitable, but they shrewdly held out just long enough to wring from the government by far the best removal treaty negotiated with the Southern tribes.

During October 1832, at the Chickasaw council house on Pontotoc Creek in northern Mississippi, tribal leaders signed a treaty with President Jackson's representatives providing for the cession of all Chickasaw lands east of the Mississippi River as soon as a suitable home in the West could be found. By the terms of the treaty, the federal government was to survey the Chickasaw nation; then each Indian family was to be assigned a homestead as a temporary residence until the Western home was found. The remainder of the land was to be sold at public auction, the proceeds to go to the Chickasaws.

Chickasaw delegations visited the trans-Mississippi territory from time to time searching for a national home. The Choctaws encouraged them to settle in their domain west of Arkansas. The federal and state governments urged the Chickasaws to make a decision, but the chiefs were not to be hurried. Finally, in January 1837, a delegation of Chickasaws and Choctaws signed the agreement known as the Treaty of Doaksville; the Chickasaws agreed to settle among the Choctaws.

Prodded by government officials, the Chickasaws began migrating west in the spring of 1837, and by 1840 most of them had arrived in Indian Territory. With a shorter distance to travel and the wise management of their removal by tribal leaders, the Chickasaw relocation was the most peaceful and orderly experienced by any of the Southern tribes. The Indian families were able to collect most of their personal property, slaves, and livestock for transfer to the West. One report told of 7,000 Chickasaw ponies gathered at Memphis, waiting for transportation to the west bank of the Mississippi. But even with their well organized removal, they did not escape suffering and disease. Cholera struck some of their camps, and many suffered from spoiled meat and grain rations issued by unscrupulous government contractors.

Seminole Relocation

The last of the Southern tribes to be colonized in the West were the Seminoles of Florida, southern Georgia, and Alabama. They were sedentary town dwellers, their government consisting of a head chief and a council with moderate power. The nation was divided into bands, each named for the captain of the band. Some of the leading band chiefs, who at the time of removal defended the right of the Seminoles to remain on the land of their ancestors, were Osceola, Alligator, Jumper, Coacoochee (Wildcat), and Micanopy.

The Seminoles first came under the jurisdiction of the United States in 1821, when Spain ceded Florida to the United States. Immediately thereafter Americans moved into Florida Territory and began demanding that the government remove the Seminoles and open up their rich coastal lands to settlement. In 1823 the Seminoles signed their first treaty with the United States. By the Treaty of Tampa they agreed to move into the swampy interior east of Tampa Bay. This satisfied the whites only briefly; in no time at all they were demanding that the federal government remove the Seminoles altogether, claiming that the Indians stole their slaves and livestock and were a menace to the settlements.

In 1832, United States Commissioner James Gadsden met with the Seminole chiefs and negotiated the Treaty of Payne's Landing, by which the tribe was obligated to move when a suitable home was found in the Western country. The Indians had three years in which to make the move, and the United States government agreed to pay the cost of removal and subsistence for one year after arrival in the West. The federal government was also to pay the nation $15,400 for the land surrendered in Florida, plus $3,000 a year for fifteen years.

A delegation of seven Seminole chiefs, accompanied by agent John Phagan, traveled to the West in search of a new home. The Creeks invited the Seminoles to settle on their lands west of Arkansas; the Seminole delegation agreed to this offer by the Treaty of Fort Gibson of 1833. By the terms of the Treaty of Payne's Landing, the Seminole grace period of three years ended in 1835. Osceola headed a faction that refused to be bound by the removal treaties, but a portion of the nation agreed to move, and federal officials made preparations accordingly. Osceola and other Seminole patriots, aroused by the removal activities, killed Emathla, one of the signers of the Treaty of Fort Gibson. Agent Wiley Thompson had Osceola arrested and placed in irons. After a brief confinement, the chief was released, and shortly afterward Osceola and a band of followers shot down Thompson, an army officer, and several civilians near Fort King. The same day, Osceola ambushed Major Francis Dade and 110 soldiers on the road near the post; only three men escaped the Seminole trap. The Fort King massacre set off the Seminole War, which lasted until 1842. No settlement was safe, and soldiers who went after the fierce Seminoles did so at great peril. Osceola promised that his warriors would fight "till the last drop of Seminole blood had moisted the dust" of their homeland.

In the meantime, peaceful Seminoles appeared every month or so to be outfitted for relocation to the West. Four hundred people departed from Tampa in April 1836. Under Osceola, the resistance faction carried on a fierce, unremitting war against the United States and the Florida settlements. In 1836, General Thomas Jesup was placed in command of troops for what the government hoped would be the final campaign against the Seminoles. Unable to bring the elusive warriors to bay, he called a peace council, and the chiefs came in under a flag of truce. In violation of the truce agreement Osceola was taken prisoner and sent to Fort Moultrie at Charleston, South Carolina. The unconquerable war chief died there in chains in January 1839, but his followers continued the war under Wildcat and Bowlegs. This protracted campaign was one of the costliest wars in American history to that date. Finally, in 1842, the hazards of flushing Seminoles from their swamp hideouts caused the federal government to call off the struggle. A community of Seminoles was allowed to remain permanently in Florida.

A census of the Seminole camps near Fort Gibson in 1842 showed that in ten years the federal government had managed to remove 3,000 Seminoles from the Old Southwest. Some came peacefully, most by coercion. The cost was high: $20 million was spent in keeping an army in the field from 1835 to 1842; 1,500 soldiers were killed; and countless others were maimed for life. For each Seminole removed to Indian Territory (man, woman, child), it cost the government $6,500. Looking at these statistics another way, for every two Seminoles removed to the West, the army paid with the life of one soldier. No one knows the exact cost in terms of Seminole lives, but it is known that the Seminole removal brought to a close one of the blackest periods in American history. The Trail of Tears of the Southern tribes and the other Eastern Indian groups who were ruthlessly uprooted to make way for the American settlers, ranks among the tragedies of the ages.

THE GREAT MIGRATION IN THE SOUTHWEST

Although the presence of populous Indian communities occupying vast tracts of rich land had arrested the region's development, between 1800 and 1820, federal commissioners had succeeded in opening substantial portions of these tribal domains to settlement. Settler-Indian competition for the remaining lands ended during the 1830s with the final cessions and removal of the tribes to the West. The opening of these tribal lands attracted vast numbers of pioneers into the Old Southwest, so that by the end of the War of 1812, its population increase matched that of the Old Northwest as a part of the phenomenal demographic surge into the Old West in the time of the Great Migration. At least one new state, Alabama, experienced a fourteen-fold increase in population in less than ten years.

Urbanization

Although most of the early immigrants to the Old Southwest were of the pioneer-farmer frontier so that—like the Old Northwest—the region was largely rural in character, the urban frontier also intruded into the Old Southwest. Kentucky's principal towns included Lexington, a leading trading and distribution center with a limited number of primary industries including tanneries, and Louisville, a port city at the Falls of the Ohio River. Tennessee's long ribbon of territory was divided into three segments, each centering on a town: Knoxville was the most important east Tennessee city; central Tennessee focused on Nashville; and Memphis dominated western Tennessee. Alabama's urban frontier centered on Mobile, an old port town on the Gulf that drained agricultural products for export (mostly cotton) from a rich interior and supplied the tributary settlements with goods and equipment. A principal interior Alabama town was Huntsville, the state capital. Mississippi's southern and western perimeter was ringed by a number of old towns, extending from Biloxi on the Gulf around the Mississippi River north to Natchez. Jackson, the state capital, was the interior's leading trade and political center.

The Plantation System

The urban frontier in the Old Southwest, however, played a less decisive role than in the Old Northwest. In the latter region, the urban frontier was the principal agent for refining out the primitive from the social milieu, metamorphosing the region into a cultural extension of the

Eastern United States, and forcing Western attributes to retreat into the New West. In the Old Southwest as well, Western attributes were purged; but the process was due less to expanding urban frontier influences than to the extension of cotton culture and the plantation system from the seaboard.

There was a progression of settlement in the region. The first comers were pioneers who opened small clearings in the wilderness and practiced subsistence agriculture. The cotton culture, which had been advancing from the seaboard since 1800, intruded into the Old Southwest by the close of the War of 1812. The plantation system, based largely on one-crop agriculture manned by slave labor, was necessarily migratory, for its practices mined the soil of natural fertility. A plantation owner or his agent customarily entered the new territory, bought up a number of small pioneer farms, integrated the scattered holdings into a large plantation, relocated his family, slaves, and equipment, and proceeded to plant cotton.

This progression caused many displaced pioneer farmers, who were unwilling to compete with slave labor, to retreat to the third province of the Old West, the Mississippi Valley. There in the emerging states of Louisiana, Arkansas, and Missouri fresh opportunities awaited them.

SELECTED SOURCES

The policy and process of tearing the Southern tribes from the land of their ancestors and driving them to Indian Territory over the "Trail of Tears" are chronicled in Grant Foreman, *Indian Removal* (Norman, 1932, 1972) and *The Five Civilized Tribes* (Norman, 1934, 1971); Morris L. Wardell, A Political History of the Cherokee Nation, 1838–1907 (Norman, 1938); *Robert S. Cotterill, The Southern Indians: The Story of the Civilized Tribes before Removal (Norman, 1954, 1974); Grace S. Woodward, The Cherokees (Norman, 1965); Angie Debo, Rise and Fall of the Choctaw Republic, 2nd ed. (Norman, 1967) and The Road to Disappearance (Norman, 1941); Edwin C. McReynolds, The Seminoles (Norman, 1957); *Arrell M. Gibson, The Chickasaws (Norman, 1971); and David H. Corcoran, The Cherokee Frontier: Conflict and Survival (Norman, 1962).

The opening of the Old Southwest wilderness and the impact of early technology on regional settlement and development are treated in Seymour Dunbar, A History of Travel in America (Indianapolis, 1915), 4 vols.; Louis C. Hunter, Steamboats on the Western Rivers (Cambridge, 1949); Charles H. Ambler, A History of Transportation in the Ohio Valley (Glendale, Calif., 1932); and Robert L. Kincaid, The Wilderness Road (Indianapolis, 1947).

The Southwest's socio-economic metamorphosis from a pioneer-farmer frontier to a predominantly plantation-type community can be traced in Thomas P. Abernethy, The South in the New Nation, 1789–1819 (Baton Rouge, 1961); *Frank L. Owsley, Plain Folk of the Old South (Baton Rouge, 1949);

* Available in paperback.

William C. Eaton, *A History of the Old South* (New York, 1950); *Ulrich B. Phillips, *Life and Labor in the Old South* (Boston, 1929); and Everett H. Dick, *The Dixie Frontier, A Social History* (New York, 1948).

Old Southwest state-making is depicted in A. B. Moore, *A History of Alabama* (Tuscaloosa, 1934); *Frederick Jackson Turner, *The Rise of the New West, 1819–1829* (New York, 1906); *Francis S. Philbrick, *The Rise of the West, 1754–1830* (New York, 1965); John A. Caruso, *The Southern Frontier* (Indianapolis, 1963); and Rowland Dunbar, *History of Mississippi* (Chicago, 1925), 2 vols.

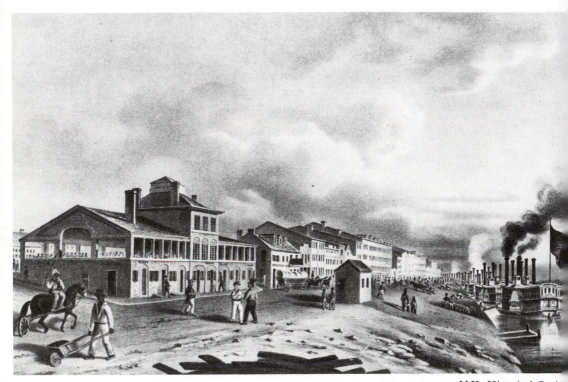

St. Louis, Missouri: View of Front Street, 1840

11

The Mississippi Valley

The third and westernmost component of the Old West was the Mississippi Valley province. It belongs in the Old West's historical context because the same frontier forces that were present in the Old Northwest and Old Southwest—and which were being altered by the impact of nationalizing currents and Eastern cultural influences and were integrating these regions into the American community—were contemporaneously at work in the Mississippi Valley. And, after the War of 1812, much of the Mississippi Valley province, like its associate regions, was populated and developed by the demographic surge known as the Great Migration.

Geographically, the Mississippi Valley consisted of a ribbon of trans-Mississippi territory that extended from the Canadian border to the Gulf of Mexico. Created from the Louisiana Purchase area, the province was tied together by the Mississippi River, which marked its eastern border. Its western border abutted the New West, and the states erected within it were Louisiana, Arkansas, Missouri, Iowa, and Minnesota.

Even after its own development had passed the frontier stage, the Mississippi Valley province continued to play a role in Western history as the forward station for American expansion to the Pacific shore, exporting settlers, goods, and culture into the New West. Political and business leaders of the region also kept the attention of the nation focused on the territories beyond Missouri, thus maintaining a continuing relationship with the New West. Of the three components of the Old West, the Mississippi Valley province remained the most Western oriented. Its people faced the West whereas those of the other regions in the Old West tended to look toward the East.

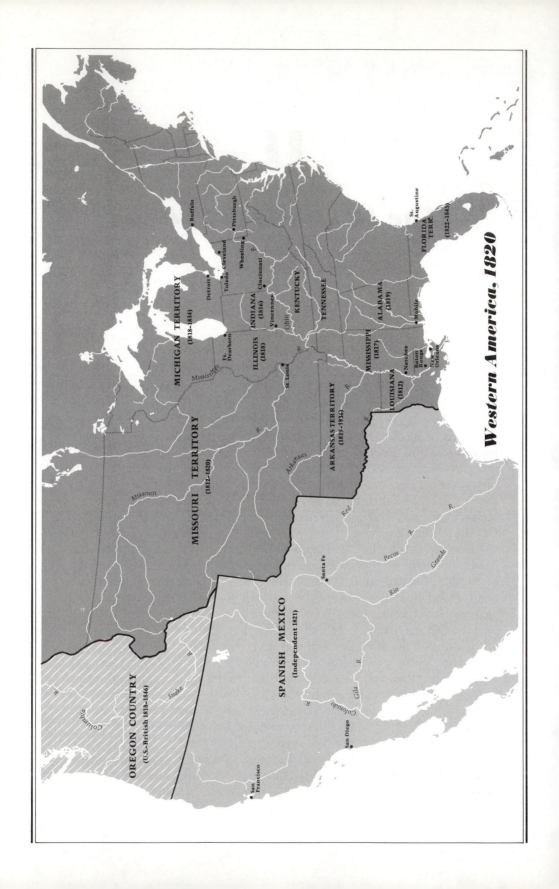

Western America, 1820

OREGON COUNTRY
(U.S.-British 1818–1846)

Columbia R.
Snake R.

SPANISH MEXICO
(Independent 1821)

San Francisco
San Diego
Santa Fe

Colorado R.
Gila R.
Rio Grande
Pecos R.
Red R.

MISSOURI TERRITORY
(1812–1820)

Missouri R.
Arkansas R.

MICHIGAN TERRITORY
(1818–1834)

Mississippi R.
Detroit
Ft. Dearborn
St. Louis

ILLINOIS
(1818)

INDIANA
(1816)
Vincennes

Toledo
Cleveland
Wheeling
Cincinnati
Buffalo
Pittsburgh

Ohio R.

KENTUCKY

TENNESSEE

ARKANSAS TERRITORY
(1819–1836)

ALABAMA
(1819)

MISSISSIPPI
(1817)

LOUISIANA
(1812)

Natchez
Baton Rouge
New Orleans
Mobile

FLORIDA TERR.
(1822–1845)
St. Augustine

AMERICAN OCCUPATION OF THE MISSISSIPPI VALLEY

American sovereignty was officially established in the Mississippi Valley segment of the Old West in December 1803, when William C. C. Claiborne took possession of the Spanish-French province of Louisiana in the name of the United States. At the time, Louisiana's French, Spanish, and American population numbered somewhat over 30,000; most of it was concentrated in the lower Mississippi Valley.

The Military Frontier

American presence in Louisiana was immeasurably strengthened by the extension of the military frontier into the new province. Two strategic areas in the lower part of the valley—the Mississippi River's mouth and the Louisiana border facing Spanish Texas—received the immediate attention of the War Department. Both locations were guarded by regular and militia troops stationed in temporary base camps. In 1819 the Adams-Onís Treaty with Spain finally established the western border of Louisiana at the Sabine River. Between 1820 and 1822, the Army built four military posts in Louisiana. To guard the Louisiana-Texas frontier, Fort Seldon was erected in 1820 on the Red River near Grand Ecore. Two years later, Fort Jesup was established at the watershed of the Red and Sabine rivers, twenty-two miles southwest of Natchitoches on the San Antonio Road. Also in 1822, the military frontier in Louisiana was extended to include two new posts near the Gulf. Fort Jackson on the Mississippi River, sixty-five miles below New Orleans, and Fort Livingstone at Barataria Bay became part of United States seacoast defenses.

Arkansas too became an important area of the military frontier extension; the construction of Fort Smith on Arkansas' western border at the junction of the Poteau and Arkansas rivers was begun in 1817. It became an important way station of the frontier. An arsenal was also erected at Little Rock to support Fort Smith and other Western posts.

At the time of American acquisition, Missouri was the center of considerable settlement and contained a population of about 10,000 people. American military officials officiated at the transfer of the Spanish Upper Louisiana posts in Missouri. In 1804 the Spanish garrison at Fort Celeste, New Madrid, was evacuated; it was promptly occupied by American troops. Guarding the western approaches to St. Louis—the metropolitan center of Missouri and Upper Louisiana—was the Spanish post of Fort San Carlos, which was occupied by American troops in 1804. Fort San Carlos accommodated the largest garrison force in Missouri until Fort Bellefontaine was erected in 1805. Established by General James Wilkinson and situated on the right bank of the Missouri River about four miles above its mouth, Fort Bellefontaine was the first post erected west of the Mississippi by the Americans. In 1808 the erection of Fort Osage, situated on the left bank of the Missouri about forty miles below the junction of the Kansas River, pushed the military frontier farther west. Originally Fort Osage was named Fort Clark after its founder, General William Clark.

North of Missouri, the military frontier extension included Fort Madison, which was built in 1808 on the Mississippi River in the southeastern corner of present-day Iowa. The principal mission of its garrison was the control of the Sac and Fox Indians. In 1819 Fort Snelling was constructed in the future state of Minnesota at the confluence of the Minnesota and Mississippi rivers. Its purpose was to establish American presence among the resident Sioux and to prevent British encroachment from Canada into important fur trading areas.

Early Governance

The national government acted promptly to provide political administration and confirm American proprietorship over the Mississippi Valley province. President Jefferson appointed William C. C. Claiborne, the American commissioner who received Louisiana from French officials at New Orleans in 1803, as first governor af the new acquisition. Congress too responded promptly to the governmental needs of the province. An act of 1804 divided the Louisiana Purchase into two territories at the 33° north latitude. The area south of 33° was designated the Territory of Orleans; the area north of that latitude was named the District of Louisiana, often called the Louisiana Territory or Upper Louisiana. In 1803, President Jefferson had named Captain Amos Stoddard, military commander at St. Louis, as commandant of the northern area and deputy governor under Governor Claiborne at New Orleans. Under authority of the 1804 statute, he directed that the District of Louisiana be temporarily administered by the Indiana Territory, of which William H. Harrison was governor.

The 1804 law was further refined by Congress in 1805, and the processes of American political organization in the Mississippi Valley were improved and extended. Under authority of these statutes the government of the Territory of Orleans was elevated to "first" or "highest class" in the territorial context. Besides a governor, territorial secretary, and judiciary appointed by the president, the territory's governmental structure consisted of a bicameral legislature, the lower house of which was elective. The citizens of the territory were also permitted to elect a non-voting delegate to Congress. Claiborne continued as territorial governor.

The government for the Louisiana Territory, as created by the 1804 and 1805 statutes, consisted of a governor, territorial secretary, and three judges appointed by the president. The capital of the territory was to be St. Louis. The focus of settlement in the territory at this time was along the Missouri River in the emergent state of Missouri. Local government for the pioneers was provided through twelve counties situated on or near the Missouri River, each with its own court. A committee of lawyers at St. Louis drafted a civil and criminal code for the territory.

Jefferson had appointed General James Wilkinson as the first governor, but before long the shadow of notoriety that dogged Wilkinson, and his conflicts with business and political leaders in St. Louis, provoked complaints against him and demands that he be removed. Finally, in 1807, Jefferson replaced Wilkinson with Alexander McNair of Pittsburgh. The most extended and capable political management of this portion of the Old West, however, came from William Clark, younger brother of George Rogers Clark and himself a peerless frontiersman and explorer. Clark became governor in 1812, and under his aegis much of the political format of the upper Mississippi Valley was consummated. In addition to serving as territorial governor, he was superintendent of Indian affairs for the Western region. His intensive negotiations with the Indian tribes did much to reduce frontier strife, diminish tribal holdings, and open new lands to settlers. His most notable accomplishment was presiding over the political organization of the Louisiana Territory.

In 1812 when the Territory of Orleans was admitted to the Union as the state of Louisiana, Congress changed the name of the Louisiana Territory to the Missouri Territory; the new region encompassed all land north of 33° and west as far as the Rocky Mountains. The focus of government for the Missouri Territory was its center, the incipient state of Missouri. In 1812, Congress made Missouri a territory of the "highest class" by adopting the Missouri Organic Act. The act provided for a territorial governor, secretary, and judiciary appointed by the president and a general assembly consisting of an elective house of representatives, a legislative council of nine members appointed by the president, and an elective delegate to Congress. Clark served as governor until the eve of Missouri statehood in 1820.

During 1819 Clark supervised the organization of the Arkansas Territory from the part of the Missouri Territory between 33° and 36°30' north, extending from the Mississippi River to the western boundary of the United States—which the Adams-Onis Treaty had set at the 100th meridian. Governor Clark also assisted in establishing several counties in the new territory. James Miller of New Hampshire was appointed the first governor.

When Missouri was admitted to the Union in 1821, the northern part of the territory was left without government. In 1834 Congress extended the western boundary of the Michigan Territory to the Missouri River to take in this area. Two years later it was again transferred, this time to the Wisconsin Territory; in 1838 Congress made it the Iowa Territory. The portion of the Mississippi Valley province comprising present-day Minnesota remained a part of the Wisconsin Territory until the latter was admitted to the Union in 1848. The following year Congress created the Minnesota Territory.

REMOVING THE INDIAN BARRIER

As in the other components of the Old West, an awesome barrier to settlement and development of the Mississippi Valley province was the presence of populous and powerful Indian tribes. On Louisiana's western border and the upper Red River resided several Caddoan-speaking peoples, who mixed with wandering bands of Choctaws and surviving remnants of other Gulf tribes from east of the Mississippi River. These Indians were no particular threat to Louisiana's settlement and development. Anglo-American pioneers regarded them a nuisance and easily exploited and brushed them aside in their march across Louisiana. Arkansas was claimed by the Quapaws and Osages, and Missouri by the Osages. Iowa's western border was populated by bands of Iowas, Otoes, and Missouris, and eastern Iowa had been pre-empted by immigrant Sac and Fox tribes from the Old Northwest. Minnesota was the domain of several Siouan tribes.

The early focus of American interest in upper Louisiana was primarily along the Missouri River and secondarily along the Arkansas River. Thus the Osages and Quapaws were among the first tribes of the Mississippi Valley province to feel the pressure of American expansion.

Problem of the Migrant Tribes

The Indian problem in the province, particularly in Arkansas and Missouri, was complicated by the presence of bands from Old Northwest tribes who had crossed the Mississippi River to escape the pressure and contaminating influence of intruding American settlements in their ancestral homeland. These included bands of Kickapoos, Delawares, Potawatomis, Shawnees, and Miamis who, under Spanish patronage, had established villages along the Missouri River and its tributaries. In addition, a band of Cherokees from Tennessee had resided along the tributaries of the Arkansas River since 1795.

Spanish officials had used the Kickapoos as mercenaries to guard their Mississippi River settlements against attacks by the Osages, and the Kickapoo-Osage wars continued into the period of American occupation. The Osages also resented the Cherokee trespass on their territory in Arkansas and regularly attempted to drive the intruders back across the Mississippi River. Inevitably these intertribal wars spilled over into the American settlements; raiding war parties in search of horses and weapons left pioneer cabins plundered and burned in their wake. Occasionally they took captives, and a mounting number of settlers were slain. In 1817 the War Department had directed the founding of Fort Smith at Belle Point, a strategic location at the confluence of the Arkansas and Poteau rivers. The principal mission of the garrison at this remote station was to abate border strife and establish peace between the Osages and Cherokees.

Early Tribal Relocations

The Indian problem of the Mississippi Valley province was further complicated by the policy of removing tribes from the Old Northwest and the Old Southwest and colonizing them on treaty-assigned permanent reservations in the Mississippi Valley province, mostly in the future states of Arkansas and Missouri. At first it appeared that this would be the principal use the national government would make of this area. Of course, in order to provide space for these Eastern tribes, the resident tribes had to be induced to surrender title to vast tracts in the Missouri and Arkansas portions of Louisiana Territory and to accept vastly reduced domains. Thus in 1808 the Osages surrendered claim to lands in Missouri and to the northern half of Arkansas; and in 1818 the Quapaws ceded their claim to lands in Arkansas between the Red and Arkansas rivers. With title cleared, federal officials began negotiations with tribes in the Old Northwest and the Old Southwest, resulting in the treaties discussed in Chapters 9 and 10.

It is significant that, in the period immediately following the War of 1812, it was clearly the intent of certain officials in the national government to use a goodly portion of the Mississippi Valley province as an Indian colonization zone for Eastern tribes. This intent manifested a lag in communication and a lack of coordination among government leaders, for, at the very time that officials of the War Department were negotiating treaties of removal with certain Eastern tribes and assigning them permanent reservations in the Mississippi Valley province, the processes of American frontier expansion were at work in the very same region. Moreover, the expansion of the settler frontier was actively aided by and abetted by leaders in the Congress. The treaties negotiated with the Kickapoos and other tribes of the Old Northwest are good examples of this conflict in national purpose, policy, and action. In 1819, when the leaders of the Indian communities surrendered their lands in the Old Northwest and accepted permanent reservations in Missouri Territory, that territory was already passing through the familiar American frontier metamorphosis and was only two years from statehood.

Other cases illustrating this dichotomy in national purpose include the Cherokee and Choctaw treaties, which assigned them vast tracts in the Arkansas Territory. In 1817 Cherokee leaders signed the first of several treaties surrendering substantial portions of their Eastern lands in exchange for a vast domain in northwestern Arkansas. Three years later Choctaw chiefs led by the redoubtable Pushmataha exchanged much of their Eastern territory in Mississippi for a new Western home that included the southwestern quadrant of the Arkansas Territory.

Two streams of development were thus occurring in this region contemporaneously, and the national government was a party to both. New territories were being created to accommodate pioneer-settler demands, and these new political entities were being prepared for admission to the Union. And western Arkansas and western Missouri were becoming a checkerboard of reservations settled by tribes from the Old Northwest and the Old Southwest. The immigrant Indians comprised a formidable barrier to the expansive American settlers, and in a very real sense they arrested the seemingly irrevocable developmental pattern common to the other provinces of the Old West. The self-governing Indian communities were states within emerging states. Inevitably, the Anglo-American settlers coveted the rich, fertile lands of the reservations. The settlers and the Indians were soon locked in a bitter contest for the reservation lands.

It was, as always, an unequal contest, for a truism of Indian-settler relations was that, when interests were in conflict, the settlers always triumphed. This was not due to innate settler merit or moral superiority— although the clergy frequently braced them with rhetorical assurances that it was God's will and that the Providential essence was on their side. More than anything else, settler victories were due to the fact that they were voters while the Indians were not. By his ballot exercise, the settler could choose the territorial delegate to Congress, through whom he had a voice in the formulation of the law and policy to serve his personal and local interests. An obsessive cause promoted by the Missouri and Arkansas congressional delegates was the clearing from their territories of those obstacles to settlement and orderly development—namely the Indian communities. Once the Indians were gone, they could achieve the ultimate for their territories—statehood in the American Union.

While their spokesmen in Washington were doing their bidding by making legal the appropriation of Indian land they so ardently coveted and arranging to relocate the resident tribes farther west in the wilderness, the Mississippi Valley settlers copied the harassment tactics being used so successfully by citizens of Alabama and Mississippi. Settler raider bands regularly terrorized the Indian communities of western Missouri and Arkansas, deliberately intending to make life so miserable for the aborigines that they would surrender their reservations and move west. Settlers burned Indian towns, violated Indian households, and ran off tribal livestock with impunity.

Local courts and friendly juries were, of course, always ready to protect presumptive settler rights in any contest over livestock and other property seized in these raids. And, if the Indians resisted and drove the intruders off, it was called an "Indian war" and justified calling federal troops from Fort Smith and other frontier posts into the reservation to quell the "uprising." On the Arkansas frontier, local citizens poached on Cherokee lands, wantonly killing game. They slaughtered buffalo for tallow and bears solely for oil, and the stench from the rotting carcasses carried into the Cherokee towns.

Creation of the Indian Territory

In 1825, Secretary of War John C. Calhoun determined to end for all time the recurring tribal relocations. He described to President James Monroe the tragedy of periodic uprooting of the tribes to serve the lust for land of the American settler. He added: "One of the greatest evils to which they are subject is that incessant pressure of our population, which forces them from seat to seat. To guard against this evil . . . there ought to be the strongest and most solemn assurance that the country given them should be theirs, as a permanent home for themselves and their posterity." [1] Jefferson and other national leaders had been accustomed to regard the land between the Atlantic Ocean and the Mississippi River as more than adequate for the settlement needs of the American people. It was surprising, therefore, to many that American expansion had thrust beyond the Mississippi River and into a new settlement region, the Mississippi Valley province. Even so, the vast empty regions of that province, for the most part north of Missouri, contained such an attractive reserve that it was inconceivable to most government leaders that the land needs of the American people would ever extend beyond the Mississippi Valley province.

Calhoun therefore recommended that President Monroe set aside the region west of Missouri and Arkansas as a permanent reserve; there the federal government could colonize the tribes remaining in the Eastern United States as well as those presently residing in Arkansas and Missouri. President Monroe and his successors followed Calhoun's recommendation. With the support of Congress, an extensive Indian colonization zone was withdrawn from settlement. Situated west of Missouri and Arkansas, it was bounded on the north by the Platte River, on the south by the Red River, and extended to the western boundary of the United States at that time (the 100th meridian) to the Arkansas River, and along that stream to the Rocky Mountains. It was restricted to the colonization of Indian tribes and was named variously the Indian Country, and, by 1830, the Indian Territory. In 1825 the Choctaws ceded their lands in the southwestern Arkansas Territory; and three years later the Cherokees ceded their lands in northwestern Arkansas and made their final move into the Indian Territory. The Missouri tribes, including the Kickapoos, relocated to an area that in 1854 became the Kansas Territory.

INTERNATIONAL TENSIONS

While the national government was seeking a solution to the Mississippi Valley province's vexing Indian problem, it also was attempting to settle some diplomatic issues with Great Britain and Spain. These issues included questions of international boundary which, when concluded, delineated the northern and southwestern perimeters of the Mississippi Valley.

Setting the Northern Boundary

The Treaty of Paris of 1783, between Great Britain and the United States, had designated the Mississippi River as the western boundary of the United States. American acquisition of Louisiana in 1803 inevitably provoked questions about the northern boundary between American and Canadian territory west of the Mississippi River. Late in 1805, General Wilkinson, governor of the Louisiana Territory, sent Captain Zebulon M.

---

[1] *American State Papers, Indian Affairs,* 2, p. 544.

Pike and twenty-one men up the Mississippi River in a keelboat to find a suitable point from which to draw this border, as well as to seek the source of the Mississippi River and to contact the Sioux and other tribes in the region. Pike explored both sides of the river, inspecting pioneer lead works on the west bank and at the mouth of the Wisconsin River and pausing briefly at the trading post of Prairie du Chien. At the mouth of the Minnesota River, Pike met in council with leaders of the Sioux and other tribes of the upper Mississippi Valley; he officially received them into the dominion of the United States. In January 1806, Pike erroneously selected Leech Lake as the source of the Mississippi River and returned to St. Louis.

Soon after the close of the War of 1812, British-American negotiations to settle the trans-Mississippi boundary question got under way in London. Albert Gallatin and Richard Rush concluded an agreement with British commissioners in October 1818; it provided that the boundary separating American and Canadian territory should begin at Lake of the Woods, intersect the 49th parallel, and extend westward along that line to the crest of the Rocky Mountains. The territory between the crest of the Rocky Mountains and the Pacific Ocean was to be regarded as jointly occupied by the United States and Great Britain for a period of ten years. Thus the 1818 agreement established firmly the northern boundary of the Mississippi Valley province.

Setting the Western Boundary

The following year, American and Spanish officials concluded the Adam-Onís Treaty, which settled a number of controversial questions that had complicated relations between the two nations for over a generation. One of these irritants to good relations was the international boundary separating the Louisiana Purchase area from Spanish Texas. The cause of imminent conflict was at the western border of the state of Louisiana—a thirty-mile-wide strip bounded by the Arroyo Hondo on the east and the Sabine River on the west. The United States claimed that Louisiana's western boundary was on the Sabine River. Spain insisted that the eastern boundary of Texas extended east to the Arroyo Hondo. To confirm this claim, Spanish officials in Texas marched 600 troops into the disputed zone during 1806 and erected fortifications at Los Adaes, near the northwestern Louisiana town of Natchitoches.

American officials in Louisiana protested the action, charging that Spain had violated American territory, and demanded that the invading army withdraw west of the Sabine River. Spanish officers at Los Adaes refused, declaring that their troops were in control of territory properly a part of Spanish Texas. Governor Claiborne replied by strengthening the small force of American regulars on the Louisiana border with Louisiana militia units. He also appealed to General Wilkinson at St. Louis to send more troops.

On September 24, 1806, Wilkinson reached Natchitoches with five companies of United States regulars. His arrival caused the Spanish officers to withdraw their troops across the Sabine River. Control of the thirty-mile ribbon of territory, which became known as the Neutral Ground, became the subject of field discussions between Wilkinson and Spanish officials from Nacogdoches. Their deliberations led to a truce. American troops were to occupy western Louisiana to the east bank of the Sabine River; Spanish troops would remain west of the Sabine River until the governments of the two nations could settle the question of title.

The question was finally concluded in favor of the American claim by negotiations between John Quincy Adams and Luis de Onís. The Adams-Onís Treaty of 1819 set the western boundary for the Louisiana Purchase area. Thus another segment in the perimeter embracing the Mississippi Valley province was established.

POPULATING THE MISSISSIPPI VALLEY

The Mississippi Valley, like its associate components of the Old West—the Old Northwest and the Old Southwest—was the creation of the federal government. Each year after 1803 the accelerating tempo of the nationalizing currents coursing through the Mississippi Valley had the effect of binding the region more closely to the nation as a whole. The success of American diplomats in setting the southwestern and northern boundaries of the province by negotiating with Spain and Great Britain is but one of several examples of how the national government removed hazards and barriers to development so as to make the region safe for settlement.

Removing the Settlement Barriers

Another manifestation of governmental commitment to the development of the Mississippi Valley was the activity of the military frontier. Troops from Fort Smith and other posts had tamed the Western border and forced a termination of the bloody frontier wars. They had opened roads and established a system of communication for the valley province, and published accounts of their surveys and explorations had increased the public knowledge of the region. Officers from the posts had regularly served in a paradiplomatic capacity by conducting councils with leaders of resident Indian tribes and negotiating treaties concerned with peace, trade, and land cessions. Military officers had also served in a para-administrative capacity in the early years of American occupation, providing direction for the infant American settlements until civilian officials were assigned to perform these essential duties. General James Wilkinson, commander of the Western army, served as governor of Louisiana Territory for two years, beginning in 1805.

A familiar sequence of processes followed the pacification of the Indian tribes of the Mississippi Valley. Federal commissioners elicited the assent of Indian leaders to treaties providing for the cession of tribal lands in

Arkansas and Missouri and for removal to Indian Territory. The Indian barrier having been erased, government employees surveyed, mapped, and plotted the ceded tracts by townships and sections and dispensed the land in small farms of 80 acres or more.

Settlement Patterns

Pioneers immigrating to the Mississippi Valley after 1803 settled in varied patterns. They tended to concentrate in the lower Mississippi Valley in the future state of Louisiana and west along the Missouri River in Missouri; settlement was very limited in Arkansas and hardly existed at all in the portion of the province north of Missouri.

American pioneers entering the Mississippi Valley after 1803 found that, in a very real sense, they were latecomers. Besides the populous Indian tribes, there resided in this province substantial communities of French and Spanish people, and over five thousand blacks—the slaves of French and Spanish plantation operators. The Mississippi Valley was thus the most varied ethnic region of the Old West. While it is true that scattered French towns survived in the Old Northwest and that there were French and Spanish settlements on the Gulf in the Old Southwest, such non–Anglo-American communities were minuscule compared to the populous French and Spanish settlements of the Mississippi Valley.

North of St. Louis in the region that eventually evolved into Iowa and Minnesota lived scattered settlements of French traders, *métifs* (people of French and Indian parentage), and Anglo-American trappers, residuals of a once-great fur industry that, for the most part, had moved west to the Rocky Mountains. Below St. Louis, close to the Mississippi River, was a string of French-Spanish settlements. Most of the 1803 population of the Mississippi Valley—about 30,000 people—was concentrated in the future state of Louisiana. Perhaps as many as 15,000 Americans, drawn by a Spanish colonization law that assured newcomers free land and religious toleration, had migrated to Spanish Louisiana during the 1790s. Most of them settled in the lower valley and in Missouri.

The Great Migration

After 1803, the rate of population increase for some portions of the Louisiana Purchase area was substantial. Louisiana's population of 30,000 mounted to nearly 77,000 by the time of the third national decennial census in 1810. Unsettled conditions associated with the War of 1812 discouraged immigration to the trans-Mississippi region for a time but, beginning in 1815, the province shared in the spectacular demographic surge, the Great Migration, that dramatically populated the three segments of the Old West. By 1820, Louisiana's population had increased to nearly 160,000; ten years later it stood at 216,000.

In 1803, Upper Louisiana had an estimated population of 10,000 people, concentrated in Missouri. At the census of 1810, Missouri tallied a population of 20,000; fed by the Great Migration, by 1820 the population had more than tripled, to over 66,000—including 10,000 slaves. Missouri continued to grow, again more than doubling by 1830 to about 141,000. As American expansion flowed on to the Pacific shore, Missouri became the gateway to the New West. Although its most important export was people, which gave rise to the name "Mother of the West," Missouri itself netted a substantial increase with each decennial census; its population doubled in every decade until the outbreak of the Civil War.

Arkansas' first population count in 1810 yielded 1,062. It increased to 14,278 in 1820, to 30,388 in 1830, and jumped sharply in 1836, the year of statehood, to nearly 70,000. In the mostly undeveloped section of the Mississippi Valley province north of Missouri, Iowa's first population count in 1840 was 43,112; and Minnesota's first census in 1850 yielded a count of 6,077.

Thus the flow of population into the Mississippi Valley concentrated on Louisiana. Handicapped on the West by the barrier of Spanish Texas, the lower part of the Mississippi Valley nonetheless remained an attractive settlement area because of its mild climate and an extensive zone of rich agricultural land still available. The fact that both sugar and cotton flourished in this part of the valley made it a prime area for the extension of the plantation-slave economy from the Old Southwest. The operation of non-agricultural enterprises at New Orleans and its tributary towns— river shipping and overseas commerce, shipbuilding, and general merchandising—provided employment for a large labor force.

In Arkansas Anglo-American settlement was thwarted for years by the Indian barrier. After the Choctaw cession of 1825 and the Cherokee cession of 1828, the Arkansas Territory's rate of development accelerated, although at no time was its growth in population and economic expansion comparable to those of Louisiana and Missouri.

Missouri was an attractive settlement zone for many reasons. The Indians were less numerous than in Arkansas and more easily removed. The navigable water highway of the Missouri River ran to the Rocky Mountains, and the state's principal river port, St. Louis, was close to the mouth of the Ohio River, providing easy communication with commercial centers as far east as Pittsburgh. The Missouri River and its tributaries watered broad stretches of fertile land. Moreover, the natural bounty of Missouri included rich, widely dispersed lead deposits, located on the Mississippi River and on the southwestern border. This vital mineral became a principal export commodity and provided gainful employment for many new settlers.

The upper segment of the province—Iowa and Minnesota—were passed over at this time; they were populated in a later age under different national and regional conditions. During the Great Migration era most of the population flowing into the Mississippi Valley originated in western Virginia, North and South Carolina, Tennessee, and Kentucky. Some of the pioneers of this period and into the 1820s were small farmers from Alabama and Mississippi who had been displaced by the expansion of the cotton-slave culture.

STATE-MAKING IN THE MISSISSIPPI VALLEY

An inevitable concommitant of American expansion into the Old Northwest and Old Southwest had been the fragmentation of each region into a group of political entities that, according to the formula established by the national government, were received into the American Union as states. The same state-making processes, manifestations of nationalizing currents, were at work in the Mississippi Valley province.

Louisiana

Louisiana was the first state to be erected in the trans-Mississippi area. When Congress in 1804 separated Louisiana from the Purchase area and designated it the Territory of Orleans, it did not regard its population of 30,000—mostly French, Spanish, and Blacks—as capable of self-government in the Anglo-American style; the act therefore made no provision for self-government. It provided only a governor and council appointed by the president. Congress also felt compelled to erase the mixed ethnic heritage of the area and to Americanize it by making English the official language. But the people of the Orleans Territory expected a greater voice in their government. Their desires were expressed in a convention held at New Orleans during June of 1804, at which Congress was urged to grant more democracy and early statehood.

Congress responded in March 1805. The new law established a government for the Territory of Orleans consisting of a bicameral legislature—the lower house elective—and an elective congressional delegate. Through the years, citizen conventions continued to urge Congress to grant statehood. Following the census of 1810, which showed that the territory had nearly 77,000 people, local citizens held a convention to draft a constitution. In 1811 Congress passed the Louisiana Enabling Act and the following year admitted the Territory of Orleans to the Union under the name Louisiana. Claiborne was elected first governor of the new state. Louisiana's capital, situated first at New Orleans and moved to Donaldsonville in 1828, eventually came to reside at Baton Rouge.

In the year of Louisiana statehood, Congress attached the ribbon of territory on the Gulf east to the Pearl River—the Florida parishes—to the new state. And, despite efforts by Congress to purge the French-Spanish heritage of Louisiana, certain non–Anglo-American elements survived in the new state constitution and legal system, which were derived from the Roman Law and the Code Napoléon rather than the common law of England. Units of local government were created along ecclesiastical lines and were called parishes rather than counties.

Missouri

Missouri was the next state added to the Union from the Mississippi Valley province. The Missouri Organic Act of 1812 provided for the familiar pattern of territorial government as a prelude to statehood, complete with an appointed governor, territorial secretary, a bicameral legislature (the lower house elective), and an elective congressional delegate. Conventions met regularly, and the delegates petitioned Congress for statehood. In 1819, when Missouri's population was approximately 67,000, Congress could no longer ignore the appeal. The Missouri Enabling Act was introduced in December 1819, and consideration of it continued into the next year. Debate on the question of admitting Missouri centered around the issue of extension of slavery into the West. Thus Missouri statehood became a *cause célèbre*, the catalyst that set off a bitter quarrel ending in one of a series of compromises constructed by national leaders to quiet the fury of divisive sectionalism.

The sectional schism erupting between Northern and Southern leaders over the extension of slavery was only the tip of a political iceberg, a highly emotionalized token of substantive economic and cultural differences. The Senate was the particular focus of this contest. The American Union, at that time was a delicate web of state and national relationships based on a constitution and law. The majority in Congress could enact certain measures, such as tariffs, that other elements in American society, particularly in the South, found oppressive. The South could thus envision a situation in which a hostile phalanx in Congress could legislate out of existence the economic and cultural mainstays of Southern life. The admission of new states that outlawed slavery, they felt, would enable just such a situation to develop. Increasingly in the North a viewpoint was developing—articulated in the campaign commitments of congressmen and senators—that the march of slavery into the West should be checked. Hence, both North and South were developing a near paranoid interest in the political evolution of the West; leaders of both sections were patently aware that each new state entered the Union with two senators and its quota of congressmen.

Prior to the climax of the Missouri question an informal adjustment or compromise system had evolved; new states were admitted in pairs—one North and one South. The scheme had begun with the admission of Indiana and Mississippi and continued with Illinois and Alabama. In 1820, each section had eleven states, and an equality of political strength between North and South had been maintained in the Senate.

In 1820, during the debate on the Missouri Enabling Act, Representative James Tallmadge of New York proposed an amendment to prohibit slavery in Missouri. The House favored the Tallmadge amendment, but the Senate opposed it, which placed the Missouri Enabling Act in limbo. Thereupon Senator Jesse B. Thomas of Illinois proposed an amendment to permit slavery in Missouri but forbid it in all other American territory north of 36°30′. Maine, a non-contiguous part of Massachusetts, was also ready for statehood and here, in 1820, the pairing pattern entered the proceedings. Henry Clay, Speaker of the House, managed the compromise and worked out details acceptable to both sides. Maine was admitted as a free state in 1820, and Congress passed the Missouri Enabling Act, including the Thomas amendment.

The Missouri constitutional convention met at St. Louis on June 12, 1820, and in six weeks produced a constitution modeled on that of Kentucky and containing a provision legalizing slavery. The proposed constitution also included a clause forbidding the entry of free Negroes. Anti-slavery spokesmen in Congress opposed admission because of the prohibition. Again Clay managed a solution, obtaining a pledge from Missouri legislative leaders never to pass an act "impairing the rights of citizens of any state"; this is called the Second Missouri Compromise. Thereupon, on August 10, 1821, Missouri was admitted to the Union as the twenty-fourth state. At first the capital was at St. Charles but was later moved to Jefferson City. Alexander McNair was elected the first governor. The state's area was increased in 1837 when the national government added a 2 million-acre tract, known as the Platte Purchase, to the northwestern corner.

Arkansas

Arkansas followed Missouri into the Union. Created as a territory in 1819, its growth was hampered until the Cherokee and Choctaw relocations in the mid-1820s, opened the more attractive portions of the territory to settlement. Much of eastern Arkansas consisted of vast swamps along the Mississippi River.

Throughout the early 1830s, citizen groups and territorial conventions appealed for statehood. Claiming a population of 70,000 in 1836, Governor William S. Fulton and legislative leaders issued a call for a constitutional convention without authority of a congressional enabling act. The convention met at Little Rock in January 1836, and drafted an organic law following closely the pattern of the Tennessee constitution and including a slavery clause. A delegation of local political and business leaders carried the constitution to Washington and presented it to Congress. Fortuitously, the Michigan Territory was also under consideration for statehood, and the pairing method was applied. The sectional balance was maintained, and Arkansas was admitted to the Union in 1836. It was the third state carved from the Mississippi Valley province.

Iowa

Most of the Mississippi Valley north of Missouri was settled and developed outside the context of America's frontier epic. However, a summary of the wilderness metamorphosis of this region is essential for fleshing out the Mississippi Valley province of the Old West and for recognizing the influence of frontier practices such as the claim associations of the Iowa Territory. Moreover, we will see in succeeding chapters how the solution to the Indian problem in both Iowa and Minnesota—the relocation to the New West—provided the setting for later obstacles to American expansion in that area.

Iowa was the home of several tribes, including the Sac, Fox, and Iowa. While the Indians of Iowa were certainly a deterrent to American settlement there, its remoteness and severe winters were even more compelling as long as land was available in more temperate areas. As late as 1820 Iowa remained the domain of the trapper, trader, and lead miner; fewer than 100 Americans resided there. The Black Hawk War of 1832 and the Sac-Fox cession of a fifty-mile-wide strip of territory along the Mississippi River in 1833 led to a rush of settlers. By 1836, Iowa's population was estimated at about 10,000.

Federal surveyors had not laid out (platted) the new tract for settlement, but settlers exercised presumptive squatters' rights; they opened farms and formed claim associations or "land clubs" to protect their interests. Officers of the 100 Iowa claim associations filed descriptions of each claim and recorded transfers. The records were to protect squatters when the federal government opened Iowa to settlement and purchasers began to appear. In 1838, when the first federal land offices were opened in Iowa, officials recognized the rights of settlers as documented by their extralegal claim associations.

Iowa was the orphan of the Mississippi Valley province. First administered as a part of the Louisiana Territory, then the Missouri Territory, and for a time classified as an unorganized territory, in 1834, Iowa was attached to the Michigan Territory; two years later it was shifted to the Wisconsin Territory. Finally, in 1838, Congress created the Iowa Territory; Robert Lucas was first territorial governor, and the capital was established at Iowa City. Ten years later, Iowa was admitted to the Union.

Minnesota

Minnesota, the northernmost portion of the Mississippi Valley during the time of early intensive American development of this province long remained the haunt of the trader and trapper. French, British, and American frontier merchants trafficked with resident Sioux and Chippewa hunters for pelts and hides. Mendota was the principal fur entrepôt and headquarters for the American Fur Company, which eventually established a trade monopoly with the Sioux. Henry H. Sibley, agent for the company in Minnesota, was the leader of the early development of Minnesota. Later lumbering came in to compete with the fur trade as a frontier enterprise. Stillwater, St. Anthony, and St. Paul joined Mendota in Minnesota's urban evolution.

Official American presence in Minnesota occurred in 1819 with the erection of Fort Snelling at the mouth of the Minnesota River. For years the most influential American official in Minnesota was Lawrence Taliferro, an Indian agent for the local tribes who was eminently successful in dealing with both Indians and traders. The Chippewas ceded most of northern Minnesota to the United States in a series of treaties negotiated between 1854 and 1863. Treaties with the Sioux between 1851 and 1860 drastically reduced their territory. On the eve of the American Civil War the Sioux were restricted to reservations.

Minnesota was administered as a part of first the Michigan Territory and later of the Wisconsin Territory. When Wisconsin was admitted to the Union in 1848, Minnesota was left with no official territorial tie until 1849, when Congress created the Minnesota Territory. At the time the population was 4,000. The new territory's first governor was Alexander Ramsey, and the capital was situated at St. Paul. In 1858, Minnesota was admitted to the Union, the last of the states to be carved from the Mississippi Valley province.

Even late into the nineteenth century, the Mississippi Valley province of the Old West was a strategic geographic and cultural connective tissue between the Old West and the emergent New West. Long after the other provinces had been "Easternized," the Mississippi Valley maintained its Western, frontier orientation. As we have indicated, its business and political leaders focused on the region across the Missouri River, maintaining a continuing relationship with the New West. In Chapters 12 and 13 we will discuss the social environment of the Old West and its effects on the cultural, economic, and political development of the New West and the nation as a whole. The Mississippi Valley province served as both conduit and filter for these effects.

SELECTED SOURCES

Early Mississippi Valley settlement and development is traced in John Monette, *History of the Discovery and Settlement of the Valley of the Mississippi* (New York, 1846, 1971), 2 vols.; Charles E. Gayarre, *History of Louisiana* (New Orleans, 1903), 4 vols.; Garnie W. McGinty, *A History of Louisiana* (New York, 1949); Cardinal Goodwin, *Trans-Mississippi West, 1803–1853* (New York, 1922); William E. Foley, *A History of Missouri, 1673–1820* (Columbia, 1972); Louis Houek, ed., *The Spanish Regime in Missouri* (Chicago, 1909), 2 vols. and *A History of Missouri* (Chicago, 1908), 3 vols.

Accounts of clearing the Mississippi Valley of settlement hazards, providing order, and removing the Indian tribes include *Ed Bearss and Arrell M. Gibson, *Fort Smith: Little Gibraltar on the Arkansas* (Norman, 1969); Grant Foreman, *Pioneer Days in the Early Southwest* (Cleveland, 1926), *Indians and Pioneers: The Story of the American Southwest Before 1830* (New Haven, 1930), and *Last Trek of the Indians* (Chicago, 1946).

* Available in paperback.

Mississippi Valley state-making is described in Edwin A. Davis, *Louisiana: The Pelican State*, 3rd ed. (Baton Rouge, 1972); Edwin C. McReynolds, *Missouri: A History of the Crossroads State* (Norman, 1962); W. Clement Eaton, *Henry Clay and the Art of American Politics* (Boston, 1957); *Glover Moore, *The Missouri Controversy, 1819–1821* (Lexington, 1953); Lonnie J. White, *Politics of the Southwestern Frontier: Arkansas Territory, 1819–1836* (Memphis, 1964); John G. Fletcher, *Arkansas* (Chapel Hill, 1947); Charles S. Syndor, *The Development of Southern Sectionalism, 1819–1848* (Baton Rouge, 1948); Cyrenus Cole, *A History of the People of Iowa* (Cedar Rapids, 1921); and William Watts, *A History of Minnesota* (New York, 1903).

"Dwelling of a Settler in Indiana" by Karl Bodmer

12

Pioneer Society in the Old West

The Old West was an integrated geographic unit, endowed with rich soils, a generally temperate climate, and thick forests; it contained vital mineral deposits important for a pioneer-agrarian society, principally lead and salt. The region's most strategic and useful resource in an age of primitive transportation technology was its river network; the Mississippi River drainage system (including the Ohio and its tributaries) provided relatively easy access into each of the region's three component provinces. The system had the effect of integrating the region's economic interests on a north-south concourse centering on the lower Gulf markets.

Until around 1828, the Old West was also an integrated region socially. The same types of frontier coursed contemporaneously through Ohio, Mississippi, and Missouri; the cyclical progression of the fur-trading frontier, stockman's frontier, miner's frontier, and military frontier were succeeded by the pioneer-farmer frontier in each region at about the same time. Pioneers in all sections of the Old West applied a common technology and methodology in transforming the wilderness to cleared farms, towns, and states. Only toward the close of the pioneer period in the Old West—around 1828—did a discernible differentiation develop among the provinces. The change occurred principally in the Old Southwest, where the introduction of the plantation-slave system displaced large numbers of pioneer farmers.

Before 1828 the Old West was a sort of crucible of pioneer experience, a testing ground for processes, technology, and values. It served as a nursery where common economic, social, and political practices were nourished and gave form, substance, a value system, and a motive force to the renewed American march into the New West.

PIONEERS IN THE WESTERN WILDERNESS

The swift populating of the Old West ranks as one of the wonders of American national development. We have seen that at the close of the American War of Independence, the region's population consisted mainly of Indians and French and Spanish settlers, the latter concentrated on the Mississippi River and the rim of the Gulf of Mexico. A limited expansion of English colonial settlements into the area west of the Appalachians had occurred in Kentucky, Tennessee, along the Gulf shore, and in the lower Mississippi Valley. This western extension continued during the War of Independence, when pioneer families, taking courage from the American military presence, followed George Rogers Clark's army down the Ohio River and established settlements at the falls of the Ohio River, at Fort Jefferson at the mouth of the Ohio River, and in the Northwest around Kaskaskia. At the same time there occurred a limited expansion of settlement in eastern Kentucky and Tennessee.

However, the most substantial westward flow began after 1790; at that time the population of the Old West numbered about 100,000. Thereafter, until 1828—the year marking the close of the pioneer period in the Old West—the region's population more than doubled during each decade. An English visitor to the Old West during 1817 commented on the seemingly unending stream of migration: "Old America seems to be breaking up and moving westward. We are seldom out of sight, as we travel on this grand track towards the Ohio, of family groups, behind and before us." [1] In 1828, the Old West's population was approximately 4 million, a demographic miracle accomplished in about 38 years.

The Pioneer Style

Pioneers breached the wilderness mostly in family groups, moving on foot or horseback. Each family required at least two pack horses to carry utensils, bedding, provisions, tools, and clothing. Pioneer men were clad in buckskin garments and moccasins, the women in loose-fitting dresses contrived from rough homespun textiles such as linsey-woolsey. The tools essential for succeeding in the wilderness were a long rifle, a shot pouch, a powder horn and bullet mold, a single-bitted pole axe—one side of the head sloped to a sharp cutting blade, the other flattened like a large hammer for driving stakes and pounding—an auger bit for boring and drilling, and a saw. The pioneer train included milk cows, often a pair of oxen, horses and a colt or two, hogs, sometimes sheep, and a crate of poultry.

Once through the rough, tumbled Appalachian Highlands, the pioneer family continued its westward passage on the rivers, usually by flatboat.

---

[1] Quoted in Henry Steele Commager and Allan Nevins, eds., *The Heritage of America* (Boston, 1949), p. 259.

This craft was about forty feet long and twelve feet wide, fitted with sides three to four feet high; there was a small cabin shelter in the center, and the boat was guided through the river currents by a sweep rudder on the stern. It accommodated the pioneer family as well as tools, provisions, personal effects, and livestock. If the pioneers selected a claim near the river, the flatboat was dismantled and used to construct their first wilderness home.

The Wilderness Farmstead

Opening a clearing in the wilderness required a sharp axe and great physical strength, and the forest was both a help and a hindrance to the pioneers. The trees provided heavy logs for constructing shelter, erecting fences, and making crude tables, stools, shelves, and other household fixtures. It was used as fuel for warming the household and for cooking. But the forest was also a hindrance, for the dense growth had to be cleared, or at least thinned, before the pioneers could sow their crops.

In the tiny clearing, the pioneer felled trees, trimmed and cut them into logs, notched the ends, and raised the logs into walls for the wilderness shelter, the log cabin. The completed cabin consisted of a structure twelve to fourteen feet wide and fifteen to eighteen feet long. Before iron nails became common on the frontier, rafters, ceiling joists, and door and window frames were held in place by oak or maple pegs driven into holes made with the auger bit. Glass was as scarce as nails, and window openings were commonly covered with heavy oiled paper, which let in some light and kept out the wind and cold. Cabin floors were either puncheon—split logs with the flat sides laid up—or packed dirt. Until latches, hinges, and other hardware items were available, pioneers set doors on wooden or leather hinges and fashioned a lock from a crude latch bar and string. The stone-hearthed fireplace was situated at one end of the cabin. Its chimney was constructed of ledge stone or of short logs plastered with clay.

Spaces between the logs in the cabin wall were packed with chinking, usually clay, to seal out the weather. The roof pitch was steep enough to provide a second-story loft for sleeping and storage. Often, to accommodate an extra large family, two cabins were constructed about ten feet apart and connected with a "dog trot"—a roofed open passageway that was used during the summer months for cooking, spinning, and weaving. The cabin roof was covered with bark strips or shakes, primitive shingles split from chunks of soft wood with an axe or froe.

The cabin interior was simply furnished. A heavy table, made from puncheon or sawed planks, several three-legged stools, open shelves, a cradle, spinning wheel, loom, a bed or two, and long pegs driven into the walls for hanging clothing comprised the pioneer's furnishings. The bed was a wooden frame laced with rope or leather straps attached to the corner walls and supported on the outside corner by a forked stake. The mattress was a tick filled with dry leaves or straw, and the bedcovers were animal skins. On the stone hearth were several simple cast-iron utensils—a large black pot suspended from an iron crane attached to the fire wall, a large skillet, and a dutch oven for baking.

The Pioneer Economy

The pioneer family household was, of necessity, a self-sufficient economic unit, producing virtually all its needs except salt, lead, and gunpowder. The women made family clothing from deer, elk, and bear skins and from textiles produced from flax, hemp, and wool. They processed the basic material by combing, carding, spinning, and weaving, producing a coarse material called linsey-woolsey. From plants, roots, bark, and walnut hulls they extracted dyes to color the cloth before cutting and sewing it into garments for the family. They also made the household soap and candles.

During the first year or so on a new wilderness claim, the pioneers derived most of their subsistence from nature. Deer, wild turkey, and bear shot by the men were staples. Bear oil supplied fat for cooking, and honey gathered from bee trees and maple sugar extracted from sap were used for sweetening. Wild fruits—particularly plums, pawpaws, and berries—and greens were used in season. Nature also provided the plants, roots, and herbs used for warding off sickness and for healing. Common ailments included bilous fever, malaria, ague, and intermittent fevers; occasionally frontier families had to cope with devastating cholera epidemics.

Of all the wilderness bounty, the deer was most useful to the pioneer during the early stages of establishing a claim in the Old West. Not only was its flesh, venison, delicious, but the skin was easy to work into a soft, pliable material for making fringed hunting shirts, leggings, and moccasins. Deerskins were so esteemed that they were widely used on the frontier as a medium of exchange. In the Missouri Territory, public officials accepted deerskins in payment of local taxes at the rate of three pounds for each dollar of taxes due. Pioneers often bartered deerskins—as well as the pelts of other animals that had escaped the sweeping harvest of the earlier fur trader—for powder, shot, salt, and other needs.

However, the pioneers' dependence upon nature for subsistence was a stage that passed quickly, for Old West pioneers were an extension of the greater American society, which was predominantly agrarian. Their intent was to emulate this society in the Western wilderness and to shift very quickly to the more dependable agricultural and stockraising enterprises. To accomplish this they had to clear fields for planting. In thickly forested areas the pioneer chopped down some trees, cleared the underbrush, burned the logs, and pulled stumps with ox teams. Often, trees were left standing but were girdled or "scotched" by cutting a deep ring through the bark around the trunk. Girdling killed the tree and permitted the sun's rays to reach the cultivated ground around the base. It was claimed that four to five years of labor were required to clear a field of ten to fifteen acres, the basic unit of tillable land required to support a family. On newly opened claims, vegetables and grains were sown amidst the girdled trees.

Crops included pumpkins, squash, cabbage, beans, potatoes, yams, corn, wheat, rye, buckwheat, oats, and barley. Hemp and flax were important textile crops. Hemp was a cash crop, from which local processors made rope and burlap for wrapping cotton bales and for making gunny sacks—containers for grains and other materials. Flax was widely used in the home manufacture of textiles.

Corn was, of course, the great staple crop of the Old West. Its uses were legion. Parched corn nourished the pioneer on the trail. Corn ground into meal on a household mill yielded flour or meal for cornbread, cornpone, and johnnycake; cooked into mush, it was eaten as hot cereal or, when cold, sliced and fried in deep fat. Corn was eaten while "in the milk" as roasting ears or "corn on the cob" or leached into hominy in lye made from wood ashes. Later, millers used water-powered commercial mills to process great quantities of shelled corn into meal; packed in large wooden barrels, it became an important export to Gulf markets, particularly New Orleans. Corn, along with rye and other grains produced in the Old West, gave rise to the trans-Appalachian distillery industry. Western whisky, from the raw "white lightning" to gentler aged-in-wood bourbon, was consumed in great quantities locally. It was also exported in barrels to Gulf markets and to the eastern United States, where it eventually displaced rum as the national beverage. Western corn was also fed to cattle and hogs to fatten them just before slaughter.

Using a primitive agricultural technology, the pioneers produced corn and other grains and vegetables for household use and export from their tree- and stump-ridden claims. A team of oxen or horses drew a crude plow, generally just an iron-tipped wooden shaft, to open the fields. The seedbed was smoothed and clods were broken by a triangular harrow—a flat wooden frame fitted with wooden or iron teeth. Grain was sowed by hand, and corn was planted in hills, usually by children. Row crops were cultivated by hand with crude chopping hoes and mattocks. At harvest time the pioneers cut the wheat, rye, and oats with a scythe and shocked the grain-laden stems for drying and curing. The grain was separated from stems and husks by driving oxen or horses over the bundles scattered on the threshing floor or by beating it with a hand flail—two long wooden handles connected by a strip of heavy leather.

The pioneer farm unit included milk cows. Bull calves were castrated and fattened for home slaughter or driven to market each autumn. A few sheep were kept, mainly for wool, and every farmstead had a herd of hogs, which roamed the forests feeding on acorns and roots. The pioneers in the eastern portion of the Old West drove their herds of cattle and hogs over the mountains to seaboard markets. In the more remote settlements, cattle and hogs were fattened and slaughtered locally; then the beef was dried or pickled in salt brine, the pork was smoked or pickled, and the meat was packed in hogsheads and, with barrels of corn meal and whisky, made up the flatboat and keelboat cargoes that were floated to Gulf markets.

Most pioneer households also included an orchard. Apples flourished in the Old West and—along with peaches and other fruits, as well as certain vegetables—were preserved by the women through drying or pickling. Salt and vinegar were essential for preserving fruits and vegetables, and apples were important as the source of the essential vinegar. Apple juice was also converted into cider, hard and soft, a frontier favorite, and fermented into a potent brandy called applejack.

OLD WEST URBANIZATION

The Old West was predominantly rural-agrarian, but an inevitable concomitant to pioneer settlement was the rise of towns. At the time of the United States' acquisition of the Old West, several urban centers existed, including New Orleans, Natchez, Vincennes, and St. Louis. Under the prodigal stimulus of expanding American settlement, these towns increased in size and importance as commercial and social centers. New towns—urban responses to the military frontier, mining frontier, and pioneer-farmer frontier—also evolved in all sections of the Old West.

Military Frontier Towns

The military frontier extension was a continuing factor in Old West urbanization. Each post, from Fort Dearborn to Fort Smith, generated an adjacent town, which drew civilian businessmen who established taverns, general stores, and other enterprises keyed to the needs of the local garrison. The post commissary was the closest and most certain market for the grain, vegetables, and livestock produced on pioneer farms, and the payment for these supplies by the post quartermaster or commissary officer was generally the only source of specie for a region.

Mining Frontier Towns

Extension of the mining frontier also produced towns. On both banks of the upper Mississippi River—on the Illinois-Wisconsin shore around Galena and on the Iowa shore at Dubuque—mining towns arose to serve the workmen who were gouging lead from the local deposits. Downriver on the Missouri shore of the Mississippi were Potosi and other mining camps. Lead mining in eastern Missouri centered on Mine a Burton at Potosi. Moses Austin, a Virginian attracted to Missouri by the Spanish immigration program of the 1790s, had received a mining grant from Spain that included Mine a Burton. In the exploitation of his mineral grant he introduced substantial improvements in mining and smelting techniques, which were widely copied in Spanish Louisiana. On Missouri's remote southwestern border, on the western edge of the Ozark Mountains, there evolved a cluster of camps centering on Minersville (the future Oronogo), antecedents of the fabulous Tri-State District of later times. Refining the lead by smelting gave rise to additional industry in the wilderness towns.

The Trading Towns

In the march of the fur trader's frontier from the Old West into the virgin hide and pelt zones of the New West, certain westerly situated towns served as entrepôts to receive the furs, pelts, and hides and to provide trade goods for trappers and traders to continue their traffic in the New West wilderness. Thus Natchitoches, on the Red River, Arkansas Post and Fort Smith, on the Arkansas River, and St. Louis, on the Missouri River, served this enterprise. Improved transportation, particularly the development of flat-bottomed river steamers, increased the importance of these towns. In 1817, steamers on the Mississippi River reached St. Louis; and two years later they were operating on the Missouri River. The vastly improved service to the fur trade reached 1,000 miles up the Missouri River and led to a minor extension of the industry; to the usual cargoes of furs, pelts, and buffalo hides and robes reaching St. Louis and Fort Smith, the hide hunters now added smoked buffalo tongues and buffalo tallow and bear oil—sometimes used as lard substitutes in the settlements—to their outbound cargoes.

The role of these river towns as entrepôts for New West commerce was altered again, in 1821, by the opening of trade with the Spanish-American towns on the Rio Grande—from Santa Fe downriver to El Paso and south to Chihuahua. Until then, the Spanish government had strictly prohibited American trade with New Mexico. But after independence from Spain in 1821, the Mexican government abolished this prohibition and a flourishing and strategic overland trade with New Mexico began. This overland commerce provided a strong urbanization impulse. Franklin, situated upriver from St. Louis on the Missouri, was the beneficiary, via traffic over the Santa Fe Trail. William Becknell, the first Missouri trader to reach Santa Fe in 1821, led a party of twenty-one traders and a large pack train of goods across the plains and over the mountains to the Rio Grande towns. The Santa Fe traders soon adopted heavy-wheeled freight wagons, drawn by teams of oxen, horses, and, later, mules, to transport their goods.

The annual flow of commerce between the Missouri export centers and the Rio Grande towns increased each year, until by 1830 its annual value exceeded a quarter of a million dollars. The principal items carried out were textiles (mostly cotton cloth), hardware, fixtures, cutlery, and glass; these goods were exchanged for furs, gold and silver bullion, Mexican silver dollars, and horses and mules. In the westward urban march, the Missouri entrepôt moved first, from Franklin upriver to Independence and, during the 1840s, to Westport, near the future Kansas City, Missouri. An alternative route to the Rio Grande began at Fort Smith. Goods were carried by river steamers to this entrepôt at the head of navigation on the Arkansas River; they were then loaded on freight wagons for the overland trek to Santa Fe along the Canadian Valley route.

This commercial dialogue between the river towns on the Missouri and Arkansas and the Mexican settlements on the Rio Grande had immediate as well as long-range effects on the development of Western America. The Santa Fe trade provided reasonably accessible markets for American manufactured goods and supplied in the exchange several valued items, including specie for a money-hungry Mississippi Valley. Local bankers and merchants commonly fragmented the Mexican silver dollars into bits—half dollars, quarters, and half quarters or bits—which they circulated as a part of the local currency. The introduction of jacks and jennies from New Mexico led to the rise of the mule-breeding industry in Missouri, soon making this Mississippi Valley state one of the world's leading producers of hybrid livestock. One long-range effect of the overland commerce was the rise of Missouri trader communities at Santa Fe, El Paso, and other Mexican towns. They established a vital American presence; the growing commercial interest of Americans in Mexican territory was to provide, in a generation, yet another confirmation of the maxim that "the flag follows commerce."

The Agricultural Towns

Although overland commerce, mining, and other enterprises had considerable influence on the extension of the urban frontier in certain portions of the Old West, the region was predominantly agrarian. Thus the principal *raison d'être* for the development of Old West towns was to serve pioneer farmers—to supply them with tools, seed, household and personal needs, and to receive, process, and market the farmers' products. Old West urban development was influenced not only by geographical situation, productivity of the tributary area, and settlement level, but also by such factors as the quality of business leadership, availability of capital and banking resources, and innovativeness of technology—all of which were contributions of the urban frontier.

THE WESTERN ECONOMY

The frontier businessman was a vital figure in urban development. Often he entered the West as a speculator who selected a townsite and promoted its settlement. Usually he operated the first business in the town, a general store where he traded tools, implements, salt, gunpowder, shot, seed, utensils, and household needs such as needles, thread, and scissors for pelts, grain, and livestock. He also provided credit, thus adding to the primitive capital resources of the region.

Frontier Enterprises

A natural move for the pioneer businessman was to open a bank, which, if successful, increased the economic resources of the area. His credit advances provided holding power for the region he served; during hard times his support often enabled pioneers to hold on to claims rather than return to the East. His banking practices, primitive and often daring, attempted to match the voracious capital needs of the Old West being generated by its phenomenal expansion and development.

Western Capital Sources

Some capital flowed into the Old West from Europe, as British, French, and Belgian interests invested in land, manufacturing, transportation and other enterprises. In addition, as the increasingly industrial East came to depend on the West as a market for manufactured goods and a source for raw materials, Eastern bankers provided some capital and credit. The national government added to Western capital resources through grants to states for roadbuilding and other public purposes and by extending credit for the purchase of land on the public domain. As the patron of the military frontier, the national government also provided specie for a region poor in currency by purchasing local grain, vegetables, and livestock to feed garrisons. Moreover, money periodically paid to troops stationed on the frontier was usually spent locally, thereby increasing the amount of currency in circulation.

Western Banking

Management of Western banking was mostly local. Among the earliest items of business considered by Western territorial and state legislatures were bank charters. Early Western banking houses included the Miami Exporting Company at Cincinnati, the Bank of Kentucky at Lexington, and the Bank of Tennessee at Knoxville. Legislative action provided for the creation of a state bank with branches in Indiana, Illinois, Missouri, Mississippi, Alabama, and Louisiana. The Indiana statute required that a branch of the Indiana state bank function in every three counties of the state. In 1818, the Kentucky legislature established a system of over forty state banks.

Commonly the initial capital reserve for each bank was established by specie paid in by bank stock subscribers. A bank's lending resources were expanded by the promissory notes it had in circulation, each one redeemable in coin on demand. Each Western bank extended credit and negotiated loans based on its specie capital reserve and promissory notes in circulation. It is estimated that with banker daring, plus specie reserve and a high volume of promissory notes, a bank could commonly expand its credit resources three- to five-fold, thus making limited capital go further. Banks also issued notes that circulated as paper money, a currency

substitute for specie. This practice encouraged both inflation and counter-
feiting. By 1818, the Kentucky state banks capitalized at about $7 million
were circulating paper money valued at four times that amount.

The United States Bank in the West

The Second United States Bank had five Western branches—at Pittsburgh, Cincinnati, Chillicothe, Lexington, and New Orleans. The management of the United States Bank was Eastern and conservative, and its
Western branches had a distinctly stultifying effect on frontier banking.
Regularly, limited supplies of gold and silver forced Western banks to
suspend specie payment on demand by holders of paper currency, even the
U.S. Bank branches. This led the Western branches of the federal bank
to discount state bank notes, often as much as 50 percent. In 1818, branches
of the United States Bank refused altogether to accept state bank notes,
destroying many state banks and creating general deflation throughout the
West. Coupled with the drastic reduction of European markets for
Western products, this situation set off the Panic of 1819 and an extended
depression. Westerners blamed the United States Bank for their ruin, and
this national fiscal institution came to be regarded as the enemy by the
people in that region.

Frontier Professions and Crafts

Besides bankers and merchants, the Old West's urban frontier required
the services of several professionals and artisans. Every town of consequence
came to include lawyers, preachers, doctors, and teachers. Lawyers and
preachers outnumbered the others, perhaps a reflection of the pioneer's
regard for the law and his compulsive preoccupation with an ambivalent
but accommodating piety. Essential artisans included a blacksmith, wheelwright, cooper, millwright, and boatbuilder.

The blacksmith was indispensable because of his talent for fashioning
iron into useful tools and implements. The wheelwright improved frontier
mobility by making and maintaining wagons and carts, and most towns
had a wagon works operated by the wheelwright and his apprentices.
Improvements in wagon construction, particularly the use of heavy wheels
with wide iron rims made land transportation easier; and Westerners
shifted from pack trains to wagons and carts to move personal effects and
goods. The principal model used by Western wheelwrights was the
Conestoga wagon, which was developed in Pennsylvania during the
eighteenth century by German immigrants. Its heavy wheels and wide iron
rims, easy running gears and braking system, and box body fitted with
wooden hoops or bows to carry a canvas cover, made it an ideal frontier
conveyance and shelter. Vehicles of this type easily negotiated boggy
crossings and could be driven through forests and over prairies where no
roads existed. The cooper built strong wooden barrels for shipping meal,

pickled meat, and whisky to Gulf markets. The millwright designed and constructed water-powered mills, which ground the grain produced on Old West farms and sawed the lumber cut from its vast forests.

Skilled boatbuilders established yards at the Ohio and Mississippi river ports and fashioned keelboats, flatboats, and river steamers. The keelboat, with its slender, rounded hull and thirty-ton capacity, was used for both upstream and downstream traffic, since it could be poled against the current. An upstream keelboat passage from New Orleans to Pittsburgh via the Mississippi and Ohio rivers required about four months to breast the currents. The flatboat could move only with the current, and after its cargo of meal, whisky, and pickled meat had been unloaded at New Orleans, the crude craft was dismantled and the timbers sold locally as construction lumber.

The application of steam power to river boats produced a revolution in the movement of people and goods on the Western waters. In 1811, Nicholas Roosevelt launched the *New Orleans*, a shallow-hulled steamboat driven by a stern paddle wheel, on the Ohio River. It made the run from Pittsburgh to New Orleans and subsequently was used to carry passengers and cargo between Natchez and New Orleans. The War of 1812 interrupted the development of steam navigation on Western waters, but in 1816 the *Washington* made a successful run upstream from New Orleans to Louisville at the falls of the Ohio River; the voyage marked the resumption of steam navigation on the Mississippi and its tributaries. Soon the time between New Orleans and Louisville by river steamer was reduced to less than two weeks; the record was a nine-day run. River steamers reached St. Louis in 1817, and two years later these craft were making stops at the Missouri River towns above St. Louis. Other Mississippi River feeders soon received steamer service; by 1824 the shallow-bottomed stern-wheelers were coursing to Fort Towson on Red River and Fort Smith and Fort Gibson on the Arkansas. During this period, steamers also reached Old Southwest towns on the Mobile and Tombigbee rivers.

Western Manufacturing

The Old West's urban frontier was nourished by a variety of enterprises. The capital cities and county seats of each state were assured a relatively stable economic base from the regular governmental business conducted in them. Other towns continued to derive their economic sustenance from the presence of the military frontier. Fort Smith on the Arkansas River and Fort Snelling on the upper Mississippi River each sustained a cluster of civilian settlements. Lead mining at Dubuque, Iowa, and Potosi, Missouri, and the associated metal refining industries, spawned a number of supporting towns. Commerce with Indian tribes for furs and hides provided the *raison d'être* for towns in Minnesota and on the western border of Missouri and Arkansas. Franklin, Independence, and Westport in Missouri and Fort Smith and Van Buren in Arkansas prospered as entrepôts for the overland trade with the Rio Grande towns.

Some of the older towns in the Old West urban frontier context, particularly along the Ohio River, developed from agrarian trade and supply centers into manufacturing communities producing a surprising variety of consumer goods. The iron ore, charcoal, and coal resources of the western slopes of the Appalachians around Pittsburgh gave rise to extensive iron works, which provided nails, hardware, and bar iron for the Old West. Factories at Cincinnati, Pittsburgh, Louisville, and Lexington converted local sands and clays into glass, bricks, earthenware jars, jugs, and other household containers. Milling, meat packing, distilling, ropemaking, and tobacco-processing industries were widely distributed among Ohio Valley towns. In the lower Mississippi Valley, plants for processing and refining sugar cane were strung across Louisiana in towns from New Orleans to Baton Rouge. Old West factories also manufactured leather goods and hats.

Yet even with the spectacular surge of the urban frontier, the Old West remained largely rural and agrarian. The high proportion of rural to urban population, coupled with improved land and water transportation and the rise of certain industries, broke much of the Old West's isolation and remoteness and produced discernible regional specialization during the late 1820s. While the pioneer-farmer commitment to household self-sufficiency continued to a large degree, the predominantly rural population in each sector of the Old West came to concentrate on a particular cash crop. The Old Northwest became a principal producer of grain and live-stock. The lower Mississippi Valley yielded sugar, cotton, and rice. Missouri's cash crop spectrum included tobacco, cotton, and grain. The frontier region to the north marketed furs, lead, and lumber.

The most intensive agricultural specialization occurred in the Old Southwest. Kentucky and Tennessee farms produced grain, livestock, tobacco, and hemp. An increasing acreage in central and western Tennessee was devoted to cotton production. A technological advance in the processing of cotton fiber made it possible to devote the agricultural lands of Mississippi and Alabama largely to the production of cotton. At this time, two strains of cotton were produced in the United States—the long staple Sea Island cotton, which is readily separated from seeds by hand or crude roller but can be grown only in the moist climate of the lower Atlantic seaboard—and upland short staple cotton. The latter strain could be produced over a wide territory, but its short fibers made it difficult to separate from the seeds. A worker could process no more than two pounds a day by hand. In 1792, Eli Whitney, a New Englander teaching in Georgia, invented the gin, which mechanically separated the seeds from the fiber of short staple cotton. Whitney's gin, powered by water or steam, could process up to 2,000 pounds of cotton a day. The device produced a revolution in American agriculture, for it made profitable the operation of large cotton plantations with slave labor.

Concomitant technological advances in cotton milling and textile production, particularly in England, created a greatly increased demand for raw cotton. In the United States the areas of intensive cotton production were greatly expanded, and soils were quickly mined of valuable nutrients. Cotton culture thus became a highly mobile enterprise, and growers regularly sought new, fresh lands. In the Old Southwest vast plantations as large as 1,500 acres were established in the rich Tennessee River valley, the Black Belt of Alabama and Mississippi, and the Yazoo Basin. Fields were tended by gangs of black slaves. This invasion of the Old Southwest by the plantation-slave cotton culture displaced many of the pioneer-farmers who had opened the Southwestern wilderness, and many migrated to Louisiana, Arkansas, and Missouri.

WESTERN SOCIETY

The frontier society of the Old West was an ethnic mélange. Its dominant population groups were persons of English, Scotch, Welsh, Irish and Scotch-Irish extraction. Communities of Germans were scattered about the region, and French Catholic settlements were situated throughout the Mississippi Valley, from Minnesota through Missouri and into Louisiana. Some French Huguenots had also settled into the Old West, particularly in the Ohio Valley. Small communities of Spaniards resided at New Orleans, Pensacola, Natchez, and the river towns of Missouri. Blacks lived in the Old Southwest and in the Mississippi Valley from Missouri south. Their status, with few exceptions, was that of slaves—valuable chattel property regularly bought and sold in the marketplace, whose principal function was to labor on the cotton, tobacco, rice, and sugar plantations. A small number of free Blacks resided in the Gulf towns and at New Orleans, where they worked as domestics, operated small businesses, and labored on the docks at the port cities.

Outside the pale of Anglo-American society, but still part of the Old West ethnic spectrum, were resident Indians. These included the Potawatomis, Miamis, Kickapoos, and other tribes in the Old Northwest; the Cherokees, Choctaws, Creeks, Chickasaws, and Seminoles in the Old Southwest; and the Osages, Quapaws, and other tribes of the Mississippi Valley. Each tribe was a self-governing community with a well established economic and religious system. Even when they succumbed to pressure from the Anglo-American settlers and their government to relocate to the Indian colonization zone west of Missouri, the tribes left a legacy in the Old West. Substantial Indian contributions included large numbers of people of mixed racial backgrounds, knowledge of the culture of certain useful plants (including corn, potatoes, tobacco, pumpkins, squash, and tomatoes), Old West place names, frontier medicine and healing, and extensive wilderness lore.

The Pioneer Family

The focus of Old West society was the family—the basic economic as well as social unit. The frontier family was strategically essential to the conquest of the Western wilderness, and it was assiduously protected by public opinion and law. Among the first statutes adopted by Western territorial and state legislatures were marriage laws, which set the age of majority at fourteen for females and sixteen to eighteen for males. Divorce required legislative action, and the parties to it were stigmatized. The ideal frontier family consisted of six to ten children who provided labor for the pioneer farm. A "barren woman" was scorned. Infant and maternal mortality rates were excessively high, and a pioneer man often buried three or more wives in a lifetime. Sex roles were well defined. By the age of fourteen, young boys had been taught by their fathers to work as men, mastering skills of building, farming, and wilderness lore; they also served in the local militia. Girls were under the tutelage of the mothers, learning the essential skills of cooking, weaving, childcare, nursing, preserving food, vegetable gardening, and caring for chickens and milk cows.

Frontier values and necessities contradicted the Eastern "sentimental veneration" for the "American Eve." On the contrary, pioneering constituted a gross exploitation of women. Frances Trollope, an Englishwoman who traveled through the Old West in 1828, observed: "the young girls, though often with lovely features, look pale, thin and haggard. I do not remember to have seen in any single instance" among the struggling pioneers "a specimen of the plump, rosy, laughing physiognomy so common of English girls." She attributed this lack of vitality to early marriage. "The slender, childish thing, without vigour of mind or body, is made to stem a sea of troubles that dims her young eye and makes her cheek grow pale, even before nature has given it the last beautiful finish of the full-grown woman." She concluded that American pioneer women "are indeed the slaves of the soil. . . . [The] life she leads is one of hardship, privation, and labour. It is rare to see a woman in this station who has reached the age of thirty, without losing every trait of youth and beauty. You continually see women with infants on their knee, that you feel sure are their grand-children, till some convincing proof of the contrary is displayed." [2]

The male was the dominant figure in the frontier family and in Old West society. His eminence was derived from the application of prodigal physical strength and vigor in transforming primal forest to productive farm, by the fact that he had the role and responsibility of defending his

[2] Frances Trollope, *Domestic Manners of Americans*, Donald Smalley, ed. (New York, 1949), pp. 117–18.

family from wilderness hazards—both as head of the household and as citizen-soldier in the local militia—and because he was the voter, selecting local and national leaders through his ballot exercise. Timothy Flint, a frontier minister, allowed that as a general rule the frontiersman was "an amiable and virtuous man. His general motive for coming here is to be a freeholder, to have plenty of rich land, and to be able to settle his children about him. It is a most virtuous motive. And I fully believe that nine in ten of the emigrants have come here with no other motive. You find, in truth, that he has vices and barbarisms peculiar to his situation. His manners are rough. He wears, it may be, a long beard. He has a great quantity of bear or deerskins wrought into his household establishment, his furniture and dress. He carries a knife or a dirk in his bosom, and when in the woods has a rifle on his back and a pack of dogs at his heels. An Atlantic stranger, transferred directly from one of our cities to his door, would recoil from an encounter with him." Flint added that the pioneer was generous to a fault, consistently hospitable to strangers, who were expected to eat at his table. "His wife, timid, silent, reserved, but constantly attentive to your comfort, does not sit at the table with you, but, like the wives of the patriarchs, stands and attends on you." Further, the pioneers "are averse to all, even the most necessary restraints. They are destitute of the forms and observances of society and religion, but they are sincere and kind without professions, and have a coarse but substantial morality." [3]

Pioneer Values

The values and attitudes of pioneer society were rent by paradoxes and contradictions. On the one hand, Old West settlers were intensely independent, self-reliant, and individualistic; and on the other, they were dependent, cooperative, and group-oriented. They were religious and irreligious, nationalistic and particularistic, compulsively devoted to self-interest and obsessively materialistic; yet on occasion they were public spirited in their emerging sense of mission to carry Anglo-American civilization to the far corners of the continent. They were anti-intellectual and contemptuous of humanistic enterprises, but supportive of education for their children, as long as it was practical and did not extend beyond the three r's.

Frontier Education

Formal education was provided by private subscription schools, with each parent paying the tuition for his children. The school term was rarely longer than three months a year, and classes were held during the winter when children could be spared from their work on the farm. The curriculum was built around writing, spelling, reading, and arithmetic—the basic skills essential in a simplistic frontier milieu. Teachers were migrant types

---

[3] Quoted in Commager and Nevins, *The Heritage of America*, pp. 266–69.

who boarded with pioneer families; they were often paid in produce and livestock. More often than not they used their teaching appointment as a base to prepare for the practice of law, medicine, or the ministry.

Social Classes

The frontier milieu tended to feed the traditions of Anglo-American political democracy and to promote a social democracy. In the early years in the Old West there were no social classes, for there was no basis for assigning or assuming social distinctions. The elite of the frontier were those endowed with superior skills, physical strength, and cunning. Birth, wealth, or learning were of no consequence. Illiterate frontiersmen scorned scholarly pursuits, pointing to their folk hero Andrew Jackson who, they calculated, would have found mastery of Greek and Latin of little value in smashing the British at New Orleans. As Eastern influences coursed through the Old West, largely through the vehicle of the expanding urban frontier, the inevitable social classes did arise. In the towns particularly, a business-professional elitism leavened and refined the coarseness of frontier society. A monolithic caste-like system evolved in the Old South-west after the entry of the plantation-slave cotton culture.

Frontier Social Life

The hardship, toil, and loneliness of pioneer life in the Old West were occasionally interrupted by social gatherings. These included houseraisings, in which families of the community gathered for the day to assist a newly arrived family erect a cabin home. Houseraising day was filled with eating, food preparation and visiting among the women, and hard labor by the men, braced by casks of cider, whisky, and applejack. The day usually closed with a frontier dance in the new cabin.

Weddings were times of great and ribald celebration and often included shivaree, a coarse serenade that was humiliating for the groom and embarrassing for the bride. Funerals, militia musters, elections, and revivals were also grand social times for frontier folk.

Frontier Religion

In the opening years of the nineteenth century the revival—an extension of the religious frontier into the trans-Appalachian region—became the principal vehicle for seeding churches and making Protestantism a compelling force in the lives of the settlers. The Roman Catholic faith of the French and Spanish settlements was the oldest non-Indian religious system in the Old West, and a limited Presbyterian, Methodist, Baptist, Roman Catholic, Congregational, and Episcopalian establishment was also present from the earliest days of Anglo-American settlement. But only Methodism was, for many years, anything more than a casual force in the day-to-day lives of the pioneers. Methodists were the most active in evangelizing the frontier before 1800. By 1782, seaboard-based missionaries from this denomination, led by the indefatigable Francis Asbury, were working in the settlements of eastern Kentucky and Tennessee. Presbyterian, Congregational, and Moravian congregations in the East maintained missionaries among the Indian tribes of the Old West in an attempt to overthrow tribal gods. But the people of the frontier, Indian and white, were for the most part apathetic or indifferent to the Christian religion. A Kentucky pastor lamented in 1798 that "the dead state of religion is truly discouraging here."

The great galvanizing personality for the extension of Protestantism in the West was James McGready, a Scotch-Irish Presbyterian from Pennsylvania. In 1788 he felt the call to make a "gospel tramp" through the South. In North Carolina his fiery style and stress on salvation won some congregations but antagonized others. The South Carolina Presbyterians found him a "pernicious distraction," burned his pulpit, and drove him away. Thereupon McGready extended his "gospel tramp" across the mountains into the pioneer settlements of Tennessee and Kentucky, where the fervor and fury of his preaching was an immediate success. Preachers throughout the West imitated McGready's emotionally charged style and message of the "total depravity of human nature, and entire separation of the soul from God." The result was religious demagoguery, with Western divines pragmatically admitting that "education displayed was a detriment, for it separated them from their congregations; the homelier the thought and the phrase, the more unresisting was the audience." [4]

The emotional virus of primitive Christianity that McGready introduced into the trans-Appalachian region led to an extended religious orgy called the Great Revival. It began in the summer of 1800, when McGready joined a group of Presbyterian ministers to conduct a week-long "religious feast" at Red River in the Cumberland region of Kentucky. Great crowds gathered in the clearing to receive McGready's spirit balm. The preaching generated an emotional fury and outburst: everyone trembled, many fainted, women shouted, men groaned, and young girls sobbed. The miracles of salvation and healing wrought at Red River were repeated many times, from the Cumberland to the Missouri. The doctrines and dogma of established denominations were scuttled; in an unabashed outpouring, Baptist, Methodist, and Presbyterian ministers cast aside denominational parochialism and preached together on the same platform, all bringing a message of the restoration of the New Testament Church and the renewal of primitive Christianity. The ultimate in ecclesiastical regeneration occurred at Cane Ridge, Kentucky, during August of 1801. There 20,000 sinners gathered in one huge encampment to bear witness to the spiritual outpourings of Presbyterian, Baptist, and Methodist preachers. The exhortations caused thousands to writhe and cry out for salvation. Freed from

[4] E. Douglas Branch, *Westward: The Romance of the American Frontier* (New York, 1930), p. 206.

inhibitions by the infectious spiritualism and obsessed with joining in the mass outpouring of sin admission and conscience catharsis, the multitude rolled in the dust, shouted, cried, uttered the "holy laugh," spoke in exotic tongues, twitched and jerked, barked like dogs, and loudly proclaimed the joy of abundant grace.

The legacy of the Great Revival included the rise of new religious bodies, among them the Disciples of Christ. It also encouraged the schismatic propensities of religious bodies functioning in the West. In 1810, valuing piety higher than learning, a group of frontier Presbyterians separated from the general body of Presbyterians over the issue of an educated clergy; they formed their own Cumberland Presbyterian Church. Before the Great Revival ended in 1805, it had provided the momentum for a militant Protestantism based on strict interpretation of the scriptures and a continuing commitment to churches modelled after the early Christian churches described in the New Testament. This form of Protestantism, known as Fundamentalism, continues to be influential in the twentieth century. On the frontier, its stress on revealed Christianity— "the call"—reduced the necessity for an educated clergy and rigidified Western anti-intellectualism.

In the post-Great Revival period, Baptists and Methodists made the greatest growth on the frontier. The Methodists were particularly success-ful because of the appeal of their stress on free will and individual respon-sibility. Also the Methodist system of ecclesiastical organization into conferences was well adapted for the broad sweeps of Western territory. Each Western conference served as a bridge to advance Methodism. The Missouri Conference was the outreach agency for seeding Methodism in the New West on to the Pacific shore. Methodism was also highly mobile because of the itinerant circuit-rider preachers who reached the most isolated households on the frontier.

Western religious bodies continued to use the revival and camp meet-ing as a periodic spiritual bracing to recover the "backsliders," win con-verts, and seed new churches. Above all else, the legacy of the Great Revival, through its saturation of the West with militant Protestantism, must receive considerable credit for imposing a subtle but overpowering social control over the Old West. Preachers and their ardent followers probably did more to establish order and impose personal restraint in the wilderness than all the sheriffs, courts, and laws.

Utopian Subcultures

The Old West's social milieu was further enriched by the presence of several utopian communities, each one a subculture separate from the surging Anglo-American stream committed to achieving a particular set of goals. Shortly after 1800 the Shakers settled in the Ohio Valley to practice a rigid celibacy and communal ownership of property in fulfillment of the Millennial or doctrine of the second coming of Jesus Christ. The principal preoccupation of the men, women, and children of the Shaker communities was preparation for the second coming, which was, according to their divines, imminent. Their Millennial doctrine was adopted by a number of other religious-oriented utopian groups in frontier America.

The Rappites were a part of this Millennial utopian stream. Their founder was George Rapp, a German peasant of considerable charisma, management skill, and energy. He believed that he had the power to miraculously transfer his followers to the Holy Land to join with Jesus Christ, and he assured them that they were the chosen people. Because the Rappites refused to conform to the established Lutheran faith, submit to compulsory military service, and send their children to state schools in Germany, they suffered persecution and were forced to emigrate. Rapp settled his followers first in western Pennsylvania at a place he called New Jerusalem; in 1815 they moved to the wilderness of Indiana on the Wabash River at New Harmonie; later they returned to western Pennsylvania.

Wherever they settled, the Rappites, through hard labor by the members and shrewd management by Rapp, were successful. The Rappite charter, drafted by the founder, established a communal society and bound his followers to obey him without question. Rapp eventually concluded that, in order to satisfy the Millennial requirements, his protégés must adopt celibacy; he also forbade the use of tobacco. Rappite artisans contrived machinery and built mills, factories, and distilleries that produced cloth, lumber, flour, and leather goods, including saddles. Their Golden Rule Distillery was famous for whisky. Rapp also entered merchandising and established several successful Rappite general stores on the frontier. By 1890, the community's assets were valued at $50 million. But notwithstanding their economic success, the Rappites held foremost the fulfillment of their Millennial commitment. Thus each night on the hour, the watchman guarding the sleeping town bellowed: "A day is past—our time runs away, and the joys of heaven are our reward."

In 1825, the British reformer Robert Owen purchased the New Harmonie colony from the Rappites to establish a planned industrial-agricultural complex based on Owen's tenets of social justice and joint ownership. Owen's experiment failed, but his interest and attempt to establish a worker's Eden in the Old West marked a noble humanistic effort in a region that was otherwise compulsively materialistic.

The principal value of these utopian colonies to the Old West was economic; the technological innovations introduced by European artisans were particularly valuable. The agricultural successes of the Rappites and other utopians made their quality farms, vineyards, and livestock herds a source of envy and emulation by Anglo-American neighbors.

Old West society for the most part was a simplistic extension of seaboard society. The Westerners' willingness to submit to a more primitive existence to occupy and tame the wilderness and their rather rapid progression from a simple to a complex lifestyle more compatible with Eastern modes, confirm that pioneering was a traumatic but transitory state. Settlers endured the ordeal because it provided opportunity for economic improvement. Rather quickly, largely through urbanization and Eastern capital, goods, management, and general culture, as well as the nationalizing currents of government and politics, change coursed through every transmontane settlement, casting the West in the Eastern image.

Although Western influence on imported Eastern institutions was rarely innovative, it did at times alter institutions, as in the case of liberalization of constitutions and extension of the franchise. Old West society was selectively receptive to new ways. Most pioneers were suspicious of the scattered Utopian communities and, for the most part, rejected the new social patterns these subcultures presented. On the other hand, they were highly receptive to evangelical Christianity, which was propagated by clergy from the Eastern United States. Even so, it is good to keep in mind that many aspects of the Great Revival were but the renaissance of an earlier stream of spiritualism, the Great Awakening, that occurred on the seaboard during the early eighteenth century.

Perhaps Western society's most important contribution to the life of the nation was its growing, expanding presence in the trans-Appalachian territory. The fruits of its prodigious labor in developing the region's rich resources materially contributed to the increase of national strength.

SELECTED SOURCES

Old West society is described and analyzed in Frank R. Kramer, *Voices in the Valley* (Madison, Wis., 1964); Robert S. Cotterill, *History of Pioneer Kentucky* (Cincinnati, 1917) and *The Old South* (Glendale, Calif., 1939); Thomas D. Clark, *A History of Kentucky* (New York, 1937); Thomas P. Abernethy, *From Frontier to Plantation in Tennessee*, 3rd ed. (University, Ala., 1967); R. C. Buley, *The Old Northwest* (Bloomington, 1951), 2 vols.; Everett H. Dick, *The Dixie Frontier* (New York, 1948); Harriet Martineau, *Society in America* (London, 1837), 3 vols.; Frances Trollope, *Domestic Manners of Americans* (London, 1832); R. W. Leopold, *Robert Dale Owen, A Biography* (Cambridge, 1940); and *Arthur K. Moore, *The Frontier Mind* (Lexington, 1957).

Religion as an alterative force in the emergent Old West society is traced in William W. Sweet, *Religion on the American Frontier* (New York, 1931), 4 vols.; Charles A. Johnson, *The Frontier Camp Meeting: Religion's Harvest Time* (Dallas, 1955); *Ray A. Billington, *The Protestant Crusade* (New York, 1953); T. Scott Miyakawa, *Protestants and Pioneers* (Chicago, 1964); and Catherine Cleveland, *The Great Revival in the West* (Chicago, 1916).

The Old West's economy, its transportation system, and urbanization are

* Available in paperback.

treated in Archer B. Hulbert, *Waterways of Western Expansion* (Cleveland, 1904); Leland D. Baldwin, *The Keelboat Age on Western Waters* (Pittsburgh, 1941); Seymour Dunbar, *A History of Travel in America* (Indianapolis, 1915), 4 vols.; Charles H. Ambler, *A History of Transportation in the Ohio Valley* (Glendale, Calif., 1932); *George R. Taylor, *The Transportation Revolution, 1815–1860* (New York, 1951); Louis C. Hunter, *Steamboats on the Western Rivers* (Cambridge, 1949); Katherine Coman, *The Industrial History of the United States* (New York, 1905); D. R. Dewey, *Financial History of the United States* (New York, 1934); Curtis P. Nettels, *The Emergence of the National Economy, 1775–1815* (New York, 1962); *Paul W. Gates, *The Farmers Age: Agriculture, 1815–1860* (New York, 1960); and *Richard C. Wade, *The Urban Frontier* (Chicago, 1959).

Painting by Thomas Cole Courtesy of Amherst College.

An Aged Daniel Boone at the Door of His Wilderness Cabin in Missouri Territory.

13

The Old West in the Life of the Nation

In the period between the American Revolution and 1828, the impact of the Old West on the nation was substantive and directive, and the region bore a peculiar and unique relationship to its parent, the national government. The land between the Appalachians and the Mississippi River was a rich territorial prize awarded to the United States by the Treaty of Paris of 1783; it became the national domain through the action of certain states in ceding their western lands to the central government and by the process of Indian removal. The Northwest Ordinance, passed by the Confederation Congress in 1787, outined the administration and future status of the Western territory and was of epochal significance in the growth of the Republic.

From the beginning, national leaders eschewed the temptation of designating the Western territory an unorganized imperial reserve to be managed and exploited solely for the benefit of the thirteen proprietary seaboard states. Instead, it was decided that the trans-Appalachian West was to be settled, developed, and organized into states, each state to be admitted to the Union on an equal footing with the original thirteen. The national government was to provide guidance and direction in the state-making process. The decision was successfully and consistently applied in the Old West, and its consummation provided the pattern and precedent for equality that was subsequently applied to American territory in the New West, and even to Alaska and Hawaii.

The results of this decision are immeasurable. One human effect was to endow the Western pioneer with a sense of being a local part of a greater democratic process, with a private and public stake in the future of the region. By the exercise of personal sovereignty through the ballot, pioneer men played a direct role in the process. Another result, the essence of the Americanization of the West, was the evolution of an almost symbiotic relationship between the pioneer—whether trapper, trader, frontier merchant, miner, or farmer—and the national government. The pioneer's part was to occupy the wilderness and establish the vital American presence; in return the national government promoted and protected pioneer interests and rights.

The pioneer as a voter sent to Congress spokesmen who expressed the Western viewpoint and expectations, which were more often than not articulated into national law and policy. The benefits of this relationship to the pioneer included protection of life, civil rights, and property, and the promotion and support of sometimes extravagant economic demands. The benefits to the federal government of supporting the pioneers and meeting their needs included extension of the national domain into the territory of another power—as in West Florida—and the acquisition of territory without purchase or a war of conquest. (Of course, the national government also used these means to satisfy the land lust of its Western section.) The pioneer served the national purpose by populating—in a strategic sense, occupying—the national territory. The concomitant political organization and economic exploitation of Western territory not only yielded individual wealth but also materially increased the strength of the nation in area, developed resources, manpower, and consolidation of the American dominion.

In the early years of the Old West, the region was wholly the creature of the national government; but by 1828, the West was strong enough politically to assert itself and provide a challenge to its creator. The interactions between the national government and the West during the first quarter of the nineteenth century in large measure determined the stream of major legislation and was the principal determinant of American diplomacy.

The government, as manager and patron of the West, responded to territorial needs through the Congress, which passed laws providing for political organization, division into states, and reception of the states into the Union in accordance with the principal of equality and the guidelines established by the Northwest Ordinances. Congress also adopted laws providing for uniform survey and recording of deeds, ending the chaos of Western land titles brought about by the blending of Northern and Southern cultural streams. The national government used its army to defeat the Indian tribes arrayed against the expanding line of American settlement and provided continuing protection through a chain of military posts extending from the Upper Mississippi Valley to the Gulf. Federal commissioners also negotiated with Indian leaders for the cession of tribal lands, enabling the line of settlement to progress, and carried out an extensive and expensive relocation of the Eastern tribes to territory beyond the Mississippi Valley province.

Congress nourished Western education for pioneer youth by providing for the reservation of tracts of public land in each township for the support of public schools. With federal grants, public roads providing the pioneer easier access into the wilderness—over which the fruits of labor could be transported to river ports for export to Gulf markets—were constructed in the Western territories and states. The enabling act of each Western territory included a provision reserving for roadbuilding a portion of the proceeds—usually 5 percent—from the sale of public lands.

In diplomacy too the national government's policy before 1828 more often than not had Western roots, mostly because the United States shared the region between the Appalachian Mountains and the Pacific with several foreign nations. It first became clear that the West was a prime mover in American diplomacy in 1786 when the Jay-Gardoqui Treaty was proposed. Spanish officials regarded the expanding American settlements in the trans-Appalachian region as a threat to their control of West Florida and Louisiana, and they had a twofold plan to throttle United States expansion: first they would close the Mississippi River to American shipping; then they sought to create a defensive buffer in the Old Southwest among the Creeks, Choctaws, and Chickasaws. In league with Spain, the warriors of these tribes could pose an awesome check on the imminent American thrust into the Mississippi Valley.

The question of navigation of the Mississippi River surfaced in 1785 during treaty discussions in New York between Diego de Gardoqui, Spanish minister to the United States and John Jay, American secretary of foreign affairs. Gardoqui offered an attractive commercial agreement, including reciprocity between the United States and Spain, and proposed that the treaty contain a mutual assistance clause whereby each nation would protect the American territory of the other against attack by another nation. In addition, Gardoqui indicated that his government would yield its claim to territory north of 31° if the United States would acknowledge Spain's right to exclusive navigation of the Mississippi River. Jay agreed, in return for commercial and territorial concessions, that the United States would "forbear" to navigate on the Mississippi for a period of thirty years.

Spokesmen for the Southern states regarded the concession as a peremptory abandonment of their interests—which extended into the lower Mississippi Valley—for the benefit of the maritime Northern states, and they sounded a vigorous protest. It became clear that the two-thirds vote of approval by the states required by the Articles of Confederation for ratification of treaties could never be obtained. It was also evident that Western interest in the navigation of the Mississippi River was a national matter of considerable moment. Jay and Gardoqui terminated their discussions.

One authority has ventured the opinion that the sectional sentiment provoked by the Jay-Gardoqui negotiations, particularly over the question of Western navigation rights, led to the inclusion in the federal Constitution of the two-thirds majority requirement for Senate ratification of treaties. It could also be said that the Jay-Gardoqui proposal for abandoning the American right to navigate the Mississippi River, a Western question, produced one of the first outbursts of sectionalism, which was soon to become a compelling force in the politics of the American Republic.

The failure of the Spaniards to close the Mississippi River to American inland commerce caused them to intensify their efforts to create an aboriginal buffer. They also established military posts on American soil on the Mississippi River's east bank—one near the site of Memphis—and operated a flotilla of warships on the river to intimidate American pioneers. We have described in Chapter 7 how Spanish officials conspired with George Rogers Clark, James Wilkinson, and other American leaders in the West to establish a separate nation under Spanish control in the trans-Appalachian region. But Spanish cabals in the American West ceased abruptly in 1795 with the signing of the Treaty of San Lorenzo. Pressed at home by the revolutionary armies of France and threatened with the loss of British support, Spain yielded to United States' demands of withdrawal from American soil. On October 25, 1795, Thomas Pinckney negotiated the Treaty of San Lorenzo, which set the United States boundary at 31° N. Spain pledged to evacuate all United States territory on the east bank of the Mississippi north of that point. The treaty also included a reiteration of free navigation of the Mississippi and granted American shippers the right of deposit at New Orleans for three years.

In 1819 the United States and Spain negotiated their final treaty relating to Western America. The Adams-Onís Treaty provided for the cession of Florida to the United States, in return for which the United States assumed $5 million in American citizens' claims against Spain. In addition, the Adams-Onís Treaty settled the boundary between American Louisiana and Spanish Territory. This latter provision had a threefold significance for American expansion into the New West. First, by accepting a boundary that began on the Sabine River, the United States surrendered its claim to Texas as a part of Louisiana. Second, having a definite western boundary simplified American administration of national territory west of Missouri. And third, by accepting 42° as its northern boundary in the New West, Spain withdrew entirely from the Pacific Northwest, leaving only Great Britain and Russia to contest with the United States for dominion over that region.

American diplomacy with Great Britain over Western questions began with the Treaty of Paris of 1783, which established the independence of the United States and recognized the Eastern seaboard colonies plus the area as far West as the Mississippi River as American territory. The treaty also provided for the free navigation of the Mississippi. When the Revolution ended, Great Britain held several posts south of the northern boundary of the United States, including Detroit and Michilimackinac; the latter was strategically located at the straits joining Lakes Superior, Michigan, and Huron. The Treaty of Paris required the British to evacuate these posts "with all convenient speed." Because they served as bases for continuing the rich fur trade in American territory and for continuing to incite the Old Northwest tribes against the Americans, the British held these posts for twelve years. The excuse for retaining them was that they were a bond for the American assumption of the claims of Loyalists (Tories) and others for damages during the American Revolution. Finally on November 19, 1794, John Jay concluded a treaty whereby the British government pledged that the posts on American soil would be evacuated no later than June 1, 1796. Among its other provisions was a commitment by both nations to the use of "concert measures" in settling the question of the northwest boundary between Canada and the United States.

The next major diplomatic settlement between Great Britain and the United States involving Western questions was the Peace of Ghent, signed December 24, 1814. It provided for a termination of the War of 1812 *status quo ante bellum* and for four mixed commissions to settle questions of boundaries and other points of issue. Thus in 1817, American and British negotiators concluded an agreement providing for the mutual demilitarization of the Great Lakes, except for patrol boats enforcing custom and tariff laws. This agreement set the pattern for the demilitarization of the international boundary all the way to the Pacific. In 1818, another British-American convention set the forty-ninth parallel, near the Mississippi River to the crest of the Rocky Mountains, as the boundary. The territory between the Rocky Mountains and the Pacific was to be jointly occupied by the two nations.

The American West also generated substantive diplomatic issues between the United States and France. During the early 1790s, when Revolutionary France was at war with Great Britain and Spain, Edmond Charles Genêt, French minister to the United States, attempted to further his nation's war effort by organizing expeditions against the Western territories of Great Britain and Spain. One of his Western agents was the influential George Rogers Clark, whom he commissioned to raise a force of frontiersmen and invade Spanish Louisiana. President George Washington protected the neutral status of the United States by demanding Genêt's recall, which ended his Western cabals.

The most spectacular Franco-American diplomatic incident with Western roots centered around the negotiations that culminated in the purchase of Louisiana. By the secret treaty of San Ildefonso, October 1, 1800, Spain ceded Louisiana to France, although Spain continued to administer this vast trans-Mississippi province. On July 14, 1802, the Spanish government ordered suspension of the American right of deposit at New Orleans. Westerners suffered economically from this obstructive ruling and appealed to their national government for relief. American officials protested to the Spanish government, with the result that the order was revoked on March 1, 1803. However, it soon became common knowledge that Louisiana had been returned to France; that nation was blamed for the suspension of deposit privileges, and Westerners feared it would be reapplied. Thereupon, President Thomas Jefferson sent James Monroe to France with instructions to negotiate the purchase of a river outlet on the Gulf, including New Orleans, to provide Western commerce with an unobstructed outlet to the sea. Monroe's negotiations culminated in the unanticipated bounty of all of Louisiana. At one stroke, acquisition of Louisiana doubled the extent of national territory and brought the Mississippi Valley under American control.

Russia too figured in the West and American diplomacy. By the terms of a Russian-American treaty of 1824, Russia accepted 54°40′ as its southern boundary in North America, and the United States acknowledged that its territorial interests in the Pacific Northwest would not extend above that line. Russia concluded a similar treaty with Great Britain the following year. Thereafter, only the United States and Great Britain were contestants for the American West territory between 42° and 54°40′.

The Old West's impact on the life of the nation increased consistently each year, mostly through the application of the principal of equality in state-making and by the viewpoints that were articulated by its senators and representatives in Congress and passed into law serving Western needs and interests. In the symbiotic exchange of nationalizing currents and regional support, the Old West received much from the national government, but it made substantial contributions to the national life as well. Aside from its contribution to the national strength derived from the demographic increase and the feverish development of natural bounty, the Old West also contributed to the national leadership. Henry Clay, John C. Calhoun, and Thomas H. Benton maintained a directive influence in Congress until the middle of the nineteenth century; and by 1840, the Old West had supplied two presidents—Andrew Jackson and William Henry Harrison—both of whom fed the American propensity to make military leadership and the martial image a primary qualification for political office.

The Old West also influenced national politics by coloring political campaigns with homespun allusions. The epitome of the simplistic, folksy appeal to the electorate is found in Davy Crockett's account of his first campaign for public office, a seat in the Tennessee legislature. In 1821, "electioneering . . . was a bran-fire new business to me. It now became necessary that I should tell the people something about the government." Crockett admitted that he knew no more about this subject than about Latin and law and "such things as that." He added that "I have never read even a newspaper in my life, or anything else, on the subject" of government. However, he commented, "over all my difficulties, it seems to me I was born for luck, though it would be hard for any one to guess what sort." The campaign began with a dinner on the ground in Crockett's own county.

> The party had everything to eat and drink that could be furnished in so new a country, and much fun and good humor prevailed. But before the regular frolic commenced, I mean the dancing, I was called on to make a speech as a candidate, which was a business I was . . . ignorant of. A public document I had never seen, nor did I know there were any such things; and how to begin I couldn't tell. I made many apologies and tried to get off for I knowed I had a man to run against who could speak prime, and I knowed too that I wa'n't able to shuffle and cut with him. He was there, and knowing my ignorance as well as I did myself, he also urged me to make a speech. The truth is, he thought my being a candidate was a mere matter of sport, and didn't think for a moment that he was in any danger from an ignorant backwoods bear hunter. But I found I couldn't get off, and so I determined just to go ahead, and leave it to chance what I should say. I got up and told the people I reckoned they knowed what I come for, but if not, I could tell them. I had come for their votes, and if they didn't watch mighty close, I'd get them too. . . . I told them I was like a fellow I had heard of not long before. He was beating the head of an empty barrel near the roadside when a traveler who was passing along asked him what he was doing that for. The fellow replied that there was some cider in that barrel a few days before and he was trying to see if there was any then, but if there was, he couldn't get at it. I told them that there had been a little bit of speech in me awhile ago, but I believed I couldn't get it out. They all roared out in a mighty laugh and I told some other anecdotes, equally amusing to them; and believing I had them in a first-rate way, I quit and got down, thanking the people for their attention. But I took care to remark that I was dry as a powder horn and that I thought it was time for us to wet our whistles a little; and so I put off to the liquor stand and was followed by the greater part of the crowd. I felt certain this was necessary, for I knowed my competitor could open government matters to them as easy as he pleased. He had, however, mighty few left to hear him as I continued with the crowd, now and then taking a horn and telling good-humored stories till he was done speaking. I found I was good for the votes . . . when we broke up.[1]

We have seen how the Old West's economic and demographic expansion increased the region's impact on politics and elections. Its growth generated issues that entered the stream of partisan contest, and the region became a regular source for the realignment of political parties. In the early years of the Old West, pioneer voters were devotees of Thomas

---

[1] Henry Steele Commager and Allan Nevins, eds., *The Heritage of America* (Boston, 1949), pp. 263–66.

Jefferson and the Democratic-Republican party, for that party consistently supported their simple needs—credit for land purchases, free navigation of the Mississippi River, and territorial expansion. The intense nationalism of Westerners, which generated the War of 1812 and the victories by Western armies over British Indians in the Northwest and British armies in the Southwest, shamed sectionalist New England, which was threatening secession, and contributed materially to the demise of the Federalist party, which had supported New England separatism.

Thereafter, Westerners had a strong voice in the collage of economic and political interests composing the single political party that survived the War of 1812. The defeat of their presidential candidate, Andrew Jackson, in 1824 led to a combination of Western and certain Eastern interests into the Democratic party. This political juggernaut swept presidential elections from 1828 until 1840, when the contesting Whig party ran a homespun campaign with a Western war hero, William Henry Harrison, as its candidate and defeated the Western-based Democratic party. The Old West and the New West continued to be factors in forcing periodic realignments of parties over such recurring issues as public land distribution, national expansion, slavery extension, and the national monetary system.

The partisan response of Western voters in presidential elections between 1796 and 1828 was as follows: in 1796 and 1800, the electoral vote of Kentucky and Tennessee was committed to the Democratic-Republican candidate, Thomas Jefferson; in the 1804 election, with the addition of the electoral vote of the new state of Ohio, the result was the same; four years later, the three Western states reported mixed returns, with a majority for the Democratic-Republican candidate, James Madison; in 1812, the four Western states of Ohio, Kentucky, Tennessee, and Louisiana supported Madison; in 1816, the electoral votes of Kentucky, Tennessee, Ohio, Indiana, and Louisiana were cast for James Monroe, the Democratic-Republican candidate; in 1820, Monroe triumphed throughout the West; but in 1824, the West's electoral vote was split, Henry Clay carrying Ohio, Kentucky, and Missouri, and Andrew Jackson victorious in Indiana, Illinois, Tennessee, Mississippi, Alabama, and Louisiana; then in 1828, the Democratic party candidate, Jackson, carried all of the West against John Quincy Adams, the National Republican candidate.

The preponderance of influence and substantive change still flowed from the East to the West but, as the West grew in economic and political power, it occasionally reacted with great force on the Eastern United States. The intense nationalism generated in the West during the War of 1812 fed the national pride and produced the emotional base for the "Era of Good Feeling" that pervaded the nation in the postwar period.

Ironically, even while the West was producing centripetal, integrating forces that destroyed the incipient sectionalism of New England and turned back the threat of its secession during the War of 1812, the West, by its presence in the national community and its compulsive expansion and development, was also producing centrifugal, disintegrating forces that threatened national unity. By 1820, the virus of sectionalism had infused Western development. Up to that time the Old West was largely undifferentiated; the pioneers of all of its sections were preoccupied with the common concerns of the Indian barrier, land policy, and free navigation of the Mississippi River. But in the 1820s the Old West's growing economic specialization—notably the expansion of the highly mobile cotton-slave plantation system of the Old Southwest—provoked the issue of slavery extension.

Debate over the admission of Missouri and the resultant Missouri Compromise fragmented the Old West, gave its future development an east-west orientation—with the Ohio River and Missouri providing the boundary for the new division—and ossified the pattern of pairing new states on a free–slave basis. Thus the Missouri Compromise marked the beginning of a continuing process of Western involvement in the growing sectional rift that was leading the nation on a disaster course. At the time, however, Clay and other national leaders regarded the Missouri Compromise as the ultimate and final solution to the recurring problem of divisive sectionalism. Their confidence grew out of acceptance of the illusion of "national completeness," a belief that, with the Old West populated, organized, and integrated into the national life, the United States had reached the westernmost limits of its development. The organized national territory was seen as adequate for the foreseeable needs of the nation. The political balance struck by the Compromise of 1820 would not be disturbed, since the problem of organizing new states west of Missouri would simply not arise.

Evidence of this illusion of "national completeness" is supplied by the comments of national leaders. Congressmen alluded to the Indian frontier colonization zone west of Missouri as a "permanent" aboriginal reserve where the tribes "are outside of us, and in a place which will ever remain on the outside." Clay subscribed to the "national completeness" view and, as a corollary to the Missouri Compromise, he set forth in an oration delivered on March 30, 1824, the plan for his American System. It was to continue the tradition set by the Missouri Compromise, integrating the nation's sections by binding the North and the South with America's new political province, the Old West, into a mutually supportive system of production of raw materials, manufacturing, and marketing. The system was to be abetted and protected by federal legislation, from which all sections would benefit. Clay's inclusion of the Old West as a co-equal component of the sectional trinity was a landmark acknowledgment of the national importance of the trans-Appalachian region. The North and the South segments of the American System model had evolved as sectional entities over a 200-year period; the American West in 1824 was only slightly more than twenty-five years old.

A further acknowledgment of the Old West as a functional component in American national life occurred in the election of 1828, the fulfillment of a cumulative process, the extension of democracy. The election is symbolic of what is perhaps the greatest legacy of the West to the nation—its role in the extension of democracy into the bastions of privilege, oligarchy, and limited franchise. The West forced a shift in the political fulcrum from Jefferson Democracy to Jacksonian Democracy, from rule by leaders drawn from the elite selected by a highly restrictive suffrage to rule by leaders drawn from the community of the "common man," selected by manhood suffrage. By 1828, all Western states had adopted universal manhood suffrage; there were only rare, mild restrictions. The Eastern states had originally limited the franchise to certain economic classes, but the backwash of Western example forced a franchise liberalization in the East too; by 1828, only minimal restrictions applied in the original states as well. In the presidential election that year Andrew Jackson was elected. He was the first president from the West and from the community of the common man.

Jackson's election was symbolic. It marked the beginning of the end of the frontier period for the Old West. By 1828, frontier processes in the Old West had largely dissipated. Its three components—the Old Northwest, the Old Southwest, and the Mississippi Valley—had been integrated into the nation, principally through the nationalizing currents and the influence of urban frontier, chief vehicle for leavening the wilderness force and purging frontier coarseness. Soon, except on its Western margins, the Old West would be only slightly different from the Eastern United States, and it would be given a new name—the Midwest. Anglo-American civilization stood poised on the Missouri border, ready to begin its march across the New West.

SELECTED SOURCES

The interplay of Western and Eastern forces that Americanized the Old West in the remarkably brief span of less than forty years may be traced in Frederick J. Turner, *The Frontier in American History* (New York, 1920) and *The Significance of Sections in American History* (New York, 1932); *Ray A. Billington, *America's Frontier Heritage* (New York, 1966); *Henry Nash Smith, *Virgin Land: The American West as Symbol and Myth* (Cambridge, 1950); Thomas A. Bailey, *A Diplomatic History of the American People* (New York, 1950); Samuel F. Bemis, *Diplomatic History of the United States* (New York, 1950); *Reginald Horsman, *The Frontier in the Formative Years, 1783–1815* (New York, 1970); *Arthur P. Whitaker, *The Spanish American Frontier, 1783–1795* (Boston, 1927); Paul A. Varg, *Foreign Policies of the Found-*

* Available in paperback.

ing *Fathers* (East Lansing, 1963); *John D. Barnhardt, *Valley of Democracy: The Frontier vs. the Plantation in the Ohio Valley, 1775–1818* (Bloomington, 1954); *Alexis de Tocqueville, *Democracy in America* (Cincinnati, 1838), 2 vols.; John A. Caruso, *The Appalachian Frontier: America's First Surge Westward* (Indianapolis, 1959); and Homer C. Hockett, *Western Influences on Political Parties to 1825* (Columbus, 1917).

PART THREE *the New West*

Yosemite National Park, California

"Big Bend" on the Upper Missouri River, by George Catlin, 1832.

14

Emergent American Dominion: Military Reconnaissance and Occupation

T<small>HE</small> United States began its absorption of the New West—the area extending from the Western border of Missouri to the Pacific Basin—on a piecemeal basis. The first piece in this new territory was acquired in 1803 by the Louisiana Purchase treaty. For a time the United States shared the New West with Spain, Great Britain, Russia, and Mexico. Through a series of treaties with these countries, the boundaries of American territory were gradually established and accepted. The Adams-Onís Treaty, 1819, momentarily set the boundary separating the territories of Spain and the United States at 42°N. Successive conventions with Great Britain established 49° as the northern boundary of the New West as far as the crest of the Rocky Mountains. The territory west of that point and north of 42°, as far as the Pacific, was subject to joint occupation and use by the United States and Great Britain.

In 1824, Russia agreed to withdraw its claim to territory south of 54°40', but continued to be a rival in the New West until 1867 by maintaining hegemony over Alaska. Mexico became independent of Spain in 1821 by a successful war of secession, thereby succeeding to suzerainty over the Spanish portion of the New West—Texas, New Mexico, Arizona, and California.

NEW WEST SETTING

When Anglo-American penetration of the New West began in earnest soon after 1803, explorers and fur traders from the East and Old West found the region already occupied by Europeans and Indians, who resided in widely dispersed communities in the wilderness. On the southern rim of the New West, the northern frontier of New Spain, the belt of Spanish towns extended from Nacogdoches on the eastern border of Texas through San Antonio to El Paso, thence north along the Rio Grande to Santa Fe and Taos, into southern Arizona (around Tucson) to California, where a string of coastal missions, presidios, and civilian communities stretched from San Diego to San Francisco. On the northern rim of the New West, south of 49° and extending from the Missouri River to the Pacific shore, British traders ranged from support bases in Canada and had established several small mercantile settlements. These were populated by British managers and mixed French-Indian *engagés*.

Aboriginal Communities

The New West's vast interior was the habitat of aboriginal peoples who displayed a considerable variety of lifestyles. The Indian colonization zone west of Missouri was populated by settlements of Eastern tribes, including Delawares, Potawatomis, Wyandots, Kickapoos, Choctaws, Chickasaws, Creeks, Cherokees, Seminoles, Quapaws, and Senecas. In the Anglo-American sense, these tribes were moderately civilized and lived by agriculture, stockraising, and frontier trade. Several immigrant tribesmen, particularly Cherokees and Choctaws, were slaveholders and operated plantations in the fertile Grand, Arkansas and Red river valleys. Immediately west of the immigrant tribes were the so-called wild Plains tribes. Having adopted the horse, they were mobile and dangerous and constituted a high-risk barrier to outsiders who ventured to pass through their domains. The Plains tribes subsisted largely by hunting buffalo, raiding, and by trading in the frontier settlements of Texas, New Mexico, and the Indian Territory, and in the British trader communities of the far north.

The Sioux nation occupied a range extending across western Minnesota into the Dakotas. For years they controlled passage up the Missouri River into the Rocky Mountains. The Cheyennes and Arapahoes dominated the territory between the Platte and Arkansas rivers, and south of the Arkansas roamed the Kiowas and Comanches. Their settlement focus was in the Wichita Mountains of southwestern Oklahoma, but their restless peregrinations took them across most of the Southwest. Kiowa-Comanche raider bands struck at settlements in a zone of depredation that extended from the immigrant communities of the Indian Territory to the Spanish towns on the Rio Grande and south across Texas into northern Mexico.

Scattered throughout the Plains were settlements of tribes practicing a mixed economy of hunting and agriculture. These included the Mandans, who resided near the great bend of the Missouri River, the Pawnees in the Platte River valley, the Omahas, Poncas, and Kansas or Kaws on the tributaries of the lower Missouri River, the Osages in the middle Arkansas River valley, and the Wichitas and Caddoes in the Red River valley. Blackfeet, Crows or Absarokas, Utes, Arikaras, and Shoshonis resided in the Rocky Mountains, but ranged seasonally onto the Plains to hunt buffalo. The northern Shoshonis played a dramatic support role in the first American reconnaissance of the Northwest through Sacajawea, the eminent young woman from this tribe who served as interpreter-guide to the Lewis and Clark expedition.

The plateau and desert country between the Rocky Mountains and the Sierra Nevadas was sparsely populated by aboriginal peoples, and each tribe developed an economic adjustment and lifestyle compatible with the generally harsh, inhospitable environment of this portion of Western America. In the north, on the Columbian Plateau, resided the Nez Perces and Salish or Flatheads. After European contact, the Nez Perces became excellent stockraisers and produced a new American breed of horse—the Appaloosa. During the nineteenth century, the Nez Perces were the most illustrious Indian patriots of the New West. Their attempts to stem the tide of American expansion into Indian lands were epitomized by the brilliant military tactician, Chief Joseph.

In the Great Basin country of Utah and Nevada resided the Gosiute, Paiute, Yuman, and Mohave tribes. The paucity of game in their territory forced them to subsist on insects, snakes, and lizards, and to burrow for nourishing roots.

Between the Pecos River and the Colorado River resided several populous and powerful tribes. Some were sedentary, others migratory. The eastern sedentary tribes of the Southwestern ethnographic province were called Pueblos after their residences—large multi-family dwellings constructed of adobe brick or stone with fortifications to fend off attacks by Utes and other marauding tribes. They practiced intensive agriculture and irrigated their crops with water drawn from the rivers near their fortified villages. The Pueblo community consisted of Keresan and Tanoan settlements on the upper Pecos and Rio Grande rivers of New Mexico, and Hopi, Acoma, and Zuñi settlements in western New Mexico and eastern Arizona. The principal sedentary tribes of the western portion of the Southwestern ethnographic province were the Pimas and Papagos, who resided on the Salt, Gila, and lower Colorado rivers. Unlike the Pueblos, the Pimas and Papagos dwelt in sizable villages of thatch houses. They too practiced intensive agriculture through irrigation.

The migratory tribes of the Southwest were Apaches and Navajos— both of Athapascan language stock—who ranged over western New Mexico and Arizona. The Apaches especially were compulsive wanderers. Fierce in battle and virtually unconquerable, they were the scourge of the Spanish-Mexican frontier and blocked American expansion into the Southwest until the last quarter of the nineteenth century. The Apache nation was divided into several bands including the Chiricahuas, Mimbreños, Jicarillos, San Carlos, and Coyoteros. The Navajos, who were somewhat less migratory than the Apaches, practiced some agriculture and were receptive to stockraising. Soon after the Spanish intrusion, Navajo families developed sizable herds of horses and sheep.

Perhaps the most populous and diverse aboriginal community in the American West resided in California. At the time of the European entry, the population of the California Indians is estimated at 150,000. The many small tribes comprising this ethnographic complex included the Modocs, Karoks, Yuroks, Shastas, Hupas, Pomos, Miwoks, and the Chuwash. They subsisted on acorns, fish, roots, and small game, and their principal craft was making baskets from native sedges. The Spanish found most of these tribes docile and readily integrated them into ecclesiastical communities so that many came to be called Mission Indians.

The Pacific Northwest tribes were also numerous and varied in culture. Their economic life centered on fishing, usually the ubiquitous salmon. The tribes of this region—which included the Klamaths, Walla Wallas, Chinooks, Salish, Umpquas, Spokans, and Yakimas—were renowned for their skill in basket and mat construction, totem-pole-carving, and the potlatch ceremony—a prodigious, competitive giving of gifts.

EARLY AMERICAN EXPLORATIONS
IN THE NEW WEST

American expansion into this vast, sparsely populated region was accomplished by both private and public action. The maritime trading frontier and the fur trade frontier seeded American interest and presence. The United States' claim to the Pacific Northwest, for example, was a direct result of wide-ranging quests by American merchant seamen for markets in the Pacific. In 1792, Robert Gray, captain of the American ship *Columbia*, searched the Northwest Pacific shore for trading stations from which to trade for sea otter pelts with coastal Indian tribes. He negotiated the turbulent waters of an estuary that led to the mouth of a great river, which he named the Columbia after his ship. In the same year, the British mariner Captain George Vancouver carried out a reconnaissance of the Pacific coast from California to Alaska. He explored Puget Sound and circumnavigated Vancouver Island. The Gray and Vancouver explorations established conflicting American and British claims to the Pacific Northwest.

The extension of the fur trade frontier into the New West was a significant prelude to the official reconnaissance of the trans-Missouri region and the ultimate integration of this region into the national territory. Early fur traders discovered the most direct routes into the Far West —the passes through the Rocky Mountains—and accumulated strategic information on that vast region. Their trails traversed both American and Spanish soil, for these hardy entrepreneurs had little regard for international boundaries. The raw knowledge of the fur men, in the form of crude maps and journals, was invaluable to the first American reconnaissance of the New West—the Lewis and Clark expedition—and to later government-sponsored explorations.

The Lewis and Clark Expedition

The region Meriwether Lewis and William Clark were to traverse from 1804 to 1806 was already partially known. In 1790, Jacques d'Eglise, a trader from St. Louis, penetrated the wilderness as far as the Mandan villages near the great bend of the Missouri River. Three years later at St. Louis, Zenon Trudeau organized the Company of Explorers of the Missouri to trade in the territory drained by the upper Missouri River. In 1794, the company sent Juan Truteau and ten traders to the Mandan villages. A Sioux party intercepted Truteau, captured his goods, and forced him to turn back. Later, the Company of Explorers sent John Evans, a Welshman, and James McKay, a Scotsman, on a trading mission up the Missouri. The information derived from these two expeditions was recorded in a journal kept by Truteau and on maps prepared by Evans and McKay. President Thomas Jefferson eventually came into possession of these papers.

On January 18, 1803, President Jefferson communicated to Congress a secret message seeking support "for a venture whose meaning and propriety were then and still remain uncertain": it was to be an expedition across foreign territory to the Pacific Northwest by way of the Missouri River and would be conducted by a detachment of the United States army. The president's interest in scientific investigation was well known, and his charade of mounting a scientific reconnaissance was meant to quiet protests by France—over whose territory the expedition would cross—and Spain—which served as trustee administrator for that territory.

The primary purpose of the projected expedition was to test a growing conviction that the Missouri-Columbia system constituted an easy water route across the continent. Gray's discovery of the Columbia River had led to a surmise that a substitute for the long-sought Strait of Annian and Northwest Passage might exist if traders could follow the Missouri River to its source, make a hopefully-brief portage to the headwaters of the Columbia River, and float down that stream to the Pacific. Such a transcontinental water route could shorten substantially the time and distance American maritime traders traveled from the Atlantic seaboard, to the south around Cape Horn, and north to the Pacific Basin for trafficking along the Pacific shore, in the Sandwich Islands, and west to the ports of China. Thus the motive for the first American exploration of the New West was largely economic; a water route through the continent could become a grand avenue of commerce, as well as provide easy access to the rich fur trade along the Missouri-Columbia river system.

When Congress responded to Jefferson's surreptitious request by appropriating $2,500, the president began preparations for the expedition. He selected Meriwether Lewis, 28—his private secretary and a captain in the United States Army—and William Clark, 32—brother of George Rogers Clark—to lead the Western reconnaissance. Both men were experienced in wilderness living, mostly from military service spent on the Western border. Jefferson's instructions to Lewis and Clark directed that they reconnoiter the Missouri River to its source, cross the drainage divide to the Columbia River, and follow that stream to the Pacific. They were to map the territory traversed and record their observations of the terrain,

plants, animals, and native peoples of the Northwest. Jefferson provided
Lewis and Clark with the maps, journals, and memoranda derived from
earlier explorations and with papers requesting Spanish officials to allow
the expedition passage west of St. Louis.

Lewis and Clark's party was recruited and outfitted at Pittsburgh
during the summer of 1803. Weapons, provisions, personal effects, instruments, and a heavy store of gifts to the Indian tribes were loaded on a
55-foot-long keelboat and two pirogues. The party consisted of forty-three
persons, twenty-nine assigned to the expedition force and fourteen soldiers
and boatmen to accompany the column to the Mandan villages on the
Missouri River and return with the river craft. The entourage was an
ethnic mix of Anglo-Americans—most of them from the Kentucky settlements—Frenchmen from the Old Northwest—to serve as guides and boatmen—and a black—Clark's servant York. En route, the column picked up
Toussaint Charbonneau and his Shoshoni wife Sacajawea, who was to
serve as interpreter and guide. She proved to be one of the most useful
members of the party. Besides Lewis and Clark, other important figures
were John Colter of Kentucky, Patrick Gass, a frontiersman and journal
keeper, John Shields, the column gunsmith, and Charles Floyd, a member
of one of Kentucky's earliest settler families and a captain in the column.

Spanish officials refused to honor President Jefferson's request for access to Louisiana, and the expedition was forced to winter on the Illinois
shore across from St. Louis during 1803–1804. The transfer of upper
Louisiana to the United States took place on March 9, 1804, and by late
spring, high water on the Missouri caused by heavy spring rains had
receded. On May 14, Lewis and Clark led their waterborne column upriver from St. Louis. Passage was slow and painfully difficult. By poling
and rowing the pirogues, rowing the keelboat and—most of the time—
towing from the bank, crewmen were able to average about ten miles a
day against the Missouri River's throbbing current; they arrived at the
Mandan villages after six months of travel.

It was the custom of the Teton Sioux to contest passage of all traffic on
the Missouri River, and on several occasions parties confronted the Lewis
and Clark column, and daring warriors attempted to seize the smaller
boats. For nearly two weeks Sioux raiders threatened from the river
bank, but Lewis and Clark's determination and the readiness of the
heavily armed men in the boats caused the Sioux to back off. This firm
stance ended the Sioux blockade on the Missouri River. Lewis and Clark
informed the Sioux and other tribes met along the route that the United
States was now ruler of this territory and that their fealty was due to that
nation.

Arriving at the Mandan villages on October 27, 1804, the expedition
erected winter quarters, which they named Fort Mandan. English traders
regularly visited the Mandan villages during that winter, and Lewis and
Clark were impressed with the English success in the fur trade of that

remote region and expressed alarm over their expanding influence among local Indians.

During the summer of 1805, the column moved upriver to the headwaters of the Missouri; they explored the drainage divide country and crossed into the Columbia River drainage. Their hopes for a short portage were dashed when they beheld the tumbled highland country lying between the navigable portions of the Missouri and Columbia rivers. They lamented that the portage consisted of over 300 miles of "land carriage," nearly 150 miles of this "over tremendous mountains which for 60 miles is covered with eternal snows." Their passage through this alpine maze of towering snowclad peaks, deep canyons, and rugged mesas was eased by Sacajawea's presence. Fortunately for the expedition, she was restored to her people, the Northern Shoshonis, who resided in this highland wilderness. From the grateful tribe Lewis and Clark received much-needed provisions, horses to transport men and gear, and valuable information on the most expeditious course to the Pacific. They explored the drainage divide country and crossed into the Columbia watershed. Following the Clearwater River to the Snake River and the latter to the Columbia, they arrived on the Pacific shore in November 1805. Near the mouth of the Columbia they erected Fort Clatsop, which served as winter quarters.

On the return, except for one diversion, Lewis and Clark followed roughly the same route they had traced to the Pacific. The column separated in the Rocky Mountains: Clark's party followed the Yellowstone to the Missouri, and Lewis led his men along the Marias River. Lewis' party met a hostile Blackfeet band, a battle erupted, and the Americans drove off the Indians. Rushing ahead of a reinforced Blackfeet war party, Lewis finally rejoined Clark below the Yellowstone on the Missouri. The expedition proceeded downstream to St. Louis, arriving there on September 23, 1806.

The results of the Lewis and Clark reconnaissance were substantial and far reaching. By their official presence in this wilderness they established the first American dominion over the land and people of upper Louisiana. Many powerful Indian nations were first introduced to Americans through Lewis and Clark's column. Their examination of the country between the Missouri River and the Columbia River disproved the theory that a relatively easy water route existed from St. Louis to the Pacific. And for the cause of national expansion to the Pacific, their land explorations, coupled with Gray's maritime explorations, provided the primary basis for American claims to the Oregon country.

Soon after the return of Lewis and Clark's column, several journals were published setting forth the vicissitudes and adventures of travel through the Northwestern wilderness and describing the land, native people, and local plants and animals. In 1807, Patrick Gass published his journal at Pittsburgh. Nicolas Biddle of Philadelphia began editing the Lewis and Clark journals in 1811; they were published three years later.

The Dunbar-Hunter Expedition

Jefferson's interest in the trans-Mississippi region included the Southwest. To obtain information on the land, resources, natural boundaries, and native peoples of that region, he was responsible for several reconnaissances, none of which had the scope and importance of the Lewis and Clark expedition. During 1804, at Jefferson's request, William Dunbar, a planter-scientist from Natchez, and George Hunter, a scientist from Philadelphia, combined to reconnoiter portions of the Red River above Natchitoches. John Sibley, an Indian agent at Natchitoches, had explored the Red River and its environs for some distance above his headquarters, and his reports were of material assistance to Dunbar and Hunter as well as to other American explorers assigned to reconnoiter the Southwest. Dunbar and Hunter were assigned a military escort of thirteen men from the regular army. The expedition explored along the Red River to the Ouachita River, then north along that stream into southern Arkansas. They proceeded north to the hot springs before concluding their explorations. The field notes of the expedition were presented to the American Philosophical Society.

The Dunbar-Hunter Red River expedition was semi-official in character. Jefferson's interest in the Southwest persisted and centered around those points in the highlands and the rivers descending to the Mississippi that he believed would in time be accepted as the western and southern boundaries of Louisiana. Therefore, during 1806 two government ventures were undertaken to thoroughly explore the headwaters of the Arkansas and Red rivers, the principal streams on the southern margins of Louisiana.

The Freeman-Sparks Expedition

The Spanish were very sensitive about American claims concerning the southern and western boundaries of Louisiana, and when reports of projected expeditions filtered through to Spanish colonial officials at Nacogdoches in east Texas and in Santa Fe, they issued warnings: no American exploration should be made until the limits of Louisiana had been positively established. For the United States to send a party of soldiers to the sources of the rivers in the disputed territory "would be an insult to Spain and would cause that nation to retaliate by forcing its return." [1]

Despite the warnings, preparations proceeded. The Red River expedition force consisted of Thomas Freeman, a surveyor and cartographer, Dr. Peter Custis, a botanist, and Captain Richard Sparks and twenty-one men, most of them regular Army personnel. Sparks organized the expedition in the American settlements along lower Red River. He planned to transport the twenty-four men, equipment, and supplies in two flat-

[1] Quoted in Arrell M. Gibson, *Oklahoma: A History of Five Centuries* (Norman, 1965), p. 47.

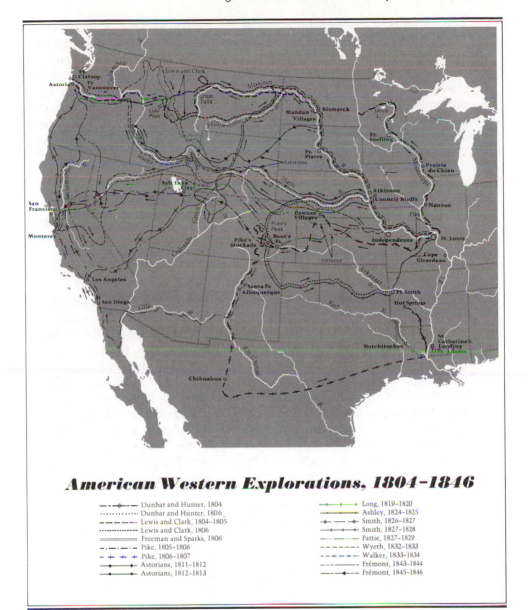

American Western Explorations, 1804–1846

—·—◇—· Dunbar and Hunter, 1804	——————• Long, 1819–1820
·············· Dunbar and Hunter, 1806	——————— Ashley, 1824–1825
— — — — Lewis and Clark, 1804–1805	—◇— — —◇ Smith, 1826–1827
················ Lewis and Clark, 1806	◀——◀——◀ Smith, 1827–1828
═══════ Freeman and Sparks, 1806	—···—···— Pattie, 1827–1829
—·—··—·— Pike, 1805–1806	— — — — — Wyeth, 1832–1833
—+—+—+— Pike, 1806–1807	—·—·—·—· Walker, 1833–1834
—◆——◆— Astorians, 1811–1812	— — — — — Frémont, 1843–1844
—●——●— Astorians, 1812–1813	—·—◀—·— Frémont, 1845–1846

bottom boats and several pirogues, all light craft, to Twin Villages, the Caddo-Wichita settlements on the upper Red River; there he hoped to trade the boats for horses to carry his party to the "top of the mountains." The Red River expedition left Natchitoches on June 2, 1806; it proceeded slowly because the river channel was choked for several miles by a vast log accumulation called "the raft." At various points along the bank Sparks visited Caddo villages. Warriors in from a hunt in Texas warned that the Spanish had learned of his purpose and that a large cavalry force was scouring the river bank to intercept him.

As the American party approached the southwestern corner of Arkansas, a Spanish column from Nacogdoches under Don Francisco Viana intercepted the Americans. Viana offered Sparks the choice of turning back to the American settlements or being arrested and detained at Nacogdoches. Faced with superior numbers, Captain Sparks ordered his men back downriver to Natchitoches.

The Pike Expedition

Another American exploratory venture launched in 1806 suffered a similar fate. Zebulon M. Pike had just returned from his reconnaissance of the upper Mississippi River country in search of the source of the Mississippi River, but in July of 1806 he led another expedition, this time to the Rocky Mountains. Captain Pike's party consisted of twenty-three men, including Lt. James Wilkinson, son of General James Wilkinson. They departed from St. Louis on July 15, traveled by boat up the Missouri, thence up to the head of navigation of the Osage River. At the Osage villages, Pike obtained horses to transport his column across the Plains. Young Wilkinson recorded that before leaving the Indian settlement, the expedition was treated to a feast of "green corn, buffalo meat, and watermelons about the size of twenty-four pound shot, which, though small, were high flavored."

From the Osage villages, Pike's men rode northwest to the Pawnee towns on the Republican River, where it was reported by Indian informants that a sizable Spanish force from Santa Fe had stopped only a few days before. Pike found the report to be true, for a Spanish flag flew over the lodge of the Pawnee chief. He later learned that the Spanish force consisted of 600 dragoons and mounted militia and was led by Don Facundo Melgares of the Santa Fe garrison. After persuading the Pawnee chief to exchange the Spanish banner for a United States flag, Pike led his men south to the Arkansas River. At the great bend in that stream, Pike detached Wilkinson and five men, ordering them to descend to the mouth of the river.

The Wilkinson reconnaissance of the Arkansas was launched on October 28, 1806. The men constructed two boats, a pirogue hewed from a cottonwood log and a light craft with a pole frame covered with elk skin and buffalo hide. Winter came early to the Southwest in 1806. Wilkinson's river craft capsized several times, dumping his meager supplies into the icy water. The little band subsisted by hunting and by trading for food from Osage bands in their winter hunting camps along the river. Ice, sometimes running from shore to shore or drifting in huge crunching floes along the Arkansas, slowed Wilkinson's descent.

On the morning of December 3, the river was completely frozen, and Wilkinson recorded that

> this circumstance placed me in a situation truly distressing, as my men were almost naked; the tatters which covered them were comfortless, and my ammunition was nearly exhausted.

Three days later the ice broke, and began to drift, and Wilkinson pushed off with it, "but," he wrote,

> as my evil stars would have it, my boats again grounded, and being in the middle of the river, my only alternative was to get out and drag them along for several miles, when we halted to warm our benumbed feet and hands. The next day several large cakes of ice had blocked up the river, and we had to cut our way through them with axes; the boats as usual grounded, and the men, bare legged and bare footed, were obliged to leap into the water. This happened so frequently that two more of my men got badly frosted.[2]

Finally, on December 31, Wilkinson's party passed the mouth of the Poteau, and deeper water and milder weather permitted an easier descent to the Mississippi River. Wilkinson's journal of the Arkansas River reconnaissance was the first report of this region. He commented on passing several Osage villages and noted a number of encroaching Cherokee, Choctaw, and Creek hunting camps. He referred to reports of rich lead mines northeast in the Osage country and mentioned meeting American trappers on the Poteau and other streams tributary to the Arkansas.

After Wilkinson went down the Arkansas, the main expedition under Pike proceeded to the Rocky Mountains by way of the Arkansas Valley. In the Rocky Mountains Pike and his men scaled one of the towering eminences; they reached an altitude of 9,000 feet before returning to camp. Pike modestly permitted the expedition cartographer to name this dominating highland Pike's Peak.

Pike led his men through the mountains in quest of the source of the Red River, reconnoitering the Royal Gorge, the Sangre de Cristo Mountains, and the San Luis Valley. During February 1807 he halted on the banks of the upper Rio Grande and directed his men to construct a stockaded shelter. On February 26, his location was discovered by a Spanish patrol of fifty dragoons commanded by Captain Ignacio Salleto. The Spaniards conducted Pike and his men to Santa Fe, where local officials exposed them to long interrogation sessions. Spanish officers relieved the Americans of their papers, powder, and shot but permitted the intruders

---

[2] Zebulon M. Pike, *Explorations and Travels Through the Western Territories of North America* (London, 1811), pp. 375–76.

to retain their weapons. Subsequently the American captives were moved to Chihuahua by way of El Paso for additional questioning. During the summer of 1807, Pike and his men were escorted to Durango, thence to Laredo and San Antonio. They were ultimately released on the yet-to-be established border separating Louisiana and Texas near Natchitoches.

The Sibley Expedition

The next American exploration of the country beyond the Mississippi Valley province of the Old West occurred in 1811. In May, George R. Sibley, Indian agent at Fort Osage, Missouri, accompanied by a servant, two interpreters, and fifteen Osage warriors, traveled to what were known as the buffalo plains. Sibley's party was gone for two months and ranged over Kansas, Nebraska, and northern Oklahoma. They made an extensive reconnaissance of the Arkansas River, tracing its tributaries, including the Salt Fork (Nescatunga), the Cimarron (Nesuketonga) or Grand Saline, and the Chikaskia. Sibley was most impressed by the Salt Plains, "glistening like a brilliant field of snow in the summer sun" on the banks of the Salt Fork. He described the area as a vast flat of salt crust, uniformly of the thickness of a wafer, on either side of the river. "This beautiful white dazzling surface (bordered by a fringe of verdant green) has the effect of looming, as the sailors call it," he noted, "producing to the unpracticed eye much delusion." [3]

Salt was an important item in frontier trade, not only for seasoning food, but also for preserving meat, and Sibley was highly optimistic about the prospects for the Salt Plains region. He recommended that federal officials open a wagon road between the Missouri settlements and the Salt Plains. While no immediate commercial development of the rich salt deposits occurred, the Salt Plains more and more became a supply point for traders, trappers, overland expeditions, and Indian tribes of the Southwestern frontier.

The Belle Point Reconnaissance

The next Western exploration was a precursor to the extension of the military frontier. For years the Osage Indians had waged a devastating war on the Western Cherokees, Delawares, Shawnees, Caddoes, and Wichitas; and in 1817, the warriors of these tribes confederated for the purpose of exterminating the predatory Osages. Settlers in Arkansas and Missouri, fearful of becoming involved in this intertribal war, appealed to the federal government for protection. In response, Secretary of War Richard Graham ordered Major Stephen H. Long of the Army Topographical Bureau to reconnoiter the country flanked by the Arkansas River and select a site for a military post. Long, with a five-man party, examined the Arkansas River upstream to the mouth of the Verdigris and decided to locate the new post, which became Fort Smith, at a place the trappers called Belle Point;

[3] Ibid., p. 50.

the site was high on the bluffs of the south bank of the Arkansas at the mouth of the Poteau. Long sketched plans for the new post, turned them over to Major William Bradford, commander of the rifle regiment that was to erect the wilderness outpost, and continued with his explorations.

From Belle Point, he moved southwest to the headwaters of the Poteau, thence across the divide into the tumbled Kiamichi Mountain country, and followed the Kiamichi River to the Red River. He coursed along the north bank of the Red River, traveled north to the "thermal springs," and continued northeast until he reached the Mississippi River settlements in Missouri in late January of 1818.

The Minnesota River Expedition

The following year Long was sent to the far north to select a site for yet another post, to establish official American presence among the Sioux of Minnesota, and to check growing British trader influence with local Indian tribes. Long's selection was situated at the Falls of St. Anthony, where the Minnesota River joins the Mississippi River; the post erected on the site was named Fort Snelling.

The Yellowstone Expedition

Also during 1819, Major Long was assigned to the Yellowstone Expedition. In a surge of interest to open and develop the country along the Missouri River and to expel the ubiquitous British trader-interlopers, Congress appropriated funds to support an extension of the military frontier into the Northwest. A 1,000-man army commanded by General Henry W. Atkinson was to proceed by steamer transport to the Mandan villages. There they were to construct a military station to serve as a support for additional posts to be erected at several points farther west, including one at the mouth of the Yellowstone River. Attached to the Yellowstone Expedition was a team of cartographers and natural scientists whose mission was to make an exhaustive scientific reconnaissance of the territory along the Missouri River. Major Long was placed in charge of the scientific party, which was transported on the steamboat *Western Engineer*.

The military flotilla ascended to Council Bluffs, where the steamers faltered due to shallow water. Army units erected quarters and the Yellowstone Expedition wintered there. Congressional interest faded, the support appropriation was not approved, and the Yellowstone Expedition was cancelled. However, Major Long was directed to lead a small party of scientists and cartographers, escorted by a military detachment, to the Rocky Mountains; he was to explore the headwaters of the eastward flowing rivers.

The Rocky Mountain Expedition

During 1820, Long led his column along the South Platte River into the Rocky Mountains. Expedition members explored the highlands and valleys, found and named Long's Peak, and traced the headwaters of the Arkansas River. Long directed his second-in-command, Captain John R.

Bell, to take twelve men and follow the Arkansas to Fort Smith. One of the notables in Bell's column was Thomas A. Say, a pioneer zoologist. Bell's men suffered great hardships on the Arkansas route, riding through the furnace heat of a scorching August sun that daily produced temperatures around 100°. When their reconnaissance was nearly two-thirds completed, they had exhausted their provisions. The intense heat had made game very scarce, and the men were reported to be casting longing eyes toward their puny horses and mules, calculating which animal they would slaughter. This drastic step was delayed when Julien, their French guide, finally killed a skunk. That night they feasted on skunk soup, enriched with a half pint of bread crumbs salvaged from knapsacks. The food restored their strength for additional marches and, while hunters ranged far and wide for game without success, they did bring in wild grapes "and some unripe persimmons, all of which were eaten."

On August 31 Bell's Arkansas River expedition camped near the mouth of the Cimarron. During the night, three privates deserted with three of the strongest horses, certain personal effects of the officers and men and, worst of all, the Say journals, which contained his notes on the plants, animals, rocks, and minerals observed along the route, his sketches and maps, and the descriptions and vocabularies of the Indian tribes encountered. Bell's men searched for the fugitives for several days without success. Grim and hungry, they continued along the river to Fort Smith, arriving there on September 9, 1820.

After dispatching Captain Bell along the Arkansas, Major Long led his ten-man detachment, which included the eminent botanist and geologist Edwin James, in search of the headwaters of the Red River. A daring five-day ride across eastern New Mexico, still a Spanish province, brought the Americans to a deep creek bed—now called Major Long's Creek—which Long incorrectly identified as a tributary of the Red. This water course was in fact a tributary of the Canadian River.

As Long's party crossed the high plains, the creek bed gradually flared until it was found to be two miles wide in some places. This highway across the Plains, a water course which Long conceived to be the Red River, was dry. For water the men gouged shallow pits in the river bed, but by the time the group arrived at the Antelope Hills, the summer heat was so intense that no amount of digging produced water. They found a substitute in wild fruit—grapes, "vines loaded with ripe fruit, and purple clusters crowded in such profusion that they colored the landscape."

Both Long and James believed that this region appropriately should be designated the Great American Desert which was "providentially placed to keep the American people from ruinous diffusion." They added,

we have little apprehension of giving too unfavorable an account of this portion of the country. Though the soil is in some places fertile, the want of timber, of navigable streams, and of water for the neces-

sities of life, render it an unfit residence for any but a nomad population. The traveller who shall at any time have traversed its desolate
sands, will, we think, join us in the wish that this region may forever
remain the unmolested haunt of the native hunter, the bison, and the
jackall [coyote].[4]

The greatest surprise and disappointment of Long's Red River expedition occurred on September 10, 1820. Dr. James recorded that on this
day the party

> arrived at the confluence of our supposed Red River with another of
> much greater size, which we at once perceived to be the Arkansas.
> Our disappointment and chagrin at discovering the mistake we had
> so long laboured under, was little alleviated by the consciousness that
> the season was so far advanced, our horses and our means so far ex-
> hausted, as to place it beyond our power to return and attempt the
> discovery of the sources of Red River.[5]

Three days later, Long's column arrived at Fort Smith to be welcomed by
Captain Bell and the Arkansas expedition party. The uncouth appearance
of the members of Long's party was reported as "a matter of astonishment
both to dogs and men."

The official reconnaissances into the New West had several long-range
effects on the private mind and public policy. Besides confirming American dominion over much of the wilderness region west of Missouri, these
government-sponsored expeditions generated maps and descriptive reports,
which provided a fund of knowledge—although it was superficial and in
many respects imperfect—about the New West. Most of the expedition
reports were published and widely read in the East. The Lewis and Clark
journals ended the hope of an easy water route through the continent,
causing national business and political leaders to seek other alternatives to
shortening the path of commerce to the Orient. Pike's journal, published
in 1810, contained his observations of life in the Spanish-American settlements along the Rio Grande and pointed to trade prospects with these
settlements.

The published accounts consistently stressed the New West's inhospitable environment, its trackless wastes, towering mountains, and
severe climate; they fixed firmly in the American mind the concept of
Great American Desert. One significant result of this image was growing
acceptance in the 1820s of the view that the limits of effective American
occupation had been reached when the Mississippi Valley province of the
Old West was integrated into the national life. "National Completeness"

---

[4] Edwin James, *Account of an Expedition from Pittsburgh to the Rocky Mountains,
1819–1820* in *Early Western Travels, 1748–1865*, ed. by Reuben G. Thwaites (Cleveland, 1905), p. 174.
[5] Ibid., p. 180.

had been achieved. The public view that a vast wasteland existed west of Missouri perhaps explains the expansive, generous gesture of national leaders in setting aside a substantial portion of the New West as a resettlement zone for the Eastern tribes. They clearly believed that low public esteem for the region would never again place the uprooted aborigines in competition with American settlers.

But, in spite of the growing low public evaluation of the New West engendered by the published accounts, American occupation and the development of the trans-Missouri region proceeded apace. The fur men were the vanguard force of the occupation.

SELECTED SOURCES

Early American entry into the New West, mostly under the auspices of the military frontier, is the subject of William H. Goetzmann's *Army Exploration in the American West, 1803–1863* (New Haven, 1959). The Lewis and Clark expedition reconnaissance is described in Reuben G. Thwaites, ed., *Original Journals of the Lewis and Clark Expedition, 1804–1806* (New York, 1904–1905), 8 vols.; *Bernard De Voto, ed., *The Journals of Lewis and Clark* (Boston, 1953); Elliott Coues, ed., *History of the Expedition under the Command of Lewis and Clark* (New York, 1893), 4 vols.; Calvin Thompkins, *The Lewis and Clark Trail* (New York, 1965); and *Richard Dillon, *Meriwether Lewis* (New York, 1965).

Southwestern explorations are the subject of W. Eugene Hollon, *The Lost Pathfinder: Zebulon Montgomery Pike* (Norman, 1949); Donald M. Jackson, ed., *The Journals of Zebulon Montgomery Pike* (Norman, 1966), 2 vols.; "Major Sibley's Diary," *Chronicles of Oklahoma*, June 1927, V; Edwin James, *Account of an Expedition from Pittsburgh to the Rocky Mountains*, vols. XIV, XV, XVI, and XVII of *Early Western Travels, 1748–1865*, ed. by Reuben G. Thwaites (Cleveland, 1905); H. M. Fuller and Leroy R. Hafen, eds., *The Journal of Captain John R. Bell, Official Journalist for the Stephen H. Long Expedition* (Glendale, Calif., 1957); and Grant Foreman, *Pioneer Days in the Early Southwest* (Cleveland, 1926).

Examples of military frontier extensions into the New West are found in *Edwin C. Bearss and Arrell M. Gibson, *Fort Smith: Little Gibraltar on the Arkansas* (Norman, 1969), and Robert W. Frazer, *Forts of the West* (Norman, 1965). The image of the New West as an arid wasteland is traced in W. Eugene Hollon, *The Great American Desert* (New York, 1966).

* Available in paperback.

Western History Collections,
University of Oklahoma Library

Monument Valley
on the Navajo Reservation, Arizona

"Long Knives on the Canadian," Early American Trapper-Explorers.

15

New West Pioneer Enterprises: The Fur Trade

By the time of the development of the New West, the fur trade was already an old American industry. As a general rule, it was the first economic exploitation of a new wilderness region. Fur-bearing animals abounded in the new land and were easily harvested. Skins and pelts were simple to process and, with reasonable care, could be kept for long periods of time. Bales of skins and pelts were easily transported to market by pack trains and in canoes, pirogues, keelboats, and other river craft. Furs were much in demand and enjoyed a stable market value.

Most of the imperialistic contesting for control of the trans-Appalachian region among European nations—from the Dutch-Iroquois drive into the West during the early seventeenth century to the French-British intercolonial wars of the eighteenth century—centered on the fur trade. Fur-trade concerns in Western America dominated the content of French, Dutch, and British treaties and laws during colonial times. The British Proclamation of 1763 was, in fact, an official gesture to set aside the trans-Appalachian West as a great fur reserve for British trading companies. And the administration of the Old West by Sir William Johnson and John Stuart prior to the Revolution was, for the most part, an attempt to provide some order in the mounting chaos of this frontier industry. British reluctance to surrender posts in the Old Northwest to the United States after the Treaty of Paris was primarily due to the desire to retain these strategically situated stations as bases for a very lucrative fur traffic with the Indians.

FEDERAL MANAGEMENT OF THE FUR TRADE

United States administration of the trans-Appalachian territory also gave considerable attention to the fur trade. The industry was intimately intertwined with tribal relations, for Indians were major suppliers of furs and pelts to American traders. Sharp or exploitive practices by traders antagonized the aborigines, provoked redress, and often generated widening frontier wars, which frequently had to be settled by federal troops. Federal laws requiring traders to obtain licenses and post bond regulated the trade, and federal rules forbade trade in certain items listed as contraband, notably intoxicants.

Federal Factory System

In 1796, Congress established the fur trade factory system. Federally managed and supplied trading stations were located at strategic points in Indian country. Each station received furs and pelts from local Indian hunters in exchange for low-cost goods. At its peak of operation, the federal factory system maintained twenty-eight government houses in the trans-Appalachian wilderness, from the upper Mississippi Valley south to near the Gulf. The principal house east of the Mississippi River was at Chickasaw Bluffs, near Memphis; west of the Mississippi was Arkansas Post, situated on the lower Arkansas River. Private traders continued to function in competition with the government houses, but their trading constituencies were severely limited.

The national government established the factory system for several reasons. First of all, officials had found it almost impossible to control the actions of the independent American trader in the wilderness, and the potential martial power of the Indian tribes in the late eighteenth and early nineteenth centuries was very great. The threat to harmonious relations with the United States posed by the wilderness trader, with his penchant for provoking the tribes by sharp trading practices, was very real. Moreover, the government found that trading houses could be used to obtain title to Indian land for the benefit of the American settler, and national leaders shamelessly did so. President Thomas Jefferson regularly admonished federal employees at the government houses to extend more and more credit to the Indians so that they would more readily cede their lands to the United States to pay their mounting debts.

Character of the New West Fur Trade

Extension of the American fur trade into the New West resembled in many ways the life cycle of that enterprise in the Old West; but there were some striking differences. It was similar in that fur traders in both regions comprised the vanguard American force entering the wilderness, establishing vital American presence in the new land. The fur trade was a prodigiously exploitive, destructive, and mobile enterprise. In their quest for virgin pelt zones, fur men ranged over the New West, quickly transforming the region from the unknown to the known. Like the Old West traders, they opened trails, discovered passes in the highland spines that laced the trans-Missouri country, and traced routes of travel that became frontier thoroughfares for later travelers. In the New West too the international rivalry continued, particularly with British commercial interests. Indian hunters also continued as a factor of consequence in the fur industry, gathering pelts and exchanging them for blankets, guns, knives, trinkets, textiles, and other trade items.

But here an important difference developed, for in the New West many Indians eschewed trader blandishments and continued their native lifestyle. Some tribes, such as the Blackfeet, even attempted to thwart the extension of the fur industry into the New West wilderness. Thus in many areas of the New West, the frontiersman had to become a trapper himself, trapping his own pelts and processing and marketing them.

But in any case, whether he became a hunter of furs for the trader, remained aloof, or even attempted to drive off the intruders, the Indian was a casualty of the fur trade. The ecological disruption caused by the fur trade extended to all levels of aboriginal society, for once traders entered the villages and accustomed them to their goods and whiskey, the Indians changed from hunters for limited local needs to commercial gatherers of ever-increasing quantities of pelts and hides to meet their expanding tastes for trader goods. This growing dependence on trader goods disturbed, and at times destroyed, aboriginal self-sufficiency. In reverberating rings, this commercial intrusion corrupted the native lifestyle, encouraged neglect of essential family, clan, and tribal duties and observances, and caused pervasive personal and social disorientation and decay. If the Indian eschewed the blandishments of the trader, saturation trapping and hunting over his range soon destroyed the wild creatures that had provided him with food, shelter, and clothing. He and his tribe were reduced to a state of poverty not of his making.

Other differences between the fur trade in the Old West and New West included improved traps and the development of other equipment and techniques that increased the number of pelts a man could harvest in a season. In addition, bonanza profits from the trade attracted an increasing number of fur men. The result was that, although the New West fur-bearing region was of greater extent than that of the Old West—which had sustained the industry for 250 years—the New West was plundered of its resources in somewhat less than 50 years. The intensity of competition for furs was fierce, not only at the international level between the British and American fur men, but also among American companies. There was rivalry of the grossest sort among the American Fur Company, the Missouri Fur Company, and the Rocky Mountain Fur Company. Still another difference was the market situation. For some time, furs shipped to St. Louis and New York had been consigned to European markets. But by 1800, a vast new fur market in the Orient, centering on Chinese ports, had opened up. The great profits derived from this commerce contributed

Vanishing Species

Wild creatures are a part of the Western milieu's natural food chain. In a state of nature, cougars, man, and other predators subsisted on bison, Big Horn sheep and other browsing animals. As man moved toward a more civilized state, he became the most destructive predator of all of nature's creatures. He disregarded the imperatives of the elemental food chain, wantonly killing many species to the threshold of extermination—largely for pelts, furs, and hides. Fortunately, in recent times that civilized state has produced a sensitive generation committed to restoration of species nearly extinct.

Brown Bear at Yellowstone
Courtesy the Northern Pacific Railway

Big Horn Sheep
Glacier National Park

Giant Alaskan Moose
*The American Museum
of Natural History*

Beaver
Canadian Government Travel Bureau

Bison
Courtesy the Northern Pacific Railway

Mountain Lion
The American Museum
of Natural History

Sea Otter and Pup
U.S. Fish and Wildlife Service

to the rapid development of the fur trade in the New West and was another reason for the intensive competition and the rapid decimation of fur-bearing animals in the Western wilderness.

EUROPEANS AND THE NEW WEST FUR TRADE

Spanish and French Fur Men

The fur trade in the New West had been developed to a limited extent before the American acquisition of Louisiana. During the seventeenth and eighteenth centuries, Spanish trappers had taken pelts in the area of the Southwest extending above Santa Fe and Taos to the valleys of the Sangre de Cristo Mountains and northwest into the Great Basin country. Each year, pack trains laden with cured pelts were driven down the Rio Grande to El Paso and south to Vera Cruz for shipment to Spain. At this time Spanish law excluded foreigners from the northern provinces. Nonetheless French trappers and traders regularly attempted to gather furs in Spanish territory and to reach the Rio Grande to trade in the Spanish-American towns. Just as regularly, they were thwarted by Spanish patrols guarding the eastern approaches to Santa Fe. Expansionist American traders suffered the same fate, as westward-ranging parties from St. Louis and Arkansas Post were all, without exception, turned back, their furs and goods confiscated.

During the French period in Louisiana, Gallic traders had used their settlements at Ferdinandina on the Arkansas River and Twin Villages on the Red River as support bases from which to trade with the fierce Kiowas and Comanches who dominated the Plains country that sweeps westward from Cross Timbers to the area near the Rio Grande. French traders dared not venture onto the Plains; but they did use Wichita and Caddo Indians as middlemen to carry trade goods to the Kiowas and Comanches in exchange for horses, mules, valuable buffalo robes, and items the native raiders had plundered from the Rio Grande settlements.

Northwest of St. Louis, Spanish and French traders carried on commerce with the Kanza, Omaha, Ponca, Pawnee, and other tribes residing on the eastern margins of the Plains. But the Missouri River, the grand water highway leading into the fur-rich Rocky Mountains, was controlled by the Sioux, and attempts by Spanish and French businessmen to tap the fur trade of that region extended no farther than the Mandan villages on the Missouri.

British Fur Men

Before the United States acquired Louisiana, two great British companies, operating from Canadian bases, were pushing relentlessly across the northern margins of the future United States. The Hudson's Bay

Company concentrated on expanding its fur empire across Western Canada to the Pacific. But in 1783, a second British company, the North West Company, was chartered at Montreal. The monopoly of Canadian territory held by Hudson's Bay Company forced the North West Company onto American soil. A principal forward supply base for the North West Company was at Fort William on Lake Superior, just north of the 49th parallel. From there agents of the North West Company came to dominate the fur trade around the Great Lakes and in the giant triangle of territory lying south of 49° between the Mississippi River and the Missouri River, including Minnesota and Iowa. Pike visited their stations on the Mississippi River in 1806 during his upriver reconnaissance.

From their trade in the territory between the Mississippi and Missouri —mostly with the Sioux—North West Company traders in the early years of the nineteenth century annually carried in trade goods valued at $60,000 and returned with pelts of deer, beaver, otter, fox, mink, bear, raccoon, fisher, and wolf valued at over $100,000. Moreover, North West Company agents traded arms to the Sioux and induced them to guard the Missouri River and thus thwart the French, Spanish, and, later, American traders moving up that stream. During their stay at the Mandan settlements in the winter of 1803–1804, Lewis and Clark observed several British traders working among the local Indians. Subsequently, American fur men came into bitter competition with agents of both the Hudson's Bay Company and the North West Company, the latter first.

EARLY AMERICAN FUR TRADE IN THE NEW WEST

As the nineteenth century opened, the fur trade of the New West beckoned irresistibly to Americans. The trans-Missouri wilderness teemed with wild creatures, and their pelts and hides had immediate and stable value. Most desired was the beaver, used in hat manufacture, followed by otter, marten, lynx, bear, deer, and elk. An increasingly popular item was the bison hide, which was carefully scraped, cured, and hand-kneaded by skilled Indian women; using a dressing of animal brains for skin tone and quality, they transformed the stiff hide into a soft, pliable, warm buffalo robe.

Commonly furs and skins passed as currency on the money-scarce frontier. Deerskin was worth forty cents a pound, a bearskin brought three dollars in trade, and a buffalo robe, six dollars. In the fur trade, pelts and skins were marketed in hundred-pound packs. A pack of beaver skins sold for $180, marten for $300, and lynx for $500.

The Southwest Fur Trade

Because the North West Company dominated the fur territory northwest of St. Louis—complete with a Sioux-ally blockade of the Missouri— American entry into the New West fur trade first began in the Southwest.

There it was simply an extension of commercial activities that had been carried on under Spanish rule.

While Spain was in control of Louisiana, officials at St. Louis had granted Manuel Lisa, a local resident, exclusive trading privileges with the Indian tribes west of St. Louis. However, the Chouteaus—a St. Louis family trading firm who were excluded from the territory by the Lisa grant—had great influence over the Osages who dwelt on the tributaries of the Missouri River. One family member, Pierre Chouteau, persuaded about 3,000 people of this tribe to move out of Lisa's franchised territory and settle in the Southwest near the Three Forks area—the junction of the Grand, Verdigris, and Arkansas rivers. Cashesegra (or Big Track) and Clermont were the chiefs of this seceding Osage group. By 1800, the Chouteaus had established several trading houses convenient to the Osage towns, including Salina on the Grand River.

Soon other French traders drifted into the Three Forks area. One of them was Joseph Bogy from Kaskaskia, who ranged out of Arkansas Post on the lower Arkansas River. Bogy gradually extended his trading operations up the river and, by 1806, had established himself at Three Forks. He prospered as a competitor with the Chouteaus for the rich Osage trade and constructed a post on the Verdigris River at the rapids, just above its mouth.

Americans, or "Long Knives" as they were called on this Southwestern frontier, first appeared on the Arkansas and Red rivers soon after 1803. Alexander McFarland, John Lemmons, William Ingles, Robert Kuyrkendall, and Benjamin Murphy were among the early pioneer fur men who operated as independent trappers and traders in the new American territory. On a Western expedition during 1812, a group of Americans were camped on the upper Red River near the Wichita villages. An Osage war party, bent on driving all intruders out of their hunting range, struck swiftly in a surprise attack. McFarland was slain, and all of the trading company goods and horses were plundered by the Osage raiders.

Following the War of 1812, a cluster of trading settlements grew up at Three Forks. Nathaniel Pryor—a member of the Lewis and Clark expedition from Kentucky—settled there, married an Osage girl, and became one of the most prosperous and influential traders on the Southwestern frontier. Other traders at Three Forks included Hugh Glenn from Cincinnati, Henry Barbour from New Orleans, and George Brand from Tennessee, who had a Cherokee wife. Each season, Indian hunters brought in their pelt catch to the Three Forks trading settlements. The Chouteaus erected a boatyard at Three Forks to construct flatboats to carry the bales of beaver, bear, panther, wolf, and the otter skins, buffalo robes, and elk and deer hides to Gulf markets. Indian hunters exchanged their furs for earrings, twists of tobacco, pipes, rope, vermillion, axes, knives, beads, cheap jewelry, bright-colored cloth, and guns and ammunition.

Soon after 1815, Chouteau expanded his operations from Three Forks toward the Great Plains by establishing a chain of trading houses extending from Chouteau Creek in central Oklahoma to the Wichita Mountains in the Southwest. His agents used these Western posts as bases for trafficking with the Kiowas and Comanches for buffalo robes. Nonetheless, by 1820, the fur trade in the Southwest had become a static enterprise. Saturation hunting had depleted the rich local fur resources; hunters were checked on the West by the uncertainty of reception by the Kiowas and Comanches, and by the international boundary that Spain forbade Americans to cross. This had an arresting effect. The industry in the Southwest became stagnant and attention was focused north to the Missouri River highway to the Rocky Mountains. Obstacles existed there, too, but each one was in the process of being overcome.

The Northwest Fur Trade

The Lewis and Clark expedition had brought back information on the great fur resources of the upper Missouri region. The expedition had also broken through the Sioux blockade and had contacted many new Indian tribes beyond the range of British traders and introduced these isolated aborigines to weapons, tools, and other trade items. On their return, they had encountered at least twelve small parties of American traders on the Missouri River. One group, which they met above the Mandan villages, consisted of Joseph Dickson and Forrest Hancock, who in 1804 had left the Illinois country to gather furs on the upper Missouri. John Colter asked to be permitted to join Dickson and Hancock, and Lewis and Clark released him from duty with the expedition.

The return of the Lewis and Clark column to St. Louis created great interest among the fur men at this bustling river port. The ever-active Manuel Lisa, who was compulsively determined to be the first in the fur trade on the upper Missouri, made preparations to launch his first enterprise into the new territory. In the spring of 1807, with goods stowed aboard a keelboat, he led a party of forty-two traders up the Missouri. Close behind was another keelboat containing rival Pierre Chouteau and his party of traders and goods. Lisa charmed his way through an Arikara blockade on the river, but Chouteau did not fare as well and was forced to turn back in the face of overwhelming Arikara strength and determination not to permit his party to pass. During his ascent of the Missouri, Lisa met Colter near the mouth of the Platte River and persuaded him to join his party. Colter accompanied Lisa to the Yellowstone. Lisa's boatmen directed the craft up the Yellowstone to the mouth of the Big Horn; there the party constructed a trading post, which Lisa named Fort Manuel.

Members of Lisa's party were sent in all directions to reconnoiter the country, to find beaver grounds and trap the furry amphibians, and to contact Indians and lead them to Fort Manuel for an exchange of pelts and trade goods. John Colter carried out the most extensive fur reconnaissance. He ranged the Yellowstone country, reached the Green River, passed through the valley of the Big Horn, crossed over the Grand Tetons, and explored Jackson's Hole. Altogether, he made a 500-mile circuit, finding rich beaver grounds and contacting both friendly and hostile Indians. Colter found bands of Crows and Flatheads who were willing to accompany him to Fort Manuel. Near the Three Forks of the Missouri, Colter and his newly made friends, who were ancient enemies of the Blackfeet, rode into a Blackfeet ambush. Colter, the Crows, and the Flatheads fought their way clear, but not before Colter suffered a serious wound. He conducted the friendly Indians to Fort Manuel, where he recuperated.

During 1808, in company with John Potts, another former Lewis and Clark expedition member, Colter returned to the Three Forks country. Again they encountered a Blackfeet band, and Colter surrendered peacefully to show his good intent and to communicate an invitation to the Blackfeet to accompany him to Fort Manuel to trade. But Potts panicked, wounded a warrior, and attempted to flee. Well-aimed arrows pierced his body. The Blackfeet then stripped Colter nude and ordered him to run. The swiftest runners in the band, each armed with a lance, took up the pursuit. Colter outdistanced all but one, and as the sole pursuer closed the gap on his quarry, Colter suddenly stopped, a move that took the warrior by surprise; he slew the Indian with his own lance, then resumed flight to the riverbank. He dove underwater and surfaced beneath a pile of drift, which screened him from his pursuers. Eventually the Blackfeet abandoned the search, and, naked and hungry, Colter made his way back to Fort Manuel. He covered the 300 miles in seven days of tortured travel.

Later that year, while trapping near the Three Forks, Colter had a third encounter with the Blackfeet, from which he escaped by climbing the sheer face of a nearby mountain. This incident convinced him of the folly of attempting to survive in the Blackfeet country, and he retired to a quieter life on a farm in Missouri.

By 1808, through his own trappers and through trade with the Crows and other friendly Indians, Lisa had accumulated a heavy cargo of furs, which he transported to St. Louis. The success of his first venture to the Rocky Mountains and his exultant reports of the prospects for the fur trade on the upper Missouri led, during 1809, to the formation of the Missouri Fur Company, which included in its membership Lisa, the Chouteaus, and William Clark.

The Missouri Fur Company became the model for other American companies engaging in the New West fur trade, for distance from markets and sources of supply, Indian hazards, and intense British competition made it virtually impossible for the lone trader to operate with any success. A company with capital and credit resources could underwrite the expense of maintaining a trapping-trading expedition for a year in the field and provide the great quantities of trade goods required to stock the remote posts on the tributaries of the Missouri. The company could engage a large force of fur men, who worked either for a share of the annual profits or as contract wage earners. It could provide the manpower to harvest furs more intensively and enable the Americans to compete more successfully with British company agents. In addition, the large force of trapper-traders in the company's employ comprised a private army that could defend itself against the almost-certain Indian attacks.

During June of 1809, the Missouri Fur Company sent its first expedition upriver. It consisted of 172 men, mostly experienced frontiersmen engaged as profit sharers or as contract wage earners, and a sprinkling of French and mixed French-Indian people employed as *voyageurs* or boatmen. The French frontiersmen were indispensable to any venture into the New West wilderness, and all fur companies included several in their rosters. "The streams were their natural element; they cordelled the keelboats up the long course of the Missouri, and their strokes pushed canoes up the small streams to the beaver lodges. They were nearly all illiterate; these voyageurs were a distinct class of frontier dwellers, volatile in temper, sentimental and contented, inured to hardship and indifferent to it." [1]

The Missouri Fur Company entourage reached Fort Manuel and scattered in small parties to establish trade stations in the wilderness and to trap beaver. The post at Three Forks had to be abandoned because of Blackfeet power and pressure, and raider bands from this tribe plundered isolated hunting camps, killed trappers, and stole their horses. One of the company's most experienced men, Andrew Henry, led a party of trappers over the continental divide in search of a beaver territory that would be free of the Blackfeet menace. The party constructed a small fort on the north branch of the Snake River in Idaho, but soon found that fur-bearing animals were scarce in that quarter and abandoned the post. The richest trapping zone was still in the vicinity of the Three Forks of the Missouri, but incessant Blackfeet pressure made any attempt to establish a permanent station there perilous if not impossible.

Blackfeet enmity was unremitting. Perhaps Meriwether Lewis' fight with a band of this tribe on the Marias River in 1806, resulting in the death of two Blackfeet, had marked the beginning of intense anti-American feeling in this tribe. Certainly John Colter's magic in escaping their deadly grasp three times had irritated and further antagonized these fierce people. The Missouri Fur Company's success in trading with and supplying arms to their ancient enemies, the Crows and Flatheads, provoked additional animus. In addition, British agents working with the Blackfeet encouraged them to check the American competitors.

For whatever reason, the Blackfeet were unalterably determined to exclude American fur men from their territory, and they succeeded in forcing the Missouri Fur Company to withdraw from the upper Missouri country. Soon after, the War of 1812 arrested American attempts to open

---

[1] E. Douglas Branch, *Westward: The Romance of the American Frontier* (New York, 1930), p. 303.

the fur trade on the Missouri. After the war, the Missouri Fur Company underwent extensive reorganization and turned its attention to the territory south of the Blackfeet range.

Astoria

The period after the War of 1812 was a new era for the Western fur trade, but before considering this phase of the subject, one more pre-war attempt to tap the fur riches of the New West should be considered. It was based on a vast and daring mercantile undertaking emanating from John Jacob Astor of New York, rated by many the "leading fur dealer in the United States." In 1808 the state of New York issued Astor a charter for the American Fur Company to engage in the New West fur trade by land and sea. Astor planned to establish a major post, Astoria, at the mouth of the Columbia River to collect furs from the coastal trade and inland stations. Traders of the Pacific mercantile fleet were to exchange furs from Astoria for silk, tea, and other items in Chinese ports, returning the Oriental cargoes to the Atlantic seaboard.

In 1810, Astor organized his Pacific Fur Company as a subsidiary of the American Fur Company; the company was to manage the West Coast trading transactions. He recruited a number of experienced fur men from Canada and the United States to organize and manage the Western enterprise at the mouth of the Columbia. Two expeditions were sent out —one by sea, the other by land. A supply ship carrying traders, goods, equipment, and supplies was to proceed to the mouth of the Columbia and construct the mother post, Astoria. A land expedition was to proceed from St. Louis via the Missouri River, cross the mountains to the Columbia, and follow that river to Astoria, opening the land route.

The maritime branch of the operation was launched from the Atlantic coast aboard the *Tonquin*, which arrived at the mouth of the Columbia during the spring of 1811. The trader complement erected Astoria as directed. The "Overland Astorians," with Wilson Price Hunt in charge, left St. Louis during March of 1811 by keelboat. Hunt's party reached the Arikara villages in June; there the Blackfeet menace at the Missouri's headwaters caused Hunt to change his itinerary. Leaving the river boats, he traded for horses, loaded the trade goods and expedition supplies and equipment on a pack train of eighty-two animals, and proceeded in a generally westerly direction, ascending the Wind River and crossing to the headwaters of the Snake River. There he directed his men to construct boats to take advantage of the westward-flowing current. Soon, however, periodic falls and rapids created such hazards to men and goods that Hunt directed resumption of land travel. Short of supplies and wearied from the long, frustrating march, the Overland Astorians divided into small survival parties and struck out across the southern Idaho desert. Most of them reached Astoria by January 1812. Their course of travel through Idaho and Oregon traced a route that in less than three decades would become the western segment of a grand transcontinental concourse—the Oregon Trail.

The Pacific Fur Company fanned out over the Columbia wilderness, erected trade stations convenient to local Indian tribes, and did some trapping in the Willamette region. During May of 1812, Astor's second supply ship arrived at the Columbia River outpost, and also in 1812, Robert Stuart led an overland party from Astoria to St. Louis. Stuart's route across the continental divide in southern Wyoming near South Pass and thence along the Sweetwater and Platte rivers became the eastern segment of the Oregon Trail.

News of the outbreak of the War of 1812 disturbed the Astorians, and in October of 1813 reports that a British naval squadron was proceeding to the mouth of the Columbia led local officials to sell Astoria and all Pacific Fur Company holdings to agents of the North West Company for $58,000. Soon after, the British warship *Raccoon* entered the Columbia. British officers took charge of Astoria and renamed it Fort George. For the time being, British fur men were pre-eminent in the Northwest.

THE BONANZA AGE OF THE NEW WEST FUR TRADE

The tempo of New West fur trading accelerated appreciably in the period following the War of 1812. Its most compelling characteristic was the fury and intensity of exploitation produced by the reckless, destructive competition among American and British companies. Each enterprise drove madly for its share of bonanza profits that ranged upwards from 50 percent. New companies and consolidated companies led to more intensive, efficient exploitation. During this period the strict Spanish control of the Southwest was replaced by a more favorable Mexican administration, opening the region to the fur men. Thus after 1821, fur men could roam freely over the New West from Missouri to the Pacific shore. In addition, this was the time of the rise of the rendezvous system, which led to the emergence of one of America's folk heroes—the Mountain Man.

Finally, during the period after 1815, the New West was thoroughly explored by agents of fur brigades in quest of new trapping grounds. They explored virgin regions, probing every nook and cranny of the New West landscape; their peregrinations added to the store of Western geographical knowledge of strategic mountain passes, desert crossings, and the most feasible and direct travel routes connecting the Mississippi Valley with the Pacific shore.

The Hudson's Bay Company

As American fur men prepared to resume operations in the New West after the war, they found several obstacles that threatened the success of their ventures. Probably the most important one was the ubiquitous British agent, who was in the employ of either the North West Company or the Hudson's Bay Company. The British purchase and conquest of Astoria during the War of 1812 had provided the Canadian-based companies with a strategic advantage for maintaining control of the fur industry west of the Rocky Mountains. In 1821, the British government required the Hudson's Bay Company and the North West Company to merge as the Hudson's Bay Company, ending the bitter intracompany strife and enabling the British to concentrate on winning the New West fur war. The consolidated Hudson's Bay Company functioned from Fort Vancouver, which was situated on the Columbia River near the mouth of the Willamette. John McLoughlin was appointed chief factor at Fort Vancouver, and under his direction, the Columbia River country was seeded with smaller trading posts. From these advance stations, British fur men ranged south into California and eastward into Utah and Wyoming.

As a tactic for discouraging the entry of American trappers into the heartland of the Northwest, McLoughlin instructed his men to create a buffer zone on a wide arc south and east of the Snake and Columbia river region; so completely trapped-out and devoid of fur-bearing animals would the area become that approaching American fur men would of necessity turn back. To consummate McLoughlin's scorched-earth buffer plan, Hudson's Bay Company agents trapped vigorously along the outer edges of a vast quadrant comprising the northwestern quarter of the present western United States.

In 1819, Donald McKenzie, one of the American Fur Company recruited from Canada for Astor's expedition who had returned to British service after the sale of Astoria, explored the Snake River valley and proceeded along Bear River and Bear Lake into northern Utah. He was the first European to collect furs in the upper interior basin country. Another British trader, Alexander Ross, extended British operations into Idaho, trapping and trading there on the tributaries of the Salmon River. Peter Skene Ogden, formerly of the North West Company and after the merger a Hudson's Bay Company agent, led a series of fur reconnaissances over the western United States. One expedition in 1825 followed the Bear River into Utah to the shore of the Great Salt Lake, only a year after its discovery by Jim Bridger. Bridger had come upon it while serving as a representative of the Rocky Mountain Fur Company. Ogden also traced out several tributaries of the Columbia River, and, in 1827, on a fur-hunting expedition that extended into central California, he reconnoitered a stream flowing eastward from the Sierras; he named it Mary's River. This became the famed Humboldt River—a principal travel artery for overland emigrants entering California in the 1840s.

Besides calculated, expansive British competition, American fur men faced the additional obstacle of a federal policy that tolerated foreign traders and trappers in United States territory and mantained an equally competitive federal factory system. As late as 1817, there were nineteen federal trading stations in operation; each one was publicly supported and supplied goods to Indian hunters at cost in exchange for furs and hides. However, the increasing political power of the independent fur companies in this period was demonstrated by their success in obtaining passage of legislation dealing with both the problem of the foreign fur traders in American territory and the competing factory system. In 1816, even before the admission of Missouri, Congress approved legislation excluding foreigners from the fur trade on American soil. In the 1820s Senator Thomas H. Benton of Missouri and Lewis Cass, government of Michigan Territory, were among the political leaders who worked for legislation favorable to the fur industry. In 1822, through the interest and work of Cass and Benton, the government factory system was abolished.

The Missouri Fur Company

For about twenty years after the conclusion of the War of 1812, three American companies dominated the fur trade west of St. Louis. The first was the Missouri Fur Company, founded in 1809 by Manuel Lisa, the Chouteaus, and William Clark. It quickly faltered in the face of Blackfeet enmity and retreated from the fur-rich Three Forks country of the Missouri River. After the disastrous trapping season of 1810, the company concentrated its operations on the safer but less productive territory between the Platte and Missouri rivers—outside of the Blackfeet range. The company underwent a number of reorganizations, and Joshua Pilcher eventually succeeded Lisa as head of this firm. By 1822, the company had 300 men in the field—some as traders dealing with Indian hunters for pelts, others functioning as trappers.

The Rocky Mountain Fur Company

The second fur enterprise operating in the New West during the postwar period was the Rocky Mountain Fur Company, founded at St. Louis in 1822 by William Ashley and Andrew Henry. The almost immediate success of this company was the result of the innovativeness of its founders and the galaxy of colorful, daring young captains—Jim Bridger, Jedediah Smith, Thomas Fitzpatrick, and James Beckwourth—Ashley recruited to lead the fur brigades throughout the New West wilderness.

Brigades of fur hunters were an invention of the Rocky Mountain Fur Company. Commanded by energetic young captains, they ranged over the country, each brigade working a territory that started on the eastern slope of the Rocky Mountains and extended west across the Great Basin to the shadow of the Sierras and beyond. Once the brigades were established in virgin beaver country, the men with their traps scattered to collect the pelts (or plews). The Rocky Mountain men did little trading, and spent most of their time taking the pelts themselves.

Each brigade member set his traps in creeks marked by beaver dams in water deep enough to drown the animal after the steel jaws of the trap closed on it. The bait was castorem, a secretion of the beaver's reproductive glands; it was liberally smeared over the tip of a wooden stake driven into the stream bed near the trap. The trapper often took an Indian wife, who helped him process the skins. Each fresh plew was stretched over a willow hoop to dry and cure. The processed beaver skins were packed in hundred-pound bundles for transport to market.

The Mountain Men

The market system developed by the Rocky Mountain Fur Company—the rendezvous—made it unnecessary for trappers to travel yearly to St. Louis or other posts to sell pelts and purchase supplies for another year's trapping. The rendezvous was an annual mobile market and fur fair that took place in a location convenient for the trappers. Many Rocky Mountain fur men remained in the wilderness for years, and the isolation marked them, producing a cultural reversion, metamorphosing them from moderately genteel Americans to proto-savages. Thus developed the image of Mountain Men—members of a subculture complete with modes of dress, behavior, values, and a language appropriate for their raw milieu and primitive lifestyle.

Although the British fur company agents were the shrewdest traders, the Mountain Men were rated "the best trappers in the wilderness beyond the rivers. These mountaineers were hard, robustly free from restraints, proud as lords." It was said that "no court or jury is called to adjudicate upon his disputes and abuses save his own conscience, and no powers are invoked to redress them save those with which the God of nature had endowed him." The Mountain Man traveled light—"the smaller his personal equipment, the greater the number of furs he could carry." [2] His equipage consisted of three horses (two used as pack animals), traps, knives, a hatchet, an iron pan or two, a coffee pot, a blanket or two, and rifle and ammunition. His supplies consisted of coffee, sugar and salt, tobacco, and whiskey. The favorite weapon of fur men was the Plains rifle or Hawken rifle, a shortened Kentucky rifle manufactured by Jacob Hawken of St. Louis.

Grizzled and clad in a worn and greasy buckskin suit, he was awesome in mien and language; his speech was described as a "medley of English, French, and Spanish, amazingly remote from grammar and beautifully profane." [3] He trapped beaver as soon as ice cleared from the snow-fed mountain streams in the spring; during the summer he prepared for the rendezvous, attended it, and spent the rest of the summer recovering from the dissipation he inflicted on his physical and nervous system at the

[2] Ibid., p. 303.
[3] Ibid., p. 304.

rendezvous. Returning to his traps in the autumn, he often ensconced himself and his Indian wife in a cozy mountain cabin for the winter.

The Rendezvous

The first Rocky Mountain Fur Company rendezvous, or fur fair, was held in 1824 on the Sweetwater River and was under the management of Thomas Fitzpatrick. Its success led Ashley to make this method of collecting furs an annual event. Henry's Fork was the site for the 1825 rendezvous. Rocky Mountain Fur Company agents loaded a great pack train of goods at St. Louis and marched overland via the Platte Trail to the prearranged site in the mountains. Of the fifteen annual fur trade fairs held between 1824 and 1838, Pierre's Hole, Ogden, and Green River were the most regularly used rendezvous sites. The goods-laden pack train reached the mountains in July, a slow time for trapping as pelts taken in the summer were not in prime condition because of the beaver's shedding season. The goods on the pack train met all the annual needs of the Mountain Men—sugar, salt, coffee, tobacco, blankets, guns, knives, traps, powder, shot, highly colored cloth and beads for the Indian wives, and much whiskey.

The rendezvous was a business occasion at which the Mountain Men exchanged their "hairy bank notes"—the beaver pelts or "plews"—for the necessities to support another year's trapping and for finery for their Indian wives. It was a social occasion too, for when the essentials were accomplished, the agents broke out the whiskey. An orgy of bacchanalian revelry followed—dancing, frolicking with Indian women, gambling, athletic contests—footraces and wrestling—and general debauchery. The appetites of Mountain Men who had been isolated and deprived of social contacts for a year inevitably led to the prodigal squandering of a collection of pelts worth a handsome sum. A year's earnings from desperate, dangerous, hellish-hard work were sometimes spent in a week-long abandoned spree.

Ashley prospered so much from the rendezvous trading system that by 1827 he retired, selling his interests in the company to a group of brigade captains that included Jedediah Smith. Three years later, Fitzpatrick, Bridger, and Milton Sublette were the principal managers of the Rocky Mountain Fur Company.

The American Fur Company

The third enterprise active in harvesting the New West fur resources during the industry's bonanza period was the American Fur Company. The irrepressible John Jacob Astor, undiscouraged by the failure of his grand Astorian plan, persisted in his determination to become pre-eminent in the Western fur trade. By 1817, Astor's American Fur Company dominated the industry in the territory south of the Great Lakes and extending to the Mississippi River. Five years later he established the Western Department of the American Fur Company at St. Louis. From this base, his agents methodically pushed up the Missouri River.

The fur-rich Three Forks country of the Missouri, still controlled by the Blackfeet, remained closed to American fur men until the 1820s. Hudson's Bay Company agents had achieved some success in trapping and trading with the Blackfeet, and Kenneth McKenzie, a Canadian, had formed the Columbia Fur Company to compete with the Hudson's Bay Company. In 1827, shrewd officials of Astor's American Fur Company purchased the Columbia Fur Company, keeping McKenzie as agent-in-charge in the Three Forks country. McKenzie then lured agents experienced in the Blackfeet trade away from Hudson's Bay Company. The following year, American Fur Company agents confidently erected Fort Union at the mouth of the Yellowstone. McKenzie's influence convinced Blackfeet hunters to trade their pelts at the new fort.

During 1831, American Fur Company agents built Fort McKenzie on the Marias River, in the center of the Blackfeet range. Company officials substituted a river steamer, the *Yellowstone*, for the slow keelboat used to supply the forts. Each year the *Yellowstone* ascended the Missouri to Fort Union with a cargo of trade goods and returned to St. Louis loaded with a prize catch. Company agents continued to use river steamers to supply their expanding grid of Northwest posts; in 1859 a company ship approached the head of navigation on the Missouri River, near the continental divide at Fort Benton.

Fur Brigade Explorations

Each of the fur companies, through the wide-ranging searches of their agents for virgin trapping and trading territories, contributed substantially to the knowledge of the geography of the New West. Rocky Mountain Fur Company brigade captains especially were skilled explorers. Their greatest scouts in this quest for new fur territory were Jim Bridger and Jedediah Smith.

In 1824, while on a trapping expedition in the Great Basin, Bridger found the Great Salt Lake. The same year, Smith rediscovered the South Pass, and, in 1826, he explored the western marches of the Great Basin, from the Salt Lake to the Colorado River. Smith followed the Colorado to the Mohave Desert, turned west across that forbidding wasteland to the Sierras, breached the mountains at Cajon Pass, and proceeded to the San Gabriel Mission in California. After a rest, he and his party moved north to the forks of the Stanislaus River, where they found rich beaver country. They collected a heavy cargo of pelts, but deep snow in the Sierras prevented them from reaching the Great Salt Lake. Thereupon, Smith left most of the party with the furs and set out with two companions. After enduring every conceivable hardship and privation, the three men arrived at the Great Salt Lake in June of 1827. A month later, Smith led a relief party to succor the men he had left in the Sierras. His column of eighteen trappers followed a now familiar route. At the Colorado crossing into the Mohave, they were attacked by a band of Mohave Indians. Ten of Smith's men died. Smith led the survivors across the Sierras into California, and in

September he was reunited with the men guarding the fur cache on the Stanislaus.

After various California adventures—including a stint in the San Jose jail from which he purchased his freedom by posting a large bond and pledging to leave California—Smith's fur column continued north, searching for a pass through the mountains. Finding none, they turned to the coast and followed it to the Umpqua River in Oregon. There Umpqua Indians plundered the camp, carried off the furs, and killed all the Americans except three, one of whom was Smith. Smith and the other survivors proceeded to the Columbia River. Hudson's Bay Company officials at Fort Vancouver interceded with the Umpquas, got the furs restored to Smith, then purchased them. Smith concluded his adventurous hazard-ridden peregrination through the Sierras by returning to the Rocky Mountain Fur Company rendezvous at Pierre's Hole. Jedediah Smith had blazed a route through the Sierras to the Pacific shore and explored the central valley of California and the rivers draining from the western slope of the Sierras. His crude maps and journals corroborated these explorations and transformed much of the New West wilderness from the unknown to the known.

Another important Western reconnaissance grew out of the attempt of Captain Benjamin L. E. Bonneville to establish a fur trade enterprise in the West. Bonneville, a captain in the United States army, went on furlough in 1832 and, backed by Eastern investors, engaged a party of trappers and established a support post near the headwaters of the Green River. Competition from established British and American companies was so intense that Bonneville's men were forced to trap over an ever-widening range. In 1833, Joseph R. Walker led a party of Bonneville trappers from the Green River post across the western portion of the Great Basin. In Nevada, Walker traced Peter Skene Ogden's discovery, the Mary's River (renamed the Humboldt), to Walker's Lake; he crossed the Sierras at Walker's Pass and entered California's San Joaquin Valley.

Bonneville's trappers suffered great hardship in the furnace-heat of the Nevada desert and the intense cold of the high Sierras. As provisions were depleted, men subsisted on the carcasses of pack horses weakened from lack of forage. They rested at Monterery, replenished their supplies, and returned to Bonneville's post on the Green River, retracing the route they had blazed to the Pacific. From the trapper's viewpoint the expedition was a failure, but it was a success in terms of exploration. Walker had found a direct route to California, the trapper trail that became the great Humboldt concourse.

THE FUR TRADER'S LAST FRONTIER

The Southwest was the first fur region in the trans-Missouri territory to receive intensive American attention. Nonetheless, after a prosperous beginning, based mostly on the commerce with the Osages at the Three Forks of the Arkansas River, the industry languished. By 1820, saturation hunting had plundered the fur resources of the region between Fort Smith and the 100th meridian—the western boundary of the United States in that sector. The boundary was a firm barrier to the extension of the American fur trade in the Southwest, for west of the meridian was Spanish territory, off-limits by force of stern law, to Americans. The interior line of demarcation separating American and Spanish territory extended north along this meridian to the Arkansas River and then west along that stream to its source in the Rocky Mountains.

In spite of Spanish prohibitions, American traders and trappers persisted in risking arrest, confiscation of property, and prison at Santa Fe or Chihuahua. The most attractive fur region in the forbidden zone was south of the headwaters of the Arkansas River in Colorado. There Pike had met two American trappers during his reconnaissance of the southern Rocky Mountains in 1807. Beginning in 1815, Auguste P. Chouteau and Jules de Munn regularly led parties of trappers from St. Louis into this fur-rich region. Both Chouteau and de Munn were discovered by a Spanish patrol in 1817 and taken to Santa Fe. Officials there confiscated their furs —valued at $30,000—and held the Missourians in jail for nearly two months before expelling them from Spanish territory.

Three Forks of the Arkansas

When Mexico achieved independence from Spain in 1821, that young nation succeeded to Spanish dominion over Texas, New Mexico, Arizona, and California. The Mexican government relaxed the stern commercial prohibitions, and Americans quickly entered these northern Mexican provinces to trade, mine, trap, and carry on other business. Both Mexican national law and provincial law regulated the activities of foreigners, but the law and its enforcement changed frequently, due to the instability of the Mexican national government and the ambivalence of the provincial administrators. Notwithstanding the uncertainty of their status, Americans in the fur trade and other commercial activities in the Mexican Southwest generally prospered. After 1821, the fur trade frontier encompassed a vast territory south of the Arkansas, extending from Fort Smith to the Pacific. The pace of activity in the trading settlements at Three Forks of the Arkansas quickened, and these tiny frontier towns became supply centers for the support of trapping and trading expeditions bound for the Southern Plains and Rocky Mountains. Goods for the Three Forks depots were moved by keelboat, and later river steamers, from St. Louis down the Mississippi and up the Arkansas to the mouth of the Grand and the Verdigris rivers. Trading stations dependent on the Three Forks depots included a chain of Chouteau posts extending from the mid-Canadian River to the Wichita Mountains, Edwards' post on the Canadian at the mouth of Little River, and Coffee's post on Red River.

Jesse Chisholm, a man of mixed Cherokee background, established a trading post on the edge of the Cross Timbers at Council Grove. He carried on a prosperous traffic with the Comanches, negotiating for buffalo robes and plunder swept up in their raids on the Texas and north Mexican settlements. Sometimes the trade included white captives, which Chisholm turned over to United States Army officers at Fort Smith and Fort Gibson; each restored captive brought Chisholm $250.

Rocky Mountain-bound trapping and trading ventures outfitted at the Three Forks depots during 1821 included the Hugh Glenn–Nathaniel Pryor expedition and the Thomas James expedition. Both groups prospered economically from their Western adventures, and both produced a published journal of experiences. The Glenn-Pryor group consisted of twenty men; one of them was Jacob Fowler, a surveyor from Kentucky, and author of the expedition journal. While working the beaver streams of southern Colorado, the trappers came upon a huge grizzly bear. Fowler's journal, cast in raw frontier style, depicted the drama and the tragedy of this wilderness encounter:

> While some ware hunting and others cooking some picking grapes a gun was fyered off and the cry of a White Bare [grizzly] was raised. We ware all armed in an instent and each man run his own cors to look for the desperet anemel. . . . Coln Glann [Colonel Glenn] with four others atemted to run but the bare being in their way and lay close in the brush undiscovered till the [y] ware within a few feet of it. When it sprang up and caught Lewis doson [Dawson] and pulled him down in an instent. Coln Glanns gun mised fyer or he would have releved the man. But a large slut [Pryor's dog] which belongs to the party atacted the bare with such fury that it left the man and persued her a few steps in which time the man got up and run a few steps but was overtaken by the bare. When the Coln maid a second attempt to shoot but his gun mised fyer again and the slut as before releved the man who run as before but as was son again in the grasp of the bare who seemed intent on his distruction. The coln again run close up and as before his gun would not go off the slut makeing an other atack and releveing the man. The coln now be came alarmed lest the bare wold pursue him and run up. . . . tree and after him the wounded men and was followed by the bare and thus the [y] ware all three up one tree. But a tree standing in rich [reach] the coln steped on that and let the man and bare pas till the bare caught him [Dawson] by one leg and drew him back wards down the tree. While this was doing the Coln sharpened his flint primed his gun and shot the bare down while pulling the man by the leg be fore any of one of the party arived to releve him. But the bare soon rose again but was shot by several other [men] wo head [who had] got up to the place of action. [Dawson's] wounds were examined. It appears his head was in the bares mouth at least twice and that when the monster give the crush that was to mash the mans head it being two large for the span of his mouth the head sliped out only the teeth cutting the skin to

the bone where ever they tuched it, so that the skin of the head was cut from about the ears to the top in several directions. All of which wounds ware sewed up as well as cold be don by men in our situation haveing no surgen nor surgical instruments. The man still retained his understanding but said I am killed, that I heard my skull brake. But we ware willing to beleve that he was mistaken as he spoke chearfully on the subgect till in the after noon of the second day when he began to be restless and some what delerous and on examening an hole in the upper part of his wright temple which we beleved only skin deep we found the brains workeing out. We then sposed that he did hear his scull brake. He lived till a little before day on the third day after being wounded, all which time we lay at camp and buried him as well as our meens would admit.[4]

The James party was made up of eleven men. On the way to the Rio Grande in 1821, they paused on the Canadian River to trade with a Comanche band. The Comanches encouraged James to return to the Plains the following year, which he did. On this second venture, James stated in his journal that he was able to trade far more packs of pelts and buffalo robes than he could carry home. A plug of tobacco, a knife, and a few strings of beads, "in all worth but little more than a dime," bought a buffalo robe, "worth at least five dollars in any of the states." [5]

The Taos Trappers

Soon after 1821, Taos eclipsed St. Louis and the trading settlements at the Three Forks of the Arkansas as the center for the Southwest fur trade. Trade goods and trappers' needs were collected there from the growing overland commerce between the western Missouri towns and Santa Fe. Mills at Taos processed local grain into flour and meal, which became a prime item to trade with the Indians for furs. In addition, distilleries at Taos produced a powerful intoxicant called "Taos lightning." Needless to say, it also was a popular fur trade item. Taos became a favorite winter resort for the Mountain Men, and every spring over 200 American trappers spread out from Taos in all directions in quest of furs. They traveled east to the Pecos, north to the headwaters of the Rio Grande, northwest into the Great Basin on the upper waters of the Colorado and Green, and south and west to the Gila and Colorado.

Changing laws and local ordinances regulating the activities of the growing Anglo community in Mexico's northern provinces included a requirement that alien trappers employ Mexican citizens as apprentices as a condition of being issued a license to take furs. By the 1830s, Mexican fur brigades ranged the southern Rocky Mountains and competed with the Anglo fur men. When a new law in 1824 limited trapping licenses to

[4] *The Journal of Jacob Fowler*, Elliott Coues, ed. (New York, 1898), pp. 41–44.
[5] Thomas James, *Three Years Among the Indians and Mexicans*, Walter B. Douglas, ed. (St. Louis, 1916), p. 217.

Mexican citizens, several Anglo trappers became Mexican citizens. Their status as citizens exempted them from taxes and other restrictive measures imposed on outsiders doing business in the Mexican provinces. James Baird of Missouri, famous for his trapping excursions into northern Arizona, was among those who took Mexican citizenship. Many other Anglos evaded or ignored the law and continued to take furs in Mexican territory without a license.

The most prominent fur men in the Southwest were William Becknell, Antoine Robidoux, Ewing Young, Céran St. Vrain, William Wolfskill, George Yount, Bill Williams, and Sylvester and James Ohio Pattie. Becknell and Robidoux trapped on the Rocky Mountains' western slope, ranging over the country drained by the upper waters of the Green and Colorado rivers. Robidoux established trading posts on the Gunnison River in Colorado and the Uinta River in Utah. Young was best known for his fur excursion of 1829, which began at Taos and ended in the San Joaquin Valley of California. Kit Carson was a member of Young's party. St. Vrain trapped in the creeks above Taos in the southern Rocky Mountains and was a co-founder of Bent's Fort on the Arkansas River. Wolfskill and Yount, after a number of successful trapping seasons in the San Juan country, in 1830 led a party of trappers on a search for new beaver grounds. They followed approximately the "Old Spanish Trail" between Santa Fe and Los Angeles; the trail swings in an extended arc across southern Colorado and skirts the Grand Canyon before dipping to the Nevada desert and the Sierra crossing into coastal California. Williams explored much of northern Arizona in his annual search for furs from his home base at Taos.

The most widely traveled of the Southwest fur men were Sylvester Pattie and his son James Ohio Pattie. They entered the fur business in 1823. After traveling some distance up the Missouri River, they turned southwesterly and proceeded to Santa Fe, where for a time they engaged in trapping, mining, and other enterprises. In 1826 James Pattie went in search of beaver along the Gila. Turning north on the Colorado, he followed that stream to the Grand Canyon, traversed a wide circuit across the Great Basin, and continued to the upper Missouri, stopping on the Big Horn and Yellowstone rivers before returning to Santa Fe. The following year he returned to the Gila with his father. They trapped beaver on that stream and, near its mouth, cached their furs. They then followed the Colorado River into the Gulf of California. The Patties stopped at the Santa Catalina Mission in Lower California, were arrested by Mexican officials for unlawful entry, and taken to San Diego prison. Sylvester Pattie died there, but the younger Pattie survived his imprisonment, was eventually released, and traveled to San Francisco before returning to the United States.

During 1831, he published an account of his Western odyssey under the title *Personal Narrative*. Moreover, the Pattie travels over the Southwest yielded a new direct transcontinental route from Missouri to Santa

Fe, down the Rio Grande to Albuquerque, west to Santa Rita, thence along the Gila to the Colorado River crossing to California. This line of travel became a thoroughfare for American trappers, traders, military expeditions, an overland mail and stage route, and a road for immigrants bound for California.

By the mid-1830s, substantive changes were occurring in the world fur market. The demand for beaver, the most prized pelt of the bonanza age of the New West fur industry, waned as manufacturers substituted silk and other materials in hatmaking—the principal use of the beaver skin. In addition, intense exploitation of the New West fur resources had drastically depleted the region's animal population, so that each year after 1835 the annual pelt harvest declined. The fur industry continued, but at a drastically reduced pace, and the buffalo robe replaced the beaver pelt as the premier item in the Western fur trade. In 1846, the American Fur Company marketed 67,000 buffalo robes. Eight years later, an estimated 250,000 buffalo were slaughtered to meet the demands of the expanding robe industry. By 1840 the colorful wilderness rendezvous or fur fair had been replaced by trading posts situated at points convenient to the remaining trappers and hide hunters. The New West fur and hide markets included Fort Hall on the Snake River, Fort Laramie on the Platte River, and Bent's Fort on the Arkansas near the mouth of the Purgatory River.

The legacy of the fur trade frontier was a colorful one, replete with daring and paradox. The irascible Mountain Men set a pattern for merciless exploitation of the region's natural bounty that was to be emulated by mining, lumbering, agriculture, and other Western industries. In less than fifty years, the fur men had plundered the New West wilderness of its pelt riches with a vengeance. Wide-ranging fur brigades had opened the New West to succeeding types of frontiers. They had seeded the New West with American presence, particularly in contested territories, and as inventive entrepreneurs they served as the vanguard force of the American thrust to the Pacific.

Americans also engaged in the fur trade on the Pacific Coast, from Alaska to Lower California, where luxuriant sea otter pelts were the principal quest. This traffic was an important part of the ever-broadening commercial development in the Pacific Basin—the maritime traders' frontier.

SELECTED SOURCES

General works depicting the exploitation of New West fur resources include Paul C. Phillips and J. W. Smurr, *The Fur Trade* (Norman, 1961), 2 vols.; Hiram M. Chittenden, *The American Fur Trade of the Far West* (New York, 1935), 3 vols.; Ora B. Peake, *A History of the United States Indian Factory*

System, 1795–1822 (Denver, 1954); *Bernard De Voto, Across the Wide Missouri (Cambridge, 1947); and Frederick J. Merk, Fur Trade and Empire (Cambridge, Mass., 1931).

British activity in the New West fur trade is the subject of Marjorie W. Campbell, The North West Company (New York, 1957); John S. Galbraith, The Hudson's Bay Company As an Imperial Factor, 1821–1869 (Berkeley, 1957); and Edwin E. Rich, The History of the Hudson's Bay Company, 1670–1870 (London, 1958), 2 vols.

Extension of the American fur trade into the Northwest is treated in Richard E. Oglesby, Manuel Lisa and the Opening of the Missouri Fur Trade (Norman, 1963); John E. Sunder, The Fur Trade of the Upper Missouri, 1840–1965 (Norman, 1965); Kenneth W. Porter, John Jacob Astor: Business Man (Cambridge, 1931), 2 vols.; and Don Berry, A Majority of Scoundrels: History of the Rocky Mountain Fur Company (New York, 1961).

The fur trade in the Southwest is detailed in Robert G. Cleland, This Reckless Breed of Men: The Trappers and Fur Traders of the Southwest (New York, 1952); David J. Weber, The Taos Trappers: The Fur Trade in the Far Southwest, 1540–1842 (Norman, 1971); LeRoy R. Hafen and Anne W. Hafen, The Old Spanish Trail (Glendale, 1954); Thomas James, Three Years Among the Mexicans and Indians, Walter B. Douglas, ed. (St. Louis, 1916); Elliott Coues, ed., The Journal of Jacob Fowler (New York, 1898); and Grant Foreman, Pioneer Days in the Early Southwest (Cleveland, 1926).

The Mountain Men have been popular subjects for study. Among the works on these exiles from Anglo-American society are Stanley Vestal, Mountain Men (Boston, 1937); LeRoy R. Hafen, ed., Mountain Men and the Fur Trade of the Far West (Glendale, 1965–71), 10 vols.; A. H. Favor, Old Bill Williams (Norman, 1962); J. Cecil Alter, Jim Bridger (Columbus, 1951); Carl P. Russell, Firearms, Traps and Tools of the Mountain Men (New York, 1967); and M. Morgan Estergreen, Kit Carson: A Portrait in Courage (Norman, 1962).

Fur men were the pioneers in the Western wilderness. Their search for new pelt zones generated considerable geographic knowledge, including maps. The exploratory aspects of their travels are traced in *Gloria G. Cline, Exploring the Great Basin (Norman, 1963); C. A. Vandiveer, The Fur Trade and Early Western Exploration (Cleveland, 1929); and *Dale L. Morgan, Jedediah Smith and the Opening of the West (Indianapolis, 1953).

* Available in paperback.

"Farewell to a Friendly Indian" by Frederic Remington.

Arrival of the Caravan at Santa Fe.
From *Commerce of the Prairies* by Josiah Gregg, 1844.

16

New West Pioneer Enterprises: Commerce by Land and Sea

Even before the opening of the nineteenth century, land and maritime traders had joined fur men in seeding the New West with American presence. Expansion of the commerce frontier, by land and sea, was a vital antecedent to the American occupation and absorption of the Western territories. The process that began with a few ships, some trading stations, and quantities of trade goods culminated in the extension of national dominion over large portions of the New West. The maxim that the flag follows commerce applied in a very real sense to the Southwest, the Pacific coastal areas, Hawaii, and Alaska. Both land-based and maritime traders introduced American goods and customs and American presence into these territories at a time when they were owned or claimed by competing nations. By word of mouth, by letters, and by published writings they shared their observations, experiences, and keen interest in the new trade areas; and their enthusiastic reports provoked widespread private and public interest in the new lands.

MARITIME COMMERCE

The maritime traders made a contribution to the American territorial advance in the New West equal to that of the fur men and land-based traders. They also opened distant new trade frontiers—in Alaska, in Hawaii, and in China—and established enduring American commercial and territorial interests in all of these remote regions.

Pioneers of the Pacific Basin

American maritime activity in the Pacific began in 1784 when Robert Morris and several associates sent the *Empress of China* from New York to Canton, via the Cape of Good Hope and Indian Ocean passage, with a cargo of ginseng. Ginseng, a root that grows wild in New England, was used as a curative by Oriental physicians. The return of the *Empress* in 1785, with a cargo of silk and tea, indicated the trade potential of Far Eastern markets. The problem for American maritime traders was to find items the Chinese would trade. Unbeknownst to the Americans, the problem was in the process of being solved, through the discoveries of Captain James Cook, the premier British navigator. In 1776 the British Royal Society commissioned Cook to survey systematically the Pacific coast of North America. It was hoped that he would find a water passage, a trade route to "bring the wealth of China and the Orient" closer to England. Parliament even offered a prize of 20,000 pounds to the discoverer of such a passage. Cook took two ships, the *Resolution* and the *Discovery*, for this venture.

Significantly, Cook's crew included a young corporal of Marines, John Ledyard of Connecticut. In 1778, Cook discovered the Hawaiian archipelago and named it the Sandwich Islands; then he inspected and mapped the Pacific coast of America without finding the water strait. The slow task of charting the many bays and inlets of the North American Pacific coastline permitted his crew much time ashore. In trading with the natives they obtained several sea otter pelts, soft brown-black skins that the aborigines fashioned into clothing. Cook's men made them into coverlets for warmth on the North Pacific cruise.

Cook returned to the Sandwich Islands to refit his ships and rest his crews. During 1779, James Cook and several crewmen were slain in a brush with the Hawaiians. The survivors sailed the vessels to Canton before returning to England. There they found the Chinese ecstatic over their coverlets of sea otter pelts. Most of the seamen took apart their coverlets and traded the individual pelts to the Chinese for an average of $120 apiece.

Making his way home to Connecticut, the perceptive Ledyard attempted to interest American businessmen in financing a trading expedition to the Pacific to take on cargoes of sea otter pelts and carry them to Canton. He described the sea otter as a creature three to four feet long with "beautiful shimmering fur" that inhabited the Pacific shore along a 6,000-mile range from the Aleutians to Lower California. The sea otters fed on shellfish under cover of thick kelp beds that floated near shore. He told Morris and other financiers that Aleut and Indian hunters searched for the sea otter in swift-moving bidarkas—small craft covered with sealskin and divided into two compartments. The steersman occupied the stern compartment and propelled the light, very maneuverable boat with a double-bladed paddle. The hunter sat in the forward cockpit. His weapon was a harpoon tipped with bone or iron and fitted with a strong sinew line.

Ledyard also reported on his visits to the Russian settlements in the North Pacific. Russian traders employed the native Aleuts to hunt the sea otter; then agents carried the pelts across the Aleutian Islands into Siberia and traded some to Chinese merchants from Peking. The remainder of each year's catch was delivered to markets in the cities of central Russia.

Ledyard's reports and the desire of American maritime interests to expand the trade with China finally bore fruit. In 1787, Boston shipping interests sent Robert Gray and Benjamin Kendrick in the *Columbia* and the *Washington* to gather sea otter skin and proceed to China. The Gray-Kendrick expedition sailed around Cape Horn into the Pacific and proceeded to the Oregon coast; it remained out of home port for nearly three years. When Gray's crew had filled the *Columbia's* holds with sea otter skins, he left Kendrick and the *Washington* on the Oregon coast and proceeded to the Sandwich Islands, took on fresh water and provisions, and set the *Columbia's* course toward the China coast, 5,600 miles to the west. In Canton Gray found a ready market and purchased a return cargo of silk and tea. Thereupon, he turned down the South China Sea, crossed the Indian Ocean, rounded the Cape of Good Hope into the Atlantic, and sailed into Boston.

Besides making a comfortable profit for himself and his patrons, Gray could claim several firsts: he was the first American trader to exploit the Pacific coast sea otter commerce; the first American ship captain to reach Hawaii; and the first American to circle the globe.

On his second trading venture to the waters of the Pacific Northwest in 1792, Gray discovered the Columbia River. His pioneering success attracted other American maritime traders to the Northwest Pacific coast. The newcomers followed the pattern set by Gray, entering the Pacific by the furious waters of Cape Horn, trading with the natives along the Northwest Pacific coast for sea otter pelts, and stopping in Hawaii for provisions en route to Canton.

Sea Otter Trade

American ships participating in the sea otter trade—most of them from New England ports—ranged in size from 100 to 250 tons. Of course, Spanish California ports of San Francisco, Monterey, and San Diego were closed to alien vessels. The stern mercantilist sanctions in force in the Spanish province of New Mexico also applied in California. In the early years of American maritime commerce, Yankee sea captains only occasionally put into Spanish California ports, and then only for very brief stops to appeal for water and wood supplies.

At times Spanish officials at San Diego and other California ports responded favorably, at other times they adamantly refused. Therefore, since American trading ships working the Pacific often were out of home port for two or three years, they customarily coasted the Northwest Pacific littoral, trading with native hunters for sea otter pelts during the spring, summer, and early autumn. Hunting slowed during the winter, and increasingly the maritime traders came to sail their ships to the Hawaiian Islands and winter in the sparkling, protected anchorage at Honolulu. The next spring they would return to the Pacific Northwest coast to continue accumulating sea otter pelts until a full cargo had been obtained.

The Sandwich Islands Establishment

One result of the practice of wintering in the Sandwich Islands was that American traders in Hawaii soon found a local plant, sandalwood, that became an important addition to their cargoes for the Canton trade. Sandalwood grew wild on the islands, and crewmen would cut the wood into short lengths and store it in bundles for transport to China. Chinese craftsmen esteemed sandalwood for carving chests, tables, and ornamental pieces. They also burned this aromatic wood as incense.

By 1820, several New England-based trading companies had established branch offices in Honolulu, each with an agent in charge. The agents received the sea otter pelts, cured and packed in casks, from the trading ships working the Pacific Northwest coast. They stowed them in warehouses near the port of Honolulu. In addition, they supervised the collection and storage of sandalwood. Increasingly, the ships took on specialized missions. Some were involved in the coastal trade, delivering their cargoes of sea otter pelts to Honolulu warehouses. Other vessels were used almost exclusively for carrying the pelts and sandalwood from Honolulu to Canton.

Each year after 1790 the sea otter commerce attracted a greater number of traders. The expanding American, British, French, and Russian trader demand for pelts led to saturation hunting by the natives, and the sea otter was annihilated in much of its Northwest Pacific range.

Eventually sea otter pelts stabilized in the Canton market at twenty to twenty-five dollars each. Pelts and sandalwood were exchanged for silk, tea, spices, porcelain, and exquisite carvings of jade and ivory. The Oriental goods were carried to American ports on the Atlantic seaboard, and were a source of great wealth for many New England families. Profits from the maritime trade often ran as high as 300 percent.

American Traders in the North Pacific

For the more efficient conduct of their business, American maritime traders introduced shipbuilding into the Northwest Pacific wilderness. Ships were frequently away from home port for two to three years, and often severely damaged in the rough North Pacific waters. Hulls were jammed by thick ice floes and, if the ships ventured too near the coastline, they were battered on rocky shoals. Crews regularly pulled their ships onto shore at low tide, turned the vessels on the side, repaired the hulls, and scraped them free of barnacles. They refitted the ships, too, replacing storm-damaged masts with new ones shaped from tall fir and spruce trees cut from the dense forests along the shore.

Many trading captains had their crews construct small coastal vessels of up to forty tons. Ships' carpenters erected miniature shipyards on the beach and supervised crewmen in the cutting of beams and planks. The smaller vessels could more easily negotiate the many shallow inlets and bays to reach the native hunters waiting on the beach to trade their sea otter pelts. The smaller craft returned frequently to the parent ship to disgorge the accumulated pelts and to take on a fresh supply of cloth, guns, knives, trinkets, and other items esteemed by the native hunters.

To maintain their dominant position against increasing foreign competition, around 1800 American traders began a limited cooperation with the Russian establishment in Alaska. Russian traders had been active in the North Pacific since the exploration of that region for Russia by Vitus Bering in the 1740s. In the late eighteenth century independent Russian traders with Aleut hunters had worked across the Aleutian chain thence to the islands off the Alaskan coast, but the scale of their operations was small. In 1796, however, the Russian imperial government issued a charter forming the Russian American Company. Thereafter, with integrated control and monopoly management, the Russians became a threatening competitor in the North Pacific.

Initially the Russian company was short on shipping and American traders contracted to buy the major portion of the company's furs. American traders also leased a large number of Aleut hunters from the Russian American Company each year. The Aleuts, the most skilled hunters in the Pacific Northwest, were taken on board in groups of forty to fifty, with their bidarkas and their gear. The Yankee captains carried them south to the waters off the coast of Lower California, where they were ashore to work the sea otter grounds. The mild climate of the more southerly latitudes enabled the Aleuts to hunt throughout the year, and their intensive harvest of pelts soon exterminated the sea otter population of the Lower California coast.

By 1812, the Russian American Company ceased to cooperate with American traders. By then the company had its own ships to carry the furs. That same year the Russian company established a large settlement of traders and Aleut hunters on the California coast north of San Francisco near Bodega Bay. It was named Fort Ross (Russ). Thereafter company officials retained the Aleut hunters for their own use.

American Traders in California

The diminishing fur range forced American traders to turn to the Spaniards, for the richest untouched sea otter territory was off the long coast of California between San Francisco and San Diego. Spain's prohibitive mercantilist policy made open trade impossible; however, the Spanish Californians were poorly supplied by the Spanish monopoly system of even the essentials of cloth and metal goods. They were therefore vulnerable to subversion by the American traders, who found a way to resolve the Californians' dilemma. Many of the California Indians were protégés of the mission system, which was controlled by the *padres*. Traders won over many of the priests by agreeing to supply the missions with essential goods in return for sea otter pelts. Mission Indians were then instructed in the methods of taking and curing sea otter pelts. Threat of interference by officials often was quieted by bribes, for Spanish officials in California were more amenable to collusion than their tougher counterparts in the New Mexican province. And so the sea otter trade continued.

Another method of dubious legality, the smuggler's art, was applied by Captain William Heath Davis of Boston in 1818. He anchored his ship, the *Eagle*, off Ortego Rancho near Santa Barbara and discussed terms with local officials. They agreed to permit him to do business in return for payment of 12½ percent of the value of the goods he proposed to land.

> Word was sent throughout the countryside that the American ship had arrived. People poured into the Ortega Rancho in creaky ox carts and on spirited California-bred horses. The place rapidly took on the air of a fiesta. Families settled in the meadow beside the stream and staked out camping spots. A large fire pit was dug by Ortega's Indian laborers. A cow was slaughtered and roasted whole on the spit. The smugglers' goods were placed on display in a thatched roof house nearby after having been brought ashore in whale boats and carried on the backs of Indians to the rancho. The place buzzed with conversation as people that saw each other only at weddings and funerals caught up on the happenings since the last event. At night a *fandango* or dance was arranged which lasted until sunrise. When the festivities broke up several days later Captain Davis was more than a thousand dollars richer in cash, and sea otter skins, also in beef and flour for the ship's food locker.[1]

Soon after 1820, the sea otter resources of the Western coast of North America had become so depleted that the rich trade died out. However, American maritime traders continued a profitable commerce with California, which, after 1822 was a frontier province of the new nation of Mexico, its ports open to trade. Vast herds of cattle on California ranches yielded hides and tallow that the traders carried to New England—the hides for a growing boot and shoe industry, the tallow for candle manufacture. American whalers entered the Pacific and used the California ports, as well as Hawaii, for refitting vessels, resting crews, and replenishing provisions. The whaler captains usually carried stores of trade goods, which they peddled in the California port settlements.

American sea traders did indeed confirm the maxim—the flag follows commerce. They first established enduring American presence and interest, private and public, along the California and Oregon coasts, north to Alaska, and west to Hawaii. Within fifty years, California and Oregon had been incorporated into the American Union; and before the nineteenth century closed, Alaska and Hawaii had been absorbed as American territory, to become states half a century later. Furthermore, the extension of the

---

[1] Robert K. Buell, *Sea Otters and the China Trade* (New York, 1968), p. 185.

maritime frontier to China created a continuing commercial interest in the Far East and enduring diplomatic and military commitments that have lasted to the present.

OVERLAND COMMERCE

We have described in earlier chapters how, from the earliest days of the Louisiana Purchase, frontier merchants at St. Louis, Arkansas Post, and Natchitoches had attempted to establish commercial relations with the Spanish-American towns in the Southwest. Their efforts were in vain for Spanish officials applied a stern mercantilist policy to New Mexico, excluding foreign traders and alien goods. The daring Americans who defied the commercial ban usually suffered arrest, confiscation of goods, and prison in Chihuahua.

William McKnight of St. Louis was one trader who attempted to enter Santa Fe and trade in 1811. He remained in a Chihuahua prison cell until 1821. Still, the northern Spanish settlements were poorly and irregularly supplied, for Mexico City was 1,500 miles distant. There was a great scarcity of many essential goods in the settlements of New Mexico, particularly cotton textiles and hardware. The journal of Zebulon M. Pike, published in 1810, recounted his 1807 tour of the Rio Grande settlements while under Spanish arrest. It told of the "scarcity of merchandise in New Mexico" and predicted that a "profitable border trade" was possible.

Beginnings of the Santa Fe Trail

Overland commerce with New Mexico did begin in 1821. In that year, William Becknell, a Missouri trader, was moving a pack train of goods from Franklin, Missouri, to trade with the Indian tribes of the southern Rocky Mountains. A Spanish-American military patrol from Las Vegas intercepted Becknell and informed him that Mexico had won its independence from Spain and trade was now permitted in New Mexico. Thereupon, Becknell turned toward the Rio Grande. In moving his pack train over the tortuous Raton Pass, his men had to labor for two days shifting heavy boulders to open a narrow trace for the goods-laden animals. The column proceeded to San Miguel and thence to Santa Fe. At the same time, two other trading parties were in the vicinity, also intent on trafficking with the Indians of the southern Rocky Mountains. One, headed by Thomas James from St. Louis, had moved by keelboat down the Mississippi and up the Arkansas River to the mouth of the Verdigris near Three Forks. There James obtained horses, formed a pack train, and marched across the Plains, roughly following the Canadian Valley route. A third party, also with a pack train of goods, led by Hugh Glenn and Jacob Fowler, had formed at Three Forks of the Arkansas River. The James and Glenn-Fowler parties also learned the tidings of the change in Mexican administration and proceeded to the Rio Grande.

The American traders were well received and found an enthusiastic market for their goods. Santa Fe, the principal Spanish-American settlement on the Rio Grande, had a population of about 2,000 and was a town of low-lying adobe buildings and dwellings. Situated about twelve miles from the Rio Grande River on a clear, rushing creek, the future center for Anglo-American commerce in the Southwest nestled at the foot of the commanding Sangre de Cristo Mountains. The town's focus was the plaza, an open quadrangle flanked by public buildings, principal of which was the governor's palace. Americans found that the New Mexicans had several attractive items to exchange for their trade goods: some quantity of gold and silver drawn from nearby mines; abundant wool processed into heavy blankets; leather goods; furs and buffalo robes; and abundant livestock, including mules.

Traders returning to the Mississippi Valley settlements carrying bags of silver representing fivefold profits on goods carried west and assurances of more trade, stirred great interest and marked the beginning of an expanding international commercial relationship that lasted until the 1840s. Soon two great trade thoroughfares, one beginning in western Missouri, the other from the settlements around Fort Smith in Arkansas Territory, converged on Santa Fe. Both trade concourses were called the Santa Fe Trail, but the designation appropriately belongs to only the northern route, as more than three-fourths of the trade flowed over it.

River steamers carried trade goods—primarily cotton textiles, glass, hardware, tools, and cutlery—from Pittsburgh and New Orleans to the Santa Fe entrepôts. St. Louis was succeeded by Franklin as the principal depot in Missouri. When a flood on the Missouri River in 1827 erased Franklin, the depot was moved to Independence on the western border of Missouri. The principal southern depots for the trade flow west of the Arkansas Territory settlements were Van Buren and nearby Fort Smith. A minor depot grew up at Three Forks on the Arkansas River above Fort Smith in the Indian Territory. Independence and the nearby town of Westport were the premier outfitting stations for the Santa Fe trade.

Highways to the Rio Grande

The northern route to Santa Fe coursed from Independence southwesterly to Council Grove on the Neosho River, then south to the Arkansas River and along that stream to the western limits of the United States. At the great bend of the Arkansas River, the trail forked. One branch ran west to Bent's Fork near the mouth of Purgatory River. At that point, the trading caravans crossed the mountains through Raton Pass to Las Vegas and into Santa Fe. A second branch of the Santa Fe Trail was blazed in 1822 by Becknell as he led a second trading expedition to Santa Fe. This time he carried his goods in three wagons guarded by twenty-one men. Near the great bend of the Arkansas River he turned south and crossed the Cimarron Desert—a forbidding arid expanse sixty miles wide—then turned west on the Cimarron River to Santa Fe. The Cimarron Desert route was a hazardous one, for there was no water for teams and drivers between the Arkansas and Cimarron rivers and it crossed the domain of the fierce Kiowas and Comanches. In 1831 the eminent explorer and fur man Jedediah Smith was slain by a Comanche war party while making the Cimarron Desert crossing. However, the advantage of the Cimarron route was in its savings of forty-eight days on a round-trip passage. It was also vastly superior to the Raton Pass route for the wagons that came to be used almost exclusively in carrying trade goods to the Rio Grande.

The southerly passage to Santa Fe ran west to Fort Smith on the Arkansas River to the Canadian and along the drainage ridge of that stream into New Mexico. Freight wagons also were used almost exclusively on the Fort Smith to Santa Fe route.

Nature of the Overland Commerce

During the spring, traders purchased "dry goods and notions"—bolts of cotton cloth, hardware, tools, cutlery, glass, and clothing—and carefully packed these items in their huge freight wagons. The wagons were one of two Pennsylvania-manufactured vehicles—the Conestoga prairie schooner with the familiar dipping canvas top—or the heavy Pittsburgh wagon —built for hauling freight over rough terrain. Later these wagons were manufactured at St. Louis and Independence. They were constructed of tough, seasoned oak and hickory and had a watertight wagon box that could float in flooded streams. Their massive running gear included huge wheels fitted with iron tires five to six inches wide to allow purchase in sand and mud. Each wagon carried a cargo of about 5,000 pounds and, pulled by eight to twelve oxen or mules, could progress an average of fifteen miles per day.

In May, when the grass on the prairies and plains was tall enough to sustain the ox and mule teams and pack train animals, the caravans formed. A caravan consisted of from five to fifty wagons with their traders and crew. The group was dominated by the tough, swaggering, loudly profane mule-skinners, perhaps 100 men or more. Each crewman was armed with rifle, pistol, and skinning knife and was expected to defend the train if attacked by hostile Indians. Before leaving, the crews established an organization for mutual protection and order on the trail. The party elected a captain, who directed the line of march, chose the night campground, designated guards, and selected the river crossings. If the caravan had more than twenty wagons, it was divided into two or four divisions, each with a lieutenant subject to the captain of the column.

Hazards on the Overland Passage

On the trail, raids by Kiowas and Comanches were a regular prospect. Also, once the ox and mule herds had been bedded down for the night there was the ever-present threat of stampedes, and thus stranded wagons, caused by sweeping sorties of Pawnee stock thieves. The eastern portion of the Santa Fe Trail crossed the territory of the Kaws and Osages. While the warriors of these tribes posed no military threat, they were capable of pilfering wagons and stealing straggling stock. Caravan outriders and night guards had to be constantly vigilant.

Most of the time the caravan crews, a paramilitary force, were able to fend off attacks and thwart theft of goods and livestock. But in some years the crossing to Santa Fe was particularly hazardous because of the presence of massed Kiowa and Comanche raiders. Appeals for protection to public officials in Missouri and Washington brought some assistance. In 1825, Thomas H. Benton, United States Senator from Missouri, obtained congressional approval of a $30,000 appropriation to be used to survey a traders' road from Independence to the Western border of the United States and to placate the Indian tribes along the trail. Implicit in this action was the commitment to provide military escort for caravans when required.

Jefferson Barracks in St. Louis was the westernmost boundary of the military frontier in that portion of the Mississippi Valley in the early 1820s. The growing volume of trade with New Mexico had produced a quickening of settlement and economic activity on the Western border. To establish the military frontier beyond the settlement line in western Missouri, and to have an operational base close to the traders' road to New Mexico, War Department officials in 1827 directed the erection of a new post, Fort Leavenworth, on the west bank of the Missouri River a few miles above the mouth of the Kaw River. This frontier station provided military escort for the trade caravans on several threatening occasions. The first formal escort occurred in 1829, when Major Bennett Riley of Fort Leavenworth marched four companies of infantry with the caravans to the Western border of the United States. The escort force camped on the Arkansas River until autumn, waiting for the traders to return. Troops from Fort Leavenworth also escorted the Santa Fe bound caravans in 1834 and 1843.

Dealing with the Mexican Bureaucracy

Once the traders had run the high-risk gauntlet of the crossing from Independence to Santa Fe—complete with Indian raids, grass fires, stampeding teams and stranded wagons, summer storms with high winds, terrifying lightning, huge hailstones, and flooded creeks and rivers—they still had to deal with local public officials before they could offer their goods in the Santa Fe marketplace. The Mexican national government and the provincial government of New Mexico levied import duties on all alien goods. The tariffs varied. At one time the duty was a flat $500 assessment on each wagon. The Missourians defeated this duty by increasing the size of their freight wagons. During most of the period of the Rio Grande commerce, the levy ran about 60 percent of the value of the goods in each wagon. Rarely, however, did the trader actually pay this high sum for the privilege of selling his goods. By blatant smuggling many traders paid no duty at all. Others, particularly in times of close surveillance, bribed the customs officers and other public officials to reduce the levy. One trader admitted that duties on American goods were distributed three ways— one-third to the traders, one-third to the officials, and one-third to the Mexican government.[2]

Josiah Gregg on the Rio Grande

Josiah Gregg, a Missouri trader, traveled four times over the Santa Fe Trail between 1831 and 1840. He was fascinated by the social milieu of the Spanish-American settlements and struck by the· singular business opportunities the Southwest offered Americans. In 1844 he published *Commerce of the Prairies*, which contains a descriptive account of his adventures on the Santa Fe Trail and the extension of American commerce into the Mexican provinces and a business guide for traders. A perceptive observer, Gregg captured the drama of life on the traders' concourse and presented a sympathetic account of Spanish-American life and culture.

Epic vignettes from *Commerce of the Prairies* chronicle the passage of the caravans from the Missouri depot to the Rio Grande: the journey's beginning, a mid-trail scene of tedium, and the quickening excitement of the approach to Santa Fe.[3] As the caravan moved out from Independence,

> The charioteer, as he smacks his whip, feels a bounding elasticity of soul within him, which he finds it impossible to restrain;—even the mules prick up their ears with a peculiarly conceited air, as if Harmony and good feeling prevail everywhere. The hilarious song, the *bon mot* and the witty repartee, go round in quick succession; and before people have had leisure to take cognizance of the fact, the lovely village of Independence, with its multitude of associations, is already lost to the eye.

At mid-passage, the boredom of trail routine was manifest.

> As the caravan was passing under the northern base of the Round Mountain, it presented a very fine and imposing spectacle to those who were upon its summit. The wagons marched slowly in four parallel columns, but in broken lines, often at intervals of many rods between. The unceasing "crack, crack" of the wagoners' whips, resembling the frequent reports of distant guns, almost made one believe that a skirmish was actually taking place between two hostile parties; and a hostile engagement it virtually was to the poor brutes, at least; for the merciless application of the whip would sometimes make the blood spirt from their sides—and that often without any apparent motive of the wanton *carrettieri*, other than to amuse themselves with the flourishing and loud popping of their lashes.

[2] Josiah H. Gregg, *Commerce of the Prairies*, Max L. Moorhead, ed. (Norman, 1954).
[3] Ibid., pp. 26, 71–72, 78.

As the caravan neared Santa Fe, its imminent arrival galvanized both natives and traders.

"Los Americanos!"—"La entrada de la caravana!" were to be heard in every direction; and crowds . . . flocked around to see the new-comers; . . . The wagoners were by no means free from excitement on this occasion. Informed of the "ordeal" they had to pass, they had spent the previous morning in "rubbing up," and now they were pre-pared, with clean faces, sleek combed hair, and their choicest Sunday suit, to meet the "fair eyes" of glistening black that were sure to stare at them as they passed. There was yet another preparation to be made in order to "show off" to advantage. Each wagoner must tie a brand new "cracker" to the lash of his whip; for, on driving through the streets and the *plaza publica*, every one strives to outvie his comrades in the dexterity with which he flourishes his favorite badge of his authority.

Commercial Expansions from Santa Fe

The dynamic character of the American commerce was reflected in the way the trade radiated out from Santa Fe. Increasingly this capital city of the Mexican province of New Mexico became a forward depot to support American traders in their search for new markets. After 1830, wagon trains moved out of Santa Fe for markets at Albuquerque, Paso del Norte, and into the settlements of Chihuahua and Sonora.

Santa Fe also nourished a commerce with the Pacific coast towns of southern California. The traders used two routes to supply the California markets. For the most part, goods were moved by pack train, for the rough terrain west of Santa Fe discouraged wagon traffic. One route followed the trail blazed by the American fur man James Ohio Pattie, which ran south from Santa Fe to Albuquerque, southwest to Santa Rita, and along the Gila River to the Colorado. The other traders' road to California carried most of the commerce and followed the "great circle" route. It is some-times called the Old Spanish Trail from the excursions of Escalante and Domínguez in the 1770s. William Wolfskill and George Yount, two Ameri-can fur men from Taos, in 1830 confirmed the Old Spanish Trail by their passage—a 1,200-mile-trek northwest from Santa Fe that led across southern Colorado, skirted the Grand Canyon, and followed the rim of the Great Basin in Utah, across Nevada, traversed the Mohave Desert, and finally crossed through the Cajon Pass to Los Angeles. Both American and Mex-ican traders formed pack trains at Santa Fe; cargoes were of locally pro-duced woolen goods and trade items from Missouri, which they exchanged in the California settlements for horses and mules.

Impact of the Overland Commerce

The volume of land commerce between the Mississippi Valley settle-ments and New Mexico was never high; at no time did it exceed a half-million dollars in annual value of goods carried out. Nonetheless, in the early years of the commerce, the return on Missouri cargoes was quite attractive. The 1824 expedition carried $25,000 worth of goods, which sold in Santa Fe for $250,000. By the mid-1830s, however, profits had declined to about 40 percent; and by the early 1840s the New Mexico market had become so saturated with American goods that only a 10 percent return was possible, a low profit yield in view of the risks. The mounting volume of imports after 1835 is indicated by the following: in 1839, 130 wagons carried $250,000 worth of goods to Santa Fe; four years later, 230 wagons brought in $450,000 worth of goods.

The vicissitudes of Mexican politics inevitably affected the Santa Fe trade. Chief of State General Santa Ana, aroused over the growing American presence and influence in the northern provinces, decreed in 1843 that all customs houses handling American goods were "entirely closed to all commerce." The ban on American trade was eased the following year and ninety wagons laden with goods from the Mississippi Valley depots reached Santa Fe. Before the trade could return to its previous volume, however, the war with Mexico occurred, and by conquest and diplomatic settlement the Mexican Southwest became United States territory.

The overland commerce with the north Mexican provinces had provided a market, albeit small, for the increasing production of a growing American industry. It was important for the Mississippi Valley, serving as a profitable enterprise for a young section of the nation that, at the time, was a region of limited economic opportunity. The Santa Fe trade also fed an ever-increasing supply of gold and silver into the Mississippi Valley economy. The region was specie-poor and the bullion and coins expanded and stabilized the section's economic life. Moreover, through their travels over the Santa Fe Trail, many Americans were exposed to the environment west of Missouri. They observed that "Great American Desert" was too harsh a designation for much of it, particularly the agriculturally attractive eastern portion traversed by the Santa Fe Trail.

American traders in Santa Fe and other Mexican communities of the Southwest also observed first-hand the weakness of Mexican administration, and realized how easy conquest would be. There were a number of resident Americans, agents for the trading companies, at Santa Fe and other Mexican towns on the commercial circuit. They knew the land, resources, the people, and how to manage the Mexican leaders. The situation seemed made for an easy conquest.

While the maritime and land traders' frontiers were establishing American presence and interest in the Southwest and Pacific Basin, federal officials were in the process of developing a public-use policy for the national domain west of Missouri. The mounting contest between Anglo-American settlers and Indians for the land in the Old West had led Congress to create the Indian Territory on Missouri's western border. During the period 1815–1845, Indian Territory was the scene of considerable settlement activity as the federal government's Indian removal program forced the Eastern tribes to vacate their Old West lands and migrate west of the Mississippi River.

SELECTED SOURCES

Overland and maritime traders, with the fur men, were the American pioneers in the New West. General studies on the traffic with the Spanish-American towns of the Southwest include *Josiah Gregg, *Commerce of the Prairies*, Max L. Moorhead, ed. (Norman, 1954); Stanley Vestal, *The Old Santa Fe Trail* (Boston, 1939); R. L. Duffus, *The Santa Fe Trail* (New York, 1930); James W. Webb, *Adventures in the Santa Fe Trade, 1844–1847* (Glendale, 1931); Kate L. Gregg, ed., *The Road to Santa Fe* (Albuquerque, 1952); Matthew C. Field, *Matt Field on the Santa Fe Trail*, John E. Sunder et al., eds. (Norman, 1960); and *Lewis H. Garrard, *Wah-To-Yah and the Taos Trail* (Norman, 1955).

Federal protection extended to the overland traders is described in Otis E. Young, *The First Military Escort on the Santa Fe Trail* (Glendale, 1952) and *Leo Oliva, *Soldiers on the Santa Fe Trail* (Norman, 1967). Extensions of the overland traffic from Santa Fe to Chihuahua and California are the subject of Stella M. Drumm, ed., *Down the Santa Fe Trail and into Mexico: The Diary of Susan Shelby Magoffin* (New Haven, 1963); Max L. Moorhead, *New Mexico's Royal Road: Trade and Travel on the Chihuahua Trail* (Norman, 1958); and LeRoy R. Hafen and Ann Hafen, eds., *The Old Spanish Trail: Santa Fe to Los Angeles* (Glendale, 1954).

Literature on the subject of the maritime traders' frontier in the Pacific Basin is limited and includes William Shaler, *Journal of a Voyage Between China and the North-Western Coast of America, Made in 1804* (Claremont, Calif., 1935); Adele Ogden, *The California Sea Otter Trade, 1784–1848* (Berkeley, 1941); John W. Caughey, *History of the Pacific Coast* (Lancaster, Pa., 1933); *Gavan Daws, *Shoal of Time: A History of the Hawaiian Islands* (New York, 1968); Edward Joesting, *Hawaii: An Uncommon History* (New York, 1972); David Lavender, *Land of the Giants: The Drive to the Pacific Northwest* (New York, 1958); S. B. Okun, *The Russian American Company* (Cambridge, 1951); S. R. Thompkins, *Alaska: Promysklennikik and Sourdough* (Norman, 1945); H. W. Clark, *Alaska: The Last Frontier* (New York, 1939); Clarence C. Hulley, *Alaska: Past and Present*, 3rd ed. (Portland, 1970); Hubert S. Bancroft, *History of Alaska* (San Francisco, 1886); and Richard H. Dana, *Two Years Before the Mast* (New York, 1960).

* Available in paperback.

Freight Wagons of the Overland Trade: Painting by Samuel Colman.

New York Public Library

The Bellevue Indian Agency on the Missouri River

17

The New West as an Indian Colonization Zone

A continuing dilemma faced by the national government in its role as manager of Western development was, on the one hand, satisfying the insatiable demand of frontiersmen for more land and, on the other, fulfilling its constitutionally assigned duty of protecting the interests of resident Indian tribes. We have seen how the irresistible flow of American settlement into the Old West and the cession treaties negotiated between federal commissioners and tribal leaders had substantially reduced the territory of the resident tribes. Government leaders, aware of the destructive effect of white contact on the tribes, knew that successive settlement waves pushing across the frontier would soon pose a threat to the remaining Indian lands. For some time they had considered resettling the Indians in the New West. President Jefferson hoped to make use of some of the Louisiana Purchase area for the creation of a permanent Indian colonization zone. After 1820, the certitude that relocated Indians would finally be free of the pressure and influence of American settlements was reinforced by the growing public sense of "national completeness." Moreover, the widely read accounts of the Pike and Long expeditions characterized much of the New West as the Great American Desert. The region became fixed in the public mind as a vast, inhospitable waste, unfit for Anglo-American pursuits and, therefore, a suitable homeland for displaced Indians.

GENESIS OF THE INDIAN REMOVAL POLICY

In 1804 an act of Congress authorized the president to begin removal negotiations, and by 1808 portions of several Indian nations from both north and south of the Ohio River began emigrating to the West, mostly to Missouri and Arkansas. The removal program was poorly coordinated, however, and American settlers regarded it their right to settle anywhere they wished. Often they squatted on lands assigned to Indians in such numbers that new territories and states were organized even before the tribes had arrived from the East. For example, the portion of Indian Country that later became Missouri received many tribes from the Old Northwest. But the area filled up with settlers so rapidly that in a short time the emigrant tribes had to be relocated again, this time west of Missouri in what was to become Kansas.

By 1830, Anglo-American settlements had drastically reduced the area of Indian Country, even though many populous tribes had not yet been evacuated from Georgia, Alabama, and Mississippi. As a consequence, Congress withdrew from settlement a strip of land west of Missouri and Arkansas; it extended from the Platte to the Red River, and to the western limits of the United States. It was designated the Indian Territory and settlement was limited exclusively to Indians.

Management of the Indian Tribes: The Indian Bureaucracy

The United States government complicated the relocation problem and management of the Indian communities within its jurisdiction by the unrealistic manner in which it conducted relations with the tribes. It simply continued the British practice—that is, it recognized each tribe as a sovereign entity, and any time a change in relations between the tribe and the United States was required, a treaty had to be negotiated by the president and ratified by the Senate. Because of the frequency of conflict between the United States and various tribes, Indian affairs were under the jurisdiction of the War Department.

The federal officer responsible for conducting Indian relations was called the Commissioner of Indian Affairs. In 1848, when the Department of the Interior was established, the Indian Commissioner was transferred to this new department. Each tribe maintained relations with the United States through delegations of chiefs, who regularly visited Washington to call on the president; and the federal government assigned an agent—somewhat like an ambassador—to each tribe. The agent's function was to maintain the Indians' friendship, distribute gifts and annuities, and watch for British and other foreign intrigue. He was required to live with the tribe to which he was assigned.

Further complicating the national government's plan to establish an Indian colonization zone west of Missouri was the fact that the newly designated Indian Territory was already occupied by tribes. The northern portion was the homeland of Kaws, Omahas, Otoes and Missouris, Poncas, Pawnees, and Osages; the southern portion was occupied by Quapaws and Osages in the east, Wichitas and Caddoes along Red River and Kiowas and Comanches in the Wichita Mountain area of the Great Plains. Many of these tribes had to be contacted by federal officials and persuaded to surrender some of their own land for the relocation of the Eastern tribes.

Much of the work of resettling the tribes west of Missouri and north of the Arkansas River in the 1820s and 1830s was handled by officials at the St. Louis Superintendency. Agents there were pressed by Missourians to again relocate the Kickapoos, Delawares, and other tribes from the Old Northwest who had been settled in Missouri after the War of 1812. Government officials relocated these tribes on new reservations in what became eastern Kansas.

Federal officials planned to colonize the more populous and powerful southern tribes—Cherokees, Choctaws, Chickasaws, Creeks, and Seminoles —in the southern half of Indian Territory. Already, in 1817, the Cherokees had been assigned territory in western Arkansas north of the Arkansas River; and the Choctaws were given lands in the territory south of the Arkansas. The growing settler population of Arkansas Territory demanded that the Indian immigrants be moved west of Fort Smith. This desire was accomplished by a treaty with the Western Choctaws in 1825 and with the Western Cherokees in 1828. At this time, however, the majority of the Cherokee and Choctaw, as well as the Creek, Chickasaw, and Seminole nations, continued to reside in Florida, Georgia, Alabama, Mississippi, and Tennessee.

ACTIVATION OF THE REMOVAL PROGRAM

The ultimate removal of the Eastern tribes to the Indian Territory was profoundly affected by the election of Andrew Jackson as president in 1828. Jackson had spent much of his life on the Tennessee frontier, and he held the typical frontiersman's attitude toward any Indians who presented a barrier to the consummation of Anglo-American purpose. His views appeared clearly in his first message to Congress; pointing to the progress made in relocating the Indians west of the Missouri and Arkansas, he asked Congress for further legislation to erase completely all occupancy of the Indian tribes east of the Mississippi.

The Indian Removal Act

The result was Jackson's wholesale removal plan, adopted in 1830. So obsessed was the president with driving the Indian tribes to the far frontiers of the United States that he gave his personal attention to the matter. It is significant that most of the Indian removals took place during his administration and that those not completed before he left office had at least been set in motion. Jackson's removal program—with its ruthless uprooting and prodigal waste of Indian life and property to satisfy the president's own compulsive desires and the demands of his constituency— has been aptly described by Indian leaders as the "Trail of Tears."

Tribal Objections to Removal

Leaders of the Southern tribes faced great pressure from government commissioners. Tribal chiefs parried this pressure by refusing to consider removal until the new tribal domains in Indian Territory were made safe for settlement. They pointed to the presence of fierce bands of Kiowas and Comanches on Indian Territory's western margins. These Plains Indians resented the prospect of Eastern Indians settling close to their hunting grounds; and they had sent to the Eastern settlements dark threats of extermination against intruders in their hunting range. Leaders of the Southern tribes also objected to the tribal boundaries within the new Indian Territory, which, they charged, were ambiguous and overlapping. The uncertain Cherokee-Creek boundary had already created friction between the leaders of those nations.

An added threat to peace and safety for Indian immigrants was the large community of Osages still residing on the Verdigris and Grand rivers in territory assigned to the Southern Indians. In 1825, the Osages had only partially vacated their old homeland there and several of their towns remained on Cherokee land. The towns served as bases for raids on Cherokee and Choctaw settlements in western Arkansas and eastern Indian Territory. Thus, before the national government could effectuate removal of the Southern Indians, its officials had first to remove the objections and quiet the concerns of the leaders of these tribes.

Work of the Stokes Commission

To accomplish this purpose and generally to expedite removal of the Southern tribes, Congress passed an act in 1832 authorizing the president to appoint a special three-member Indian commission. Jackson selected Montfort Stokes of North Carolina, Henry R. Ellsworth from Connecticut, and John F. Schermerhorn of New York as members. The group became known as the Stokes Commission, after the chairman, who was the former governor of North Carolina. Fort Gibson at the mouth of Grand River was designated headquarters for the Stokes Commission. The War Department provided the Stokes Commission with a military arm, for its work would be accomplished by the use of force if peaceful means failed. Military action was thought likely, especially in dealing with the warlike Osages, Kiowas, and Comanches.

Major Henry Dodge had been ordered to recruit a battalion of heavily armed cavalry, called the Mounted Rangers, for service in the Illinois-Wisconsin Black Hawk War of 1832. By the time this special force had been raised and trained, its services were not required east of the Mississippi River. The secretary of war therefore ordered three companies of Mounted Rangers—one headed by Captain Jesse Bean, another by Captain Nathan Boone, and the third by Captain Lemuel Ford—to Fort Gibson to assist the Stokes Commission in establishing peace on the Indian Territory frontier and settling the immigrant tribes. Ellsworth was the first commissioner to arrive at Fort Gibson, reaching Grand River on October 8, 1832. His party included three distinguished guests: on the way west while on Lake Erie, he had met Washington Irving, America's most prominent writer; Charles Latrobe, an English naturalist and author; and Count Albert de Portales, an Italian nobleman. When Ellsworth invited the trio to accompany him to Indian Territory, promising high adventure (including a buffalo hunt), they accepted. Upon arrival at Fort Gibson, Commissioner Ellsworth learned that Captain Bean and his Mounted Ranger Company had preceded him by three weeks and had already been sent on an assignment. Bean's mission was to explore the lands contiguous to the upper waters of the Cimarron, Washita, and Canadian rivers in search of bands of Kiowas and Comanches; he was to invite them the next year to a peace council with the Stokes Commission at Fort Gibson.

Colonel Mathew Arbuckle, the commandant at Fort Gibson, sent two Indian scouts to intercept Bean's Rangers with instructions to wait for Ellsworth and his guests. Accompanied by an escort from the Fort Gibson garrison, the party caught up with Bean on the Arkansas River above Three Forks on October 14. The combined force moved up the Cimarron and turned south to the Canadian into central Indian Territory. Bean's frontier reconnaissance lasted until October 24. By the time that he ordered his column back to Fort Gibson, Irving and Latrobe had hunted buffalo, deer, and wild turkey and captured wild horses. Their experiences furnished material for two books of colorful and dramatic descriptions of life on the Indian Territory frontier during the 1830s. *The Rambler in North America* by Charles Latrobe is perhaps not as well known to Americans as Irving's classic, *A Tour on the Prairies*.[1]

By early 1833 the three members of the Stokes Commission were all at Fort Gibson and ready to carry out their duties, the first of which were fairly simple. The Seneca Indians needed a home. This once-powerful tribe from New York, like so many others, had been pushed across the frontier by the settlers; its population was reduced by war, disease, and general contamination by the whites until only a pitiable remnant survived. Just prior to 1833, the Senecas had resided near Sandusky in Ohio, but in 1831 they had ceded their Eastern lands to the United States. The Stokes Commission had to find them a home in Indian Territory and for a band of Shawnees—reduced in numbers and power like the Senecas— who had recently affiliated with this tribe. The commissioners assigned the Senecas and Shawnees a 127,000-acre home north of the Cherokee nation between the Missouri border and the Grand River.

[1] Materials subsequently discovered in the papers of Count de Portales have been edited and published under the title *On the Western Tour with Washington Irving: The Journals and Letters of Count De Pourtales*, George F. Spaulding, ed., Seymour Feiler, tr. (Norman, 1968).

The commission had also been instructed to look into reports that the Quapaws were destitute and needed help. In 1818 this tribe had ceded to the United States all claim to land south of the Arkansas River and east of the Kiamichi River. The commissioners found that about 200 impoverished Quapaws were living among the Caddoes on the Red River. They negotiated a treaty with the Quapaw chiefs, in which they agreed to locate on a 96,000-acre reserve north of the Senecas, between the western boundary of Missouri and the Grand River.

The Stokes Commission was also able to settle the Cherokee-Creek boundary controversy relatively easily. Cherokee and Creek leaders met with the commissioners at Fort Gibson and produced an amicable solution. A new border was drawn between the two nations, which gave the Creeks some of the land between the Verdigris and Arkansas rivers that had been claimed by the Cherokees.

Dealing with the Osages, however, was a very different matter. Whereas the Stokes Commission had found harmony and conciliatory attitudes in their negotiations with the Cherokees, Creeks, Senecas, Shawnees, and Quapaws, they met only hostility and obstruction from the Osages. In February 1833, the commission held its first council with the Osage tribal leaders at Chouteau's Post on Grand River near Salina. The proceedings recessed briefly and resumed at Fort Gibson in March. For three weeks the Osage chiefs bitterly denied Cherokee and Creek charges that they had burned cabins and stolen the horses and other property of immigrant Indians. Repeatedly, the commissioners attempted to persuade Osage leaders to set a time at which they would move their villages from the Cherokee nation to the northern domain assigned them by the treaty of 1825. Finally, on April 2, the Osages struck their lodges, left Fort Gibson, and headed west to hunt buffalo. Later that spring came reports that the Osages were holding scalp dances on the Verdigris, celebrating the taking of over 100 trophies and five captives.

Gradually the authorities pieced together a story of ghoulish barbarity. When the Osages arrived on the buffalo range they had picked up a fresh trail, which led them into the Wichita Mountains to a place later known as Cut Throat Gap. Finding an undefended Kiowa village, the Osage warriors had terrorized the women, children, and the few old men who were present; they plundered the lodges, killed over 100 Kiowas, decapitated the bodies and placed the heads in brass camp kettles, burned the village, and returned to the Verdigris loaded with plunder and captives.

The Kiowa captives provided the Stokes Commission with a possible link with the wild tribes. Two unsuccessful attempts had previously been made to establish contact with the Kiowas and Comanches. The first was Captain Bean's reconnaissance of 1832. The next year, Colonel James B. Many, with two companies of Mounted Rangers, had been sent west to the Wichita Mountain area in search of Kiowa and Comanche camps to deliver an invitation from the Stokes Commission.

Among the Osage captives was a Kiowa girl named Gunpandama and a boy called Tunkahotohye. Hugh Love, a trader on the Verdigris, purchased the children from the Osages—paying $75 for the boy and $140 for the girl. The Stokes Commission negotiated with Love for the prisoners, hoping to use them as the means of gaining access to the unapproachable Kiowas and Comanches. Preparations for a third expedition to the buffalo country centered around the delivery of the captives, but the Kiowa boy died before the commissioners had completed negotiations with Love. They did manage to obtain Gunpandama for $200.

The Dragoon Expedition

Probably the busiest time in Fort Gibson's history was the first six months of 1834. The activity was directed toward establishing tranquility in the Indian Territory in order to assure leaders of the Southern tribes that life and property were safe there. In the early months of the year, General Henry Leavenworth succeeded Arbuckle as commander at Fort Gibson. He sent out detachments of troops to establish a line of posts on the frontier west of Fort Gibson for the purpose of checking raids into the Eastern settlements. The troops constructed three cantonments—Camp Arbuckle at the mouth of the Cimarron, Camp Holmes at the junction of Little River and the Canadian, and Camp Washita at the mouth of the Washita River. Each post was connected to the command center at Fort Gibson by a system of military roads patroled by horsemen who maintained surveillance from the Cherokee nation in the north, through the Creek nation, south into the Choctaw nation, and to the Red River.

Next, the military force in the Indian Territory was strengthened by the arrival of a new type of unit called Dragoons. The First Dragoon Regiment was organized late in 1833 and was commanded by Colonel Henry Dodge. A core of experienced men for the unit came from the disbanded Mounted Rangers. Captains Bean, Ford, and Boone—key officers in the new regiment because of their frontier experience—were joined by Lieutenant Jefferson Davis (later president of the Confederate States of America) and Lieutenant Colonel Stephen Watts Kearny, a hero of the Mexican War. Most of the recruits were from Boston, New York, Philadelphia, Baltimore, and St. Louis.

After a very brief training period, the Dragoon Regiment prepared for an expedition to the buffalo country. To date, it was the most colorful and awesome military force mustered on the Southwestern frontier. The splendid Dragoon trappings and accoutrements were calculated to produce a lasting impression on the wild Kiowas and Comanches and to intimidate them into making a peace treaty with the United States. General Leavenworth's sparkling column, with guidons flying, rode out of Fort Gibson on the morning of June 15, 1834. A wagon train contained commissary supplies, ammunition, gifts for the Indians, the Indian captive Gunpandama, and a guest of General Leavenworth, George Catlin, the Philadelphia artist. The line of march was over the new military road to Camp Holmes, and thence to Camp Washita.

Disaster stalked the Dragoon expedition from its first day. Summer heat came early to the Southwest in 1834, and the proud Dragoons suffered in their heavy uniforms. By the time the regiment arrived at Camp Washita, nearly half of the men were ailing—some from heat stroke and exhaustion, others from a gastrointestinal malady. A few miles west of Camp Washita, so many officers and men had been stricken that a field hospital called Camp Leavenworth was established on the prairie. Here General Leavenworth, who was dying from injuries received in a fall from his horse while chasing a buffalo calf, ordered Colonel Dodge to select 250 effective men and proceed to the Wichita Mountains.

Nonetheless, Dodge did succeed in drawing the Kiowas, Comanches, and Wichitas into council. His return of Gunpandama established good relations with the chiefs; the gifts he lavished on the tribal leaders helped too, and by patient negotiation he extracted from them a promise to remain peaceful and to come to Fort Gibson for a treaty council with the Stokes Commission. Catlin, although ailing, rode west with Dodge; he visited the Indian villages while Dodge's councils were in progress, sketched the people and camp scenes, and kept a daily journal. He later published both the journal and sketches in a two-volume work titled *Letters and Notes on the Manners, Customs, and Condition of the North American Indians*.

The Dragoon column straggled back to Fort Gibson during August; their line of march to and from the buffalo country was marked by graves. The Dodge-Leavenworth expedition paid a high price for its success in pacifying the tribes of the Plains. Of the 500 proud young troopers who rode west from Fort Gibson on that sunny June day in 1834, only about 350 returned.

Negotiations with the Plains Tribes

During September 1834, chiefs of the Comanches and Wichitas came to Fort Gibson as promised for a council with the leaders of the Cherokees, Creeks, Choctaws, other immigrant tribes, and the Osages. Unfortunately, by this time the authority of the Stokes Commission to negotiate treaties had expired, and Colonel Dodge and other officials could only praise the Indians for their interest in peace and invite them to attend a grand council the following summer. The tribal leaders made declarations of goodwill and pledges of peace and promised to be present at the council.

Arbuckle returned to Indian Territory in late 1834 and resumed command at Fort Gibson. Early the next year he, Montfort Stokes, and Francis W. Armstrong, the superintendent of Indian Affairs, were named commissioners to negotiate treaties with the Plains tribes. Arbuckle sent Major R. B. Mason and a Dragoon detachment to select a meeting site. Mason chose a location on the Canadian River in central Indian Territory;

it was designated Camp Mason. His men cut a road from Fort Gibson to Camp Mason, constructed brush arbors to protect the delegates from the summer heat, and increased the comfort of the conferees by building puncheon benches. A commissary train brought supplies for feeding the Indian guests, who had begun gathering at the council grounds in late July. The commissioners arrived with a 150-man escort from Fort Gibson in early August and negotiated for several weeks with the Kiowa, Comanche, and Wichita chiefs.

The treaty signed there pledged the Plains tribes to live at peace with their new neighbors, the Southern tribes. Since traffic to the Rio Grande towns was increasing, the commissioners also exacted an assurance of unmolested passage for traders through the buffalo range. The Kiowas, however, departed Camp Mason before the treaty was ready for signing. To assure complete peace on the Plains, the cooperation of this powerful tribe was necessary, and government agents continued to seek a treaty with the leaders of these fierce people. They were successful in 1837, when a delegation of Kiowa chiefs came to Fort Gibson and signed a treaty with terms similar to the one negotiated with the Comanches and Wichitas.

REMOVAL OF THE SOUTHERN TRIBES

Meanwhile, one by one, the leaders of the Southern tribes were submitting to the ever-mounting pressure of federal commissioners and signing treaties providing for the surrender of their Eastern lands and removal to new domains in the Indian Territory. Successive treaties with the Cherokees, Choctaws, Seminoles, Creeks, and Chickasaws assigned to them virtually all of the southern half of Indian Territory—a vast region extending from 37°N to the Red River, and from Fort Smith west to the 100th meridian, nearly all of the present state of Oklahoma.

The Cherokee nation and outlet absorbed the northern third of this portion of Indian Territory. The entire southern half of this segment, bounded on the north by the Arkansas and Canadian rivers and on the south by the Red River, was shared by the Choctaws and Chickasaws. Much of the territory between the Cherokee nation on the north and the Choctaw-Chickasaw nations on the south became the territory of the Creek nation. A ribbon of territory between the North Fork of the Canadian and the Canadian River west of the Creek nation became the lands of the Seminole nation.

The Removal Treaties

Colonization of the Southern tribes in the Western wilderness was not accomplished by a single treaty. Rather, at least three treaties were negotiated between the federal government and each tribe before removal was consummated. As we saw in Chapter 10, in no case did the Southern Indians willingly evacuate the land of their ancestors. In some cases the relocation was quiet; in others, particularly the Creeks and Seminoles, bloody campaigns were carried out by regular United States troops and state militia units against Indian patriots and their followers. Federal and state armies rounded up the insurgent Indians, shackled the more recalcitrant, and literally drove them to Indian Territory at the point of bayonets.

The Trail of Tears

The removal treaties contained clauses obligating the national government to pay the cost of removal for each tribe (except the Chickasaws, who were required to pay the cost of their own relocation). Although federal officials were pledged to supervise the removals, they assigned to private contractors the function of supplying rations and transportation for the immigrating Indians. The result was intense suffering, due to poor planning by government agents and the callousness of the removal contractors. Far too many immigrants were caught on the overland trail in midwinter and had to endure freezing temperatures, deep snow, treacherous ice, and sudden thaws that mired the removal columns in deep mud. Cholera and smallpox also devastated the parties. Conditions were made all the more deplorable by the rations of spoiled meat, corn, and flour supplied by the contractors. The suffering and hardship endured by the Southern Indians on their "Trail of Tears" decimated the tribal populations and reduced every nation by at least one-fourth.

INDIAN PIONEERS IN THE SOUTHWEST

As the Southern Indians recovered from the trauma of removal and adjusted to the Southwestern wilderness, they turned to establishing the essentials of orderly existence, including government and economy. For some time they had lived near European and American settlements, and the proximity had resulted in cultural and genetic interaction. By the time of removal each nation had a large community of people of mixed parentage, who tended to be the principal carriers of change. On the eve of their removal, the Southern Indian nations had established organized governments with functioning executive, legislative, and judicial branches. They maintained schools, in some cases with strong missionary support. Increasingly, they had sustained themselves by stockraising, agriculture, and trading, relying less and less upon the primitive arts of hunting, fishing, and gathering. Most Southern Indians had adopted so-called citizen dress—the costume of the white settlers residing adjacent to their nations. Many of the prosperous mixed Indians were slaveowners. In many ways the political, economic, and social patterns of Southern Indian society on the eve of removal were similar to those of their Anglo-American neighbors.

The Cherokees, Choctaws, Chickasaws, Creeks, and Seminoles energetically transformed the Southwestern wilderness and planted there constitutional government, formal education, economy, slaveholding, and certain other familiar Anglo-American practices. The Southern Indians must therefore be regarded as just as important carriers of Anglo-American culture into the New West as the frontiersmen residing in the adjacent border settlements of Missouri, Arkansas, and Texas.

The Five Indian Commonwealths

Like other new settlers, the Southern Indians, many with slave labor, established farms, ranches, and plantations in the primal valleys, uplands, and prairies of the Indian Territory. They founded towns, businesses, and newspapers, and began river steamer, stage, and freight transport systems. The leaders created functioning governments with constitutions to guide their nations. Activities of the tribal governments were concentrated in their national capitals—Tahlequah for the Cherokees, Doaksville for the Choctaws, Tishomingo for the Chickasaws, North Fork Town for the Creeks, and Seminole Agency for the Seminoles.

The governmental pattern created by the Cherokees was similar to that used by the other tribes. The Cherokee nation was governed by a constitution, which divided the government into three coordinate divisions: an elective principal chief, an elective bicameral legislative branch called the national council, and an appointive judiciary of a supreme court and lesser courts. The nation was divided into local government units called districts, similar to counties; each one was administered by a set of elective officials, including commissioners and a sheriff.

Educational Advances

The Cherokees maintained a public school system for the nation's youth. It offered elementary and grammar school work and was directed by a national superintendent of public instruction. Books and other learning materials were published in both English and Cherokee—in the Cherokee syllabary invented by Sequoyah during the 1820s. The *Cherokee Advocate*, a weekly newspaper printed in both English and Cherokee, was published at Tahlequah beginning in 1844.

Samuel A. Worcester, a teacher supported by the American Board of Commissioners for Foreign Missions who had been jailed in Georgia for teaching in Indian schools, established Park Hill, a missionary settlement near Tahlequah. The compound included a school, church, and the Park Hill Press, a publishing house established by Worcester with printing equipment he had brought to Indian Territory from the East. Park Hill Press did a thriving business publishing books, pamphlets, the *Cherokee Almanac*, and other items.

Similar governmental and educational developments occurred among the other nations in Indian Territory. The Southern Indians were the first pioneers, even preceding the Texans, to establish the familiar agricultural frontier in the New West. Cotton produced on Indian Territory plantations was shipped from landings on the Arkansas and Red rivers aboard river steamers to ports on the Gulf. Grain and livestock from Indian Territory farms and ranches made their way to markets on the Southwestern border in Missouri, Arkansas, and Louisiana.

EXTENDING THE MILITARY FRONTIER

The creation of an Indian colonization zone was the first substantive use which the national government had made of the New West. The growing sense of "national completeness" caused government leaders to superimpose on the Indian colonization zone a comprehensive system of permanent military defenses, primarily to guard the Western approaches to the nation's settled interior.

The Southwestern Posts

Fort Smith, erected in 1817 at the junction of the Arkansas and Poteau rivers at Belle Point, was the first American outpost on the Southwestern frontier. To keep the military frontier in the vanguard of American settlement, the War Department had in 1824 directed the establishment of two new posts west of Fort Smith—Fort Gibson at the mouth of Grand River and Fort Towson on Red River near the mouth of the Kiamichi River. The quickening of economic activity and settlement on Missouri's western border produced by the growing Santa Fe trade led to the establishment in 1827 of Fort Leavenworth on the Missouri River near the mouth of the Kaw.

In 1834 the military frontier was extended beyond the Fort Gibson–Towson defense line by the erection of camps Arbuckle, Holmes, and Washita. Also in 1834, the military Southwest was strengthened by the establishment of Fort Coffee, which was situated on the south bank of the Arkansas River about twenty-five miles upriver from Fort Smith. Its principal function was to provide a forward station on the Arkansas River in the Indian Territory from which to watch for runners of contraband goods, particularly whiskey, which federal law prohibited in the Indian nations.

The Cass Frontier Defense Plan

Until 1836, there had been a minimum of coordination in the military frontier extension. That year a comprehensive plan of frontier defense conceived by Secretary of War Lewis Cass was proposed to Congress. In appealing for appropriations to finance the plan, Cass told Congress that the time had "arrived when a systematic plan for the protection of our frontiers, ought to be devised and adopted." [2] Cass proposed that the War Department be authorized to establish a chain of posts along the Indian

---

[2] Quoted in Edwin C. Bearss and Arrell M. Gibson, *Fort Smith: Little Gibraltar on the Arkansas* (Norman, 1969), p. 142.

frontier on a line from Fort Towson on the Red River—the international boundary for the United States—northward through Fort Gibson–Fort Smith to Fort Leavenworth and terminating at Fort Snelling in the far north. Interstitial posts would be constructed and the entire frontier defense system would be connected by a major military road.

Cass pointed out that since most of the Eastern Indian tribes had been colonized in Indian Territory, the posts and garrisons close to their former settlements in the East were no longer required. The military interests of the nation would be better served by locating the major portion of the regular cavalry and infantry units in the proposed frontier defense system in the New West. Besides guarding the interior of the nation against the threat of foreign invasion from the West, the defense chain would provide internal order on this far-flung frontier, maintaining peace between indigenous tribes and the intruding immigrant tribes. Cass pointed out that, with the colonization of the Eastern tribes in the New West, there were then nearly 250,000 Indians concentrated in the Indian Territory. He warned that the presence of such an "immense body of Indians . . . placed on the borders of our settlements" [3] was a threat to the security of the Mississippi Valley and the nation. His frontier defense plan would discourage the buildup of Indian military power for retaliatory strikes to the East.

Congress approved certain portions of the Cass frontier defense plan. New posts constructed in the Indian country included Fort Wayne in the Cherokee Nation and Fort Scott, situated strategically on the upper edge of the new Osage nation in the northern segment of Indian Territory. In addition, the proposed military road connecting the chain of New West posts from Fort Towson on the Red River to Fort Snelling on the upper Mississippi River was surveyed and constructed.

By the 1840s, the sense of "national completeness" was replaced by a revivified American expansionism. The military frontier, as in the Old West, kept pace with the surge of renewed settlement and development. The obsolescence of the Cass frontier defense line was demonstrated in 1842 by the establishment of Fort Washita, erected west of the old line on a site selected by General Zachary Taylor above old Camp Washita. Nine years later, Fort Arbuckle was established by Captain Randolph B. Marcy in the western Chickasaw nation. It guarded the eastern segment of the California Road, a new thoroughfare connecting the Mississippi Valley settlements with the Pacific shore.

In the period before the Civil War, the military frontier was further extended across Indian Territory by the erection of two additional posts. In 1858 Major Earl Van Dorn directed the founding of Camp Radziminski on the southern approaches to the Wichita Mountains to serve as a support base for cavalry operations against the Kiowas and Comanches.

[3] Ibid., p. 143.

The following year Major William H. Emory supervised the erection of Fort Cobb on the upper Washita to provide the army with a permanent station in the heart of the Kiowa-Comanche range.

Role of the Military Frontier

The military frontier, superimposed over the New West's Indian colonization zone, performed many significant services for the nation and for the immigrant Indians. The infantry and cavalry troops stationed at the posts along the New West's defense chain from Fort Snelling to Fort Towson were in the field much of the time, guarding the Eastern Indians from the retributive attacks of angry Kiowas, Comanches, Osages, and other resident tribes. The troops also materially assisted the immigrant tribesmen in locating on their new domains. They built roads and established communication systems—the first mail service in the New West was provided by the military. Troops regulated trade in the Indian Territory, inspecting the credentials of traders and maintaining surveillance on the rivers and trails, watching for contraband. Post officers often hosted councils at which federal officials negotiated treaties with tribal leaders. Besides providing protection and pushing back obstacles to settlement, troopers on the line explored, surveyed, and mapped the unknown regions of the New West.

Almost every military station provided an impetus to urban development. Near each post there grew up a crude civilian settlement of shops and stores maintained by traders and tavern keepers and residences for families of the men at the post. Thus the station's presence generated a satellite settlement that eventually became a town. The legacy of the old forts is preserved in the names the towns still bear. Post personnel often added to the satellite community's population, for discharged soldiers might take up residence there. In addition, the posts provided markets, for local commissary officers purchased substantial quantities of grain, meat, and vegetables from local stockraisers and farmers.

The Hitchcock Mission

The importance of the interaction between the military frontier and Indian Territory communities is in dramatic evidence in two incidents—the Hitchcock mission and the pacification of the Leased District. The removal treaties with the Eastern tribes had contained clauses obligating the government to pay the cost of relocating each of the tribes, including feeding and clothing the Indians during the emigration and supplying provisions for one year after arrival in the West.

Government officials had for the most part delegated the feeding and transporting of the Indians to private contractors, and those Indians who survived the "Trail of Tears" claimed that much of their suffering and high death rate was due to the callousness of contractors who enriched themselves at the Indians' expense. Critics claimed that "at so much per head it was entirely a business proposition with the contractors." In their hands, "the removal of the Indians was not a great philanthropy, but was carried out with the same business considerations that would characterize the transportation of commodities of commerce from one point to another." [4]

Vast sums of public money were paid to contracting firms newly formed to render this service for the government; it was later revealed that most of the contractors were friends and relatives of officials high in the government. The contracts customarily called for the following: "the ration of bread shall be one pound of wheat flour, Indian meal, or hard bread, or three quarters of a quart of corn; the meat ration shall be one pound of fresh meat, two quarts of salt to every hundred rations. The transportation shall be one six-horse wagon and 1500 pounds of baggage to from 50 to 80 persons. The provisions and transportation shall be of the best of their kind. The average daily travel shall not exceed twelve miles." [5]

Angry protests by tribal leaders and charges of profiteering and fraud caused the federal government to investigate the removal contractors. Major Ethan Allen Hitchcock was ordered to look into the complaints. Concerning his appointment, John R. Swanton has said: "Since . . . the national administration was willing to look the other way while this criminal operation [the removal] was in progress, it made a curious blunder in permitting the injection into such a situation of an investigator as little disposed to whitewash iniquity as was Ethan Allen Hitchcock." [6]

Major Hitchcock began his investigation of removal abuses during November, 1841. A highly perceptive investigator, he confided to his journal that news of his mission had preceded him, and there was much curiosity about his business in Indian Territory. He added that one of the contractors who had settled on the border "came here so poor that a man with a $400 claim against him was glad to settle for $100. Now he owns a considerable number of Negroes and has offered $17,500 for a plantation." Major Hitchcock's exhaustive investigation yielded evidence of "bribery, perjury and forgery, short weights, issues of spoiled meat and grain, and every conceivable subterfuge was employed by designing white men on ignorant Indians." [7]

Hitchcock took his findings to Washington; there he prepared a report with 100 exhibits attached and filed the heavy document with the secretary of war. "Committees of Congress tried vainly to have it submitted to them so that appropriate action could be taken; but it was stated that too many

[4] Quoted in Arrell M. Gibson, *Oklahoma: A History of Five Centuries* (Norman, 1965), p. 188.

[5] Ibid.

[6] Quoted in Grant Foreman, ed., *A Traveller in Indian Territory: The Journal of Ethan Allen Hitchcock* (Cedar Rapids, Iowa, 1930), p. 7.

[7] Ibid.

friends of the administration were involved to permit the report to become public. It disappeared from the files and no trace of it is to be found." Swanton's comment on the fate of the Hitchcock report was "the fact that it did not allow the report to be made public and its mysterious disappearance from all official files proves at one and the same time the honesty of the report and the dishonesty of the national administration of the period." [8]

Pacification of the Leased District

In the period before the Civil War, pacification of the Leased District was the most demanding assignment of the military frontier in the Indian Territory. The Kiowas and Comanches were inveterate raiders, and treaties with the United States were little understood and less respected by these fierce people. Kiowa-Comanche depredations extended into lower Coahuila in Mexico and west to the Rio Grande settlements in New Mexico. Their sweeping raids on Texas ranches and the Mexican towns netted horses, mules, and captives—especially women and children—whom they carried to their villages in the Wichita Mountains.

During the 1850s the military power of these tribes threatened the increasing American traffic crossing the Plains to the Rio Grande and to the Pacific shore. Travelers referred to the passage through the Kiowa-Comanche range as the "dreaded crossing." The United States government, therefore, undertook the pacification of the southern Plains; they planned to conquer the Kiowas and Comanches and concentrate them on a fixed military reservation guarded by federal troops. In accordance with their plan, government officials in 1855 leased from the Choctaws and Chickasaws the southwestern quadrant of Indian Territory between the 98th and 100th meridians. The area was bounded on the north by the Canadian and on the south by the Red River. Federal officials designated it the Leased District, intending to use it as a military reservation for the Plains tribes.

Two campaigns were carried out against the Kiowas and Comanches before the Civil War—one by a Texas Ranger force under Captain John S. Ford, the other a United States cavalry strike led by Major Earl Van Dorn. In the late spring of 1858, Ford's men followed a Comanche raiding party from Texas into the Wichita Mountains. Finding the raiders' village they struck in a surprise attack, killed seventy-six Indians, dispersed the survivors, and burned the settlement. During September of the same year, a federal cavalry column operating from Camp Radziminski scoured the Leased District for hostile bands. On October 1, Van Dorn's Tonkawa scouts found a Comanche camp at a watering point known as Rush Springs, near the eastern border of the Leased District. The troopers struck during the night, killing sixty Indians.

[8] Ibid., p. 12.

Momentarily the tribes of the Leased District were inactive, and the military frontier extension into the lair of the Kiowas and Comanches appeared to have accomplished its mission. During 1859 Fort Cobb was erected on the upper Washita River, strategically near the Kiowa and Comanche villages. In the same year, the federal government established the Wichita Agency near Fort Cobb to administer the new reservation. Most Kiowa and Comanche bands residing in the Leased District ignored the agency and the assistance its staff sought to provide in agriculture and stockraising. The most important function of Wichita Agency at this time was the reception of tribes from Texas.

For several years a collage of once-populous Texas tribes—the Waco, Tonkawa, Anadarko, Tawakoni, Ioni, Keechi, Caddo, and some Comanche bands—had resided on the Brazos Reserve in northwest Texas. In the 1850s the line of Texan settlements had reached the rim of this reservation, and the Texans were demanding that the Indians be removed or face extermination. Hurriedly, Agent Robert S. Neighbors collected the Brazos Reserve tribes—about 1,500 people—and, escorted by an Army force commanded by Major George H. Thomas, conducted them to a new home in the Leased District near the Wichita Agency.

CANNIBALIZING THE INDIAN TERRITORY

Well before the Civil War, the Indian Territory's status as a permanent Indian colonization zone off-limits to white settlement was challenged by the renewed expansion of American settlements into the New West. By the 1850s, settlers were agitating for the opening of the entire Indian Territory. Their demands were articulated in a number of bills introduced into Congress providing for the extinguishment of tribal titles and the opening of Indian Territory to settlement.

The tribes of the northern part of Indian Territory—Potawatomis, Wyandots, Kickapoos and others, vestigial remnants of once great tribes from the Old Northwest—were weak, disorganized, and poorly led. Thus they were easy marks for federal government pressure to sign treaties surrendering their communally owned reservations and accepting individual allotments. By doing so tribal rights and title were abrogated, and vast tracts were opened to white settlement.

The Kansas-Nebraska Act

The tribes of the northern half of Indian Territory were the first casualties of the renewed settler juggernaut that was pushing its way into the New West. The Kansas-Nebraska Act of 1854 removed from Indian Territory the region north of 37° and created from it the Kansas and Nebraska territories. Most of the tribesmen of this part of the old Indian colonization zone were allotted small individual tracts. The surplus lands of each Indian reservation were opened to white settlement.

The Neosho Statehood Plan

The portion of Indian Territory between 37° and the Red River, and west of Fort Smith to the 100th meridian, was the domain of the Southern tribes. It too was coveted by the settlers. At the same time that the Kansas-Nebraska bill was approved by Congress, that body was considering a bill, introduced by Senator Robert W. Johnson of Arkansas, to organize three territories in the southern half of Indian Territory. Johnson's proposal provided for a survey of the national domains of the Cherokees, Creeks, Choctaws, Chickasaws, and Seminoles, the assignment of allotments to each tribal citizen, and the sale of surplus land to settlers. The bill required the creation of three territories—Cherokee, with its capital at Tahlequah; Muskogee, with the capital at Creek Agency; and Chatah, with the capital at Doaksville. As soon as the mixed Indian-settler population of the three territories had made satisfactory progress in self-government, the three territories were to be fused into the state of Neosho. Johnson's bill failed and the southern half of Indian Territory was spared, at least momentarily. The defeat of the proposal was primarily due to the intense opposition of highly articulate Southern Indian leaders who had spent much time in Washington working against its adoption. Unfortunately, the subsequent folly of these same Indian leaders in signing alliances with the Confederate States of America provided the federal government with sufficient diplomatic leverage in 1866 to begin the process of diminishing the much-coveted Indian Territory lands of the Southern tribes.

While Indian pioneers from the eastern United States were being colonized over a large segment of territory adjacent to Missouri and Arkansas, Anglo-American pioneers were beginning to occupy other portions of the New West. Texas was the focus of their interest in the period 1820 to 1836.

SELECTED SOURCES

Colonizing the Indian Territory is the subject of *Grant Foreman, *The Five Civilized Tribes* (Norman, 1934) and *Indian Removal* (Norman, 1932); Angie Debo, *Rise and Fall of the Choctaw Republic* (Norman, 1934) and *The Road to Disappearance* (Norman, 1941); Grace S. Woodward, *The Cherokees* (Norman, 1963); Edwin C. McReynolds, *The Seminoles* (Norman, 1957); and *Arthur H. DeRosier, *The Removal of the Choctaw Indians* (Knoxville, 1970).

Pacification of the Indian Territory is traced in *George Catlin, *Letters and Notes on the Manners, Customs, and Condition of the North American Indians* (London, 1842), 2 vols.; Grant Foreman, *A History of Oklahoma* (Norman, 1942), *Advancing the Frontier* (Norman, 1933), and *Fort Gibson*

* Available in paperback.

(Norman, 1936); and *Arrell M. Gibson, *Oklahoma: A History of Five Centuries* (Norman, 1965).

The subject of Indian pioneers in the Southwestern wilderness is treated in Morris L. Wardell, *A Political History of the Cherokee Nation, 1838–1907* (Norman, 1938); Althea Bass, *Cherokee Messenger* (Norman, 1936) and *The Story of Tullahassee* (Oklahoma City, 1960); Carolyn Foreman, *Park Hill* (Muskogee, Okla., 1948); and Lester Hargrett, *Bibliography of the Constitutions and Laws of the American Indians* (Cambridge, Mass., 1947).

The military frontier's extension across Indian Territory is discussed in Robert W. Frazer, *Forts of the West* (Norman, 1965); Edwin C. Bearss and Arrell M. Gibson, *Fort Smith: Little Gibraltar on the Arkansas* (Norman, 1969); Francis Paul Prucha, *A Guide to the Military Posts of the United States, 1789–1895* (Madison, 1964); and William B. Morrison, *Military Posts and Camps in Oklahoma* (Oklahoma City, 1936).

Reduction of Indian Territory to accommodate the demands of the American settler during the 1850s is depicted in George W. Manypenny, *Our Indian Wards* (Cincinnati, 1880) and Katharine Turner, *Red Men Calling on the Great White Father* (Norman, 1951).

Courtesy San Antonio Chamber of Commerce

The Alamo, "Cradle of Texas Liberty."

18

American Expansion in the New West: Texas

THE comforting credo the "national completeness" was shattered during the 1820s by a renewed burst of American expansionism. Beginning in Texas, the virus of territorial acquisition spread across the New West to the Pacific shore. Before it spent itself, it had completely marked out the geographic perimeter of the American nation and absorbed the lands within it.

Texas, claimed by Spain on the basis of sixteenth-century explorations, was a neglected frontier of New Spain for nearly 150 years. La Salle's reconnaissance of the Mississippi Valley and Texas Gulf coast in the 1680s, however, caused a quickening of Spanish interest. During that decade, officials in New Spain directed an extension of the Spanish mission and presidio frontier into Texas as a check to the French. The religious and military settlements confronting the French town of New Orleans and Natchitoches in adjacent Louisiana included San Antonio de Bexar, La Bahia, and Nacogdoches; they were linked by a system of military express roads radiating from Laredo on the Rio Grande. Nacogdoches, near the Louisiana border, was the terminus for the Camino Real ("royal road") that bore northeast from Laredo.

The Spanish were surrounded in a defensive colonial zone in south central Texas; along the Gulf near the Sabine on the east was the border of French Louisiana. North of San Antonio was a deadly aboriginal barrier, populated by wandering bands of Lipan Apaches and Comanches. Although the Spanish were able somewhat to pacify the Apaches by establishing the mission of San Luis de Amarillas on the San Saba River, the Comanches were unconquerable, an ever-present threat to the settlements from San Antonio into Coahuila in Mexico.

When France ceded Louisiana to Spain in 1762, Spanish officials moved their defensive apparatus for guarding the approaches to New Spain forward to the Mississippi Valley. France recovered Louisiana in 1800, although Spain continued to administer the province until 1803 when the United States acquired this vast trans-Mississippi territory. Thereupon the Spanish retired west of the Sabine and again manned their Texas defenses.

The region west of Louisiana was mostly open country, free of mountain barriers and of easy access. It had a temperate climate and rich soils, abundant grass, water, wood, and game. From the Sabine to the Rio Grande six major rivers emptied into the Gulf, permitting easy penetration of the interior. All these features made this Spanish frontier province singularly attractive to American frontiersmen, especially since they found the East Texas environment quite similar to their Mississippi Valley milieu.

EARLY AMERICAN PENETRATION OF TEXAS

Americans regularly entered Texas after 1790. Traders carrying passports issued by Spanish officials in Louisiana trafficked with the tribes of eastern Texas, and Anglo hunters roamed west to the Brazos to capture wild horses for the Spanish troops in Louisiana. A limited number of American farmers also migrated into eastern Texas lands. A few of the latter were Anglo squatters, but the heaviest immigration to Texas before 1821 consisted of portions of Indian tribes from the East and New West who had undertaken a self-imposed exile to escape contamination from the expanding settlements and to evade management by federal officials. During the 1790s, large bands of Cherokees, Shawnees, Delawares, and Kickapoos drifted along the middle border country southward into east Texas and settled in villages near the Sabine. Welcomed by Spanish officials, the aboriginal expatriates subsisted largely on agriculture, frontier trade, and hunting. Several intermarried whites resided with these Indian immigrants, particularly the Cherokees from Tennessee. In a strong sense, the American agricultural frontier was already established in Texas by 1821.

Spanish Texas in this period lured restless American adventurers seeking action, fame, fortune and, sometimes, empire. These border renegades, with their small private armies, were called "filibusterers." Aaron Burr's aborted scheme of empire apparently included the conquest and occupation of Spanish Texas.

The Nolan Entrada

One of the most active Americans on the Southwestern border was Philip Nolan. Throughout the 1790s Nolan, armed with passports from Spanish officials in Louisiana, made regular ventures into Texas. His activities had a shadowy color, for he was a close friend of the notorious General James Wilkinson. In 1800, Nolan led a party of twenty men to the Middle Brazos and captured 300 wild horses. On his return to the settlements, he was intercepted by a Spanish patrol. The officer in command suspected that Nolan had entered Texas as an agent for an American conspiracy and that his purpose was to map the country and provoke the tribes to attack the Spanish settlements. Nolan was slain in the confrontation, and several of his men were captured and taken to prison in Mexico.

American Filibusterers in Texas

Proof of Nolan's association with an American conspiracy for the conquest of Texas is inconclusive. However, it is known that by 1821 at least two other American-based filibustering armies had made overt attempts to conquer portions of Texas. An attempt at revolutionary overthrow of New Spain, led by Padre Miguel Hidalgo, was crushed in 1811. Among the followers of the priest who took up residence in exile in the American border towns of Natchitoches, New Orleans, and Natchez was Bernardo Gutiérrez de Lara. In league with Augustus McGee, a former U.S. Army lieutenant, Gutiérrez conceived a plan for the conquest of Spanish Texas. In 1812, the Gutiérrez-McGee army of 500 men invaded Texas and swept through the country, capturing Nacogdoches, Goliad, and San Antonio. The invasion force then lost its momentum, McGee died, and most of the invading host was hunted down and destroyed by Spanish troops.

The signing of the Adams-Onís Treaty in 1819 sparked a second invasion of Texas. This pact between the United States and Spain, which set the boundary separating the two nations on the Sabine River, amounted to an American renunciation of claims to Texas. But expansive Anglos in the Southwest regarded Texas as a legitimate part of the Louisiana Purchase territory; they based their claim on La Salle's explorations on the Texas Gulf coast. In bitter protest to the renunciation of American claims to Texas, Dr. James Long, a Natchez physician, mustered a small private army and invaded Texas in 1821. Long's force captured Nacogdoches, and he announced the independent Republic of Texas. Operations along the border continued when the invaders captured Goliad; but Long's attempts to obtain recognition of his conquests were in vain. While in Mexico City he died; his Texas Republic scheme failed.

AGE OF THE EMPRESARIOS

The Spanish-American population of Texas in 1820, numbering about 4,000, was scattered in tiny settlements from San Antonio south to the Gulf. In that year, officials in Texas—in an attempt to increase the population and thus strengthen the eastern border against recurring invasions from the United States—implemented a law that permitted aliens to enter Texas and settle at certain locations.

The Austin Grant

Moses Austin was the first person to seek to benefit from this law. Born in Connecticut and a former resident of Virginia, Austin had moved to Spanish Missouri in the 1790s. There he received a land grant and developed a profitable lead mining and smelting enterprise. At the time he had been a Spanish subject; his citizenship changed after the United States acquired the Louisiana Territory.

During 1820, Austin traveled to San Antonio and applied for a grant of land. His colonization plan, which was approved by local Spanish officials, permitted Austin to settle 300 American families on a tract situated between the Colorado and Brazos rivers. Each immigrant was to swear allegiance to the Spanish government and its laws and, if not already a communicant, to become a Roman Catholic. Austin died in 1821 before he could complete arrangements for the Texas colony. His son, Stephen F. Austin, continued his work and became the most important figure in the subsequent Americanization of Texas.

A successful revolt in New Spain during 1821 resulted in Mexican independence. That year and the next, Austin spent much time in Mexico City seeking confirmation of his father's grant. Continuing revolutionary ferment and changing governments slowed the process, and not until 1823 did Austin finally receive approval of a land grant between the Guadalupe and Colorado rivers.

Austin's success led other Americans to apply for land grants in Texas, and the Mexican national government adopted the Colonization Law of 1823. It established a settlement system directed by the *empresario*, the manager of a tract of Texas land. His principal function was to attract and settle colonists on his grant. The amount of land assigned each settler varied according to changing national and state laws; but, as a general rule, each colonist could obtain *uno labor* of 170 acres for farming and *uno sitio* —a square league of 4,439 acres—for stockraising. In return for his services in populating Texas, each *empresario* who brought in 200 families received fifteen *sitios* and two *labors*. The cost to the settler for nearly 5,000 acres was only about $200 in small instalments; it was, in fact, more of a fee to offset costs of survey, title issue, promotion, and other expenses incurred by the *empresario*. The law required that each colonist swear allegiance to the Mexican government and its laws and become a Roman Catholic.

American Migration to Texas

During 1821, the first wave of the American settler tide reached Texas, bound for the Austin grant. As other *empresarios* were awarded land by the Mexican government, their tracts were populated too. The panic of 1819 had created wide distress, and many Americans were restless for fresh opportunity.

The greatest Texas attraction was, of course, the promise of nearly

5,000 acres of virtually free land for each settler. In the United States, after July 1, 1820, the system of selling public-domain land on credit was abolished. By federal law the minimum unit of sale had been reduced to eighty acres at $1.25 an acre, to be paid in cash at the time of purchase. Federal land sales dropped drastically, due to the drift of homeseekers to Texas as well as the depressing effect of the Panic of 1819. In 1819, settlers had purchased over 5,000,000 acres of public land. A year later, when the no-credit system went into effect, public land sales dropped to 1,100,000 acres; in 1821 only 800,000 acres were purchased.

The *empresarios* widely advertised their Texas lands in the United States, England, and other European countries. Most of the settlers came from the United States—Missouri, Arkansas, Tennessee, Kentucky, Mississippi, and Alabama being the principal suppliers of Texan immigrants. By 1830, the population of Texas exceeded 30,000.

Americans and Mexican Law

Offsetting the necessity to change national allegiance and adopt the Roman Catholic religion, the immigrants received, besides substantial grants of land, the privilege of importing goods into Texas duty free for six years. Thus settlers, most of them from the United States, could obtain tools, textiles, and other needs at stateside prices.

Mexican law prohibited slavery, but Austin persuaded the Mexican government to lift the ban for the benefit of the colonists residing on his grant, a privilege that was extended to colonists settling on other *empresario* grants. The 1827 Coahuila-Texas constitution also prohibited slavery, but Austin induced the legislature to enact a law authorizing owners to negotiate contracts with their slaves—classed as indentured servants. The contracts committed servants to serve an apprenticeship of ninety-nine years.

The national constitution of 1824 created a federal system for Mexico, and initially Texas was part of a state comprised of Nuevo Leon, Coahuila, and Texas. Soon Nuevo Leon was separated from this tripartite political community; thereafter until independence, Texas was half of the state of Coahuila-Texas.

In 1827 Coahuila-Texas adopted a state constitution that divided the state into three departments—Saltillo, Monclava, and Texas. The state law-making body was the congress, in which the department of Texas was allocated two seats. Members of the Coahuila-Texas congress were chosen indirectly by electors. The state governor, chosen by popular vote, appointed the head official or political chief for each department. No provision was made for the governance of the *empresario* colonies. Therefore the *empresario* had, theoretically, political and administrative control over his grant. In practice, each grant was self-governing. By custom the grant obligated the *empresario* to maintain civil order, appoint commissioners—whose duties included locating towns—and organize a militia.

Besides maintaining local law and order, the *empresario* grant militia was expected to defend the settlements against Indian attack.

While each *empresario* grant was self-contained and self-governing, the *empresarios* and their colonists looked to Austin and his colony for leadership. He regularly intervened with Mexican officials in Coahuila and Mexico City on matters of common interest. In a sense he was the *de facto* governor or political chief of the Texas colonies. His duties were heavy, his frustrations taxing. He stated to a friend that he had "a perplexed, confused colonization law to execute, and an unruly set of North American frontier republicans to control who felt that they were sovereigns, for they knew that they were beyond the arm of the Government or the law, unless it pleased them to be controuled." [1]

Few Americans in Texas took seriously their obligations to change national allegiance and church membership. Their patent disregard for the authority of the Mexican government was a matter of grave concern for the British minister to Mexico. During 1825 he presciently warned that Americans in Texas "are increasing daily, and though they nominally recognize the authority of the Mexican government, a very little time will enable them, to set at defiance any attempt to enforce it ... [the settlers] are American-Backwoodsmen, a bold and hardy race, but likely to prove bad subjects and most inconvenient neighbors." [2]

The Mexican regulations, mild enough considering the benefits received by the Americans, were nonetheless grossly evaded or ignored. Most Americans in Texas were from the frontier and were strongly Protestant. They worshipped as they pleased—in some cases quietly in private homes, in others in open public service—flagrantly violating Mexican law and their oath at entry.

MEXICAN REACTION

Many *empresarios*, by indiscriminately promoting their Texas lands in the United States and Europe and by openly speculating on these lands, also contravened the grant laws. But infractions by settlers and *empresarios* usually went unheeded. Enforcement was emasculated by the strife and chaos caused by changing governments and changing laws in the national capital. One observer, commenting on the desperate political situation in Mexico City, stated that Mexican officials generally gave "no heed to Texans but went on with their petty game of putting down one and setting up another, until it became almost impossible to follow." [3]

[1] Quoted in E. Douglas Branch, *Westward: The Romance of the American Frontier* (New York, 1930), p. 361.

[2] Quoted in Frederic L. Paxson, *History of the American Frontier, 1763–1893* (New York, 1924), p. 307.

[3] George P. Garrison, *Texas: A Contest of Civilizations* (New York, 1903), p. 98.

The Fredonian Rebellion

One *empresario* incident, however, was so boldly threatening that even the strife-ridden Mexican government could not ignore it. The Fredonian Rebellion and the Mexican reaction to the incident must be regarded as the first in a continuum of events that led to Texan insurgency, secession, and, finally, independence.

In 1825, the Mexican government awarded Hayden Edwards an *empresario* grant in the Nacogdoches area. Several grants had already been assigned in that part of east Texas. Moreover a considerable area of the land was occupied by Mexican settlers and a goodly number of American squatters. Edwards, by the terms of his grant, was required to respect the property and civil rights of persons already established in the area. Apparently he was careless in managing his grant and encroached on the established land rights of prior settlers in the process of locating colonists on what he regarded as his *empresario* grant. Those dispossessed by Edwards' peremptory action complained to Mexican officials, who annulled Edwards' grant.

In retaliatory fury, Edwards, with his brother Benjamin, raised a private army of 200 Americans and in late 1826 captured Nacogdoches and proclaimed the Republic of Fredonia. Shortly thereafter, a combined Mexican army and militia force from Austin's grant marched on Nacogdoches, smashed the revolt, and dispersed the Fredonian army, forcing Edwards to flee across the Sabine River into Louisiana.

Militarization of Texas

In the aftermath of the Fredonian Revolt, the Mexican government directed General Manuel de Mier y Terán to inspect the *empresario* communities of Texas. He reported "grave danger" to Mexican interests in Texas and acknowledged that he was troubled by the "sense of superiority" assumed by the immigrants toward Mexican law, culture, and citizens. Terán recommended the military occupation of Texas, with the garrisons situated close to American settlements to maintain much-needed surveillance. He also urged that Mexicans be encouraged to settle in Texas to balance the alarmingly disproportionate American population.

The Mexican government's response to General Terán's report and recommendations was to adopt, between 1830 and 1832, a series of laws aimed at restricting the American population in Texas and generally tightening Mexican control of that province. The statutes closed the Texas border to American immigration and, for the most part, terminated the *empresario* system. Mexican troops, many of them convicts serving out their sentences in army service, were stationed in Texas. The statutes also directed the strict enforcement of the tariff laws on imports into Texas by the colonists. All Texas ports were closed except Anahuac, at the head of Galveston Bay; there troops were stationed to assist the customs collectors in enforcing Mexican revenue laws.

The Texan Response

Settler reaction to these laws was prompt and direct. Americans continued to migrate to Texas in spite of the prohibition, and with limited troops to guard a thousand-mile border, Mexican officials found it impossible to enforce the ban on American immigration. Americans had grown accustomed to importing goods, primarily from the United States, duty free and regarded this a right. The Mexican intent all along had been that it was a temporary privilege to ease the expense of becoming established in Texas. In 1832, enforcement of Mexican tariff laws at Anahuac led to a local revolt. Colonel John Bradburn, an American in Mexican government service, commanding a company of Mexican troops, arrested several local residents on charges of evading the revenue laws. A small force of armed settlers marched in Anahuac, forced Bradburn and the Mexicans to retreat, and freed the American prisoners. This incident marked the establishment of a pattern whereby the Texans sought to rectify their grievances against the Mexican government by resort to arms.

TEXAN INDEPENDENCE

American leaders in Texas, such as Stephen F. Austin, saw in the ferment of Mexican politics some hope for gaining a redress of their grievances by peaceful means. They blamed their difficulties on President Anastacio Bustamente who, in consummate disregard for the federal constitution of 1824, was seeking to establish a highly centralized system of rule. Following the Anahuac incident, representatives of the Texan settlements met at Turtle Bayou and adopted a resolution supporting rebel leader Antonio Lopez Santa Ana, who claimed to be engaged in a crusade to overthrow the harsh centralized rule of Bustamente and restore the constitution. By the Turtle Bayou Resolution of 1832, the Texas colonists "sang fulsome praises" of Santa Ana's "character and work, which four years later it must have sickened them to recall." [4]

Texan Particularism

Later the same year, a convention of delegates representing the *empresario* settlements met at San Felipe. Austin presided at the meeting. The delegates drafted a statement of support for Santa Ana and praised his actions aimed at restoring the Constitution of 1824 and the federal system. In addition, the convention generated a petition to the Mexican government. It urged tariff reform, to permit free importation of tools, machinery, and textiles needed in the Texas settlements, the repeal of the law banning American immigration, and separation from Coahuila. The separation was desired, according to the delegates, because of language and geographic differences and the oppressive underrepresentation of Texas

[4] Ibid., p. 180.

in the Coahuila-Texas congress. William H. Wharton was designated to carry the petition to Mexico City, but because of continuing political ferment and disorder in the national capital, Mexican officials paid scant heed to it.

Official disregard of Texan interests led Austin and other local leaders to call a third convention in April 1833 at San Felipe. This body drafted a constitution for the proposed Mexican state of Texas and prepared a petition similar to the one drafted the preceding year. This time Austin himself was delegated to carry the documents to Mexico City. Like Wharton before him, he had little success in obtaining the attention of Mexican officials. And in the daily disorders and struggle for power in the national capital he observed firsthand the futility of seeking prompt remedy of Texan grievances. He shared his views in letters to friends, including a recommendation that the Texas convention proceed unilaterally to establish the Mexican state of Texas. His letters were intercepted, he was thrown in jail, and was unable to return to Texas until September 1835.

Mexican Recrimination

Santa Ana became president of Mexico in 1833. Two years later he formally abolished the federal system and developed a plan for the complete political centralization of Mexico, the states to become departments in a new unitary system. The states of Zacatecas and Coahuila-Texas were the principal opponents to Santa Ana's plan; both states were determined to preserve the Constitution of 1824. In May 1835, Santa Ana's armies, in several bloody battles, smashed all resistance in Zacatecas. The only surviving opposition to Santa Ana's centralization plan, therefore, was in the Texas portion of Coahuila-Texas. In 1835, Mexican authorities prepared to integrate Texas into the new unitary system. They began by placing a force of troops at Anahuac to support the customs collector in the enforcement of Mexican revenue laws. Texan troops mustered from the *empresario* militia companies marched on Anahuac, expelled the Mexicans, and closed the revenue station.

Thereupon Santa Ana increased the Mexican military force in Texas, assigning infantry, cavalry, and artillery units to watch the larger towns for seditious activity. Wherever possible, arms held by the settlers were confiscated. This practice led to the Battle of Gonzales on October 2, 1835. A Mexican column was ordered to Gonzales to seize a cannon, ostensibly used by local citizens as defense against Indian attacks. A Texan militia force determined to retain the cannon, intercepted the Mexican troops, defeated them, and forced a retreat.

Texan Insurgency

The Battle of Gonzales was the clarion call for insurgent activity all across south Texas. Swift-moving Texan volunteer forces struck the Mexican garrisons at Victoria, Goliad, and Anahuac and captured large quantities of arms, ammunition, and quartermaster supplies. The shattered Mexican army, dispersed in companies throughout the *empresario* settlements, rushed to San Antonio to join the major Mexican garrison force. Austin collected the scattered volunteer troops and set up a siege of San Antonio.

Word of events in Texas spread throughout the Mississippi Valley, and American volunteers rushed across the Sabine to aid the Texans. Numbered among the arrivals were two volunteer companies from Mississippi and Louisiana. On December 11, 1835, after fierce fighting in San Antonio, General Martin Cos, commander of Mexican forces in Texas, capitulated. His surrender agreement included the pledge "not to resist further the struggle for the Constitution of 1824" and to evacuate his army south of the Rio Grande.

Austin and other Texan leaders proceeded to organize a provisional Mexican state government compatible with the Constitution of 1824. This presumptive state government, directed by a governor and council, assumed jurisdiction over all territory embraced by the Texas portion of the Mexican state of Coahuila-Texas. The principal concern of that government was the creation of an army to defend the insurgent state against the expected retaliatory action of General Santa Ana. For this purpose the state council named Sam Houston as commander-in-chief of the Texas state army. Houston, a Tennessean and a close friend of Andrew Jackson, had served in the United States Congress and as governor of Tennessee. He had only recently arrived in Texas after an extended sojourn among the Cherokees in Indian Territory.

The Alamo Incident

In February 1836, Santa Ana marched to Texas at the head of a 5,000-man army. His forces scattered across south Texas striking at the American settlements, then massed for an attack on San Antonio. This town was defended by a force of 187 men commanded by Colonel W. B. Travis and including Jim Bowie, Davy Crockett, and several Mexican-Americans. At the Mexican approach, the Texans retreated to the thick-walled Alamo mission and endured a siege that extended from February 23 to March 6. On the last day, the Mexican army took the Alamo by storm and put to death every surviving male defender. The sole survivors were three women and three children, but the price of victory was high for Santa Ana. The Mexicans suffered over 1,000 casualties, 500 of whom died.

Texan War of Independence

Santa Ana's invasion of Texas metamorphosed Texan sentiment; instead of status as a state in the Mexican federal system, the Texans desired independence. A Texas convention met March 1, 1836, at Washington-on-the-Brazos; Richard Ellis of Pecan Point on the Red River was elected president of the convention. In its deliberations, the convention charged that the "Mexican government had broken faith with colonists by failing to secure them that constitutional liberty and republican government, to which they had been habituated . . . had rendered the military superior to the civil power; had commanded them to give up their arms; had invaded their country by land and sea . . . and had continually exhibited every characteristic of a weak, corrupt, and tyrannical government." [5] On March 2, the convention declared Texas independent of Mexico and proceeded to establish a republic, producing a constitution modeled closely after that of the United States.

Santa Ana determined to break up the insurrection by marching his troops in large bodies—of at least regimental strength—through the country, terrorizing the Texans by burning their homes, confiscating livestock, and making examples of captured adults by executing them. Most settler families fled before the destroying host.

On March 20, General Jose Urrea, the Mexican commander operating on the Gulf coast between Matamoras and the Brazos, captured near Goliad a Texan force of about 400 men commanded by J. W. Fannin. Santa Ana directed the execution of the prisoners: 330 Texans died before Mexican firing squads at Goliad.

Santa Ana personally led a force of 1,500 men. Houston, with 700 Texans, remained close to Santa Ana's column but repeatedly fell back before the Mexican general's advance toward the Gulf. On April 21, near a point where Buffalo Bayou joins the San Jacinto River, Santa Ana paused. In a swift movement, Houston's Texans overran the Mexican encampment, administering a devastating defeat and capturing General Santa Ana. The president of the Texas Republic, David G. Burnet, on May 14 signed, with the captive Santa Ana, the Treaty of Velasco. The Mexican general agreed to end hostilities, evacuate his troops from Texas, and do his utmost to "secure recognition" of the Texas Republic, the borders of which were to extend to the Rio Grande.

THE TEXAS REPUBLIC

During September 1836, President Burnet called an election to select officials in the republic's government, ratify the new nation's constitution, and obtain a popular expression on the question of annexation to the United States. Houston, the hero of San Jacinto and a popular idol, easily won the presidency over Henry Smith and Austin. The constitution received overwhelming approval, as did the question of annexation.

The Texas Republic had a life of nine years, during which time the consuming passion of most Texans was annexation to the United States. This goal colored every aspect of Texan national life. However, the familiar

[5] Ibid., p. 214.

expansion pattern of frontiersmen—entering a territory, establishing American presence, generating the inevitable nationalizing currents, and absorbing the territory into the American community—was arrested by domestic and international pressures. The pressures forced national leaders strongly committed to Texan annexation to follow an oblique, patience-wracking, and, at times, subtle course in the consummation of their goal. Even President John Quincy Adams, who as secretary of state had presided over the abandonment of American claims to Texas in his negotiations with Luis de Onís in 1819, made a serious attempt in 1825 to purchase Texas from Mexico. Four years later President Jackson attempted and failed in the same enterprise.

Times had indeed changed. Naked overt appropriation of territory into the American nation—as in West Florida—was no longer feasible or possible. The compelling desires of Jackson and other devotees of Texan annexation had to be tempered by realistic considerations of national politics and sectional issues. The New England-based Abolitionist crusade had injected the issue of slavery into Western expansion. Increasingly, annexation of Texas was looked upon in the North as a calculated effort by Southerners to extend slavery west of the Sabine. Clearly the Democratic Party had to find a *quid pro quo* to silence Northern opposition to annexation. In addition, the international pressures that caused Jackson and other national leaders to proceed cautiously toward Texas included the very real prospect of war with Mexico.

Momentarily, the best the Texas Republic could expect was diplomatic recognition. Yet President Jackson approached even this step with uncharacteristic delicacy. He delayed according recognition to the Texas Republic until his Democratic protégé, Martin Van Buren, had triumphed in the 1836 election. The United States government recognized the Republic of Texas on March 3, 1837. France, Great Britain, and the Netherlands also extended diplomatic recognition.

Vicissitudes of the Texas Republic

During its national life the Texas Republic faced two constant threats: reconquest by Mexico and destructive Indian raids, particularly from the Comanches. The Texas government was therefore required to maintain a disproportionately large army and a navy of ten ships. Raising the funds for defense and other public functions was a second major problem facing the republic. The new nation tried many means to achieve fiscal solvency, including tariffs, ad valorem taxes, issues of land scrip funded by the vast public domain, and issuance of bonds, which were sold to American and European investors. Most of its national life the republic was on the brink of bankruptcy; its debt in 1845 was nearly $12 million. However, in spite of all its security and fiscal problems, the Texas Republic preserved its national existence, and it continued to be a popular settlement region for immigrants from the United States and Europe, particularly from Germany. By 1845, the Texas population had increased to nearly 145,000.

The preservation of Texan national existence was due to the spirit of its citizens and the quality of public leadership. Houston served as chief executive until December 1838, when Mirabeau B. Lamar succeeded to the presidency. Houston returned to lead the republic in 1841; in 1844 he was succeeded by Anson Jones, last president of Texas. Houston's leadership was directed most toward international concerns and an unremitting commitment to the tortuous negotiations for annexation. Lamar, who was internally oriented and intensely nationalistic, complicated the life of the republic by his imperialist adventures.

Texan Expansion to the Rio Grande

Mexico refused to recognize the independence of Texas and made it clear that its only policy toward the territory north of the Rio Grande was reconquest. Mexican forces invaded Texas in 1841 and 1842. Each time, Texan army units forced the invaders to retreat south of the Rio Grande. At the same time, Republic armies were attempting to fulfill the claim that Texan national territory extended west to the Rio Grande. In 1841 Colonel Hugh McLeod led nearly 300 Texans west to establish Texan suzerainty on that river. The hard march over plains and deserts so exhausted the Texans that they were easily captured by New Mexican forces and taken prisoner into Mexico; more than half of the Texans perished from the ordeal. A second expedition to New Mexico in 1843 fared little better. This time the men were intercepted by an American patrol guarding the Santa Fe Trail, disarmed, and forced to return to their homes.

Texas Indian Policy

The Indian policy of the Texas Republic was basically no different from that of the United States. The confederated Indian community of eastern Texas, consisting mainly of Cherokees, occupied rich farming lands coveted by the Texans. Republic officials accused the Indians of conspiring with Mexican agents and in 1839 used this as justification for a bloody campaign to drive the Indians from Texas. Cherokees, Kickapoos, Shawnees, and other confederated tribesmen fled south to Mexico and north across the Red River into Indian Territory.

In addition, the rapid increase in the Texas population, due in part to the continued liberal land policy of the *empresario* period, led to expansion of Texan settlements north and west of San Antonio into the Comanche range. There Indians and settlers engaged in a long and bloody contest for the land that was not completely decided until 1874. The government spent considerable sums maintaining an Indian defense on the northwestern frontier; the line was manned by companies of mounted Texas Rangers.

Annexation by the United States

Houston's greatest accomplishment as a Texas leader was the skill with which he forced annexation by the United States through great patience, tenacity, and a good deal of playacting. The timidity of American leaders in facing the issue squarely led him to feign attachment to the British, who were genuinely interested in Texas as a source of cotton and a market for manufactured goods. To cultivate Texan leaders, British agents interceded with Mexico to gain a pledge of no further invasions of Texas and received assurances that if Texans rejected annexation by the United States, Mexico would recognize its independence.

The threat of Texas becoming a British economic enclave in North America forced American officials to press for annexation. In early 1844, President John Tyler believed that he had softened Northern objections to annexation by stressing the national over sectional benefits that would accrue to the nation by annexation. Sadly for the cause, Secretary of State John C. Calhoun indiscreetly commented, before the negotiations had been concluded, that Texas properly was a new territory for the extension of slavery. This contradiction of Tyler's assurances to the contrary scuttled the treaty. On June 8, 1844, the Senate rejected the Texas annexation treaty by a vote of 35 against to 16 in favor.

The presidential campaign of 1844 retrieved annexation from its antislavery limbo; the victorious Democratic Party provided the expansionist rhetoric, which included something for all contending groups in its campaign pledge of "Reannexation of Texas and Reoccupation of Oregon." It has been said that the election "revealed that the South, in general was for both slavery and expansion; the West was for territorial expansion, and not greatly concerned over slavery; the East had a strong minority opposed to both." Texas advocates regarded the election of 1844 as a mandate for the annexation of Texas, and "Northern Democrats, conciliated with the promise of the admission of Oregon, were willing to let that interpretation stand." [6]

Thus braced, President Tyler resorted to a joint resolution, which required that only a simple majority in each house of Congress approve the measure. The joint resolution calling for the annexation of Texas passed both houses of Congress during January and February of 1845, winning with some strength in the House, 120 to 98, but barely passing the Senate 27 to 25. On March 1, 1845, Tyler signed the resolution. By the terms of the annexation agreement, Texas would enter the Union as a state and retain both its public lands and the responsibility for paying the republic's debts. Texas officials submitted a state constitution, which included a slavery clause compatible with the Missouri Compromise, and entered the American Union on December 29, 1845. It was the first American state to be carved from the New West, albeit under rather

[6] Branch, *Westward*, p. 370.

special circumstances. As confirmation of renewed American expansion, its absorption provided a national momentum that was ready to carry American dominion to the Pacific shore.

SELECTED SOURCES

American colonization of Texas under the Spanish and Mexican immigration programs may be traced in Hubert H. Bancroft, *History of the North Mexican States and Texas* (San Francisco, 1883–1889), 2 vols.; Eugene C. Barker, *The Life of Stephen H. Austin* (Nashville, 1925) and *Mexico and Texas, 1821–1825* (Dallas, 1925); Mattie A. Hatcher, *The Opening of Texas to Foreign Settlement, 1801–1821* (Austin, 1927); and *Barnes F. Lathrop, *Migration into East Texas, 1835–1860* (Austin, 1949).

The Texan war of secession against Mexico is the subject of William C. Binkley, *The Texas Revolution* (Baton Rouge, 1952); W. H. Calcott, *Santa Ana: The Story of an Enigma Who Was Once Mexico* (Norman, 1936); and George L. Rives, *The United States and Mexico, 1821–1848* (New York, 1913), 2 vols.

The vicissitudes of the Texas Republic are traced in *Llerena Friend, *Sam Houston: The Great Designer* (Austin, 1954); *William R. Hogan, *The Texas Republic; A Social and Economic History* (Norman, 1946); Stanley Siegel, *A Political History of the Texas Republic, 1836–1845* (Austin, 1956); and Noel M. Loomis, *The Texan–Santa Fe Pioneers* (Norman, 1958).

Annexation of Texas by the United States is discussed in O. P. Chitwood, *John Tyler: Champion of the Old South* (New York, 1939); Justin H. Smith, *The Annexation of Texas* (New York, 1941); James M. Callahan, *American Foreign Policy in Mexican Relations* (New York, 1932); Ephraim D. Adams, *British Interests and Activities in Texas, 1838–1846* (Baltimore, 1910); Joseph H. Schmitz, *Texan Statecraft: 1836–1845* (San Antonio, 1845); and *Frederick Merk, *Manifest Destiny and Mission in American History* (New York, 1963).

* Available in paperback.

Emigrants Crossing the Plains.

19

American Expansion in the New West: Oregon

THE quickening American settler drift into the New West after 1820 forked at the Missouri border. One stream moved southwesterly into Texas, the other northwesterly to Oregon. By late 1845, the absorption of both Texas and Oregon into the American community was assured, leading Congressman Edward Hannegan of Indiana to comment that "Texas and Oregon were born the same instant, nursed . . . in the same cradle." [1]

In the early stages of American expansion to the Pacific Northwest, the term "Oregon Country" referred to a vast territory—all the land west of the continental divide, including southwestern Canada, the future states of Washington, Oregon, and Idaho, and a portion of Montana and Wyoming.

Oregon was therefore a gargantuan province and contained extreme contrasts of climate, topography, resources, and demography. Sweeping toward the Pacific shore in awesome succession—from the arid, dry-as-desert interior milieu to the humid, fogshrouded ocean shore—were towering highlands, deep canyons cut by the surging Snake and Columbia rivers, scrambled rock and sand sinks, and expansive plateaus leading to the towering Cascades that guarded the rich windward valleys. The Oregon Country's natural bounty included dense forests, rich soils, minerals, timber, game, fur-bearing animals, and streams teeming with salmon.

This bonanza land, which infected the highly susceptible American frontiersmen with "Oregon Fever," was populated by unfamiliar aborigines

[1] Quoted in E. Douglas Branch, *Westward: The Romance of the American Frontier* (New York, 1930), p. 387.

with exotic names—Flatheads, Nez Perces, and Coeur d'Alines in the arid region between the Rocky Mountains and the Cascades, and Yakimas, Chinooks, Umpquas, Salish, and Nisquallys along the streams of the interior valleys.

PROPRIETORSHIP OF THE OREGON COUNTRY

Until 1819, four nations had a stake in the Oregon Country. Russia based its claims on the southward extension of the Alaskan-based fur trade. The explorations of Spanish mariners from the Pacific ports of Mexico were the basis for Spanish claims. British rights were derived from the maritime reconnaissances of James Cook and George Vancouver, the land explorations of Alexander McKenzie and Simon Fraser, and occupation by Canadian-based fur traders of the territory as far south as the Columbia. American claims originated in Pacific Northwest explorations and discoveries of Robert Gray and other maritime traders, the Lewis and Clark explorations, and the occupation of the Columbia River valley by representatives of the American Fur Company at Astoria.

The Oregon Country in Diplomacy

Spain withdrew from the Oregon Country in 1819 by assenting to the Adams-Onís Treaty, which set the northern boundary of Spanish territory in North America on the 42nd parallel, the future northern boundary of California. By this treaty, Spain also ceded to the United States its "rights, claims, and pretensions to all territories north of the treaty line." Russia pulled back to 54°4' by successive diplomatic agreements with the United States and Great Britain concluded during 1824–1825. The United States and Great Britain in 1818 negotiated a convention establishing the 49th parallel as the boundary of their respective territories west of the Mississippi River and as far west as the drainage divide of the Rocky Mountains. From the mountains to the Pacific, the two nations agreed to jointly occupy the region between 42° and 54°40'; the nationals of both nations were to have equal rights of access and use of the Oregon Country. This arrangement was continued indefinitely by a pact concluded in 1827, although a proviso was inserted that either party could terminate the joint occupation with due notice.

British-American Joint Tenure

Americans were the first to occupy the Oregon Country by founding Astoria in 1811, but after the War of 1812 the rapid extension of the Canadian fur trade to the Columbia River enabled the British to attain a seemingly insurmountable advantage. The center of British power in the Oregon Country focused on Fort Vancouver, the Hudson's Bay Company post situated in what is now Washington, on the north bank of the Columbia River six miles above the mouth of the Willamette.

John McLoughlin, chief factor of the post and acknowledged "King of Oregon," was the principal force in creating this dominant economic enclave. McLoughlin developed local mills, shops, a shipyard, and farms to support the wide-ranging sorties of his fur brigades. Tough, hard driving, and imperious, McLoughlin was also benevolent and compassionate; he often sheltered and succored the early American arrivals in the Oregon Country.

Hudson's Bay Company fur agents, headed by the redoubtable Peter Skene Ogden, maintained commercial supremacy over a vast trading and trapping territory bounded on the east by the Rocky Mountains and extending southward into the Great Basin and northern California. Everywhere in the region, British agents thwarted the American fur men's advance by monopolizing the fealty of Indian hunters; they gave the tribesmen regular gifts and paid higher prices for furs than the Americans offered. In addition, McLoughlin's men established the buffer of "scorched earth" described in Chapter 15, exterminating the game by saturation hunting. A few American fur men, including Jedediah Smith, entered the Hudson's Bay Company domain and visited Fort Vancouver, but it was only to rest before returning to their Rocky Mountain rendezvous stations.

THE OREGON BOOMERS

The joint occupation and equal use privilege guaranteed by the British-American conventions was effectively negated by the British economic imperialism. The Hudson's Bay Company's assiduous monopoly of the fur trade was a patent manifestation of British intent to exclude Americans from the Oregon Country. Thus, for the first time, that vanguard of frontiersmen—the fur trader—who had opened so many territories for American settlers was checked.

American missionaries, on the other hand, were readily accepted by the British managers at Fort Vancouver, for their ostensible purpose was to minister to the local Indian tribes, and they posed no economic threat. Three men—John Floyd, Hall J. Kelley, and Nathaniel J. Wyeth—created the setting for the missionary frontier advance into the Oregon Country. Their fervor to Americanize Oregon, expressed through writings, speeches, promotional work, and sustained attempts to influence public policy as the drama of the British-American contest for the Columbia River valley unfolded, exceeded the spiritual vigor and application of the missionaries themselves.

Congressman John Floyd

Through the accounts of his cousin, Charles Floyd, and other members of the Lewis and Clark Expedition, Congressman John Floyd of Virginia developed an abiding interest in the Oregon Country. In fact, he became infatuated with a region he had never seen. By 1820, Floyd was using the Congress as a forum to express this interest, attempting to promote official action by holding hearings on the "American mission" in the Pacific Northwest. He produced lengthy reports on the subject and urged Congress to adopt a resolution supporting American occupation of Oregon.

Floyd's activity undoubtedly influenced John Quincy Adams' attempt, in 1824, to apply the strengthened American claim to the Pacific Northwest, established by the 1819 treaty with Spain. Adams proposed to British representatives that the northern boundary established in 1818 be extended from the continental divide to the Pacific shore along the 49th parallel. At this time, the British so completely dominated the region that Adams' proposal was rejected. Most other public officials, comfortable in the illusion of "national completeness," were passively indifferent to national expansion in any direction and paid little heed to Congressman Floyd.

Hall J. Kelley

Publication of the Lewis and Clark journals in 1814 by Editor Nicholas Biddle, head of the U.S. Bank, caught the attention of many readers, one of them Hall J. Kelley, a New England schoolmaster. Kelley developed an obsession for Oregon that matched Congressman Floyd's, and for the remainder of his life, he worked indefatigably for the cause of American occupation of Oregon. He became an authority on the subject and lectured to audiences all across New England on the promise of Oregon and the commanding necessity for prompt American occupation of this territory.

Kelley busily circulated petitions urging official assertion of American territorial rights in Oregon and submitted them to Congress. He formed the American Society for Encouraging the Settlement of the Oregon Territory and published a pamphlet entitled *A Geographical Sketch of That Part of North America Called Oregon*. In 1829 Kelley stated that "the time is near at hand, and advancing in the ordinary course of Providence, when the Oregon country shall be occupied by enlightened people, skilled in the various improvements of science and art." [2] Failing to generate any substantial interest or official action, in 1832 Kelley undertook a personal inspection of Oregon. He approached his "Pacific Eden" over a circuitous route—traveling to New Orleans, he sailed to Vera Cruz, proceeded to Mexico City, crossed to the Pacific side of Mexico, then struck a northerly course by land and sea to San Diego.

In California Kelley was joined by Ewing Young, the fur man, and the pair continued to Oregon. Young soon saw the folly of attempting to compete with the British fur monopoly along the Columbia and settled in the Willamette Valley, content with farming and stockraising. He helped to form the Willamette Cattle Company and brought in 800 head of cattle from California.

[2] Quoted in ibid., p. 374.

Kelley was antagonized by McLoughlin, who scorned his New Englander's dream of an American agricultural community in Oregon. Embittered, he returned home to continue lecturing and writing for the Oregon cause, adding an appealing anti-British twist by denouncing the "iniquitous Hudson's Bay Company" and warning his listeners of the threat of a permanent British establishment in Oregon.

Nathaniel J. Wyeth

One of the persons influenced by Kelley was Nathaniel J. Wyeth, a Cambridge, Massachusetts, businessman. He organized a company to establish a timber and salmon industry on the Columbia River and to trade for furs. His plan was to ship furs, pickled salmon, and wood products by ship to New England markets. In March 1832, Wyeth dispatched a ship to the Columbia from Boston, loaded with supplies and equipment; he then traveled overland with a party of twenty employees. On the Missouri border, he formed a pack train to carry the expedition's trade goods and equipment and engaged William Sublette, a Mountain Man, to guide his party to the Pierre's Hole rendezvous site near Henry's Fork of the Snake River. There Wyeth traded for furs and disposed of his goods; his men also had some success in trapping beaver in nearby streams.

The Boston party continued to the Columbia, arriving there in October, but Wyeth received the disheartening news that his support ship, with its cargo of essential equipment and supplies, had been lost at sea. With the assistance of McLoughlin the New Englanders wintered near Fort Vancouver and returned to the East in the spring.

In 1834, Wyeth repeated his earlier effort, first sending out a supply ship, then traveling to Independence, Missouri, to form a train of goods bound for the Rocky Mountain Fur Company rendezvous. Wyeth's westbound party included Jason Lee and other members of a Methodist missionary group assigned to Oregon. At the fur rendezvous, competing suppliers thwarted Wyeth's attempt to dispose of his goods, forcing him to halt at Soda Springs near the Snake River, where his men erected Fort Hall for the storage of the huge caravan of trade goods. Wyeth then continued to the Columbia, and, at the mouth of the Willamette River, he established Fort William as headquarters for his salmon- and lumber-processing enterprises and as support station to the fur trade he intended to develop on the lower Willamette. This time Wyeth's supply ship reached the Columbia with the equipment and supplies required to establish these industries.

Nonetheless, in spite of prodigious efforts by Wyeth and his men, the trapping, fishing, and lumbering enterprises failed. Subtle, and at times overt, interference from British agents at Fort Vancouver was certainly a significant reason for the failure. In 1836 Wyeth abandoned Fort William, sold Fort Hall to the Hudson's Bay Company, and returned to Boston. While Wyeth's bold Columbia River enterprises had foundered, his activities received more than passing notice, and his efforts added materially to the growing tide of private and public interest in the Oregon Country. And, inadvertently, Wyeth performed a singular service to the cause of American expansion into the Oregon Country on his second journey to the Columbia by transporting Jason Lee's Methodist missionary party. The missionary frontier was able to intrude into a region that was closed to the American fur men by the stern British monopoly of the Pacific Northwest fur trade.

THE MISSIONARY FRONTIER IN OREGON

The deceptively noncompetitive missionary frontier was energized in 1831 by the appearance of four Flathead Indians from the Oregon Country in St. Louis. During their Eastern sojourn, the Indians commented that their people desired instruction by missionaries. What might have been an idle remark circulated through religious circles in the Mississippi Valley and became rich copy for national religious newspapers and magazines. Editors transformed the Flathead comment into a plaintive heathen call from the Northwest wilderness. It became a holy charge as pastors transmitted the tidings to their congregations. The mission boards of several religious bodies interpreted the Indian appeal as comparable to St. Paul's "Macedonian call." [3]

Methodist Missions

The first religious body to respond with a definite plan for establishing missions in the new territory was a consortium of Methodist congregations in New England and New York. Their mission board raised funds, collected material required for operating a religious establishment in the wilderness and selected Jason Lee, a prominent clergyman, to lead the Oregon Mission to carry the gospel to the tribesmen of the Pacific Northwest. Accompanied by his nephew, Daniel Lee, and a small party of mission workers, Lee departed from New York in 1833. The following spring at Independence, Lee's party joined Wyeth's column for the overland crossing. They reached the Columbia in mid-September and, like other Americans before them, were assisted by McLoughlin.

Lee established a mission school and church at French Prairie in the upper Willamette Valley; the school became the headquarters for several additional Methodist stations, the most important one situated at the Dalles. The Methodist church and school at French Prairie ministered largely to employees of the Hudson's Bay Company at Fort Vancouver and their families. Methodist mission schools for the Oregon Indians were boarding schools, providing a curriculum consisting of instruction in English and religion and vocational training in sewing, cooking, farming, and

[3] Acts 16:9.

animal husbandry. After three years, the Methodist mission schools had an enrollment of nineteen students.

Presbyterian Missions

The Methodists were followed to Oregon in 1835 by the Presbyterians, who were sponsored by the American Board of Commissioners for Foreign Missions, an ecumenical effort of Eastern Congregational, Presbyterian, and certain Dutch Reformed congregations. American Board missionaries had already achieved considerable success among aboriginal peoples. Their greatest efforts had been concentrated among the Southern tribes, particularly the Cherokees and Choctaws.

Their outstanding men were Samuel A. Worcester—the missionary teacher to the Cherokees who had adapted Sequoyah's syllabary of the Cherokee written language to textbooks and the scriptures—and Cyrus Kingsbury and Cyrus Byington—missionaries to the Choctaws who had founded schools and churches in the Choctaw nation in both the East and the West, and reduced the Choctaw spoken language to written form. Under their supervision, books, newspapers, and other printed materials were produced in Choctaw. American Board missionaries were also established in Hawaii, where they had founded schools and churches for the Polynesians of that archipelago. The board maintained a college in Connecticut, Cornwall Academy, where the promising students from the Cherokee, Choctaw, and Hawaiian missions continued their studies.

During the 1820s, American Board missionaries in Hawaii occasionally accompanied traders to the Oregon coast. As a result of these reconnaissances, they recommended that the American Board establish missions among the Pacific Northwest tribes. The board, stirred by these recommendations and the "Macedonian call" from St. Louis, in 1834 selected Samuel Parker of Massachusetts as the clergy representative, Dr. Marcus Whitman, a physician, and three mission workers to travel to Oregon and select mission sites. In April 1835, the group reached Independence, where they joined a fur-trade train bound for the mountains. At Green River rendezvous, Whitman turned back to the Old West to obtain supplies and recruit additional mission personnel. Parker and the three workers continued to Oregon, stopping at Fort Vancouver and the Methodist community on the Willamette before exploring the territory for mission sites.

While in the East, Whitman stopped in New York and married Narcissa Prentice. He recruited Henry H. Spalding and his wife, William H. Gray, and Miles Goodyear. The Whitman party returned to the West with two wagons laden with supplies. At Fort Hall, Whitman abandoned one wagon and converted the other to a two-wheeled cart and proceeded to Fort Boise. The increasingly rough terrain forced the party to abandon the cart at Fort Boise, and they proceeded by pack train to Fort Vancouver.

Subsequently, the American Board mission was established at Waiilatpu, near the junction of the Columbia and Snake rivers. Waiilatpu served as the center for several smaller mission stations in areas near the tribes on the tributaries of the Snake and Columbia rivers.

Roman Catholic Missions

Roman Catholics also responded to the call for missions in the Oregon Country. The first stream of missionaries issued from Canada during 1838. Fathers François Blanchet and Modeste Demers, guided by Hudson's Bay Company men, founded missions at Cowlitz on Puget Sound and at Nisqually, midway between the Sound and the Columbia River. Shortly thereafter, Roman Catholics in Missouri joined the missionary drift to the Oregon Country. Their most famous representative was Father Pierre Jean De Smet who, by 1842, had established the most successful of all Christian missions in the Pacific Northwest. De Smet's principal work was among the Flatheads and Pend Oreille, in the Coeur d'Aline and Bitterroot mission districts. The Catholic missions in this period far exceeded the Protestant missions of the Oregon Country in sustained commitment, service, and results. More than any other reason, this fact is attributable to the Catholics' singlemindedness in their charge. The Protestants were torn by mixed interests.

Missions and American Settlement

Whether by design or inadvertence, the Protestant missionary frontier in the Oregon Country became the precursor of American expansion and settlement. In order to activate their vocational training programs, the missionaries imported cattle, horses, and mules from California. They established flourishing orchards and broad fields of grain. These training farms, undertaken to instruct a few Indian students in farming and stock-raising techniques, demonstrated the fertility of the soils and the generally favorable conditions existing in the Oregon Country.

The Protestant missionaries have been accused of following an ambivalent course—of working for the Americanization of the Oregon Country while fulfilling the missionary charge to the local tribes. Jason Lee has been called an expansionist, a missionary with "a colonizer's heart and a pioneer's shrewdness," intent upon importing New England values and that region's "superior brand of American culture to the Pacific." It is claimed that he conceived his true mission to be providing "New England farmers a foretaste of Heaven" by attracting them to Oregon.[4] It must be said that the accusations contained more than a grain of truth. The expanding mission staffs increasingly spent their time developing farms and livestock herds for their personal benefit to the detriment of their ministry to the Indians. One tribal leader commented to McLoughlin at Fort Vancouver: "They or we must die. Not only do they spoil our

---

[4] Branch, *Westward*, p. 373.

forests and drive away our game, thus depoiling us of food and clothing, but with their accursed morals and religion they sow broadcast the seeds of disease and death. Shall we kill them or let them kill us?" [5]

Missionary workers corresponded with families and sponsoring church congregations in the East, and their letters are replete with superlatives describing the bounty of Oregon Country. Often these letters were shared with newspaper and magazine editors, who published them for a wider reader constituency. Missionaries also regularly returned to the states to raise money for the support of their work in the Oregon Country and to recruit additional workers for the missions. Whether or not they were intended to be, these fund-raising junkets served as promotional campaigns for Oregon. From the Mississippi Valley to the Atlantic seaboard, in churches and public buildings at every stop on the missionary itinerary attentive audiences listened to the appeal for funds to support missions in the Oregon Country, and each address was laced with vivid descriptions of the wonders of the Oregon Country and the promise of the new land.

In 1838, four years after the founding of the mission at French Prairie, Jason Lee journeyed to the East on a fund-raising venture; he returned to Oregon with fifty men, women, and children, certainly more persons than were needed for the Methodist mission staffs in the new country.

AMERICAN OCCUPATION OF OREGON

In spite of the enthusiastic response of the Eastern public to the missionary lectures and letters from mission residents, there was a wide gap between interest and action. Probably the expanse of largely unoccupied territory—2,000 miles—that separated the settlements on the western border of Missouri from the Columbia was intimidating. Previously the advancing frontiers of settlement had been contiguous with settled areas or separated by only a short distance. A 2,000-mile crossing was undoubtedly an awesome deterrent. Potential Oregon settlers had the wish but not the will. And because the frontiersmen had not established themselves in the Oregon Country in sufficient numbers to activate those vital nationalizing currents that could so swiftly absorb the territory into the American dominion, the federal government remained generally passive toward Oregon.

The Slacum Mission

During the 1830s, Senator Lewis F. Linn of Missouri replaced Congressman Floyd as the principal Oregon advocate in the Congress. He regularly urged American occupation of the Pacific Northwest. His activity

---

[5] Quoted in John W. Caughey, *History of the Pacific Coast of North America* (New York, 1938), p. 222.

finally influenced President Jackson in 1836 to send Lieutenant William A. Slacum to Oregon as his official observer. Slacum's investigation of the territory along the Columbia and his observations on the activities of the British and Americans there were contained in a report on Oregon. In it Slacum reiterated Senator Linn's oft-repeated warning that only by prompt action could the United States thwart the British threat of total engulfment of this province. Slacum's report was submitted to Congress in 1837, causing Linn to urge immediate military occupation of Oregon. The bill did not pass, but the report and the work of Linn's committee added to growing public interest in Oregon.

Clearly, the comfort of "national completeness" was hard to shake. Most politicians were content and remained passive on the question of expansion. The flurry Linn provoked led one congressional leader to impatiently admonish that "Nature has fixed limits for our nation; she has kindly interposed as our western barrier mountains almost inaccessible, whose base she has skirted with irreclaimable deserts of sand." [6] Some of the more perceptive men in Congress saw the necessity for maintaining the established sequence in national expansion and adopted a pose of "wise and masterly inactivity" until the "footloose and fecund frontiersman" had created by his presence in the new territory the *raison d'être* for public action.

The Wilkes Mission

A more substantial quickening of public interest and action toward Oregon did occur after 1840. In 1841 Captain Charles Wilkes, commander of the Pacific naval squadron, led a topographic expedition to the Columbia. He mapped the Oregon coast and rivers and sent reconnoitering parties into the interior. Wilkes' report included the comment that the Protestant missionaries were "more interested in land grabbing than in uplifting the Indians." [7] The report led to the appointment in 1842 of Elijah White as United States Indian agent for the Oregon Country; his special assignment was to protect tribal interests. White was the first resident American government official in the Pacific Northwest. Also in 1842, the War Department ordered John C. Frémont to explore the trans-Rocky Mountain West, including Oregon. The published reports and maps emanating from Frémont's Oregon explorations were timely and served to foster a growing public and private demand. In addition, between 1841 and 1843, several bills were introduced into Congress providing for American occupation of Oregon and for the erection of forts along the route to Oregon. One such bill passed the Senate in 1843 but was defeated in the House.

---

[6] *Annals of Congress, Debates and Proceedings in the Congress of the United States,* 17th Cong., 2 Sess., 1822–23, p. 598.

[7] Caughey, *Pacific Coast,* p. 236.

American Settlement in Oregon

The Panic of 1837 created great hardship for many Americans and generated a widespread restlessness. For many, it also created a daring that made a journey of 2,000 miles not too far to travel for a fresh start. Expanding citizen interest in Oregon as the land of promise and opportunity was manifested by the formation of Oregon immigration societies in Massachusetts, Missouri, Ohio, Michigan, and Pennsylvania. The Oregon Provisional Emigration Society of Lynn, Massachusetts, for example, sought to recruit several hundred "Christian families" to migrate to Oregon to lead the Indians to Christianity and develop the country.

The first Oregon immigrants who had no missionary connection, numbering about thirty, gathered at Independence, Missouri, in 1841. They were absorbed by a caravan made up mostly of persons bound for Mexican California to settle on a grant recently assigned to John Marsh of Massachusetts. John Bartleson was designated captain of the immigrant column, which became known as the Bidwell-Bartleson party. Thomas Fitzpatrick, the Mountain Man, had been engaged as guide. On August 10, the Bidwell-Bartleson train reached Soda Springs near Bear River. There thirty-two immigrants continued to Oregon, the remainder proceeding to California. At Fort Hall the Oregon immigrants transferred their possessions and supplies from wagons to pack animals and proceeded to the Columbia. The next year more than 100 settlers ventured over the Oregon Trail, which by this time was a well-marked immigrant concourse beginning at Independence, Missouri, or at Council Bluffs in southern Iowa.

The Oregon Trail followed the Platte River to its north fork, ran along the North Platte to the Sweetwater, passed through South Pass into the Green River valley to Fort Bridger, proceeded northwest along Bear River by way of Soda Springs to Fort Hall near the headwaters of the Snake River, followed the Snake past Fort Boise to the Columbia, and, finally, traveled down that stream to the Willamette Valley. The 2,000-mile journey required an average of six months, the immigrant trains covering twelve to twenty miles each day. Fur trade posts at Fort Bridger near Green River, Fort Hall on the upper waters of the Snake, and Fort Boise became important havens of rest and strategic supply stations for the Oregon traffic.

Ox, horse, and mule teams were used to pull the immigrant wagons, although oxen were preferred because of their demonstrated ability to withstand harsh conditions of plains and mountain travel that caused horses and mules to falter. Each wagon contained household effects, tools, and implements—particularly a plow, seeds, clothing, bedding, and cooking gear to use along the trail. Each caravan was followed by herds of horses and cattle to stock the pioneer farms in the wilderness. As the caravans progressed toward the mountains, the oxen weakened from the punishing pull in summer's heat over increasingly rough terrain, forcing the pioneers to lighten the cargo in each wagon. Of necessity, they discarded valued but dispensable chests, bedsteads, and other household impedimenta, retaining the tools, bedding, camp gear, and supplies. The immigrant road from Independence to Fort Boise was well-marked by the abandoned litter of the wagon trains.

During the first crossings, when immigrant trains were small, the pioneers, faced with almost impassable terrain between Fort Boise and the Columbia, abandoned their wagons, and proceeded by pack trains. As the immigrant trains increased in size, enough men and animals were available to handle the wagons by ganging the teams for crossing summits and downgrades and, in tumbled terrain, easing the vehicles with ropes into the deep canyons. The pioneers could thus retain their wagons all the way to the Willamette Valley.

POLITICAL ORGANIZATION OF THE OREGON COUNTRY

In 1843, over 1,000 Americans passed over the Oregon Trail; there were 800 the following year; and, in 1845, the Oregon-bound tide swelled to over 3,000. By the end of that year, 5,000 Americans had arrived in Oregon, compared to a resident British population of less than 1,000. Most of the American settlements were situated south of the Columbia in the Willamette Valley, while the British were concentrated north of the Columbia River around Fort Vancouver. During 1844, Americans began settling north of the Columbia and, in 1846, the Oregon provisional government organized a county there. Urbanization of the Oregon Country proceeded as a string of towns sprang up along the Willamette Valley from Portland—near the site of Wyeth's Fort William—across the Columbia River from Fort Vancouver, south through Champoeg, Oregon City, French Prairie, and Salem.

The Champoeg Government

The increasing American population gave rise to law-and-order problems and, inevitably, legal questions of marriage, probate, and land titles. Between 1841 and 1843, the Oregon settlers held several public meetings leading to a convention in July 1843, at Champoeg. There the so-called Champoeg government was organized. The delegates drafted a frame of government or compact, based in essence on the Northwest Ordinance of 1787 and the Iowa statutes; it contained an antislavery clause. The Oregon compact created a provisional government with elected officials, established guidelines for the organization of counties and local governments, and included rules governing land tenure and other pressing matters. Messengers carried petitions to Washington urging that Congress recognize the Oregon provisional government and absorb the Pacific Northwest into the American community.

The Oregon settlers' plea reached Washington at a propitious time. In Congress, advocates of American occupation of the Pacific Northwest vied for center stage with proponents of Texan annexation. Oregon supporters, backed by the certitude of American occupation of the Pacific Northwest to the Columbia, waxed expansive. Some pressed for national absorption of the territory to the 49th parallel, others to 54°40′. In 1843, Marcus Whitman returned to the East on mission business. His several public speaking appearances and private conversations with national officials, all addressed to the urgency of prompt official assertion of American territorial rights in Oregon, transformed Whitman from an obscure mission physician to a public hero.

The Oregon Treaty

A report that the interest of President John Tyler was being diverted from Oregon to California caused the Oregon advocates great concern. Secretary of State Daniel Webster had just settled the Maine boundary through negotiations with British representative Lord Ashburton. The Oregon boundary had also been a possible subject for consideration, but was submerged; it was claimed that Tyler was willing to set the American boundary at the Columbia in return for British support of his attempt to purchase California from Mexico. Linn and other expansionists in Congress regarded the acceptance of the Columbia boundary as a shameful retreat. "Oregon conventions" were held in the major Eastern cities to protest this rumored action.

The presidential campaign of 1844 provided the solution for the American expansionist dilemma in both the Northwest and the Southwest. Lewis Cass of Michigan, Edward A. Hannegan of Indiana, and other Old West Democratic leaders saw in Oregon the *quid pro quo* for Texan annexation. Their support for the well-established political device of pairing free state–slave state absorption led to their party's acceptance "Reannexation of Texas and Reoccupation of Oregon" as the theme for the presidential campaign of 1844.

James K. Polk, Democratic victor in that election, braced by the majority electoral support for expansion, threw down the gauntlet to the British in his inaugural address, stating that American title to Oregon was "clear and unquestionable." Moreover, in his first message to Congress, Polk urged that joint occupation of the Pacific Northwest be terminated.

The election results also set into motion definitive diplomatic action. Preliminary discussions of the Oregon boundary in 1844 had included an offer by British minister Richard Pakenham to extend the 49th parallel to the Columbia River and, from that point, for the river to serve as the boundary. However, internal pressures in Great Britain—particularly the dependence of British manufacturers on the United States as a market and source of cotton—and American expansionist fulminations of "Fifty-four Forty or Fight!," caused the British to alter their diplomatic course.

Also of considerable import was the fact that long, intensive exploitation of the Columbia River valley by the Hudson's Bay Company had largely exhausted its fur resources. The value of Fort Vancouver as a trade center was considerably diminished; in 1845, company officials had moved the post from the Columbia north to Vancouver Island.

During 1846, the national government devoted considerable attention to Oregon matters. This time Pakenham offered to extend the 49th parallel boundary all the way to the Pacific. On June 15, he and Secretary of State James Buchanan concluded the Oregon Treaty.

Creation of Oregon Territory

Settlement of the Oregon boundary question led Congress to approve funds for the fortification of the Oregon Trail. Thereupon the War Department directed the army to establish Fort Kearny—near Grand Island on the Platte River, 310 miles northwest of Fort Leavenworth—and Fort Laramie—a former trading post on Laramie Creek, 337 miles northwest of Fort Kearny. Congress also considered a bill creating the Oregon territorial government in 1846, but Southern Congressmen attacked the antislavery clause, delaying final consideration. The expanding war with Mexico thereafter absorbed the attention of government officials.

The event that redirected official attention to Oregon was the massacre at Waiilatpu Presbyterian Mission carried out by Cayuse Indians on November 29, 1847. The missionaries were blamed for a killer measles epidemic that was raging among Indian children at the mission. Whitman, his wife Narcissa, and twelve mission workers were slain. Messengers from Oregon rushed to the Eastern United States with a memorial pleading for relief, protection, and official action on Oregon's territorial status. Public expressions of sympathy for the Whitmans and indignation over the massacre induced Congress to reconsider the bill creating the territorial government. It was finally approved in August 1848.

There were at least three far-reaching results of the absorption of Texas and Oregon into the American community. First, the illusion of "national completeness" was shattered. Second, immigrant roads that carried the sweeping American settler tide to the Rio Grande and the Columbia crossed a region off-limits to whites and reserved exclusively for the Eastern tribes. The War Department did not even try to enforce the provisions of the Indian Intercourse Act, which forbade white entry and crossing of the Indian country. Travelers observed firsthand that a goodly portion of the territory west of Missouri and Arkansas, which had been assigned to the transplanted Indians and described as desert, was, in fact, a fertile, attractive region. To the settlers, Indian Territory was an annoyance, an impediment to easy communication between the East and West coasts. Third, and last, the addition of Texas and Oregon made inevitable the fulfillment of the American nation's presumed continental destiny—the acquisition of New Mexico, the Great Basin, and California.

SELECTED SOURCES

General accounts tracing American expansion into the Pacific Northwest include Hubert H. Bancroft, *History of the North West Coast* (San Francisco,
1884), 2 vols.; David Lavender, *Land of the Giants: The Drive to the Pacific
Northwest* (New York, 1958); *Earl Pomeroy, *The Pacific Slope: A History*
(New York, 1957); Dorothy O. Johanssen and Charles M. Gates, *Empire on
the Columbia* (New York, 1957); and Oscar O. Winther, *The Great Northwest* (New York, 1947).

The influence of boomers and the missionary frontier on the American-
ization of Oregon is traced in Cornelius J. Brosman, *Jason Lee: Prophet of
the New Oregon* (New York, 1932); Fred W. Powell, *Hall Jackson Kelley:
Prophet of Oregon* (Portland, 1917); Clifford M. Drury, *Marcus Whitman*
(Caldwell, 1937) and *Henry S. Spalding* (Caldwell, Idaho, 1936); John U.
Terrell, *Black Robe: The Life of Pierre-Jean DeSmet* (Garden City, 1964);
and Nard Jones, *The Great Command: The Story of Marcus and Narcissa
Whitman and the Oregon Country* (Boston, 1960).

American settlement and development of the country along the Columbia
are discussed in Bernard De Voto, *The Year of Decision, 1846* (Boston, 1943);
*David Lavender, *Westward Vision: The Story of the Oregon Trail* (New
York, 1963); LeRoy R. and Ann W. Hafen, *To the Rockies and Oregon,
1838–1843* (Glendale, 1952); and W. J. Ghent, *The Road to Oregon* (New
York, 1929).

The diplomatic settlement for the Oregon Country is traced in Norman
Graebner, *Empire on the Pacific* (New York, 1955); *William H. Goetzmann,
*When the Eagle Screamed: The Romantic Horizon in American Diplomacy,
1800–1860* (New York, 1966); and Frederick Merk, *The Oregon Question:
Essays in Anglo-American Diplomacy and Politics* (Cambridge, 1967).

* Available in paperback.

A Store in Salt Lake City, *ca.* 1857.

20

American Expansion in the New West: New Mexico, California, and the Great Basin

AMERICAN absorption of Texas and Oregon nearly completed the contiguous territorial format of the New West. There remained only the vast southwestern quadrant extending from the Great Basin to the California shore of the Pacific. However, expansionists were beginning to encounter growing opposition to the consummation of their goals from the increasingly powerful antislavery community, which regarded each New West territorial increment as a province for Southerners to seed their abominable institution. The antislavery bloc in Congress had been able to thwart the annexation of Texas for nearly a decade, and expansionists ultimately triumphed only because of the fortuitous readiness of Oregon to be received into the American Union as a free territory.

The expansionists, led by President James K. Polk, were obsessively committed to extending American dominion over the Southwest, in order to round out the geographic perimeter of the United States and to provide the nation an unbroken face on the Pacific from Puget Sound to San Diego. Much of the southwestern territory in question belonged to Mexico. By the 1840s, naked appropriation of territory of another nation was anachronistic and unbecoming of a maturing nation. Polk and other expansionists had to temper their lust for territory with concern for the American image among European nations, particularly Great Britain and France. They also had to contend with the growing fury over slavery and expansion. In order to accomplish their expansionist designs, and at the same time offset domestic and foreign criticism, Polk and his advisers therefore turned to an alternative policy; they attempted to acquire the desired territory through peaceful diplomatic negotiation and purchase.

Failing this, the president was prepared, as the ultimate means, to resort to military conquest.

THE AGE OF MANIFEST DESTINY

The expansionist cause during the 1840s was abetted by a surging national-ism that momentarily caught up the American public in its emotional sweep. Newspapers, lecture platforms, and many pulpits echoed a jingoist line that crystallized into a doctrine designated Manifest Destiny—the idea that it was divinely ordained that the United States extend its en-lightened institutions and law, its elevating Anglo-American force, to the far corners of the continent in order that benighted, deprived peoples could achieve fulfillment. A goodly portion of the American nation adopted this Manifest Destiny spirit as their holy charge, their sanctified national mission. Moreover, it provided expansionists with the essential rhetoric to embroider the naked takeover of desired foreign territory if peaceful means failed. And, if resort to war were necessary, Manifest Destiny would serve as a salve to the national conscience.

American Pioneers in New Mexico

American interest and presence, a vital preliminary to national ap-propriation of territory in both the Old West and the New West, had been established in the Southwest. As a Spanish frontier territory and later a Mexican province, the New Mexican portion of the southwestern quadrant extended from the western edge of the Great Plains to the Colorado River.

After 1821, American fur men and overland traders entered New Mexico. In the early days of the fur trade in the Southwest, over 200 Mountain Men customarily wintered at Taos in northern New Mexico. The town also served as their principal support base, from which each spring they ranged north into the Rocky Mountains, west into the Great Basin, and southwest to the Gila and Colorado hunting areas. As the fur trade faded, many mountain men took up permanent residence in New Mexico; some of them married Mexican women, became Mexican citizens, and turned to trade, particularly with the California settlements. Others farmed, raised livestock, and mined copper, gold, and silver. A few of the more enterprising developed grain and lumber mills and distilleries that yielded the potent and infamous Taos Lightning.

Like the Taos trappers, several American traders from Missouri and Arkansas took up permanent residence and citizenship in New Mexico, marrying Mexican women, and conforming to the prescriptions of the Roman Catholic church. The principal Anglo communities were at Taos and Santa Fe, although several Americans resided in the Rio Grande settlements around El Paso. As the overland commerce was extended to Chihuahua, a small colony of Americans, most of them agents for Missouri and Arkansas-based trading companies, gathered there. Less than a score of Frenchmen and Britons, mostly Scots, also resided in the Rio Grande settlements; most of them were engaged in mining.

New Mexico, because of its semi-arid desert and mountain environment, lacked appeal to American agrarian settlers, and the Mexican colonization laws did not induce the heavy agricultural immigration that they did in Texas. At the time of the American conquest of New Mexico, the Anglos numbered slightly fewer than 1,000 people out of a total Mexican and Indian population of perhaps 50,000. Nonetheless, while the American colony was small compared to the Mexican-Indian population, Anglos did exercise a pervasive influence over New Mexican affairs through their economic power and family connections. They comprised a force to be reckoned with and were to play a strategic role in the bloodless conquest of New Mexico in 1846. New Mexico was very important in the Manifest Destiny–generated expansionist surge through the Southwest, for its territory served as a land bridge between the Mississippi Valley and the Pacific shore.

American Pioneers in California

California was the prize most desired by American expansionists because of its ocean frontage on the Pacific Basin and, hence, its accessibility to the China trade. Spaniards from New Spain were, however, already established there. Belatedly, during the middle of the eighteenth century, the Spanish had occupied California in order to thwart the Russian drive down the Pacific shore from Alaska. Serious Spanish colonization began in 1769 with the founding of San Diego and the initiation of the Spanish mission frontier. Representatives of the Franciscan order, led by the revered Junípero Serra, founded nine missions in California, from San Diego to Santa Clara on San Francisco Bay. Military establishments—presidios—scattered from San Diego to San Francisco, braced the Spanish hold on California.

Spanish pioneers too founded civil settlements and sustained themselves by farming, stockraising, and mining. The political administration of California, manned by officials from New Spain, centered on the capital at Monterey. Colonial California was, however, dominated economically and politically by the Franciscan padres, who collected the local Indians about the missions and instructed them in the vocational arts of weaving, carpentry, masonry, farming, and stockraising.

Spanish mercantilist policy banned foreign commerce from California, but the cumbersome and expensive Spanish trade monopoly produced only irregular and uncertain supplies. Serious shortages of manufactured goods among the California settlers made them easy marks for alien smugglers, mostly Americans, who carried on a profitable clandestine commerce with Spanish California after 1795. Yankee traders found most Spanish officials willing to suspend the stern ban on trade with outsiders in exchange for a share of the trade profits. California was a neglected Pacific frontier of New Spain.

During 1822, the independent Mexican government extended its jurisdiction to California and assigned a governor and other officials to administer the territory. Monterey continued as the capital of California. There the governor and his aides attempted to enforce the laws of Mexico regulating trade, immigration, and other public matters. However, the chaos of Mexican politics, the ever-changing governments and alternating administrative policy, and the general neglect of the northern Mexican provinces of Texas, New Mexico, and California cast the people on their own resources for political direction. As in Texas and New Mexico, Mexican immigration to California after independence from Spain was minimal.

The Mexican policy of open trade legalized a rich commerce, dominated by American maritime traders, that was already well established in Spanish times. At certain seasons, as many as fifty American ships were anchored in San Diego, Yerba Buena, and other California harbors. The traffic consisted of manufactured goods from the eastern United States, carried to Mexican California ports and exchanged for cowhides, tallow, pelts, and other local items. The growing volume and legalization of American trade after Mexican independence led the trading companies to establish offices and warehouses manned by Anglo agents in the principal port towns of California. Thus began the seeding of vital American presence.

British maritime traders, based at Lima, Peru, and other Pacific ports, increasingly participated in the California trade, and by 1840 they were pressing the Americans for commercial preeminence in this rich province. The intense commercial rivalry foreshadowed a complicated diplomatic British-American contest for control of the Pacific Basin frontier.

At the same time that American presence was being established by the maritime traders, it was being strengthened by the overland traders. Increasingly, after 1830, the trade goods brought to Santa Fe by freight wagons from the Mississippi Valley entrepôts on the western border of Missouri and Arkansas were loaded on pack trains and moved over the Old Spanish Trail to California markets. The land traders thus added their presence and interest to the growing American population in California and increased the national stake in the area.

The bucolic calm of Mexican California, and its mission-dominated economy, with stockraising the principal enterprise, was shattered during the 1830s by a change in Mexican land policy. Beginning in 1832, local officials began the secularization of the missions; the process, mostly completed by 1838, broke the power of the missions and opened vast tracts of agricultural and grazing land for lay exploitation. Thereafter, Mexican citizens were allocated huge grants of land. And, even though certain tracts of the appropriated mission properties were reserved for the Indians, in most cases they were easily exploited and shorn of their lands.

The shift in Mexican California from a mission-dominated economy to a lay-dominated economy had a galvanizing effect on expanding American interest in California. No longer was the interest confined to trading frontier enterprises. As in Oregon, distance had been the principal deterrent to the American agrarian frontier's occupation of California; nearly 2,000 miles separated the Missouri border settlements from the Pacific. Anglos had rapidly settled Mexican Texas because it was readily accessible from the Mississippi Valley, but the 2,000-mile crossing to California was an awesome undertaking. However, again as in the case of Oregon, the Panic of 1837 created hardships for many Americans, who became willing to risk the journey and the geographical separation in order to make a fresh start in a rich country.

In Oregon, the missionary frontier had seeded American presence and promoted settlement; in California the traders' frontier served a similar purpose. The material successes of American businessmen in California were personified by Thomas O. Larkin, who was rated as one of the wealthiest men on the Pacific. He, and others like him, provided irrefutable proof of the opportunity waiting in the new land. Many members of the American colony in California were consummate promoters, who ardently desired that their fellow countrymen join them and share in the California bonanza. They transmitted their ecstatic accord for this "Pacific paradise" through letters, articles, and books published in the eastern United States. By the time of the American occupation of California in 1846, a substantial collection of California "boomer" literature had been published.

The first important promotional piece to be published in the American press was Robert Shaler's *Journal of a Voyage from China to the Northwestern Coast of America Made in 1804*, which appeared in the *American Register* in 1808. In it Shaler praised California's harbors, climate, and resources. Larkin was the most ardent of the California promoters. He arrived on the Pacific Coast in 1831, made a sizable fortune as a trader, and was appointed American consul at Monterey. He also served as California correspondent for several Eastern newspapers, including the *New York Sun*, the *New York Herald*, and the *Journal of Commerce*. His reports from California contained detailed, enthusiastic accounts of the land, resources, and climate and the abundant opportunities they afforded for Americans. John Marsh, a New Englander, worked as a frontier trader, settled for a time at Santa Fe, and in 1836 reached Los Angeles. He received a grant of land from Mexican officials and wrote regular letters to newspaper editors in the border towns of Missouri and Arkansas, promoting migration to his tract in California.

Richard Henry Dana arrived on the California coast as a sailor aboard the *Pilgrim* in 1834; the ship was engaged in the hide and tallow traffic. Two years later, he returned to his native New England, and in 1840 he published *Two Years Before the Mast*, a descriptive account of his experiences as a sailor in the American merchant marine in the 1830s. The book contained rich glimpses of life in coastal California. Alfred Robinson, agent for the Bryant and Sturgis Company on the Pacific Coast, published *Life in California* in 1846; it was a serious, unvarnished account of the California opportunity. The published letters, articles, and books on California were widely read in the eastern United States and must bear some credit for developing among restless Americans the interest, will, and commitment to migrate to California.

In the drama of American occupation of California, special note must be made of John A. Sutter, a German of Swiss citizenship who migrated to California in 1839. Sutter applied to Mexican officials at Monterey for a grant of land and was assigned a vast tract on the American River, near its juncture with the Sacramento. There he developed a thriving settlement, complete with fortress, a mill, shops, and a general store. Sutter's workmen opened broad fields for planting grain and tended the herds of cattle and horses that the Swiss immigrant obtained from Mexican ranchmen. Sutter's north California establishment, which he named New Helvetia, was located at the end of most of the trails through the Sierra passes. Sutter, like McLoughlin at Fort Vancouver, succored many a near-starving American immigrant train as it descended into the California valleys. New Helvetia remained an important center for American activity in northern California until the conquest in 1846.

The overland trails to California had already been marked by the American fur men in their furious search for new pelt zones. Their wilderness traces became concourses for the American settler tide. We noted in Chapter 15 that Sylvester and James Ohio Pattie had opened the southern route from Santa Fe to the Gila and west to the Colorado into San Diego. Ewing Young had established a second route, the Great Circle or Old Spanish Trail, from Santa Fe to the Pacific shore; it led through Cajon Pass into Los Angeles. Jedediah Smith and James Walker had reconnoitered the land between the Great Salt Lake and the high Sierras, searched out the passes, and found the routes into California's interior valleys.

Most overland traffic to California originated on the Missouri border at Independence, followed the Oregon Trail to Fort Hall, then turned southwest, skirting the northern edge of the Great Salt Lake to the Humboldt River; it followed the Humboldt across the Nevada desert and approached the Sierras by way of the Walker River or Truckee River, crossing at Truckee Pass into California's interior. A second route, favored by some because the northern trail was often closed for six months by deep snows, started at Fort Smith, went west over the trader's trace along the Arkansas and Canadian valleys into New Mexico to Santa Fe, thence proceeded southwest to Santa Rita and followed the Pattie route to San Diego via the Gila.

In 1841, the first wave of the American agrarian migration reached the Pacific shore, the fruits of intense promotion by California boosters. The chain of events that led to the Bidwell-Bartleson party centered around

Antoine Robidoux and John Marsh. Robidoux, a St. Louis trader based at Taos, had explored much of the Great Basin, the Sierras, and the interior valleys of California in his quest for furs. During 1840, on a visit to the Missouri settlements, Robidoux is reported to have publicly related the bounty of California and its promise. At that time, Missouri editors were publishing the letters of John Marsh, urging settlers to join him on his California land grant. Robidoux's glowing reports of the California opportunity, combined with Marsh's published invitations to settle in California, led to the formation of the Western Emigration Society.

Local interest generated by the society attracted sixty-nine persons, who collected at Independence in the spring of 1841 with wagons, livestock, plows, and provisions in preparation for the crossing to California. The immigrants elected John Bartleson, a Missouri farmer, captain of the column. Bartleson subsequently faltered in his leadership and was replaced by John Bidwell, a young schoolteacher, so the first California immigrant train has been designated the Bidwell-Bartleson party. Thomas Fitzpatrick, the eminent Mountain Man, guided the wagon train to Fort Hall. There, half the members continued to Oregon. Those determined to hold to the original California commitment were now without a guide; they turned southwest, skirting the upper edge of the Great Salt Lake. Rough terrain and wornout animals that were weakened by lack of grasses, forced the Bidwell party to abandon the wagons and pack their equipment and supplies on the backs of the surviving horses and oxen. This first California immigrant column suffered every conceivable hardship on the trail—furnace heat on the Nevada desert, chill in the Sierras, worn-down livestock and wornout and tattered clothing, long periods of torturing thirst, and exhausted provisions that forced them to slaughter even the skinny oxen to keep from starving. Following the Humboldt River to the Humboldt Sink and crossing the Nevada desert, the weakening and at times wavering California-bound immigrants ascended the Sierras along the Walker River. They crossed to the Stanislaus River, and descended into the San Joaquin Valley to Marsh's grant, arriving there in early November 1841.

A second group of California immigrants, the Rowland-Workman party, numbering twenty-five, started west in 1841, following the southern route via Santa Fe and the Gila to the Colorado and on to California. Thereafter, until 1845, an annual average of fifty American immigrants entered California by the overland trails. In 1845, over 250 persons reached California that way; and the following year, the number was probably doubled.

The 1846 immigrations included the ill-fated Donner party, a group of seventy-nine people from Sangamon County, Illinois, many of the members of the families of George and Jacob Donner. Divisive disputes over routes and trail routines slowed the Donner column, and they had progressed only to the east slope of the Sierras by late autumn; the other immigrant trains for that overland crossing season had already negotiated the mountains. Most of what followed was predictable. Deep snow stalled their progress and forced the party to halt at Donner Lake. The terrible Sierra winter produced indescribable suffering, each immigrant facing the grim choice of death by freezing or starvation. Their livestock, the final food resort, had been lost in the highland winter storms. A small group of the stronger immigrants moved out on crude snowshoes over snow ten feet deep in a desperate attempt to reach the transmontane valley settlements. Only seven survived the effort. When rescue parties reached the beleaguered camp, they found only forty-six survivors, who were sustaining themselves on the corpses of their perished comrades.

By 1846, California's population consisted of 7,000 Spanish-Americans, 100 other Europeans, mostly British, and 700 Americans. Each year the American segment of the California population increased, and this Mexican province inevitably was faced, like Texas, with an Anglo-American occupation. One observer has commented that "the fact that this territory belonged to Mexico was no more of an obstacle than was Mexican ownership of Texas. . . . The Mexican War hastened the annexation of California but did not cause its conquest. This was under way before the war began. The peaceful penetration that carried the frontier of the United States into Texas and Oregon was at work and must have produced the same results in California." [1]

American Pioneers in the Great Basin

The Great Basin was the third portion of the New West's southwestern quadrant occupied by Americans during the expansionist decade of the 1840s. The unique force that carried American dominion to this vast intermontane area was a blend of the missionary frontier and agrarian frontier; it was exclusively the work of a new militant religious sect spawned in the Old West—the Church of Jesus Christ of Latter Day Saints, popularly designated the Mormons.

Joseph Smith, the founder of Mormonism, was from Vermont, but had moved to western New York, where, in the period 1823–1830 he experienced a series of metaphysical contacts and visions that yielded revelations and a personal mission. The visions directed Smith to produce and publish the Book of Mormon and to form the Mormon sect as the agency to activate the divine revelations and mission assigned to him. The Mormon Church began to function in June 1830, at Fayette, New York. Smith's doctrines, which became the sacred ordinances for the Latter Day Saints, included the teaching that American Indians were descended from the lost tribes of Israel; therefore, unlike most other American frontier groups, Mormons regarded Indians with a great deal of sentimentality.

Smith's community of followers grew rapidly. They regarded him as

---

[1] Frederic L. Paxson, *History of the American Frontier, 1763–1893* (New York, 1924), p. 367.

the prophet. What he declared to be the order of things for Mormons—on spiritual questions, the economic and social order, and later on polygamy, as well as where they should reside—was accepted as divine mandate not to be questioned. The revelations for founding the new order, interpreted by Smith to the Latter Day Saints, included formation of a theocratic society founded on stern Old Testament patriarchal domination and certain communal practices based on the tithe and common storehouse. The vigorous appeal of Mormonism generated intense and sustained evangelical activity. Missionaries from the sect ranged through the settlements and towns of America and Western Europe, particularly Great Britain, seeking converts and conducting them to the American Zion that Smith had planned for the Latter Day Saints.

Mormonism's tight-knit social organization and the economic success gained through communal sharing provoked envy and alarm among the bigoted "Gentile" (non-Mormon) communities near the settlement in western New York; in 1831 Smith relocated his people to Kirtland, Ohio. There he developed the plan for Zion, where the faithful would gather. He selected Independence, Missouri, as the Zion, headquarters for the Mormon church. During 1832, the Latter Day Saints began collecting at this Missouri border town. Their rapid growth, hard work, economic success, and close social organization, which excluded outsiders, as well as their religious zeal, provoked suspicion and envy among Gentile neighbors and stirred them to harass the Saints. Thereupon, Smith directed his followers to evacuate Independence and move to a sparsely settled section in northern Missouri at a place Smith called Far West. In a short while the line of agricultural settlement reached Far West, and the Mormons received the increasingly familiar bigoted, suspicious response from their Gentile neighbors. The newcomers smarted under Mormon exclusiveness, coveted the Saints' success in farming and business, and vented their resentment by burning and looting Mormon barns, households, and businesses. The Saints retaliated in kind. In one Gentile raid at Far West, eighteen Mormons were slain.

The Missouri governor's order to the state militia to "exterminate" the Mormons caused Smith in 1839 to seek a new home for his people. He found it on the Mississippi River in western Illinois, at the abandoned village of Commerce, which he purchased and renamed Nauvoo. By 1842, the Mormons had transformed this derelict community into a thriving, prosperous town of nearly 15,000 people, one of the largest urban centers in Illinois. The "virulent intolerance" of frontier society followed the Mormons to Nauvoo, so their residence in western Illinois was brief. But during their stay, Smith refined the Latter Day Saint's doctrine, perfected his sect's ecclesiastical and lay organization, and introduced, as a divine mandate, the practice of polygamy.

It seems clear that economic success and the growing population at Nauvoo inflated Smith's sense of power. The fact that he had gained concessions from the Illinois legislature—including special privileges for the governance of Nauvoo under the Mormon system—led him to further politicize the Latter Day Saints by considering the possibility of announcing his candidacy for the United States presidency in 1844. This bold step added to the mounting public resentment. Gentile neighbors were already antagonized by the Mormons' assumed superiority as a chosen people and felt threatened by their demonstrated superiority in agriculture, stock-raising, and business. Smith's action in instituting the practice of polygamy as a divine ordinance outraged local puritan sensibilities and inflamed the growing anti-Mormon bias. During June 1844, Smith and his brother were arrested on a charge of suppressing freedom of speech by their alleged direction of the seizure of a local rival newspaper. Public officials placed them under guard in the Carthage, Illinois, jail. A mob seized and executed the prisoners.

The prophet's death and the threat to Mormon life and property posed by local raider bands caused the Saints to abandon their homes and businesses at Nauvoo and, once more, flee to a safer place. Most of the exiles followed Brigham Young, Smith's successor as head of the sect. However, some Saints differed with the orthodox group led by Young, particularly on the question of polygamy, and remained in the East. A large party of Mormons migrated to Texas, but most of the Saints from Nauvoo followed Young. The new Mormon prophet led the Saints like a latter-day Moses into the New West wilderness in search of Zion, where they could be free of meddlesome, repressive Gentiles. They settled briefly at Council Bluffs; by 1846, an estimated 10,000 Mormons had collected there. Young and the council made plans for a migration that they expected would take them to some remote, protected spot in the Western wilderness, far beyond the settlements.

While the Mormons were collecting at Council Bluffs and preparing to search for a Zion in the New West, the Mexican War began. War Department officials urged Young and the council to recruit a military unit of their young men to serve in the Army of the West, under Colonel Stephen W. Kearny. Young approved the request, for it would provide the means for Mormons to make the Western crossing at government expense. Moreover, the pay received by the Mormon recruits, under the tight communal system, could be used to pay the expenses of others. Therefore, army officials were permitted to recruit the Mormon Battalion, a force of 500 young Saints, who marched to the Pacific under the aegis of the Army of the West.

During the spring of 1847, Young formed a reconnoitering party of 150 persons and 73 wagons, laden with plows, tools, seed, and supplies; with a large herd of livestock, they headed west from Council Bluffs. Young established a paramilitary organization for the column and placed himself in command. The Mormon scouts followed the Platte River into the Rocky Mountains, proceeded through South Pass to Fort Bridger, then turned southwest over the Uinta and Wasatch ranges to the rim of the Great Salt Lake Basin, arriving there on July 24, 1847. Young declared this region to be the Promised Land where the Saints would establish Zion.

Meanwhile, Mormon leader Parley Pratt had collected 230 Saints and led them to New York. There Mormon Samuel Brannon took charge, transported the exiles by ship to the California coast, and led them inland to New Hope, on the Stanislaus River. Brannon then hurried overland to contact Young, meeting him on the trail to the Great Salt Lake. He urged Young to proceed to California and establish Zion there, but Young refused and continued his reconnaissance of the Great Basin. Brannon's colony remained at New Hope, but continued its spiritual affiliation with the Salt Lake community.

Young set the advance party members to developing the New Zion site at Great Salt Lake. Fired by the Mormon stress on virtue of labor, the Saints opened fields to produce food and erected shelters for the incoming migrations. While construction of the Salt Lake City Mormon headquarters began during the late summer, Young returned to Council Bluffs to supervise the relocation of the remaining Mormons to Salt Lake City. The great westward migration was carefully planned and efficiently executed. Young directed the establishment of supply stations along the line of travel to sustain migrants and teams and thus reduce the ordeal of the passage.

The Saints' first winter in the Great Basin was a time of great hardship, accentuated by the problems of feeding the growing population produced by the flood of new arrivals. When the grain supply was exhausted, the pioneers subsisted on roots and wild plants. Subsequently, rigid control of the agrarian society and the fruits of its labor by church officials and the use of communal fields and storehouses produced a public surplus and modest prosperity. By 1850 the Mormons had successfully occupied the Great Basin, and intensive proselytizing in the eastern United States and Western Europe yielded a steady stream of converts. Mormon scouts were kept busy searching the Southwest for settlement sites, the principal consideration being the availability of a stable, sustained flow of water for irrigation. Latter Day Saints' settlements radiated north from Salt Lake City into Idaho, west to Nevada, south into northern Mexico, and southwest across the Sierras near the Cajon Pass in California.

Soon Mormonism had prospered sufficiently from the tithe-and-communal-business practice to enable Young and the sect managers to establish an immigration fund. Missionaries advanced both American and European converts expenses to pay transportation costs to Zion. The European flow was received at New York and New Orleans and conducted to Salt Lake City by Mormon agents. Recruits repaid the transportation advance after becoming established in the Great Basin settlements. By 1850 the Mormon population in the New West numbered between 15,000 and 20,000 and was distributed among nearly 100 settlements. Each new community setting forth from Zion moved as a group, following the old New England congregational pattern and settling on a site selected beforehand by experienced Mormon scouts. In the early stages, each Mormon town in the New West was almost exclusively communal; gradually greater individual enterprise was tolerated, with the ecclesiastical establishment at Salt Lake City maintaining a strong, continuing oversight.

The polity for directing Mormon affairs was ecclesiastical, that is, the Saints were governed by church officials. Young dominated the theocratic establishment. In 1849, the Saints took steps to create a civil government, not to supersede the religious apparatus, but to supplement it. A Mormon convention met in Salt Lake City and drafted a constitution creating the provisional state of Deseret. In an election held under the provisions of the Deseret constitution, church officials were chosen to fill the elective positions in the new provisional government. Young was elected governor. Deseret officials sent a memorial to Congress urging acceptance of the work of the Salt Lake City convention and admission to the American Union. Congress deferred consideration of the request.

From the American agrarian viewpoint, the Mormons had occupied the most unattractive portion of the New West. Their energy and industry, their peculiar cooperative response to the semiarid Great Basin country, provided convincing proof that even the most scorned portion of the Great American Desert could be occupied and turned to prosperous exploitation. Mormon experience with irrigation and water management was instructive and precedent setting. And Mormon settlements, situated conveniently to the great immigrant concourses, were strategic demographic and economic bridges connecting the East with the Pacific shore.

THE MEXICAN WAR

By 1846, American presence had been well established in New Mexico and California, and the occupation of the Great Basin was assured. Local action by Anglo residents had begun to generate nationalizing currents, and leaders of the national government—particularly President James K. Polk—ached to absorb the southwestern quadrant of the New West into the United States. California and New Mexico were only nominally bound to Mexico, and Anglo settlers found the same conditions in those territories that they had seen in Mexican Texas. American residents were daily witnesses to the administrative ineffectiveness and military weakness of the Mexican government. Revolutionary ferment, political chaos and uncertainty in Mexico City sapped the young nation's vitals and robbed it of the will and means to properly manage its frontier territories. But the efficiency-inclined Anglos regarded this political malaise with grand contempt as a despicable waste of human and natural resources for which they had little patience.

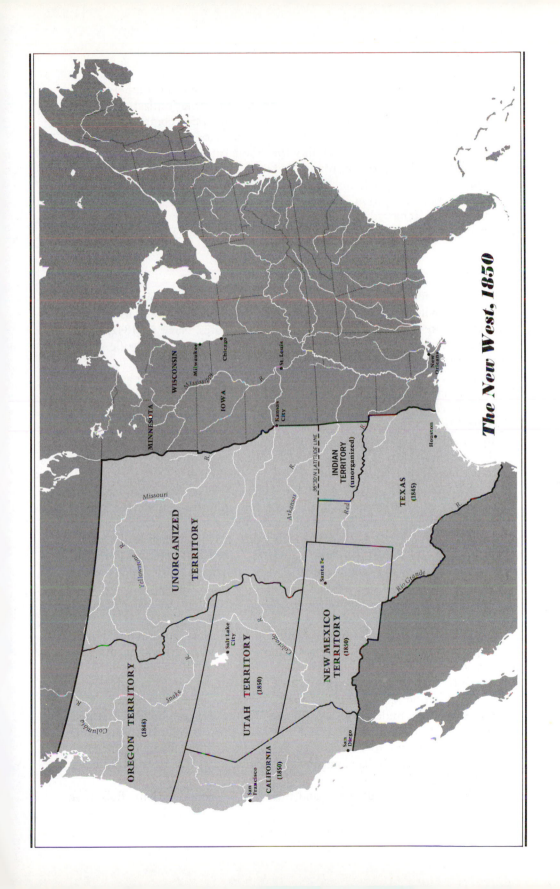

The New West, 1850

MINNESOTA

WISCONSIN
Milwaukee
Chicago

IOWA

Mississippi R.

St. Louis

Kansas City

New Orleans

Houston

TEXAS
(1845)

INDIAN TERRITORY
(unorganized)

36°30' LATITUDE LINE

Red R.

Arkansas R.

Missouri R.

UNORGANIZED TERRITORY

Yellowstone R.

Santa Fe

Rio Grande

NEW MEXICO TERRITORY
(1850)

Salt Lake City

Colorado R.

UTAH TERRITORY
(1850)

OREGON TERRITORY
(1848)

Columbia R.

Snake R.

San Diego

San Francisco

CALIFORNIA
(1850)

President Polk was determined to obtain the southwestern territory, but he believed it was too risky to wait for the Americanization process that had brought Texas and Oregon into the American community to run its course in California and New Mexico. Two factors lent urgency to quick annexation. One was the possibility that the great public wave of intensive nationalism—the spirit of Manifest Destiny—that supported his expansionist policy and that, for the time being had throttled the opponents of territorial acquisition in the New West, would spend itself before his goal was achieved. The second factor, and an even greater threat to expansionist goals in Polk's view, was the growing British interest in California.

The British Threat

For some time, national leaders had been concerned over expanding British activity on the Pacific Coast. Their uneasiness was demonstrated by a precipitate act committed by the United States Navy in 1842. Commodore Thomas A. C. Jones, commander of the American Pacific squadron, was under orders to occupy strategic points in California in case of hostilities between the United States and Mexico; he was also assigned to counter any threat of British activity against California. During 1842, Jones received communications, which he regarded as convincing proof that the critical time had arrived, and swept into the harbor at Monterey. He sent an armed force ashore, occupied the capital city of California, and raised the American flag. Learning of his error, Jones quickly apologized to Mexican officials, hauled down his flag, and withdrew.

Thomas Larkin, who served the double role of American consul at Monterey and Polk's confidential agent for California, submitted regular warnings of expanding British influence and activity in California. According to his reports, British agents were active among the Mexican population and the British navy had strengthened its forces in the Pacific. British traders were becoming increasingly competitive with Americans for the California maritime commerce. Hudson's Bay Company officials from Fort Vancouver had established a trading settlement on San Francisco Bay.

British investors also held $50 million in Mexican government bonds. Reports came to Polk of several schemes discussed by British agents with Mexican officials to liquidate this debt. One plan allegedly provided for the outright cession of California to Great Britain by the near-bankrupt Mexican nation. Another called for the creation of an independent California republic under British patronage. It was even rumored that British agents were pressing for the transfer of California to colonial status under British protection, to be managed by creditors through an organization similar to the East India Company and used as a base for British commerce in the Pacific Basin.

Pressed by both domestic and international considerations, Polk took several steps to ensure success for his expansionist goals. During late 1845, he ordered Commodore John D. Sloat, commander of the Pacific naval squadron of seven warships, to be ready to occupy key California ports. The president also reinforced American forces in the Pacific by sending Commodore Robert R. Stockton to California waters with additional warships. At the same time, to counter the growing British influence in California, Polk and Secretary of State James Buchanan sent secret messages to Larkin directing him to encourage the people there to look to the United States for protection if they decided to separate from Mexico. And Larkin was instructed to promote separatist activity.

In 1845 the War Department sent an expedition of sixty heavily armed men overland under the command of Captain John C. Frémont. (One member of the force was the frontier guide Kit Carson.) Frémont's mission, ostensibly a scientific one, was to reconnoiter and map the Great Basin and Cascades region. The column arrived at Sutter's Fort on the American River in September. Leaving his men in camp, Frémont proceeded to Monterey, where he met with Larkin and received permission from Mexican officials to winter in California. In the spring of 1846, Frémont was pressed by Mexican officials to evacuate his camp near San Francisco Bay and leave California. After some delay, the party turned north toward Oregon.

Additional steps taken by Polk during 1845 to brace his expansionist plan included the strengthening of naval forces in the Gulf of Mexico off Vera Cruz and the increase of American army forces in Texas. The Texas forces were then stationed on the Nueces River and were commanded by General Zachary Taylor.

The Slidell Mission

Next Polk resorted to diplomacy in an attempt to consummate his expansionist goals. In early 1845 when the United States annexed Texas, Mexican officials declared it a hostile act, the "fruits of an extended American conspiracy," broke diplomatic relations with the United States, and recalled the Mexican minister in Washington. In the absence of an official diplomatic relationship, Polk encountered some difficulty in obtaining Mexican consent to receive his special envoy to present his proposals for resolving the Mexican-American impasse. Finally, receiving an indication of Mexican willingness to discuss negotiations, Polk selected John Slidell of Louisiana to discuss with Mexican officials the long-standing claims questions. Revolutionary disorders in Mexico had destroyed a considerable amount of American property, and by an 1843 treaty the Mexican government had acknowledged responsibility for nearly $2,500,000 in claims. After three instalments, the Mexican government defaulted; by 1845, American property losses had mounted to over $5 million.

Slidell could offer to the Mexican government the assumption of payment of claims by the United States if Mexico would acknowledge the

Rio Grande as the international boundary. The Texas Republic had claimed the Rio Grande as the southern and western boundary under the terms of the Treaty of Velasco; at the time of annexation, the United States had assumed the river to be the new American border. However, Mexico persisted in claiming that the Nueces River was the Texas boundary. Polk's special envoy was also empowered to offer Mexico $25 million for California and the Southwest.

Slidell reached Mexico during late 1845, at a time when one revolutionary government was being overthrown and replaced by another. Neither government would receive Slidell and discuss Polk's proposals. When word reached the president that Slidell's mission had failed, he ordered General Taylor to occupy the territory between the Nueces and the Rio Grande. By the spring of 1846, the army had established fortifications on the Rio Grande opposite Matamoras.

The Declaration of War

In discussions with his cabinet, Polk stated that war with Mexico was likely, he "welcomed it," and "in making peace we would if practicable obtain California and such other portions of the Mexican territory as would be sufficient to indemnify our claimants on Mexico and to defray the expenses of the war." When Mexico did not respond militarily as promptly as he expected, Polk prepared a message to Congress urging a declaration of war against Mexico because "the United States had enough grievances to justify a war for their satisfaction." [2]

On May 9, the day before Polk's war message was to be delivered, the president was informed that on April 24 a Mexican force had crossed the Rio Grande, attacked an American patrol, and killed several Americans. The president altered his war message. In requesting a declaration of war, he reiterated American grievances against Mexico, pointed to the shedding of American blood on United States soil, and stated, "War exists ... by the act of Mexico herself." [3] On May 13, 1846, Congress approved the declaration of war, adopted a bill calling for 50,000 volunteers, and appropriated $10 million to support the enlarged fighting force. Most of the initial troops were raised in the South and the West; volunteers responded in such numbers that they oversubscribed all enlistment quotas.

Campaigns Against Mexico

The United States army campaigned on three fronts. The first front was opened by General Taylor on the lower Rio Grande on May 9, 1846, and by February 23, 1847, the battle line had extended south into Mexico

---

[2] Quoted in Frederic L. Paxson, *History of the American Frontier, 1763–1893* (New York, 1924), p. 354.

[3] Quoted in Thomas A. Bailey, *A Diplomatic History of the American People* (New York, 1940), p. 269.

as far as Buena Vista. Taylor's troops first engaged the Mexican army in two battles on the Rio Grande, at Palo Alto and Resaca de la Palma on May 9 and 10, and drove the enemy from the Rio Grande. Then, on May 15, with reinforcements, Taylor crossed into Mexico. A large Mexican army led by General Santa Ana confronted Taylor on two occasions. On September 21, American forces drove the Mexican army from Monterrey; and on February 22 and 23, 1847, in the bloodiest engagement of the interior front, Taylor defeated Santa Ana at Buena Vista. Taylor waited at Buena Vista for reinforcements and supplies before proceeding to Mexico City. The support never arrived. Instead, two additional fronts had been opened by American forces; one, converging on Mexico City from the Gulf, drew on Taylor's elite units. Taylor's reduced army was thus forced to carry out a holding action in central Mexico.

The second new front extended from the upper Rio Grande to the Pacific. Polk regarded the rapid conquest of this region as essential to American possession of the territory when the war ended. Moreover, no strong resistance to American occupation of New Mexico and California was expected, largely because of the influence of American residents in these north Mexican provinces. To fulfill this military objective, the War Department directed Stephen Watts Kearny, a colonel and soon to be a brigadier general, to organize at Fort Leavenworth a combined military force of 2,700 dragoons, Missouri volunteers, and Mormons. The force, including an artillery battery of sixteen guns, was designated the Army of the West. The First Regiment of Missouri Mounted Volunteers, the largest component of the Army of the West, was commanded by Colonel Alexander W. Doniphan, a prominent Missouri attorney. Kearny's mission was to occupy the territory between the Rio Grande and the Pacific.

The army departed from Fort Leavenworth on June 30, 1846. As he approached the capital at Santa Fe, Kearny called on James Magoffin and other American traders to persuade New Mexico Governor Manuel Armijo to offer no resistance. They were successful, and American forces entered the capital of New Mexico on August 18, 1846. Kearny established a government for New Mexico and distributed troops throughout the territory to serve as an occupation force. He ordered Doniphan's Missouri regiment to march south, destroy Mexican military resources between Albuquerque and Chihuahua, then move east to link up with General Taylor.

Doniphan's army of 800 men moved down the Rio Grande; near El Paso it defeated a Mexico army at the battle of Brazito and took El Paso. From the Rio Grande, the Missourians marched on Chihuahua, smashing that interior Mexican city's defenses at the Battle of Sacramento on February 28, 1847; it then proceeded east to Taylor's holding line at Buena Vista.

Kearny and 300 dragoons began the overland march to California on September 25, 1846, via the Gila River route. On the trail, they met Kit Carson, a member of Frémont's force, who was carrying tidings of American successes on the Pacific. The pattern of the California conquest was complex indeed! In the early spring of 1846, Marine Lieutenant Archibald Gillespie, bearing secret messages from Washington, had arrived in California. He first contacted Larkin, then rushed north to overtake Frémont. Near Klamath Lake, he found Frémont. After a private conference, Frémont turned his column back toward San Francisco. Beginning on July 9, Commodore Sloat sent marines and sailors ashore to occupy Monterey and other principal California port towns.

When Frémont and his men returned to the American settlements in California, a group of about fifty traders, trappers, and settlers from the Sacramento and American River settlements—led by William Ide—on June 15 declared an independent California republic. They raised a crude flag with a bear figure, which lent the name "Bear Flag Revolt" to their action. Frémont joined the rebels, supplying them with arms and provisions from coasting American warships. Robert Stockton arrived to replace Sloat as naval commander and deployed the Pacific squadron offshore to support the southward march of Frémont's mixed army of 150 men. The co-ordinated land-sea campaign resulted in the near bloodless capture of all Mexican California towns from San Francisco to Los Angeles. Each town was occupied by a small force of marines, sailors, and recruits from the Bear Flag community. Lieutenant Gillespie was placed in command at Los Angeles.

Upon receiving Carson's report of the California conquest, Kearny ordered all but 100 dragoons back to Santa Fe. Relying for support on the approaching Mormon Battalion, which had arrived in Santa Fe during October, Kearny resumed the march to San Diego with the diminished column led by Carson. After a punishing passage of the Mohave Desert, the Americans were caught in a deadly ambush on the approaches to San Diego by a Mexican army. Only the timely arrival of a relief force of marines sent from San Diego by Commodore Stockton saved Kearny's men from annihilation. The army continued to San Diego, arriving there in January 1847. Mexican revolts against American military rule at Los Angeles and other west coast towns had threatened the conqueror's hold on California, but these were put down by mid-January of 1847, and thereafter the residents submitted to American occupation. United States military strength on the Pacific was augmented during January 1847 by the arrival at San Diego of the Mormon Battalion.

The third and last front of American military operations against Mexico was established at Vera Cruz, where, on March 7, 1847, General Winfield Scott launched an amphibious operation against this principal port city. An intensive siege, supported by heavy fire from artillery batteries positioned on the heights around the city, forced the capitulation on March 29. Scott's army marched on Mexico City and was blocked regularly by Mexican armies that inflicted heavy losses on the invaders. President Polk's determination to succeed on this front was fired by his conviction that only by inflicting a humiliating defeat on the Mexican nation—culminating in the capture of the capital city—could the United States force the cession of the southwestern territory he and his expansionist followers so obsessively desired. Driven by great pressure from his commander-in-chief, Scott pushed his troops unmercifully. They fended off the fierce Mexican challenges, and on September 17, 1847, captured the prize—Mexico City.

The Diplomatic Settlement

Traveling with Scott's army was Nicholas Trist, a representative of the Department of State. His assignment was to negotiate the terms of the conqueror. On February 2, 1848, he concluded with Mexican officials the Treaty of Guadalupe-Hidalgo. It provided for the cessation of hostilities and the cession to the United States of all the southwestern territory desired by President Polk. By this treaty, the boundary separating the United States and Mexico was set on the Rio Grande, from the Gulf of Mexico west to a point just above El Paso; thence it ran west to the Gila River, crossed the Colorado River and ended at the coast, one league south of San Diego. The United States agreed to pay Mexico $15 million and to assume $3,500,000 in claims. On March 10, 1848, the Senate ratified the Treaty of Guadalupe-Hidalgo by a vote of 38–14 .

American expansionist goals had been achieved. Except for a small parcel of territory south of the Gila, which was subsequently purchased from Mexico, the geographic perimeter of the contiguous United States was completed. The tribute exacted from the American nation by this victorious war of conquest was the blood of 12,000 of its citizen-soldiers and $100 million. This sobering cost nagging at the national conscience was salved by the mystical balm of Manifest Destiny, by the tangible achievement of expansionist goals, and by the fresh economic opportunity the fruits of conquest afforded its materialistically driven citizens.

SELECTED SOURCES

The American occupation of the Southwest is detailed in the following works, arranged according to area. NEW MEXICO. Hubert H. Bancroft, Arizona and New Mexico, 1530–1888 (San Francisco, 1888); Hobart Stocking, The Road to Santa Fe (New York, 1971); David J. Weber, The Taos Trappers: The Fur Trade in the Far Southwest, 1540–1846 (Norman, 1971); Charles L. Camp, ed., George C. Yount and His Chronicles of the West (Denver, 1966); Stella M. Drum, ed., Down the Santa Fe Trail into Mexico: The Diary of Susan Shelby Magoffin (New Haven, 1963); and James O. Pattie, The Personal Narrative of James O. Pattie of Kentucky (Cincinnati, 1831). CALIFORNIA. Hubert H. Bancroft, History of California (San Francisco, 1884–1890), 7 vols.; Andrew Rolle, California: A History (Rev. ed., New York, 1969); Robert G. Cleland, A History of California: The American Period (New York, 1922); John W.

Caughey, *California: A Remarkable State's Life History* (3rd ed., New York, 1970); and Walton Bean, *California: An Interpretive History* (New York, 1968). THE GREAT BASIN. Hubert H. Bancroft, *History of Utah* (San Francisco, 1889); Wallace Stegner, *The Gathering of Zion: The Story of the Mormon Trail* (New York, 1964); Ray B. West, *Kingdom of the Saints* (New York, 1957); and *Leonard J. Arrington, *Great Basin Kingdom: An Economic History of the Latter Day Saints, 1830–1890* (Cambridge, 1958).

American operations during the Mexican War and the diplomatic settlement are the subject of Milo M. Quaife, ed., *The Diary of James K. Polk During His Presidency* (Chicago, 1910), 4 vols.; Justin H. Smith, *The War with Mexico* (New York, 1915), 2 vols.; *Otis A. Singletary, *The Mexican War* (Chicago, 1960); Jesse Reeves, *American Diplomacy Under Tyler and Polk* (Baltimore, 1907); James M. Callahan, *American Foreign Policy in Mexican Relations* (New York, 1932); *Frederick Merk, *Manifest Destiny and Mission in American History* (New York, 1963); and *A. K. Weinburg, *Manifest Destiny: A Study of Nationalist Expansion in American History* (Chicago, 1963).

* Available in paperback.

Wagon Trains at Independence Rock, by W. H. Jackson.

California Placer Mining, 1852.

21

The New West's Economic Development to 1861

B_Y 1848, the United States had absorbed all of the New West territory except a small strip on the southern New Mexico-Arizona border, which was purchased from Mexico in 1853. At this time, the New West was sparsely populated, and settlement was concentrated around the outer rim of this vast territory. The land immediately west of Missouri, the Indian Territory, had been colonized by aboriginal peoples, most of them from east of the Mississippi. South, in Texas, only the eastern portion of this vast new state had been settled. Southern Arizona was populated by a string of Spanish-American settlements on the Santa Cruz River around Tucson. A thin line of settlement extended along the Pacific coast in California and Oregon. Except for a tongue of settlement running north of El Paso along the Rio Grande to Santa Fe and Taos, the Mormon settlements in the Great Basin, and a scattering of Indian tribes, the New West's heartland was unoccupied.

The economic pulse of this vast trans-Missouri territory, extending from the 49th parallel south to a line on the Rio Grande and Gila rivers, was slow. Agriculture, stockraising, desultory mining, and overland and maritime commerce were the principal industries, and over much of the New West's interior, there was only the residue of the once-great fur industry. Trapping and trading with Indian hunters for pelts continued but on a much-reduced basis. By the 1840s, beaver had given way to the buffalo robe as the most important product. The industry centered at Bent's Fort and other trading stations on the western edge of the Great Plains near the Rocky Mountains.

THE MINING FRONTIER

In 1848 the fortuitous discovery of gold on the American River in northern California drastically quickened the New West's economic pulse and produced pervasive, sweeping alterations in the settlement and development of the region. The riches of the Sacramento encouraged a comprehensive mineral reconnaissance of the New West, which produced discoveries of gold and silver in Washington, Idaho, Nevada, and Colorado, and intensified established mining operations in the older mineral districts of New Mexico and Arizona.

The rush of miners to the new mineral regions rapidly populated many sections of the New West and stimulated essential supportive industries—particularly agriculture and stockraising—that in many cases outlived the mining frontier and became permanent enterprises. Much of the New West was arid and unattractive to settlers from the East, and under normal conditions, settlement of the frontier would have been slow and uncertain. The mineral strikes prevented this outcome, and the rate of occupation and development in some areas was little short of phenomenal. The rapid peopling of portions of the New West, so out of step with the anticipated rate, had an immense and near-immediate impact on the national life and exerted strong pressure for nationalizing currents, to which a reluctant federal government finally yielded.

In the frontier progression from the Old West into the New West, mining had long been a well-established enterprise. The gold fields of North Carolina and Georgia and the lead mining regions of western Illinois, Wisconsin, and eastern Missouri had produced experienced miners. The prospector-miner characteristically occupied a position in the vanguard of the agrarian frontier, often crowding the fur trader as leader of American occupation of the West.

Early Mining in the New West

The great California gold strike had several New West mining frontier antecedents. The first California gold was found by Mexican miners, near Los Angeles in 1842. But even earlier, during the 1830s, rich lead deposits were discovered on Missouri's southwestern border. The ore was close to the surface—from the grass roots down to fifty feet—making extraction easy; and it was very pure, virtually free of silver and other mineral traces, which made smelting simple. Pioneer miners could easily smelt the ore (galena) cubes over wood fires. Miners followed the ore beds west of the Missouri border into southeastern Kansas—which at the time was located within Cherokee Neutral Lands—and south into Indian Territory, opening a small but rich mineral field in the New West.[1]

The eastern section Indian Territory abounded in salt deposits. Springs and wells along the Grand and Illinois rivers yielded a heavy saline

---

[1] Cherokee Neutral Lands were an 800,000-acre tract in southeastern Kansas assigned to the Cherokee nation by the Treaty of New Echota of 1835.

solution that pioneer processors evaporated in huge saucerlike iron kettles over slow-burning fires; they produced a prime grade of salt readily marketed on the southwestern frontier and at New Orleans. Blacksmiths at Doaksville, Boggy Depot, Tahlequah, and other Indian Territory towns fired their forges with bituminous coal mined from shallow pits on the western slopes of the Kiamichi Mountains in the Choctaw nation.

An important antecedent to the opening of the California gold fields was the Spanish mining frontier in the interior of the Southwest. These pioneers from New Spain developed gold and silver mines in New Mexico and Arizona and a rich copper field at Santa Rita in western New Mexico in the eighteenth century. During the Mexican period, some quantities of gold, silver, and copper were mined in New Mexico and Arizona. The gold and silver entered the Santa Fe trade and were important exchange items for the manufactured goods carried to the Rio Grande settlements; they provided much-needed coin and bullion for the specie-hungry Mississippi Valley.

The Sutter's Mill Strike

The discovery that became the great energizing force for the rapid demographic and economic development of the New West occurred January 24, 1848, on the American River in northern California. James W. Marshall, a recent American immigrant, had settled at New Helvetia and entered the employ of John Sutter. In early 1848, he was directed by his employer to erect a water-powered sawmill. Marshall selected a mill site on the American River, fifty miles above Sutter's settlement and near the forested western slopes of the Sierras. After completing the mill structure, workmen excavated a mill race to divert the river's flow to power the mill. Marshall noticed bright yellow flecks in the water flowing through the diversionary channel. He extracted samples of the hard goldlike particles, which after tests proved in fact to be gold.

News of the discovery on the American River set off a human stampede from the coastal settlements. Workmen, ministers, clerks, crewmen from ships anchored in the harbors, lawyers, all manner of men were galvanized by the tidings, abandoned their tasks, and rushed to the gold field. The California coastal towns were nearly depopulated by this first surge of the mining frontier to the American River. The electrifying news of Marshall's discovery also coursed along the channels of commerce in the Pacific Basin to Oregon and the Pacific coast of South America, and to the Sandwich Islands, China, Australia, and New Zealand. During 1848, an estimated 10,000 goldseekers arrived in California—American farmers from Oregon, Mexican miners from Sonora, Hawaiians, Chinese, and Australians. They found rich minerals all along the American River and its tributaries; during 1848 they extracted an estimated $10 million worth of gold.

In June 1848, Thomas Larkin at Monterey sent reports of the strike on the American River and gold samples, which reached the eastern United

States in September. During the summer, Colonel R. B. Mason, the principal American official in California, visited the gold field, and in August he sent an official report of his findings, with gold samples, to President Polk. In December 1848, the president incorporated Mason's report in a message to Congress, providing official and public confirmation of the momentous events in California.

Eastern newspapers published the Larkin and Mason reports, precipitating a national gold fever. The lure of the "new El Dorado" swept like an epidemic through New England, the Middle Atlantic States, and the South; it coursed into the Old Northwest, the Old Southwest, and the Mississippi Valley. Its virus even intruded into the rim of the New West itself as goldseekers collected in the Texas and Indian Territory settlements. Parties of Cherokees, Choctaws, and Chickasaws prepared to venture to the California gold fields. Word seeped across the Atlantic, and goldseekers in the British Isles, France, and other European nations made ready for the passage to California, although the greatest goldseeker outpouring came from the United States.

The California Gold Rush

The first wave of California-bound immigrants collected at the Atlantic Coast ports and at New Orleans for the six-month passage around Cape Horn to California. A shorter but more expensive route used by many was to take a steamship to Panama, make a land crossing of the Isthmus, and board another steamship bound for San Francisco. During December and January, sixty-one ships debarked from Atlantic ports laden with miners.

An estimated 100,000 Americans rushed to California during 1849, three-fifths of them via the less expensive overland passage. All during the winter of 1848–1849, the overland migrants collected at the New West border towns of Independence and Fort Smith or at San Antonio and other Texas towns. The timely publication of Captain John C. Frémont's journal and map of explorations into Utah and California during 1843–1844 provided guidance in the Western wilderness.

The trails followed by the Forty-niners included a road leading from San Antonio to El Paso and running along the Gila to the Colorado River; from there it went west to San Diego and continued north to San Francisco and the Sacramento River. Another immigrant route, the California Road or Doña Ana Road, had been established in 1849 by Captain Randolph B. Marcy. It extended west from Fort Smith, Arkansas to Santa Fe or, alternatively, to Doña Ana; from there it followed the Gila River route to San Diego and north to the gold fields. Several parties of Argonauts followed the by-then familiar Santa Fe Trail from Independence to the Rio Grande, then traveled by the Old Spanish Trail to Los Angeles, or from Santa Fe struck out in a southwesterly direction to hit the Gila route. By far the Western concourse carrying the greatest volume of overland traffic to the gold fields was the well-established northern trail—the Oregon–California Road—that began at Council Bluffs or Independence; crossing the Rockies through South Pass, it reached Fort Hall, then turned southwest and followed the Humboldt to the Sierra crossing.

The demographic fruits of the California gold rush surpassed even the phenomenon of the Great Migration into the Old West. By 1852, California had an estimated population of 250,000. From 1848 to 1858, California was a "poor man's camp"; miners, working singly or in partnership, with a small grubstake and simple equipment, could and did function with some success. It was the period of placer mining—a method of gathering the free gold in small nuggets and dustlike particles. Washed from mother lodes in the Sierras by creeks and rivers to the succeeding hills and lowlands, the gold was dispersed in stream beds and in gravel and soil along the banks.

Placer gold could be mined by simple labor and a relatively primitive technology. Pioneer miners used the pick, shovel, pan, and sluice to collect the mineral. Gold, which is seven times heavier than the associated materials, was easy to separate from the sand, gravel, and soil. Washing the ore-bearing material from the stream bed or from shallow pits along the bank in a shallow pan or in a sluice separated the nonauriferous material and concentrated the gold. Miners also "creviced" nuggets of gold found in a rock face by prying the mineral loose with a knife or bar. The California Mining Bureau reported that the most productive period of placer mining was between 1848 and 1853, when an annual average of $65 million worth of gold was mined. The first decade of California mining produced a half-billion dollars' worth of gold.

The California Mining Camps

The flow of thousands of miners across the western slopes of the Sierras led to successive strikes and produced a rapid urbanization of the gold fields, but most of the mining towns growing up around a new strike had a short life. When the placer gold supporting the mining camp was exhausted, the miner residents moved on to new mineral districts, the abandoned camp more often than not becoming a ghost town. However, several northern California towns that were founded as mining camps developed permanent economic bases and survived the gold-rush period. The principal survivors were Sonora, Columbia, Placerville, Sonoma, Marysville, Sacramento, Stockton, and Oroville.

In the "poor man's camp" or placer era of California mining, a mining camp society came to flower that had been developing on the American mining frontier since colonial times. When pioneer prospectors found a productive gold field, they customarily

> organized a mining district and adopted laws determining the number of running feet of river bottom each claimant was entitled to and the distance up the hills on either side that claims might go; they

decided how much work the finder must do to establish a claim and how much to hold it. They recorded on their informal books the claims and transfers and did the work so well that when laws caught up with the prospectors, it was generally enough to give legal effect to the agreements already in force. . . . Mining law upon the American frontier was a spontaneous growth, embodying some of the experience of Welsh and Spanish miners, but mostly representing the practical adjustments reached on the ground by men used to self-goverment.

Frontier mining law differed from the statutes governing the distribution of public domain lands to farmers "in that it was not the work of non-resident legislators or social theorists." [2] Much of the locally derived mining law of the New West was, in 1866, incorporated into federal statutes.

The California mining frontier, which was far ahead of the national-izing currents that would eventually reach the area, produced immediate law-and-order problems. Mining camp residents met this need by creating extralegal miners' courts and private law enforcement systems—vigilante committees, which maintained surprisingly adequate protection for life and property. The patterns and precedents regulating law-and-order sys-tems, courts, and extralegal management of mining claims and settlement of property disputes were followed in the areas to which the mining fron-tier subsequently expanded.

In the California gold fields, wealth was easily gained and just as easily lost. Essentials in food, clothing, equipment, and entertainment were scarce and oppressively expensive. Through every gold camp there pulsed an essence of desperation; each man was driven by the selfish fear of losing out to his neighbor in the intensively competitive quest for quick, Midas-like riches. One Forty-niner vignette illustrates the hetero-geneous composition of the "poor man's camp."

Take a sprinkling of sober-eyed, earnest, shrewd, energetic New En-gland businessmen; mingle with them a number of rollicking sailors, a dark band of Australian convicts and cutthroats, a dash of Mexican and frontier desperadoes, a group of hardy backwoodsmen, some pro-fessional gamblers, whisky-dealers, general swindlers, or "rural agricul-turists" . . . and having thrown in a promiscuous crowd of broken-down merchants, disappointed lovers, black sheep, unfledged dry-goods clerks, professional miners from all parts of the world, and Adulamites gen-erally, stir up the mixture, season strongly with gold fever, bad liquors, faro, monte, rouge-et-noir, quarrels, oaths, pistols, knives, dancing and digging, and you have something approximating to California society in early days. [3]

[2] Frederic L. Paxson, History of the American Frontier, 1763–1893 (New York, 1924), p. 373.

[3] Quoted in E. Douglas Branch, Westward: The Romance of the American Frontier (New York, 1930), pp. 437–38.

Except for a very few, California mining society generally lacked women. Far and away the favorite of the gold camps was Maria Dolores Eliza Rosanna Gilbert, Countess de Landsfeld, better known as Lola Montez. Billed as a dancer and actress and acknowledged as an overpowering seductress, Lola Montez was characterized by male casualties of her charms as temperamental, tempestuous, violent, and irresistible. She arrived in San Francisco in 1851, her arrival having been announced several weeks beforehand. The docks of the port were jammed with hungry males lusting for a glimpse of this "distinguished wonder."

By the mid-1850s, pioneer miners were encountering increasing difficulty finding free gold in the northern California placers. Much gold remained, but its extraction required mining on a larger scale and capital to finance the expensive excavation of deep shafts and tunnels to expose the ore veins—the mother lodes—that had fed the gold dust and nuggets into the placer deposits along the creeks and rivers. As the placer gold played out, prospectors turned to various other activities. Some went to work as day laborers for the mining companies formed to exploit the ore deposits. Others returned to their homes, some with a stake, others broke. Many Forty-niners remained in California and resumed farming, stock-raising, and other vocations they had followed before being smitten with the gold mania.

Some miners, still obsessed with the gold bug, crossed the Sierras and scattered over the New West from Arizona and New Mexico northward. They coursed through the Great Basin and Rocky Mountains into the Columbia and Snake river country, a restless pack of prospectors; each used the experience he had gained in California and was driven by the eternal hope and conviction that at the turn of a canyon in some remote Western mountain wilderness he would make the bonanza strike. The mining frontier's peripatetic sweep across the mountain fastnesses of the New West in search of riches did in fact lead to several important gold and silver discoveries.

The Nevada Mines

One of the first gold discoveries outside of California was made on the eastern slope of the Sierras in Nevada in 1850. Limited amounts of gold were found in Six Mile Canyon near Mount Davidson. Lake Washoe, at the base of Mount Davidson, gave the name Washoe District to the cluster of tiny mining settlements that grew up there after the 1850 discovery. Over 200 miners worked this area throughout the decade and—while no one made a bonanza strike—each found enough gold to make the search tantalizing. One of the annoyances miners faced in working the Washoe District was the regular appearance of a "blue stuff," which they cast aside.

In 1850, Peter O'Reilly and Pat McLoughlin were working a claim in

Six Mile Canyon. Soon they were joined by Henry T. Comstock, who bought them out. At about this time, an assay was run on ore from the Washoe District; it estimated that each ton of ore would yield $1,595 in gold and $4,791 in silver—the scorned "blue stuff." When the assay reports became public knowledge, a rush to the Washoe occurred. In a few weeks, 20,000 miners arrived at the new bonanza field, about half of them from the nearby California mines. The richest claim was the Comstock Lode, which spawned Virginia City, the principal camp in the district. Virginia City was described as the most abandoned, promiscuous, slovenly, non-descript settlement in the New West:

> Frame shanties, pitched together as if by accident; tents of canvas, of blankets, of brush, of potato sacks, and old shirts, with empty whisky barrels for chimneys; smoking hovels of mud and stone . . . holes in the hillsides . . . pits and shanties with smoke issuing from every crevice; piles of goods and rubbish on craggy points, in the hollows, on the rocks, in the mud, on the snow—everywhere—scattered broadcast in pellmell confusion.[4]

The high cost of processing the silver ore led prospectors to search for and establish mineral claims capable of substantial production. They would then customarily sell out to mining speculators, who formed companies that provided the capital to import, install, and operate the machinery required to mine and process the ore. By 1860, nearly forty companies, capitalized at over $40 million, were operating near Virginia City. Although high wages held some miners in the Comstock mines, many were entrepreneur prospectors who preferred the "poor man's camp" and placer mining. They drifted up and down the canyons and over the mountains of the New West searching for new fields. Out of the prospectors' meanderings and their mineral reconnaissances came additional placer discoveries.

The Colorado Gold Rush

One of the new discoveries occurred in the Rocky Mountains of Colorado. Prospectors had been searching this region for signs of minerals for nearly a decade, when in 1858, prospectors found gold at the mouth of Cherry Creek, a tributary of the South Platte River. The rush that followed is called the Pike's Peak Gold Rush, although the mountain was in fact fifty miles away. During 1858, an estimated 50,000 goldseekers rushed to the eastern slope of the Colorado Rockies to found a string of mining camps, including Boulder, Golden, Black Hawk, Central City, and Denver.

The "poor man's camp" era—the time when prospectors with limited grubstakes worked the placers with pick, shovel, pan, and sluice—was brief in the Colorado field. Placer traces followed to the parent source generally revealed that the gold was embedded in quartz and rock formations that

---

[4] Ibid., p. 494.

required heavy machinery and large work crews for mining and processing. Thus, corporate mining quickly succeeded placer mining in the Colorado gold fields.

The New Mexico–Arizona Mines

In the Southwest, gold had been mined in the Ortiz Mountains near Santa Fe since 1828. Between 1846 and 1850, New Mexican mines annually yielded gold valued at $3 million. Following the American conquest, the copper mines at Santa Rita were periodically worked as well; and soon after 1846 American miners in Arizona were working small gold and silver mines near Tubac. More extensive prospector reconnaissance led to small strikes on the Gila River—twenty miles east of Yuma in 1858—and six years later above Yuma on the Colorado River at Ehrenburg and La Paz. Tubac was the mining center for Arizona before the Civil War. In the 1860s Apache pressure reduced activity in Arizona and forced abandonment of several mining communities.

Mining in the Northwest

During the early 1850s prospectors reached the upper waters of the Columbia and Snake rivers. In 1855, they found gold near Fort Colville, the old Hudson's Bay Company post above the great bend of the Columbia. The arrival of miners from the Oregon and Washington settlements caused the mineral search to continue eastward. Discoveries of gold on the Clearwater branch of the Snake River in 1860 led to the founding of Lewistown, Orofino, and Pierce City.

SUPPORTIVE INDUSTRIES

As we have indicated, the lure of gold and silver broke through the agrarian preoccupation of America and produced the rapid settlement of many parts of the New West that would have been passed over in the usual frontier progression. Mineral discoveries led to patterns of occupation and urbanization of the wilderness that differed from those of the Old West. Miners who feverishly worked their claims from dawn to dark each day had no time to maintain the traditional frontier self-sufficiency; they were dependent on others for food and other essentials. The mining towns thus generated many supportive industries that had a further stimulating effect on the settlement and development of the New West. Many of the supportive industries, particularly stockraising and farming, survived the mining period and became permanent enterprises. The principal supportive industries that grew up along this far-flung mining frontier were stockraising, agriculture, lumbering, some manufacturing, and transportation.

Stockraising

Stockraising was an essential supportive industry for the mining frontier of the New West, providing cattle and sheep to feed the miners, and horses, mules, and oxen to transport the goldseekers from the eastern settlements to California and between the various parts of the mining fields. These animals also supplied the motive force to turn the crude ore crushers and, using the "horse whim," to hoist the minerals from shallow diggings. Huge quantities of freight—food, clothing, tools, and machinery —were delivered to the mining camps in heavy wagons drawn by horse, mule, and ox teams.

Stockraising was one of the earliest industries established in the New West. The Spanish missions, presidios, and settler communities had introduced cattle, horse, and sheep herds into New Mexico, Arizona, Texas, and California. Spaniards and Mexicans also introduced mule breeding, which was carried to Missouri by the Americans who worked the Santa Fe trade. Eastern Indians—notably the Cherokees, Choctaws, Chickasaws, and Creeks—and Anglo-American settlers established stockraising on the eastern margins of the New West from Indian Territory south into Texas. American breeds of cattle and horses mixed with Spanish breeds and produced large, tough, wide-foraging horses and cattle capable of withstanding the hardships of open-range existence. The great post–Civil War cattle industry of the New West had its foundations in Texas and was derived from this blending of Spanish and Anglo-American streams of stockraising.

Before 1851, stockraisers in the Indian Territory and Texas marketed their cattle and horses at St. Louis, Arkansas Post, Shreveport, and New Orleans. There are even reports of drives of Texas cattle to Cincinnati in 1846 and to Chicago in 1856. Many Texas stockraisers drove their steers to Galveston, loaded them on ships, and marketed them in Cuba. The California cattle industry, which had been the basis for a thriving hide and tallow trade during the Mexican period, was drained after 1848 by the heavy demand for cattle in the mining camps. The resultant scarcity caused stockmen in the Indian Territory and Texas to transfer their interest from eastern markets to the Pacific Coast. After 1850, herds of cattle and horses from ranches on the eastern margins of the New West were regularly driven to the gold camps of California. Oregon stockraisers also marketed cattle and horses in the neighboring California mining districts. Stockmen moved into the grasslands along the Platte River after 1850; there they fattened their herds and drove them to the new mining camps in the Colorado Rockies.

Sheep also figured prominently in the New West livestock industry. Spanish pioneers had introduced flocks of sheep into New Mexico, Arizona, Texas, and California. Many Southwestern Indian tribes, particularly the Navajoes, had become sheep raisers. By 1840, wool was New Mexico's chief trade item in the commerce between Santa Fe and the Missouri settlements and with California. Sheep raising also was well-established on the west Texas border around the Spanish-American settlements at Ysleta and El Paso. Anglo-Americans introduced new sheep breeds into the Southwest, including the Merino, which mixed with the Spanish-American *chaurro* breed and produced a larger animal that yielded more wool. During the California gold rush, large flocks of sheep were driven from New Mexico over the Old Spanish Trail and other routes to California to feed the miners.

The Mormons introduced stockraising into the Great Basin and the industry brought them considerable profit. Their settlements, situated near several of the important trails, served as way stations where goldseekers could exchange wornout, footsore oxen, horses, and mules for fresh teams from the Mormon herds.

The early food and transportation needs of the mining fields were supplied by outside stockraisers who drove their herds of cattle, sheep, horses, and oxen over great distances to the mining camp markets. It was not long, however, before a local stockraising industry grew up near the mines. Many of the ranching operations that became important in the postwar period had their beginnings on the mining frontier in this bonanza era.

Agriculture

The modern foundations of agriculture in the New West were established by the Spanish mission frontier that extended from Mexico into Texas, New Mexico, Arizona, and California. Pioneer padres of the eighteenth century found that many communities of sedentary peoples practiced agriculture with irrigation; they altered the Indian irrigation system and applied to this northern frontier the land-use techniques that had been developed in arid Mexico. In addition, the padres introduced new grains, vegetable crops, and fruit-bearing trees, including the olive and citrus. Thus, by the time of the American conquest, agriculture was already well-established in portions of the Southwest.

On the eastern margins of the New West, there was a corridor of well-watered territory endowed with productive soils; it extended from the Platte River southward across east Texas to the Gulf of Mexico. The section of this humid strip between the Platte and Red rivers was the eastern segment of Indian Territory. Before 1861, three important developments in the extension of the agricultural frontier occurred in this region. First, by the mid-1820s, Cherokees, Choctaws, and other colonized tribesmen had occupied the center of this rich wilderness territory and were producing bountiful crops of grain and cotton. Second, at the same time, the part of the humid corridor south of Red River in Texas had been occupied by Anglo-American immigrants, who also opened farms and plantations and established grains and cotton as the staple crops of the region. And third, beginning in 1854, the part of the Indian Territory north of 37° was opened to Anglo-American settlement. The flow of the agrarian frontier across this new land led to the organization of Kansas and Nebraska territories.

The American sweep to Oregon too was part of the extension of the agrarian frontier. Pioneers in the Willamette Valley opened farms to produce grain and other familiar American food crops. The American Oregonians were not, however, the first to exploit the rich lands of the Pacific Northwest; for although the Hudson's Bay Company was primarily concerned with the fur trade of the Columbia region, it also promoted agriculture on a limited basis. Employees—many of them French and Indian mixed engagés from Canada who had completed their term of contract service with the company—were permitted to select farm sites and settle down with their families. A few engagé families lived in tiny farming settlements on the upper waters of the Snake and Columbia rivers, but most of them resided south of Fort Vancouver in the Willamette Valley at French Prairie.

Officials at Fort Vancouver provided each family with seed, wheat, two oxen, two milk cows, plows, and other farming implements. Because of the importance of locally produced grain, vegetables, and beef to support the Fort Vancouver operation, Chief Factor John McLoughlin attempted to recruit farmers from the British Isles; a few did come out to the Columbia region. As the fur trade faded, many free trappers, including several Americans, settled with their Indian wives along the Willamette. One of these was Ewing Young.

In the Great Basin, the Mormon occupation succeeded mostly because of the Saints' ability to adapt established agricultural practices—through irrigation—to desert conditions and because church managers maintained rigid discipline over members of the sect. Latter Day Saints' doctrine held that land, water, timber, and other resources were the common property of the church, rules for their use to be determined by church managers. Mountain Men who had roamed the Great Basin from the earliest days of the New West fur trade were highly skeptical of its agricultural promise. Jim Bridger reportedly offered $1,000 for the first ear of corn grown at Salt Lake.

Under Brigham Young's driving leadership, the Mormons established a communal irrigation system. They dammed streams flowing from the Wasatch Range and excavated canals to divert the water to ditches, which served the producing fields. The agricultural land near Salt Lake City was surveyed and divided into five- and ten-acre tracts and distributed by lot. Each assignee was required to fence his field with stone or poles and to maintain the water ditch that served it. Irrigation permitted intensive use of the land: wheat, corn, vegetables, flax, hemp, cotton, sorghums, and alfalfa were the principal crops produced on these pioneer irrigated Mormon farms.

Young imported trees, shrubs, plants, and seeds from California and other places for the production of additional food crops as well as for ornamenting the new Zion rising in the New West wilderness. The Mormon experience in urbanization and irrigation at Salt Lake City became the model for Latter Day Saints' expansion in other sections of the Great Basin.

In the period between 1840 and 1848, California agriculture was in the process of being Americanized by the growing number of agrarian immigrants from the United States arriving on the West Coast. John Bidwell, one of the better-known Americans, had acquired a grant of 20,000 acres on Butte Creek, where he grew wheat and fruit with marked success. Other Americans were making similar progress in adapting to farming in the new land. But the discovery of gold in 1848 caused widespread abandonment of agricultural beginnings. Grain was left to rot in the fields, orchards withered, and mills stood idle from lack of corn and wheat as the transplanted husbandmen joined mechanics, sailors, townsmen, and others in the rush to the gold fields. One observer said that "the proportion of labor employed for digging gold . . . was altogether too great for the true interest of California." The "gold mania had blinded men's eyes to the surer profits to be derived from producing more useful commodities." [5]

As the gold excitement subsided, many farmers returned to their fields to produce food for the mining camp market. A goodly number of them found in farming the El Dorado that had eluded them in the gold fields. For example, near Sacramento in 1850, an acre-and-a-half truck patch yielded tomatoes worth $18,000. As more miners abandoned mining for farming, an increased volume of vegetables, fruits, and grain replaced the miners' monotonous fare of dried beans and salt pork. Until 1853, Californa suppliers imported wheat to feed the miners. Renewed agricultural production yielded sufficient wheat in 1855 so that no grain imports were necessary; and in 1856, California's wheat surplus permitted the export of 70,000 barrels of flour to Peru.

European immigrants attracted to California by the gold rush increasingly turned to agriculture, particularly truck gardening for the mining camp market. French, German, and Italian immigrants established vineyards and marketed their grapes in the mining camps. American pioneers introduced cotton production and sericulture—making silk from mulberry trees and silkworms.

Lumbering

Until the California gold rush and the subsequent mineral reconnaissance of the trans-Missouri region, lumbering was only a minor New West industry. Logs from the prime walnut stands in the territory of the Creek nation in Indian Territory were carried by barge to New Orleans and shipped to Europe for fashioning into gun stocks in French and German

[5] Katherine Coman, *Economic Beginnings of the Far West* (New York, 1912), vol. 2, p. 291.

factories. Oak, hickory, and ash were lumbered from the hardwood forests on the eastern rim of the New West for use in the carriage works at Independence and Fort Smith. They were used in the manufacture of heavy freight wagons used to carry goods to the Western settlements.

The grand coastal forests of the Pacific Northwest were exploited for masts and planking in refitting merchant ships engaged in the Pacific Basin commerce. John McLoughlin erected several water-powered sawmills near Fort Vancouver and introduced lumbering along the Columbia. The dense Oregon forests supplied logs that pioneer American lumbermen converted into planks for constructing houses and barns and for fencing. The new mining camps also required great quantities of lumber for constructing shelters for miners, mill structures such as mine tunnel supports, cribbings for mine shafts, and ties for car tracks. A great deal of wood was consumed in the manufacture of charcoal, which was used in smelting.

Before the wood products industry established itself in the Sierras considerable quantities of lumber were imported. In 1849, New England sawmill operators shipped 5 million feet of lumber from Bangor, Maine, to the California gold fields. The ships that carried the lumber also included water and steam sawmill equipment in their cargoes. Soon every mining camp of any size had at least one sawmill. Lumbermen cut the fir, pine, and cedar on the Sierra highland slopes. They also tapped the redwood forests in the Coastal Range; redwood planks were the cheapest wood material available for fencing and for plank roads. The heavy consumption of lumber products by the mining camps and saturation cutting by the lumbermen soon deforested many of the highland timber areas around the gold camps.

Manufacturing

In spite of its primitiveness and isolation, the New West developed several rudimentary manufacturing enterprises before the Civil War, most of them for the support of the mining frontier. Resourceful Mormons scrapped iron from hubs and tires of wagons abandoned along the trails and melted and cast the metal parts for flour and lumber mill machinery and for making plows and other agricultural implements. By 1850, the Mormons had sixteen sawmills, eleven grist mills, several sorghum mills, a tannery, a pottery plant, and a woolen mill. By their energy and initiative, the Saints came to dominate the trade of the Great Basin and Pacific slope by the distribution of their industrial products and foodstuffs from their irrigated farms.

California manufacturing in this period was heavily committed to producing heavy machinery for the mining frontier. Wheat ships brought pig iron and scrap metal as ballast to West Coast ports to supply the growing metal fabrication industry. By 1860, sixteen foundries and machine shops in San Francisco produced steam engines and hoisting equipment and milling machinery for the local mines as well as for export to the mining fields of Nevada, Utah, and Arizona. Coal for the California metal furnaces came from mines in the Cascades and at Puget Sound.

Transportation

The New West's quickening economic pulse, produced by the phenomenal expansion of the mining frontier, the concomitant occupation of remote sections of the trans-Missouri region, and the rise of industries to support the mining frontier, created compelling transportation needs. Subsequent political organization into territories and states provided the New West with a strong voice in Congress with which to articulate these needs. This input energized the familiar nationalizing currents, which were soon expressed in laws providing federal guidance and fiscal support for the development of transportation systems to serve Western needs. Technological advances, including the application of steam power to water and land transportation and advances in electromagnetic communication, abetted the process.

Wide use of steam-powered flat-bottomed river boats materially improved service on several Western waterways, even though the character of the streams in the New West's vast interior prevented penetration by river steamers for any great distance. The rivers of the trans-Missouri region for the most part had broad, shallow, sandy bottoms; several of them, such as the Canadian, carried a flow of water only at certain seasons of the year. The deepest penetration by water in the New West was via the Missouri River. During the 1830s, fur trade steamers reached Fort Union at the mouth of the Yellowstone; and by 1859 had reached Fort Benton at the head of navigation near the great falls of the Missouri.

River steamers could course the Rio Grande for nearly 200 miles inland. In California, steam-powered craft plied the Sacramento River system. In the Pacific Northwest during the 1850s, river steamers operated on the Columbia between Astoria and Portland and the Cascades. Steam passage was interrupted at the Cascades rapids by a portage and resumed to the Dalles rapids; above this point, shippers used sailboats. In the far Southwest, steamers ascended the Colorado River from the Gulf of California to Fort Yuma and the upper river gold mining towns of Ehrenburg and La Paz.

The Arkansas and Red rivers were also important water arteries to the interior from the lower Gulf region. However, log obstructions in the beds of these streams slowed passage, and at one location completely blocked passage to the head of navigation. The Great Raft on the Red River above Natchitoches—a natural accumulation of log and brush debris —blocked the channel. Beginning in 1824, Congress appropriated funds to improve navigation on the Red, Arkansas, and Missouri rivers. The river clearance program was under the supervision of Captain Henry Shreve. Shreve's men, using his machine called "Uncle Sam's tooth-puller" for extracting the snags and sunken trees—the bane of river pilots—removed the Great Raft from the Red and doubled the extent of navigable water on that stream. Thereafter, at seasons of high water, supply steamers could reach Fort Towson and occasionally the mouth of the Washita to deliver provisions to nearby Fort Washita. Shreve's men also cleared the Arkansas River of navigation obstacles as far as Fort Gibson and the Missouri River as far as the mouth of the Yellowstone.

The growing use of ocean steamers and the need to provide faster communication with the Pacific Coast led Congress in 1847 to approve a subsidy to support steamship mail service to California. William H. Aspinwall, the contractor, was braced by a federal subsidy, which by 1851 annually amounted to nearly $800,000. He put in service a small fleet of steamers to provide both mail and passenger service on a guaranteed twenty-five-day schedule twice each month. The ocean steamship mail service began in 1849. The eastern branch ran from New York to the Panama Isthmus. Passengers and the mail were then loaded on pack trains, crossed the 47-mile-wide isthmus and re-embarked for San Francisco on the Pacific side. In 1855, the Panama Railroad linked the Gulf and Pacific steamer ports.

However, by far the greatest percentage of California-bound, ocean-borne passengers and freight went by the much longer and slower Cape Horn route. The great profits made hauling food, machinery, and other essentials to the Pacific Coast ports for distribution to the gold fields had a pervasive effect on American shipping and shipbuilding. This influence was particularly important in the case of the clipper ship. This swift craft, developed by American shipbuilders after the War of 1812, had become a fixed model by the 1830s. The fast-moving, streamlined vessel with its "bow turned inside out" was acknowledged the "greyhound of the sea." The clipper, which often weighed as much as 500 tons, was more heavily sparred and carried more sail than the conventional sailing ship.

A conventional sailing ship required from 150 to 200 days to make the 16,000–mile run from New York to San Francisco via Cape Horn. The clipper ship average for this passage was 110 days, and several clippers made the run in just over 90 days. The fastest clippers on the California passage were the *Flying Cloud*, the *Lightning*, and the *Sea Witch*. Huge profits from carrying supplies, mining machinery, and passengers to California after 1849 promoted a shipbuilding surge in the New York and Boston yards. Between 1850 and 1854, 350 clipper ships were completed and sent to sea.

Railroad Beginnings

Maritime connections between Atlantic and Pacific ports touched only the periphery of the New West's territory. Inland water transportation, except for the Missouri River, penetrated only its rim. Providing transportation service for its vast interior remained an awesome problem. By 1850, national political and business leaders acknowledged that the railroad—with its capability for spanning the territory between the Missouri border and the Pacific slope with a main line, while trunk or arterial connections served the scattered intermediate settlements—was the solution to the New West's transportation needs.

European railroad technology had been readily adopted in the eastern United States, beginning with horse-drawn cars on tracks of wood fitted with iron strips. The development of iron rails—steel rails were not widely used until after 1861—and steam locomotives encouraged leaders at Baltimore, Charleston, Philadelphia, and Boston to develop coastal and westward lines. By 1833, a Southern railroad connected Charleston with Western settlements in the lower Appalachians; the Boston and Albany line was completed in 1841; and eleven years later the Philadelphia to Pittsburgh railroad was operational.

During the 1850s, Chicago became the nation's railroad center: the Chicago and Northwestern, Chicago, Rock Island and Pacific, Chicago, Burlington and Quincy, and the Illinois Central all radiated out from the city. In 1854, the Rock Island became the first railroad to reach the Mississippi; and the following year it was the first to bridge the river.

Sectional competition in the railroad drive to the Mississippi Valley and the New West led Southerners to develop lines from the Atlantic ports of Norfolk and Charleston to Richmond, Chattanooga, and Memphis on the Mississippi River. One dramatic effect of the new east-west orientation of railroad expansion into the Mississippi Valley was to threaten the historic north-south concourse of commerce in wheat, corn, and meat products from the Northwest and Mississippi Valley, along the natural waterway system of the Mississippi River, to New Orleans, and thence to New York and other northeast ports.

The Hannibal and St. Joseph Railway was the first line to build across Missouri; it reached the western border in 1859. Throughout the early 1850s, local railroad construction occurred in Iowa, Missouri, Arkansas, Louisiana, and Texas. The Panic of 1857 slowed this development, but by 1861 several rail termini were well-established on the border of the New West. The railroads were ready to proceed toward the Pacific shore.

Support for a transcontinental railroad began during the mid-1830s. Samuel B. Harlow of Massachusetts was an early promoter of this cause. In 1845, Asa Whitney of New York presented a memorial to Congress urging approval of a transcontinental rail line, financed with grants of land from the public domain, to run from the Great Lakes to the Pacific Coast. Whitney said that such a railroad would assure the American pre-eminence in trade with the Orient. After 1846, leaders in the national government had accepted the idea of a railroad connecting the Mississippi Valley with the Pacific shore. The principal Western railroad advocates in Congress were Senator William Gwin of California and Senator Stephen A. Douglas of Illinois. Both urged the adoption of legislation providing for grants of land from the public domain to help finance the construction of a transcontinental railroad. The Illinois Central Railroad Act of 1850 served as the precedent for federal land grants to subsidize railroad construction.

Intense competition developed between the North and the South for the route of the proposed transcontinental railroad. Out of the growing sectional controversy over this issue, Congress appropriated $150,000 in 1853 to fund the exploration and survey of the New West to determine the "most practicable and economical route between the Mississippi and the Pacific coast." The surveys included one from St. Paul to Puget Sound, between the 47th and 49th parallels; another along the 38th parallel via Salt Lake City; a third along the 35th parallel from Fort Smith by way of Albuquerque to Los Angeles; and a fourth along the 32nd parallel from the Texas settlements to San Diego. No survey of the Platte and South Pass route was made at this time. Captain John C. Frémont, in 1843–1844 and 1845–1846, had explored the territory embraced by this potential railroad route. He and other explorers of this course differed on several points; but they all agreed that the South Pass route through the Rocky Mountains was the most feasible. Frémont described South Pass as a sandy plain extending for 120 miles with a gradual and regular ascent.

In 1855, in an attempt to satisfy all contesting advocates of Western railroad routes, Senator Douglas introduced a bill in the Congress providing for three transcontinental railroads—one to be constructed along the northern route, another on the central course, and a third on the southern route. The Douglas bill passed the Senate, but died in the House. Secretary of War Jefferson Davis, spokesman for the South on the railroad location issue, ardently supported the 32nd parallel route connecting New Orleans and San Diego. The bitter sectional contest over the route of the proposed transcontinental railroad during the 1850s created an impasse in Congress. In the meantime, however, Congress did approve appropriations to finance temporary expedients to meet the New West's pressing transportation needs; these included wagon-road construction, mail subsidies for overland stage lines, and a scheme to use camels in the arid Southwest.

The Camel Experiment

The most exotic attempt to overcome the problem of transportation in the arid Southwest involved camels. Secretary of War Davis supported the dromedary experiment for which, in June 1856, a train of seventy-five camels from the Levant arrived in San Antonio. Army detachments tested the camels for every conceivable transportation use. Most of the officers involved in the experiment were impressed by the ability of the animals to function as pack and draft animals under the most trying desert conditions. Lieutenant Edward F. Beale enthusiastically praised the ability of these slow-moving beasts, laden with heavy packs, to go long distances without water; and he noted that their padded feet were superior to the fragile hoofs of mules and horses for travel in arid lands.

Despite supportive field reports, the camel experiment failed to win wide public support. And until after 1861, federally funded wagon roads and federal mail subsidies to steamship and stage companies were the principal stopgap expedients used to meet the pressing transportation and communication needs of the New West. The wagon roads opened in the New West before 1861 included: a road connecting Fort Benton on the Missouri River and the mining settlements on the upper Columbia River via Mullan Pass; a road from Fort Kearny over the South Pass to the California boundary; one from El Paso to Fort Yuma; and a road from Fort Defiance, New Mexico, to the Colorado River near the Mohave Indian villages.

Western Stage and Freight Lines

Both passenger and freight traffic flourished on the new wagon roads, on the Santa Fe Trail, and the other earlier established concourses. Before railroads came to the New West, freighting—the supply of Western communities by wagon caravans drawn by ox, horse, and mule teams—was a thriving industry. Freighting companies were a strategic lifeline for the army posts of the expanding military frontier, remote Indian agencies, and the camps of the mining frontier. In California, freighting companies carried provisions, machinery, and supplies over the rough trails from the Pacific ports to the Sierra mining camps. In the Great Basin the Mormons dominated the supply and distribution industry.

Russell, Waddell, and Majors was the premier freighting firm serving the territory between Missouri and the Rocky Mountains. This company's caravans coursed along the Platte and the tributary routes to supply the scattered army posts, Indian agencies, and mining camps. One company report made in 1860 announced that 18,000 heavy freight wagons operated west of Missouri to supply the expanding needs of the wilderness settlements.

The stage line, supported by a federal mail subsidy, also served to integrate the New West into the life of the nation before the railroad era. Between 1848 and 1861 routes opened by transportation companies operating passenger stage and mail lines laced the New West. These pioneer commercial carriers used both stagecoaches and light wagons drawn by horse and mule teams. Mail and passenger service between Independence and Salt Lake City began in 1848. The following year the Mormons formed the Great Salt Lake Carrying Company to extend the mail, passenger, and freight service to the Pacific Coast. By 1850, mail and passenger coaches also operated between Independence and Santa Fe and San Antonio and Santa Fe. This was not a particularly rapid service, for the stage moved only during daylight; the driver and passengers camped at night to rest the teams.

Federal subsidies for New West mail service began in 1850 when Samuel H. Woodson received a federal contract for $19,000 a year to carry

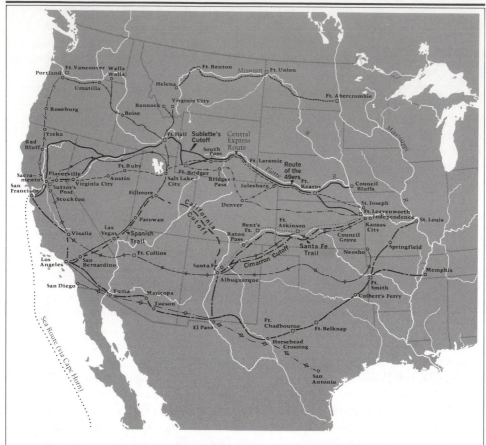

Stage, Mail, Freight and Immigrant Routes in the New West

–––◆––– Kansas and Stockton Express	––•––•–– California Stage Co.
––––––––– Butterfield Overland Express 1858–1861	– – – – Spanish Trail
·–◇––◇–· San Antonio Express	–+–+–+– C.O.C. and Pike's Peak Express
– – – – – The Pony Express, Telegraph and Overland Mail	–·–––·–– Leavenworth and Pike's Peak Express
▪▪▪▪▪▪▪▪▪ Fort Abercrombie to Helena	–·–··–·– Santa Fe Trail
———————— Salt Lake City to Los Angeles	–x–x–x– Sacramento to Portland
+–+–+–+ Salt Lake City to Virginia City and Umatilla (Ben Holladay)	·············· Independence to Sante Fe
	———— Route of the 49ers

Map labels: Ft. Vancouver, Walla Walla, Portland, Umatilla, Helena, Ft. Benton, Missouri, Ft. Union, Ft. Abercrombie, Roseburg, Bannock, Virginia City, Boise, Yreka, Ft. Hall, Sublette's Cutoff, Central Express Route, Red Bluff, South Pass, Ft. Laramie, Platte R., Route of the 49ers, R., Council Bluffs, Sacramento, Placerville, Ft. Ruby, Austin, Ft. Bridger, Bridger Pass, Julesburg, Ft. Kearny, San Francisco, Virginia City, Salt Lake City, St. Joseph, Sutter's Post, Fillmore, Denver, Ft. Leavenworth, Independence, St. Louis, Stockton, California Cutoff, Council Grove, Parowan, Bent's Ft., Ft. Atkinson, Kansas City, Visalia, Las Vegas, Spanish Trail, Raton Pass, Santa Fe Trail, Neosho, Springfield, Los Angeles, San Bernardino, Ft. Collins, Santa Fe, Cimarron Cutoff, Memphis, San Diego, Yuma, Albuquerque, Ft. Smith, Maricopa, Colbert's Ferry, Tucson, El Paso, Ft. Chadbourne, Ft. Belknap, Horsehead Crossing, San Antonio, Sea Route (via Cape Horn) the mail by pack train from Independence to Salt Lake along the Platte route. The next year, George Chorpenning received a federal contract providing for an annual payment of $14,000 to carry the mail from Salt Lake City to Sacramento. Local stage lines in California distributed the mail received from ocean and land carriers.

In 1857, the Postmaster General announced bidding on the first transcontinental mail service. John Butterfield joined with the Adams, American, National, and Wells Fargo companies to form the Butterfield Overland Mail Company and received the federal contract providing for an annual subsidy of $600,000 for six years. The company was required to provide semimonthly mail delivery of no longer than twenty-five days from San Francisco to the eastern termini. The Butterfield Overland Mail Company selected a southern route, claiming that only on that all-weather itinerary could the contract be fulfilled. Terminals at St. Louis and Memphis joined at Fort Smith, on the border of Indian Territory. The route ran southwesterly across the Choctaw and Chickasaw nations to the Red River crossing at Preston; from there it proceeded to El Paso, Fort Yuma, San Diego, and San Francisco.

Elaborate preparations were required to make the line operational. The Butterfield Overland Mail Company purchased 250 Concord coaches for the 2,795-mile run from San Francisco to Saint Louis. Each coach was fitted with wide-rimmed wheels to negotiate the soft soil and sand of southwestern trails, leather straps for springs, and accommodations for nine passengers, the mail, and a driver. Along the route, the company established way stations ten to fifteen miles apart; each had a cabin, corral, relay stock of horses and mules, and employed a stock tender. Freight service on the line furnished way stations with hay and grain for horses and mules and provisions for passengers. Vehicles were to provide expedited service; that is, they would move day and night in continuous progress from one terminal to the other, changing drivers and teams at intervals.

Service on the Butterfield Overland Mail line began on September 15, 1858. The first eastbound coach made the passage in 24 days, 18 hours, and 35 minutes. The Butterfield Overland Mail was a triumph of organization to deliver the mail between St. Louis and San Francisco, likewise "a feat of endurance" for passengers, who paid a $200 fare. From the federal government's viewpoint, the service had to be justified on the basis of national need, for receipts from mails averaged only $28,000 a year.

Two slower transcontinental mail and passenger lines served California on the more northerly course. One ran from St. Joseph, Mo., to Stockton by way of Albuquerque; another from Independence to Salt Lake to Placerville. The latter run required thirty-eight days; the former, sixty days.

Continuing demand by Westerners for improved communications service led to the introduction of another temporary, stopgap expedient—the Pony Express. Senator William Gwin of California conceived the plan, which was developed by the firm of Russell, Waddell, and Majors. The Pony Express was a private mail-carrying venture, unsupported by federal subsidy. The company established a series of relay stations an average of fifteen miles apart on a route between St. Joseph and Placerville-Sacramento, California. They recruited a corps of lightweight daring riders— "orphans preferred." The original postal rate was five dollars an ounce; it was later reduced to one dollar an ounce.

Service began on April 3, 1860, with riders simultaneously departing from Sacramento and the Missouri border. The Pony Express Company had promised subscribers a ten-day mail delivery. The record run was 10 days, 17 hours. Riders averaged ten miles an hour on a 100-mile course per rider. While it was never a financial success, the venture was exciting and focused public attention on the communication needs of the New West. The Pony Express became obsolete after a little over a year of operation by the application of a technological advance in communications to the New West's needs. The Morse electromagnetic telegraph had been perfected in 1844. By 1858, the telegraph line from New York to St. Louis had reached Independence. Work on the line from California progressed, and the east and west crews met at Salt Lake City on October 24, 1861. Thereafter, instantaneous communication linked the Atlantic and the Pacific over a line 3,595 miles long.

In a brief span of thirteen years—from the California gold rush to the outbreak of the Civil War—Americans had accomplished a miracle of expansion, occupation, and development in the remote regions of the New West. These vanguard pioneers required the nationalizing currents of political organization, which only the national government could provide, to match their prodigious economic effort. Reluctantly, the national government responded.

SELECTED SOURCES

Mining was the dominant Western industry in the New West before 1861. The flow of the mining frontier across the trans-Missouri region is discussed in *Rodman W. Paul, *California Gold: The Beginning of Mining in the Far West* (Cambridge, Mass., 1947) and *Mining Frontiers of the Far West, 1848–1880* (New York, 1963); Otis E. Young, Jr., *Western Mining: An Informal Account of Precious Metals Prospecting, Placering, Lode Mining, and Milling on the American Frontier from Spanish Times to 1893* (Norman, 1970); William S. Greever, *The Bonanza West: The Story of the Western Mining Rushes, 1848–1900* (Norman, 1963); *John W. Caughey, *The California Gold Rush* (formerly *Gold Is the Cornerstone*) (Berkeley, 1948); Owen C.

* Available in paperback.

Coy, *The Great Trek* (Los Angeles, 1931); Archer B. Hulbert, *Forty-Niners* (Boston, 1931); *Arrell M. Gibson, *Wilderness Bonanza* (Norman, 1972); Grant H. Smith, *The History of the Comstock Lode, 1850–1920* (Reno, 1943); LeRoy R. Hafen, ed., *Colorado and Its People* (New York, 1948), 4 vols.; William J. Trimble, *The Mining Advance into the Inland Empire* (Madison, Wis., 1914); Rufus W. Wyllys, *Arizona: The History of a Frontier State* (Phoenix, 1950); Warren A. Beck, *New Mexico: A History of Four Centuries* (Norman, 1962); and Charles H. Shinn, *Mining Camps: A Study in American Frontier Government* (New York, 1965).

The supportive industries that were nourished by the development of the mining frontier in the New West are discussed in Katherine Coman, *Economic Beginnings of the Far West* (New York, 1912) 2 vols.; *Oscar O. Winther, *The Transportation Frontier* (New York, 1964); W. Turrentine Jackson, *Wagon Roads West* (Berkeley, 1952); Roscoe and Margaret Conkling, *The Butterfield Overland Mail* (Glendale, Calif., 1947), 3 vols.; Henry P. Walker, *The Wagonmasters: High Plains Freighting from the Earliest Days of the Santa Fe Trail to 1880* (Norman, 1966); Roy S. Bloss, *Pony Express: The Great Gamble* (Berkeley, 1959); and *Ray Allen Billington, *The Far Western Frontier, 1830–1860* (New York, 1956).

Missourians Going to Kansas to Vote.

22

The New West's Political Evolution to 1861

THE sweep of the mining frontier across the New West in the decade between 1848 and 1858 made an immense and almost immediate impact upon national economic and political life. The demographic phenomenon created clusters of mining camps, which early coalesced into expectant political communities. Far ahead of governmental nationalizing currents, New West pioneers formed local extralegal governments and, as their needs increased, appealed to Washington for acceptance and guidance in the state-making process.

National leaders, however, assumed a hesitant, slow, and reluctant posture toward these emerging Western governments. The failure of the federal government to respond promptly to local appeals for recognition and guidance caused many Western communities to hold conventions, write state constitutions, conduct elections, and form functioning provisional governments without federal help. The national government was thus regularly confronted with the *fait accompli* in Western state-making.

NATIONAL INERTIA

There were several reasons for the national leaders' hesitancy in responding to the New West demands for action. First, the rapidity with which portions of the New West had been occupied was inconceivable to many officials. There were still those who languished in the myth of "national completeness"; and it was difficult for them to comprehend that great numbers of American frontiersmen had indeed breached the barrier of the Indian Country and crossed the towering Rocky Mountains to the Pacific. Second, certain national leaders genuinely believed that absorbing the territory west of Missouri would disperse and dissipate the energy and force of the young nation over too wide an area. Third, spokesmen in several states expressed the fear that a bloc of New West states might threaten the established political and economic power of the East. They pointed to the telling effect the population drain—spurred by the recurring gold and silver strikes—had already had on the East. They warned that the process would heighten and produce more damage to Eastern interests if the national government established additional states in the trans-Missouri region. They believed that state-making would create stability and orderly process in the West, thus increasing the region's attractiveness.

There were, of course, men of limited view in high place who were overwhelmed by the sheer distance separating the Atlantic and the Pacific. They regarded with anxiety the problem of managing the vast New West and favored allowing the Far West to organize itself into a political entity independent of the United States. General Zachary Taylor, who was elected president in 1848, took this position in the early days of his administration.

Sectionalism and State-Making

However, the most compelling reason for the reluctance to move promptly to provide political organization for the New West was the growing alienation between North and South over the question of the extension of slavery. The issue colored and limited any national government move to develop the West in the pre–Civil War period. From 1820 to 1861, every new Western territory seeking admission to the Union had to "stand and wait" while Congress reiterated the bitter sectional question of whether the West should be slave or free. Politicians from both the North and the South were edgy and wary of the political consequences of New West state-making.

The Wilmot Proviso

The sectional impasse over Western expansion and slavery crystallized in the Wilmot Proviso. In August 1846, Congressman David Wilmot of Pennsylvania proposed an amendment to a war appropriation bill that President Polk had requested. The substance of the resolution, subsequently identified as the Wilmot Proviso, was to exclude slavery from any territory that the United States might acquire from Mexico. Although it was rejected at the time, the Wilmot Proviso reappeared regularly in Congress as that body debated various matters concerning the conduct of the Mexican War, including the ratification of the Treaty of Guadalupe-Hidalgo.

NATIONALIZING CURRENTS

Momentarily prevented by sectionalism from responding directly to Western political needs, the national government responded obliquely. Federal officials managed to activate throughout the New West some of the less controversial nationalizing currents, such as funding for construction of wagon roads and subsidy of mail—both of which nourished improved transportation systems—and directing the extension of the military frontier. Considering the times, this qualified form of support was the best the federal government could provide.

The Military Frontier and State-Making

An important antecedent to civilian organization of the New West was the entry and expansion of the military frontier into the region. As in the Old West, the military frontier established the first official national presence in many parts of the New West. It fulfilled the traditional functions: erecting military posts—many of which became urban centers in the new land—establishing roads and communication systems, surveying and mapping the wilderness, guarding the international boundaries, and protecting the frontier settlements from Indian attack.

The military campaign against the tribes resisting the invasion of their territory by swarming hordes of miners, stockraisers, farmers, and town builders forced the Indians to accept reduced hunting territory and reservations. Vast areas of the New West were pacified and opened to peaceful settlement. And, as in the Southwest, the military frontier provided the first governments.

One of the duties of General Stephen W. Kearny as commander of the Army of the West was to establish American government in the conquered territory. Following the bloodless conquest of New Mexico, he promised the Spanish and Indian populations security of life and property, freedom of religion, and other benefits of citizenship in the new order. He also organized for New Mexico a government that was a mixture of military and civilian rule. He appointed Charles Bent governor and directed a group of attorneys attached to the Army of the West to compose a code of laws for the territory. The leader of the group was Francis P. Blair; their work became known as the Kearny Code. Troops erected Fort Marcy at Santa Fe to quarter an army of occupation. Governor Bent's administration was braced by a strong military force commanded by Colonel Sterling Price. Seeing the situation was well in hand, Kearny, accompanied by a Dragoon force, proceeded to California in late 1846.

Revolts in the Southwest

On January 19, 1847, many people from the Spanish-American and Indian settlements between Santa Fe and Taos rose in rebellion against American rule. The rebels were stirred by Mexican malcontents, notably Pablo Montoyo, a New Mexican politician, and Tomasito, a leader of the Taos Indians. The two men exploited the resentment of residents against exactions by the American army of occupation. Most of the latter were Missourians who insolently appropriated beef, grain, and Mexican women.

In a swift strike, the rebels assassinated Governor Bent and nearly twenty other Americans at Taos.

From Fort Marcy, Colonel Price led a force of 500 men—some of them Spanish-Americans—against the insurgents. On January 24, his force defeated the rebel army of 1,500 at La Cañada. The survivors fled to Taos, where they took refuge in the thick-walled pueblo until a punishing artillery siege and heavy fighting within the enclosure ended the revolt. Fifteen Taos revolt leaders were tried by jury and sentenced to hang. Price's summary response had restored order to New Mexico, and the mixed civil-military government established by General Kearny continued to function until 1850.

In California, General Kearny faced stiff opposition in his attempt to execute a War Department order to take over that territory as military governor. Following the American sweep through California before Kearny's arrival, Commodore Robert F. Stockton had organized a government for California and had named Captain John C. Frémont military governor. Both Stockton and Frémont ignored Kearny's orders from the War Department. When, on February 15, 1847, Kearny received confirmation of his orders to establish the California government and serve as military governor, Frémont persisted in his refusal to step down. Kearny had Frémont placed under military arrest for insubordination; an army court martial subsequently found him guilty and directed that he be dismissed from the service. President Polk permitted Frémont to resign his commission instead. California too was governed by a mixed civilian-military group supported by a small army of occupation. Kearny and his successor military governors directed the territory during the transition to a purely civil government.

Fortification of the Overland Highways

After 1848, there was a conspicuous change in the direction of the military frontier. From the times of earliest advance of American settlements across the Old West to the Western border of Missouri, the military frontier had always moved in the vanguard of the agrarian frontier. For the most part it had maintained military posts in a north-south pattern extending from the Canadian border to the southern limits of the United States. The classic orientation of the frontier defense was confirmed during the 1830s by the partial consummation of the Cass frontier protection plan. The Cass plan had established a string of military posts from Fort Snelling on the upper Mississippi to the Red River on the southern boundary of the United States. At that time the fortification line was located on the western border of the Mississippi Valley province of the Old West, serving as a buffer between the settlements and Indian Territory. In the 1840s, however, the rapid occupation of the New West between the Rocky Mountains and the Pacific Coast had created a broad, sparsely settled interstice—consisting mostly of the Great Plains—between the Missouri border and the Rocky Mountains. This noncontiguous settlement forced the military frontier to alter its course from the traditional north-south to an east-west concourse in order to protect the roads into the Far West settlements.

Soon after 1846, War Department officials directed the construction of posts at strategic points along the lines of travel into the New West. Fort Smith, as the parent post in the Southwest, supported military stations along the southwestern routes to New Mexico and California. Intermediate posts for protecting the California Road and the Doña Ana Road were Fort Washita and Fort Arbuckle in Indian Territory, Fort Stanton—situated between the Pecos and the Rio Grande—Fort Bliss and Fort Fillmore —which were intermediately situated—and Fort Yuma on the Colorado River. Several protected lines of travel also radiated from Fort Leavenworth on the western border of Missouri. Fort Riley and Fort Mann in Kansas, and Fort Union and Cantonment Burgwin in New Mexico, provided protection from Indian attack on the Santa Fe Trail to the Rio Grande. Northwest along the trail to Oregon and California, Fort Kearny and Fort Grattan in Nebraska, Fort Bridger and Fort Laramie in Wyoming, and Fort Hall in Idaho guarded this great immigrant concourse.

The military in the period between 1848 and 1861 also established a number of military posts as operational bases from which to strike at tribesmen who might obstruct the advance of settlement in the New West. In western Indian Territory and western Texas the War Department established twenty posts to check Kiowa and Comanche raids in Texas and northern Mexico. These included Fort Cobb, Fort Belknap, Fort Chadbourne, Fort Davis, Fort Phantom Hill, Fort Quitman, Fort Stockton, and Fort Worth. The military occupation of New Mexico Territory, which until 1862 embraced all of the territory west to the Colorado River, included Fort Craig, Fort McLane, Fort Thorn, Fort Breckenridge, Fort Buchanan, Fort Defiance, and Fort Mohave. These posts were to provide military strength near the Utes, Apaches, and Navajoes. Discovery of gold in Colorado led to the establishment of bases in the Rocky Mountains at Fort Garland, on the Colorado–New Mexico border near La Veta Pass, and at Fort Wise, near Bent's Fort on the Arkansas River. Fort Wise provided the United States army with a strategic presence near the Cheyenne and Arapaho tribes, who were being pressured by the Colorado gold seekers.

In California, one post, Fort Bragg, was established to protect the Indians of Mendocino County from the rapacity of American settlers. The remainder of the interior California posts were concentrated in the gold regions—Fort Crook, Fort Jones, Fort Humboldt, Fort Miller, Fort Reading, and Fort Ter-waw—and were established to protect the miners against retaliatory attacks by Indians who had been driven from their lands by the rapidly expanding mining frontier.

During the 1850s, Oregon and Washington also each received a cluster of military posts to contain the Indian tribes threatened by the advancing agricultural and mining settlements. The principal posts in Oregon were Fort Dalles, Fort Stevens, Fort Umpqua, and Fort Lane. In Washington, Fort Steilacoom, Fort Taylor, Fort Walla Walla, Fort Bellingham, Fort Cascades, Fort Chekalis, and Fort Colville provided regular and militia forces support for campaigns against insurgent Indians. During the 1850s, some settlement entered the eastern edge of the Dakotas as well. It was protected by the military frontier at Fort Abercrombie in North Dakota and Fort Lookout, Fort Pierre, and Fort Randall in South Dakota.

Pacification of the New West Tribes

The military frontier's conquest of the New West tribes was all but complete by the close of the 1870s; the capitulation of the indomitable Apache leader Geronimo in 1886 was a dramatic epilogue to a long and bloody chronicle that divides itself into three periods. The first period—from 1848 to 1861—was by far the most important in terms of the accomplishment of objectives, especially compression of Indian lands. The second—1861 to 1865—was a time when, curiously, Union troops raised to fight Confederates were used to wage war on New West Indian tribes. And the third—1866 to 1878—which is popularly regarded as the most important period in the process, was in fact a time for consolidation, for following up the advantages gained by the military frontier during the more productive first and second periods.

The accelerated pace of settlement and development in the New West after 1848 required the compression of many Indian tribes into reduced territories. In some cases the Indians submitted quietly. More often they resisted; and the campaigns waged by both regular and militia forces to accomplish American objectives resulted in the near annihilation of several tribes. Before that occurred, however, the government attempted to deal with the Indian problem as it had done so many times before—by treaty.

Federal officials placed the tribes of the northern Great Plains and Rocky Mountains under the management of the Upper Platte Agency at Fort Laramie and appointed Thomas Fitzpatrick agent. In 1851, he held council at Fort Laramie with the leaders of several of the tribes under his jurisdiction, including Mandans, Gros Ventres, Assiniboines, Crows, Blackfeet, Cheyennes, and Arapahoes. Spokesmen for these tribes signed treaties whereby they agreed to permit the United States to build military posts in their territory. They pledged that their warriors would commit no depredations on the immigrant trains crossing their territory, and they accepted reduced hunting grounds. The treaties of Fort Laramie marked the beginning of the compression of tribal lands in this area and the assignment of the tribes to smaller, fixed reservations. By this pact, the Mandans and Gros Ventres accepted reservations east of the Yellowstone, the Assiniboines west of the Yellowstone, the Crows west of Powder River, the Blackfeet were assigned a range in northwestern Montana, and the associated Cheyennes and Arapahoes agreed to remain in a territory situated between the North Platte and Arkansas rivers along the east slope of the Rocky Mountains. In return for these concessions, the signatory tribes were to receive a cumulative annuity of $50,000 for fifty years; the term was later reduced by the United States Senate to fifteen years.

During the 1850s, there were some military confrontations in this north Plains region. These were brought about by Sioux attacks on traders, overland traffic, and the settlements that intruded into the eastern edge of the Dakotas. In late 1854 a Brule Sioux party was attacked by a small United States force under Lieutenant John Grattan; the attack was allegedly punishment for depredations on overland traffic. The Sioux reacted by killing every man in Grattan's column. In August 1855, General William S. Harney led a force of 1,200 troops against the Brule Sioux, engaged them at Ash Hollow on the North Platte, and defeated them.[1] The bitter contest between the Sioux and settlers for control of the land west of Minnesota and Iowa also required regular action by United States troops. A temporary peace was achieved in 1859, when American commissioners concluded a treaty with the Yankton Sioux; by its terms the tribe ceded to the United States a large tract in southeastern Dakota.

In the Southwest, in western Indian Territory and in Texas, United States army troops and the county militia known as Texas Rangers maintained constant pressure on the Kiowas and Comanches. One of the many battles with these fierce people that took place during the 1850s occurred on October 1, 1858, at Rush Springs in the Leased District. Major Earl Van Dorn and a cavalry force made a surprise attack on a Comanche village and inflicted a punishing defeat on these southern Plains raiders.

Soon after the conquest of New Mexico, General Kearny and various officers of the Army of the West met with Navajo, Pueblo, Ute, and Apache leaders, who acknowledged American suzerainty. However, the great increase in mining activity and the mounting immigrant traffic across their lands antagonized the tribes of New Mexico. Soon their reprisals against trespassers and their increasing raids on the settlements required troops to remain in the field most of the time to contain the aroused Indians. Jicarilla Apaches, Utes, and often Mescalero Apaches raided the settlements of northern and eastern New Mexico and preyed on immigrants crossing their country.[2]

During 1854, Jicarilla and Ute war parties threatened Taos. Troops

---

[1] The Brule and Yankton Sioux are of the Dakota group of the Siouan linguistic community, which also includes the Santee and Teton. The Dakota group occupied a territory extending from eastern Minnesota to northern Nebraska across North and South Dakota into Montana.

[2] The Apache are divided into several tribal groups, which include the Querecho-Vaquero (Mescalero, Jicarilla, and Lipan), the Chiricahua (Chiricahua), and the Gila (Mimbreño). The Querecho-Vaquero group resided in northern and southeastern New Mexico and western Texas, the Chiricahua and Gila groups in southwestern New Mexico, southern Arizona, and northern Mexico.

from Fort Union, commanded by Colonel Phillip St. George Cooke, accompanied by the New Mexico militia under Kit Carson, pursued the Ute and Jicarilla raiders into their mountain fastnesses, located their villages, and destroyed great quantities of provisions, blankets, and equipment; the troops recovered some booty and horses and dispersed the Indians. Northern New Mexico remained relatively quiet thereafter until the opening of the Civil War.

Eastern New Mexico was also troubled by the Mescalero Apaches during the 1850s. The tranquility of this portion of the Southwest was further threatened by the Comanches who, deflected from their traditional raiding territory in Texas and northern Mexico by the new, stiffer military frontier defenses, ranged into the Pecos Valley, at times threatening settlements near the Rio Grande. Campaigns by United States regular forces led by Captain Richard S. Ewell pacified the Mescalero Apaches during 1855. The wily Comanches continued to elude the forces sent against them.

Western Apache and Navajo marauders also preyed on the new mining camps of New Mexico and Arizona, sometimes extending east to the Rio Grande where they caused the abandonment of some towns. On one occasion the Navajoes even attacked Fort Defiance and held it under seige. The Western Apaches and Navajoes were not tamed until the coming of the California Column during the Civil War.

In California the rate of Indian destruction and absorption of tribal lands was shocking. The gold rush disturbed the northern California tribes, many resisted, and they were nearly annihilated. The Indian population declined from an estimated 150,000 in 1848 to 30,000 in 1861, a reduction approximating genocide. The conquest of the Modocs is a case study in this aboriginal annihilation. The Modocs occupied the Tule Lake region on the California-Oregon border, where they were caught in a squeeze between the southward expanding Oregon settlements and the northward flow of the mining frontier in California. Heavy traffic from the Oregon towns to the California mining settlements coursed through the Modoc territory. During the early 1850s, attacks by warriors from this tribe on immigrant and supply trains yielded considerable plunder and claimed an estimated 100 American lives. California and Oregon militia, supported by regular troops, were determined to remove this barrier to easy passage between the two settlement areas. Their furious retaliatory campaigns in the Tule Lake area reduced the Modoc population by at least a half and made the tribe an easy mark for dispersal and, eventually, removal to far-off Indian Territory in the postwar period.

The Whitman massacre of 1847, described in Chapter 19, stirred deep resentment among the Washington and Oregon pioneers and set off an Indian-settler conflict that lasted until nearly 1860. After the Waiilatpu Mission attack, 500 volunteers marched through the Cayuse country, pressing tribal leaders to surrender the warriors involved in the massacre. Five men were tried, found guilty, and, on June 3, 1850, hanged. However, incidents continued to mount in the familiar Indian-settler contest for the land. Cession treaties compressed tribal hunting and fishing territories; the rush of miners across eastern Washington and Oregon increased the pressures on the tribes and aggravated the problem. Indian raids on American settlements throughout Washington and Oregon led to joint retaliatory campaigns by regular and militia troops and, often, a further reduction in tribal living space. Between 1850 and 1855, a series of actions against the Shastas and other tribes near the Rogue River drastically reduced the aboriginal population in that area, opened new lands to settlement, and cleared the overland passage to California. Regular and militia forces battered the tribes of the Puget Sound area and put an end to Indian resistance to settlement expansion.

The surge of the mining frontier to the east also caused the Snakes, Palouses, Coeur d'Alenes, Spokanes, and Yakimas to take the warpath. In 1858, Colonel E. J. Steptoe and 150 militia, campaigning in the Palouse country, were attacked and nearly wiped out at Pine Creek by a large force of Spokanes. Later that year, Colonel George Wright and 600 regulars marched through the country to crush the rising Indian resistance. On September 5, on the Spokane Plains, his troops defeated a force of warriors from several tribes and captured and slaughtered 800 Indian horses. On October 5, at a council at Walla Walla, Wright met with leaders of the Snake, Coeur d'Alene, Spokane, Yakima, and Palouse tribes. He demanded that the tribes turn over to him four insurgent leaders; they did so; he executed them and established peace east of the Cascades.

Compression of Indian Lands

The most extortionate action by the federal government in the process of New West Indian land compression before 1861 was accomplished against the tribes of the northern half of Indian Territory. These Indians, most of whom were colonists from the Old Northwest, were casualties of the national plan for a transcontinental railroad to connect the western border of Missouri with the Pacific Coast. Proponents of the Platte route were troubled by the obvious advantages of the proposed southern railroad course along the 32nd parallel. The territory between New Orleans and San Diego had milder winters and lower mountains with less abrupt grades than the region through which the northern transcontinental line would pass. In December 1853, the southern route became even more attractive when federal officials concluded the Gadsden Purchase Treaty with Mexico; the treaty provided for the acquisition of a strip of territory south of the Gila River. It contained a superior roadbed for the southern line. Moreover, the southern route traversed a continuous zone of organized states and territories from Louisiana across Texas and New Mexico into California.

Advocates of the northern route found the right-of-way blocked by the Indian Territory "which now stood as a monument to the short sight of those who in 1825–41 built it up as a perpetual western boundary to the states. There were none now who thanked God for the American Desert and the Indian tribes that prevented straggling of the people across the continent. Instead a demand arose that the Indian Frontier be abolished, that the tribes of the border be made to cede their lands again, and that the right-of-way for the agricultural frontier be acquired west" [3] of Missouri.

Thus in 1853, Commissioner of Indian Affairs George W. Manypenny was directed to begin negotiations with the tribes occupying the northern half of Indian Territory. He traveled to the Indian Territory and opened councils with the leaders of the tribes whose lands comprised the barrier to the railroad advance. He urged tribal leaders to abrogate treaties containing solemn pledges that "forbade the creation of any organized territory" within the lands granted them by their removal treaties. He found that there were few squatters in this part of Indian Territory; he declared that in no way was the region under "pressure of population which had in the past given a justification to many of the removals. . .-. It was a political demand that he was serving, to remove the obstacle to railroad building." [4] The commissioner reported that "without enthusiasm" the Omahas, Otoes, Missouris, Sac and Fox, Kickapoos, Delawares, Shawnees, Kaskaskias, Peorias, Piankeshaws, Weas, and Miamis signed the 1853 treaties and accepted compensation and territory elsewhere. About half the tribes refused to cede all their lands; in compromise, they accepted reduced reservations within the limits of their old domains. In July 1853, the General Land Office opened a branch in Kansas for the sale of the Indian lands opened by the Manypenny treaties. Feeling regret and some shame for what he had pulled off so successfully, Manypenny wrote: "By alternate persuasion and force some of these tribes have been removed, step by step, from mountain to valley, and from river to plain, until they have been pushed halfway across the continent. They can go no further; on the ground they now occupy the crisis must be met, and their future determined." [5]

WESTERN STATE-MAKING

While the military frontier proceeded with the fulfillment of its mission to remove the aboriginal barrier to peaceful occupation of the New West, the national government, sensitive to the prevailing sectionalist furor, reluctantly approached the task of providing political organization for the region. Some formal political organization already existed on the eastern rim of the New West where Texas, a republic for nine years, had been received into the American Union in 1845.

---

[3] Frederic L. Paxson, *History of the American Frontier, 1763–1893* (New York, 1924), p. 431.
[4] Ibid., pp. 431–32.
[5] Ibid., pp. 431–32.

Moreover, north of Texas was the Indian Territory, a region usually overlooked and unacknowledged in assessing the New West's political composition in 1848. The southern half of the territory had been assigned to the Cherokees, Choctaws, Creeks, Chickasaws, and Seminoles. These Southern tribes were the prime carriers of Anglo-American culture into the New West wilderness. Each of the tribes had created functioning governments—all except that of the Seminoles based on written constitutions—even before state government was established in Texas.

The structure and operation of the Cherokee national government illustrates the level of political organization functioning among the immigrant tribes in the period prior to the signing of the Treaty of Guadalupe-Hidalgo. The Cherokee constitution, which remained the organic law for this Indian nation until tribal governments were abolished in 1906, copied the American pattern of separation of powers. It provided for an executive branch composed of an elective principal chief and assistant chief, an elective bicameral legislative branch—the national council—and a judiciary—an appointive supreme court and district courts created by the national council. Other elective officials included a national treasurer and a national superintendent of public instruction. All elections for public officers were *viva voce*. The Cherokee constitution included a bill of rights, defined eligible voters as male Cherokee citizens eighteen years of age and over, and set qualifications for officeholders. The first requirement was that all legislative, executive, and judicial officials had to be Cherokee by blood. The national capital was at Tahlequah. Land in the Cherokee nation was held in common, and any tribal citizen had the right to exploit the national domain. The nation maintained a public school system and other public services.

Compromise of 1850

In early 1848, there were no officially organized state or territorial governments west of Texas and the Indian Territory. There did exist several pockets of *de facto* governments: in Oregon local government had been created by the agrarian frontier extension; in the Great Basin the Mormons had established a theocracy; and in New Mexico and California, mixed military-civilian governments had evolved from the rapid expansion of the mining frontier. Spokesmen for the New West provisional governments urged Congress to legitimatize local political activities.

President Polk had attempted to settle the question in the 1840s, but he was stymied by the force and fury of the great debate over the Wilmot Proviso. The increasing stridency of Free Soil leaders was manifested in their insistence that settlement of the question of slavery expansion was an essential antecedent to providing government for the New West. They urged that slavery be excluded from all territory conquered from Mexico, whereas Polk favored extending the Missouri Compromise line to the Pacific shore. During 1848, bills to establish territorial government for

New Mexico, California, and Oregon were considered by Congress. Only Oregon, which had been functioning since 1843 under a provisional government and which banned slavery, received its territorial status. The Southwest was held in abeyance.

California was administered by a military governor and remained essentially in a state of military occupation. The southern part of the territory continued to be governed by the Spanish-Mexican *alcalde* (mayoral) system. In northern California "each mining town was an out-and-out democracy, and remarkably successful in running its own affairs." Brigadier General Bennett Riley, military governor in 1848, visited the mining fields and reported that officials elected by the miners were "preserving order and regularity almost everywhere, and that while there had been exercise of judicial powers which no law conferred upon these mining-camp executives, the general results had been to bolster society." [6] The California population, fed by the rapid surge of the mining frontier along the northern Sierras, was approaching 100,000 in 1850. Because Congress failed to respond promptly to their needs for a broad civil government organization, Californians met in convention several times during 1848–1849. The conventions produced resolutions urging Congress to act on their behalf; they also considered establishing a provisional government. In February 1849, a block of settlements formed an integrated government for the San Francisco district.

Zachary Taylor, elected president in 1848, was reluctant to intensify the sectional controversy raging over the question of slavery expansion. While initially he favored allowing the Far West to organize itself into a separate political entity independent of the United States, he soon changed his view and took steps to provide leadership for the Southwest. He instructed the California military governor, General Riley, to encourage Californians to draw up a constitution and apply for immediate statehood, thus avoiding the territorial stage of state-making and, hopefully, a prolongation of the slavery expansion argument.

Thus in September 1849, a constitutional convention met at Monterey. William Gwin of Tennessee, a leader in the California statehood movement, was prominent in the convention. The delegates drafted a constitution containing a clause banning slavery, and the draft was approved by a territory-wide referendum in the autumn of 1849. California voters also elected state officials and two United States senators. The confrontation of California's readiness for statehood, abetted by the president, could not be ignored by Congress. The California statehood bill became part of the hard-won sectionalist compromise concluded in 1850.

The statehood ferment was also at work in New Mexico and Utah. Anglo- and Spanish-American politicians in New Mexico joined forces during 1849; they held several conventions, which produced petitions and

[6] E. Douglas Branch, *Westward: The Romance of the American Frontier* (New York, 1930), p. 440.

memorials urging Congress to end military government and authorize an exclusively civil government. At that time, the New Mexico Territory, which stretched as far as the Colorado River and included present-day Arizona, had a population of nearly 62,000. In 1850, in response to the statehood current coursing throughout the New West, a popularly elected convention drafted a constitution banning slavery and establishing a provisional state government. New Mexico's status, however, was complicated by a Texas claim—dating from the days of the Texas Republic—that its western boundary was the Rio Grande River; if the claim were accepted, Texas would, in effect, absorb the eastern half of New Mexico. The boundary question, as well as New Mexico's stand against slavery, forced Congress to consider New Mexico's request for statehood in the context of the great compromise then being fashioned by congressional leaders.

The Mormon-dominated Great Basin had a population of about 15,000 by 1850. The Church of Latter Day Saints had provided the region with a strong, theocratic government. Brigham Young, president of the Mormon Church, and the Council of Twelve Apostles managed both the ecclesiastical and secular life of the Great Basin. In March 1849, a convention of Mormons met at Salt Lake City and wrote a constitution creating the provisional state of Deseret. In elections held under this constitution, Deseret citizens chose Brigham Young governor and elected a legislature and a congressional delegate to promote Mormon statehood in Washington. The state of Deseret claimed all the territory south of Oregon between the Rocky Mountains and the Sierras. The Deseret proposal received the same delayed treatment accorded the California and New Mexico statehood plans.

Pressed by these extralegal activities of Western politicians, during 1850 Congress began the tortured attempt to soothe the bitter sectional passions that the New West demands had precipitated in both the North and the South and to forge a definitive Western settlement. The effort brought together the nation's greatest living statesmen—Henry Clay, John C. Calhoun, and Daniel Webster.

Clay and Webster worked mightily for a solution. Through the force of personality and the persuasiveness of their oratory they triumphed. Clay initiated the concept of clustering Western issues, rather than considering them piecemeal. To soften Southern objections to California's admission as a free state—which negated the Missouri Compromise—and in order to leave open the question of slavery in New Mexico and Utah, he offered the South a stronger fugitive slave law and protection of slavery in the District of Columbia. An obstacle to Clay's plan was President Taylor, who adamantly pushed for the admission of California independent of all other issues. His death on July 9, 1850, and the succession of Millard Fillmore, who was favorably inclined toward the compromise, augured success for the omnibus settlement.

What Clay had so valiantly begun, Senator Stephen A. Douglas pressed to completion. During September 1850, President Fillmore signed the series of bills comprising the Compromise of 1850. For the time being, the political organization needs of the New West were being met. California was admitted as a free state. Texas surrendered its claims to New Mexico in return for federal assumption of $10 million of the Texas Republic debt. New Mexico and Utah were organized as territories "without mention of slavery," implicitly permitting the question to be settled by popular sovereignty. Utah's territory was considerably reduced from the claims of the provisional state of Deseret; it retained an area approximately the size of present-day Utah and Nevada and parts of Colorado and Wyoming.

Oregon Statehood

While Congress was concluding a political settlement for the Southwest, Northwest politicians demanded that the organizational needs of their region also receive attention. Congress had recognized Oregon's provisional government, with its slavery ban, during the late summer of 1848; it created the Oregon Territory, which embraced all of the land west of the Rocky Mountains between the 42nd and 49th parallels. Oregon's first territorial governor was Joseph Lane.

Agitation for statehood continued to be strong, and the Oregon delegates regularly introduced statehood bills in Congress. Congress took a preliminary step in 1853 by detaching the portion of the Oregon Territory north of the Columbia River and creating the Washington Territory. Nonetheless, when, by 1857, Congress still seemed disinterested in statehood, determined Oregon citizens approved a legislative proposal calling for a constitutional convention. The convention met in Salem and drafted a state constitution, which was ratified in September of 1857. Following elections for selecting a governor, legislature, United States senators, and a congressional representative, the *de facto* Oregon state government began functioning in July 1858. This implementation of a state government without official sanction finally forced Congress to admit Oregon to the Union on February 14, 1859.

Washington Territory

The region north of the Columbia River had been organized into counties by the Oregon provisional government and, for a brief period was a part of Oregon Territory. The first Washington census, conducted in 1850, yielded a count of 1,050 people, who supported themselves by farming, lumbering, and coal mining. They also established salmon fishing and packed salted fish in barrels for shipment. The principal market for Washington products were the California mining camps.

After 1850, Washington pioneers regularly petitioned Congress for separation from the Oregon Territory, and in 1853, Congress created the Washington Territory. Isaac Stevens was appointed the first territorial governor. When Oregon was admitted to the Union in 1859, its present eastern boundary was established; and the area east to the Rocky Mountains—which includes Idaho and portions of Montana and Wyoming—was attached to the Washington Territory. The present-day boundary of Washington was set when Idaho became a territory in 1863.

Kansas and Nebraska Territories

No decade in the nation's history produced a greater amount of political organization than the 1850s. We have seen that the principal precipitant was the rapid expansion of the mining frontier and that the inevitable result was local demand for Congress to provide political organization. However, in another portion of the New West during the 1850s the impetus for settlement was the intense free soil–slavery expansion contest. Partisans on both sides of this cause were fired with an evangelical zeal that matched the Argonauts' "gold fever." Each side was determined to populate the two new territories on the border of the New West in such numbers as to overwhelm their antagonists. It is intriguing that, whereas in the initial stages the political organization of the mining frontier was consistently unofficial and extralegal, Congress actually created the milieu for the free soil–slavery expansion contest by providing, in the Kansas-Nebraska Act of 1854, guidelines for settlement and organization.

The lands included in the Kansas and Nebraska Territories had only recently been taken from the tribes of the northern portion of Indian Territory. The legislation to direct the settlement and development of the lands grew out of a bill introduced in January 1854, by Senator Stephen A. Douglas of Illinois. The measure organized the recently ceded lands west of Missouri and Iowa into the Nebraska Territory. Southern interests regarded the bill a threat to slavery access and opposed it. Thereupon, Douglas modified the bill to provide for the creation of two territories, Nebraska and Kansas, to be divided on the 40th parallel. The Douglas bill included the proviso that the slavery question would be settled by popular sovereignty in each of the territories, and, when it became tacitly understood that the slave interest could be expected to control the southern territory of Kansas and the free-soil interest the northern territory of Nebraska, the measure was approved, in May 1854.

The Nebraska Territory took in the region between the 40th and 49th parallels west from the Missouri River to the continental divide. The Kansas Territory was located between the 37th and 40th parallels west to the same point. The first governor of the Nebraska Territory was Francis Burt of South Carolina. He died soon after reaching the new territory and was succeeded by Thomas B. Cuming of Iowa. Andrew Reeder of Pennsylvania was appointed first governor of the Kansas Territory.

The Kansas-Nebraska Bill, the opening of Kansas and Nebraska to settlement, and the subsequent disorder and chaos "broke the charmed silence" of the Compromise of 1850 and "let loose all the attack upon slavery that the old leaders had hoped to stifle." [7] The tacit understanding

[7] Paxson, *American Frontier*, p. 434.

that Nebraska would be a free-soil state led the antislavery partisans to concentrate their settlement energies on Kansas. Their contest with slavery partisans produced a bloody border conflict. The Civil War in its most depraved form raged in Kansas six years before the outbreak of that great sectional contest in 1861.

Senator David R. Atchison of Missouri was the leader of border partisans who were determined to make Kansas a slave state. Most of the proslavery settlers were Missourians. Their numbers were augmented at election time by outsiders—mostly Missourians—entering Kansas to cast their ballots for the slavery cause. Equally determined, to make Kansas a free-soil state, were political and social action groups in the East. These coalesced into Emigrant Aid Societies, which were formed to subsidize free-soil immigrants. Eli Thayer, a Massachusetts Abolitionist, was the leader of this movement. Although some free-soil partisans emigrated from New England, most came from Ohio, Indiana, Illinois, and Iowa. By 1855, the population of the Kansas Territory was 8,500, and it continued to increase throughout the decade. The effects of the concentrated effort to populate Kansas are evident in the 1860 figures. Nebraska's population stood at 28,840; that of Kansas at 107,200.

Between 1855 and 1857, free soilers and slavery protagonists established rival governments in Kansas. Both groups attempted to gain acceptance into the Union. Free-soil settlers met at Topeka in 1855, drafted a constitution banning slavery, and appealed to Congress for admission. In 1857, slavery advocates adopted the Lecompton constitution. Prior to their submissions to Congress, both constitutions were approved by strong majorities of Kansas voters, demonstrating the hazards of popular sovereignty. President James Buchanan submitted the Lecompton constitution to Congress, urging its approval and admission of Kansas as a slave state. Congress stipulated that the Lecompton constitution first be submitted to a territorial referendum, with the promise of statehood if approved. This time the Lecompton constitution was overwhelmingly defeated.

Friction between free-soil and slave communities soon led to bloodshed. On May 21, 1856, Southern raiders struck Lawrence, the center of free-soil sentiment. The Abolitionist zealot John Brown led a free-soil raid against the proslavery settlements and killed five persons in the Pottawatomie Massacre. These incidents set off an orgy of retaliatory raiding, burning, and killing across the Kansas frontier, brigandage that conditioned the people of this beleaguered New West commonwealth to the fury of the Civil War that was soon to spill across its border.

Turbulence in the Great Basin

The political organization of the Great Basin also produced conflict. After the creation of the Utah Territory in 1850, Brigham Young was appointed territorial governor. The remainder of the appointive territorial officers, however, were non-Mormons. Inevitably friction developed between the officials—particularly members of the judiciary—and the Mormons. In 1857, President Buchanan deposed Young as chief executive and appointed Alfred Cummings, a non-Mormon. Two incidents that followed this action seriously impaired statehood prospects for the Great Basin.

In the first incident, threats of local resistance to the accession of Governor Cummings caused the War Department to order a force of 2,500 troops under Colonel Albert Sidney Johnston to Utah. Danites, Mormon militia, harassed Johnston's column, threatening the supply train, running off livestock, and setting fire to the grass ahead of the column's advance. Young finally yielded, Cummings was permitted to enter Salt Lake City, and the army withdrew. Also during 1857, a wagon train of 140 California-bound emigrants from Arkansas and Missouri passed through the Utah Territory. While they were camped at Mountain Meadows in southwestern Utah on September 7, they were struck in a surprise attack by Indians and Mormons. All the adults were killed, although the children were spared. The Mountain Meadows Massacre and the official adoption of polygamy by the Latter Day Saints' Church in 1852 created widespread public revulsion and strong anti-Mormon sentiment, which caused the Congress to hold Utah statehood in abeyance.

Kansas Statehood

In 1861, with the Southern opposition departing to participate in the emerging Confederate States of America, Congress went through one last burst of activity to provide political organization for the New West. On January 29, 1861, a Republican-dominated Congress accepted the antislavery constitution for Kansas, which had been prepared by a free-soil convention at Wyandotte the preceding July, and granted statehood to this embattled territory.

Nevada Territory

The mining frontier expansion along the eastern slope of the Sierras in western Utah Territory generated local demands for the establishment of a government closer to and more compatible with mining camp needs. At this time the mining settlements contained a population of over 20,000. On March 2, 1861, Congress created the Nevada Territory, and appointed James W. Nye of New York territorial governor.

Colorado Territory

The entry of the mining frontier into the southern Rocky Mountains in 1859—the Pike's Peak gold rush—rapidly populated the area and led to local demands for political organization. In 1859, Kansas Territory organized the mining region into five counties. Leaders from local extralegal governments in the mining camps met at Denver to establish a provisional government for the area. They produced a constitution and gave the name Jefferson Territory to their proposed miner's state. Under authority of this constitution, elections were held during October of 1859, to select a governor and legislature. The population of Jefferson Territory was nearly 35,000. In early 1861, Congress responded to the urgings of representatives from Jefferson Territory and created the Colorado Territory, with William Gilpin named first governor.

Dakota Territory

Beginning in 1849, an area west of Minnesota and north of the Nebraska Territory began to develop. The population at that time has been estimated at 1,000. The Minnesota Territory absorbed this settled area in 1857, but with Minnesota statehood the following year, the pioneers in Dakota Territory met at Sioux Falls to organize a provisional government and elect a governor and legislature. The Dakota provisional government urged Congress to extend official organization; finally persistent requests led Congress in March 1861 to create Dakota Territory—an area between the 43rd and 49th parallels, extending from the Minnesota border to the continental divide. The first governor was William Jayne of Illinois.

The decade of the 1850s was a time of phenomenal change in the New West. Rapidly its territory was occupied by mining frontier expansion and the rise of supportive industries; concomitantly governments were organized and the Indian barrier was reduced. The readiness of that technological marvel, the railroad, to proceed from the Mississippi Valley to the Pacific shore, produced the setting for consummation of the most extravagant dreams of the political and economic expansionists.

In 1861, the great sectional contest—precipitated in large measure by the pressing demands of the New West for prompt political organization—shattered the American Union and arrested the momentum of New West development. The New West did not escape this epochal struggle; as we shall see in the next chapter, it was in a sense, the prize for Confederate conquest. Its men fought in the Union and Confederate armies; its soil was bloodied by fierce battles; and its eastern portion—the Indian Territory and Texas—was punished by the victorious Union government for its alignment with the Confederacy by being forced to undergo the pain of Reconstruction.

SELECTED SOURCES

The impact of sectionalism on Western state-making in the period between 1848 and 1861 is discussed in Avery O. Craven, *The Growth of Southern Sectionalism, 1848–1861* (Baton Rouge, 1953); Ray P. Orman, *The Repeal of the Missouri Compromise* (Cleveland, 1909); Charles B. Going, *David Wilmot, Free Soiler* (New York, 1924); Chaplain W. Morrison, *Democratic*

Politics and Sectionalism (Chapel Hill, 1967); and *Holman Hamilton, *Prologue to Conflict: The Crisis and Compromise of 1850* (Lexington, 1964).

The role of the military frontier in fortifying and pacifying the New West and compressing the lands of the Indian tribes is the subject of Edwin C. Bearss and Arrell M. Gibson, *Fort Smith: Little Gibraltar on the Arkansas* (Norman, 1969); Robert W. Frazer, *Forts of the West* (Norman, 1966); Averam B. Bender, *The March of Empire: Frontier Defense in the Southwest, 1848–1860* (Lawrence, 1952); and R. M. Utley, *Frontiersmen in Blue* (New York, 1968).

Two first-rate works tracing the political organization of portions of the New West, both by Howard R. Lamar, are *The Far Southwest, 1846–1912: A Territorial History* (New Haven, 1966) and *Dakota Territory, 1861–1889* (New Haven, 1956). Sources on the creation of New West territories and state-making during the period 1848–1861 include *James C. Olson, *History of Nebraska* (Lincoln, 1955); David Lavender, *Land of the Giants: The Drive to the Pacific Northwest* (New York, 1958); John W. Caughey, *History of the Pacific Coast* (Lancaster, 1933); *Earl S. Pomeroy, *The Pacific Slope* (New York, 1965); LeRoy R. Hafen, *Colorado and Its People* (New York, 1948), 2 vols.; Morton Ganaway, *New Mexico and the Sectional Controversy, 1846–61* (Albuquerque, 1944); George W. Fuller, *A History of the Pacific Northwest* (New York, 1921); and Andrew F. Rolle, *California: A History* (rev. ed., New York, 1969).

* Available in paperback.

Confederate General and Cherokee Leader Stand Watie.

23

The Civil War in the West

BY 1861, the national government had provided some form of political organization for all of the New West. Beginning on the western border of the Mississippi Valley province, the first tier of organized political units consisted of the Dakota Territory, the Nebraska Territory, the state of Kansas, Indian Territory, and Texas. The New West's broad interior—the Great Plains, Rocky Mountains, and the Great Basin—had been carved into the Colorado Territory, the New Mexico Territory, the Utah Territory, and the Nevada Territory. West of the Sierras, Congress had divided the Pacific littoral into the Washington Territory and the states of Oregon and California. Except in the cases of Texas and Indian Territory, this organization had occurred between 1850 and 1861.

Settlement and development in the New West did not slow perceptibly because of the Civil War, but continued—mostly because of the expanding mining frontier. This growth created local demands that established territories be fragmented into smaller political units that would be more responsive to local demands. And the national government, now freed of the impeding Southern bloc in Congress, continued to create additional states and territories. It is ironic that the process of state-making and territorial organization—which acted as a nationalizing current and was carried on over Southern objections during the 1850s—was primarily responsible for provoking sectional animus to the breaking point in 1861. By that year, eleven states and territories (excluding Indian Territory) had been organized in the New West. Eleven Southern states withdrew from the Union and created the Confederate States of America.

CONFEDERATE GOALS IN THE WEST

Southern leaders had two broad goals: (1) to separate from the United States in order to pursue an independent national life, free of the pressures and threats of the Abolitionist crusade and the laws of Congress; and (2) to absorb that part of the New West recently denied it as an area for expanding its institutions, particularly slavery. The attempt of the Confederate States to fulfill its goal of independent existence was challenged militarily by the federal government, leading to the Civil War. And the attempt of the Confederacy to fulfill its Western objective involved the New West in the Civil War.

Confederate planners developed a bold and broad design for the New West. As a tributary area, its primary purpose was to provide a continuous land corridor across Texas, Indian Territory, New Mexico, and California to the Pacific shore. The gold and silver mines of Colorado and Nevada and the transportation and communication routes crossing Utah and connecting with California also made these intermediate territories attractive to Southerners; they were considered as secondary areas for Confederate expansion.

Role of Texas and Indian Territory

Each territory and state south of the Missouri Compromise line had a role to play in the Confederate design for the New West. Texas, a slave-holding state, was expected to yield stores of foodstuffs and fibers from its rich farms and ranches. In addition, its population of nearly 605,000 augured substantial manpower for the Confederate cause.

Indian Territory was a surprisingly promising region for the supply of Confederate essentials. Confederate supply officers' survey of Indian Territory resources reported that its farms, plantations, and ranches could provide beef, hides, horses, and grain, as well as salt and lead—items particularly important for the new nation. The report claimed that the rich mines on Indian Territory's northeastern border yielded sufficient lead to supply the total small-arms needs for all the Confederate armies in the field. The combined population of the five Indian commonwealths—the Cherokee, Seminole, Creek, Choctaw, and Chickasaw nations—was nearly 100,000. The South saw the nations as a source of troops to guard the Western border.

A compelling strategic consideration for incorporating this border province into the Southern orbit was its location between Union Kansas and Confederate Texas. It was expected that control of Indian Territory and its network of military posts—from Fort Smith in the east through Fort Gibson and Fort Cobb—would defend the Western approaches to Arkansas, Texas, and Louisiana against invasion through Kansas. In addition, the Indian Territory's waterway system—the Arkansas and Red rivers

—and its major highways—the Texas Road, the Butterfield Road, and the California Road—were vital communication and transportation links with the Far West.

Role of the Southwest

New Mexico Territory, with its population of 95,000, was expected to provide some manpower for the Confederate cause, but its chief value was as a land bridge connecting Texas and Indian Territory with California and the Pacific. Moreover, New Mexico Territory's producing gold, silver, and copper mines attracted strong Confederate interest.

California, with its population of 380,000, was the jewel of the Confederate design for the New West. The gold from its mines and its increasing agricultural production, notably in grains, weighed heavily in Confederate planning. But above all, California was essential to the Confederacy because of its long, port-studded front on the Pacific. Southern commercial intercourse with Europe was thwarted by the Union blockade of Atlantic and Gulf ports. Possession of the California ports would enable the Confederates to export cotton and other products to European markets and to import the manufactures necessary for national existence.

Gold and silver from New West mines would provide the Confederate States with a stable base for its currency and the specie with which to purchase essential goods from Europe. Thus, what the South lost through the Compromise of 1850 and the slavery-excluding political organization process of the 1850s, it sought to recover as an independent nation.

During early 1861, the Confederate cause in the New West was furthered by the withdrawal of federal troops from much of the region. Until the government could raise and train new armies to crush the Confederacy, its limited regular forces were required in the eastern United States to protect the nation's capital and to guard against a threatened Confederate invasion. The War Department pulled its troops from many stations in the New West and rushed them to the East. The weakened federal position in the New West thus made Confederate goals easier to accomplish. In addition, Union withdrawal of military forces affected local morale, and, in some areas, made the people susceptible to Confederate blandishments. Confederate forces occupied many abandoned Western posts and took over the task of protecting the local settlements from Indian attack.

Early in the war, pro-Southern activity by Texas militia companies forced the surrender of all federal posts, troops, and supplies in that military department. Federal troops were permitted to leave the state. By March of 1861, Texan armies were crossing the Red River preparatory to occupying Fort Washita, Fort Arbuckle, and Fort Cobb. The threat led War Department officials to order speedy evacuation of all Indian Territory posts; companies from Fort Smith, Fort Washita, and other frontier stations—about 750 infantry and cavalry—collected in central Indian Territory and, led by Colonel William H. Emory, hastily retreated to Fort Leavenworth in Kansas for reassignment to the eastern United States.

In the New Mexico Territory too, federal officials directed abandonment of the Arizona posts and the concentration of troops at Fort Fillmore and Fort Craig on the Rio Grande and at Fort Union, which guarded the roads from the East to Santa Fe. The plan was to maintain federal troops at those posts until replacement companies of local volunteers had been recruited and trained. In California too, as volunteer troops were recruited and trained, they gradually replaced the regular troops being transferred to the East. There was widespread defection among federal officers in the New West, particularly in New Mexico. Some resigned their commissions to join the Confederate service, devastating the morale of regular troops and thus reducing their effectiveness in this time of crisis.

Consummation of the Confederate Design

The Confederate States of America undertook to absorb the states and territories of the southwestern quadrant of the New West into its orbit by local legislative action, resulting in secession ordinances, diplomacy, intrigue, and in some cases, conquest. Texas, a slave state, enthusiastically withdrew from the American Union and joined the Confederacy. The secession movement began there in late 1860, when a convention of delegates met at Austin and drafted a declaration providing for nullification of the annexation ordinance of 1845. In an election held February 23, 1861, state voters approved the proposition. Texas was admitted to the Confederacy on March 1 of that year.

Indian Territory was divided into five semi-autonomous Indian republics. The United States had maintained relations with the five "civilized" nations through treaties. The Confederate States used the same device to absorb this strategic border province into the Southern community. Indian slaveholders, who were mostly of mixed parentage, dominated tribal affairs and already had expressed sympathy for the Southern cause. The Confederate government appointed Albert Pike of Arkansas commissioner to negotiate alliance treaties with the five nations. During the spring of 1861, he traveled to the Indian Territory and, between May and October, concluded negotiations with the leaders of the five Indian commonwealths. Each treaty terminated all relationships with the United States, provided for complete withdrawal from the American community, and accepted the nation in question as a dependent territory of the Confederacy. Each Indian nation pledged to support the Confederate cause by raising armies. During the late summer of 1861, Pike traveled to the Leased District and negotiated Confederate treaties of alliance with the Wichita Agency tribes—mostly Wichitas and Caddoes—and with several Comanche bands.

In southern New Mexico Territory, there were two widely separated pockets of settlement. The first, located on the Rio Grande above El Paso, was Mesilla, a settlement of mixed Spanish-Americans and Texans, where destructive Apache raids were a constant threat to life and property. The settlers received scant attention from the territorial government at Santa Fe, and they resented the gross neglect of their needs by territorial and federal officials. In southwestern New Mexico Territory, isolated mining settlements along the Santa Cruz River from Tubac to Tucson, on the Gila, and above Fort Yuma on the Colorado River, faced the same problems of neglect by the territorial government at Santa Fe and federal officialdom and attacks by the Apaches. The two military posts in the area, Fort Breckenridge and Fort Buchanan, provided only minimal protection from the Apaches, and these forts were abandoned by Union troops in 1861. Like miners in other sections of the New West, the pioneers of this western region formed simple, extralegal governmental associations and urged separate territorial status for their area and the formation of a government closer at hand and more responsive to their needs. Sylvester Mowry, a local mine owner, was elected by the settlers of western New Mexico Territory to travel to Washington to urge better administration and protection. His pleas for more responsive government and improved protection were ignored by federal officials.

In this setting of resentment, the settlers of Mesilla and Tucson joined together in a convention at Mesilla in March 1861. Designating it a "convention of the people of Arizona," the delegates denounced the United States and the New Mexico Territory for neglect and adopted a secession ordinance urging absorption of "Arizona" into the Confederacy. The remaining settlements of the New Mexico Territory, which had federal troops quartered nearby at Fort Craig and other posts, were uncommitted. This remaining area became the focus of Confederate military conquest.

In early 1861, California was divided on the question of preserving the Union. It is estimated that 30 percent of its population was Southern-born, and the Democratic party was strong there. The state's senators, William M. Gwin and Milton S. Latham, were pro-Southern Democrats. Many California Democrats favored dividing the state so that the six southern counties could join the Confederacy. There was also some particularistic sentiment—supported by certain Democrats and Republicans—to establish an independent republic. This proposition was appealing because many Californians considered that the federal government had grossly neglected the state by failing to improve ties with the Pacific Coast through prompt completion of the transcontinental railroad. News of the firing on Fort Sumter on April 12, 1861, however, crystallized the strong latent Union sentiment. Mass meetings at San Francisco and other northern California towns forced a timid legislature to adopt strong resolutions of support for the Union cause. California's sustained commitment to the Union was manifested by the raising of 16,000 volunteer troops. Nonetheless, for most of 1861, secession sentiment remained strong in the southern part of the state and fostered many an intrigue to bring California into the Confederacy.

From the Southern viewpoint, Colorado, Nevada, and Utah were peripheral in importance to the states and territories comprising the southern corridor to the Pacific. Although some Southern sentiment was expressed in the Nevada and Colorado mining camps, it was never a serious threat. On April 24, 1861, when Southern sympathizers raised a Confederate flag at Denver, an angry Union group tore it down.

In Utah, citizens were still smarting from the federal invasion of 1857, and they alleged harassment by appointive federal officials of the territorial government. Mormons felt that their theocratic establishment was threatened, and they resented the scorn heaped upon them for their practice of polygamy. Embittered by thwarted statehood ambitions, which would end rule by unsympathetic appointed gentiles and restore Mormon dominance, the Saints were sullen. Federal officials were aware of their glowering resentment and considered them vulnerable to Confederate blandishments. Therefore, throughout the Civil War, the War Department maintained a military occupation of Utah.

WESTERN MILITARY OPERATIONS

Military operations in the New West during the war were an extension of the larger conflict in the eastern United States. Battles between Confederate and Union armies in the trans-Missouri region were principally the result of Southern attempts to fulfill the design for incorporating the land corridor to the Pacific into the Confederate community. What could not be achieved by local legislation through secession ordinances, intrigue, and diplomacy, the Confederate government sought to accomplish by armed conquest. And the Union government's equal determination to thwart consummation of the Confederate design and to reconquer Indian Territory and other strategic zones, accounts for the intense military activity in the region between the Missouri-Arkansas border and the Colorado River. For convenience, the Civil War operational zones in the New West can be divided into the middle-border sector—mostly Indian Territory—and the Rio Grande sector.

Middle Border Sector

On April 12, 1861, Confederate batteries shelled the federal garrison at Fort Sumter, South Carolina, opening the Civil War. Confederate officials believed that their river defenses could check Union attempts to penetrate the South via the Mississippi River. They therefore expected Federal armies to either move along the Western frontier from bases in Kansas and drive through Indian Territory's Grand River Valley, or to travel along the Telegraph Road in southwestern Missouri, and strike at the Confederate rear with columns moving eastward along the Arkansas and Red rivers.

To defend against this threat, military authorities in Louisiana, Arkansas, and Texas raised troops for a Western border defense to be stationed at Indian Territory posts. Fort Smith was to be the command center. Three regiments, one each from Louisiana, Texas, and Arkansas, were commanded by General Ben McCulloch of Texas. Four regiments from the Indian nations—one from the Creek and Seminole nations, one from the Choctaw and Chickasaw nations, and two from the Cherokee nation—were led by General Albert Pike. Altogether, the seven regiments comprised the border defense force. McCulloch's brigade reached Fort Smith during the summer of 1861.

The first combat on the border between Confederate and Union armies occurred in southwestern Missouri. Claiborne F. Jackson, Confederate governor of Missouri, along with his staff, had been forced out of the state capital at Jefferson City by a strong Union force from St. Louis. He re-established Missouri's Confederate government at Carthage on the southwestern border. General Sterling Price, commanding a force of 1,700 Missouri troops, defended Jackson's government. When reports that a large Union army was marching into southwestern Missouri reached McCulloch, he moved his troops north from their Indian Territory camps in support of Price. On August 9, Generals Nathaniel Lyon and Franz Sigel marched their Union army out of Springfield to storm the Southern defenses at nearby Wilson's Creek. The next day the armies locked in a fierce, bloody contest—the Battle of Wilson's Creek—which the Confederates won.

Following the defeat at Wilson's Creek, Union commanders received reinforcements and prepared to conquer the border region held by the Confederates. General David Hunter led the restored Union army south and, in a series of engagements during October of 1861, he drove the Confederates out of southwestern Missouri. McCulloch's frontier defense force fell back to the Confederate camps on the Indian Territory–Arkansas border, while Hunter paused to await reinforcements for a thrust along the Western border.

The only actions on the border for the remainder of 1861 grew out of the determination of anti-Confederate Indians, Creeks, Seminoles and Cherokees led by Creek Chief Opothleyaholo, to remain neutral. Opothleyaholo established a settlement for his neutral followers—about 8,000 men, women, and children—on the Deep Fork River in the Creek nation. Confederate leaders, equating neutrality with sympathy if not active support for the Union cause, regarded Opothleyaholo's settlement on the Deep Fork as a menace to the security of Indian Territory. On two different occasions, Confederate Indian companies and Texan cavalry, jointly commanded by Colonel Douglas H. Cooper, attempted to drive the neutral Indians from Indian Territory. Each time, Opothleyaholo's fighters defeated their Confederate attackers, first at the Battle of Round Mountain on November 19 and again at Chusto Talasah on December 9.

Cooper appealed for reinforcements from Fort Gibson and Fort Smith and received 1,600 cavalry. On December 26, 1861, the strengthened Confederate force reached Opothleyaholo's camp at Chustenalah in the upper Creek nation. The troops ringed the neutral Indian encampment and, at a signal, swept like a tide over the battlements. The defenders fought bravely, as before, but with no sources of supply and their ammunition severely depleted by the two earlier battles, they were unable to hold their positions. Confederate troops stormed through the camp, captured most of the wagons, equipment, and livestock, and scattered Opothleyaholo's people over the heavily timbered hills of northern Indian Territory. A fierce snowstorm swept over the countryside the night after the battle, causing great suffering for the survivors. Eventually they reached Union Kansas, and soon thereafter, warriors from Opothleyaholo's formerly neutral community, dressed in the Federal uniform of troops of the First and Second Union Indian Brigade, returned to Indian Territory determined to wreak vengeance on their Confederate tormentors.

In early March 1862, the Union army resumed its drive against Confederate border defenses. The renewed Union offensive caused Confederate commanders in the trans-Mississippi Department to rush men, artillery, and supplies to check the advance. General Earl Van Dorn replaced McCulloch as commander of Western frontier troops. On March 6, Union and Confederate armies collided near the Indian Territory–Arkansas boundary at Elkhorn Tavern. The Union army triumphed in the Battle of Pea Ridge, which lasted for two days and inflicted massive casualties upon the Confederates. Colonel Stand Watie, with his regiment of Cherokee Mounted Rifles, won one of the few victories attributed to the Confederates in this bloody contest; the Cherokee troops captured the strategically positioned Union artillery batteries that had rained death and destruction on the Southern ranks. Watie's men also held their position on the broad Confederate line and helped cover the general withdrawal.

The Union victory at Pea Ridge sealed the doom of the Confederate cause in the West and cut mightily into its human and material resources. General Ben McCulloch, who was regarded as the border's finest soldier, was among the slain. In their retreat, Confederate troops had to abandon great quantities of subsistence and forage stores, muskets, ammunition, heavy guns, and tents. Survivors falling back to Fort Smith and Fort Gibson deserted in large numbers, and many joined the Union army. Gloom permeated the border. Never again would Confederate recruiters meet with much success there. Confederate units continued to carry out strikes from bases in Indian Territory along the Missouri-Kansas border. Some produced momentary successes, but never permanent results. After the Pea Ridge disaster, Federal commanders took advantage of Confederate weakness in the West to complete the conquest of that region.

During the spring of 1862, Union forces in Kansas were bolstered by Wisconsin and Ohio volunteer cavalry and infantry and an artillery battery from Indiana. These troops and two Kansas brigades, plus two Indian regiments recruited from the refugee camps of Opothleyaholo's followers, were formed into the Indian Expedition. Colonel William Weer commanded the force. During the spring of 1862, the Indian Expedition marched down the valley of Grand River, defeated Confederate defenders under General T. M. Hindman and Colonel Watie at Locust Grove, conquered the Cherokee nation, occupied Tahlequah, and took Chief John Ross captive. The slow pace of the conquest of Indian Territory led Union officials in the West to place General James G. Blunt in charge of the border operations, and his tenacious campaigning led to the conquest of Fort Gibson in April of 1863.

During that summer, a large Confederate force led by Cooper moved on Fort Gibson. Blunt marched his troops out to meet the Southern army, and, at the Battle of Honey Springs—fought on July 17—his superiority in artillery forced Cooper to withdraw. Thereupon Blunt took the offensive. He crossed the Arkansas River into the Choctaw nation and captured and burned the Confederate depot at Perryville, opening the road to Fort Smith. Blunt then marched his army east, easily taking this post on September 1.

The fall of Fort Smith to Union forces ended major engagements in Indian Territory. Thereafter, Union and Confederate regiments on the border were drained, most of the men being reassigned east of the Mississippi to the armies of General Ulysses S. Grant and General Robert E. Lee. Union and Confederate commanders maintained just enough troops on the Western border to protect their established positions in a holding action. The joint reduction in military strength created for the remainder of the war a stalemate, out of which evolved bloody, internecine strife and guerilla warfare. The Arkansas–Canadian River line became the boundary separating Union and Confederate forces.

Three types of guerilla bands functioned on the border in the period between 1863 and 1865: the free companies, the Quantrill band, and Stand Watie's raiders. The free companies were comprised of local renegades who were outcasts from the Indian nations. These depraved brigands flourished in the anarchic milieu of the border, stealing cattle and horses and plundering and burning both Union and Confederate Indian communities. The depredations of the free companies added to the disorders plaguing this border region during the last two years of the war.

Colonel Charles C. Quantrill had been commissioned by the Confederate government to raise a private army to prey on the Union border settlements of Kansas and Missouri and to counter the Jawhawkers, private raider bands from Kansas. Quantrill built a dreadful reputation on the border. His most notorious coup was the sacking of Lawrence, Kansas, on August 21, 1863, in which over 150 Union men died. But Quantrill and his bushwhackers were indiscriminate in their raiding and attacked Union and Confederate settlements with equal satanic fury. From time to time the Quantrill band roamed through Indian Territory and northern Texas, spreading destruction and slaughter wherever they rode.

Stand Watie's activities were distinguished from those of the Quantrill band and the free companies by their concentration on military objectives. His men destroyed dwellings and barns only when they were used by the enemy for headquarters, billeting troops, or storing supplies. His favorite target was the Union supply line between Fort Scott and Fort Gibson. He preyed on this lifeline not only because of its military aspects, but also because the plunder he swept up in his raids could be distributed among Confederate Cherokee and Creek Indian refugees scattered in camps along Red River in the Choctaw nation and in north Texas. Watie's raids made feeding the garrison at Fort Gibson, plus the 16,000 Cherokee, Creek, and Seminole refugees who had collected there, a serious problem for Union officials. Watie tormented the garrison and refugees with the prospect of mass starvation by harassing and, at times, cutting the post's lifeline, the military road that ran from Fort Scott to Fort Gibson.

During the spring of 1864, the Confederate War Department reorganized its Western armies, creating the Indian Cavalry Brigade, consisting of the First and Second Cherokee Regiments, the Creek Squadron, the Osage Battalion, and the Seminole Battalion. Watie was placed in command and appointed brigadier general. He was the only Indian to achieve this rank in either the Union or the Confederate armies. Watie's troops were active until the end of the war. From his base south of the Canadian, he sent squads into Union territory to harass and raid. Federal details sent out to cut hay for the thousands of cavalry mounts at Fort Gibson were always in peril. Finally, to feed the starving horses and mules, Union officers sent great herds of livestock under heavy guard to graze on the prairie flats near the post. Watie's raiders regularly swooped down to drive the animals across the river, with the result that the cavalrymen at Fort Gibson became foot soldiers.

After the conquest of Arkansas and Fort Smith, Union officers attempted to provision the fort by sending supply steamers up the Arkansas River. During June of 1864, Watie's scouts discovered the slow-moving *J. R. Williams* toiling upstream toward the Fort Gibson landing on Grand River. At Pleasant Bluff, just below the mouth of the Canadian, Watie swept from ambush and captured the vessel with a cavalry charge. Great quantities of provisions, uniforms, and medical supplies fell to the Confederates by this feat.

Watie's greatest stroke occurred during September 1864, at the Cabin Creek crossing on the Fort Scott–Fort Gibson military road in the Cherokee nation. A huge supply train of 300 wagons accompanied by a strong military guard was en route from Fort Scott to Fort Gibson. The Cherokee general attacked and captured the train and, by a skillful decoy, eluded a

Union relief column from Fort Gibson, driving his prize into Confederate territory where the stores of food, medical supplies, clothing, and blankets were distributed among the Confederate Indian refugee camps.

Confederate defenses in Indian Territory served to insulate Texas from attack by Union armies from the north. Federal commanders did, however, make three attempts to invade the state from the Gulf of Mexico. In December 1862, a Union army captured Galveston but was driven off by Confederate counterattacks. The following September, a Federal force invaded Texas via the Sabine Pass, but it too was forced to retire. During 1864, a Union column proceeded from New Orleans and ascended the Red River, intent on breaching Texan defenses from the north. This plan failed too, because of the defeat of the Federal force in Louisiana.

Rio Grande Sector

During the Civil War in the West, the Rio Grande sector was a point of convergence for armies from Texas, Colorado, and California. In July 1861, Colonel John R. Baylor and a force of 300 Confederates occupied Fort Bliss near El Paso, then marched to Mesilla, which was already a Confederate community by local declaration. Nearby at Fort Fillmore 400 Union troops were garrisoned. Baylor's advance caused Federal officers to order abandonment of the post and retreat upriver to Fort Craig. The Texans overtook the fleeing Union column, forced its surrender, and Baylor declared himself governor of the Confederate Territory of Arizona.

During November 1861, General Henry H. Sibley mustered a Confederate brigade at San Antonio and marched to El Paso to complete the conquest begun by Baylor. Captain Sherod Hunter, commanding a mounted company, advanced in a swift move to Tucson, reaching the Santa Cruz settlements in February 1862. He integrated the scattered mining towns into the new Confederate Territory of Arizona and prepared to move on Fort Yuma.

After the Fort Fillmore disaster, General Edward R. S. Canby, Union commander of the Department of New Mexico, accelerated the training of New Mexico volunteers and advised the War Department of New Mexico's peril. He urged that reinforcements be rushed to the Rio Grande. He also informed the governor of Colorado Territory of the expected Confederate thrust from Mesilla up the Rio Grande and requested military assistance. Canby concentrated the Union troops in New Mexico at Fort Craig and Fort Union in order to guard the southern and eastern approaches to Santa Fe. Nearly 4,000 men, one-fourth of them regulars, waited for Sibley to advance on Fort Craig. On February 21, 1862, Canby sent his troops against the approaching Confederates. At Valverde, Sibley's brigade—fewer than 1,800 infantry and cavalry—inflicted a humiliating defeat on Canby's much-larger army and forced the survivors to flee to Fort Craig. Sibley then flanked the post and proceeded upriver, easily taking Albuquerque and Santa Fe. Texas troops occupied Santa Fe and raised both the Confederate and the Texas state flags over the Governor's Palace. The latter was a symbolic act: what they had unsuccessfully tried several times as citizens of the Texas republic and what they had had to abandon by the Compromise of 1850, the Texans finally had achieved by conquest.

After a few weeks' rest, Sibley sent most of his brigade east to take Fort Union, then to march over Raton Pass into Colorado; they were intercepted before reaching Fort Union. Canby's warning of the Confederate invasion and his appeal for aid to Colorado officials had received quick attention. Colonel John P. Slough mustered the First Colorado Volunteer Regiment and, by forced marches through heavy snowstorms, moved his men over the passes into New Mexico. They passed Fort Union and continued along the Santa Fe road. On March 26, 1862, the Colorado troops made first contact with Sibley's brigade. Major John M. Chivington, commanding an advance battalion, encountered a small Confederate forward detachment and forced it to yield. Two days later the full complement of both armies met at Glorieta Pass, twenty miles southeast of Santa Fe. A bloody, close-in engagement took a heavy toll of the ranks of both armies, but the Confederates forced the Union troops to yield and appeared to have won the battle.

Chivington, however, had moved a large flanking force over the highlands and around the main Confederate position to the enemy's rear. There the Colorado volunteers found the Southern supply train of 73 wagons and 600 horses and mules. They captured the train from the light guard, burned the wagons laden with precious subsistence and ordnance supplies, and bayoneted the horses and mules. Shorn of food and ammunition reserves in a barren territory, Sibley's brigade altered its course from advance to retreat. The Confederates fell back to Santa Fe, then rushed down the Rio Grande into Texas, eluding Canby's cavalry along the river.

The third convergence on the Rio Grande sector came from the Pacific Coast, where the First California Volunteer Regiment—soon to be known as the California Column—was commanded by General James H. Carleton. The regiment had first been used in southern California to suppress Confederate intrigues. During the spring of 1862, the California Column was ordered to the Rio Grande to campaign against the Confederate invaders from Texas. Carleton's men crossed from the coastal towns of southern California to Fort Yuma and advanced on Tucson, reaching that mining settlement on May 21, 1862. The small Confederate garrison there fled eastward before them. Carleton established martial law over the mining camps of southern Arizona, declared himself military governor, and resumed the march to the Rio Grande. However, Sibley's battered brigade had reached Texas before the California Column could arrive at Mesilla.

On September 18, 1862, Carleton succeeded Canby as commander of the Department of New Mexico. Between them, the two men had restored to the Union the territory between Mesilla and Fort Yuma, and the Confederacy's grand design for the New West had failed.

The Civil War produced a thorough militarization of the New West that was to extend into the postwar period. In 1861, President Lincoln called on the Western states to raise volunteer infantry and cavalry regiments to man the many forts abandoned during 1861 as regular troops were concentrated in the East. Other duties assigned the volunteer regiments included guarding the Pacific Coast at shore stations and protecting the overland telegraph, mail, and freight routes. Above all, the volunteer regiments mustered in the New West states and territories were to be kept in constant readiness for duty in the East.

MILITARIZATION OF THE WEST

Every state and territory in the New West north and west of Texas and Indian Territory raised troops for Union service. Kansas volunteer regiments participated widely in Civil War operations, particularly in the Indian Territory sector. California volunteer troops were very widely used by War Department officials. A few California companies served in the East with regiments from Massachusetts and other Union states, and the California Column occupied New Mexico. A large California force performed duty in Utah, and California volunteer infantry and cavalry companies occupied posts in the state of Oregon and in the Washington Territory until local regiments could be formed. Oregon eventually raised a cavalry regiment, and the Washington Territory organized an infantry regiment. Volunteer companies also were raised in the Colorado, Nebraska, and Nevada territories.

The Indian Campaigns

The extensive militarization of the New West between 1861 and 1865 had long-range effects on the region's Indian tribes. Since they were being held as reserves for Eastern combat and had no Confederates to fight after early 1862, the volunteer troops were frequently used against the Indians. Infantry and cavalry regiments throughout the New West continued the process of aboriginal conquest and compression of tribal territory that the military frontier, manned by regulars, had begun in the period between 1848 and 1861. Moreover, the Civil War was not a total war for the New West, and settlement and development continued in the area during the period. Mining frontier expansion was primarily responsible for keeping this developmental process alive, as discoveries of rich mineral deposits in Idaho and Montana during 1862 and 1863 precipitated a new gold rush. The movement of great numbers of people and ever-increasing quantities of machinery and general freight across Indian land precipitated incidents.

In addition, the general business of the war—the flow of guns, ammunition, uniforms, and other essentials for equipping and maintaining the New West volunteer military establishment—added to the traffic from the Mississippi Valley into Colorado, the Great Basin, the Northwest, and the Pacific Coast. The Confederate attempt to drive through to the Pacific had closed mail, immigrant, and freight routes in the Southwest, diverting the traffic to northern routes and adding more to the volume of activity there. These factors, as well as the occupation of additional tribal lands by new mining settlements, placed tremendous pressures on the New West tribes. They resisted, and the period between 1861 and 1865 was a bloody time of Indian conquest, pacification, and compression of tribal lands—a process made more direct and effective by the militarization of the New West.

Bosque Redondo Concentration

The most extensive operations against New West tribes were carried out in the Department of New Mexico. General Carleton was determined to pacify the military constituency, which he ruled with an iron hand braced by his declaration of martial law and his presumptive claim as military governor. His California troops were supported by New Mexico volunteer companies; together they manned existing military posts in New Mexico and Arizona and established new ones as the situation required. Carleton ordered his officers in the field to hold no councils with the Indians but to kill the warriors "wherever and whenever found" and to take the women and children prisoner. On the Pecos River at Bosque Redondo, Carleton's men established a reservation on which they concentrated many of the New Mexico Indians. They erected Fort Sumner near the reservation to provide surveillance over the Indian prisoners.

Mescalero Apaches were the first tribesmen to be relocated at Bosque Redondo. New Mexico volunteer companies commanded by Colonel Kit Carson and several California units campaigned relentlessly against this southeastern New Mexico tribe. To support the Mescalero roundup, troops reoccupied Fort Stanton and converted it into an operational base. Carson's men maintained a constant pressure on the Mescaleros, destroying villages and food stores and regularly engaging the warriors in combat. During March of 1863, almost 500 Mescaleros surrendered and accepted assignment to Bosque Redondo.

The Navajoes of western New Mexico and northern Arizona were next to feel the fury of Carleton's conquest. California and New Mexico troops entered their territory, burned villages, destroyed grain fields and orchards, captured sheep, cattle, and horses, and created a wasteland among the Navajo villages. In early 1864, Carson invaded their natural bastion, Canyon de Chelly, and campaigned so extensively that finally the Navajoes capitulated, evacuating their homeland and moving to Bosque Redondo.

By late 1864, nearly 9,000 Indians, mostly Navajoes and Mescaleros, were concentrated on the Bosque Redondo Reservation.

During the 1850s, the Western Apaches, mostly Chiricahuas and Mimbreños, had been pressed by the extension of the mining frontier into western New Mexico and southern Arizona and by the increase of California-bound traffic through their lands. Their retaliatory raids had threatened to prevent expansion of the mining frontier in their territory and to close the overland passage to California. These proud and fierce people were highly mobile and unremittingly committed to thwart the American attempts to cross and occupy their territory. They were the most difficult of all the Indians of the Department of New Mexico to deal with, and at no time did Carleton's program of conquest and containment at Bosque Redondo succeed with them.

The California Column had its first combat with the Western Apaches in 1862. Chiricahua and Mimbreño warriors preyed on the column in its advance to the Rio Grande, killing scouts and messengers caught away from the main column. At Apache Pass an advance force of about 125 men was faced by about 300 Indians. The California troops were pinned down and were saved from annihilation only by the gunners, who lobbed howitzer shot into the highland battlements occupied by the Indians. Between 1862 and 1865, Union troops and Western Apache warriors fought many battles. Countless Indians were slain, in the process taking their toll of troops and settlers. But for Carleton's men it was like fighting phantoms; the swift-moving Apaches struck here, there, and were eternally a threat, unconquerable. Although they campaigned constantly against them, the California and New Mexico troops were unable to establish military dominance over the Western Apaches.

Troops from the Department of New Mexico also campaigned northeast of Santa Fe, against the tribes of the Southern Plains. The lifeline for the military establishment on the Rio Grande was the road between Fort Leavenworth and Santa Fe over which, nearly every month, caravans of mule-drawn freight wagons toiled to supply provisions, ammunition, and other essentials for Union troops in the Southwest. Kiowa and Comanche bands preyed on the caravans and on several occasions succeeded in cutting the supply line. New Mexico troops established Fort Bascom on the Canadian River in eastern New Mexico as a cavalry support station to guard the Fort Leavenworth road. During the autumn of 1864, Carleton directed Carson and a force of 350 men and two howitzers to remove the Kiowa-Comanche threat to his supply line.

Ute and Jicarilla Apache scouts located a large Kiowa-Comanche encampment on the Canadian River in the Texas Panhandle near the ruins of an old trading post called Adobe Walls, and on November 25, Carson struck the village in a surprise attack. Fierce defensive counteraction nearly overwhelmed Carson's ranks. He later admitted that his men were saved by the howitzers, which were loaded with grape shot and fired at point-blank range, turning the Indians and forcing their retreat.

Sand Creek Massacre

The expanding mining frontier in Colorado Territory, proliferation of ranches along the Platte River, and the general increase of traffic crossing the Plains into the settlements on the eastern slope of the Rocky Mountains led to demands that the Cheyenne-Arapaho range, which had been assigned by the Treaty of Fort Laramie in 1851 and extended from the Platte to the Arkansas, be reduced. In 1861, leaders of these tribes signed the Treaty of Fort Wise, in which they accepted a much-reduced reservation in southeastern Colorado. The new Cheyenne-Arapaho domain, designated the Sand Creek Reserve, was bounded by Big Sandy Creek and the Arkansas River and was about ninety miles wide. It was described as the "most dry and desolate region of the whole" and, from the settler viewpoint, it was ideal, as it was isolated from the principal east-west roads into the Colorado Territory. Fort Lyon was erected on the reserve to serve as the center for managing the Indians. The Cheyennes and Arapahoes retained the right to hunt on unoccupied portions of the ceded territory.

The Indians, who depended upon the buffalo for subsistence, found their Sand Creek Reservation intolerable. The increasing traffic across the buffalo range to the Colorado settlements diverted the herds, and the animals became increasingly difficult to find. The tribesmen turned to raiding ranches along the Platte and depredating stage and freight traffic between Fort Kearny and Denver.

In early 1864, Colorado Territorial Governor John Evans sent word to the Cheyennes and Arapahoes to return to their reservation or "suffer the consequences." During that autumn, 500 Cheyennes, led by Black Kettle, returned to the Sand Creek Reservation. On November 29, Chivington, now a colonel in the First Colorado Volunteers, marched 900 men to the Sand Creek Reservation for a surprise attack on Black Kettle's village. Two hundred Cheyenne men, women, and children died in the carnage. The federal commissioner of Indian Affairs denounced Chivington's action as a massacre in which Indians were "butchered in cold blood by troops in the service of the United States."

Compression of Indian lands in the Colorado Territory also occurred in 1863. The Utes were then occupying the attractive San Luis Valley of southern Colorado. Their raids on the Colorado settlements led to retaliatory strikes by the Colorado volunteer troops, which had been raised as Union Army reserves and were fresh from their victory over Sibley's Confederate brigade. Intimidated by this intensive campaigning, Ute leaders met with federal officials in October 1863, and exchanged their San Luis Valley lands for a new domain west of the continental divide and remote from the settlements. The militarization of Colorado, produced by the Civil War, momentarily pacified the territory, substantially reduced the Indian barrier to settlement and development, and drastically compressed tribal lands in the territory.

Campaigns in the Northwest

Replacing California volunteer companies, cavalry and infantry regiments raised in Oregon and Washington manned the Pacific coastal defenses and interior posts. They sharpened their field and fighting skills for possible combat in the Eastern United States by continuing the pressure on the Spokanes, Snakes, Cayuses, and other tribes who lived east of the Cascades. After the opening of new gold fields in Idaho and Montana during 1862 and 1863, these troops guarded the roads and protected the heavy immigrant and freight traffic.

Campaigns in the Great Basin

South into Utah and Nevada, the Shoshonis, Bannocks, and Utes, like other New West tribes, were pressed and provoked by the increased traffic over their lands, and the extension of the mining frontier that occurred during the war. Raider bands from these tribes attacked mail stations and preyed on the stages and freight caravans operating between the Platte River and Fort Bridger. Their strikes especially threatened isolated ranches and mining camps, and Union officials feared that the widening sorties would cut the transcontinental telegraph line.

Brigham Young, president of the Mormon Church, offered to raise a militia force to guard the stage and freight routes and the telegraph line east of Salt Lake City. Until California volunteer troops reached the Utah Territory, federal officials reluctantly accepted Young's offer. The Mormon mounted company was in service from May 1 to August 14, 1862. It escorted the mail stages and freight caravans through the troubled zone, patrolled the telegraph line, and campaigned against hostiles along the headwaters of the Snake River and into the Tetons.

California volunteer troops, numbering 700 and commanded by General P. E. Connor, entered Utah during October 1862, and established Fort Douglas near Salt Lake City. Detachments campaigned against Shoshoni and Bannock raiders that were preying on mining camps and Mormon agricultural settlements. In the Bear River campaign of January 1863, Union troops killed 368 Indians and took 160 women and children captives. This action destroyed Indian power in northern Utah and southern Idaho and removed a threat to the Oregon road. California and Nevada troops garrisoned Fort Bridger and other posts along the immigrant passage, guarded the telegraph line, and convoyed mail stages and freight caravans.

In western Utah and Nevada, Pahvants, Utes, and Goshutes during the same period attacked mail coaches and freight caravans and cut down isolated prospecting parties. Intensive campaigning by California and Nevada troops also conquered these tribes during 1863. Thereupon, federal officials negotiated treaties with them and other Great Basin Indians, providing for peace with the United States and pledges to permit safe passage for mail stages, freight caravans, and immigrant trains through their territories.

The conquest treaties also contained clauses permitting construction of a transcontinental railroad across tribal lands and compressing some tribal territories to permit the establishment of new mining and agricultural settlements. In return for these considerations, the government pledged to protect the signatory tribes and to issue at once to all tribal members gifts of clothing, provisions, and other goods, and to pay each tribe for twenty years an annuity in goods ranging in value from $1,000 to $5,000. These campaigns by the reserve Union volunteer armies brought peace to the Great Basin.

The Sioux War

Two additional incidents, widely separated but a part of this bloody drama of aboriginal conquest during the period between 1861 and 1865, should be considered at this time to complete the context of Indian suppression and compression. Each of them will also provide useful information for future reference.

The first incident occurred on the Minnesota frontier, where the press of pioneers onto lands assigned by federal treaty to the Santee Sioux and consequent tribal disillusionment with the United States government for its failure to fulfill treaty guarantees, led to a destructive war. Little Crow was the principal leader of the Santee Sioux uprising, in which it is estimated that 700 settlers were slain. The Sioux were defeated by regular and volunteer troops, their leaders arrested and, on December 26, 1862, thirty-eight of them were hanged at Mankato. The remaining Sioux prisoners were sent to Western reservations, where they joined the Western Sioux and became a source of great military concern to the United States during the next decade.

The Kickapoo War on Texas

The other incident occurred in west Texas in 1862, at the Battle of the Concho. In 1861, about 600 Kickapoos resided in south-central Kansas. Both Union and Confederate agents had attempted to muster the warriors from this tribe into their frontier armies; but the Kickapoos nourished a bitter hatred for the United States and its citizens and, wishing to be free from the solicitations of both Union and Confederate agents, decided to join a band of their tribe living in the north Mexican state of Coahuila. The band had resided in Mexico since Texas Republic President Mirabeau Lamar had directed the Texas army to drive out the Cherokees, Kickapoos, and other Indians living along the Sabine River.

During the summer of 1862, the Kickapoos abandoned their Kansas villages, proceeded west, and then turned south just beyond the 100th meridian, taking every precaution to escape detection by Texas Confederate patrols. They traveled without incident until, during late December 1862, they arrived on the Little Concho River in southwest Texas. While they were camped to rest and to restore their horses, the Indians were sighted by a mounted Confederate battalion assigned to frontier defense against the Comanches. The Texas troops noted the Indians' large herd of horses and struck at it. Warned of the danger, the warriors rallied quickly, recovered the horse herd, then drove back repeated cavalry charges. After sixteen Texans had been shot from their saddles, the battalion retreated. The Kickapoos gathered their camp gear and hastened on to Mexico.

The Mexican government made a grant of land to the Kickapoos in the state of Coahuila on the Remolino River in return for which the Kickapoos undertook to defend the northern frontiers of Mexico from Comanche and Apache raiders. This group of aboriginal émigrés—known subsequently as the Mexican Kickapoos—in retaliation for the unprovoked attack on the Concho, carried on a ruthless war against the Texans from their bases in Mexico. They were quieted only after Colonel Ranald Mackenzie and the Fourth Cavalry made their famous raid into Mexico in 1873 (see Chapter 24).

RECONSTRUCTION IN THE WEST

General Robert E. Lee surrendered to General Ulysses S. Grant at Appomattox Court House on April 9, 1865, thus ending the Civil War. Confederate General E. Kirby Smith, commander of Southern troops west of the Mississippi River, capitulated on May 20. However, the conflict on the Western border did not cease until June 23, when Stand Watie tendered his sword to federal commissioners at Doaksville in the Choctaw nation; he was the last Confederate general to surrender.

Texas Reconstruction

The Civil War had scourged parts of the West, and two of its components—Texas and Indian Territory—had to undergo Reconstruction for their support of the Confederate cause. Before it could resume its former place in the American Union, Texas, as one of the Confederate states, had to follow the formula set by the Radical Republican Congress in the Reconstruction acts. This formula included military occupation by Union troops, the banning of Confederates from participation in state government, the freeing of slaves, and alterations in the state constitution. A decade of Republican rule in the state ensued.

Indian Territory Reconstruction

The Reconstruction process for Indian Territory was similar, except that treaty rather than law set the pattern. Before the Confederate Indian commonwealths could resume their former relation to the United States, leaders of the vanquished Choctaw, Seminole, Creek, Chickasaw, and Cherokee nations were required to sign the Reconstruction Treaties of 1866. These pacts pledged each Indian nation to revise the tribal constitution, abolishing slavery and granting tribal citizenship to freedmen with all the rights of Indians and making provision for them in land and other benefits. In addition, each nation was required to grant railroad rights-of-way to chartered companies for the construction of north-south and east-west lines across Indian Territory.

The Reconstruction Treaties also required each of the Indian commonwealths to cede vast tracts of their domains to the United States as a sort of reparations of war. The areas ceded were the western half of Indian Territory on which the federal government settled tribes from Kansas, Colorado, Texas, Nebraska, Iowa, California, Idaho, Arizona, and Mexico —casualties of the American occupation of the New West.

SELECTED SOURCES

The Civil War in the West was fought on two broad fronts—the Middle Border sector, centering on the Indian Territory, and the Rio Grande sector. A record of engagements between Union and Confederate armies in the Middle Border is found in Jay Monaghan, *Civil War on the Western Border, 1854–1865* (Boston, 1955); *Edwin C. Bearss and Arrell M. Gibson, *Fort Smith: Little Gibraltar on the Arkansas* (Norman, 1969); Alice Nicholas, *Bleeding Kansas* (New York, 1954); Albert Castel, *A Frontier State at War: 1861–1865* (Ithaca, 1958); William E. Connelley, *Quantrill and the Border Wars* (Cedar Rapids, 1910); and Richard S. Brownlee, *Gray Ghosts of the Confederacy: Guerrilla Warfare in the West, 1861–1865* (Baton Rouge, 1958).

Operations in the Rio Grande sector are detailed in Ray C. Colton, *The Civil War in the Western Territories* (Norman, 1959); William A. Hall, *Turmoil in New Mexico, 1846–1868* (Santa Fe, 1952); Martin H. Hall, *Sibley's New Mexico Campaign* (Austin, 1960); Max L. Heyman, *Prudent Soldier: A Biography of General Edward R. S. Canby* (Glendale, 1959); and William C. Whitford, *Colorado Volunteers in the Civil War: the New Mexico Campaign in 1862* (Denver, 1906).

Indian campaigns carried out by Union and Confederate armies are described in Donald J. Berthrong, *The Southern Cheyennes* (Norman, 1963); *Stan Hoig, *The Sand Creek Massacre* (Norman, 1961); Fred B. Rogers, *Soldiers of the Overland . . . General Connor and His Volunteers in the Old West* (San Francisco, 1938); Aurora Hunt, *Major General James Henry Carleton* (Glendale, 1958); *Arrell M. Gibson, *The Kickapoos: Lords of the Middle Border* (Norman, 1963); and Robert H. Jones, *The Civil War in the Northwest: Nebraska, Wisconsin, Iowa, Minnesota and the Dakotas* (Norman, 1960).

* Available in paperback.

The Washita Massacre, 1868: The 7th Cavalry Commanded by Colonel George Custer.

General William T. Sherman in Council with Indian Chiefs at Fort Laramie, 1867.

24

Pacification and Consolidation of the Western Tribes

The national government, having preserved the American Union during 1865 by the final triumph of its armies over the forces of the insurgent Confederate States of America, turned its attention to completing the military conquest of the Western Indian tribes. This process, begun in 1848, had already substantially reduced the Indian threat to American expansion in the New West and had opened vast new areas to settlement and development.

The first phase in the conquest and compression process took place, as we have seen, between 1848 and 1861 and was carried out largely by regular troops. Their efforts were particularly successful in California, Oregon, and Washington where, except for scattered pockets of resistance, the Indian was no longer a factor to be reckoned with by the beginning of the war. The war itself produced an even more comprehensive militarization of the New West. Volunteer infantry and cavalry regiments, raised in the region's new states and territories, kept themselves in combat readiness for service in the East by campaigning against Indians. Their actions, comprised the second phase of the conquest that took place from 1861 to 1865. They further reduced Indian military power and compressed tribal territories, pacifying the Shoshonis, Bannocks, Utes, and other tribes residing near the Oregon-California roads. Their campaigns against the Cheyennes and other tribes of the Colorado, Nevada, and Utah territories scattered the Indians and reduced their domains. In New Mexico and Arizona, General James H. Carleton's conquest and containment policy at Bosque Redondo had emasculated the Mescalero Apache and Navajo will to resist. The Western Apaches had yet to be dealt with decisively.

As the national government prepared to undertake the third phase of

New West aboriginal conquest and compression—which extended from 1865 to 1878—federal officials could, for the first time since American independence, conclude with some certitude that the time was near when the Indian would no longer be a military threat and a barrier to the consummation of American purpose. In carrying out the third and what was expected to be final phase of the conquest of the New West tribes, the national government had immediate and long-range concerns.

POSTWAR ABORIGINAL SETTING

An immediate concern was pacifying the vast territory of the New West's heartland—the Great Plains, which extended from Canada to the Rio Grande. This country was the buffalo range and the domicile of America's most powerful surviving aborigines. Fierce Northern Cheyennes and Sioux dominated the Northern Plains; Southern Cheyennes and Arapahoes ruled the Central Plains; and Kiowas and Comanches roamed over the Southern Plains. These tribes had often felt the lash of American military might during the Civil War period of tribal conquest and compression, but in 1865 they still retained control of vast domains. Each tribe possessed superb fighting power and a strong will to resist American occupation. Federal officials, on their side, felt compelled to clear the Plains hunting range in order to open a wedge for the advancing transcontinental railroad, which soon would link the Mississippi Valley with the Pacific shore.

Management of the New West Indians once conquest had been accomplished was a long-range concern of the national government. The mauling these tribes had received at the hands of volunteer troops during the Civil War—particularly the Southern Cheyennes at the Sand Creek Massacre—had provoked some protest in the eastern United States, and in 1865 a congressional committee was appointed to investigate the Indian situation and to recommend a definitive policy for final settlement of the problem. Senator J. R. Doolittle of Wisconsin was named chairman of the seven-member investigatory body. The Doolittle committee traveled over the West, interviewing Indians, pioneers, and military men and observing conditions firsthand.

But even while the Doolittle committee prepared for its Western mission, federal officials, particularly the military, were faced with the immediate necessity of opening the central corridor through the Plains to assure unimpeded railroad construction. It was hoped that this task could be accomplished peacefully, by diplomacy. During early 1865, federal agents attempted to contact the Plains tribes and to lure their leaders into councils to discuss the government's proposition. Only the Kiowas, Comanches, and Kiowa-Apaches from the Southern Plains and a few Cheyenne and Arapaho bands from the Central Plains responded to the government invitation to a council.

Most of the Cheyenne and Arapaho bands had been scattered by the

Sand Creek incident and had settled along the Smoky Hill River in western Kansas. Sympathetic Brule, Oglala Sioux, and Northern Cheyenne warriors joined them during 1865 to cut a swath of gore and destruction through the area from central Nebraska to South Pass. Cheyenne, Arapaho, and Sioux war parties destroyed stations on the transcontinental telegraph line and killed several operators; they raided ranches and preyed on the stage and freight lines and immigrant trains on the Platte route. Access to Denver was closed for a time, and Julesburg, a stage and freighting center in northeastern Colorado, was raided twice during 1865. Federal cavalry and infantry columns pursued the raiders for two months over dim trails into northern hideaways. Fierce counterattacks and sweeping strikes at supply trains, which stampeded the horses and mules and caused the loss of essential provisions and reserve ammunition, forced the military to withdraw.

Little Arkansas Council

While conflict raged on the Central and Northern Plains, federal commissioners and leaders of the Southern Plains tribes convened on October 10, 1865, in a council at the mouth of the Little Arkansas River in western Kansas. Thomas Murphy, head of the Central Indian Superintendency, John B. Sanborn, and General William S. Harney represented the United States. Tribal leaders present included Black Kettle for the Cheyennes, Ten Bears for the Comanches, and Satanta for the Kiowas.

The government did achieve a portion of its objective to create a railroad corridor between the Platte and Arkansas rivers. By the Little Arkansas Treaties, the signatory tribes ceded to the United States their claims to the territory north of the Arkansas River and agreed to settle on diminished territories south of that stream. The Cheyennes and Arapahoes were assigned a domain between the Arkansas and Cimarron rivers in southwestern Kansas and northwestern Indian Territory; the Kiowas and Comanches agreed to a range between the Cimarron and Red rivers, extending across western Indian Territory and the Texas panhandle between the 98th and 103rd meridians. The terms of the Little Arkansas Treaties also included a provision that the Kiowa-Apaches would confederate with the Cheyennes and Arapahoes.

Fort Laramie Council

During 1865, federal commissioners also attempted to negotiate with the Sioux and Northern Cheyennes, in order to complete the railroad corridor through the Central Plains. General Grenville Dodge managed to meet with some Sioux bands and drew from them a pledge of peace, but he was unable to contact a sufficient number of band leaders to negotiate a definitive treaty. Finally, during June of 1866, a delegation of Brule and Oglala Sioux, headed by Red Cloud, met with American officials at Fort Laramie. American demands upon the Northern Plains tribes included assent to improvement and fortification of a traders trace known as the Bozeman Road, which ran from Fort Laramie to the Virginia City, Montana mines. The Bozeman Road coursed northwesterly along the Powder River on the east side of the Big Horn Mountains, then ran across the headwaters of the Yellowstone and over Bozeman Pass into the mining country. Because it traversed the prime buffalo-hunting range of the Sioux, Red Cloud refused to hold discussions with United States officials on any subject until the federal government abandoned its plan to improve and fortify the Bozeman Road. On this note, the Fort Laramie council of 1866 ended.

Powder River War

During 1866 Colonel Henry B. Carrington led a force of regular cavalry and infantry into the Powder River country to guard the Bozeman Road. His troops erected three posts along the road—Fort Reno, Fort Phil Kearny, and Fort C. F. Smith. Red Cloud's warriors made travel on the Bozeman Road risky, and freighters and miners traversed it at great peril. So intense was the Sioux pressure on this artery that, on several occasions between 1866 and 1868, they choked off all travel. Sioux parties also closely watched the military posts on the Bozeman Road and made it difficult for troops to escort caravans over the road and guard the posts at the same time. Fort Kearny, particularly, was in a state of siege most of the time.

Two incidents from a long list of engagements along the Powder River road illustrate the determination of the Sioux to exclude the Americans from their essential hunting grounds. Sioux raiders regularly preyed on details sent out from the post to cut wood; on December 21, 1866, an Indian band cut off a wood detail near Fort Kearny. When Captain William J. Fetterman led a cavalry force of eighty men to rescue the wood cutters, Sioux raiders decoyed the riders into a trap, and every man was slain. Soldiers on the Bozeman Road regarded the Fetterman Massacre as a senseless waste of lives. Captain Fetterman had proudly declared, when ordered to rescue the wood cutters, that with eighty men he could ride through the entire Sioux nation. Some months later, on August 2, 1867, at the Wagon Box Fight, the attitude was different. Thirty troopers commanded by Captain J. N. Powell were guarding a crew of wood cutters working near Fort Kearny when the inevitable Sioux attack came. Captain Powell's response to the raid indicated the new respect the troops had for Sioux warriors and the caution they now employed in combat. Rather than answer the Indians' challenge to pursue them on horseback, Powell directed his men to circle the wood wagons, which were turned on their sides and used as impromptu fortresses to protect the riflemen while they rebuffed the fierce Sioux charges. Powell's men held off the Sioux until relief arrived from Fort Kearny.

CONQUEST AND COMPRESSION

Conflict also continued on the Southern Plains, in spite of the Little Arkansas Treaties, which contained pledges of mutual peace and protecttion. The soil of the new Kiowa, Comanche, and Cheyenne domains was bloodied by the contest between Indians and intruders. The reduced hunting ranges assigned the tribes by the Little Arkansas Treaties were endangered by the failure of the Senate to ratify these pacts. Moreover, the refusal of federal officials on the Western border to protect the tribal territorial rights guaranteed by these pending treaties put the Indians under heavy pressure from land-hungry settlers pressing into the eastern margins of the assigned domains. The flow of traffic along the rivers and the old trails across these tribal ranges increased; American hunters trespassed and slaughtered the buffalo—so essential to the survival of these tribes—for the hides.

Within two years, it was apparent to federal officials that the tribal domains assigned by the Little Arkansas Treaties would have to be reduced to satisfy the expanding land desires of settlers and railroad builders. Widespread trespass and intrusion on treaty-assigned ranges were clear violations, which irritated the Indians, and, when federal troops failed to protect their rights, the tribes assumed this function themselves.

Retaliatory strikes by Southern Plains Indians against intruders caused federal commanders to campaign against the tribes. During April 1867, General Winfield Scott Hancock led a large cavalry and infantry force across western Kansas. On the Pawnee Fork, his troops captured and burned a Cheyenne village of 250 lodges. The infuriated Indians, in retaliation, stopped almost all travel across western Kansas; survey parties for the Kansas Pacific Railroad were held up for a month. Constant and intense campaigning against the Kiowas, Comanches, and Cheyennes throughout the summer of 1867 made the Indians ready for a truce, which came in October 1867, at a grand council on Medicine Lodge Creek.

The Doolittle Report

While federal troops were attempting to contain the Northern Cheyennes, Sioux, Southern Cheyennes, Kiowas, and Comanches—to maintain the railroad construction corridor through the Central Plains—the ultimate solution for the New West Indian problem was being forged in Washington. The Doolittle committee had completed its investigations and published its findings under the title *Report on the Condition of the Indian Tribes*. The committee concluded that the bloody Western conflict was, in most cases, due to unlawful settler intrusion, white hunter trespass on tribal territories, and precipitate actions by over-zealous military officers. The committee further stated that it was no longer feasible to allow the New West tribes a free, roving existence. To prevent Indian wars and to establish peace in the West, the Indians would have to give up the nomadic life, accept limited reservations, and "walk the white man's road."

Medicine Lodge Council

The Doolittle Report was used by leaders in both the legislative and executive branches of the national government as the basis for developing the final answer to the Indian problem. During 1867, Congress created a peace commission to negotiate with Western tribal leaders for the assignment of fixed, limited reservations. Members were Commissioner of Indian Affairs Nathaniel G. Taylor, Senator John B. Henderson of Missouri (chairman of the Senate committee on Indian affairs), Samuel F. Tappan, John B. Sanborn, General Alfred Terry, General William S. Harney, and Colonel Christopher C. Augur.

Messengers first made contact with leaders of the Southern Plains tribes, in summoning them to a council in October 1867 with the peace commission on Medicine Lodge Creek, seventy miles south of Fort Larned in southwestern Kansas, just north of the Indian Territory border. Principal Indian spokesmen at the Medicine Lodge Council included Stumbling Bear, Satank, and Satanta for the Kiowas, Ten Bears and Little Horn for the Comanches, Wolf's Sleeve and Brave Man for the Plains Apaches, and, for the Cheyennes and Arapahoes, Black Kettle, Whirlwind, and Tall Bear. This was the most colorful assemblage ever gathered on the Southern Plains. Buffalo-hide tipis were scattered along the stream banks for miles. Over 7,000 Indians gathered to watch their chiefs match wits with the federal commissioners and to receive gifts of cloth, paint, and beads sent to them, according to the issue sergeant, by their Great White Father in Washington. The importance of the Medicine Lodge Council was indicated by the presence of several newspaper correspondents who covered the proceedings. One of them was Henry M. Stanley from the *Missouri Democrat*, who later gained prominence by trekking through Africa to find Dr. Livingstone.

Although the treaties negotiated during the Medicine Lodge Council are very important historically, it is the Indian oratory, reflecting the pathos of harassed people, that provided a rare insight into the characters of these raiders of the Plains. The American commissioners warned that the buffalo would soon disappear and that, for their own good, the chiefs must lead their peoples to settled lives on reservations in Indian Territory and set examples by taking up farming and peaceful living. Ten Bears and Satanta made the most forceful responses.

The first to speak was Satanta, the Kiowa chief who was acknowledged as

> the orator of the plains. . . . He was a tall man and good-looking, with plenty of long shiny black hair, dark piercing eyes, a consuming vanity, and a quick temper. His presence was commanding and he was able to sway the councils of his people. He was respected, too, as a warrior.

He faced the commissioners and declared:

> All the land south of the Arkansas belongs to the Kiowas and Co-
> manches, and I don't want to give away any of it. I love the land and
> the buffalo and I will not part with any. . . . I have heard you intend
> to settle us on a reservation near the [Wichita] mountains. I don't
> want to settle there. I love to roam over the wide prairie, and when
> I do, I feel free and happy, but when we settle down we grow pale
> and die. . . . I don't like that, and when I see it, my heart feels like
> bursting with sorrow. I have spoken.

Ten Bears spoke next:

> The Comanches are not weak and blind, like the pups of a dog when
> seven sleeps old. They are strong and far-sighted, like grown horses.
> . . . There are things which you have said to me which I did not like.
> They were not sweet like sugar, but bitter like gourds. You said that
> you wanted to put us upon a reservation, to build us houses and make
> us medicine lodges. I do not want them. I was born upon the prairies,
> where the wind blew free, and there was nothing to break the light
> of the sun. I was born where there were no enclosures and where
> everything drew a free breath. I want to die there, and not within
> walls. I know every stream and every wood between the Rio Grande
> and the Arkansas. I have hunted and lived over that country. I lived
> like my fathers before me, and like them, I lived happily.[1]

Despite these rhapsodic utterances, the will of the commissioners
prevailed, and before the council closed, the chiefs had assented to drastically reduced ranges. By the terms of the Medicine Lodge Treaties, the
Kiowas and Comanches were assigned a reservation in the Leased District
on lands taken from the Choctaws and Chickasaws by the Reconstruction
Treaties of 1866. The 1,200 Kiowas and 1,700 Comanches received a
3 million-acre domain. In addition 300 Kiowa-Apaches confederated with
the Kiowas and Comanches and agreed to settle on their reservation. The
Cheyennes and Arapahoes were assigned a reservation in the Cherokee
Outlet, bounded by the Cimarron and Arkansas rivers. Those tribesmen,
numbering about 2,000 Cheyennes and 1,200 Arapahoes, actually settled
south of the designated reservation on the North Canadian River. An
executive order in 1869 established a new Cheyenne-Arapaho reservation,
containing nearly 5 million acres, south of the Outlet line and between
the 98th and 100th meridians; it extended to the Kiowa-Comanche line
on the Washita.

In 1872, the Cheyenne-Arapaho domain was reduced by about 600,000
acres. At that time federal officials established a reservation on the Washita
River for about 1,100 Wichitas, Caddoes, absentee Delawares, and remnants of the Texas tribes—Keechies, Anadarkoes, Ionies, and Wacoes.

---

[1] Quoted in Arrell M. Gibson, *Oklahoma: A History of Five Centuries* (Norman,
1965), pp. 238–39.

These Indian settlers had been colonized in the Leased District before the Civil War.

Federal commissioners working separately from but in coordination with the peace commission, accomplished additional tribal relocations and concentrations in Indian Territory between 1869 and 1884. During 1870, negotiations with the Osages led to the exchange of their lands in southern Kansas for an Indian Territory reservation situated between the 96th meridian and the Arkansas River; the following year, 1,500 Osages returned to Indian Territory. During 1872, the Kaws disposed of their Kansas reservation and relocated in Indian Territory on a 100,000-acre tract in the northwest corner of the Osage Reservation on the Arkansas. Between 1867 and 1876, federal commissioners relocated remnants of the Sac, Fox, Iowa, Shawnee, and Potawatomi tribes from Iowa and Kansas onto a 480,000-acre tract west of the Creek nation between the Cimarron and North Canadian rivers.

In the Cherokee Outlet, west of the Osages and Kaws, federal commissioners resettled Poncas, Otoes, Missouris, and Pawnees from Kansas and Nebraska. The Tonkawas, a Texas tribe that had been resident in the Leased District for several years, were moved in 1884 to a reservation in the Cherokee Outlet on the Salt Fork River. In addition, the Cherokees accepted about 1,000 Delawares and 700 Shawnees from Kansas into their nation proper. In northeastern Indian Territory, on surplus lands of the Quapaws, Senecas, and Shawnees, the federal government relocated Wyandots, Miamis, and Ottawas from Kansas.

Fort Laramie Council

After the Medicine Lodge Council negotiations, the federal peace commission turned to the Northern tribes. Commissioner Taylor had urged Red Cloud and other Sioux and Northern Cheyenne leaders to meet with the commission in September 1867, at Fort Laramie. Red Cloud made it clear that he would not meet with the commission until the federal government withdrew troops from the Powder River hunting range and abandoned the Bozeman Road. Finally, during April of 1868, Sioux and Northern Cheyenne leaders did meet with the peace commission at Fort Laramie. The treaties negotiated at the council provided that the federal government would abandon roads and military posts in the Sioux hunting range. In return, the Sioux and Northern Cheyennes accepted fixed reservations in the Dakota, Montana, and Wyoming territories, with a hunting annex in the Big Horn–Powder River region. The Northern Plains tribes pledged peace with the United States and unimpeded passage for railroad construction, including the Northern Pacific.

Federal Policy Changes

With the new concentration of Indian population on tribal reservations, some of the additional policy changes called for in the Doolittle

Report could be effectuated. To achieve tighter management over the aboriginal peoples, the federal government in 1871 ended the historic practice of conducting its relations with the Indian tribes by treaty. This practice had ascribed to each tribe a functional sovereignty that, in view of the drastically reduced power status of the Indian nations, federal officials regarded as a fiction and a cumbersome and bothersome process. Thereafter, the tribes were subject to all the laws of Congress and the administrative decrees of executive officials, particularly the Commissioner of Indian Affairs. All treaties negotiated before 1871 were to remain in force. The Board of Indian Commissioners was created in 1868 to watch over the federal bureaucracy in its management of Indian affairs. A nonpolitical agency with advisory and investigatory powers, its work softened the callousness of bureaucratic management and occasionally exposed maladministration in Indian affairs.

For about ten years after 1868, the federal government followed a dual, ambivalent course in administering the Indian nations—the differing approaches were the so-called "peace policy" and the "force policy." Shortly after his inauguration, President Ulysses S. Grant met with a delegation of nationally prominent churchmen, most of whom were Quakers (Society of Friends). These religious leaders pointed out that a century of force had failed to solve the Indian problem. Grant was impressed by their argument and offered this challenge: "If you can make Quakers out of the Indians it will take the fight out of them. Let us have peace." [2] He invited the leading religious denominations to recommend from among their members persons whom the president could appoint as agents to the tribes. One of the outstanding and courageous agents so appointed—considering the hazards he exposed himself to—was Laurie Tatum, who was assigned to the fierce Kiowas and Comanches. As it turned out, the Indians paid little heed to the Quaker agent's stress on nonviolence, but they respected Tatum, protected him, and treated him with great affection.

War Department officials, however, had no illusions about the Indians' propensity for nonviolence, particularly the Great Plains tribes. William T. Sherman, Philip Sheridan, Ranald Mackenzie and other field commanders were convinced that the Kiowas, Comanches, Cheyennes, Arapahoes, Sioux, and Western Apaches were still untamed, and that they would remain on reservations only after their war-making potential had been completely destroyed. Therefore, while "peace policy" agents worked on the reservations, attempting to lead their aboriginal charges "along the white man's road," the military developed a stand-by "force policy." New military posts were constructed at strategic points over the Great Plains, in the Rocky Mountains, and in the Southwest as support bases for regular cavalry and infantry units, which were held in readiness to strike at errant tribesmen.

[2] Quoted in ibid., p. 252.

The goal of the federal government, as set forth in the Doolittle Report, was to metamorphose New West Indians into law-abiding wards, to erase tribal lore and native customs, and, finally, to lead them along the road to white civilization; the Indians were to become self-sufficient farmers in the image of the typical American rural family. To achieve this aim the agent was expected to see that the men were instructed in farming and animal husbandry, the women taught household crafts, and that schools were established for instructing Indian youth in basic learning and vocational skills.

Most of the tribesmen settled peacefully on their assigned reservations and gave the agents no particular trouble, except for their determined efforts to continue intertribal visits, horse racing, gambling, feasts, and dances, and their calculated attempts to avoid farming and other detribalization programs. The buffalo-hunting Plains tribes, however, followed a course of active resistance. They remained belligerent and continued to raid the settlements in states and territories near their reservations. The Southern Plains tribes were the first to receive the recriminative fury of the "force policy."

Taming the Southern Tribes

The federal government had failed to deliver the gifts and rations promised by the commissioners at Medicine Lodge Council; Kiowa, Comanche, Cheyenne, and Arapaho warriors claimed that the failure of the United States to keep its pledge excused the tribes from observing the treaties, and during 1868, small predatory bands, well-mounted and heavily armed, raided the frontiers of western Kansas, Nebraska, and Texas. Troops found it almost impossible to confront the scattered, fast-moving war parties. In the late summer of 1868 General Alfred Sully finally located a village of Kiowas and Comanches in the North Canadian valley; but the strength of the encampment caused him to beat a hasty retreat to Fort Dodge.

Federal commanders on the Western frontier determined on a winter campaign; it was expected that this stroke would be effective for several reasons. First, the Indians would be concentrated in large villages for winter quarters. Second, they would not be expecting trouble, for federal troops usually left them alone during the colder months, mostly because the Indians were quiet at this time. And third, the Indians would be unable to defend themselves as effectively as during the spring and summer because their horses would be weakened by a sparse diet of winter forage.

The winter campaign was planned to initiate at Fort Supply, on the Cherokee Outlet at the junction of Beaver River and Wolf Creek. Federal troops from Fort Lyon, Colorado, Fort Bascom, New Mexico, and the Nineteenth Kansas Cavalry were to join the Seventh Cavalry at Fort Supply. However, in late November 1868, a heavy snowstorm swept into the Southern Plains and delayed the troops converging from Colorado, New

Mexico, and Kansas. Colonel George Armstrong Custer, commander of the Seventh Cavalry, was anxious to move on the hostile bands before they learned of the winter campaign. He led his troopers—complete with military band—and three scouts—California Joe and two Osage trackers—south over the cold, snow-covered Plains of western Indian Territory. On the morning of November 27, 1868, Custer's scouts located a large Indian village on the upper Washita. The Seventh Cavalry surrounded the settlement, smashed it with a roaring dawn attack, and caught the sleeping Indians by such complete surprise that only the slightest resistance was possible. The massacre that followed was identified in the official reports as the Battle of the Washita. Cheyenne Chief Black Kettle, who had miraculously escaped the Sand Creek Massacre in eastern Colorado in 1864, was among the 102 Cheyenne warriors, and numerous women and children slain in the Washita Massacre. Custer's troopers also slaughtered the village herd of 800 Indian ponies, burned every lodge in the encampment, and gathered up over fifty women and children as prisoners.

General Sheridan followed up the Washita campaign with a thrust south into the Leased District. From their base at old Fort Cobb, 1,500 troops rounded up scattered bands of Kiowas and Comanches, forcing the Indians to establish their camps near Fort Cobb, where the soldiers could watch them. While in the area, Sheridan selected the site for a new post on the edge of the Wichita Mountains; he named it Fort Sill. Sheridan's devastating winter campaign and the relentless watch his troopers maintained over the tribes appeared to pacify the warriors. But an undercurrent of discontent was evident by 1870 and threatened to flower into a full-scale uprising. Congress had cut the appropriations for purchasing rations for the reservation tribes, and the agents had to permit small bands of Indians to go to the Plains to hunt buffalo. The warriors were sickened and angered at what they saw. A high demand for buffalo hides and robes in Eastern markets had attracted white hunters, who roamed up and down the Plains slaughtering thousands of bison each day, taking only the hides and leaving the carcasses to rot.

Another disturbing influence that produced great unrest among the tribes was the fact that several bands had not yet come to the reservation to surrender to the military. The deadliest group still free was the hostile Quahada Comanche band led by the famous Quanah Parker, son of a Comanche chief and a white girl captive from Texas. Warriors from the Quahada band frequently slipped into the Kiowa-Comanche reservation and taunted the peaceful Indians, calling them cowards and "squaws"— the epitome of Indian derision—and invited them to join Quanah in his resistance to white domination. Beginning in 1870, small war parties began slipping away from the reservation to attack the settlements. Usually the warriors made their way on foot to make detection more difficult. Once across the Red River, they prowled about the ranches and stole horses and weapons. Then, armed and mounted, they began their work of death and destruction. One of the more famous raids was carried out in 1871 by a party of Kiowas led by Satanta, Satank, and Big Tree. Near Jacksboro, Texas they plundered and destroyed a wagon train.

There were raids more destructive than the Jacksboro incident, but its aftermath was of fundamental significance for the future of the Plains warriors. The three leaders, Satanta, Satank, and Big Tree, were arrested soon after their return to the reservation and held for trial in Texas. This procedure marked a drastic departure from the established practice and became a precedent; thereafter, hostile leaders were held personally responsible for actions of their warriors. Satanta, Satank, and Big Tree were shackled and hauled by wagon across the Red River. Satank slipped his bonds, attempted to kill one of his guards, and was shot by the cavalry escort. Satanta and Big Tree were tried and sentenced to death as punishment for the mass killings at Jacksboro, but the Texas governor commuted the sentences to life imprisonment. The Kiowas petitioned state and federal officials to parole their chiefs. Finally, federal officials agreed to use their influence to gain freedom for Satanta and Big Tree, in exchange for which the Kiowas and Comanches were to remain on their reservation and keep the peace. The agreement set the release date for late in 1873. The tribes scrupulously observed the terms, and Satanta and Big Tree were paroled as promised.

The return of the famous raider chiefs to the Kiowa-Comanche country seemed to be a signal for renewed depredations. The year 1874 was a bloody one on the southwestern frontier; the many engagements between war parties and wide-ranging cavalry units based at military posts and camps in Indian Territory and Texas during this year are known in military history as the Red River Wars. Federal commanders launched a major offensive during 1874 to end once and for all the martial strength of the Southern Plains tribes. General Nelson A. Miles was placed in command of a force that contained eight troops of cavalry—including Colonel Mackenzie's famed Fourth Cavalry—four companies of infantry, a battery of artillery, and a company of guides and scouts, principally Delawares. His orders were to comb the region between the Cimarron and Red rivers for hostile tribesmen. Between August and December 1874, Miles' army maintained a relentless pressure on the Indians; one by one the renegade bands came into Fort Sill to surrender. The last to capitulate were the Quahada Comanches, led by Quanah Parker.

Three things happened to each band: the troops at Fort Sill appropriated the Indian ponies, disarmed the warriors, and arrested the chiefs. Satanta, having broken parole, was returned to Texas prison. Seventy-two raider chiefs were placed in irons and hauled under heavy guard to military prison at Fort Marion in St. Augustine, Florida. Finally, the warriors of the fierce Southern Plains tribes, leaderless, disarmed, and stripped of their horses, were thoroughly pacified. They settled down to the dull routines of reservation life, demoralized by the drastic change in life confronting them but studiously thwarting the attempt of the agents to lead them along the "white man's road."

Taming the Northern Tribes

Next, the War Department turned its repressive "force policy" on the tribes of the Northern Plains. The Fort Laramie Treaty of 1868 was followed by a general increase in activity north of the Platte River, associated with the survey and construction parties of the railroads. Inevitably, incidents occurred between Indians and workmen, immigrants, and soldiers; according to the Sioux the trouble was due to trespass and general disregard for the Indian rights guaranteed by the Fort Laramie Treaty. The increased activity on the Northern Plains disturbed the buffalo and made hunting more difficult; the Indians had to range over a widening circuit to find the buffalo. Hunters in the employ of railroad companies also killed buffalo to feed the rail construction crews, and hide hunters wantonly slaughtered the huge, hairy beasts for the skins, leaving the carcasses to rot. The tribesmen, who were dependent upon the buffalo for food, shelter, and clothing, were incensed. The federal officials on the Plains actually encouraged extermination of the buffalo—the "Indians' commissary." As long as there were buffalo to hunt, the Indians would have an excuse to leave the reservation. Once the animals were gone, it was reasoned, they would become dependent upon government rations and farming for subsistence. Military commanders claimed that all too often the Indian mixed the buffalo hunt with raids on immigrant trains and rail construction crews.

Throughout the period between 1868 and 1876, Sioux and Northern Cheyenne warriors had brushes with the military. One of the most dramatic was the Battle of Beecher's Island. During September 1868, Colonel George A. Forsyth rode out from Fort Wallace in western Kansas with fifty men to scout for hostiles. He rode into eastern Colorado, where, while camped on the Arikaree River, they were surrounded by a large Sioux and Cheyenne party. Forsyth's men set up a sand-pit breastworks on an island in the river and fought an eight-day battle; they were nearly wiped out before the Indians withdrew. The defenders were able to turn back charge after charge only because of their superior firepower provided by new repeating rifles and a large supply of ammunition.

The time of reckoning and repression approached for the Northern Plains peoples just as it had for the Southern Plains tribes. Incidents leading up to the climax began in 1874. The first of them was precipitated when prospectors ranging from the mining frontier in Montana and Idaho claimed that they had found rich gold deposits in the Black Hills, in the heart of the Sioux Reservation in Dakota Territory. During 1874, Colonel Custer led the Seventh Cavalry through the Black Hills, ostensibly to answer Sioux protests and expel intruders, but really to escort a geological reconnaissance to confirm the gold find. The Sioux were also pressed from the north by the construction of the Northern Pacific Railway which, by

Indian Patriots

Anglo-Americans, fired with the presumptive holy mandate to occupy and develop the continent, found their mission challenged and their expansionist momentum periodically checked by a human barrier. They compounded a soothing conscience balm for their bloody, genocidal campaigns, which removed the tribal obstructions by casting the Indian in the black image of a pagan enemy of Christian civilization, a

Osceola (1808–1838). Seminole.
University of Oklahoma Library

Sitting Bull (1834–1890). Sioux.
The Bettmann Archive

Black Hawk (1767–1838). Sac.
The Newberry Library, Chicago

Quanah Parker (1845?–1911). Comanche.
The Bettmann Archive

skulking, bloodthirsty savage, a
fiend of hell.

From the Indian viewpoint,
leaders and warriors who defended
aboriginal lifestyles, tribal lands,
and group values—which they
regarded as superior to the Anglo-
American alternative—were patriots no less than those hallowed
heroes who resisted tyranny, appropriation, and the quenching
of freedom in another historical
context.

Chief Joseph (1840–1904). *Nez Perces.*
The Smithsonian Institution

Geronimo (1829–1909). Apache.
The Bettmann Archive

Satanta (1831?–1878). Kiowa.
University of Oklahoma Library

Big Foot (1838?–1890). Sioux.
Dead in the snow
at Wounded Knee.
The Smithsonian Institution

1872, had reached the Missouri River at the Mandan villages. Miners entered the Black Hills during 1875 in increasing numbers. The Sioux threatened retaliation against the intruders, and federal officials attempted unsuccessfully to purchase the Black Hills.

Sioux bands left their reservations in protest and reportedly were preparing to sweep through the country and destroy the intruding prospectors. Federal officials sent messages to the Indians, ordering them to return to their reservations by February 1, 1876, or face military action. The bands who received the message ignored it. The principal leaders in the Sioux nation at this time were Crazy Horse—Red Cloud's successor to Oglala martial leadership after the latter determined on a course of peace following the Fort Laramie Council—and Sitting Bull, leader of the Hunkpapa group of Teton Sioux.

During the winter of 1875–1876, federal commanders on the Northern Plains planned a punitive expedition into the Sioux country. Three columns were to converge on the principal Sioux concentration, believed to be on the Big Horn River and its tributaries. One column under General George Crook was to move north out of Fort Fetterman, Wyoming, into Montana. A second column under Colonel John Gibbon was to march east from Fort Ellis, Montana. The third column, commanded by General Alfred Terry, and including the Seventh Cavalry led by Colonel Custer, was to move from Fort Abraham Lincoln in Dakota Territory west to the Big Horn. Crook marched his column out of Fort Fetterman along the old Bozeman Road in March of 1876. On two occasions his men came upon scattered Sioux villages; they destroyed over 100 lodges, but fierce Indian counterattacks slowed his advance toward the rendezvous on the Yellowstone. After the first encounter, in March, Crook returned his men to Fort Fetterman to recuperate. His contacts with the Sioux were inconclusive, but they held him up, destroyed the element of surprise, and made impossible the co-ordination required for the success of the overall campaign. Nonetheless, the other two columns met on the Yellowstone at the mouth of Powder River, and scouting reports confirmed that a large encampment was situated in the valley of the Little Big Horn.

Terry sent Custer and twelve troops of the Seventh Cavalry to close retreat at the south end of the valley; on June 25, he came upon the Indian settlement. Dividing his column into four sections and placing three in positions to check flight from the village, he led the fourth section—consisting of 225 men—along the Little Big Horn River toward the village. En route, Sioux and Northern Cheyenne defenders intercepted the attack force. Custer and every trooper in his section were slain. The dispersed sections of the Seventh Cavalry were pinned down and saved from extinction only by the timely arrival of elements from the main force.

Sioux exultation at the victory over the Seventh Cavalry was brief. Massed federal troops forced the Sioux and Northern Cheyennes to abandon their encampment on the Little Big Horn and relentlessly pressed the retreating Indians. Band leaders surrendered and led their people back to the reservations. Crazy Horse was shot down during 1877 in what was reported as an escape attempt. Sitting Bull and a group of followers fled to Canada; they returned to the Sioux reservation in Dakota Territory during 1881. By the end of 1876, the Northern Plains, like the Southern Plains, were quiet and peaceful. The tribes had been subdued, the aboriginal barrier to settlement and development had been removed. The military conquest of the New West tribes was nearly completed. Peripheral resistance to American dominion, posed by the Modocs, Mexican Kickapoos, Nez Perces, Utes, and Western Apaches, was dealt with in summary fashion by the federal military establishment.

The Conquest of the Modoc

The surviving members of the Modoc tribe resided on the Klamath Reservation on the California-Oregon border. In 1869, President Grant appointed Albert B. Meacham, a Methodist leader, the "peace policy" agent for the Oregon tribes. Meacham's strong commitment to lead the Klamath Reservation Indians along the "white man's road" and his intensive suppression of tribal ways antagonized the Modocs. Kenitpoos, better known as Captain Jack, led a group of protesting Modocs off the reservation in 1870. When local citizens became alarmed and appealed for protection, troops were rushed to the troubled zone. The Modocs took refuge in the Lava Beds near Tule Lake and successfully defended themselves.

In April of 1873, Modoc leaders met in council with a peace commission which included General Edward R. S. Canby and Meacham. During the proceedings, the Indians killed Canby and wounded Meacham. Thereupon, a force of 1,500 troops moved in for the kill, and Captain Jack surrendered on June 1, 1874. An army court martial tried and convicted him and three other Modoc leaders. They were executed by hanging. The resistive Modocs were shipped off to Indian Territory as prisoners-of-war and were settled on Quapaw Agency lands. In 1909, the Modocs were permitted to return to the Klamath Reservation, although about fifty chose to remain in Oklahoma—the former Indian Territory.

The Conquest of the Kickapoo

Beginning in the spring of 1865, the Mexican Kickapoos, claiming that Texas had declared war on the tribe by the attack at Concho River, launched a ten-year offensive against Texas. The campaign was unmatched for calculated vindictiveness and destruction of life and property. Before Kickapoo vengeance was finally satisfied, marauding bands from the Coahuila sanctuary across the international boundary had destroyed millions of dollars' worth of property, killed hundreds of Texas citizens, carried countless children into captivity, and completely desolated entire counties on the Texas side of the Rio Grande. The war also embroiled the United

States in a dispute with Mexico, when United States armed forces trespassed on Mexican soil; the incident provoked a diplomatic tiff that involved an embarrassed Congress, the secretary of state, and the president.

In response to petitions, letters, and memorials from distressed Texans along the Rio Grande, the national government in 1873 gave serious attention to the Mexican Kickapoos. Colonel Ranald S. Mackenzie, fresh from victories over the Comanches in the North, arrived on the Rio Grande in the spring of 1873 with his famous Fourth Cavalry and orders to smash the Kickapoos. On May 17, the cavalry moved out of Fort Duncan and crossed the river into Mexico to make a surprise attack on the Kickapoo settlement near Nacimiento on the Remolino River. Scouts had reported that most of the warriors were away hunting and raiding. The next day, the troopers reached the Remolino and struck the villages in a lightning-swift attack. In a matter of minutes the settlement was a shambles. The troopers burned the dwellings, "ruin and desolation now marked the spot—a cyclone could not have made more havoc or a cleaner sweep"[3] where scarcely an hour before had stood the prosperous villages of the Mexican Kickapoos.

Mackenzie's mission had been accomplished. The soldiers gathered fifty women and children captives and beat a hasty retreat to the Rio Grande. The captives were held at Fort Gibson as bait to lure the warriors to Indian Territory. Shortly thereafter, 317 Kickapoo husbands, parents, and relatives of the prisoners moved from Coahuila to Indian Territory. Agents settled them on lands on the Sac and Fox Reservation. Nearly 400 Kickapoos remained in Mexico, but they had been generally pacified by the Mackenzie raid.

The Conquest of the Nez Perces

Extension of the mining frontier into Idaho and Montana during the 1860s displaced many tribes occupying the territory between the Rocky Mountains and the Cascades; it also produced the inevitable compression of Indian lands. One tribe, the Nez Perces, who had an unbroken record of peace with the United States, was grossly exploited during this period. A treaty with the United States, negotiated in 1855, had guaranteed perpetual tenure of their territory on the tributaries of the Snake River. But soon the press of settlement led to demands for Nez Perces land and, in 1863, federal commissioners negotiated a treaty with selected tribal leaders providing for the cession of the Wallowaw Country, esteemed by the Nez Perces for its salmon-filled streams and the rich pastures it provided for their herds of cattle and horses. This treaty assigned the tribe a small reservation at Lapwai near Lewiston.

The Nez Perces living in the Wallowaw Country refused to move. During 1877, settlers trespassed on Nez Perces areas; the Indians killed

---

[3] Arrell M. Gibson, *The Kickapoos: Lords of the Middle Border* (Norman, 1963), p. 243.

thirteen intruders, and federal troops came to drive the Indians to Lapwai. Chief Joseph collected his Nez Perces band of 200 warriors, with their women and children, and fled to evade the military dragnet. This small band roamed over Idaho, Wyoming, and Montana on a 1,300-mile sweep, pausing occasionally to inflict embarrassing defeats on the pursuing army. At the Battle of Big Hole, Nez Perces warriors defeated Gibbons' troops. Tenacious columns led by Crook, Gibbons, and General O. O. Howard continued the pursuit and finally forced the Nez Perces to a stand in the Bear Paw Mountains of north central Montana. On October 4, 1877, after a five-day battle, to save the women and children from freezing, Chief Joseph surrendered. Federal authorities sent the Nez Perces to Indian Territory and settled them in the Cherokee Outlet on the Salt Fork River. In 1885, they were returned to the Northwest to the Colville Reservation in Washington.

The Conquest of the Ute

Repression of old tribal ways by government agents produced a revolt on the Ute Reservation in western Colorado. The victims of earlier conquest and relocation, the Utes, who numbered about 3,600, occupied a tract on the White River west of the Continental Divide. Portions of the reservation contained timber, some minerals, and scattered rich agricultural lands. Colorado statehood in 1876 fired the citizens to a strong desire for the lands embraced within the reservation. Politicians campaigned on the slogan "The Utes Must Go!" Ouray, the principal tribal leader, urged the Utes to bend a bit and rely more on farming so as to protect their claim to the White River Reservation.

In 1879, Agent Nathan Meeker established a program of comprehensive detribalization for the Utes. Douglas, an old warrior chief, led a revolt that resulted in the killing of Meeker and eleven other whites. Ute warriors later defeated an invading military force of nearly 200 men, killing 14 soldiers. Thereupon, a large federal and state militia force marched through the Ute country and mercilessly drove the Indians to a new reservation in Utah Territory at Uintah and Ouray. Only a small group of Utes were permitted to remain in southwestern Colorado.

The Conquest of the Apache

The Western Apaches were the last New West Indians to capitulate. By 1871, the federal government was ready to deal decisively with these peoples. Vincent Colyer, representing the Bureau of Indian Affairs and the Board of Indian Commissioners, traveled to the Southwest and laid out four reservations—one in the New Mexico Territory and three in the Arizona Territory—for concentrating the Apaches. He assigned the fierce Chiricahuas and Mimbreños to the San Carlos Reservation on the Gila River. Next, federal officials attempted to send word to the scattered Apache bands to direct them to locate promptly on the reservations.

General Crook, with a large force of cavalry and infantry, ranged across New Mexico Territory and Arizona Territory, pressing the scattered bands to comply. Most Apaches submitted to reservation life, but a few restless ones watched for the opportunity to escape the reservation confines. Beginning in 1874, Victorio, a Mimbreño Apache who had served with Mangas Coloradas, led the bolder spirits, rarely numbering over fifty, on destructive raids against the scattered settlements and ranches of the Southwest. Over 2,000 troops were in the field most of the time between 1874 and 1880, pursuing this wily Apache predator. In 1880, he was slain in northern Mexico by Mexican frontier troops.

The elderly Nana succeeded Victorio and led the raiders briefly until Geronimo emerged as the leader. Geronimo's depredations in the Southwest led to massed operations against him in 1883; he was forced to surrender and return to the reservation. In 1885, he again left the reservation at the head of a band of fewer than 50 men and about 100 women and children. Over 4,000 troops, operating in small parties, searched for this renegade Apache band. Finally in 1886, Geronimo surrendered. Following the capitulation, federal officials shipped the war leader and nearly five hundred other Apaches to military prison at Fort Pickens in Pensacola, Florida. In 1887, the Apaches were removed to Mount Vernon Barracks, Alabama, where a fourth of them died of tuberculosis and other diseases. Finally, federal officials moved them to the Kiowa-Comanche Reservation in Indian Territory and placed them under the guns of Fort Sill. Their status as prisoners-of-war continued until 1913.

THE RESERVATION ERA

For many tribes, the reservation era covered the period 1867–1887. It was an ordeal to be endured. In this twenty years, the federal government expected to accomplish the magical transformation of the New West tribes from free, roving raiders into settled peaceful, law-abiding wards made self-sufficient by the adoption of agriculture and stockraising. The reservation was the focus for tribal management and reformation. The agency staff included the Indian agent, who was expected to direct the transformation process, a clerk, reservation farmers, teachers, and a squad of Indian police recruited from among the warriors of the tribe. The latter were responsible for maintaining order, confiscating whisky, and reporting on white intruders. Various religious denominations were permitted to place missionaries among the tribes, for the federal government regarded conversion as vital to leading the Indians along the "white man's road."

The Detribalization Process

American society directed an almost paranoiac defensiveness toward ways that differed from established Anglo-American cultural values and practices. Tribal lifestyles were thus regarded as threatening, unChristian primitivism, and the government was expected to throttle and expurgate them. The agent was assigned the task of eradicating tribal practices that included polygamy, native religion, dances, rituals, and rites. It was his duty to require his charges to abandon Indian garb and take up "citizen dress." Native languages were to be suppressed. In the detribalization process, Indians who persisted in the old lifestyle were punished by having rations withheld. Children in the reservation schools who faltered and used the Indian language were punished. Comanche children complained bitterly that teachers literally "whipped the Comanche out of us."

The quality of agents was fairly high during the period of the "peace policy," which ended in 1877. Thereafter, the agents and vocational and educational staffs assigned the task of leading the Indians along the "white man's road" were partisan appointees, and quality deteriorated accordingly. One writer has charged that most of the agents were corrupt, that their staffs consisted of "instructors in agriculture who had never farmed, clerks who couldn't write, and teachers too dissolute or incompetent to hold positions in other schools." [4]

The quality and substance of the missionary effort among the reservation tribes was also low. American religious bodies seemingly found the "Chinaman on the banks of the Yangtze . . . a more romantic and challenging figure" for missionary effort than the pitiable Indian of the New West. One federal official arraigned the nation's churches for their feeble interest in the reservation Indian, claiming that the churches and mission societies of America expended millions on foreign missions annually and less than $10,000 on American Indians. The few churches that responded to the reservation opportunity often confused the Indians by their sectarian devisiveness. Chief Joseph would not permit missionaries among his people, declaring that "They will teach us to quarrel about God as the Catholics and Protestants do. . . . We may quarrel with men . . . but we never quarrel about God. We do not want to learn that." [5]

Moreover, many Indian leaders were quick to detect the contradictions and duplicity of American society, which provoked their scorn toward missionary gestures. A Sioux leader, when asked to permit missionaries to work among his people, answered "it is your people, who you say have the Great Spirit's book, who bring us the fire-water. It is your white men who corrupt our daughters. Go teach them to do right, and then come to us and I will believe you." [6]

Pan-Indian Movements

Reservation life produced widespread malaise among the Indians, and out of their melancholy, disorientation, and cultural shock many sought their own solutions to the problem of finding a way to face the new order.

[4] William T. Hagan, *American Indians* (Chicago, 1961), pp. 127–29.
[5] Ibid.
[6] Ibid.

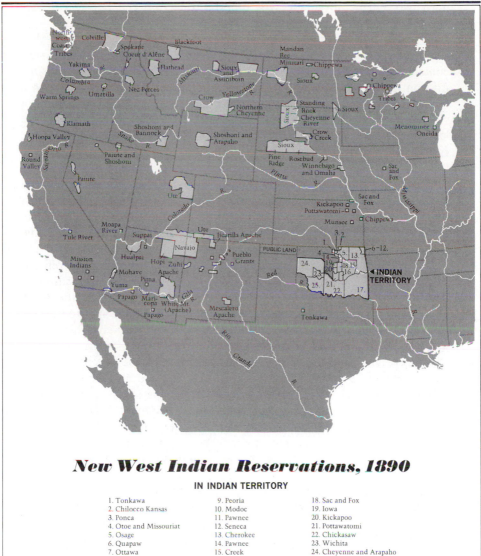

New West Indian Reservations, 1890

IN INDIAN TERRITORY

1. Tonkawa
2. Chilocco Kansas
3. Ponca
4. Otoe and Missouriat
5. Osage
6. Quapaw
7. Ottawa
8. Wyandotte
9. Peoria
10. Modoc
11. Pawnee
12. Seneca
13. Cherokee
14. Pawnee
15. Creek
16. Seminole
17. Choctaw
18. Sac and Fox
19. Iowa
20. Kickapoo
21. Pottawatomi
22. Chickasaw
23. Wichita
24. Cheyenne and Arapaho
25. Kiowa and Comanche

Two pan-Indian movements, the Ghost Dance and the peyote cult, are manifestations of this attempt.

During 1889, a Paiute Indian in Nevada named Wovoka (Jack Wilson), experienced a series of visions in which he reported metaphysical contact with the Great Holy Force Above. This "force" assigned him the mission of transmitting to the Indian a new way of life that included a return to the old tribal ways, purification rites, and the eschewal of violence, whisky, and white ways in general. As a reward to them for following the new way, the Great Force would destroy all that oppressed the Indian—the agents, schools, missionaries, and the plow. And the world the Indians cherished would be restored: Grass would again cover the prairies; the buffalo would be restored; and the free, happy life of old would return. The restoration promise of Wovoka's teachings swept across the reservations of the New West. Because communicants participated in a special group movement that transfixed them and produced a mild, mass hypnosis, the ritual was given the name Ghost Dance Religion.

The most tragic incident produced by what alarmed federal officials called the "Ghost Dance Craze" occurred on the Sioux Reservation in South Dakota in late 1890. Local officials there charged that the aging Sioux chief Sitting Bull was encouraging the Ghost Dance among his people for ulterior purposes. They ordered his arrest, and the venerable warrior was slain in the process. Hundreds of Sioux fled the reservations in fear and anger. One band under Big Foot was pursued by the Seventh Cavalry. On December 29, 1890, while this band was camped at Wounded Knee Creek, the soldiers attempted to search the Indians for weapons. A fight broke out, the troops opened fire on the encampment with their new rapid-firing Hotchkiss guns, and 150 Indians were slain. Another fifty received serious wounds, and perhaps as many as 100 Indians, scattered over the countryside, died from freezing. Twenty-nine soldiers died at Wounded Knee.

The reservation Indians who followed Wovoka's prescriptions performed the Ghost Dance and waited for the restoration; but to their dismay, the agents, teachers, missionaries, and the plow remained. However, before their disillusionment was complete, a new way came to them from the Southwest, principally by way of the Kiowa-Comanche Reservation in Indian Territory. The new practice was the peyote cult, a holy rite centering on the peyote button, the fruit of the mescal cactus. It produced in the communicants a mild hallucinatory state, whereby they could transmit themselves from the ennui of daily reservation life—its poverty, degradation, and suppression of tribal values—to a satisfying level of quiet peace and freedom. The peyote cult was a mixture of native religion and certain Christian concepts and rituals; the ceremony was a kind of sacrament of communion, in which the worshipers substituted peyote for the bread and wine. The cult flowered into the Native American Church and, like most Indian ways, was regarded as a mystical threat; it was suppressed by the Bureau of Indian Affairs and banned by most state governments, forcing it underground where, predictably, it increased its appeal and following.

Allotment in Severalty

By 1887 it was evident that the national government was not accomplishing its goals of cultural transformation. Critics claimed that the reservation system was a curse for the Indian and America's shame. These "institutionalized slums" were the subject of Helen Hunt Jackson's *Century of Dishonor* (1881), which stirred the public conscience. Federal officials blamed the failure of the detribalization process on the Indian land system. The Indians held their reservation lands in common, with the title vested in the tribe. This arrangement tended to nourish tribal government which, although suppressed, continued to function. Federal officials concluded that the way to break tribal resistance and communal strength would be to abolish reservations and assign each Indian an allotment of land in fee simple. They believed that private ownership of land—that is, allotment in severalty—would accomplish what twenty years of reservation life had not.

Congress therefore passed the Dawes Act (1887), which provided for the assignment to each Indian of 160 acres of reservation land, which would be held in trust by the federal government for twenty-five years. The Dawes Act was the ultimate act in the tribal land compression process; and it was applied to virtually all reservation lands that held promise for agricultural development. Thus, the reservations in the desert and mountain regions, which, at the time, were not coveted by the Anglo-American settler, escaped the allotment process. In Indian Territory all of the reservations, except the domains of the Five Civilized Tribes, were liquidated under the terms of the Dawes Allotment Act. Each member of the Kiowa, Comanche, and other tribes was assigned an allotment. The surplus lands, amounting to several million acres, were opened to homesteaders. The allotment system cruelly cast the Indian adrift in the dominant white society.

The aboriginal peoples of the New West were casualties of the rapid Anglo-American occupation of the trans-Missouri territory. After the Civil War, a compelling motivation for the federal government's intensive program of pacifying the tribes and compressing their lands was to enable transportation companies to extend their railroad routes from the Mississippi Valley to the Pacific Coast.

SELECTED SOURCES

General studies on the Indians of the New West, their conquest and assignment to reservations include *William T. Hagan, *American Indians* (Chicago,

* Available in paperback.

1961); Angie Debo, *A History of the Indians of the United States* (Norman, 1970); *Alvin M. Josephy, *The Indian Heritage of America* (New York, 1968); and Frederick W. Hodge, ed., *Handbook of American Indians North of Mexico* (New York, 1959), 2 vols.

The drama and pathos of tribal conquest are presented in Donald J. Berthrong, *The Southern Cheyennes* (Norman, 1963); *Mildred P. Mayhall, *The Kiowas* (Norman, 1962); Stanley Vestal, *Sitting Bull: Champion of the Sioux* (Norman, 1957); Ernest Wallace and E. Adamson Hoebel, *The Comanches: Lords of the South Plains* (Norman, 1952); Robert C. Carriker, *Fort Supply, Indian Territory: Frontier Outpost on the Plains* (Norman, 1970); William H. Leckie, *The Military Conquest of the Southern Plains* (Norman, 1963); *Arrell M. Gibson, *The Kickapoos: Lords of the Middle Border* (Norman, 1963); and *Douglas C. Jones, *The Treaty of Medicine Lodge* (Norman, 1966).

Works on the reservation period include D. S. Otis, *The Dawes Act and the Allotment of Indian Land* (Norman, 1973); William E. Unrau, *The Kansas Indians* (Norman, 1971); *Robert M. Utley, *The Last Days of the Sioux Nation* (New Haven, 1963); and *Helen Hunt Jackson, *A Century of Dishonor*, Andrew F. Rolle, ed. (New York, 1881, 1965).

The Completion of the Transcontinental Railroad,
Promontory Point, Utah, 1869.

Pacific Express Rounding Cape Horn, Idaho.

25

Technological Conquest
of the New West:
The Railroad

By the 1850s, the New West was on the threshold of a transportation revolution. Already a grid of rail lines connected the Atlantic seaboard with the Mississippi Valley. The railroad's conquest of distance and time was impressive; it took less than a week to move freight and passengers from the eastern United States to the western border of Missouri. But there the railroad thrust languished as Northern and Southern political leaders bitterly debated whether the extension to the Pacific shore should follow a northern or a southern course. In 1861 the issue was resolved by the Southern secession, and only a year later—with the national government locked in savage combat with the insurgent South—Congress adopted legislation to permit the resumption of railroad construction toward the Pacific.

Meanwhile, New West transportation needs continued to be met by primitive overland stage and freight services and by slow, expensive maritime voyages to West Coast ports. The outbreak of sectional hostilities in 1861 forced the Butterfield Overland Mail and other stage and freight enterprises serving the Southwest to transfer their routes to the central and northern regions. During the war most of the mail and passenger stage service and freighting west of Missouri was combined into a transportation empire controlled by a man named Ben Holladay. Holladay first became involved in Western transportation during the Mexican War, when he managed a freight company that supplied the Army of the West in its march from Missouri to New Mexico and California. In 1862, he purchased the giant Russell, Majors and Waddell Company. Subsequently he expanded and consolidated New West transportation services so that, by 1866, he controlled over 3,000 miles of stage and freight facilities west of Missouri. Holladay stages served accessible major centers such as Denver and Salt Lake City, as well as remote Northwest communities such as Virginia City, Montana, and Walla Walla, Washington. Holladay also dominated the freight business between Missouri and the Great Basin and maintained maritime service to Panama, Oregon, and China.

THE FIRST TRANSCONTINENTAL RAILROAD

The demands of the nation at war between 1861 and 1865 made development of New West railroad facilities impossible. But the railroad momentum was so strong that, even in these times of dire national stress, it would not lay quiet. The legacy of Asa Whitney, Stephen A. Douglas, and other pioneer promoters was about to bear fruit. The essential preliminaries had already been completed during the 1850s, when the national government had financed a comprehensive survey of the New West (*see* Chapter 21). Engineers from the War Department had searched the Northwest, the Southwest, and the vast center of the New West for the most feasible route for the transcontinental railroad. The explorations had generated a vast corpus of geographic and cartographic data, and the possible means had been analyzed and evaluated.

Rail connections already existed at several points on the western border; there they remained, expectantly, impatiently awaiting continuation of roadbed construction. The Hannibal and St. Joseph Railway had reached Missouri's western border in 1859, and the Missouri Pacific was building a line between St. Louis and Kansas City, which was to be completed in 1865.

Pacific Railway Act

On July 1, 1862, Congress passed the Pacific Railway Act, authorizing the Union Pacific Company and the Central Pacific Company to construct the first transcontinental railroad over a right-of-way 400 feet wide; it was to follow a course across the New West on the central route from Omaha to Sacramento.

The act also contained a subsidy clause to offset the problem of reluctant private financing of roadbed construction. Unlike the new line, the railroads that ran from the Atlantic to the western border of Missouri crossed settled areas, which provided promise of passenger and freight use sufficient to warrant local private investment. Many state and municipal governments had issued bonds to support railroad construction, and limited federal support had been provided some of these lines in the form of grants of public land along the railroad right-of-way. But the transcontinental extension would cross vast empty areas, and the anticipated limited passenger and freight use discouraged private investment. The Pacific Railway Act, therefore, provided two forms of federal aid for financing construction of the transcontinental line. First, each of the railroad companies was to receive ten sections of public lands on alternate sides of the track for each mile of completed roadbed. An amendment to the Pacific Railway

Act, adopted in 1864, increased this to twenty alternate sections for each mile. Second, the Union Pacific Company and the Central Pacific Company were to receive government loans in the form of federal bonds paid on the following scale: $16,000 per mile of roadbed over level terrain; $32,000 per mile of roadbed in the upland, plateau country of the Great Basin; and $48,000 per mile of roadbed in the mountains. Interest and principal on the bonds were both payable in thirty years. The companies then raised funds to finance roadbed construction by converting the bonds to cash in the nation's financial markets.

The Pacific Railway Act designated the construction territory for each company. The Union Pacific was authorized to build the roadbed from Omaha to the California border, and the Central Pacific from Sacramento to the eastern California border. This clause of the statute was amended twice: in 1864, the Central Pacific construction territory was extended 150 miles into Nevada; and two years later it was further extended eastward to the point where its tracks joined those of the Union Pacific.

The Builders

The men whose leadership made possible the building of the nation's first transcontinental railroad were pioneers in an emerging age of determined entrepreneurs. Their driving energy, callous exploitation of human, natural, and capital resources, and sublime successes established management patterns that were emulated by the emerging American business community for the rest of the nineteenth century. Several men—including the notorious Oliver Ames of Massachusetts—served as president of the Union Pacific, but the firm's driving spirits were Thomas C. Durant, vice-president and executive officer, and the Union Pacific chief engineer, General Granville M. Dodge. Central Pacific managers were four Sacramento businessmen—Collis P. Huntington, Mark Hopkins, Leland Stanford, and Charles Crocker—and the company's chief engineer, Theodore P. Judah.

The Central Pacific, which was organized in 1861 under a California charter, was the first to begin construction. Supply problems for both companies were immense, but, besides wartime shortages of essential materials and machinery, the Central Pacific faced the additional problem of remoteness; materials and equipment had to be shipped by sea around Cape Horn. However, by 1863, Judah's energetic management resulted in the accumulation at San Francisco of 6,000 tons of rails—enough for sixty miles of track—along with locomotives and rolling stock. Judah marked out the route from Sacramento across the Sierras, and by July of 1864, the the Central Pacific had built thirty-one miles of track. During 1867, its roadbed crossed the Sierras 100 miles east of Sacramento. The Central Pacific crews worked in the near-inaccessible Sierra terrain, with its steep grades, hard granite faces, and deep canyons. It required heavy blasting with nitroglycerin, monumental filling, long tunnel excavation, extensive bridgework, and the construction of forty miles of snowsheds to lay the bed through the mountains.

The Labor Crews

Central Pacific managers faced a serious labor problem as well, for white workers were expensive and difficult to keep because of the draw of the new mining fields. During 1866, rail officials began importing great numbers of Chinese laborers from Canton. Each of them was paid $35 a month. Leland Stanford claimed that the Chinese workmen were as "efficient as white laborers" and that "without them it would be impossible to complete the western portion of this great national highway." [1] Within a year, over 7,000 Chinese were laboring on the Central Pacific branch of the transcontinental line.

Union Pacific officials broke ground at the transcontinental line's eastern terminus at Omaha during December 1863; but the war so sapped the nation's energy and attention at that time that this proved only a ceremonial act. It was not until July 10, 1865, that Union Pacific workmen laid the first rail. When General Dodge first sent his crews into the field, machinery, materials, and workers were carried by steamboat up the Missouri River to Council Bluffs. In 1867, however, the Chicago and Northwestern Railroad had reached Council Bluffs; thereafter, that line hauled construction materials to the Omaha depot. Because the Missouri River had not yet been bridged, supplies still had to be ferried across to the Union Pacific railhead.

Dodge formed a labor army of Irish immigrants and discharged soldiers that, at the peak of construction during 1868, numbered 10,000. He carefully organized the crews according to their function. Survey parties ranged ahead of the construction crews, traveling along the Platte, through Lone Tree Pass, and across the Wyoming Basin and Wasatch Range; they marked a route that followed the lowest grade and necessitated the fewest curves. To the disappointment of the citizens of Denver and Salt Lake City, the designated routing missed both cities.

Building the Transcontinental Railroad

Grading crews pressed hard on the heels of survey parties. Dodge established a daily quota of three to four miles of roadbed that had to be readied for tracklayers. Behind the construction crews on the newly completed track moved locomotives pulling hundreds of freight cars from the Missouri River depots; they were loaded with ties, rails, and other construction essentials. Forty-freight cars were required to supply the material for one mile of track.

One of Dodge's greatest problems was the ever-present Indian threat. Sweeping strikes by Sioux and Cheyenne raiders kept the crews on constant alert. Troops guarded the engineering and survey parties and construction gangs, but the long spread of activity made total surveillance impossible.

[1] E. Douglas Branch, Westward: The Romance of the American Frontier (New York, 1930), p. 530.

Every workman was armed and became a defender in the moment of danger, dropping his shovel or maul and taking up his rifle. Indians rode ahead of the grading crews, pulled up surveyors' stakes marking the route, hit undefended survey parties, and attacked the construction line, driving crews back and burning equipment and supplies. Squads of hunters sent out to shoot buffalo to feed the work crews were cut off and slain. Dodge did his best to suppress reports of Indian attacks and keep them out of Eastern newspapers, for workmen were difficult enough to recruit and hold on the job.

Yet, in spite of Indian hazards and construction obstacles of towering mountains, deep canyons, and broad river beds, the Union Pacific line irresistibly, determinedly progressed westward. By the close of 1865, Dodge's men had completed forty miles of track west of Omaha. During 1866, they laid 260 miles of track; and in the following year, in more difficult terrain, they laid 240 miles of track. On November 13, 1867, Union Pacific rails reached Cheyenne, Wyoming. Union Pacific crewmen had completed 1,038 miles of track, Central Pacific 742 miles of track.

Completing the Transcontinental Railroad

On May 10, 1869, the Union Pacific and Central Pacific crews met at Promontory Point, Utah. Two special trains packed with officials and guests—one from San Francisco, the other from Omaha—arrived on the summit during the morning. Elaborate oratory and ceremony marked the joining of the final section of track, including the placing of the "last tie"—a highly polished piece of hardwood bound with silver and fitted with a silver plaque—and the driving of the "last spike"—which was cast from twenty-dollar gold pieces. In the final act of this grand transportation drama, the two locomotives eased forward until their guards touched, trainmen broke bottles of champagne over the engines, and the master of ceremonies proclaimed "This railroad unites the two great oceans of the world." [2]

EXPANDING THE NEW WEST RAILROAD GRID

By 1893, five transcontinental railroads linked the Mississippi Valley with the Pacific shore. Completion of the first of these, the Union Pacific–Central Pacific, in 1869, spurred the engineers and work crews of the other four lines to greater competitive fury in their rush into the New West wilderness.

Texas and Pacific

The Texas and Pacific, headed by Thomas A. Scott, was chartered by Congress to build a line from Marshall, Texas—at the head of navigation

[2] Ibid., p. 539.

of the Red River—east to Shreveport, west to Fort Worth, and thence to El Paso and along the 32nd parallel to San Diego. West of El Paso, the Texas and Pacific Company was to receive a federal subsidy of twenty alternate sections for each mile of track. Texas and Pacific work crews reached Dallas in 1873, when the financial panic of that year forced an end to construction.

Southern Pacific

In the meantime, the Central Pacific Company created the Southern Pacific Company and received authority from Congress to establish a line through California from San Diego to San Francisco; the company received a federal land-grant subsidy of twenty sections for each mile of track completed. The charter also permitted the construction of lines from the coast to the eastern border of the state to two crossings on the Colorado River: the first, at Needles, was reserved for the Atlantic and Pacific—the line that was chartered to build along the 35th parallel; the second crossing, at Yuma, was reserved for the Texas and Pacific—the line assigned the 32nd parallel route from Marshall. Delayed construction across Texas by the Texas and Pacific Company, however, led Southern Pacific officials during 1876–1877 to apply to the governments of the Arizona and New Mexico territories for charters authorizing them to construct a roadbed along the 32nd parallel.

Following the financial collapse of 1873, the Texas and Pacific was reorganized under the leadership of Jay Gould, who entered into a pact with Southern Pacific officials: the Texas and Pacific would build to El Paso, while the Southern Pacific would receive the Texas and Pacific land-grant subsidy in New Mexico and Arizona; the latter company would also continue construction of its line to El Paso. The tracks of the two companies joined in 1882. Congress, however, failed to approve transfer of the Texas and Pacific land grant to the Southern Pacific. As officials of the latter line were determined to build to the Gulf of Mexico and into the Mississippi Valley, they proceeded with construction east of El Paso toward San Antonio. Before the end of 1882, by absorbing several local lines, this transportation goliath had established connections east of El Paso with San Antonio, Houston, and New Orleans.

Atlantic and Pacific

In 1866, Congress chartered the Atlantic and Pacific, granting to it the twenty alternate sections per mile of public land and authority to build along the 35th parallel to the Pacific. Atlantic and Pacific rail connections extended from St. Louis to Springfield, Missouri. Company officials planned to route their line southwesterly across Indian Territory to a point on the 35th parallel and to proceed thence to Needles on the Colorado River by way of Albuquerque. Financing difficulties, however, slowed construction;

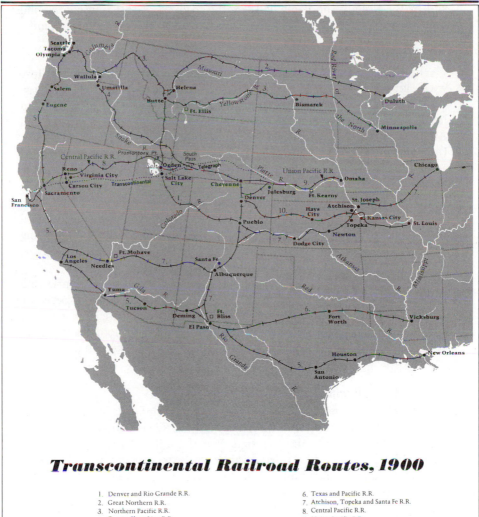

Transcontinental Railroad Routes, 1900

1. Denver and Rio Grande R.R.
2. Great Northern R.R.
3. Northern Pacific R.R.
4. Oregon Short Line R.R.
5. Southern Pacific R.R.
6. Texas and Pacific R.R.
7. Atchison, Topeka and Santa Fe R.R.
8. Central Pacific R.R.
9. Union Pacific R.R.
10. Kansas Pacific R.R.

and by the time of the Panic of 1873, the roadbed of this transcontinental line had proceeded no farther than the Cherokee nation town of Vinita.

Atchison, Topeka and Santa Fe

Portions of the Atlantic and Pacific grant west of Indian Territory were eventually acquired by the Atchison, Topeka and Santa Fe Railway Company. This line—chartered in 1858 by the Kansas legislature and headed by Cyrus K. Holliday—was authorized to build a railroad from Atchison on the Missouri River to Topeka, the capital of Kansas. In 1863, the company received a 3 million-acre public land subsidy that extended across Kansas; nine years later it completed construction to the Colorado border. From that point, company officials hoped to cross the Colorado Territory to the rich mining fields and to build southwest across New Mexico to the Rio Grande. Rival, Colorado-chartered railroads thwarted the Santa Fe Company's designs on the mining fields; but by rushing construction into New Mexico, the Santa Fe won control of the strategic Raton Pass, which enabled it to proceed to Albuquerque.

In 1880, the Santa Fe negotiated for the still-unused Atlantic and Pacific right-of-way and land grant along the 35th parallel. Proceeding to the Colorado River, it crossed at Needles and connected up with the Southern Pacific tracks in 1883. Negotiations with Southern Pacific management enabled the Santa Fe Railway to enter California and establish connections with the Los Angeles–San Francisco line.

Northern Pacific

In 1864, Congress chartered the Northern Pacific Railway Company to build a railroad from Duluth, Minnesota, on Lake Superior, to Seattle. The federal land-grant subsidy assigned to the railroad exceeded all other railroad land grants: it awarded twenty alternate sections of public land for each mile of track completed in the states it crossed and forty sections in the territories—a total of 40 million acres. The Northern Pacific was capitalized at $100 million to fund the very difficult and expensive construction west of Minnesota. Jay Cooke and Company of Philadelphia handled much of the early Northern Pacific financing, selling company bonds to American and European investors.

By 1873, Northern Pacific tracks had reached Bismarck, North Dakota. The financial panic of that year closed Cooke's banking house and ended for the foreseeable future fiscal support to continue construction. The Northern Pacific languished in the Dakota wilderness for five years. In 1878, Henry Villard, a prominent Civil War journalist—who by the 1870s dominated the Columbia Valley traffic by his control of the Oregon Central Railroad and the Oregon Steam Navigation Company—moved to connect his Northwest transportation empire with the Northern Pacific. By 1881, he had raised funds sufficient to buy control of the Northern Pacific; two years later he connected the Northern Pacific line with his

Northwest transport grid. In 1887, construction on the Northern Pacific main line was completed to Seattle.

Great Northern

One additional transcontinental line was completed before 1900. In 1878, James J. Hill, a freight company owner at St. Paul, and a group of his associates obtained control of the bankrupt St. Paul and Pacific Railroad, which included a 3 million-acre federal land grant in Minnesota. Hill renamed the line the Great Northern and proceeded to construct a roadbed, north of the Northern Pacific's, from Lake Superior to Seattle. West of Minnesota, Hill had no federal subsidy in the form of loans or land grants; but by practicing judicious and conservative management of the construction process, his Great Northern line reached Seattle in 1893.

Granger Lines

Other east-west lines of more limited scope were constructed in the New West after 1866. They included the Kansas Pacific and a group of Chicago-based railroads called the "Granger lines." The Kansas Pacific, a branch line of the Union Pacific, received federal land grants and loans similar to those accorded the parent line. The Kansas Pacific right-of-way extended from Kansas City on the western border of Missouri to Denver. In 1870, it reached Denver and was connected to the Denver and Pacific, a branch line Colorado businessmen were constructing to join the Union Pacific main line at Cheyenne. The "Granger lines"—the Chicago, Burlington and Quincy, the Chicago, Milwaukee and St. Paul, the Chicago and Northwestern, and the Chicago, Rock Island and Pacific—radiated west of Chicago and tapped many agricultural, stockraising, and mining areas not directly served by the major transcontinental lines. They drew grain, beef, and pork into Chicago processing plants, primarily from the Northern and Central Plains; the Rock Island line also developed a vast rail complex in the Southwest. The Chicago and Northwestern connected with the Northern Pacific in Montana in 1894; and the Chicago, Milwaukee and St. Paul made its way to Seattle in 1909.

Border Lines

East-west railroads extending from southwestern Missouri, Arkansas, Louisiana, and Texas into the New West included the Fort Smith and Western and the Choctaw and Gulf, which served the mining and lumber industries of Indian Territory and connected with Gulf ports in Louisiana and Texas. The Atlantic and Pacific, reorganized as the St. Louis and San Francisco Railway Company—better known as the Frisco—in 1882 resumed westward extension of its line from Vinita in the Cherokee nation, into the Creek nation, and to the rich oil center at Tulsa. In 1898 the Frisco proceeded to Quanah, Texas, by way of Oklahoma City.

The Chicago, Rock Island and Pacific Railway Company—one of the

"Granger lines" mentioned above—entered the Southwest during the 1880s; following the pattern of many major railroads, it absorbed smaller lines and improved connections with more direct tracks, so that by 1890 it, and the Santa Fe Railway Company, dominated the traffic between the Union Pacific and Southern Pacific main lines. During the 1880s, the Rock Island completed a line across the Oklahoma Panhandle and another line south across the Indian Territory to Terrel, Texas; by absorbing the Choctaw and Gulf line in 1902, it acquired major connections with Gulf markets.

During the 1880s the Santa Fe Railway Company also built a line across central Indian Territory to connect with Houston on the Gulf. Other interior north-south lines on the eastern margins of the New West connected the Missouri River towns with Gulf markets; these included the Missouri, Kansas and Texas Railway—the Katy Line, which crossed Indian Territory into Texas at Colbert's Ferry in 1872 with connections on the Gulf at Galveston Bay—and the Kansas City Southern, which ran between the Missouri River and New Orleans.

Interior Lines

The New West's heartland was served by a group of interior lines that included the Denver and Rio Grande. Construction on that line began at Denver in 1871; its competitive thrust to Pueblo, in eastern Colorado Territory, checked the Santa Fe Railway Company's attempt to enter the rich Rocky Mountain mining territory. The Denver and Rio Grande was headed by William J. Palmer, who planned his line to Mexico City. Defeated by the Santa Fe in the construction rush for Raton Pass, however, Denver and Rio Grande officials routed their line into the highly profitable mining region around Leadville via the Royal Gorge of the Arkansas River.

CHANGING RAILROAD TECHNOLOGY

By 1900, the New West's railroad grid was complete, and three decades of transportation development had produced changes and improvements in railroad technology and service. Steam locomotives, in the early days of New West railroading, were fired by wood and some coal. But as mining companies opened the bituminous coal resources of the Indian Territory and other Western fuel regions, engineers came to fire their locomotives almost exclusively with coal.

Track Gauge

For years, the track width or gauge was a subject of some controversy. Pre–Civil War experience with variant track widths in the East had provided the impetus for a movement to establish a uniform or standard gauge of four feet, eight and a half inches. This standard would permit an easy interchange of freight and passenger cars from one line to another without the expensive and time-consuming necessity of reloading freight, mail, and passengers. The transcontinental lines were required by the federal chartering statutes to construct roadbeds with standard gauge track.

However, there were advocates of narrow-gauge track—which varied from three feet to three feet six inches—among the railroad builders establishing lines in the rough mountain and plateau country of the New West. There, it was argued, narrow-gauge tracks would permit easier purchase on the sharp curves and steep grades and allow use of lighter equipment. The Denver and Rio Grande Railway was the principal carrier using narrow-gauge track. By the 1880s, most of the narrow-gauge lines had added a third track to permit use of the line by standard equipment.

Specialized Carriers

Other improvements in railroad technology included differentiation of the freight car and enlargement of its capacity to forty tons. After 1867, technicians developed the refrigerator car, which made it possible to ship fresh fruit, vegetables, and meat from the West to Eastern markets. Special cars were designed with feed bins and water troughs to transport cattle, sheep, and hogs over great distances; oil tank cars were improved— the crude, upright wooden containers being replaced by horizontal steel cylinders—and coal carriers were fitted with hopper bins for easy unloading.

Passenger cars also were improved. Chair cars with lounging seats were rated first class; the "Zulu cars" with their austere wooden seats, used for hauling immigrants to the West, were designated second-class passage. In 1865, George Pullman began improving the primitive sleeping car, creating a palatial chamber on wheels. After 1870, dining cars replaced many eating stops, so that the trains could make continuous progress.

RAILROADS AND WESTERN DEVELOPMENT

Railroad building in the New West had an immense influence on the nation's private financial community and on Western urbanization and settlement. To link the Mississippi Valley with the Pacific shore, Western railroads crossed vast empty spaces. Optimists anticipated the day when the entire trans-Missouri region would be dotted with prosperous farms, ranches, and towns, the citizens using the railroad for marketing farm and ranch produce and for importing increasing consumer needs. Railroads, of course, were expected to promote the settlement that would accomplish this goal; but such work required much expensive time, and railroad officials were concerned with immediate profits. One way to achieve quick returns was by profiteering from the construction process itself. Officials of the first transcontinental line set the pattern for other railroad builders to follow.

Railroad Financing

In 1864 Union Pacific officials established Crédit Mobilier of America, a Pennsylvania corporation to serve as the construction company for the transcontinential line west of Omaha. Crédit Mobilier would build, for example, a mile of track in the West at a cost of $30,000, billing the Union Pacific for $50,000. The profit was then distributed among Crédit Mobilier's stockholders. Union Pacific officials and holders of Crédit Mobilier stock were thereby able to control and divert the vast proceeds from the conversion of government bonds to construction money. In 1868, Crédit Mobilier paid dividends of nearly $342 for each $100 share of stock; one source commented that the profit was "not excessive" in view of the risk of investment.

Crédit Mobilier came to flower while Oliver Ames of Massachusetts was president of the Union Pacific Railway Company. It was exposed in 1872, and Ames' brother and shareholder, Congressman Oakes Ames, was censured by the House of Representatives for distributing "shares of Crédit Mobilier stock among those influential members of Congress" [3] and officials in the executive branch of the national government, where maximum benefits to the company were assured. Central Pacific officials, using the Central Pacific Contract and Finance Company, employed the same method to draw grand cash returns from construction of the western branch of the first transcontinental railroad.

Railroads and Urbanization

Western railroad building imprinted New West urban geography by the creation of construction camps along the right-of-way. Progress of the Union Pacific and other transcontinental lines required great labor forces; the Union Pacific at its time of peak construction in 1868 employed 10,000 laborers. The eating, sleeping, and entertainment needs of this vast labor army were met by the railhead town, a highly mobile settlement not unlike the camps of the expanding mining frontier; these towns evolved along the right-of-way at intervals of twenty to thirty miles. The settlements were, of course, temporary, and as soon as construction had been completed to the camp site, the buildings were razed, the materials, equipment, and town dwellers were loaded on flat cars and hauled to the next base camp, where the urban process was repeated. The railhead settlements provided shelter, food, and entertainment for the railroad construction crews.

Like the early mining camps, the railhead towns were gerry-built; buildings were tents, wooden frames covered with canvas, or rough wooden shacks.

> Along the disreputable street, deep with dust or mud in the center, and flanked by the hitching rails for horses, were the stores and houses. The wooden fronts ascending to a parapet above the roof made an

[3] John P. Stover, *American Railroads* (Chicago, 1961), p. 75.

ambitious showing that was often belied by their canvas backs. Saloons, dance halls, and gambling dens were innumerable. After work there was nothing to do but wait for tomorrow, and while away the time with the parasites who swarmed along the line.

One commentator called these railhead towns "Hell on wheels." He added that "Hell would appear to have been raked to furnish them," and the tinhorns, soiled doves, and depraved promoters "must have naturally returned after graduating here." Robert Louis Stevenson described the railhead towns as "roaring impromptu cities full of gold and lust and death." [4] Most of them were shifting, brawling, momentary urban incidents abrading the prairie's peace. Several, including North Platte, Laramie, Cheyenne, and Elko, survived as railroad division points.

Railroads and Western Promotion

Railroad expansion across the New West also had substantive impact on the region's settlement and concomitant development. In earlier times the flow of population from settled areas had been mostly motivated by personal necessity and ambition. Word-of-mouth reports by frontiersmen returning to the settlements and letters from the frontier had detailed opportunities and promise in the new land and stimulated Easterners to migrate.

In the early days of the nation, land companies had attempted without much success to promote Western settlement. The earliest successful formal promotion of Western settlement occurred during the 1820s when the *Empresarios* resorted to advertising in Eastern newspapers to stimulate the settlement of Texas. California boomers and Oregon missionaries also had some success in luring migrants from the eastern United States to the Pacific. These pioneer promotional efforts, however, were keyed to attracting population to particular regions of the New West.

After 1866, on the other hand, railroad promotion of settlement in the New West was comprehensive, as the various lines sought to attract settlers to the vast empty spaces in the Northwest, the Southwest, and the Central Plains and mountains. The period between 1866 and 1900 was thus a time of sustained, saturation promotion by all the Western railroads; for it was advantageous for the lines to have settled constituencies from which to derive the full traffic potential. Railroads with Western land grants also promoted settlement to market their vast tracts along the right-of-way. By the time Congress ceased making land grants in 1871, the national government and several states had granted Western railroads 180 million acres. The land was sold for an average of $5 an acre.

To promote Western settlement, the railroads maintained immigration bureaus in the eastern United States and Europe, particularly in Great

---

[4] Quoted in Frederic L. Paxson, *History of the American Frontier, 1763–1893* (New York, 1924), p. 497; quoted in Henry Steele Commager and Allan Nevins, eds., *The Heritage of America* (Boston, 1951), p. 842.

Britain, Germany, and the Scandinavian countries. Bureau staffs published handsome immigrant guides that described opportunities in the New West. These booklets contained maps, instructions on how to purchase railroad lands, and, if the line was not a land-grant railroad, informed readers on how to obtain a homestead on public domain lands. The Burlington and several other railway companies operating in the West even conducted agricultural research in dry-farming methods and published their findings to assist settlers in coping with the special problems of exploiting the arid Plains of Nebraska and Colorado.

The immigrant guides grossly exaggerated the New West's bounty. A piece of boomer literature published by the Northern Pacific in 1872 to promote settlement on its Montana lands assured immigrants that "the only illness which touched residents of Montana was the distress of over-eating, resulting from excessive indulgence of appetites heartened by the invigorating atmosphere." Similar tracts by Rock Island and Santa Fe stylists promoted Southern Plains settlement, describing this region of wind-swept prairie and abrupt weather changes as the "banana growing belt of the Greater Southwest, where rich soils and gentle climate combined to produce every crop known in the states and territories, and where the gentle breezes that blow are zephyrs of pure delight." [5]

This extravagant prose had its effect, luring a steady stream of home-seekers from the eastern United States and Europe, populating the Plains and mountain valleys of the New West, and producing up to tenfold increases in population of established states and territories between 1870 and 1900. This heavy flow of settlement also forced the creation of new states and territories so that, by 1900, the political format of the New West was virtually completed. Besides populating the remote regions and providing access to markets and sources of supply, the New West railroads created new sources of employment. Vast numbers of workmen were required to operate the trains and to maintain the far-flung grid of railroad lines. The railroads, in fact, brought the first labor unions to the New West.

Railroads and Politics

During the Western railroad age that ended in 1900, the Western lines dominated regional politics and became powerful forces in the New West's territorial and state governments. It is not surprising, therefore, that they consistently secured the passage of legislation favorable to railroad interest. During this period, the railroads also established a strong influence in the Congress, thereby obtaining favorable national legislation and often dictating policy on the government's management of the New West, especially on questions of public-land utilization and Indian affairs.

A prime example of pervasive railroad power and influence in national

[5] Branch, *Westward*, p. 552; Fred Wenner, *Homeseeker's Guide* (Guthrie, Okla. Terr., 1892), p. 3.

affairs was the adoption by Congress of legislation further compressing New West Indian lands. The Dawes Allotment Act of 1887 is case in point. Railroads operating in Indian reservation areas found these communally held tribal estates barriers to more intensive settlement, contrary to the railroads' interest. The railroads regarded the low man-to-land ratio of Indian Territory as a waste of railroad potential. One official of a line crossing the territory complained of the tribal citizens' modest use of his facility; he commented that from Kansas to Texas his railroad ran through a "long tunnel" of nonproductive passage. However, in order to open the 45 million acres of Indian Territory to settlement, it was necessary to destroy the tribal governments and to convert the vast tribal estates to small individual allotments. Settlers could then homestead on the surplus lands. Passage of the Dawes Allotment Act and amendments accomplished this purpose.

Increasingly after 1865, the New West served as a bonanza region for the investment of Eastern and European capital. Railroads were among the first Western enterprises to receive the energizing flow of these capital resources. Their conquest of the region's vast plains, mountains, plateaus, and deserts had been little short of phenomenal, so that the New West's rail grid of less than 1,000 miles of track in 1865 had increased to over 100,000 miles of track before the close of the century. The railroad companies established the pattern and tradition for Eastern capital control of the New West's economy, which was extended to mining, lumbering, stockraising, corporate farming, and other primary industries. Thus, until the middle of the twentieth century, the New West was a captive region, its economic status shaped by its absentee fiscal masters and its development confined to supportive enterprises for the benefit of the increasingly industrialized eastern United States.

SELECTED SOURCES

The prime general source on American railroad development is *John F. Stover, *American Railroads* (Chicago, 1961). Other general works on this subject include Robert E. Riegel, *The Story of Western Railroads* (New York, 1926); Howard Fleming, *Narrow Gauge Railroads in America* (New York, 1949); Roger Burlingame, *March of the Iron Men* (New York, 1938); Seymour Dunbar, *A History of American Travel* (New York, 1915), 4 vols.; Benjamin Botkin and Alvin F. Harlow, eds., *A Treasury of Railroad Folklore* (New York, 1953); John W. Starr, *One Hundred Years of American Railroads* (New York, 1928); Stewart H. Holbrook, *The Story of American Railroads* (New York, 1947); Ira J. Clark, *Then Came the Railroads: The Century from Steam to Diesel in the Southwest* (Norman, 1958); Julius Grodinsky, *Transcontinental*

* Available in paperback.

Railway Strategy, 1869–1893 (Philadelphia, 1962); and Lucius Beebe and Charles Clegg, Hear the Train Blow (New York, 1952).

Studies of particular rail lines include Nelson Trottman, History of the Union Pacific (New York, 1925); John D. Galloway, The First Transcontinental Railroad: Central Pacific, Union Pacific (New York, 1950); Wesley S. Griswold, A Work of Giants (New York, 1962); Glenn D. Bradley, The Story of the Santa Fe (Boston, 1920); L. L. Waters, Steel Rails to Santa Fe (Lawrence, Kansas, 1950); William S. Greever, Arid Domain: The Santa Fe Railway and Its Western Land Grant (Stanford, 1954); V. V. Masterson, The Katy Railroad and the Last Frontier (Norman, 1953); Robert G. Athearn, Rebel of the Rockies: A History of the Denver and Rio Grande Western Railroad (New Haven, 1962); and James B. Hedges, Henry Villard and the Railways of the Northwest (New Haven, 1930).

Kansas Stockraising in the 1890s.

Western History Collections,
University of Oklahoma Library

Virginia City, Nevada.

26

Plundering the New West's Natural Bounty

Soon after the conclusion of the Civil War, the obstacles to the full economic and political development of the New West had been removed. Military conquest had erased the Indian barrier that had checked American occupation of great portions of the trans-Missouri region. Aboriginal patriots, who had fiercely defended their domains, mouldered in their graves or languished on government reservations.

The railroad had conquered the New West's vast distances. Its continental grid spread from the Mississippi Valley to Pacific and, with intersecting interior lines, from the Canadian border to Texas. It provided even the region's most remote sections access to markets for their minerals, lumber, and livestock and agricultural produce. The New West's rich natural bounty, demonstrated by scattered exploitation between 1848 and 1865, increasingly attracted essential supplies of investment capital. An expanding technology, spurred in part by war industry mustered for the Union's great effort during the war—augmented by generous importation from Europe—provided improved tools, mechanical items, and processes for application to the peculiar problems of concluding the conquest of America's great Western frontier.

Moreover, the federal government, continuing the historic pattern of nationalizing currents, contributed materially to Western development. Its military establishment crushed the resistive Indian tribes and segregated them in remote places where they could no longer obstruct the advance of the American exploitive frontier. Congress rendered prodigious support to New West transportation expansion by generous public-land subsidies and low-interest loans for railroad construction. In addition, it regularly responded to the land needs of miners, stockgrowers, lumbermen, and farmers by enacting special legislation for dispensing the vast national domain in the West.

By 1900 this fortuitous combination of essentials had produced a miraculous transformation of the West into a complex of mines, ranches, farms, cities, new territories, and states. The development process had virtually completed the political format of the American nation.

THE HUNTERS

Among the first spoilers in the New West's exploitive age that took place between 1865 and 1900 were the commercial buffalo hunters. Before the Civil War an estimated 15 million American bison roamed the Great Plains from Canada to the Rio Grande. So great were their numbers and so overpowering their influence that the range of these giant hairy beasts was known as "Buffalo Country." One writer claimed to have "traveled through buffaloes along the Arkansas River for 200 miles, almost one continuous herd, as close together as it is customary to herd cattle." [1]

For centuries buffalo had sustained the Plains tribes. Tribal lifecycles, migrations, religions, seasons, and cultures generally revolved about the animal. Resourceful Indian women utilized every part of the animal. They dried the meat for winter use, saved the tallow for seasoning and cooking grease, dried sinews and separated them into thread and bowstrings, and rubbed hair from the outer hide and wove it into ropes and coarse cloth. Gall was saved for yellow paint, and buffalo-dung chips were used as fuel in a treeless country. They cleaned the intestines, tied the ends, and used them for carrying water. Hides were stretched, dried, tanned, sewn together, and used as tipi covers. The tanned hides were used for making bullboats, clothing, footwear, bags for packing camp gear, and riding paraphernalia; they braided strips of hide into lariats. Green hides were stretched and fitted over frames for warriors' shields.

Warm buffalo robes required the most careful and skilled attention. The men killed the animals at the season when the hair was longest. Women stretched the hide on pegs, scraped off the flesh and softened it—kneading the inner surface with a mixture of buffalo brains and water until it was cured into a soft, pliable robe. The Plains Indians especially esteemed the albino or white buffalo and considered it sacred. Anglo-Americans valued them highly too; an Anglo hunter killed one during 1874 and sold the robe to a Dodge City trader for $1,000.

The Hide Industry

The transcontinental railroads brought the commercial buffalo hunters to the Great Plains. The railroads also provided a means for shipping

[1] Quoted in Arrell M. Gibson, *Oklahoma: A History of Five Centuries* (Norman, 1965), p. 277.

hides and meat—hindquarters, tongues, and "jerked" or dried meat—to Eastern markets. By 1875, a growing demand in the East had caused a rapid expansion of the hunting industry on the Plains. Furriers converted the thick winter pelts into coats and lap robes, and harness and bootmakers tanned the leather for footwear and carriage equipage. The hide hunters became involved in feverish competition, wantonly slaughtering the bison for the harvest of hides and leaving the carcasses to rot. Soon, the Plains were littered with the bones of countless buffalo. The new Sharps .50 caliber, breechloading rifle assured marksmen of kills at 1,500 yards.

Many of the big names in the American West scouted for buffalo in the West. These included Buffalo Bill Cody, Pawnee Bill Lillie, Wild Bill Hickock, Pat Garrett, and Billy Dixon. Dixon recalled in his *Autobiography* that

> the hunting was started by a firm of eastern hide buyers, whose agents came to Hays City and other towns near the buffalo range and offered prices that made hide-hunting a profitable occupation. The first offers were $1.00 for each cow hide and $2.00 for bull hides, which enabled us to make money rapidly. As the slaughtering increased and buffalo grew scarcer, prices were advanced, until $4.00 was being paid for bull hides by the fall of 1872. . . . Generally there were three or four men in each outfit, each having contributed his share for necessary expenses. They went where the range was best and buffalo most plentiful. A dug-out worth having was one with a big open fireplace, near the edge of a stream of good water, with plenty of wood along its banks. We often occupied the same dugout for a month or more. Then, as the buffalo grew less plentiful, we shifted our camp and built a new dug-out, which was easily and quickly done. From where the buffalo were killed on the range, we hauled the hides to market. . . . I always did my own killing, and generally had two experienced men to do the skinning. A capable man could skin fifty buffalos in a day, and usually was paid fifty dollars a month. I have paid as high as twenty cents a hide to a good skinner. We often killed the buffalo the day before they were to be skinned.[2]

Extermination of the Bison

Dodge City was the great entrepôt on the Southern Plains for the buffalo-hide industry. In a single season, Robert Wright, a local trader shipped 200,000 hides over the Santa Fe Railway, plus 200 cars of hindquarters and two cars of smoked buffalo tongues. The Kansas Pacific Railway and the Santa Fe Railway annually carried a million hides to Eastern markets. Bismarck, in the Dakota Territory, was one of the principal markets for buffalo hides taken on the Northern Plains, and the Northern Pacific Railway Company was the main carrier in this area.

In 1877 a herd of 40,000 buffalo was reported on the North Canadian

[2] Olive H. Dixon, *The Life of Billy Dixon* (Dallas, 1927), pp. 61–62.

River near Fort Supply. Commercial hunters so reduced it that the next year Cheyenne and Arapaho hunters ranging from their reservation in western Indian Territory in search of their winter meat supply, found few animals. In 1879, the Indian hunt was virtually a failure. In only two years, saturation hunting had obliterated the great southern herd. A small herd was sighted in the Oklahoma Panhandle in 1885, and the last wild buffalo on the Southern Plains, "a lonely old bull," was killed at Cold Spring in Cimarron County in October 1890.

Between 1879 and 1883, hundreds of thousands of buffalo ranging through the Dakotas and Montana were slaughtered by commercial hide hunters. The camps lined the Missouri, the Yellowstone, and its tributaries, "cutting off the buffaloes from water; and a cordon of camps along the international border prevented the herds from escaping into Canada. . . . one scant carload [was] transported east in the spring of 1884," marking "the almost complete extermination of the northern herd." This phenomenal decline of the once-great herds was explained by the reports of kills made by commercial hunters. One Kansas newspaper announced that "the best kill on record . . . is that of Tom Nickson, who killed 120 at one stand in forty minutes, and who, from September 15th to October 20th, killed 2,173 buffaloes." [3]

For years, bleached bison skeletons littered the Great Plains. Starving homesteaders eked out a scanty subsistence by collecting the bones and selling them to dealers in the railroad towns. Hundreds of carloads of buffalo bones were shipped to fertilizer plants for making phosphates and to sugar refineries for conversion to carbon.

THE RANCHMEN

Pacification of the Western tribes and extermination of the buffalo opened the Plains to stockraising. This industry, already well-established in scattered portions of the New West before the Civil War, underwent a drastic expansion after 1865; it became one of America's billion-dollar postwar industries. The principal emphasis was on production of beef cattle and oxen. The latter strong, slow-moving draft animals were still widely used by freighting firms serving mining and agricultural settlements remote from the railroads and by farmers for pulling plows through the tough prairie sod.

Horse and mule production was also important. Ranchmen required great numbers of horses to supply mounts for their riders to herd cattle. Sheepraising continued to be a leading enterprise and underwent an expansion after 1865 similar to cattleraising. Near the close of the nineteenth century, sheep were competing with cattle for the diminishing

---

[3] E. Douglas Branch, *Westward: The Romance of the American Frontier* (New York, 1930), p. 568; quoted in Gibson, *Oklahoma*, p. 279.

Western ranges. Also in certain portions of the New West—particularly on the Edwards Plateau in southwest Texas—ranchmen managed vast herds of goats for mohair.

Origins of the Industry

Between 1865 and 1900, the most romantic and dramatic form of stockraising in the New West was cattle ranching. The early phase of postwar beef production is called the range-cattle industry because animals were managed, from breeding to marketing, on the West's vast open-range pastures. Ranchmen paid little attention to providing shelter or winter feeding for their stock. Cattle grazing on the open range were watched over by mounted herdsmen, the cowboys. The principal type of cattle during the range-cattle period was a mixture of well-established Spanish-Mexican cattle and Anglo cattle imported into Texas and Indian Territory during the early part of the nineteenth century. Through many generations of breeding, there had evolved a rangy, long-horned, multi-colored critter that was capable of wide foraging in all seasons and adapted to the climatic vagaries of the Great Plains. Range-cattle industry management included branding—burning the owner's registered mark onto each animal's flank—castrating the bull calves, and spring and autumn roundups to separate the herds, brand the calves, and segregate the steers for market.

Great Plains pastures consisted of hardy grasses that formed a protective sod cover; they were predominantly buffalo, grama, and mesquite grass and a mixed prairie-grass growth that cured out in the autumn and provided nutritious winter forage. On the Southern Plains, cattle fattened on the fruit of the mesquite tree, beanlike pods that ripened in early autumn.

The Trail Drives

The postwar range-cattle industry was spawned in Texas. At the close of the Civil War, Texan ranges, largely untouched by foraging Union and Confederate armies, were crowded with an estimated 5 million head of cattle. Locally, each animal was worth only $3 to $5; but the war had drained Eastern livestock resources and created a critical beef shortage there. In Chicago and Cincinnati, buyers were paying $35 to $40 a head.

During 1866, several Texan cattlemen, attracted by this favorable market condition, attempted to deliver their herds to railheads on the Missouri border. Their northern passage crossed Indian Territory and traced the first of the great cattle highways—the East Shawnee Trail. It entered Indian Territory at Colbert's Ferry on the Red River, ran to Boggy Depot in the Choctaw nation, then coursed up the Texas Road to Baxter Springs, Kansas, and on to Sedalia, Missouri—a railroad town on the Missouri Pacific Railroad. On the southwestern border of Missouri, the drovers encountered serious trouble. Texas cattle were carriers of stock diseases, to which they were immune, but which infected local cattle.

Settlers on the border intercepted the intruding herds, stampeded them, and fought several hot battles with the Texans. Only a few herds reached Sedalia during 1866.

Joseph McCoy, an Illinois stockraiser, developed a plan for marketing Texas cattle without meeting with border obstructions. The Kansas Pacific Railroad was building a line across Kansas to connect Kansas City with Denver. At Abilene, a tiny settlement on the railroad in north-central Kansas well beyond the line of settlement, McCoy constructed loading pens and accommodations for the cowboys. He advertised the depot and market in Texas, and during 1867 drovers reached Abilene. It was the first of the famous Kansas cow towns; that year 35,000 head of cattle were loaded. The next year, ranchers marketed 75,000 Texas longhorns at Abilene.

Texas cattlemen moved their herds to Abilene over the West Shawnee Trail, which forked from the East Shawnee Trail at Boggy Depot and ran north and a bit west of the Creek nation settlements into Kansas. The most famous of the Indian Territory cattle highways linking Texas ranches with the Kansas cow towns was the Chisholm Trail, named for Jesse Chisholm, a mixed Anglo-Cherokee trader who had blazed a freight trail from the Leased District to the mouth of the Little Arkansas River near Wichita. Crossing at Red River Station, the Chisholm Trail closely followed the 98th meridian across Indian Territory to the Kansas cattle markets.

The railroads that carried Texas cattle to Eastern markets also brought homesteading farmers West. Their fenced-in lands soon closed the trails to Abilene and the adjacent open range required to sustain the herds while they awaited buyers. The cattle market was forced to move farther west. The Santa Fe Railroad, which was also building across Kansas, ran south of the Kansas Pacific; it was, therefore, the nearest rail line for the Texas drovers. Newton, Ellsworth, Wichita, Hunnewell, and Caldwell—each had its heyday as a ripsnorting cow town. The last of this tradition, Dodge City —the "Queen of the Cow Towns"—was the most notorious of them all.

The western movement of the cow towns influenced the direction of the Indian Territory cattle trails linking Texas ranches with northern markets. The fourth livestock highway, the Dodge City or Great Western Cattle Trail, crossed the Red River at Doan's Store and angled northwesterly across Indian Territory to Dodge City. Texas drovers moved over 300,000 head of cattle up the trails in 1870 and 600,000 the following year. During the first ten years of the northern drive, nearly 5 million longhorns crossed Indian Territory on their way to the Kansas cow towns.

A fifth passage used by Texas ranchmen to move herds north was the Goodnight-Loving Trail, named for Oliver Loving and Charles Goodnight, two pioneer Southwestern stockmen. In the early years the trail was used by Texas ranchmen to move steers to markets at the Indian reservations and military posts of New Mexico Territory. It began near Fort Concho and proceeded to the Horsehead Crossing on the Pecos, thence into eastern

New Mexico. During the late 1870s, the Goodnight-Loving Trail became a busy concourse for moving Texas cattle to stock the new ranges of the Central and Northern Plains.

The northern drive to markets in the Kansas cow towns diminished during the 1870s. The march of agricultural settlement across Kansas closed the cattle trails and converted the raucus cow towns into tranquil, law-abiding nester (homesteader) settlements. Also, by 1880 Texas cattlemen, through the M.K.T. and other Southwestern rail lines, had local access to shipping facilities to Eastern markets. At the same time, the range-cattle industry was expanding rapidly northward into western Kansas, western Nebraska, eastern Colorado, and the Dakotas and Montana. Increasingly, the Texas cattlemen moved their surplus animals north to stock the new ranges.

Ranching on the Great Plains

Finally, a productive and profitable use had been found for one of America's most scorned regions, the Great American Desert. By 1885, the Great Plains, from Canada to the Rio Grande, was a checkerboard of cattle ranches. The rapid expansion of the range-cattle industry—from a profitable enterprise dominated by Texas ranchmen to a corporate empire of bonanza proportions extending over nearly half of Western America— was abetted by steadily growing markets in the increasingly urbanized eastern United States—with its swelling immigrant population—and in Europe. Technological advances also contributed to this trend, particularly development of refrigeration units for railroad cars and ships; the latter opened new overseas markets for Western beef.

Homesteaders had not entered the Great Plains in appreciable numbers, and cattlemen, indulged by the federal government, had free use of the grass. Stockraisers worked out their own customs for establishing ranges on the public-domain pastures. In this semi-arid region, the ranch base had to supply water for the stock, usually from creeks or rivers. By open-range custom, a cattleman was acknowledged to control all the grassland drained by a particular watercourse back to the divide, the upland point separating the waterflow.

Eastern and European capital, attracted by promised profits of up to 50 percent, flowed into Western stockraising ventures. Interest was flamed by glowing prospectuses from newly formed cattle companies and by promotional writings, including James S. Brisbin's *The Beef Bonanza: or How to Get Rich on the Plains* (1881). Huge cattle corporations based on absentee funding and control were formed. As the number of ranches increased, the range-cattle industry became intensely competitive and exploitive of both law and resources. Local managers of cattle corporations were pressed to produce profits, at virtually any cost, for stockholders. Thus, they appropriated additional range on the public domain to accommodate larger herds. The Arkansas Land and Cattle Company controlled a million acres of grass in Colorado. In Wyoming, the Swan Land and Cattle Company, financed primarily by Scottish investors and capitalized at $3 million, dominated a stockraising estate of half a million acres. In Texas, where the state controlled the public domain, Charles Goodnight's J.A. Ranch, situated in the Panhandle, extended over a million acres; on the fabulous XIT Ranch, also in the Texas Panhandle, nearly 200,000 head of cattle grazed on 3 million acres.

Like the mining frontier, the cattleman's frontier on the Great Plains gave birth to extralegal associations for mutual protection. Stockraisers formed associations and adopted rules to regulate roundups and brand registration, to protect their herds against rustlers, to provide predator control, and to function as a lobby to obtain favorable legislation from state and territorial legislatures and from Congress. In this grassland wilderness, they were a law unto themselves, and they maintained a law-enforcement corps that sometimes included inspectors and range detectives.

Several associations employed crews of gunmen, mostly Texans, as a sort of private militia to intimidate nesters and others who threatened their position of eminence on the range. Two of the most successful ranchmen coteries were the Wyoming Stock Growers' Association and the Cherokee Strip Live Stock Association. Asa S. Mercer's *Banditti of the Plains* (1894) is an exposé of the ruthless, predatory actions of the Wyoming Stock Growers' Association.

Decline of the Range-Cattle Industry

During the mid-1880s, the range-cattle industry on the Plains quickly faded. One cause was the homesteader's invasion. The farmer-pioneer had the legal right to make entry on a 160-acre claim on the public domain, fence off the ranges with barbed wire, and close the water to cattlemen. It seemed that no amount of threats, harassment, burning, and shooting could dislodge him. He stubbornly held to his prairie claim.

Thereupon, many cattlemen exploited the law by filing their own claims to water and pasture sites under the Homestead Act and other federal statutes for dispensing the public domain. They also induced their cowboys to file on adjoining claims; then, for a price, the cowboys turned title to the land over to the ranchmen. The result was great waste and flagrant exploitation of the law, as many cattlemen brought under their direct ownership land they had been using for years as open range. Charley Coffee, an old trail driver from Texas who had settled on a ranch in Wyoming, found another way to thwart the encroaching homesteader. When nesters entered his range, he said: "We couldn't shoot, for they weren't like Indians, so the only way I could get even was to go into the banking business." [4] By making generous loans at high interest to suffering nesters

---

[4] Quoted in *Letters from Old Friends and Members of the Wyoming Stock Growers' Association* (Cheyenne, n.d.), pp. 25–29.

and taking mortgages on their homesteads, Coffee in due time was able to foreclose; he thereby held under fee-simple ownership the same land he had earlier used as open range.

Coupled with the nester, the great destroyer of the range-cattle industry on the Plains was the climate. In the rush for profits, corporate ranch managers had overstocked the ranges, and by 1885 saturation grazing had drastically reduced the rich grassland resources. Droughts during 1885 and 1886 further depleted the pastures. To relieve pressure on the sun-scorched ranges, stockmen shipped lean, hungry cattle to market in such numbers that they glutted the slaughter centers at Chicago and at Eastern cities. Bonanza beef prices plummeted, and many Great Plains cattle corporations were bankrupted. The range-cattle industry's doom was sealed in 1887, when, during January, the worst blizzard in history struck the Great Plains. Sustained snows and high winds created 30-foot drifts and produced temperatures of 50° below zero. The average herd loss was 40 percent; on some individual ranch losses it was as high as 80 percent.

The cattle raisers who survived the market collapse of 1886 and the droughts and the ruinous blizzard of 1887, were forced to make substantive adjustments. Recovery problems were compounded by increasing competition for the land. By the 1880s, sheepmen were moving their flocks out of the Rocky Mountains onto the western edge of the Plains in search of autumn and winter pastures. The nester tide was sweeping from the East, homesteading choice claims on the public domain. The blizzard had forced from stockmen reluctant respect for the Plains milieu.

A new order of cattle raising arose on the Plains as ranchmen increasingly shifted from reckless, bonanza open-range ranching to the judiciously managed stock-farm type of operation. This form of management included maintaining a herd size compatible with range resources and climatic vagaries. Wider use of Shorthorn, Hereford, and Polled Angus bulls, and segregation of stock within barbed-wire enclosures improved herd quality and produced prime steers for market. More and more, Great Plains stockmen resorted to winter feeding and, on exposed ranges, sheltering cattle from winter storms.

The Cattleman's Last Frontier

Growing competition for public-domain lands in the Great Plains led several cattlemen to establish ranches in the Indian Territory, which in many respects became the ranchman's last frontier. During the era of the northern drive, Texas cattlemen had allowed their herds to fatten on the grasslands adjacent to the trail; and beef contractors supplying the reservations of western Indian Territory had used these ranges to bring their herds to prime condition before releasing them to the tribes.

Large-scale ranching came to Indian Territory around 1880. Anglo cattlemen negotiated grass leases with the Cherokee, Choctaw, Chickasaw, Creek, and Seminole nations; but the pastures in these areas were limited since already many of the tribesmen were established in stockraising and needed the grass for their own herds. Cattlemen had better success in finding new ranges on the reservations in western Indian Territory. By 1890, a portion of every reservation west of the Five Civilized Tribes was under lease to cattlemen. In the Kiowa, Comanche, and Cheyenne-Arapaho reservations, virtually every acre of grass was leased to ranchmen. During 1882, through their agent John D. Miles, the Cheyennes and Arapahoes negotiated an agreement with seven cattlemen, organized as the Cheyenne-Arapaho Stock Growers Association, for use of 3 million acres at two cents per acre per year. The syndicate grazed 200,000 head of cattle on the vast reservation range. Their operation included publishing a newspaper called the *Cheyenne Transporter*, whose columns were mostly devoted to subjects of interest to stockraisers—such as brand registration and identification and the problem of cattle rustling.

The most extensive ranching enterprise in the Indian Territory during this period was in the Cherokee Outlet. While the eastern third of the outlet had been taken from the Cherokees by the federal government for the purpose of relocating tribes, about 6,500,000 acres of choice grassland remained unused. In the late 1870s, cattlemen began occupying, more or less permanently, certain ranges in the Outlet. Their numbers increased each year, with the result that this sixty-mile wide ribbon of grassland extending from the Arkansas River to the 100th meridian became one of the most famous ranges in the West. Cherokee nation officials at Tahlequah soon learned of the cattleman's appropriation of their land and sent representatives west with authority to collect grazing fees. At first, the annual levy was twenty-five cents per head, but later it was increased to forty-five cents. The grazing tax collected from Outlet stockgrowers became such an important source of revenue for the Cherokee government that the treasurer of the nation came each year to Caldwell, Kansas, established an office, and sent his deputies riding through the outlet to collect grazing fees.

To gain exclusive use of the Outlet and to protect their ranges from rustlers, a group of cattlemen met at Caldwell in 1883 and established the Cherokee Strip Live Stock Association. Its membership consisted of over 100 individuals and corporations owning a total of more than 300,000 head of cattle. A five-year lease at $100,000 a year was negotiated with the Cherokee nation for the exclusive use of the Outlet; the lease was renegotiated in 1888 for $200,000 a year. Association officers hired brand inspectors to police the range for rustlers and to inspect and record livestock shipments. They adopted roundup schedules and rules, surveyed and mapped the outlet, assigned particular ranges to members, and made rules for fencing ranges.

Even here, however, the cattlemen were not spared their eternal nemesis, the nester. The Dawes Allotment Act of 1887 was applied to the Cheyenne-Arapaho Reservation, and the vast cattle ranges were liquidated by federal officials who ordered removal of all ranch enclosures. Surveyors divided the grasslands into 160-acre tracts, and in 1892 the reservation was opened to homesteaders. The following year, the same fate befell the Cherokee Outlet.

Western Sheep Growing

A less romantic but no less profitable stockraising enterprise, which flourished in the New West after 1865, was sheepraising. Before the Civil War, flocks established on New West ranges by Spanish, Mexican, and Indian herdsmen were improved in quality by the introduction of new breeds by Anglo sheepmen. A growing postwar demand for wool and mutton by Eastern textile factories and slaughterhouses led to a phenomenal expansion of sheepraising in the New West. Flock quality was further strengthened by the introduction of Merino, Shropshire, Cotswold, and Lincoln breeds from Europe. Several sheep ranch proprietors, particularly those in Nevada, imported Basque herdsmen from the Pyrenees to manage their flocks.

By 1900, nearly 25 million sheep ranged over the upland grasslands of Texas, California, New Mexico, Arizona, Utah, Wyoming, and Colorado. Cowmen scorned sheepmen and their flocks, claiming that "woolies" destroyed the range by close feeding and tore up the sod with their sharp hoofs. The presence of the sheep supposedly contaminated pastures so that cattle would not graze on them thereafter. But the profits from sheepraising were too lucrative for sheepmen to capitulate to the cattlemen, and, despite pressure and destructive raids, they persevered and ultimately forced cattlemen, reluctantly, to share New West pastures with them.

THE MINERS

The New West's mining frontier, energized in 1848 by the strike at Sutter's Mill, flowed from California across the Sierras and Great Basin into the Rocky Mountains in the 1850s. Opening mineral fields in Nevada, Colorado, New Mexico, and Arizona, the frontier maintained its momentum even during the Civil War. In this era, the quest of an army of peripatetic prospectors was gold and silver. Virtually every section of the mountain and plateau region yielded some rewards of precious metals for the seekers. Recurring discoveries were the principal factor in populating remote regions of the New West and provided the basis for the creation of new territories and states. In addition, the mining settlements attracted the supportive industries of agriculture, stockraising, and freighting, which, in most cases, were more permanent than mining.

Mining Patterns

By the mid-1860s, a three-stage pattern, which was applied to most of the New West mineral districts, had emerged. First came the placer period, based on the mining of free gold in nugget and dust form, as described in Chapter 21. Placer discoveries set off the gold rushes, and intensive working of the placers with pans, sluices, and rocker devices soon exhausted the stream bed deposits. Hydraulic mining was resorted to in the second stage. Workmen fed water under pressure onto the slopes above the exhausted placer deposits, washing soil, rock, and mineral material to the lowlands where processing separated the gold from associated materials. The third stage, quartz or hard-rock mining, began when prospectors had traced the source of the mineral to the mother lode, which was usually in a mountain side or straight down beneath the surface, imbedded in quartz and rock. This sort of mining required excavation of tunnels or shafts to provide access to the ore veins and was accomplished by use of drills, blasting powder, hoisting devices, and other heavy equipment, as well as large labor crews.

In addition, ore thus extracted had to undergo a milling process to separate the gold and silver from its nonmetallic associates; this processing required huge rock-crushing equipment and chemicals. In this final stage, the independent prospector often became a day worker for a mining company formed by outside capitalists. Sometimes he remained employed only long enough to accumulate enough wages for a grubstake to enable him to prospect for new placer deposits. Increasingly after 1875, however, prospectors simply accepted their fate and became permanent day workers.

Flow of the Mining Frontier

In the postwar era of New West mining, production continued in the established fields of California, Nevada, Colorado, and the Southwest, and wider prospecting opened new bonanza regions. Thus the mining frontier spread into Idaho, Montana, South Dakota, Wyoming, and Utah to exploit the placer strikes.

California's Sierra mining region continued to be the heaviest producer of gold. Authorities estimate that its first half billion dollars worth of this precious metal came from placer mining, which was practiced until about 1855. During the succeeding hydraulic mining stage, another half billion dollars worth of gold was produced. Quartz mining yielded yet another half billion dollars worth.

Across the Sierras in Nevada, the focus of activity was still the rich Comstock Lode in the Washoe District of Mount Davidson. Production in these mines rose and fell regularly. During the late 1860s, when the silver and gold deposits at the upper levels were nearly exhausted, mine managers contemplated abandonment. Then deeper shafting to the 1,500-foot level located rich ore bodies. These levels were exhausted during the 1880s, and again abandonment was forestalled by shafting below the 1,600-foot level, which exposed paying ore bodies.

Deeper mining, however, tapped underground waters and flooded the mines. Moreover, heat in the mine workings increased at deeper levels. The comfortable temperature of 68° at 500 feet rose to 81° at 1,000 feet, 101° at 1,500 feet, and an unbearable 111° at 2,000 feet. Workmen could control the water by pumping, but little could be done about the heat. At the lower levels men were able to work in the drifts—the lateral tunnels that followed the vein of ore—only for brief periods before retreating to cooler regions. During the 1860s, Adolph Sutro, a mining engineer, proposed that a tunnel be excavated completely through Mt. Davidson in order to drain the Washoe District mines and to cool the shafts, drifts, and mineral galleries. After twelve years of intermittent progress, the Sutro tunnel was completed in 1878 at a cost of $3 million. The tunnel, dug at the 1,600-foot level, was four miles long, fifteen feet wide, and twelve feet high.

Prospectors working the Nevada highlands opened other fields. Although none of them matched the fabulous Comstock—which in a half century of production yielded a billion dollars worth of gold and silver—in aggregate they were substantial producers. The later mining areas included the Reese River gold field, the Esmeralda district, the White Pine district, and the Base Range district; all were opened between 1860 and 1865. Aurora, in the Esmeralda district, had a population of 10,000 in 1864. The Base Range district around Eureka, Nevada, produced $40 million in silver, $20 million in gold, and $10 million in lead in fourteen years.

Colorado prospectors scattered from the pioneer mining center at Denver in all directions. In 1860 at California Gulch, miners found Colorado's richest gold placer, which drew 10,000 miners to Oro City. After five years, the placers faded, little deep prospecting was done, and the mining life of California Gulch seemed ended. In 1864, prospectors found rich silver deposits in the Argentine district centering on Georgetown; by 1867 the region had become the principal Rocky Mountain silver center. Miners then returned to California Gulch; in 1873, using deeper prospecting methods, they exposed rich gold and silver bodies that overnight made Leadville Colorado's chief mining camp. Additional strikes during the 1870s produced the famous Cripple Creek diggings, the Gunnison district —which centered on the Tin Cup and Gold Cup mines and produced gold, silver, and lead—and the Aspen district silver mines. A social aspect of Colorado mineral development was the importation of foreign workers, including skilled Cornish, Irish, and Austrian miners.

The mining frontier's sweep into the Northwest began in Idaho during 1860; there gold placers were discovered in the north near Clearwater River and in the south at Boise Basin. The mining rush that followed led to the founding of the Orofino Creek district, with Pierce as its principal settlement. Lewiston, at the junction of the Snake and the Clearwater rivers, served as the major supply center for the Idaho mines. The Salmon River mines were opened in 1861. Additional mining frontier extensions in Idaho included the Wood River district in 1879; some gold, but mostly silver and lead, were found. Idaho's great bonanza strike occurred in 1882

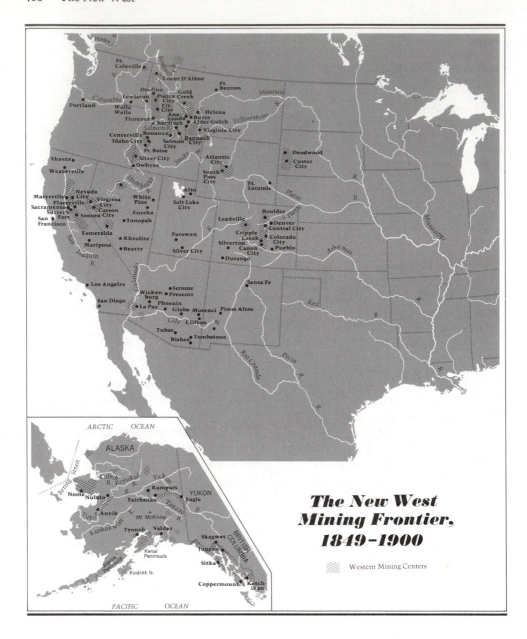

The New West Mining Frontier, 1849–1900

Western Mining Centers

with the Coeur d'Alene rush, which was based on rich gold placers. The Coeur d'Alene mines yielded first gold, then silver, followed by lead and zinc; in sixty years they produced a billion dollars worth of metal.

Prospectors from the Idaho camps ranged over Utah, Wyoming, and Montana, finding gold placers in each of the three territories. In 1862, John White, from the Colorado and Idaho mines, made a major placer discovery on Montana's Grasshopper Creek; the strike quickly attracted 500 miners and led to the founding of Bannock. There followed the fabulous Alder Gulch strike, which gave rise to Virginia City, Montana's premier gold mining camp. The latter settlement had a population of 15,000 by 1864. Successively, prospectors developed the Helena and Butte districts. The latter contained perhaps the richest and most variegated mineral deposits in the entire New West. From 1860 to 1950 Montana mines yielded an estimated $3 billion worth of metals.

The last big rush for gold in the contiguous United States occurred in the Black Hills of South Dakota. This highland formation was sacred to the Sioux. During the 1850s, traders found scattered gold placers but kept them secret. The mining frontier flow across the Northwest finally reached this area during 1865; scattered prospecting took place, resulting in the discovery of some placer gold. Several large parties of miners attempted to enter the Black Hills that year but were turned back by military authorities attempting to enforce the Sioux treaties, which protected them against trespassers.

In 1874, Colonel Custer explored the Black Hills at the head of a mixed military-civilian expedition. Several members of the party found gold, reports of their discoveries were widely published in newspapers, and the following year intruding prospector parties found gold placers. Two years later, the Black Hills gold rush took place, as thousands of miners swept into the forbidden territory. The principal placers were on French Creek and Whitewood Creek. At Gold River Gulch, Deadwood, Lead, and other mining camps soon developed. The bonanza quartz mine of the Black Hills was the Homestake. By 1924, a quarter of a billion dollars worth of gold had been extracted from the Black Hills field.

In New Mexico, gold had been found in widely scattered small placer deposits throughout the territory. The local geology made finding the mother lodes, which fed the placers, difficult; in most cases only deposits close to the surface were located and worked. Lack of water also handicapped wide application of the familiar placer, hydraulic, and quartz mining processes in New Mexico. The Elizabethtown field was the most productive gold region before 1900. During the 1860s, silver was found in great quantities; the principal districts at Magdalena and Socorro were succeeded during the 1870s by the opening of rich silver mines in the Silver City district.

Development of Arizona's mineral wealth was slowed by the Apache presence. Pioneer miners produced gold and silver along the Santa Cruz,

Gila, and Colorado rivers during the 1850s and 1860s. In 1879, the territory's richest mines were opened at Tombstone; this notorious field produced gold and silver valued at over $30 million in a single decade.

Western Base Metal Mining

During the latter part of the nineteenth century, as the raw material needs of the industrial East grew, more and more miners exploited the New West's base metals, especially copper, lead, and zinc. Industrial demand for copper was growing rapidly. In 1882, the first electric generating plant in the United States was installed at New York City. Copper was needed for transmission wires and generator armatures. The mining frontier responded to this need by extracting vast quantities of copper ore. During 1875, Montana prospectors in the Butte district opened the world's richest copper mine, the Anaconda. In the Southwest, copper had been mined at the Santa Rita mines of western New Mexico from Spanish times. Arizona's mineral promise was assured in 1875 when prospectors opened rich copper mines centering on the Copper Queen mine at Bisbee.

Lead and zinc also were increasingly in demand, and the mines of Colorado, Idaho, and Montana produced vast tonnages of these minerals. Also, on the New West's eastern border, in the Tri-State District—southwest Missouri, southeastern Kansas, and northeastern Indian Territory—miners opened vast deposits of lead and zinc. The Tri-State District became the world's leading lead and zinc field; in a fifty-year period it produced a billion dollars' worth of these metals.

Fossil Fuel Exploitation

Another extractive industry, which responded to the expanding needs of an increasingly industrialized society of the late nineteenth century, was limited exploitation of fossil fuels—coal and petroleum. Rich bituminous coal deposits in the Indian Territory had been used from earliest frontier times to fire blacksmith forges. The railroad expansion produced a double market and drastic expansion of coal mining, particularly in the Choctaw nation. Railroads not only consumed vast quantities of coal to fire the steam boilers of their locomotives, they also provided the means to transport the coal to industrial markets. Deposits in Kansas, Colorado, and other Western states and territories were also widely used to supply the vast milling and smelting needs of the expanding mining frontier.

Late in the nineteenth century, petroleum had limited but important uses: as an illuminant (in the form of kerosene, coal oil, rock oil), as a lubricant (axle grease), and as medicine. Pioneer wildcatters (drillers) opened wells on the border of southern Kansas and northern Indian Territory and converted the crude to coal oil and axle grease. Natural gas associated with petroleum production was piped to frontier towns on the Western border and used to illuminate city streets and homes and to heat buildings. An essential concomitant industry for the mining frontier's mineral and fossil fuel production was refining. The crude ores had to be processed and separated, smelted, and then molded into blocks or "pigs" of pure metal. Wood, charcoal, coal, and natural gas were used to fire the smelter furnaces of the refinery plants situated near the mines.

Of all the industries of the New West's exploitive frontier, mining and refining were the most destructive and harmful to the natural milieu. Highly competitive mining extracted minerals at an ever-increasing rate to feed the great industrial maw of the eastern United States. These irreplaceable resources—which had required millions of years of natural processes to accumulate in deposits—were sapped by saturation mining. Each mining district became a wasteland. The landscapes were pitted with prospect holes, deep shafts and tunnels, the surface scarred with mine dump piles and punctuated with vast depressions created by cave-ins, as supports in mined-out galleries rotted and collapsed. Forests near the mines were obliterated, bare mountain sides exposed to the elements; the trees were sawed into timbers and boards to provide mine cribbing, supports, and lumber for mill structures and mining camp shelters. Great quantities of wood, sometimes converted to charcoal, were required to fire the steam boilers that turned the mine machinery and to smelt the ore. Noxious fumes from the smelter furnace stacks corroded trees, shrubs, and grasses, destroying all plant and animal life for miles around. Mine and mill waters, charged with deadly minerals and chemicals, fed into the creeks and rivers, killing fish, migratory waterfowl, and the land creatures that drank from the poisoned waters.

THE LUMBERMEN

Western forests received only limited attention before 1900 as a source of lumber for the eastern United States, for that market was still mostly supplied by pine stands in the Old Northwest and Old Southwest. Some lumber from Rocky Mountain and Pacific Northwest forests was shipped east over the railroads, and lumber from Northwest forests was often shipped by water to Atlantic ports. But most of the New West forest production before 1900 was absorbed locally. Railroad construction required vast quantities of lumber for ties and bridging, and new and expanding settlements consumed millions of board feet of lumber each year for houses, business buildings, and farm and ranch structures. Mining absorbed vast amounts of lumber for shaft cribbing, mineral gallery supports, mine-, mill-, and smelter-building construction, and fuel for steam boilers and smelting furnaces. Plank lumber was used to construct New West roads over bogs and sandy spots.

Lumbering the Pacific Northwest Forests

The federal government through nationalizing currents in the form of special legislation, subsidized the lumber industry—just as it had the railroads and other Western enterprises. The Timber and Stone Act of 1878 was applied to uplands classed as unfit for cultivation in Nevada, California, Oregon, and Washington. It permitted a lumberman to file a claim for 160 acres of forest and to purchase the tract for $2.50 an acre. Using dummy entrymen, much as cattlemen on the Great Plains had done, lumbermen acquired millions of acres of prime public-domain forest land before the act was repealed in 1891. Large-scale lumbering in the Pacific Northwest began after the region was laced by railroads connecting the lush forests with the Eastern markets.

Lumbering the Indian Territory Forests

One of the first New West forest areas to be opened by lumbermen for Eastern markets was the dense pine and hardwood stands of eastern Indian Territory. This timber had long been the source of building material, furniture, and fuel. Water-powered sawmills were already in operation there before the Civil War. Then, in 1868, steampowered mills were introduced, and six years later the railroads established a thriving commercial lumbering industry. The first important lumber center was on the M.K.T. line at Stringtown in the Choctaw nation. Pine logs were cut in the mountain and plateau forests and were hauled to the huge steam mill. Rough, heavy logs came out of the plant as planed lumber, ready for construction use.

The principal products fashioned from Indian Territory forests were railroad ties, bridge timbers, shingles, telegraph poles, fence posts, staves, cordwood, lath, mining timber, and construction lumber. Lumberjacks slashed away at these primeval forests, producing annual lumber shipments running into the millions of board feet. They took their heaviest toll in the pine forests, although ash, cottonwood, oak, hickory, cypress, walnut, and cedar also were used. The magnificent walnut stands in the Creek nation were cut into logs, sawed into blocks, and sent to Germany for making gunstocks.

THE PLOWMEN

Agriculture was established in the New West before 1865, but on a widely scattered basis. An agrarian belt had developed on the trans-Missouri border —a ribbon of farms extending from eastern Dakota Territory south through eastern Nebraska, Kansas, Indian Territory, and Texas. Irrigated agriculture flourished in the river valleys of New Mexico and Arizona, the Great Basin, and California. In the Pacific Northwest, farmers practiced a mix of humid-type and irrigated agriculture.

The Farmer's Last Frontier

Between 1870 and 1900, major agrarian attention focused on the long-scorned Great American Desert, the vast semi-arid grasslands that lay between the 98th meridan and the Rocky Mountains and extended from Canada to the Rio Grande. This province of low rainfall and generally variant climate was unlike any region ever approached by the American agricultural frontier. Its conquest by the plowmen required special laws, special technology, and special attitudes.

Distributing the Western Public Domain

Agricultural interest in the Great Plains was instigated during the 1870s and 1880s by intensive promotion by the railroads and by the immigration bureaus maintained by territorial and state governments. Nationalizing currents in the form of supportive legislation for dispensing this vast grassland included application of the Preemption Act of 1841, whereby a squatter could buy, free of competitive bid at public sale, 160 acres at the minimum price of $1.25 an acre. The Homestead Act of 1862, made it possible to obtain an additional 160 acres, requiring five years' residence on the claim and payment of an entry fee of about $15. Yet another 160 acres could be added to the Great Plains farm by fulfilling the requirements of the Timber Culture Act, passed in 1873: planting forty acres of trees on the tract. This requirement was reduced to ten acres five years later. In eleven arid states, the Desert Land Act of 1877 permitted acquisition of a section of land after payment of $1.25 an acre and irrigation of a portion of the tract.

Settlers could also purchase land distributed to the states under the Morrill Land Grant Act of 1863; this statute subsidized the establishment of the agricultural colleges to promote training and research in agronomy. States received 30,000 acres of land scrip for each senator and representative, and the states often sold the land to speculators, who resold it to settlers for $5 to $10 an acre.

Land-grant railroads too sold agricultural tracts to settlers at an average price of $5 an acre. Land-grant railroad companies also supported the agrarian frontier's occupation of the Great Plains by selling land to settlers on credit, usually seven-year mortgages at 7 to 10 percent interest. In addition, Eastern and European investors formed loan and mortgage companies to provide funds to settlers; they charged 10 to 12 percent interest on loans for purchasing tools, equipment, and stock.

Technology and New West Agriculture

Postwar technology was especially crucial to the agrarian conquest of the Great Plains. Its peculiar milieu—usually treeless, mostly covered by deep sod grasses, having marginal rainfall and scarce surface water—required special equipment, tools, and methodologies. Rarely was water found above 200 feet; often it was as deep as 500 feet. During the 1870s, American industry developed well-drilling equipment capable of tapping the Plains deep-water strata and pumping equipment, which—combined with the windmill—could raise the water to the surface. Even these wells provided only enough water for household use, stock, and irrigating a vegetable garden. The scarcity of fencing material on the Plains complicated the problem of keeping livestock out of growing crops. In 1874, this need was met by the introduction of barbed wire.

The Plains' carpet of deep-rooted buffalo, grama, and mesquite grasses required special tools to open fields for planting. The heavy sod plow developed was of two types—the Jack Rabbit plow and the Nebraska plow. Both were pulled by a two-horse or double-ox team and worked on the same principal, although the Nebraska plow was the shorter and lighter of the two. Instead of a moldboard, commonly found on regular turning plows, the sod plow had steel rods that were set four inches apart and curved like a moldboard. The tough sod was cut vertically and horizontally in shallow furrows by a knife-like blade set near the point of the plow. Plow rods turned the sod bottom-side-up in long ribbons or slab-like layers.

Dry-farming methods had to be devised to offset the region's marginal precipitation—which was generally ten to twenty inches a year—and uncertain climate. Research demonstrated the efficacy of deep plowing as a phase of dry farming; turning Plains soils twelve to fifteen inches deep brought subsurface moisture to the plant roots by capillary action. Frequent harrowing broke up the soil and retarded evaporation. Other phases of dry farming included allowing fields to lie fallow and the use of new varieties of drought-resistant corn, wheat, barley, rye, and feed crops.

Problems of Great Plains Agriculture

But it was not only the technology of Plains farming that was different. Special mental attitudes were required to succeed on the Great Plains, including the ability to accept a drastically changed milieu. Treeless grasslands stretched in monotonous, sweeping expanses from horizon to horizon. Unstable meteorology often produced unceasing winds, abrupt overnight weather changes—from mild sunshine to "blue northers" and blizzards—tornadoes, and crop-destroying hailstorms. Cyclical climate patterns interspersed wet years with dry years and searing droughts. Mixed with these vicissitudes were prairie fires, and periodic grasshopper plagues—hordes of swarming insects that devoured corn and other crops, invaded households, ate curtains off the windows, and fouled the wells. Moreover, nature limited the Plains farmers' choice of crops, forcing them more and more into a highly speculative one-crop agriculture. The concentration on grain crops, usually wheat, subjected them to market fluctuations that were increasingly influenced by national and international factors over which they had no control. The farmers who survived the agricultural conquest of the Great Plains adopted a gambler pose and engaged in a highly competitive, intensive exploitation of Great Plains soils.

Between 1870 and 1900, the agricultural conquest of the American West—centering on the Great Plains—was completed. During that period, the nation's farms tripled in number and "more farm land was brought under cultivation ... than in the entire previous history of the nation." [5] Most of this increase occurred in the region between the 98th meridian and the Rocky Mountains. After 1870, the agrarian establishment of the entire nation shifted gradually from subsistence to commercial agriculture. Nowhere was the trend—and its results—more conspicuous than on the Great Plains. Intensive exploitation of this region disturbed, and in some sections irreparably altered, the region's ecology. Reckless farming stripped the natural grass cover, which would have been better left to the stockraiser for grazing, and mined the soil's natural fertility. Exposed to the elements, millions of acres of Great Plains cropland became hopelessly eroded and gullied. An estimated one-third of the region's top soil was lost to wind and water erosion, setting the stage for the dismal dust-bowl disasters of the early twentieth century.

The exploitive frontier's assiduous plundering of the New West's rich natural bounty produced some positive as well as negative results for the region and the nation. Its outpouring of primary mineral and timber materials, fibers, and foodstuffs was supportive of the rapidly expanding Eastern industrial establishment and thereby contributed materially to emerging national strength. In addition, the bonanza opportunities of the exploitive frontier attracted ever-increasing numbers of settlers to the New West. Their persistent demands for political organization led the federal government reluctantly to complete the state format of the trans-Missouri region.

SELECTED SOURCES

The tragedy of the extermination of the bison is the subject of *Wayne Gard, *The Great Buffalo Hunt* (New York, 1959); James H. Cook, *Fifty Years on the Old Frontier* (New Haven, 1923); Olive H. Dixon, *The Life of Billy Dixon* (Dallas, 1927); and Carl C. Rister, *The Southwestern Frontier* (Cleveland, 1928).

From the vast literature on the subject of Western ranching, the following works cover most phases: Edward E. Dale, *The Range Cattle Industry* (Norman, 1929); Louis Pelzer, *The Cattlemen's Frontier* (Glendale, 1936); *Lewis Atherton, *The Cattle Kings* (Bloomington, 1961); *Gene M. Gressley, *Bankers and Cattlemen* (New York, 1966); Wayne Gard, *The Chisholm Trail* (Norman, 1954); *Robert R. Dykstra, *The Cattle Towns* (New York, 1968); and William W. Savage, Jr., *The Cherokee Strip Live Stock Association* (Columbia, 1973).

Mining, fossil-fuel extraction, and agriculture in the exploitive age are discussed in Otis E. Young, Jr., *Western Mining: An Informal Account of*

* Available in paperback.

[5] John P. Stover, *American Railroads* (Chicago, 1961), p. 98.

Precious-Metals Prospecting, Placering, Lode Mining, and Milling on the American Frontier from Spanish Times to 1893 (Norman, 1970); *Arrell M. Gibson, Wilderness Bonanza (Norman, 1972); William S. Greever, The Bonanza West: The Story of the Mining Rushes, 1848–1900 (Norman, 1963); S. G. Bayne, Derricks of Destiny (New York, 1924); Carl C. Rister, Oil! Titan of the Southwest (Norman, 1949); Gilbert C. Fite, The Farmer's Frontier, 1865–1900 (New York, 1966); Fred A. Shannon, Farmer's Last Frontier (New York, 1945); *Walter P. Webb, The Great Plains (Boston, 1931); and W. Eugene Hollon, The Great American Desert (New York, 1966).

A Fur Trapper's Camp in the New West.

A Settler Caravan Leaving the Great Bend of the Arkansas River, 1872.

27

State-Making in the New West

Western state-making, based on the principle of equality with states formed earlier, had been a regular and primary concern of the national government from the earliest days of the republic. In the thirty-year period after 1790, much of the Old West was integrated into the American Union almost automatically and substantially in accord with the guidelines of the Northwest Ordinance. Of all the Old West states, Missouri had the most difficult time because of the controversial issue of slavery extension—the *cause célèbre* of New West state-making until 1861. The admission of Texas, the first state carved from the New West, was held up for nine years, largely because of this question. We have related how the flow of the agrarian frontier into the Northwest and the sweep of the mining frontier across the Southwest generated local demands to Congress for political organization in the years before the Civil War. The reluctance of national leaders to respond promptly to these demands was closely related to the growing alienation between the North and South over the slavery extension issue.

Leaders of both North and South were wary of the political consequences of creating additional states in the New West and proceeded with considerable caution. In 1848 Congress created the Oregon Territory, which had been functioning with a *de facto* government for five years, and in 1853 the Washington Territory was organized; both of these new territories were closed to slavery. In 1850, an agonizing sectional compromise was contrived for the Southwest: California was admitted as a free state, and the organization of Utah and New Mexico Territories was permitted on the basis of popular sovereignty. Four years later, on the Missouri border, Congress created the Kansas and Nebraska territories; again, its work was tinctured with the slavery question, and the territories were allowed to organize on the principle of popular sovereignty. Although with some difficulty, Congress was able to admit Oregon to the Union as a free state in 1859. And, finally, in 1861, with Southern obstructionists removed from the national government, Congress admitted Kansas and created the Nevada, Dakota, and Colorado territories. In spite of a bitter sectional debate and a recurring impasse, a surprisingly large amount of New West territory was accorded some form of political organization before the Civil War.

THE CIVIL WAR STATES AND TERRITORIES

During the Civil War, Congress continued to work on the political organization of the New West. New issues, questions, and conditions replaced the slavery arguments. Whereas before 1861, Western state-making was used to serve the interests of sections, thereafter it was more frequently exploited for particular partisan interests. And, unless it served some partisan purpose, no state in the New West received the swift and certain access to statehood accorded the Old West. The infusion of political opportunism and of new divisive issues deferred completion of the political format of the contiguous United States until 1912.

Arizona, Idaho, and Montana Territories

During the war, Western state-making was exploited by the Union government to further its war policy and constitutional goals. To smother Confederate sentiment in Arizona and New Mexico, to reward local Union support, and to follow up the reconquest and occupation of the Southwest by the California Column, Congress in 1863 separated the western half of the New Mexico Territory and established the Arizona Territory. Also in 1863—in response to the gold rush in eastern Washington Territory and the rapid occupation of the Boise Basin, Salmon River district, and other Northwest mining regions—Congress reduced the Washington Territory and created the Idaho Territory. The great Alder Gulch discovery and the rise of Virginia City, Montana, led Congress the following year to separate the eastern section of the Idaho Territory and to create the Montana Territory.

In late 1863 and early 1864, at President Abraham Lincoln's urging, Congress also passed enabling acts for the Nevada, Colorado, and Nebraska territories. This action was based on the expectation that the wilderness outposts were ready to provide Republican support in the upcoming presidential election and to ratify the proposed thirteenth amendment to the constitution.

Nevada Statehood

In Nevada, where the statehood movement had been strong since 1860, the enabling act was warmly received. Delegates were selected and a constitutional convention began its deliberations in late 1863. Throughout early 1864, national Republican leaders regularly pressured the convention to complete its work in order that Nevada citizens could participate in the November elections. So urgent was the need for Nevada's electoral support that the text of the proposed constitution was telegraphed to Washington for approval, at a cost of nearly $3,500. On October 31, 1864, Nevada, which had a population of fewer than 40,000 people, was admitted to the Union.

Nebraska Statehood

The Nebraska Enabling Act was received with mixed feeling. Both local Democratic and Republican parties had favored statehood in early territorial days. In 1860, the Nebraska territorial legislature had authorized an election for a statehood convention; but because the population was only about 30,000, citizens voted against establishing a state government at that time. Statehood advocates continued to press, and when Congress passed the Nebraska Enabling Act in 1864, they made preparations to call a constitutional convention. Territorial Democrats, however, faced with certain submersion in a state government dominated by local Republicans strongly supported by the national party, opposed statehood. They warned that the expenses of government, presently borne by Congress, would, with statehood, become a local responsibility and necessitate an increase in taxes. The convention met but failed to produce a constitution.

Statehood advocates persevered and, in 1866, submitted a constitution to Congress. Nebraska's proposed organic law contained a clause restricting suffrage to free, white males. The "Republican Congress was surprised and disappointed to see a constitution coming from a presumably safe territory like Nebraska that did not reaffirm the position" [1] of the Radical Republican majority. The bill was amended to forbid abridgement of franchise— a change approved by Nebraska leaders—and was passed. President Andrew Johnson vetoed the Nebraska statehood bill, but Congress overrode the veto, and Nebraska was admitted to the Union on March 1, 1867.

Colorado Political Vicissitudes

In the early days of territorial life, Colorado citizens had strongly desired statehood. Pioneer miners had formed *de facto* governments as a step toward this goal. Jefferson Territory had been created to fuse the scattered mining camps and to improve chances for recognition by Congress. When Congress created the Colorado Territory in 1861, this Rocky Mountain community had a population of nearly 40,000. In response to the enabling act of 1864, the Colorado assembly adopted a joint resolution favoring statehood and authorized an election to select delegates to the constitutional convention. But by the time the convention assembled in

---

[1] James C. Olson, *History of Nebraska* (Lincoln, 1966), p. 126.

1864, citizen support had waned. Established mining fields appeared to be petering out, no new mineral discoveries of consequence had been made, and great numbers of discouraged prospectors were moving on to the new Idaho and Montana placers. Many citizens believed that with the decline in mining, Colorado could not support a state government. Also, as in Nebraska, Colorado Democrats were faced with minority status in a state government dominated by local Republicans braced by the Radical Republicans in Washington. They therefore opposed statehood. In an election held during 1864 Coloradans overwhelmingly rejected a constitution and statehood.

A year later a referendum on statehood carried by 200 votes, while a proposal to include black suffrage in the state constitution was defeated. This exclusion antagonized many Radical Republicans in Congress who had earlier been friendly to Colorado statehood. Moreover, the national shame of Chivington's Sand Creek Massacre of the Cheyennes hung heavily over the territory. Even so, a majority in Congress approved the Colorado statehood resolution. President Johnson, however, refused to proclaim Colorado statehood on the grounds that the convention had deviated from the requirements of the enabling act. He vetoed several Colorado statehood bills—one in 1867 failed on override in the Senate by only three votes. Thus Colorado statehood, caught in the troubled arena between Congress and the chief executive, was held in limbo for nine more years.

Wyoming Territory

A product of the stream of political organization accomplished during this period was the Wyoming Territory. For much of its early history, Wyoming had been a strategic crossing on the overland thoroughfare to the Pacific shore. The South Pass had long provided travelers the easiest access through the towering Rocky Mountain cordillera. Wyoming was a borderland in the mining-frontier expansion. Prospectors from the Idaho and Montana mines found traces of gold along the creeks draining Wyoming's mountain valleys; the sources of the Sweetwater yielded the most productive placers. By 1865, several mining settlements centering on South Pass City had grown up.

Until 1868, Wyoming was administered as a part of the Dakota Territory; the present state encompasses four former Dakota counties. Jurisdictional conflicts developed as the remote mineral settlements on the Sweetwater organized local governments based on mining-camp law. In 1865 Wyoming's pioneer miner settlements combined to form a *de facto* government independent of the Dakota Territory and petitioned Congress for recognition of their separate status.

The building of the Union Pacific Railroad across Wyoming broadened the settlement, which, by 1868, centered on Cheyenne and Laramie. Leaders of Wyoming's *de facto* government continued to pressure Congress to detach Wyoming from the Dakota Territory and establish a separate territorial government. Congress acquiesced on July 25, 1868. In organizing their territorial government, Wyoming citizens took the innovative and revolutionary step of granting suffrage and service on juries to women.

The creation of the Wyoming Territory substantially completed the territorial format for the New West. Except for the division of the Dakota Territory and the addition of No-Man's Land to the Oklahoma Territory, the present boundaries of the trans-Missouri region's political components were established. At this point, however, the New West state-making process faltered. After 1870, almost every territory had to endure a tortured and peremptory congressional scrutiny before gaining admission to the Union.

COLORADO STATEHOOD AND NATIONAL POLITICS

By 1870, only six states had been carved from the vast territory of the New West. There remained ten territories—Dakota, Montana, Idaho, Washington, Wyoming, Colorado, Utah, New Mexico, Arizona, and Indian Territory—at various stages of preparation for statehood. Territorial status was recognized as a second-class, colonial-type of political existence. Executive and judicial officers in each territorial government were appointed by the party in power in Washington. These men, "owing nothing to the people whom they governed . . . reflected that detachment in their official acts." [2] Territorial appointments were cherished by the national parties, for they comprised a rich source of patronage. And Congress maintained its control of local affairs through its power of review over the laws passed by territorial legislatures. Just as Eastern capitalists increasingly shaped Western economic life, so Washington politicians dominated its political life.

In this long period of political colonialism in the Western territories—it lasted from 1870 to 1912—only two reforms of consequence occurred in territorial management. During 1873, the administration of territories was shifted from the Department of State, where it had resided since 1789, to the Department of the Interior. And after 1890, the much maligned "carpetbag government"—rule by appointive outsiders—was replaced by a greater measure of home rule through the appointment of local men to the territorial offices.

During the decade of the 1870s, only one territory—Colorado—was admitted to the Union. Its struggle to achieve admission exposed several new, restrictive trends in the state-making process that had their basis in the Republican party and the Congress. The long Republican domination of national affairs began in 1861 and led to the formation of a strong Republican party in each territory—a firm local power base braced by the

---

[2] E. Douglas Branch, *Westward: The Romance of the American Frontier* (New York, 1930), p. 587.

national party. The local party consisted of two supporting groups: the intensely committed Grand Army of the Republic—an organization of Union veterans that zealously supported the party of Union—and the corps of high appointive territorial officials. Twice in the period between 1861 and 1912 there was a Democratic interruption in this strong Republican trend—the presidential interludes of Grover Cleveland, 1883–1887, and 1893–1897—but they did little to arrest the solidification of Republican strength in the Western territories.

Congressional Conditions

Historically, the only statehood condition set by Congress was the assurance that a republican form of government would be maintained. The Northwest Ordinance had also excluded slavery from the Northwest Territory. In the case of Missouri, Congress had deferred statehood until a section of the state constitution forbidding entrance of free blacks had been expunged and admitted the state only on condition that slavery be excluded from Western territory north of 36° 30′. Beginning in 1850, Congress required that the question of slavery be decided by local popular sovereignty. Although held back by sectional pressures in the period 1848–1861, Congress generally came around to approving the actions of Westerners in organizing *de facto* governments, confirmed territories, and received several states into the Union. It was accepted that Congress had no means of controlling the actions of a state once it had been admitted to the Union.

During the Civil War, however, Congress was dominated by Radical Republicans, who took a different stance. The Reconstruction Acts set congressional prescriptions and established complicated formulas and conditions under which seceding states could be readmitted to the Union. This new directorial attitude became a traditional posture for the Congress even after Reconstruction had been completed, and it persisted in the setting of elaborate and, at times, extreme conditions for the admission of Western territories. During Reconstruction, the Southern states had to overcome the handicap of the taint of treason; after Reconstruction, the Republican-controlled Congress found new handicaps that the Western territories had to overcome before being admitted to the Union. These barriers to statehood included polygamy in Utah, deviant cultures in Indian Territory, New Mexico, and Arizona, and climate and resource limitations that would make it difficult for certain territories to provide adequate support for the essential structures of state government.

To further complicate state-making in the West, there developed a contest over the constitutional question of congressional supremacy in the admission process. The constitution provides that Congress is the sole judge of the elections, returns, and qualifications of its members and that Congress has the power to exclude or expel members. A new state's relation to the federal community could thus be consummated only by its representatives and senators being received by Congress. Moreover, since the 1840s Congress had regularly delegated to the president the authority to admit a territory by proclamation when, in his judgment, it had met the conditions set forth in the enabling act. The president's continued performance of this function was of great moment during the Johnson administration and was a central issue in the disputed presidential election of 1876, the outcome of which hinged on Colorado statehood.

Colorado Statehood and the Election of 1876

During the 1870s, Colorado, because of an increase in agriculture and stockraising, developed a varied economy. These industries supplemented mining and provided greater economic stability for a more permanent population. In addition, new mineral discoveries during the early 1870s exceeded all previously known strikes. The wonders of Leadville and other mineral districts produced a drastic increase in population; in the five years after 1870, the population of the Colorado Territory grew from 40,000 to over 150,000. Naturally, local politicians resumed the press for statehood, and a reluctant Congress, faced with a close presidential election in 1876, passed an enabling act for Colorado in March of 1875. Clearly, Colorado was to play a role in the 1876 presidential election similar to that played by Nevada in 1864. A convention produced the Colorado constitution, and President Ulysses S. Grant issued a proclamation admitting Colorado to the Union in the summer of 1876. The proclamation allowed Coloradans to participate in the presidential election, and the three Colorado Republican electoral college votes proved crucial in Rutherford B. Hayes' victory over Democrat Samuel J. Tilden.

Subsequently, the Democrats in Congress challenged Colorado's admission on the grounds that Congress had no power to delegate authority to admit a state. In early 1877 House Democrats contested the seating of Colorado's Republican congressman-elect, arguing that Colorado was still a territory. If the Democrats view were sustained, Colorado's three electoral votes could not be counted, and President-elect Hayes would lack a majority and be forced to vacate the presidency. The Democratic challenge failed, however, and Hayes was sustained in his victory when the House seated the Republican representative from Colorado.

THE OMNIBUS STATES

Both parties in the Congress well remembered the effect of Colorado statehood on the presidential election of 1876. "It is small wonder that in ensuing Congresses, members of both parties looked upon new states with reference to their influence on presidential aspirations, and that Democrats resolved not to increase the burden of votes that might be cast against them." For a period of nearly twelve years after the election of 1876, the Democrats maintained a majority in the House of Representatives. Leaders of that party were unremittingly committed to blocking the admission of Republican-dominated territories. During Cleveland's first administration, the "blockade was from the other side, with a Republican Senate suspicious of every statehood proposition that might turn out Democratic." [3]

Meanwhile, the Western territories continued the metamorphosis from wilderness to settled, prosperous communities as mining, agriculture, stockraising, transportation, and urban development proceeded at an unprecedented rate. Before 1860, the demographic phenomenon of swift occupation of portions of the New West created clusters of mining camps that coalesced into expectant political communities. After 1870, the mining frontier was joined by the agricultural frontier in continuing this demographic sweep across the New West. Of the six territories to be admitted in 1889–1890—Washington, Montana, Idaho, Wyoming, and North and South Dakota—most had undergone a tenfold population increase between 1870 and 1890; several had experienced a twentyfold increase. This sustained population increase and the concomitant economic expansion inevitably produced strong local demands that Congress recognize the Western territories' more advanced condition and grant statehood.

Washington

In the Washington Territory, railroad connections between Seattle and the Mississippi Valley, growing trade with China, and the development of lumbering, shipbuilding, stockraising, agriculture, and commercial fishing combined to produce a stable economic base. Its population in 1870 of nearly 25,000 had increased by 1889 to over 350,000. A strong but unsuccessful statehood movement occurred in 1878 at the Walla Walla convention. Throughout the decade of the 1880s, statehood advocates urged action by Congress, but to no avail. The "congressional blockade" was unyielding.

Montana

Montana Territory was first populated by the mining rush of the 1860s, which produced the fabulous Virginia City, Bannock, and ultimately Butte. The Northern Pacific Railroad crossed the territory and, besides providing an essential transport facility for Montana's growing mineral production, it also stimulated agriculture and stockraising. Montana Territory's population had increased from 21,000 in 1870 to over 140,000 in 1889. Statehood advocates were active throughout the 1880s; the most important although unsuccessful effort took place at the Helena convention in 1884. Congress was completely unresponsive to the statehood appeals from Montana Territory.

[3] Frederic L. Paxson, *History of the American Frontier, 1763–1893* (New York, 1924), p. 556.

Wyoming and Idaho

Belatedly included in the state-making spree of 1889–1890, Wyoming and Idaho underwent increases in development and settlement generally commensurate with those of the adjoining Northwest territories. Stock-raising, mining, some agriculture, and railroad development were the principal industries of these two territories, each of which received substantial population increases from 1870 to statehood in 1890. Idaho, with a population of 15,000 in 1870, had nearly 90,000 people in 1890; and during the same period, Wyoming increased from 9,000 to 63,000.

North and South Dakota

Dakota Territory was fed by three streams of settlement. The mining frontier was concentrated in the southwest in the Black Hills. Agricultural settlement predominated in the eastern part of the territory, where pioneer farmers produced rich yields of wheat and corn. The Plains grasslands of central and western Dakota Territory were occupied by ranchmen. The population of what is now North Dakota increased from 2,000 in 1870 to nearly 120,000 in 1889; for the same period, South Dakota, with 12,000, increased to nearly 350,000. Dakota statehood advocates met in convention at Sioux Falls in 1883 and again in 1885, produced constitutions, and urged Congress to act. The Republican Senate complied by regularly passing bills for the division of the territory into two states, but in each case the action was negated by the Democratic House.

The strength of the Republican showing in the 1888 election threatened the Democratic hold on the House. Thereupon, both parties turned to promoting statehood for various Western territories in an attempt to outdo the other and thus receive the credit for favoring statehood. In early 1889, the House considered a bill to admit the Dakota Territory. It was amended to include the Washington, Montana, and New Mexico territories. When the bill reached the Senate, New Mexico was eliminated and the Dakota Territory was divided into the proposed states of North Dakota and South Dakota. The so-called Omnibus Bill, providing for the admission of Washington, Montana, and North and South Dakota, passed Congress and the four states were admitted to the Union during 1889. Wyoming and Idaho territories, omitted from this state-making orgy, each proceeded to produce a constitution without congressional sanction and to demand consideration. In 1890, Congress admitted both territories.

THE DRAGOONED TERRITORY—UTAH

Congress had created the Utah Territory in 1850. It was populated mostly by Mormons, hard-working, intensely committed disciples of Joseph Smith who had miraculously converted the Great Basin desert into a prosperous community of irrigated farms, ranches, and industries. Every phase of Mormon life was dominated by the Church of Jesus Christ of Latter Day

Saints, a theocratic establishment governed by President Brigham Young and his council. Mormons practiced several curious and—in American society's strongly entrenched conformist Protestant view—deviant doctrines. One of these doctrines was plural marriage. Gentiles would perhaps have begrudgingly tolerated the Mormons' thrift, industry, and economic success in transforming Utah's desert wasteland into a thriving garden, but—trapped in a twisted, puritanical, monistic context—they denounced polygamy as un-Christian, un-American, and the ultimate in human depravity. Mormon leaders ardently desired statehood, for only then could they manage their affairs free of Gentile meddling, but from the beginning federal officials made it clear that a *sine qua non* for statehood was the abolition of polygamy.

Mormon Incompatibility

Mormon difficulties with the federal government began during the 1850s when their leader, Brigham Young, was replaced as territorial governor by a Gentile. Thereafter, until statehood in 1896, all major territorial executive and judicial appointive officials were Gentiles, who produced continuous local conflict by regularly insulting Mormon men and women, lecturing them on the evils of polygamy, and doing all in their power to coerce Mormons to abandon this "nauseous practice." Relations between Gentile territorial officials and Mormons reached such a bitter impasse in 1857 that the Mormon militia threatened to expel all Gentiles. Federal officials ordered a large force of regular troops to Utah, and bloody combat seemed inevitable. At the crucial moment, however, territorial officials and Mormon leaders struck a truce, the federal troops were withdrawn, and a troubled peace came to the territory.

Union officials feared that Mormon dissidents might be vulnerable to Confederate blandishments and, during most of the Civil War, federal troops—a California regiment—maintained a military occupation of the Utah Territory. Congressmen, even with all their war concerns, and reflecting the puritanical values of their constituents, found time to strike a blow for monogamy by passing a law in 1862 making bigamous marriages a federal offense in the territories. But "since Mormon juries could not be expected either to indict or convict on this charge, and there were few Gentiles there, the law became a dead letter." Gentile officials turned to other forms of harassment. They claimed that "the curse of polygamy" was the Utah Territory's major problem, and declared it their solemn public duty to clean up this "Augean stable," to purge plural marriage from American soil. In their simplistic approach to transforming Latter Day Saints culture, these territorial officials had failed "to dissect [Mormon] . . . institutions and determine where the church stopped and the state began." [4]

[4] Paxson, *American Frontier*, p. 570.

After the war, perceptive federal prosecutors hit upon the ploy of proceeding against polygamists by attacking the Mormon church law that regulated plural marriage. During October of 1871, Young and several other Mormon leaders were arrested and tried on charges of "lascivious cohabitation." They were convicted in the lower courts, but, on appeal, the territorial supreme court ruled that the defendants should be released because of lack of jurisdiction.

The Mormons, well-inured to harassment and public scorn from their tortured times in Missouri and Illinois, did not take this sustained maltreatment supinely. The council applied the great economic resources of the church to defend Mormons against prosecution in the territorial courts. A steady increase in Gentile migration to the Utah Territory after the war threatened to become a tide that would overcome the Mormon numerical advantage and erase their domination of the elective offices of the territory, particularly the legislature. To check the threat of conquest by suffrage, Mormons extended voting privileges to women, thereby more than doubling their electorate.

The campaign against polygamy in the Utah Territory intensified during this period. It took on the dimension of a national crusade as the *New York Herald* and other leading newspapers demanded its expurgation. Like the South, Utah was required to undergo a comprehensive social reconstruction as a condition of admission to the Union. Intemperate Radical Republicans went after Mormons with the same zeal that they went after ex-Confederates. A disproportionate amount of Congress' time between 1870 and 1896 was devoted to composing legislation to bring the stubborn Mormons to heel. One bill receiving strong support provided for prosecution of polygamists without jury trial. Another would have partitioned Utah and assigned segments of it to adjoining states and territories. Yet another measure would have disqualified polygamists from holding public office.

The Utah Commission

Finally on March 22, 1882, Congress passed the Edmunds Act, which was the work of Senator George Franklin Edmunds of Vermont. It provided for a fine of $500 and a prison term of up to five years for polygamists. The act banned polygamists from voting, holding public office, and serving on juries. A bill of attainder section of the statute declared children born of polygamous marriages after 1883 illegitimate. The Edmunds Act also created the Utah Commission, a five-member body to preside over the "cleansing" of Mormon institutions. Its duties included registration of voters and management of territorial elections. The commission took oaths of conformance, hoping thereby to exclude substantial numbers of Mormon voters by reason of polygamy and thus enable Gentiles to win control of the territorial assembly and adopt supporting legislation. In 1880, the Utah Territory's population was 144,000, of which 120,000 were

Mormons. By hard work and zealous application of the oath process, the Utah Commission was able to exclude only 12,000 men and women as polygamists.

Brigham Young, the vigorous and shrewd leader of the Mormons from their earliest days in Utah, died in 1877. John Taylor succeeded him as president of the Latter Day Saints Church. He submitted to the Utah Commission, subscribing to the oath under protest. Mormons were daily hounded by the Utah Commission and their agents. Posses of federal marshals invaded Mormon privacy and subjected them to coercion, harassment, and insult. Their industry faltered, their farms, ranches and businesses suffered from neglect caused by this federal invasion of their domain. Many church officials and thousands of Mormons went into hiding or fled Utah.

Federal prosecutors vigorously pushed polygamy trials under the Edmunds Act. By 1885, over 500 Mormons had been indicted, and 289 were serving jail terms. Stern enforcement of the Edmunds Act and the denial of franchise, jury service, and public office excluded the Saints' elite and emasculated Mormon leadership. Amendments to the act tightened the Mormon noose by delegating to the Utah Commission authority to seize Mormon church property and place it in the hands of court designates. They were thus deprived of the funds necessary to defend their members against prosecution.

Utah Statehood

President Taylor died in 1887. Mormon moderates gained control of Saints society, and at once they began to bend to the will of their federal oppressors. A convention of 1887 produced a constitution prohibiting polygamy. Congress was unimpressed, however, for plural marriage was still a church doctrine. The Utah Territorial assembly in 1888 adopted a law forbidding polygamy, and in 1890, a convocation of the Mormon church repealed the plural marriage doctrine. Three years later, President Benjamin Harrison—on the recommendation of the Utah Commission and in response to pressure from Mormon leaders—proclaimed amnesty for all Mormons who had followed the Edmunds Act since 1890.

In 1894, Congress passed the Utah Enabling Act, delegates were elected to a constitutional convention, which met in Salt Lake City and produced a constitution repudiating polygamy. President Cleveland signed the Utah Statehood Act on January 4, 1896, a merciful gesture that ended the Mormon commonwealth's legal agony.

THE TWIN TERRITORIES

With the admission of Utah, only New Mexico, Arizona, Oklahoma, and Indian Territory remained outside the pale of American statehood. This vast southwestern bloc extended from the Arkansas border to the Colorado

River and contained heavy concentrations of Indian and Spanish-American peoples with lifestyles unlike the approved patterns of Anglo society. National leaders adopted a superior, condescending posture toward these culturally disparate territories and required their Americanization as an essential condition for statehood.

In the late nineteenth century, the United States, through annexation and conquest, acquired the overseas territories of Hawaii, Puerto Rico, and the Philippines. The "white man's burden" attitude derived from the administration of these colonial areas was also applied by Congress to the deviant Southwest. During this period, Albert J. Beveridge of Indiana was chairman of the Senate Committee on Territories. His management policy for the Southwestern territories was ultra-conservative and his attitude contemptuous and imperious. He took a dim view of admitting the dissimilar Southwestern communities to the Union until the Americanization processes were completed. Because Oklahoma Territory received a heavy infusion of Anglo-American homesteaders between 1889 and 1900, it was the first, in the judgment of Congress, to become Americanized and therefore received the earliest attention in the state-making process.

By treaty commitment to scores of Indian nations, the federal government was obligated to preserve the area embraced by the present state of Oklahoma as a permanent tribal domain. However, these treaty assurances were threatened by the late 1870s. Most of the arable, well-watered regions of the trans-Missouri territory had been settled, and land hungry settlers began to cast covetous glances at the Indian Territory. By federal law, the future Sooner State was off-limits to settlers, except for cattlemen with grazing leases in the western part and permit holders among the Five Civilized Tribes.

The railroads were prominent in the movement to open Indian Territory to settlement. The M.K.T., Frisco, Rock Island, and Santa Fe lines crossed the Indian country and linked Missouri and Kansas trade centers with the greater Southwest. Except in the mining and timber regions of eastern Indian Territory, the sparsely settled nations and reservations made only small use of these lines. The railroad companies were hopeful that Indian Territory would soon be settled with a farmer on every quarter-section and thriving towns along the tracks.

Equally interested in opening the territory to settlement were officials of banking and mercantile firms in St. Louis, Kansas City, Topeka, and Wichita, who saw therein the rich prospects for investments and markets. Because railroad, banking, and commercial combinations were generally unpopular with the public during this period, a direct campaign by these interests to open Indian Territory to settlement would have aroused suspicion. Therefore, the homeseeker, who more closely accorded with the image of American democracy, was selected as a likely stalking horse for the business interests. Once the territory was opened, it was agreed, all would benefit.

Authority for removing the barriers to settlement, however, still had to come from Congress. The railroad lobby, one of the real powers behind the scenes in the national government, was responsible for most of the bills introduced in Congress between 1866 and 1889 proposing to open Indian Territory to settlement. Each proposal met vigorous opposition from tribal delegations, missionaries working among the Indians, traders, intermarried citizens, and others interested in maintaining the status quo in the Indian country. One of the most powerful groups working against opening Indian Territory was the cattleman's lobby.

The Boomers

The origins of triumph for the advocates of opening the Indian country appeared in 1879. Out of the railroad strategy sessions emerged a class of professional promoters called boomers. T. C. Sears, an attorney for the M.K.T., announced early that year that he and Elias C. Boudinot, the Cherokee attorney, had examined the treaties, laws, and land-title questions for Indian Territory. He claimed that they had found that 14 million acres of land in Indian Territory belonged to the public domain of the United States and was subject to entry by qualified homeseekers. "These lands are among the richest in the world," Sears declared. "Public attention is being called to them and my opinion is that, if Congress shall fail to make suitable provision for the opening of the Territory within a short time, the people will take the matter into their own hands and go down there and occupy and cultivate these lands." [5]

On February 17, 1879, the *Chicago Times* published an article written by Boudinot on the Indian Territory land question. The Cherokee attorney reiterated his claim that 14 million acres in the Indian country awaited the homeseeker. An accompanying map showed this vast tract as situated in the Kiowa, Comanche, and Cheyenne-Arapaho reservations, the Unassigned Lands—the so-called Oklahoma District contained nearly 2 million acres— and Greer County, then in dispute with Texas. Special attention was given to the Oklahoma District. Boudinot's article was widely copied by newspapers all over the United States. This article, Boudinot's many speeches on the subject, and a massive distribution of boomer literature describing the wondrous opportunities awaiting the homeseeker in Indian Territory had the desired effect. Three Oklahoma colonies were organized during the spring of 1879: one at Topeka, one in north Texas, and a third at Kansas City. Leaders of these colonies were Charles C. Carpenter, David L. Payne, and William L. Couch.

Carpenter, an adventurer of the Buffalo Bill Cody type, had once guided a caravan of intruders into the forbidden Black Hills country in the Dakota Territory. Indeed, his success there led him to hope for an

---

[5] Quoted in Arrell M. Gibson, *Oklahoma: A History of Five Centuries* (Norman, 1965), pp. 288–89.

equally fortunate outcome in the Indian Territory. Carpenter soon faded from the Indian Territory scene, but Payne and Couch persevered. Payne established a string of homeseeker camps along the Kansas border, near Arkansas City, Caldwell, and Hunnewell. Collectively these were called Payne's Oklahoma Colony. He regularly visited the camps, made speeches, and kept the hopes of his followers high with a newspaper called the *Oklahoma War Chief*. Between 1879 and 1884, Payne led several boomer raids into the "Promised Land." Each time federal cavalry from Fort Reno arrested Payne and the colonists and escorted them back to Kansas. Payne was aware of the publicity value of these boomer raids and always took along newspaper reporters on his excursions. At Payne's death in 1884, Couch succeeded to the leadership of the Oklahoma Colony and continued the boomer raids.

The boomer colonies and the movements into Indian Territory were a sustained protest against the barriers to settlement, and these demonstrations evoked widespread public interest and sympathy. The campaign to popularize the Indian country and to win support for removing the barriers to settlement was having a telling effect. Boomer charges of inequity in the use of Indian lands—primarily of cattlemen being treated as a privileged group—won over the Knights of Labor and other organizations. One labor leader declared: "The cause of the Oklahoma colonists is the cause of the poor man, the laborer." [6]

Congress finally responded by authorizing the opening of the Unassigned Lands, a 2 million-acre tract in the center of the Indian country; the opening was to take place in 1889. Because the Indian Territory lands had been popularized by the boomers and since the Unassigned Lands represented such a small settlement area, officials responsible for the opening realized there would be many more homeseekers than claims. To equalize opportunity, it was decided to settle the area by the land run. The rule against trespassing on Indian Territory lands was lifted three days previous to the opening to allow homeseekers time to gather on the four borders of the Unassigned Lands; in a short time homesteader camps crowded to the southern boundary in the Cherokee Outlet, east in the Sac and Fox country, south along the Canadian in the Chickasaw nation, and west in the Cheyenne-Arapaho country.

Opening Oklahoma Territory

Monday, April 22, 1889, dawned clear and bright. Fifty thousand homeseekers thronged the borders of Captain Payne's New Canaan, awaiting the starting signal. Then from the detachment of United States cavalry assigned for the day to supervise the race for homesteads there emerged a booted trooper: "Riding to a high point of ground, where he could be seen for miles each way with a flag in one hand and a bugle in the other, the

[6] Quoted in ibid., p. 292.

signal officer took his position. At precisely 12 o'clock he raised the bugle to his lips and gave the signal blast, long and loud, waving and dropping the flag at the same moment. Then began the race for homes.... It was a race free to all. None was barred." [7] By evening, nearly all of the 10,000 homestead claims as well as the town lots in Guthrie, Kingfisher, Oklahoma City, and Norman had been staked out.

Congress in its rush to open the Unassigned Lands had failed to provide for territorial government, and for well over a year the settlers, by grass-roots democracy and vigilante action, provided the law and order for this raw frontier community. In May of 1890, Congress adopted the Oklahoma Organic Act, establishing the traditional territorial government and including two provisions important to the growth of the Oklahoma Territory. First, it stipulated that all reservations in western Indian Territory, when opened to settlement, would be automatically annexed to Oklahoma Territory. The act also attached No-Man's Land to Oklahoma Territory. This ribbon of land, which became the Oklahoma Panhandle, had been a sort of territorial orphan. Its eastern boundary was established at 100° by the Adams-Onís Treaty in 1819; its southern boundary came from the annexation of Texas in 1845 and the Compromise of 1850, which cut off Texas at 36° 30'; the western boundary was set at 103°, by the organization of New Mexico Territory in 1850; and its northern boundary was established by the organization of Kansas Territory in 1854, which had a southern boundary at 37°.

Under authority of the Dawes Allotment Act, President Harrison appointed a commission to liquidate the lands of the tribes of western Indian Territory. This group was called the Cherokee Commission or the Jerome Commission—the latter from the name of its chairman, David H. Jerome, former governor of Michigan. The Jerome Commission negotiated allotment agreements with each of the tribes and assigned each tribal member a 160-acre allotment—except for the Kickapoos, who, because of their raids on Texas and their generally uncooperative attitude, were punished by being assigned only 80 acres each. The remaining land on each reservation was declared surplus, purchased by the federal government, and opened for homesteading. In 1896 the United States Supreme Court awarded Greer County—situated on Oklahoma Territory's southwestern corner and claimed by Texas—to the Oklahoma Territory.

From 1889, Oklahomans strove for statehood, but it was eighteen years after the first land run before this goal was achieved. Most of the American states created from the classic pattern set by the Northwest Ordinance began life as territories, and the land areas designated for future statehood were already established. However, the formation of Oklahoma only began with the Unassigned Lands. From this nucleus, the territory grew piecemeal through the years by land runs, congressional action, a lottery, and a court decision, until, in 1906, the Oklahoma Territory encompassed all of

[7] Quoted in ibid., p. 294.

present western Oklahoma. Every year from 1889 to 1907, statehood conventions were held in various towns over the territory. Regularly this sentiment crystallized into statehood proposals introduced in the Congress.

Congress deferred for several reasons. One was a consideration of geography. Oklahoma Territory occupied an area of about 40,000 square miles. Most of the states of the trans-Missouri region were at least twice this size. Certain congressional leaders held that the Oklahoma Territory should not receive statehood with such a limited domain. Politics entered the picture, too. Early Republican successes in local elections raised hopes among national Republican leaders that a safe Republican state could be established in the traditionally Democratic Southwest. Uncertainty caused Republican leaders to wait to see how strong and permanent their party's showing in the Oklahoma Territory would be.

Liquidation of Indian Territory

In addition there was the problem of Indian Territory—the community of five Indian nations, each pursuing a lifestyle regarded as incompatible with established American practices. By 1900, it was apparent that fusion of the Twin Territories was inevitable. First, in the view of Senator Beveridge and other obscurantists, joining Indian and Oklahoma territories would mix the dominant Anglo-American culture with the deviant Indian cultures and produce the Americanization they expected. And second, the early Republican majorities in the Oklahoma Territory elections had declined as increasing numbers of Southern homeseekers migrated to the new land. It was acknowledged that Indian Territory would be overwhelmingly Democratic. Therefore, rather than risk the rise of two Democratic states on the southwestern border, Republican leaders decided to fuse the Twin Territories into a single state, the reverse of their action in the case of Dakota Territory.

Before Congress could execute this plan, however, it had to prepare Indian Territory for fusion. This involved changing the Indian land system and liquidating the tribal governments. In 1893, Congress adopted a law amending the Dawes Act and making the Five Civilized Tribes subject to land allotment. The Dawes Commission, headed by Senator L. Dawes of Massachusetts, was to transform the common-ownership land system of Indian Territory to fee-simple ownership through the process of allotment. The Curtis Act, adopted in 1898, provided for the liquidation of tribal governments, none of which were to extend any longer than 1906. Leaders of the Cherokee, Choctaw, Creek, Seminole, and Chickasaw nations, however, were content with their situation, and for years they resisted every attempt by the federal government to interfere with what they regarded as the best possible arrangement for their people. They valiantly thwarted the attempts of the Dawes Commission to allot their lands. For five years they succeeded, but finally succumbed to the great power of the federal government and coercion by the Dawes Commission.

In 1897, beginning with the Choctaws and Chickasaws, tribal leaders began signing allotment agreements. Leaders of the Five Civilized Tribes were able to assure the assignment of all land to tribal members, except tracts reserved for townsites and other public purposes. There was thus no surplus land for homesteading in Indian Territory as there had been in Oklahoma Territory.

Leaders of the Five Civilized Tribes, dreading fusion with Oklahoma Territory, made a strong effort to form a separate Indian state to be called Sequoyah. In 1905, a constitutional convention met at Muskogee and drafted a constitution. When tribal leaders submitted the Sequoyah Constitution to Congress, that body finally was ready to act with finality on the Twin Territories. Congress passed the Oklahoma Enabling Act in 1906, providing for a constitutional convention of delegates elected from the Twin Territories to meet at Guthrie. Conditions in the Enabling Act included the requirement that the capital of the new state be at Guthrie, a Republican stronghold in Oklahoma Territory, and that prohibition of alcohol apply to Indian Territory and the Osage nation for twenty-one years.

Oklahoma Statehood

Alfalfa Bill Murray chaired the convention. The delegates composed a constitution that included many reforms from the Populist-Progressive legacy—initiative and referendum, a weak executive, power centered in the legislature, an elective judiciary, the long ballot, and alcohol prohibition, which was extended to the entire state. The convention almost included women's suffrage, but one of the delegates warned that such a step would surely "unsex" the female citizens of the new state. On November 16, 1907, President Theodore Roosevelt signed the Oklahoma Statehood Proclamation, and the forty-sixth state entered the Union.

NEW MEXICO AND ARIZONA

Following the admission of Oklahoma in 1907, only two territories—New Mexico and Arizona—remained in the contiguous New West. Both had endured a long period of colonial status. New Mexico Territory had been established in 1850, Arizona Territory in 1863. Through the years, statehood advocates had been active. Their principal antagonist was Senator Beveridge; he scorned both territories, referring to them as "backward areas," each "stifled by their Spanish heritage," "not equal in intellect, resources or population to the other states in the Union," their principal handicap that they were not "sufficiently American in their habits and customs." [8]

By 1890, New Mexico and Arizona had a widespread system of railways: the Santa Fe and Southern Pacific and local connecting lines linked

[8] Howard R. Lamar, The Far Southwest, 1846–1912 (New Haven, 1966), p. 17.

the territories with both the Mississippi Valley and the Pacific shore. Moreover, as a result of their long tutelage period, both territories had citizens experienced in politics and government. Their economies were expanding through additional development in mining, stockraising, and agriculture. By 1900, the New Mexico Territory had a population of nearly 200,000, the Arizona Territory about 125,000.

The Americanization Process

Both territories had received some congressional notice as other New West territories were considered for statehood. The Omnibus Bill of 1889 —which admitted North Dakota, South Dakota, Washington, and Montana—in its original form had included New Mexico. Every session, Arizona and New Mexico territorial delegates introduced statehood bills in Congress. An Arizona enabling act passed the House in 1892 but fell before the Senate because Republican leaders were "opposed to free coinage views" of Western senators. During 1893, at least five bills for Arizona and New Mexico statehood were introduced and turned aside. An omnibus bill to admit Arizona, New Mexico, and Oklahoma passed the House in 1902, but Senator Beveridge led its defeat in the Senate. He favored admitting "American" Oklahoma Territory, but persisted in his opposition to New Mexico and Arizona, referring to the latter as a "mining camp."

Shortly thereafter, Beveridge changed his position somewhat and agreed to support New Mexico and Arizona statehood on the condition that the two territories be joined into a single state. In 1906, an omnibus bill calling for the fusion of the Oklahoma Territory and Indian Territory into one state and the Arizona and New Mexico territories into another passed Congress. The Oklahoma portion of the statute was activated, the Twin Territories joined as the state of Oklahoma, and admission was accomplished the following year. However, the proposed merger with New Mexico was bitterly opposed in Arizona; it was claimed that the opposition came from a heavy increase in the Anglo-American mining population, which held a strong prejudice against Spanish-Americans.

New Mexico-Arizona Statehood

Finally in 1910, Congress passed an enabling act to permit New Mexico and Arizona to enter the Union as separate states. During the following year, conventions in both territories drafted constitutions. Congress found the New Mexico constitution sufficiently conservative to authorize its admission on January 6, 1912. The Arizona constitution, however, contained a recall provision that included the judiciary. President William H. Taft, a former jurist, objected to this section and returned the constitution to the Arizona convention for revision. The objectionable section was altered and, on February 12, 1912, he signed the proclamation admitting Arizona. Once safely in the Union, Arizona leaders restored recall of judges to the state constitution.

The admission of Arizona concluded state-making in the contiguous West. The political format of the vast territory from the Appalachians to the Pacific had been completed. There remained two territories in the maritime frontier—Hawaii and Alaska. Belatedly involved in the state-making process, these last two were incorporated into the American Union nearly half a century later.

SELECTED SOURCES

General studies that trace the vicissitudes of New West state-making include Earl S. Pomeroy, *The Pacific Slope* (New York, 1965); Howard R. Lamar, *The Far Southwest, 1946–1912: A Territorial History* (New Haven, 1966); Leonard Arrington, *The Changing Structure of the Mountain West, 1850–1950* (Logan, Utah, 1963); and John W. Caughey, *History of the Pacific Coast* (New York, 1938).

Absorption of New West territories into the American Union is traced in J. Sterling Morton and Albert Watkins, *History of Nebraska* (Lincoln, 1913), 3 vols.; James C. Olson, *History of Nebraska* (Lincoln, 1966); Richard A. Crabb, *Empire on the Platte* (New York, 1967); Elmer Ellis, *Henry Moore Teller: Defender of the West* (Caldwell, 1941); Robert G. Athearn, *High Country Empire* (New York, 1960); LeRoy R. Hafen, *Colorado and Its People* (New York, 1948), 2 vols.; Oscar O. Winther, *The Great Northwest* (New York, 1947); G. W. Fuller, *A History of the Pacific Northwest* (New York, 1931); Hubert H. Bancroft, *History of Washington, Idaho, and Montana, 1845–1880* (San Francisco, 1890); Joseph Schafer, *A History of the Pacific Northwest* (New York, 1922); J. W. Hulse, *The Nevada Adventure: A History* (Reno, 1965); J. G. Scrugham, *Nevada: A Narrative of the Conquest of a Frontier Land* (Chicago, 1935), 3 vols.; C. J. Brosnan, *History of the State of Idaho* (New York, 1918); J. M. Hamilton, *From Wilderness to Statehood: A History of Montana* (Portland, 1957); E. S. Meany, *History of the State of Washington* (New York, 1909); T. A. Larson, *History of Wyoming* (Lincoln, 1965); Howard G. Lamar, *Dakota Territory, 1861–1889* (New Haven, 1956); Lewis F. Crawford, *History of North Dakota* (New York, 1931); Doane Robinson, *History of South Dakota* (Rapid City, Ia., 1904); Leonard Arrington, *Great Basin Kingdom* (Cambridge, 1958); Orson F. Whitney, *History of Utah* (Salt Lake, 1904), 4 vols.; Warren A. Beck, *New Mexico: A History of Four Centuries* (Norman, 1962); Rufus K. Wyllys, *Arizona: The History of a Frontier State* (Phoenix, 1950); and Arrell M. Gibson, *Oklahoma: A History of Five Centuries* (Norman, 1965).

The Continuing Stream of Settlement: Custer County, Nebraska, *ca.* 1886.

Bound for the Klondike Gold Fields: Chilcoot Pass, Alaska, *ca.* 1898.

28

The Pacific Territories— Hawaii and Alaska

America's last frontier was the Pacific Basin, an oceanic province disposed in a broad triangle formed by Hawaii, Alaska, and the coastal states of California, Oregon, and Washington. Through the progression of American dominion into the Pacific Basin during the nineteenth century, Hawaii and Alaska became an extension of the New West frontier. The familiar Americanization processes, derived from Old West experience and refined in the contiguous New West, were applied, with some variations, to Hawaii and Alaska. Thus, American presence, established by the maritime traders and succeeded by expanding private and public interest, activated nationalizing currents that led to the acquisition of Hawaii and Alaska and ultimately—through the state-making process—to their integration into the American Union.

HAWAII

The Hawaiian archipelago has a land area of nearly 6,500 square miles distributed over the principal islands of Kauai, Oahu, Molokai, Maui, Lanai, and Hawaii. Situated approximately 20° north of the equator and 2,100 miles west of San Francisco in the trade-wind climatic zone, the islands bask in a mild climate. Hawaii's aboriginal people were bronze-skinned Polynesians who lived an easy life based on farming—which yielded abundant crops of bananas, breadfruit, yams, a starchy root called taro, and sugarcane. They also raised hogs and fowls, fished, and engaged in inter-island trade. Their original homeland was in the South Pacific—probably in the Society Islands. By the time of their discovery by Europeans, contact had been lost with Tahiti, and the Hawaiians were living an isolated oceanic existence.

Coming of the Haoles

Westerners discovered Hawaii rather belatedly. The British navigator, Captain James Cook of the *Resolution* and the *Discovery* chanced upon the islands during a search for a water passage through North America. This search for the Northwest Passage was Cook's third and last voyage of discovery. On January 18, 1778, Cook first touched at the island of Kauai. The inhabitants came out to the ships in small crafts to exchange garden produce and pigs for trade goods, mostly iron nails. Cook named the archipelago the Sandwich Islands after the Earl of Sandwich, First Lord of the Admiralty, then continued to the Northwest Coast of North America. After a fruitless search for the water strait during 1778, he returned to the islands to refit his ships, rest his crews, and take on provisions and water. During early 1779, on the beach at Kealakekua Bay, on the island of Hawaii, the islanders became enraged at demands that they return a ship's cutter they had stolen. In the ensuing melee, they killed Cook and several sailors and drove the survivors back to their ships. After completing the repair and refitting of the *Resolution*, the crewmen lifted anchor and departed the Sandwich Islands.

Cook's contact with the islands had several results. He introduced such Western goods as iron, livestock—goats and a boar and sow to improve local stock—and melon, onion, and pumpkin seeds. His crewmen consorted with native women, beginning a mixed population and introducing venereal disease, which became one of the scourges of the islands. Cook's North Pacific reconnaissance also assured future Western interest in the islands, for while in the Northwest, his men trafficked with local Indians for sea otter pelts. At Canton, it was soon found, these exquisite furs were much esteemed by Chinese merchants. Thus did the Sandwich Islands become the principal winter resort for maritime traders collecting sea otter pelts on the Northwest coast of America.

Official British interest in the Sandwich Islands continued. During the 1790s, George Vancouver—who had served as a young midshipman on Cook's last two voyages—made three more visits to Hawaii. He introduced cattle and sheep and urged the island chiefs to cede their lands to Great Britain. Kamehameha, ruler of the island of Hawaii, agreed, and on February 25, 1794, Vancouver raised the British flag over this largest of the Sandwich group; his crewmen nailed a copper plate announcing the cession to Kamehameha's door. The British government subsequently failed to confirm the cession.

By the 1780s, news of the rich Chinese market for sea otter pelts had attracted trading ships from France, Great Britain, and the United States to the Pacific Basin. Often, these ships remained away from their home ports for three years at a time. During the spring and summer, they coasted the Pacific Northwest, trading with Indian hunters for pelts; then they wintered in the Sandwich Islands, refitting their ships, resting their crews, and taking on stores of food, water, and wood. In 1804, ships from Russian

American Fur Company stations in Alaska first appeared in the islands to trade for cargoes of foodstuffs. Thereafter, for many years, Hawaii was the principal source of pork and other provisions for the Russian fur outposts in the Northwest.

American Maritime Traders Frontier

American maritime traders, most of them from New England, came to dominate the sea otter trade and the Hawaiian scene. *Haoles*—the native designation for aliens—used all the islands as winter stations; but after 1793, they concentrated on Oahu. A navigable channel through the reef provided access to a natural anchorage that could accommodate over 100 ships. Deep water close to shore permitted construction of wharves and warehouses. The port town of Honolulu evolved, which became the commercial, political, and social center of the Sandwich Islands.

Hawaii's natural and human resources increasingly were exploited by traders. The islands' productive farms yielded vast quantities of vegetables, fruit, and pork for the ships calling at Honolulu and other ports. The forests and sparkling streams supplied wood and water for ships' galleys. Hospitable native women provided companionship and pleasure for ship-bound crewmen, and increasingly, Hawaiian seamen, *kanakas*, were employed on the trader ships. American traders noted that the natives used a wood called iliahi from the upland forests to make musical instruments and ground the wood's aromatic heart into a powder for perfume. Americans collected cargoes of *iliahi*, which they called sandalwood, and carried it to Canton. Chinese craftsmen used it to carve fine chests and other decorative pieces and for conversion into pleasantly scented incense and perfume. The sandalwood trade increased American interest and profits in the islands.

Americanization of Hawaii

Hawaii's growing *haole* population, most of it American, had substantial effects on island life. Most *haoles* were seamen who preferred the easy life of these exotic islands to the harsh regimen aboard ship. The trading companies at Honolulu and other island ports required large numbers of Western employees to manage the docking and loading of ships, vessel supply and repair, and to receive sea otter pelts and stores of sandalwood in warehouses for transshipment to Canton.

In addition, many Americans were employed by the *aliis*, the island chiefs. They were much in demand as carpenters, sailmakers, boatbuilders, and gunsmiths. Increasingly, at the urging of the island chiefs, the maritime traders brought arms and ammunition to Hawaii, and Americans were employed to train Hawaiian troops and to maintain weapons. One island potentate had five Western advisers and an arsenal of three six-pound cannons, forty swivel guns, and a large supply of muskets. Kamehameha, chief of the island of Hawaii, had fifty Westerners in his retinue and possessed a large arsenal. In return for skills and service, island chiefs granted to each *haole* adviser a large tract of land, with servants and the right to take as many wives as he liked.

Unification of Hawaii

Gradually, the *haoles* turned from carpentry and boatmaking to state-making, and the combination of Western arms and advisers produced the unification of Hawaii. For centuries, the island chiefs had warred on one another, but contesting troops, armed with lances, shark's tooth knives, and slingshots, had never been able to win decisive battles. No island chief had ever achieved pre-eminence in the archipelago. The chief of Hawaii—the Big Island—was the shrewd and intelligent Kamehameha. Between 1782 and 1810, with the assistance of Western arms and advisers, trained troops, and a flotilla of gunboats, he conquered or forced tribute status from all the island chiefs and declared himself King of the Sandwich Islands—thereafter called the Kingdom of Hawaii after his home island.

Kamehameha maintained his power by requiring subdued island chiefs and their families to reside apart from their subjects at his court. He appointed governors for the islands—sometimes from his corps of *haole* retainers. The unification of Hawaii was timely and boded well for its continued independent existence. Kamehameha became wealthy by making the sandalwood trade and the supply of ships a royal monopoly. He also levied several royal imposts, including a tax on the sexual relations of Hawaiian women and *haole* sailors. When he integrated the island of Oahu into the kingdom, he established his royal residence at Honolulu and charged all ships entering the harbor an anchorage fee of $60.

In 1819, Kamehameha Nui ("the Great") died at the age of seventy. He was succeeded by his son Liholiho, who was proclaimed Kamehameha II. He ruled in partnership with the powerful Queen Regent Kaahumanu. Her influence was particularly decisive in Hawaiian affairs of state, for she continued the Westernization of Hawaii Kamehameha I had begun. She abolished the practice of commoners prostrating themselves before the *aliis* and the king. The powerful *kahunas*, or priests who presided over the native religion, regularly attempted to thwart the rising *haole* influence. Through intercession of Kaahumanu, a royal order directed destruction of images and abolition of the elaborate *kapu* system—the taboos. As Queen Regent, she set a precedent for women ruling the kingdom. She also assured the success of Western missionaries.

American Missionary Frontier

Missionary interest in Hawaii was derived from several *kanaka* seamen who had made their way aboard American trading vessels to home ports in New England. Several were enrolled as students at Cornwall Academy, an interracial school maintained at Cornwall, Connecticut, by the American Board of Commissioners for Foreign Missions—an ecumenical association of Congregational, Dutch Reformed, and Presbyterian churches. The academic success of the Hawaiian students stirred the interest of American Board officials, and it was decided to return the converts to the islands, accompanied by an American Board missionary party.

Congregational ministers Hiram Bingham of Vermont and Asa Thurston of Massachusetts were selected to head the mission. Their party, which included teachers and a printer, mechanic, physician, and several *kanaka* converts, reached the Kingdom of Hawaii in March of 1820. With royal permission, Bingham and Thurston established the first missions at Kailua and Honolulu. From these parent stations, they seeded mission schools and churches throughout the islands.

Queen Regent Kaahumanu greatly aided the missionary cause. When she became gravely ill, missionaries restored her to health and she was converted. Thereupon, she enthusiastically pressed other Hawaiian leaders to abandon the native religion and to join the mission church. Very quickly the American Board missionaries established the puritan tradition in Hawaii. They sought to purge Hawaii of its worldliness, paying particular heed to the abolition of bare bosoms, "lewd dancing," sexual freedom, and royal incest. In 1823, the royal household promulgated a moral code that included laws prohibiting gambling, dancing, fornication, and the sale of liquor; it also required strict observance of the Sabbath. Temperance societies flourished.

Missionaries reduced the Hawaiian language to written form, using the English alphabet. The mission press was kept busy publishing hymnals, translations of books of the Bible, and religious tracts. By 1838, nearly 100 Protestant workers manned the scattered island missions, and thousands of Hawaiians attended churches and schools. In 1854, missionary leaders formed the Hawaiian Evangelical Association; nine years later the association admitted Hawaiian clergymen.

Other religious groups also came to the islands. In 1827, French Catholic missionaries arrived. Partly because of covert Protestant missionary pressure, they were expelled by Hawaiian officials four years later. They returned in 1837, but the royal government, now overtly influenced by the American Board missionaries, banned absolutely the Catholic religion. During the 1850s, Mormons reached the islands and established several missionary settlements. Latter Day Saints produced the Book of Mormon in Hawaiian and established churches and schools. During the 1860s, Episcopalian missionaries arrived.

The period between 1820 and 1860 was a time of great social, economic, and political change for the kingdom, due largely to expanding American presence and influence. The missionary frontier contributed substantially to the Americanization of Hawaii, as missionaries basked in royal patronage and used their favored position to influence the monarchs to formulate law compatible with American Board morals. Their schools produced an educated Hawaiian and part-Hawaiian elite, trained in American sectarian and secular traditions. In addition, the sons of many American missionaries departed the church fold for the worldly pursuits of Hawaiian business and politics.

Hawaiian Economic Diversification

While American missionaries were reshaping Hawaiian society, American businessmen were producing concomitant economic and political change. A development that had an immense impact on the Hawaiian economy was the movement of the New England whaling fleet into the North Pacific. Whaler crews not only hunted and killed the whales; they also rendered oil from the blubber of the huge pelagic mammals in large pots on the decks; sometimes they dried the bones as well. Whale oil was used as an illuminant, and whale bone was used in the manufacture of women's garments, buggy whips, and surgical instruments. During the winter season, as many as 100 whaling ships were anchored at Honolulu, Lahaina, and Hilo, creating lively disorder—particularly in Honolulu, where 3,000 crewmen jammed the streets. Hawaiian maids flocked to the shores to exchange favors for silks, satins, and perfumes. Whaler crews enriched the townspeople and shocked the missionaries, who warned that "the Devil is busily engaged."

Trading continued to flourish. Goods for the islands and Far East markets were stored in vast warehouses at Honolulu. Of all the ships calling at Hawaiian ports, 80 percent were American. But an economic development of even greater magnitude for the future of Hawaii was the rise of commercial sugarcane culture. This enterprise expanded so rapidly that by 1850 the native labor supply was inadequate, and American sugar growers imported 200 workers from China. When their labor contracts expired, many of the coolies left the sugar plantations and established small businesses in the towns. Others turned to raising rice, which also became an important export crop. The continuing shortage of agricultural laborers during the 1860s led American planters to begin the importation of Japanese workers. In addition, they brought in Portuguese, Russians, Blacks from the United States, and additional Chinese. Japan continued to supply the greatest number of plantation laborers; by 1896, the Japanese in Hawaii numbered nearly 25,000. Increasingly, Hawaii's society was becoming pluralistic.

The Changing Hawaiian Government

During this period (1820–1860), there also occurred a comprehensive restructuring of the Hawaiian government. Graduates of the mission schools and mixed Hawaiian-American descendants of traders began to agitate for political change. This indigenous pressure and mounting American influence in 1840 produced a constitutional monarchy. The constitution contained a bill of rights, provided for an elective national bicameral assembly, and committed the royal government to land reform. Commoners were granted the right to own land. Until this time, the land of the islands was regarded as crown property, and it was held by commoners and *haoles* only at the pleasure of the monarch. To activate this section of the constitution, the national assembly and the royal household carried out the Great Mahele, or land distribution. Small tracts were assigned to commoners in fee simple, and the royal family gave up all rights to the land except the reserved crown estates. In addition, the national assembly adopted laws creating a cabinet, a civil service, and a judiciary, and granting suffrage to all native males.

American presence and influence in Hawaiian affairs was manifested in the management of the new constitutional monarchy. John Ricord, a lawyer from New York, was appointed attorney general of the kingdom; William Lee, also from New York, was named chief justice of the Hawaiian Supreme Court; and Robert C. Wyllie, a Scottish immigrant from the United States, served as minister of foreign affairs. The most powerful man in Hawaii during the early constitutional period was Gerrit Judd from New York. He had been assigned to the Hawaiian mission as a physician. During his missionary assignment, he had learned the Hawaiian language, then become a royal adviser. By the 1840s, he was supreme, a *de facto* prime minister. He controlled the royal treasury, developed the land-distribution plan and—being an ardent American annexationist—formulated the royal policy that excluded official French and British influence in the kingdom. Another American, James J. Jarvis, published the weekly *Polynesian* in Honolulu; in 1844 it became the official organ of the royal government.

Another manifestation of mounting American presence and activity in Hawaii was in land ownership. An 1841 law permitted governors of the islands to lease land to foreigners for no more than fifty years. Nine years later, a change in the land code permitted foreigners to buy land. By the end of the century, *haoles*, mostly Americans, owned three-fourths of the island kingdom's land.

By 1840, American private interests in the Kingdom of Hawaii had reached a point that required public action by its government. British and French gestures toward Hawaii were threatening the entrenched American position. Naval commanders from these nations zealously watched for excuses to commandeer Honolulu and other ports with gunboat squadrons, under the pretext of protecting the lives and property of their own nationals. On two occasions during the early 1840s, British and French naval forces occupied Hawaiian ports and forced *de facto* cessions of the island kingdom. The British and French governments disavowed these actions, but they created an ideal context in which the American government could respond in a protective way to the compelling private interests of *its* citizens.

Extension of Nationalizing Currents to Hawaii

During 1842, royal Hawaiian representatives traveled to Washington and warned American officials that if the United States did not extend protection to Hawaii, the royal government would probably have to accept annexation by Great Britain or France. Thereupon, officials in the Tyler administration issued a statement that no nation should seek exclusive commercial or colonial privileges in Hawaii. In addition, it was declared, American interests there were paramount and the United States would oppose the attempt of any nation to appropriate the island kingdom. In effect, the national government extended the Monroe Doctrine to Hawaii. Great Britain and France subsequently issued statements promising to respect the independence of Hawaii.

Nationalizing currents, activated by American presence and expanding interests, were pulsing toward Hawaii, much as they had in Texas and Oregon. The American government's 1842 declaration precipitated a movement in the United States to annex Hawaii. During the 1840s, the American nation had completed its territorial face on the Pacific shore, commerce with the Far East was increasing, and Congress was willing to support the development of a larger fleet in the Pacific. In 1854, Secretary of State William L. Marcy and Hawaiian representatives negotiated a treaty providing for the annexation of Hawaii. The Senate rejected the pact for several reasons, one being the opposition of Louisiana sugar growers. The next year Marcy attempted to bind Hawaii commercially to the United States with a reciprocity treaty. This proposal also failed in the Senate, due, again, to the influence of the Louisiana sugar planters. In 1867, Secretary of State William H. Seward and Hawaiian representatives concluded another reciprocity treaty, which the Senate rejected yet again.

Hawaii was finally integrated into American economic life in 1875, when the Hawaiian reciprocity treaty devised by Secretary of State Hamilton Fish was approved. It provided for mutual reduction of tariffs, and Hawaiian sugar was to enter the United States duty free. Later integrative treaties with Hawaii included a pact concluded in 1887, which granted to the United States the use of Pearl Harbor as a naval station.

The Hawaiian Republic

In the year of the Pearl Harbor treaty, leaders in the Hawaiian national assembly adopted a reform constitution that established legislative preeminence and drastically reduced royal prerogative. Queen Liliuokalani, who had ascended the throne in 1890, opposed the restrictive constitution, and in 1892 she appealed to native Hawaiians to support her in restoring royal supremacy. The reform party, braced by powerful business interests, mostly American planters, formed a committee of public safety. Its leaders appealed to John L. Stevens, the American minister and an annexationist, for protection.

Anchored in the quiet waters of Honolulu Bay was the *U.S.S. Boston*. At Stevens' request, the warship's commander sent ashore a heavily armed party of 162 marines and sailors, with two field pieces and Gatling guns. Ostensibly, their mission was to protect American lives and property, but officers placed the men embarrassingly near the royal palace. Thus, by a bloodless coup, the insurgent reform party dispatched the monarchy. On January 18, 1893, the day after the fall of Queen Liliuokalani, Stevens recognized the new government on behalf of the United States. The committee of public safety created a provisional government, which in turn proclaimed the Republic of Hawaii. The Queen officially submitted on February 1, 1893, and Stevens declared Hawaii a United States protectorate and raised the American flag over the capital. Sanford Dole, who was descended from missionary stock, was selected as president of the new republic.

American Annexation

Hawaii's new government sent a five-man commission to Washington to offer the island to the United States. Annexation sentiment on the continent was divided largely along partisan lines: the Republican party favored absorption of Hawaii into the American community; the Democratic party opposed it. Early in 1893, Hawaiian representatives and State Department officials concluded an annexation treaty. Republican President Benjamin Harrison submitted the treaty to the Senate, but before its consideration was completed, the Democratic Grover Cleveland was installed as president. Responding to his party's opposition, Cleveland withdrew the treaty and commissioned James H. Blount to investigate conditions in Hawaii.

At Honolulu, Blount lowered the American flag and withdrew the marine-sailor detachment. In his report to Cleveland, Blount charged that Stevens had exerted unwarranted interference to bring about Queen Liliuokalani's overthrow, and he claimed that Hawaiians were opposed to annexation. Braced by Blount's findings, Cleveland refused to support the annexation treaty, and for most of the decade, the Republic of Hawaii drifted in the limbo of mainland partisan politics.

Expansionists, of course, continued to urge Hawaiian annexation. Most of the American press favored annexation. Editors pointed to growing Japanese military strength and the continued colonial ambitions of Great Britain and warned the public of the threat these nations posed to the established American interests in the Pacific, centering on Hawaii. One of the most influential persons of the decade was Alfred Thayer Mahan, an American writer, an internationally recognized authority on naval affairs, and an advocate of Hawaiian annexation. In 1890, he published *Influence of Sea Power on History,* in which he articulated the thesis that control of the seas determines a nation's destiny. In the Hawaiian context, Mahan urged that the United States, as an established naval power in the Pacific, required land stations to support its fleet, and that Hawaii was the most strategically located naval support station in that vast water hemisphere.

The Republicans won the presidential election of 1896, and President William McKinley was committed to fulfill his party's expansionist desires.

In 1897, a new annexation treaty was defeated in the Senate, but the Pacific expansion cause received a strong assist the following year from the Spanish-American War. American operations against Spanish territory in the Pacific confirmed Mahan's thesis that the Hawaiian archipelago was required to provide the first line of defense for the mainland facing the Pacific and to protect America's mounting Far East interest. During the war, American bases in Hawaii were the principal support stations for the movement of ships and troops to the battle zone.

Public exultation over Commodore George Dewey's victory over the Spanish at Manila on May 1, 1898, provided the fortuitous setting for action by the annexation advocates. Senate Democratic opposition to annexation was offset by Republican resort to the joint resolution—the method followed by Congress in the case of Texas. A joint resolution for annexation passed the House on June 15, the Senate on July 6, and, on August 11, 1898, the Republic of Hawaii was absorbed by the United States.

The American nation approached fulfillment of its destiny in the Pacific Basin frontier by the acquisition of Hawaii. Soon after annexation Hawaiians began to demand full status in the American Union, but federal leaders deferred statehood for over half a century. In the meantime, consummation of national destiny in the Pacific Basin occurred with the acquisition of Alaska.

ALASKA

Alaska, the nation's largest state, embraces an area equal to one-fifth of the contiguous United States. This gargantuan territory is rimmed by the Coastal Range from its southern extremity to the Bering Strait. In the Bering Strait area, the Coastal Range is a mixture of mountains and glaciers, some which are larger than Rhode Island. Alaska's vast interior is comprised of plains and intermontane plateaus and is drained by the Yukon River. Most of the northern interior—in the perma-frost area—is covered with tundra-type vegetation; the lower interior and coastal range are cloaked with dense coniferous forest growth. Only the southern coast enjoys a mild climate; there marine West Coast climatic influences prevail. In most of Alaska's interior, the climate provides, at most, from one to four months of above-freezing average temperatures; no month of the year averages above 50°. In the interior, south of the Arctic tundra zone, is a belt of subarctic climate, characterized by long cold winters and brief cool summers.

The Russian Outpost in America

Alaska began its modern life as a Russian fur outpost. In 1728, Peter the Great commissioned Vitus Bering, a Danish navigator serving in the Russian Imperial Navy, to explore the North Pacific. From his base at Kamchatka, Bering probed the Siberian coast as far as the Bering Strait.

On a second expedition, in 1741, Bering proceeded south of the strait and explored the Alaskan coast. Russian fur men, the *promyshlenniki*, from Kamchatka, followed up Bering's discoveries, moving into the North Pacific in small trading ships. From temporary stations in the Aleutian Islands, the *promyshlenniki* visited the offshore Alaskan islands and traded with native peoples.

The first permanent Russian settlement in Alaska was established in 1784 on the island of Kodiak by Gregory Shelikov and a party of traders. Shelivok's manager at Kodiak was Alexander Baranov. Baranov established the Russian technique of Alaskan fur gathering whereby each *promyshlenniki* brought under his control a band of Aleut hunters. The Aleuts, the island-dwelling aborigines of the Aleutian group, were regarded as superior to all other native hunters. They stalked the sea otter, seal, and other fur-bearing creatures from small, swift-moving skin-covered craft called bidarkas. Russian traders—each with his own retinue of Aleut hunters—were carried by trading ships from Kodiak into the Alaskan bays and inlets; they were set ashore to collect furs and were picked up when their hunting was finished.

The Russian American Company

In 1799, the Russian government chartered the Russian American Company and granted it a monopoly of the Alaskan trade. Baranov was appointed resident manager. Saturation hunting soon obliterated the sea otter and other fur-bearing animals on Kodiak and adjacent islands, forcing Baranov to seek new fur territory on the Alaskan mainland. Sitka became the favored station in the string of Russian mainland settlements.

Baranov also imported agricultural workers, seeds, livestock, and implements from Russia and attempted to develop an agricultural colony at Sitka. The Russian American Company was perennially short of food, and Baranov hoped to produce sufficient grain and beef to sustain the scattered trading settlements. The agricultural colony failed, mostly because of unfavorable soil and climate conditions. In 1802, Tlingit Indians massacred the Russians at Sitka. With the help of naval vessels, Baranov recaptured Sitka, dispersed the Tlingits, and founded a new settlement. In 1808, he moved his headquarters from Kodiak to Sitka.

The continuing problem of providing adequate food for the Alaskan settlements led Baranov to trade sea otter pelts to Yankee ship captains for cargoes of grain and salted meat. In 1812, he established the Fort Ross (Russ) settlement near Bodega Bay in northern California and colonized it with agricultural workers. The California colony did not produce the quantities of grain and beef required by the Alaskan traders, but it did enable Baranov to purchase mission-produced grain from the padres. Even so, most of the food required came from Hawaii.

In spite of food shortages, Baranov continued to found new trading settlements in Alaska; and by 1840, the Russians occupied twelve towns—including Sitka, Kodiak, and Unalaska—the principal Alaskan coastal areas and adjacent islands south of the Yukon River. In 1824 and 1825, Russian treaties with the United States and Great Britain established the southern limit of Russian Alaska at 54°40′. British fur brigades from the Hudson's Bay Company at Fort Vancouver on the Columbia River had moved across British Columbia and, by 1830, were seriously competing with the Russian traders for the resources of southern Alaska. To check this intrusion, Russian American Company officials established the fortified settlement of Wrangell on the Stikine River near the boundary.

By 1820, the Tlingits, Haidas, Tsimshians, Timehs, and other Alaskan tribes were under nominal Russian control. Missionaries assisted the company in the aboriginal conquest by maintaining missions among the tribes. Several thousand Indians were converted to the Russian Orthodox faith. Nonetheless, throughout the Russian period, the Tlingits persisted in resistance and were a perennial threat to the settlements. Their power gradually declined, however, which was more the result of smallpox and venereal disease than the force of Russian arms. As saturation hunting erased the fur resources of coastal Alaska, Russian traders moved to the interior and established new pelt territories. In the later years of the occupation of Alaska, company officials diversified their exploitation of the region's natural bounty. Shipbuilding became an important industry, and expansion of the company's North Pacific fleet enabled it to compete with New England whalers in Bering Strait waters. In addition, the Russian American Company received a profitable annual return from leasing skilled Aleut hunters to American maritime traders, who used the natives to gather sea otter pelts in clandestine forays into the bays and inlets of Spanish California.

In keeping with their desire to shift from near total reliance on the fur trade to other exploitive enterprises, Russian American officials also made an extensive mineral reconnaissance of Alaska. Geological expeditions found small quantities of gold in placers on the Kenai Peninsula and promising signs of lignite coal at several coastal locations. The company imported mining machinery from the United States and miners from Germany and opened a coal mine at Port Graham on Cook Inlet. The crew of 131 workers produced about thirty-five tons daily; the output was used as household fuel at Sitka. After the California gold rush, Alaskan ice became another important source of income for the Russian American Company. Until 1852, ice for San Francisco had to come from the eastern United States around Cape Horn; that year the American ship *Bacchus* reached Sitka and took on a cargo of 250 tons from the company ice houses at $25 a ton. Thereafter, Russian Alaska supplied ice to American towns on the Pacific coast.

Russianization of Alaska

Sitka was the center for Russian culture in Alaska. Baroness Wrangell and Princess Maksoutoff, wives of government officials assigned to Russian

America, attempted to emulate the elegance of the St. Petersburg court in the North Pacific wilderness. There were facilities there for the military, civil, and business establishment, the Cathedral of St. Michael, and Baranov Castle. The Russian American Company maintained the Colonial Academy to train surveyors, navigators, printers, and accountants for service in Alaska, and Lady Etolin's school for young ladies provided instruction in needlework, social graces, and household arts. In 1841, the Russian Orthodox Church established the Sitka Seminary. Nonetheless, Russian Alaska did not attract a substantial migration from Russia. In 1845, there were only 700 Russians and 1,500 people of mixed parentage scattered throughout the Alaskan coastal and island settlements. Isolation was certainly one important limiting factor. Mail from St. Petersburg arrived only once a year, and an exchange of letters required two years.

The Russian American Company's exploitation of Alaska's natural and human resources was cruel and thorough. Its early reliance on the fur trade had, by 1840, exhausted the readily accessible pelt regions: "gone were the roistering days of the old *promyshlenniki*, prodigal of life, contemptuous of danger, who had plundered and murdered the natives, had robbed them of their women, had exposed themselves recklessly to every hazard, had endured the ravages of scurvy, and had suffered shipwreck or perished at sea." [1] The Russian population in Alaska remained sparse, and in spite of serious attempts at diversification, the company was unable to develop a substitute enterprise as glamorous and profitable as the fur trade. Moreover, the company had built up a debt of nearly $6 million to Russian and international suppliers.

By 1840, there were increasing manifestations of Russian American Company disinterest in Alaska. One was the sale of Fort Ross on the California coast to John Sutter for 30,000 piastres. Another was an agreement between the Russian American Company and the Hudsons' Bay Company, which leased to the latter the southeastern Alaskan mainland, including the port of Wrangell on the Stikine River.

Mounting Russian disinterest in Alaska was matched by growing American interest in this North Pacific territory. American maritime traders had trafficked for pelts in Russian Alaska, they had carried meat and grain to the Russian American Company trading settlements, and had leased Aleut hunters. After 1820, American whaling ships were also a part of the growing American presence in the North Pacific, and in 1852, the American Russian Company of San Francisco was formed to engage in the Alaskan ice trade.

Russian-American cooperation was carried into the early 1860s through a scheme to establish telegraphic communications between San Francisco and St. Petersburg; a cable was to be laid across California, Oregon, Washington, British Columbia, and Alaska to the Bering Strait. Work on

[1] Stuart R. Tompkins, *Promyshlennik and Sourdough* (Norman, 1945), p. 150.

the Alaskan telegraph during 1865 progressed as far as the upper Yukon Basin at a cost of over $3 million. The following year, word came of the completion of the Atlantic cable and the Pacific project was abandoned. Sections of the telegraph were used for local communication in the northern wilderness. An important side effect of the Alaskan telegraph project was that its promotion in the United States attracted wide American interest in this northern territory.

American Acquisition of Alaska

During the 1860s, Edouard de Stoeckl, Russian minister to the United States, regularly hinted to Secretary of State William H. Seward that his government would consider sale of Alaska to the United States. It was no secret that the Russian government wished to sell the territory for a sum sufficient to liquidate the Russian American Company debt, estimated at the time to be $6,500,000. The British-sponsored Hudsons' Bay Company had a primary interest in Alaska through its lease of the southeastern section and the port of Wrangell from the Russian American Company. Russia, however, still smarted from its defeat at the hands of the British in the Crimean War and was willing to favor the United States.

Seward and Stoeckl agreed upon a purchase price of $7,200,000, and the Alaskan Purchase Treaty, signed on March 30, 1867, was readily approved by the Senate. However, when the House of Representatives came to consider the appropriation to consummate the purchase, considerable opposition developed. After much lobbying and some alleged bribery by the treaty managers, the House approved the appropriation. On October 18, 1867, General L. H. Rousseau, representing the United States, and Captain T. Postchouroff, representing the Russian government, concluded transfer ceremonies at Sitka—including lowering the Russian flag and raising the American flag.

Early American Management of Alaska

At the time of transfer, national leaders were uncertain as to what to do with Alaska, and for years it was ruled by executive order. President Andrew Johnson placed Alaska under the War Department, and the new territory was controlled by the army until 1877. Under military rule, 500 infantry and artillery personnel were scattered at six posts in Alaska; the principal stations were at Sitka and Wrangell. In 1868, the population of Alaska consisted of about 500 Russians, 1,500 people of mixed backgrounds, 300 Americans and other nationals, and perhaps 30,000 Indians, Aleuts, and Eskimos. Customs and fur-trading license questions were under the jurisdiction of courts in Washington, Oregon, and California.

Scarcely a month after the transfer, Americans at Sitka produced a charter providing for a local government of an elective mayor and council. A school was also organized. The military government recognized the action and authorized the Sitka mayor's court to settle local questions of law and order. The first American newspaper, the *Alaskan Times*, was founded at Sitka on May 1, 1868, by Thomas J. Murphy.

After the American takeover, Alaska became the scene of intensive activity by the exploitive frontier that at this time was prodigally plundering other portions of the New West. San Francisco businessmen formed several firms to engage in the ice trade, trade for furs with the Indian tribes, and hunt seals. The Secretary of the Treasury, who controlled Alaskan hunting permits, granted one of the San Francisco firms, the Alaska Commercial Company, exclusive rights to hunt seals on the Pribilof Islands for twenty years. This company also engaged in the land fur trade and maintained regular steamer service to several Alaskan ports. Whaling and salmon fishing were also important enterprises during the early American exploitive era in Alaska. The first salmon canneries were established on Prince of Wales Island and at Sitka in 1878–1879; by the turn of the century, there were fifty-five canneries on the Alaskan coast. This industry was controlled by corporations from the states, which moved their crews into the Alaskan settlements each canning season, then returned them to the states when the catch had been processed.

Alaskans charged that the canning corporations, the Alaska Commercial Company and other states-based enterprises, were opposed to territorial government for Alaska since local control would apply regulations and taxes to these businesses. The Alaska Commercial Company and other firms profiting from the status quo maintained a lobby in Washington—focused on the Senate—to thwart any change in Alaska's governance. Thus, proposals to attach Alaska to Washington as a county in order to improve local civil government, to survey Alaska and divide the land into homesteads and promote agricultural settlement, and to protect natural resources were defeated in the Congress. Local residents appealed regularly to Congress for a territorial government, but without success. By 1877, the War Department had withdrawn its troops from Alaskan posts. Thereafter, the only United States official in Alaska was the customs collector at Sitka; he administered the territory until Congress passed the Alaskan Government Act in 1884. Even then, Alaska continued to be a neglected land.

The Mining Frontier in Alaska

It was the extension of the mining frontier to Alaska that finally broke the power of the exploitive corporations and brought civil government to the northland. In the early 1870s, gold was found in western British Columbia, and 13,000 miners rushed to the scene. Prospectors worked along the Stikine River into coastal Alaska. Wrangell, the port of entry for the miners, became a boom town. Prospecting across southeastern Alaska led, in 1880, to the discovery of gold quartz formations along the Gastineau Channel. Juneau was the principal settlement for this field.

While as yet no great amounts of gold had been found, enough placer mineral was taken each year to maintain interest. Then, in 1896, the northland's big strike occurred in the Canadian portion of the Yukon, the Klondike district, about 100 miles from the Alaskan boundary. The rush to the Klondike field lasted from 1897 to 1900 and attracted an estimated 100,000 gold seekers. Dawson City, center for the Klondike field, had a population of 30,000 by 1900.

At first the Klondike was a "poor man's camp." Harsh winters and frozen ground prevented prospectors from working their placers more than two months a year to a depth of about four feet. Gradually they applied the Siberian mining method—using fires to thaw the ground—which made it possible to work the diggings twelve months of the year. In the frozen ground, miners could shaft and tunnel without worrying about cave-ins or water filling their workings. Some miners used steam piped into the shafts and tunnels to work the ore beds. By 1900, large companies with steam shovels, mechanical separators, and dredges entered the Klondike, and the "poor man's camp" era ended. An estimated $200 million in gold was taken from the Canadian Klondike during the rush period.

Prospectors moved from the Canadian Yukon into Alaska and found gold at several locations, using methods that had proved successful in the Klondike. In 1898 one of the most spectacular fields was developed at Nome, on the seashore and tundra where Anvil Creek empties into the Bering Sea. Within two years, Nome had a population of 10,000. At the same time, prospectors were opening the rich Fairbanks field. The Klondike, Nome, and Fairbanks gold rushes popularized and populated Alaska. This north Pacific province doubled in population—to nearly 65,000— during the decade between 1890 and 1900. The broad prospector reconnaissance for gold also led to the discovery of copper, lead, and coal, and of several oil seeps—spots where petroleum oozes up out of the ground.

Miners working the Copper River area near Chitina found rich copper deposits. In 1900, J. P. Morgan and Simon Guggenheim established the Kennecott Copper Company, to exploit the Copper River lodes. The company built one of Alaska's first railroads, which ran from Cordova to Chitina. Ores from the Copper River mines were refined at smelters in the Puget Sound area.

District of Alaska

The sweep of the mining frontier across Alaska produced familiar results. Miners founded towns and demanded organized government. Juneau, with a population of 1,000, was the leader in this movement. During 1881, several Alaskan conventions produced petitions urging Congress to act. M. D. Ball, Collector of Customs at Sitka, was selected as the delegate to go to Washington and appeal to Congress. Ball was not taken too seriously at first, but he persevered; and in 1884, Congress passed the Alaska Organic Act. It provided for appointment of a governor, judiciary, and other essentials of a territorial-government apparatus; but curiously, the law designated Alaska a "district" rather than a territory. J. H. Kinkhead was appointed governor.

Both Alaska and Hawaii had to wait nearly sixty years for acceptance into the American Union. Their non-contiguous locations and non-Anglo cultures were the principal reasons for holding statehood advocates in abeyance for so long. The ultimate reception of Alaska and Hawaii in the twentieth century was the result of the West's new national economic and political leadership, of technological advances—particularly in air travel and instantaneous communication—and of a realization of the strategic importance of these Pacific Basin territories to the national defense.

SELECTED SOURCES

American expansion into the Pacific Basin leading to the acquisition of Hawaii and Alaska is discussed in R. S. Kuykendall, *The Hawaiian Kingdom* (Honolulu, 1967), 3 vols.; Norris Potter and L. M. Kasdon, *Hawaii, Our Island State* (Columbus, 1964); Chevigny Hector, *Russian America: The Great Alaskan Venture, 1741–1867* (New York, 1965); and Clarence C. Halley, *Alaska, Past and Present* (Portland, 1970).

The Americanization, annexation and absorption of Hawaii into the American Union is the subject of *Gavan Daws, *Shoal of Time: A History of the Hawaiian Islands* (New York, 1968); A. G. Day, *Hawaii: Fiftieth State* (New York, 1960); and Edward Joesting, *Hawaii: An Uncommon History* (New York, 1972).

The Americanization, acquisition and absorption of Alaska into the American Union is the subject of S. B. Okun, *The Russian American Company* (Cambridge, 1951); H. W. Clark, *Alaska: The Last Frontier* (New York, 1939); Ernest Gruening, *The State of Alaska* (New York, 1954); *A. W. Shiels, *Russian America and the Purchase of Alaska* (Bellingham, 1949); Merle Colby, *A Guide to Alaska* (New York, 1941); and J. P. Nichols, *Alaska: A History of Its Administration, Exploitation, and Industrial Development During Its First Half Century Under the Rule of the United States* (Cleveland, 1924).

* Available in paperback.

Mansion in Oklahoma: Homesteader Family
and Dugout Home Near Guthrie, *ca.* 1889.

29

Pioneer Society
in the
New West

THE New West's social milieu was in most respects a continuum of Old West society. The types of frontiers formed and perfected in the Old West, in recurring patterns, carried American dominion across the trans-Missouri region and out into the Pacific Basin. However, in the New West there occurred an alteration in tempo and order of progression of the frontiers. The agrarian frontier, which had been an early and predominant economic and social force in Old West development, lagged behind in the New West and did not become a noticeable contributor to that region's social evolution until after 1870. Instead, it was the mining frontier that served as the most important instrument for populating and developing the trans-Missouri region.

THE AGRARIAN LAG

During the antebellum years, agriculture was practiced on the New West's eastern margins in Indian Territory and Texas, in the Pacific Northwest, and at irrigated locations in the desert Southwest and the Great Basin. In addition, some farming developed around the mining camps as supportive enterprises. But the trans-Missouri region's vast interior remained mostly untouched by the plowman until relatively late in the New West's pioneer period.

Deterrents to Agrarian Occupation

This lag in the progress of the agrarian frontier was caused by several factors. One of the most important was the isolation from any but relatively local markets; in most of the New West, there was no river transport grid comparable to the Old West's Mississippi Valley waterway with its easy access to the Gulf of Mexico.

Another deterrent was the sustained competition for land. One source of competition was the Indian. The interior of the New West was populated by large concentrations of aborigines. Some tribes, including the Siouan peoples of the Northern Plains, the Cheyennes and Arapahoes of the Central Plains, and the Kiowas and Comanches of the Southern Plains, were indigenous. Other tribes, including the Cherokees, Choctaws, Nez Perces, Modocs, and many more were colonists recently resettled on reservations from the eastern United States and the Far West in order to make room for the expanding Anglo-American settlements. Several of the tribes resisted fiercely and were a serious military threat to the occupation of the region by the agrarian frontier. The other principal competitor for the New West's interior lands was the stockman. During the post–Civil War bonanza period of the range-cattle industry, cattlemen had occupied much of the trans-Missouri region's choice land and established highly profitable ranching empires. Farmers found ranchmen belligerent antagonists, often as dangerous as Indians.

Yet, perhaps the most compelling deterrent to the flow of the agrarian frontier into the New West was the character of its physical environment as well as its popular image. The trans-Missouri region was unlike any American territory yet broken by the plow. It required tools, methods, and crops unfamiliar to the Old West farmer, and, as experience proved, demanded special human attributes of commitment, toughness, and tenacity to survive and succeed. Moreover, the interior was generally lacking in both surface water and the forest cover needed to provide wood for building material, enclosures, and fuel. And the continuing popular image of the region as an arid wasteland—the Great American Desert—fixed on the public mind by early nineteenth-century explorer's accounts—gave the farmer-pioneer a strong reason to hesitate.

Removing the Deterrents

By 1870, these deterrents were in the process of being overcome. An expanding railroad grid provided some access to markets, helped reduce isolation, and contributed materially to comprehensive agrarian occupation. Continuing military action by the United States army conquered the resisting interior tribes, who as vanquished people were forced to cede to the national government their claim to vast portions of the interior and to accept fixed residence on drastically diminished reservations. After 1887, the General Allotment Act further reduced the Indian reservations and opened additional agricultural lands to the farmer.

Federal officials assisted by checking the gross appropriation of vast tracts of New West public domain land by stockmen and enforcing a ban on ranch enclosures on public lands. Laws for dispensing the public domain in small parcels, favorable to the farmer, caused widespread displacement of stockmen in this region. Similarly, technological developments leading to the production of cheap barbed wire and improved well-drilling and

pumping equipment overcame other pressing problems for immigrating farmers. New grain strains and advances in agricultural technology, particularly plowing, were of considerable consequence in abetting the belated flow of the agrarian frontier into the New West's midland.

The Special Role of the Publicists

Throughout its history as a territorial component of the American community, the New West has often been the subject of promotion campaigns. Its advocates had to undertake calculated, planned, directed settlement to overcome the deterrents of distance, isolation, environmental problems, and a negative public image. Publicists labored mightily to alter the image of the New West from that of a desert wasteland to the "Garden of the World."

Their first success was Texas. Promotional efforts by *empresarios* and their agents in the East and Europe, provoked wide public interest in the new Eden beyond the Sabine through public lectures, newspaper articles, and advertisements; their efforts had an appreciable effect on the rapid populating of Texas. Spokesmen for the missionary frontier in Oregon performed a similar function. Their published letters and personal appearances in Eastern churches and lecture halls exulted in the promise of the American nation on the Columbia. They warned of the British threat should the nation not act promptly, stirring patriotic concern and feeding the growing expansionist sentiment that was soon to flower into Manifest Destiny. Publicists also used the British threat to jab their reluctant government to annex Texas and to acquire California when, in fact, the prospects for British absorption were real. In Hawaii, as well, Americans exploited the British threat to national interests in the Pacific Basin to provoke action by the federal government.

The American public still regarded Great Britain as a national enemy, and the publicists' stress on British territorial ambitions in Texas, California, Oregon, and Hawaii struck a responsive chord. Therefore the publicists generated a wide public interest and protective attitude toward the New West that crystallized into Manifest Destiny, the nationalist surge that demanded from the reluctant federal government a war of conquest against Mexico. The war itself, in turn reinforced American interest in the New West and began to erode the idea of national completeness.

Besides provoking public action, early Western publicists also stimulated widening private interest in the trans-Missouri territory. Before 1840, however, they concentrated on certain portions of the New West and specific enterprises; finding no redemptive quality in the vast interior, they mostly ignored it. Except for the promotional writings and speeches pertaining to Texas and Oregon, which dealt largely with their agricultural promise, most publicists stressed the New West's mercantile prospects. The writings of Thomas Larkin and other California pioneers were widely read in the eastern United States and attracted some Americans to the Pacific shore; but their emphasis on business opportunities contained little appeal to the farmer. The Josiah Gregg's popular *Commerce of the Prairies* was a literary guide to the Southwest as a trade territory for businessmen.

To appeal to the general public, which was largely agrarian, Western publicists had to stress the agricultural promise of the New West's interior, and after 1840 they accomplished this by developing an expansive rhetoric that combined the heady doctrine of the nation's imperial destiny of continental empire, the bold commercial design of the "Road to China and India" for maritime traders based at Pacific Coast ports, and the conversion of the Great American Desert image to the "Garden of the World."

Thomas Hart Benton, a United States Senator from the border state of Missouri, was the pioneer New West prophet who conceived a broadened expansionist doctrine that included a constructive role for the New West interior. Throughout his long public career, Benton looked to the Pacific and was a consistent supporter of Western interests. In Benton's view, national completeness was public folly; America's destiny was to extend to the Pacific shore. The degree to which the nation absorbed, settled, and developed the territory west of Missouri would determine its ultimate position among the advanced nations of the world. By 1840, Benton had found a place for the New West interior in his doctrines of continental destiny and the mercantile highway to China and India. The promise of the railroad to connect the western border of Missouri and the Pacific shore with swift, regular transport led him to advocate the creation of a land bridge—a block of states extending across the New West's interior. This political and economic connective tissue linking the eastern United States with the Pacific Basin entrepôts to the maritime "Road to China and India" would be traversed by the continental railroad. Each of the constituent states could then contribute to the national strength.

Benton's polemical genius transformed, for attentive Eastern audiences, the desert into a garden. He averred that much of the territory west of Missouri was "rich like Egypt and tempting as Egypt." [1] The bosom of the succeeding highlands, he said, contained mineral treasures required by the nation's growing industrial establishment. And even the deserts of the Great Basin could be made to flower by application of bountiful artesian waters to the parched but productive soils. Benton's idyllic transformation of the Great American Desert to a "Garden of the World" supported by the railroad was taken up by other publicists. Asa Whitney, a New York merchant who had resided in China for two years, became an enthusiastic advocate of transcontinental railroad development. In his view the transportation conquest of the New West would provide the United States

---

[1] Quoted in Henry Nash Smith, *Virgin Land: The American West As Symbol and Myth* (Cambridge, 1950), p. 37.

an advantage over the European nations in developing the rich Far East trading areas. Collateral benefits to the nation would include agrarian settlement and development of the area of the land bridge.

Probably the most intensely committed evangelical New West publicist was William Gilpin, a Philadelphian who had traveled over much of the trans-Missouri territory and become infatuated with its promise. Gilpin was a prodigious writer on the West; his best-known work is *The Mission of the North American People* (1860, 1874). His promotional treatises, derived from the premise that "the untransacted destiny of the American people is to subdue the continent" echoed Benton's "Garden of the World" myth.[2]

Senator Stephen A. Douglas succeeded Benton as the public voice for the New West. He energetically promoted its settlement and development, primarily under the aegis of railroad expansion. Douglas argued that the handicap of the New West interior was less a matter of limitations of climate and soils than of inaccessibility. The fortuitous technological marvel, the railroad, overcame the problem of isolation and opened new vistas for the pioneer. Douglas "considered the individual farmer with his primitive agriculture to be the ultimate source of social values and energies" for the nation. Therefore, he concentrated on the agrarian occupation of the New West under the "creative power of the railroad." [3]

Horace Greeley, publisher of the New York *Tribune*, was another consistent advocate of the New West. He regarded it as a prime supportive region for the increasingly industrialized and urbanized East. In his view, the American nation should develop the trans-Missouri region's natural bounty, particularly minerals; but its agricultural prospects should not be neglected. Greeley held that the territory embraced by the Great American Desert could be utilized to solve grave social problems facing the nation, serving as a safety valve for the poor of the Eastern cities. Transplanting struggling city laborers to Benton's "Garden of the World" and converting them to yeomen farmers would purge them of poverty, depravity, and dependence!

After 1865, publicists continued to promote the interior West as a garden spot. In order to muster evidence to counter the Great American Desert image, they shifted their rhetoric from the metaphysics of continental destiny to the new science. In 1867, Ferdinand V. Hayden completed a federally sponsored scientific reconnaissance of portions of the New West. He reported to the Secretary of the Interior his conviction that there was a direct correlation between annual rainfall and vegetative cover, particularly trees. Therefore, in order for the Western farmer to succeed, he should plant both grain crops and trees. According to Hayden's formula, ten to fifteen acres of trees on each quarter-section in the arid regions

---

[2] Ibid.
[3] Ibid., p. 34.

would increase the annual rainfall to a level sufficient to sustain crops. He wrote ecstatically in 1871 that "Never has my faith in the grand future that awaits the entire West been so strong as it is at the present time." [4] Additional surveys and demonstrations by scientists determined to confirm the prophets' claims produced the simplistic maxim that "rain follows the plow." Thus, when the yeoman farmer exposed virgin prairie sod to the elements, an unfathomable concatenation of natural processes would produce sufficient rain for crops to prosper. During the 1870s, as settlers occupied the grasslands of western Kansas and Nebraska, rains came regularly, and the new science seemed confirmed. However, a bitter experience awaited settlers during the 1880s. Sustained, searing droughts demonstrated that Great Plains meteorology was cyclical in character, that it ignored trees and the plow, and that the two decades after the Civil War had been a period of abnormally wet years.

After 1870, publicists for railroad companies and immigration bureaus of the Western states and territories continued to write in the "Garden of the World" tradition. The vast quantities of promotional literature they produced and distributed attracted settlers to the West. They took greater literary liberties than the pre–Civil War prophets; their copy lacked the style and grace of the latter, and they often resorted to gross exaggeration in broadcasting the New West's agrarian promise.

During the postwar period, only one negative voice of consequence was raised to the "Garden of the World" myth. John W. Powell, director of federal surveys in the West during the 1870s, in 1878 published his *Report on the Lands of the Arid Regions*. He warned that agricultural techniques workable in the nation's humid regions were not applicable to the arid West; he took the position that a 160-acre homestead was inadequate to support a family. He directly challenged the myth and insisted that most of the New West's interior was semi-arid to desert in character and would so remain. Powell urged a utilization of the trans-Missouri territory that was compatible with the region's natural limitations; he declared that in most of it only stockraising should be practiced. He recommended that in view of the realities of the region, particularly the limited rainfall, Congress should enlarge the size of the Western homestead to 2,560 acres.

Powell's finding clouded the buoyant optimism of New West advocates. Bankers, speculators, railroad officials, and Western congressmen successfully opposed the land-use reforms recommended by Powell. Congressman Thomas M. Patterson of Colorado, speaking against the reform proposals coming from the Powell survey, warned fellow legislators that approval would destroy the yeoman farmer in the West and that the region "would in a few years be filled with baronial estates, with an aristocratic and wealthy few." [5]

[4] Ibid., p. 181.
[5] Ibid., p. 199.

PIONEERS IN THE GARDEN OF THE WORLD

Removal of the deterrents to agricultural settlement in the New West interior and intensive promotion of the region by publicists precipitated agrarian interest. After 1870, farmers occupied the Great Plains at a rate little short of phenomenal; several trans-Missouri territories received ten-fold population increases between 1875 and 1885. Most settlers entering the interior during the seventies and eighties were poor. Loans and the development of cash crops eventually made it possible for many to remain on their homesteads and adapt to this anomalous prairie-plains environment; but in the early harsh days of opening a claim, survival was a clear and constant question.

The Pioneer Household

Pioneers used tents or canvas-covered wagon boxes for shelter until they had completed their dwellings made from the resources of the new land. If there was a timbered canyon on their claim, the homesteaders cut logs and constructed a crude cabin along the pattern of the Old West wilderness dwelling. Most of the new country was grassland, and the majority of settlers built sod houses, dugouts, half-dugouts or sod fronts dug into a low hill. The sod house was the most widely used structure.

As in the Old West, erecting the dwelling was a cooperative effort. A sod-house raising or "bee" was a social event of some consequence. One pioneer recalled that "neighbors for miles around gather" at the claim of the newly arrived family "and put up his house in a day. Of course there is no charge for labor in such cases. The women come too, and while the men lay up the sod walls, they prepare dinner for the crowd, and have a very sociable hour at noon." [6]

Sod house dimensions were generally twelve feet wide by sixteen feet long. Experience on the Plains had shown that building a sod structure any larger would prevent the walls from settling straight up and down, thus causing them to fall either in or out. In laying a sod wall, pioneer builders took ribbons of sod about four inches thick and two feet wide, sliced from the earth by the sharp-bladed sod plow; with a spade these were cut into blocks two and a half feet long. They placed the sod blocks grass side down in overlapping joints, like bricks. It was believed that the thick sod walls kept the interior cool in summer and warm in winter. The roof, framed with poles, was usually slightly rounded, shaped like the top of a freight car. First the roof frame was covered with tarpaper, and often a rim of sod was placed around the outer edge; then the entire surface was covered with six inches of soil to hold the tarpaper down. Homesteaders claimed that this type of roof shed water very well. If the settler's family was too large

---

[6] Quoted in Clark C. Spence, *The American West: A Sourcebook* (New York, 1966), pp. 228–29.

to be accommodated in one sod house, he simply erected a second one nearby.

Scarcity of surface water led Plains farmers to drill wells—some over 300 feet deep—and to pump the water to the surface with windmills. Some excavated cisterns—small covered caverns with plastered walls and bottom —or small ponds near the eaves of the house to catch runoff from rains. Most ground water of the interior region was charged with minerals, particularly gypsum, and was rated "hard"; homemade soap would not lather or make suds in it. Each household had wooden rain barrels placed at the corners of the sod house; the mother and daughters used the rainwater for washing their hair and some clothing.

During the hardscrabble days, settlers often found it difficult to gather even sufficient fuel for cooking. Wood on most claims was scarce, and chief reliance was placed on "cow chips." Homesteaders found that a bucket of dry cow dung, kindled by dried grass tapers, made a hot bed of cooking coals. Through heavy use, this fuel became scarce across the country; and many families placed sideboards on their wagons and went onto the great cattle ranges on cow-chip gathering expeditions. Each family member would take a washtub with a rope tied to one handle and drag it across the range. When full, the tub was emptied into the wagon. One settler recalled that his family accumulated a winter fuel pile fifty feet long, twelve feet wide, and eight feet high.

Homesteader fare was simple and reflected well the resourcefulness of the people. Game was abundant. In 1894 one settler killed a wagonload of turkeys in one day at Boiling Springs in the Cherokee Outlet. Another pioneer reported that after a severe snowstorm he went along the creeks near his claim gathering prairie chickens and quail in a grain sack. Coveys of these game birds had frozen during the cold. He thawed and dressed them and fed his family through a lean period. A native fruit was the sand plum, which made excellent pies and jellies and was of great value to the settlers. When a household ran out of canning jars, the remaining plums were cooked into a batter, spread on cloths made from flour sacks, dried in sheets, removed from the cloths, rolled up, and put away for the winter. During hard times pioneer families even subsisted on boiled kafir corn— grain sorghum—and it "became a polite art that first winter to . . . gracefully spit the hulls out while at the table." [7]

Most settlers had a milk cow and were able to milk several additional animals because of a curious custom that developed in some areas. Many ranchers allowed homesteaders to milk all the cattle they could drive up from the open range. When the ranch crews branded calves in the spring, the cowboys made the rounds of the homesteads, branding the calves of

[7] Quoted in Arrell M. Gibson, *Oklahoma: A History of Five Centuries* (Norman, 1965), p. 307.

the cows bearing their employer's mark. Cattlemen did not object because the settlers cared for their range cows and calves during the severe winter weather.

Lacking money, nesters bartered butter and eggs for salt, sugar, and coffee, and it was common to trade a horse or cow for a year's supply of flour. The men gathered buffalo bones on the prairie and sold them to fertilizer companies at $7 to $9 a ton. Some settlers cut cedar posts on the uplands and sold them to ranchers at two cents per post. After their own crops were in, many fathers and sons followed the wheat harvest northward across Kansas and Nebraska into the Dakotas to earn extra money to stock and equip their farms. Harvest wages were $1.50 a day, $3.00 for a man and a team.

Pioneer Education

Two of the earliest concerns of new settlers were the establishments of schools and churches. In the absence of territorial or state support for education, they built and maintained schools through public subscription. Men donated their labor for hauling material and erecting the buildings. Some of these pioneer schoolhouses were made of sod; others were constructed of split cedar posts placed in vertical picket walls. The only textbooks were books that parents had brought from the East. One student remembered that "spelling, ciphering and geography matches, with an occasional 'speaking' relieved the monotony of the regular school life." Students at one school carried drinking water from a spring situated a quarter of a mile from the schoolhouse, and it was considered a treat to go for water. "Two privies were located on the back of the school yard, you held up two fingers in a 'V' shape to get permission to leave the room." During pioneer days, school ran for only three months of twenty days each, and teachers received about $25 a month. "One teacher was given a cow . . . as a consideration for teaching a fourth month." [8]

The agrarian frontier in the trans-Missouri region showed a hunger for learning, albeit simplistic, which extended beyond childhood. Providing rudimentary education for adults—most of them deprived in their youth— took many forms. In the coal camps of Crawford County, Kansas, and south into the Choctaw nation, itinerant teachers held night classes to teach English, reading, and writing to immigrant Russian, Polish, Italian, and Greek miners. A popular form of adult education used up and down the Plains was the camp school. A description of the operation of a camp school near Granite in Greer County, Oklahoma Territory, illustrates the curriculum, as well as student and public interest in this type of adult education.

T. E. Jones, the local schoolmaster, was "an ardent prohibitionist and

[8] Ibid., pp. 307–308.

very much a promoter." Each summer for four weeks he conducted a camp school for adults on the south side of a mountain in a "beautiful grove near a gushing spring of pure, cold water." [9] The curriculum consisted of instruction in reading, writing, oratory, singing, and temperance. Jones' salary was derived from the enrollment fee of $3 per student and from income earned from the franchise issued him by the town to operate the concessions at the three-day graduation ceremonies and picnic that concluded the camp-school term. Students camped near the shady grove, where out-of-doors classes were conducted, or boarded with families in Granite. During the 1897 session, fifty persons enrolled.

The day began each morning at 7:30 A.M. when Jones sounded "assembly" on the trumpet. After students had endured twenty minutes of rigorous calesthenics, he distributed songbooks and the student body sang for half an hour. A stanza from one song went:

> Somewhere tonight in a cold, dreary world
> wanders a boy I cherish so,
> treading the dark and unbidden road
> Leading to misery, pain, and woe.
> Once he was pure as the saints in white,
> noble and manly, my joy and delight,
> Facing a future so happy and bright
> But now, oh my God, he's a drunkard tonight!

The day's academic instruction then began. Jones passed each student books for reading and for memorizing speeches. While half the class remained at the platform and received guidance from the instructor, the other half scattered to various parts of the grove, each finding some secluded spot in the shade to read the assignment, memorize the speech, and practice delivery. Jones instructed each student on reading, as well as the oratorical arts, including voice, enunciation, emphasis, and gesture.

Camp school closed with graduation ceremonies and a three-day picnic. Most of each commencement day was consumed by student orations. Jones awarded a silver medal, a gold medal, and a "grand gold" medal to students rendering what he judged superior performances. Pioneer families from fifty miles around gathered for the closing exercises, and businessmen from the town provided lumber to build a large platform and seats. The local school board loaned the school organ for group singing. Jones was allowed to sell concessions for the merry-go-round, cold-drink stands, doll racks, a shooting gallery, and peanut and popcorn venders. The concessions opened during the morning and afternoon recesses between orations and in the evening. One student recalled that "The audience listened with rapt attention" to the orations, most including a strong temperance appeal, "but it is

⁹ Arrell M. Gibson, ed., *Edward Everett Dale: Frontier Historian* (Norman, 1975), p. 13.

doubtful if our efforts had the slightest effect upon the consumption of liquor." [10]

Pioneer Religion

One of the most socially compelling culture sets carried by Old West pioneers into the trans-Missouri region was a religious system, spawned by the Great Revival, which centered on sects propagating evangelical, primitive Christianity. The principal denominations seeded in the New West by the late-arriving agrarian frontier were Baptist, Methodist, Cumberland Presbyterian, and Disciples of Christ or Christian—soon to proliferate the conservative Church of Christ group. Virtually all these sects practiced an intense congregationalism that vested ecclesiastical authority in the local body of believers as represented by the church elders. This mode of church polity and the stress on revealed Christianity—"the call"— reduced the necessity for an educated clergy and, in the absence of resident ministers, permitted laymen to perform most religious functions, including preaching. In addition, the religious bodies established in the New West continued the Great Revival tradition of literal interpretation of the Scriptures and commitment to follow the simple New Testament church model. That these sectarian progeny of the Great Revival had changed little in the nearly three-quarters of a century since the Cane Ridge outpouring discussed in Chapter 12 was confirmed by the comment of an aged clergyman who had evangelized both Old West and New West settlements. He averred that the pioneers' religious "character" had been "formed before they emigrated thither, and they have been slightly or not at all modified by their change of residence." [11]

In the early days of pioneering the New West's interior, there were few church buildings, and settlers worshiped in schoolhouses or in homes. One pioneer recalled that "Every one went to these meetings." The periodic revivals were occasions of wide social interest. "They were outstanding, regardless of the denomination of the preacher. We had what was called free or shouting Methodists, regular Methodists, Baptists, and Christian evangelists "who received little pay and stayed with the neighbors." [12]

Militant Protestantism, which had dominated Old West pioneer society, comprised a force of considerable and continuing consequence in the New West. Yet it was unable to exercise its accustomed pervasive influence, for its values, based on puritan restraint, had to compete with the more permissive values of the established mining and stockraising frontiers. Thus, while it was less of a force for molding New West society than it had been in the Old West, it remained a continuing, competitive force. Cer-

[10] Ibid., p. 14.

[11] Earl Pomeroy, "Toward a Reorientation of Western History: Continuity and Environment," *Mississippi Valley Historical Review* 41 (March 1955): 593.

[12] Quoted in Gibson, *Oklahoma*, p. 308.

tainly pioneer religion's persistent, unyielding commitment to strict interpretation of the Scriptures and its stress on revealed Christianity rigidified
emerging Western anti-intellectualism. It has remained a prime source for
New West social and political conservatism well into the twentieth century.

Pioneer Diversions

Pioneers settling on the grass-carpeted prairies of the trans-Missouri
region had more leisure than Old West settlers. There were no forests to
clear, and they were liberated from the eternal contest with ubiquitous
sprouts that had to be grubbed from the soil after each planting season.
Also the growing one-crop emphasis—usually either cotton or wheat—
required only intensive seasonal attention, permitting settlers time for other
activities, which had not been the case in the multi-activity, self-sufficient
agrarian frontier of the Old West.

With more leisure, pioneers sought diversions compatible with their
puritan values. One was the literary society, which conducted public meetings at the schoolhouse or in homes twice a month; it was directed by the
local schoolmaster. Programs included musical numbers, humorous readings, dramatic productions performed by children and adults, and orations
and debates by the men. Favorite readings presented by local literary society
entertainers were "Spartacus to the Gladiators," "Curfew Must Not Ring
Tonight," and "The Face on the Barroom Floor." Debate subjects included
"Resolved, that fear of punishment has a greater influence over human
conduct than does the hope of reward."

During the 1870s, the Chautauqua, traveling troops of singers, speakers,
ventriloquists, magicians, and other performers, became a popular national
entertainment medium. After the railroads laced the trans-Missouri territory, Chautauqua troops accepted bookings at the principal Western settlements. Pioneers often traveled fifty miles by team and wagon to partake
of Chautauqua diversion; usually the families camped near the Chautauqua
pavilion during the week-long program.

A Chautauqua company touring the South Dakota settlements in 1897
was billed as an "opportunity for culture, education and inspiration."
Methodist, Baptist, and Presbyterian women's groups maintained cook
tents to feed the crowds. The morning program included a lecture on "Your
Boy," which provided parents with insights on "how they should raise
their boys so they would grow up to be good men." Afternoon offerings
included the Chautauqua Ladies Quartet, illustrated lectures with colored
chalk, and a woman in a "spangly dress" reciting "The Charge of the Light
Brigade." The day's program closed with the featured billing, the favorite
of the Chautauqua circuit, Reverend T. De Witt Talmadge, whose rich,
sonorous tones assured man's promise as a Christian. His closing line was
"No matter what others may choose, give me a Christian's life, a Christian's
death, a Christian's burial, and a Christian's immortality." Thunderous
applause coaxed him back to the stage, and the audience waved handker-

chiefs, white ones studded with farmer's red bandannas; "the Chautauqua salute," was the "greatest honor" a performer could receive.[13]

Another popular pioneer diversion was the itinerant medicine show, which mixed entertainment with the sale of patent medicines. The entertainment used to draw a crowd included magicians, who delighted the populus with feats of legerdemain and mystic sleight of hand, musical numbers, tumbling, feats of strength, demonstrations of hypnotism and ventriloquism, and phrenology lectures. Virtually every show troop included a minstrel group, for show managers regarded the blackface comedians indispensable to the sale of medicine; their antics brought easy laughter and "laughter greased the gullets of fools and opened their pocketbooks." [14]

In the medicine-show format, the health lecture followed the opening round of entertainment; in some cases, this "pitch" or "spiel" was so morbidly colorful and appealing that it was entertaining too. The medicine man was a type. He had to have poise and stage presence, and to succeed he had to know regions and people, their prejudices, and their assumed needs. Above all else, he had to be able to "scare hell out of a man." Commonly he posed as the "poor man's friend," the "people's doctor." That these pioneers in advertising were persuasive is attested to by one medicine-show patron: "Why, a man could enter that medicine show tent a picture of health but depart a terrible sick man with a bottle of cure-all clasped tightly in his hand and new hope in his heart." [15] To sell his tonics, pills, linaments, and exotic oils, the medicine man first had to persuade his listeners not only to recognize but to feel the symptoms of disease. He managed this by placing medical displays on the stage: jars of alcohol containing livers, kidneys, and hearts; and huge anatomical charts with the vital parts and circulatory system printed in lurid reds, purples, and blues. Hookworms and tapeworms, obtained from a slaughterhouse by the bucketful and curling in jars of alcohol, were favorite lecture pieces and always a crowd pleaser.

By the 1890s, medicine men were attracting crowds in Western towns by providing free medical demonstrations, diagnosis, and treatment. Painless dentistry became a common prop of the late-nineteenth-century frontier medicine shows. The Big Sensation Medicine Company of Nebraska maintained a sideshow attraction billed as the "King of Forceps," operated by a man-and-wife team. Both were huge; she held the patient, and he pulled. This gargantuan team also had a fifteen-minute spot on the main program in the big tent. A member of the Big Sensation troop recalled that "the band played loudly to drown the howls of pain while the King of Forceps worked." [16] A Texas medicine show was also well-received by the natives

---

[13] Quoted in Henry Steele Commager and Allan Nevins, eds., *The Heritage of America* (Boston, 1951), pp. 932, 938.

[14] Arrell M. Gibson, "Medicine Show," *The American West* 4 (Feb. 1967): 34–39.

[15] Ibid.

[16] Ibid.

because of its free clinic. One patron reported he saw the healer "rub rheumatism out of a fellow's knee, give free treatment to three men with Bright's Disease, cut a tumor off Bill Syke's neck, pull three ingrowing toe-nails off the left foot of a total stranger, cut a cataract out of Jeff Spencer's right eye, and pull sixty-seven teeth without pain, besides selling $13 worth of medicine." [17]

A quieter and more common pioneer diversion and social outlet was the Sunday visit. While the men hunkered in the dooryard discussing crops and weather, the women quilted, patched worn clothing, and sewed garments. At such times, according to one chronicler, the "women's tongues often moved faster than their fingers as they discussed the local news and gossip." [18]

Pioneer Ways

Superstitions and taboos were powerful individual and group behavior determinants in New West agrarian society. There was an injunction against killing frogs in a pond, for such an act would cause cows using the water to give bloody milk. It was believed by some people that pain suffered by an infant at tooth-cutting time was eased by tying a mole's tooth around the baby's neck. And old men often carried potatoes in their pockets to ward off rheumatism.

The puritan values of New West agrarian society banned certain female parts and functions as subjects of public discussion. A "woman did not break her leg but a 'lower limb'." Edward Everett Dale, the eminent frontier folklorist, commented that with "floor-length skirts and the use of the term 'limb' it almost seemed that it was a social error for a woman to admit that she had legs! . . . To refer to an unmarried woman's future child was a grave social error. . . . Such words as 'belly,' 'boar,' and 'pregnant' were never used in mixed company." When a woman was pregnant the euphemism "in a family way" was used to describe her state.[19]

In legal matters too, pioneers had their own peculiar practices. Often settlers substituted local arbitration for "going to the law" to settle disputes over land, property boundaries, or stock ownership. The two parties to the dispute beforehand agreed to settle the matter by private arbitration. The local arbitration panel consisted of three men: each party to the dispute appointed one man, and these two chose the third. The extralegal frontier tribunal investigated the matter in dispute, heard the evidence, and rendered a decision, which both parties had agreed to accept as final.

AGRARIAN LAG AND WESTERN CULTURE

As we have indicated, the agrarian frontier did not occupy the trans-Missouri region in strength until after 1870. By that time miners, stock-

[17] Ibid.
[18] Edward E. Dale, The Cross Timbers (Austin, 1966), pp. 145–46.
[19] Ibid., p. 117.

men, and other Anglo-American groups, as well as other ethnic and religious communities, had become entrenched in the New West social milieu. The result was that farmers were unable to dominate the social scene as they had in the Old West.

Agrarian Antagonists

Nonetheless, the pioneer farmers were the principal carriers of Anglo-American culture. In the Old West, they had been the focus of society. While other enterprises developed there, most were supportive of agriculture, and farmers were paramount in the economy and society. The agrarian-based Old West society created and nourished values and institutions that crystallized into culture sets regarded as the essence of American society. These culture sets included a special type of family—protected by custom and law—a religious system centering on sects propagating evangelical, primitive Christianity, and social controls based on puritanical restraints and taboos that combined to produce a repressive, conforming society. The lag in the agrarian frontier's flow into the New West slowed that region's cultural consolidation and integration with the rest of the nation.

The values of the Anglo-American groups—miners, stockraisers, lumbermen, and railroad builders—occupying the New West before the agrarian advent, inevitably flavored the region's culture and tempered the late-coming farmer values. For one thing the miners, stockmen, and other agrarian antecedents often were refugees from the Old West's puritanical, repressive society, and their values were accordingly more permissive. They were not fixed on the soil. Their enterprises were intensely exploitive, and, after they had plundered a given tract of minerals, grass, or timber, they moved on. Their periodic movement imparted a quality of restlessness, impermanence, and mobility to New West society. Farmers, conversely, by the nature of their enterprise, were committed to the land in a fixed, permanent way. The interplay of miner-stockman restlessness, impermanence, and permissiveness with agrarian stability, permanence, and behavioral repression produced inevitable social and political tension and confusion and no little social disarray.

Ethnic and Cultural Diversities

Similarly, farmers had to share the New West social stage—a racial mélange—with variant ethnic and religious groups. Western society, although dominated by Anglo-Americans, was seasoned with varied European elements of recent origin, a mixed Oriental community, a growing Black community, a substantial Mexican-American community, and a large Indian community. The Anglo-American community compiled a grim record of repressing peoples of unlike physical and cultural attributes. Following a cruelly ambivalent course, they imported workers from other nations and the eastern United States, exploited them, then rejected and suppressed them when their cheap, unskilled labor was no longer required. To no group was this repressive pattern applied more assiduously than to Asian immigrants.

Chinese were the first Orientals to reach the West in large numbers, several hundred arriving soon after the California gold rush in 1849. After 1865, thousands of Chinese were imported to build the Western railroads. The Central Pacific Railroad was constructed almost exclusively with Chinese coolie labor. In the early years of Chinese immigration, most laborers settled in California. By 1870, over 120,000 Chinese resided in the United States, mostly on the Pacific Coast.

As California's white working population increased, the low-paid Chinese laborers came to be regarded as a threat to desirable wage and working standards. During the 1870s, labor agitators—primarily Dennis Kearny and the California Workingman's party—braced with the slogan "The Chinese must go," precipitated mass Sinophobia—fear of Chinese. The Chinese became, besides an economic threat because of their willingness to work for low wages, a social threat as well. Chinese settlements were a "health menace." They "lived in squalor . . . [were] responsible for gambling and prostitution." The Chinese worshiped "strange gods," and subsisted "under tong governments." [20] On several occasions, California mobs from north of San Francisco to San Diego destroyed Chinese restaurants and laundries. The bloodiest outbreak occurred during 1871 in Los Angeles, where a mob killed twenty-two Chinese people. State laws and municipal ordinances sought to legally segregate and repress the Chinese. This strife and oppression drove many Chinese from rural areas into the larger California coastal cities, where they established protective enclaves; others migrated to other parts of the West.

But wherever they went, the Chinese suffered discrimination and repression. Idaho miners excluded them from most camps, and in those places where they were permitted to settle, they had to pay a discriminatory residence tax of four dollars a month. They were forbidden to engage in placer mining, except on claims that white men did not want. One Idaho commentator said he never knew a Chinese "to refuse payment on a debt; but he knew of hundreds of cases where whites cheated them." Chinese feared to go into the courts for "not one judge or jury in a hundred would give a decision in favor of an Oriental where he obviously was entitled to it." [21]

In the Montana Territory, there were nearly a thousand Chinese by 1869. Local miners permitted them to mine gold only from unwanted claims, so they supported themselves by operating restaurants and laundries in the mining camps. In Nevada, local ordinances and practices permitted Chinese to work as household servants, operate restaurants and laundries, and peddle wood in the mining towns. They were described as "peaceful,

---

[20] John W. Caughey, *History of the Pacific Coast* (New York, 1938), p. 321.
[21] William S. Greever, *The Bonanza West* (Norman, 1963), p. 269.

quiet, tractable, industrious, free from drunkenness, seldom disorderly, and likely to ignore the worse insults or injuries. By law, they could not testify in a Virginia City court." [22]

Chinese arrived in Colorado soon after completion of the transcontinental railroad. They were banned from most mining camps and mostly settled in Denver, where they operated restaurants and laundries. Colorado bigotry toward peoples of deviant cultures was manifested during 1880 by degrading editorial references to the Indians, Chinese, and Mexican-Americans in the state. The Denver editor claimed that Colorado was "ruined through Chinese labor." Newspaper stress in Denver during 1880 on the Chiense menace to wages and social conditions inflamed three thousand citizens to attack and burn the local chinatown, killing countless Chinese and scattering the survivors. Under pressure from the Western state and territorial governments, Congress in 1882 passed the Chinese Exclusion Act, which banned immigration of Chinese laborers to the United States.

Throughout the nineteenth century, the West received demographic infusions from all over Europe. French, German, and British immigrants flocked to California during the gold rush. Promotional activities in Europe by American railroad representatives stressing opportunities in the West— particularly on federal land grants held by railway companies—attracted thousands of immigrants from Sweden, Norway, Denmark, Germany, and other European nations to the "Garden of the West" on the Great Plains. Portuguese, Italian, Hungarian, Rumanian, and Czech immigrants settled on the Pacific Coast during the latter nineteenth century to man the fishing fleets and to labor on the truck farms of the Sacramento delta and other agricultural regions. Many succeeded as owners of farms, vineyards, and wineries. Mining company officials holding leases to rich coal deposits in the Choctaw nation of Indian Territory and southeastern Kansas imported thousands of Italian, Polish, Czech, Welsh, and Russian miners. And sheepraisers recruited Basque herdsmen from northern Spain to tend their growing flocks on the Western ranges. These immigrants further seasoned Western society and added a dimension of color and creativity to the monistic and generally bland Anglo-American culture.

Blacks were present in large numbers in Indian Territory and in Texas from the 1820s; they were the slaves of Indian and Anglo-American planters. Many free Blacks also participated in the fur trade and in other antebellum frontier enterprises. When the status of slaves changed after the Civil War, many Blacks worked in the Western mines, served as freighters, and were employed as cowboys and trail drivers on the ranches. Others enlisted in the all-Black cavalry and infantry regiments that were formed after the war. They saw action on the Plains as "Buffalo Soldiers" in the final Indian conquest during the 1870s. Other Blacks were lured from the South by

[22] Ibid., p. 95.

colonization societies that urged freedmen to go West and take up free land under the Homestead Act. They began settling Nebraska and Kansas during the 1870s, and, after 1889, Black homesteaders participated in the land runs that opened Oklahoma Territory to settlement.

The monistically-inclined agrarian frontier found the New West social milieu additionally diversified by the presence of a large Mexican-American population concentrated in Texas, New Mexico, Arizona, and California; by the close of the nineteenth century, it numbered about half a million. Most Mexican-Americans residing in United States territory were of mixed background—mestizos—a blend of Spanish and Indian. Major American contact with Mexican-Americans began shortly after the United States acquired the Southwestern quadrant of the New West. Soon after 1848 large numbers of Anglo-Americans—the natives called them Gringos—began arriving in the former Mexican territory. The intruders "considered themselves representatives of a superior race" and were "overt in their rapacity" toward the Mexican-Americans, "consistently disregarding Mexican rights and generally holding the Greasers—their condescending designation for the natives—in contempt." [23]

The Anglo-Americans arrogantly displaced the natives, taking over choice farming, mining, and ranching locations throughout the Southwest. Nowhere was this practice more blatant than along the Rio Grande. Gringos began arriving in the El Paso area around 1850, appropriating the prime farming land along the river, the adjacent grasslands, and rich salt deposits. Displaced Mexican-American families from San Elizario and El Paso established new settlements in southern New Mexico Territory, at Mesilla, Doña Ana, and Paraje. There they opened new ranches and grain and vegetable farms irrigated by *acequias*—canals tapping the waters of the Rio Grande. The Mexican-American settlers prospered and lived generally secure in the tenure of their holdings for over a generation. Then around 1885, they were confronted by renewed Anglo pressure. Cattlemen, displaced on the Great Plains grasslands by intruding homesteaders, entered New Mexico in large numbers. After appropriating the better-watered public domain pastures of the territory, they began to cast covetous eyes on the river-bottom plots of the Mexican settlers. The natives found the Anglo law difficult to understand, and few had taken the trouble to perfect their land titles under United States law. A bit of bullying by rough-talking, gun-brandishing cattle-company riders generally was sufficient to flush Mexican settlers from their land. Thereupon, stockmen appropriated the properties by having their cowboys file on the land at the local branch of the General Land Office.

Increasingly, after 1865, the Mexican-American element became a submerged subculture in the New West social order. From San Antonio to

[23] Arrell M. Gibson, *The Life and Death of Colonel Albert Jennings Fountain* (Norman, 1965), p. 52.

San Diego, dominating Anglos inflicted repressive and discriminatory treatment upon Mexican-Americans similar to that accorded the Chinese. In the Southwest during the turbulent, lawless 1870s and 1880s, Anglo gunmen contemptuously averred that "like Chinese," Mexicans did not count, and refused to record "Greasers" in their ghoulish count of casualties tallied by the notches on their sixshooters; and they were accorded general public immunity for killing Spanish-Americans. Mexican-Americans also had to endure unequal treatment before the law. They were segregated in the towns and socially discriminated against. In Texas, even the cemeteries were segregated. Anglo-American employers permitted them to perform only menial tasks at pitiably low wages, and politicians shamefully exploited them as voters to advance their petty partisan causes.

The Indian added another dimension of ethnic diversity to the New West's social milieu. Following the conclusion of the Indian wars and the concentration of the tribes on reservations, an estimated 300,000 aborigines, members of over a hundred tribes, resided in the trans-Missouri territory. Most were concentrated on reservations in Indian Territory, North and South Dakota, Montana, Utah, New Mexico, and Arizona. Except for the so-called Five Civilized Tribes—the Cherokees, Creeks, Seminoles, Choctaws, and Chickasaws—of eastern Indian Territory, most Indians remained outside the stream of Anglo-American society, studiously resisting the acculturation programs imposed on them by federal agents and determinedly pursuing their tribal lifeways. After 1887, under authority of the Dawes Act, federal officials liquidated many of the western reservations and assigned each Indian an allotment averaging 160 acres in size. Allotment cruelly cast the Indians adrift in an Anglo-American dominated society, which they could not comprehend and with which they could not cope. The Dawes Act provided that after the Indian had been assigned an allotment, he would be granted citizenship in the American community; but most allottees were of the restricted class, which continued their ambivalent repressive wardship relationship with the federal government. Thus there was little opportunity for developing viable aboriginal self-determination, and many allottees were easy marks for exploitation by Anglo-American farmers and stockmen who—with federal bureaucratic collusion—leased allotments from the Indians for an annual pittance. Thus most Indian allottees continued to be as poverty-stricken as they had been under the reservation system. In large measure, allotment stripped them of all that had meaning for them—communally owned land, tribal government, and esteemed native ways of life. In the new order, they were subject to local, state, and national laws, which they did not understand.

Religious Diversity

There was great contrast between the religious orders of the Old West and the New West. In the first segment of Western America settled and developed by the agrarian frontier, a high degree of religious uniformity existed through the pervasive and enduring force of the Great Revival. When the agrarian frontier belatedly entered the New West to establish its culture sets—including militant Protestantism—it found the region's religious universe already pre-empted by well-established deviant faiths. The New West's religious spectrum included a variety of religious systems that were extensions of the variant ethnic and social systems. These included a strong Roman Catholic establishment in the Southwest, extending from Texas across New Mexico and Arizona into California; it was the legacy of the long Spanish occupation of the region. In the Pacific Basin territory of Alaska, there was a Russian Orthodox establishment. Exotic Oriental religions, imported by the Chinese and other Far East immigrants, centered on the Pacific Coast. Mormonism, with its theocratic polity and polygamous practice, dominated the Great Basin. There was a scattering of strong Mennonite and Lutheran enclaves in Texas and the Pacific Northwest imported by German and Scandinavian immigrants. And, on the New West's eastern border, flourished pockets of Russian Orthodox, Greek Orthodox, and Roman Catholic communicants—immigrants imported by mining companies exploiting the Kansas and Indian Territory coal fields. Moreover, there was a continuum of Indian religion that seemed to strengthen among the tribes in direct proportion to the efforts of federal agents to suppress it.

Religion was a paramount concern of militant, Protestant-oriented Anglo-American society in the nineteenth century. Its intolerance and bigotry toward unlike faiths and its obsessive commitment to orthodoxy and conformity strengthened private and public Americanization programs. Protestant religious bodies carried out extensive and sustained evangelical crusades in an attempt to alter the New West's variant ecclesiastical milieu. Their pressure on Congressmen led to repressive national law and policy aimed at expurgating the objectional features of Mormonism and forcing Indians to abandon their native religion.

Western Culture and Environmental Determinism

Despite efforts of the agrarian frontier to saturate the New West with its monistic culture, the region's entrenched pluralistic lifestyles persisted. This was one reason for the lag in the region's cultural consolidation and integration, a lag that continued even into the twentieth century. As latecomers to the trans-Missouri region, rather than dominating the region's culture as they had in the Old West, the pioneer farmers only tinctured it.

An important reason for the inability of the agrarian frontier to assume its accustomed societal pre-eminence was the environment. First, Great Plain's milieu limited farming and determined its direction toward cash crops, particularly small grains; this fact made the region's agriculture nearly totally dependent upon national and world markets. Natural limitations of wood and water, erratic climates, and unsurpassed natural disasters created continuing agrarian hardship. The region became increasingly less attractive as a farming area from the viewpoint of accustomed Old West agricultural practices, and the dream of owning a fertile farm in the "Garden of the World" became a cruel myth for most pioneers in America's midland. Secondly, the New West's natural environment was a rich storehouse of minerals: gold, silver, essential base metals, coal, oil, natural gas, timber, and other resources vital for the growing Eastern industrial establishment. The region's seemingly infinite resource base and its escalating exploitation created a diversity of economic patterns. Stock-raising, mining, lumbering, and other enterprises were well-established before pioneer farmers arrived in large numbers. All of these frontiers continued to function with considerable success after the agrarian advent.

So it was that the farmer had to share the stage with these established enterprises. To make matters worse, the continuing bonanza opportunities provided serious diversions to the plodding, demanding, frustrating labor of developing a successful farm on the Great Plains. The strength of the agrarian frontier was further diluted as increasing numbers of its young men were attracted to the competing enterprises. They left the farms to work in the mines, on the ranches, in the lumber camps and, around the turn of the century, in the new oil fields. Even employment in railroad construction was preferred by many over farming; at least it provided a certain monthly income.

Throughout the latter part of the century in the New West, the lure of quick wealth produced restlessness and mobility, which infected the staid farming communities. Lord James Bryce observed this atmosphere during his tour of the American West during the 1880s. He commented that the "most enterprising and unsettled Americans" were in the West:

> They have left their old haunts, broken their old ties . . . they are resolved to obtain the wealth and success for which they have come. They throw themselves into work with a feverish yet sustained intens-ity. . . . Everything is speculative. . . . No one has any fixed occupation; he is a storekeeper today, a ranchman tomorrow, a miner next week I found the waiters in the chief hotel in Denver . . . saving their autumn and winter wages to start off in the spring 'prospecting' for silver 'claims' in the mountains. . . . This venturesome and shifting life strengthens the reckless and heedless habits of the people.[24]

There was a sustained commitment to the exploitive frontier, which came into full flower during the period between 1865 and 1900. Its credo, nourished by compulsive American materialism, was derived from the confidence, the assurance, that the West's natural resource base was infinite. This view, well-established in the folk-wisdom of the Old West, was con-vincingly corroborated time and again in the New West. With bold action, fierce competitiveness, and great destructive fury the hunter, ranchman,

---

[24] James Bryce, *The American Commonwealth* (New York, 1927), Vol. 2, pp. 892–93.

miner, lumberman, and, to some degree the farmer, exploited the New West's wildlife, mineral, forest, and soil resources with total disregard for elementary natural processes and blatant disrespect of nature. By 1900, this furious assault on the New West landscape had produced a pervasive disturbance of the region's natural order—deforestation, polluted streams, extermination of several species of wildlife, a scarred earth, and skimmed mineral riches. In little more than a generation vast segments of the primeval wilderness were transformed into irredeemable wasteland. And fixed on the West was a cult of waste that continued well into the twentieth century.

Lord Bryce, a witness to this prodigious spoliation, commented that Americans attacked the wilderness with "passionate eagerness" pouring strenuous effort "towards the material development of the greatest quantity of ore, to scatter cattle on a thousand hills, to turn the flower-spangled prairies . . . into wheat fields . . . this is the end aim of their lives, this is their daily and nightly thought." [25]

SELECTED SOURCES

The interplay of the New West's diverse ethnic and cultural entities and the sublimation of the altering force of the agrarian frontier and its stereotyped cultural sets—which account for the lag in New West cultural integration—is an elusive subject. Information on this tantalizing phenomenon, in bits and pieces and in large blocks of germane material, can be digested from the following: Earl Pomeroy, "Toward a Reorientation of Western History: Continuity and Environment," *Mississippi Valley Historical Review* 41 (March, 1955); *Clark C. Spence, ed., *The American West: A Source Book* (New York, 1966); *D'Arcy McNickle, *Native American Tribalism: Indian Survivals and Renewals* (New York, 1973); *William L. Katz, *The Black West* (New York, 1973); Jennings C. Wise and Vine Deloria, Jr., *The Red Man in the New World Drama* (New York, 1971); W. Eugene Hollon, *The Southwest: Old and New* (New York, 1961) and *The Great American Desert: Then and Now* (New York, 1966); *Philip Durham and Everett L. Jones, eds., *The Frontier in American Literature* (New York, 1966); D. S. Otis, *The Dawes Act and the Allotment of Indian Lands* (Norman, 1973); William S. Greever, *The Bonanza West: The Story of the Western Mining Rushes, 1848–1900* (Norman, 1963); James B. Bryce, *The American Commonwealth* (New York, 1889), 2 vols.; *Henry Nash Smith, *Virgin Land: The American West as Symbol and Myth* (Cambridge, 1950); Louis Pelzer, *The Cattlemen's Frontier* (Glendale, 1936); Fred A. Shannon, *Farmer's Last Frontier* (New York, 1945); and *Gilbert C. Fite, *The Farmer's Frontier, 1865–1900* (New York, 1966).

* Available in paperback.

[25] Ibid., p. 895.

Pioneer Religion: A Baptism in the Pond.

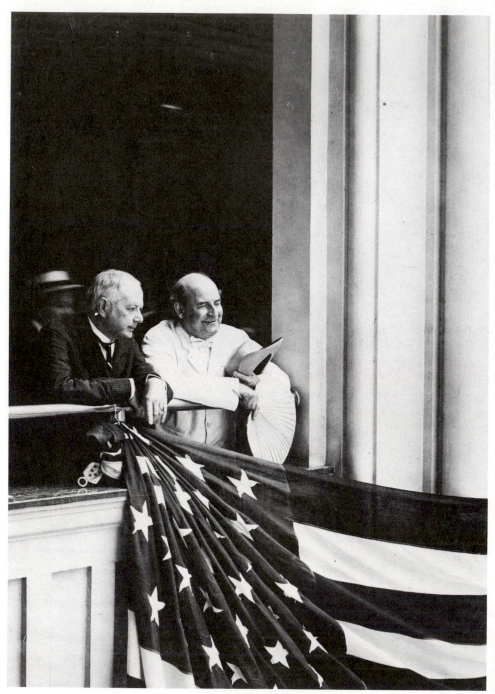

William Jennings Bryan of Nebraska.

30

The New West in the Life of the Nation

THE New West's influence on national affairs was minimal before 1900. The familiar symbiotic relationships between frontiersman as agent and national government as patron did evolve in the trans-Missouri region, and they generated the usual nationalizing currents. The patron national government, however, was slower to respond than it had been for the Old West, and, consequently, the New West developed more slowly. By the time the region was ready for national attention, Eastern and Old West economic, social, and political interests had fused into an amalgam that the New West found difficult to break through. Collusion between these two older sections held the New West in abeyance as a colonial, tributary region and kept it on the threshold of the national community for much of its life.

In the early nineteenth century, national leaders were preoccupied with Old West development and gave little attention to the trans-Missouri region. They were patently reluctant to face directly the question of what use to make of the territory west of Missouri. Their reluctance was derived, as we have said, from the pervasive view of national completeness, the illusion that, with the Old West organized and integrated into the national life, the United States had reached its feasible limit of effective occupation. Therefore, it was believed, the sectional peace struck by the Compromise of 1820 would not be disturbed; the problem of organizing new states west of Missouri would simply not arise.

Moreover, the public was disinterested in the New West, viewing it as a vast inhospitable wasteland unsuited to traditional American pursuits. The Lewis and Clark journals contained regular references to the vast emptiness, low rainfall, harsh terrain, and difficult access of the territory northwest of the Missouri settlements. Pike's journal of his peregrinations

561

across the Southwest confirmed the conditions of anomalous geography and difficult access and encouraged the public to view the entire trans-Missouri territory as a desert. Published reports of Long's reconnaissance along the Platte into the Rocky Mountains and his return to Fort Smith across the southern Plains rigidified this concept of the New West. Long characterized this region the "Great American Desert." Scientists in the Long party held little hope for American occupation of the melancholy arid terrain sweeping from the Missouri border to the face of the Rocky Mountains. In the established context of American expansion, these pessimistic reports chilled private interest, momentarily checked the momentum of frontier progression, and colored public attitudes and policy toward the New West for a century.

Reluctance by federal officials to regard the New West as a region capable of being integrated into the national life on the basis of equality with the Old West produced hesitancy and uncertainty as to what to do with the territory. Inevitably, an imperialist policy was applied to it, which affixed to the region a colonial status and image that persisted until after 1900. By 1830, federal officials had devised two uses for the New West, both confirming the national-completeness view. First, national leaders determined to erect a permanent north-south frontier defense line across that portion of the New West adjacent to the border of the Mississippi Valley province. Second, they planned to create in the New West territory an Indian colonization zone.

Secretary of War Lewis Cass conceived a plan for strengthening national defenses by creating a line of permanent stone fortifications—a sort of early-day Maginot Line—from Fort Snelling on the north to Fort Towson on the Red River, then the southern border of the United States. The fortifications were to protect the nation from enemy invasion by land from the west, just as its Atlantic seaboard defenses guarded the nation from an oceanborne attack. During the 1830s, the Cass frontier defense plan was activated, and a line of posts from Fort Snelling through Fort Leavenworth, Fort Scott, Fort Gibson, and Fort Smith to Fort Towson were connected by military roads.

As a second exercise in imperialist management, federal officials reserved a vast tract—bounded by the Platte on the north and Red River on the south—as a permanent Indian settlement area. They reasoned that because the New West was an arid region unfit for Anglo-American pursuits, the harassed Eastern tribes could be colonized in the Indian Territory, where they would be free of settler intrusion. Between 1820 and 1845, virtually all of the Eastern tribes were resettled in the New West.

Yet, notwithstanding the government's attempt to apply imperial management to the territory west of Missouri, the American frontiering process would not rest. Federal officials had underestimated the pioneer's propensity for expansion. As early as 1803, frontiersmen were poised on the Missouri border ready to apply the expansion formulas that had populated and developed the Old West, to continue the drama of American expansion into the New West.

The familiar fur-trade frontier, military frontier, and agrarian frontier were soon after in evidence, and each, as in the Old West, played its particular directive role in occupying the wilderness, establishing American presence and interest, and activating the essential nationalizing currents that ultimately bound the most remote regions of the New West to the American Union. But in the New West, additional frontiers were significant in establishing American presence, interest, and dominion. The civilized Indian frontier settled and opened the southwestern wilderness; Cherokees, Choctaws, Creeks, Seminoles, and Chickasaws were the first settlers in the New West. They planted constitutional government, public education, agriculture, and slavery in the New West just as surely as their Anglo-American neighbors did in Texas. The missionary frontier was also of strategic importance in establishing American presence and ultimately national dominion in Oregon and Hawaii. The overland traders' frontier seeded American presence in the Southwest, and the maritime trader's frontier performed the same function on the Pacific Coast and in Hawaii and Alaska.

The mining frontier was the most important part of the expansion process in the New West. The 1848 discovery of gold on the American River in northern California drastically quickened the New West's economic pulse and produced pervasive, sweeping alterations in its settlement and development. The riches of the Sacramento encouraged a comprehensive mineral reconnaissance of the New West, which produced discoveries of gold and silver in Washington, Idaho, Nevada, Colorado, Montana, and the Dakotas and intensified established mining operations in the older mineral districts of New Mexico and Arizona. The rush of miners rapidly populated many sections of the New West and stimulated essential supportive industries.

The New West's Great American Desert image, which made the region generally unattractive to settlers from the East, was overcome by the recurring mineral strikes, and the rate of settlement and development in some areas was little short of phenomenal. The rapid settlement was out of step with the anticipated rate and pace of American frontier progression and had an immense and near immediate impact on the national life. It forced a response in nationalizing currents, to which a reluctant federal government finally yielded late in the century.

Frontiersmen ignored the federal government's commitment to national completeness and its plan for limited imperialist use of the trans-Missouri region. They were supported by a growing community of advocates, who applied their oratorical and literary talents to shattering the desert image and replacing it with the picture of an attractive region worthy of private and public enterprise where the American destiny of continental empire could be fulfilled. By generating a public attitude of protectiveness toward the New West and a sense of continental destiny to extend to the Pacific, the publicists fed a progression of influence that led from citizens to leaders in the legislative and executive branches of the government; eventually, the public will was translated into national action leading to territorial absorption.

The New West's new, more favorable geographic image generated wide public interest in the region and, after 1870, contributed materially to its rapid settlement. However, the colonial status affixed to the territory continued to influence the attitudes of federal officials in their management of the region; they were particularly reluctant to receive states created from New West territory into the American Union. The Old West, closer to the seat of the nation's economic and political power, had received prompt and sustained supportive action; the New West, more remotely situated, had to persevere to receive attention.

Until 1861, the New West's impact on national affairs was negative, its influence indirect. It was, in fact, a source of continuing sectional friction, an intruder on the national calm. The surge of Western development forced national leaders to resort to the painfully contrived Compromise of 1850 to maintain section peace. The intrusion of the railroad into the West during the 1850s and the issue of its route to the Pacific became a question as laden with sectional fury as slavery. The sectional contest for control of the New West, the grim realization by Southerners by 1860 that they had lost the struggle, and their frustration at this defeat was a factor of considerable consequence in Southern secession. During the Civil War Confederate leaders looked upon the West as a territorial prize and worked out a broad design for its conquest and incorporation into the Southern orbit. What the South had lost politically, it sought to recover militarily. Both during and after the Civil War, the New West was exploited for partisan advantage. In 1861, much of the region was still in the territorial state of political evolution, a colonial type of existence that was bearable only if it was not extended unduly.

The infusion of new issues, questions, conditions, and blatant political opportunism into the state-making process delayed completion of the political format of the contiguous portion of the New West until 1912. The issue of non-contiguity delayed statehood for Alaska and Hawaii until 1959. The central government exploited New West state-making to serve partisan interests. Congress admitted Nevada in 1864 in order to assure the Republican party of necessary electoral votes and ratification of the thirteenth amendment; Nebraska statehood was a part of the legislative-executive struggle centering on President Andrew Johnson's impeachment; and Colorado was admitted in 1876 to cast its three electoral votes for Rutherford B. Hayes. Increasingly after 1876, both Republican and Democratic parties looked upon new Western states with reference to their influence on presidential elections; for thirteen years no Western territory was admitted to the Union, although several had met basic statutory requirements and were eligible for statehood.

Congress, habituated to the exercise of awesome power over the Southern states during the Reconstruction period, continued this tradition in its management of the Western territories. Thus Congress often set extreme and irrelevant conditions for statehood consideration or required territories to remedy local problems as a condition of consideration. These "conditions" included abolition of polygamy in Utah and "Americanization" of deviant cultures in Indian Territory, New Mexico, and Arizona. Congressmen became so tedious and picayune in their review of the statehood appeals of the Western territories that, in the case of Oklahoma, they went so far as to select the site for the state capital and prohibited the sale of alcoholic beverages in the eastern half of the state for twenty-one years.

The only time before 1900 that the New West exercised a direct influence over national politics occurred during the agrarian revolt that flowered in the 1890s. A current of rural discontent, generated by drastic postwar changes in farm economics, coursed from the Old West into the newly established agrarian community on the Great Plains. Growing application of technology to farming, increased size of farm holdings, and expanded production meant that the nation needed fewer farmers to sustain its burgeoning industrialized cities. The self-sufficient family farm became a highly competitive commercial enterprise, based on production of staples—cash crops, which, for the New West, were mostly small grains. Farm prices, particularly for grain and cotton, were increasingly influenced by production in new foreign farming areas and by international market conditions.

Agrarian problems in the New West were acute. Many settlers had been attracted to the region by the writings of Western publicists who had portrayed the Great Plains as the "Garden of the World" covered by family farms. But rather than becoming independent farmers, New West settlers were increasingly caught up in a web of dependence in the new-style agrarian economics, of reliance on staple-crop production that required expanded holdings and expensive equipment in order to compete in the fluctuating world market. They became dependent upon bankers for capital to obtain more land and essential equipment. Remoteness placed them at the mercy of the railroads, which charged "all the traffic would bear." And they had the added problem of operating in a mercurial climate, facing the regular prospect of drought, destructive hailstorms, and other natural disasters. Caught in a hopeless cycle of high freight charges, exorbitant interest rates, crushing debt, mortgage foreclosure and bankruptcy, the settlers faced tenancy as the final prospect. By 1890, over 25 percent of New West farms were operated by tenants, a mocking denouement to the self-sufficient farmer ideal.

Resort to political action was complicated by the region's diverse economic groups and their variant interests. The New West farmers were unable to present a unified voice for the region as they could in the Old West agrarian frontier in an earlier age. They shared the voter community with railroad workers, miners, stockraisers, lumbermen, and maritime workers on the Pacific coast. In this collage, the farmer was only a part, there was no visible common interest to provide the means for concerted action, and this condition weakened the general political force of the West. Walter P. Webb epitomized the New West farmers' melancholy, desperate state: "Far from markets, burned by drought, beaten by hail, withered by hot winds, frozen by blizzards, eaten out by grasshoppers, exploited by capitalists, and cozened by politicians" they turned to radical action in an attempt to force government to provide some relief.[1]

During the 1870s, some common agrarian interest was generated by the Grange, a nonpolitical organization that fused farmers throughout the nation in a common cause of economic and social improvement. This movement materially influenced New West farmers to agitate for state and territorial legislation to regulate railroads, bankers, and the middle men who covertly sapped farmers' profits. The California Farmers' Union challenged the Central Pacific Railroad's monopolistic practices, and the Texas Farmers' Alliance actively promoted railroad and bank control. Western legislatures imitated the farm states in the Old Northwest in setting railroad, elevator, and bank rates and adopted codes of regulatory laws. The railway companies challenged these laws in Munn v. Illinois in 1876, but the Supreme Court upheld state power to regulate, creating chaos in transportation. Freight tariffs varied from one state to another, and in the Wabash case of 1886, the court reversed the Munn decision and ruled that a state did not have the power to regulate traffic moving in interstate commerce. Thereupon, Congress reacted on behalf of the regulatory advocates by adopting the Interstate Commerce Act in 1887, which created the Interstate Commerce Commission. While initially not as effective as Western advocates desired, the commission eventually provided some regulatory relief for the agrarian community.

Widespread debt default and mortgage foreclosure in the New West during the 1880s led agrarian reformers to support schemes to inflate the currency, which would make it easier for debt-ridden settlers to meet their obligations to bankers on mortgages and equipment loans. Thus Westerners supported the Greenback movement and joined the anti-monopolist-Greenback party fusion that coalesced into the Populist party. A meeting of agrarian leaders at Cincinnati in 1891 led to the Populist party convention at Omaha the following year; it was the first political meeting of consequence ever held in the New West. At the Omaha convention, Populist leaders developed a platform calling for government ownership of railroads, free coinage of silver, a graduated income tax, the secret ballot, and popular election of senators. In the presidential election of 1892, Western voters supported the Populist party's presidential candidate, James B. Weaver of Iowa.

[1] Walter P. Webb, *The Great Plains* (New York, 1930), p. 503.

During the 1890s, Populists were successful in electing United States senators in South Dakota and Kansas and, in coalition with minority Democrats, consistently won state offices in California, Idaho, Kansas, Nevada, and North Dakota. Populist voter strength in elections was augmented by the silver-mining interests, who were attracted by the party's stand on coinage of silver. William Jennings Bryan of Nebraska was among the few New West political leaders to gain national prominence. In 1896 he was the Populist and Democratic party candidate for president. The Democratic party appropriated some of the Populist program into its platform, and modest farm prosperity after 1896 caused Populism—the New West's first political surge of consequence—to wane.

Throughout the nineteenth century, there was a sustained reluctance to accept the New West into national life as an equal of the East and Old West. Early hesitancy and uncertainty as to what use to make of this vast trans-Missouri territory was succeeded by timidity, derived from the anxiety of national leaders that succumbing to western demands for political organization would prejudice the sorely won sectional peace. Subsequently, there developed a growing concern in Congress that, by providing political organization for the New West, it risked the creation of a colossus that could disturb the political relationship of the East and the Old West. Thus Western political promise was aborted, and not until the middle of the twentieth century was the New West able to challenge its Eastern master, assert a determinative role in national politics, and make substantial contributions to American life.

SELECTED SOURCES

The struggle of the New West to receive prompt reception into the national life during the nineteenth century is an epic of frustration. General works that cover various phases of this protracted struggle incllde Robert E. Riegel and Robert G. Athearn, *America Moves West* (New York, 1971); LeRoy R. Hafen, W. Eugene Hollon, and Carl Coke Rister, *Western America: The Exploration, Settlement, and Development of the Region beyond the Mississippi* (Englewood Cliffs, N.J., 1970); Frederic L. Paxson, *History of the American Frontier, 1763–1893* (Boston, 1924); Ray Allen Billington, *Westward Expansion: A History of the American Frontier* (New York, 1974); Kent Ladd Steckmesser, *The Westward Movement: A Short History* (New York, 1969); and Thomas D. Clark, *Frontier America: The Story of the Westward Movement* (New York, 1959).

The publicists' impact on the American private and public mind and action is analyzed cogently in *Henry Nash Smith, *Virgin Land: The American West as Symbol and Myth* (Cambridge, 1950). The West and national lore are treated in *Leo Marx, *The Machine in the Garden: Technology and the Pastoral

* Available in paperback.

Ideal (New York, 1964), and *Roderick Nash, *Wilderness and the American Mind* (New Haven, 1967).

Studies on regions of the New West and their effect on national development include *Walter P. Webb, *The Great Plains* (Boston, 1931); W. Eugene Hollon, **The Southwest: Old and New* (New York, 1961) and *The Great American Desert: Then and Now* (New York, 1966).

PART FOUR *the* **West in the Twentieth Century**

Hoover Dam on the Colorado River

Oil Rig at Raccoon Bend on the Texas Gulf Coast.

31

Western Economic Maturation

ONE of the spectacular developments in American national life during the twentieth century has been the transformation of the West from a colonial outback to a mature, coequal region of the country. Especially since 1950, the West has exercised an increasingly directive influence on national affairs and, on occasion, has been preeminent in shaping policy and providing leadership for the nation. This Western metamorphosis is due to a dynamic combination of factors centering on a drastic population increase and continuing development of the region's rich resource base.

The West has received substantial population increases in every decade of the new century; its rate of growth in each ten-year period is at least 40 percent—twice the national average. By 1970, the Western population exceeded 50 million, about 26 percent of the national population. More than half of it is concentrated in Texas and California. Such sustained population increases have had immense effect on Western economy, society, and politics. The new population created an expanding reservoir of skills and professions that provided the region much-needed business, social, and political leadership.

A concomitant increase in capital has occurred. During the bonanza period of Western development, capitalists for the most part remained in the East and exercised absentee direction over their Western investments. Increasingly after 1900, they moved to the West to participate directly in the developmental process. Besides contributing to the economic strength and diversification of the regional economy, this population movement had important ramifications for the political realm and abetted the West's emergence as a force in the councils of the nation.

EVOLUTION OF THE MODERN WESTERN ECONOMY

Between 1915 and 1970, the Western economy was radically altered through wide application of new technology, infusion of management talent, expansion of capital resources, and diversification—primarily in manufacturing. The region's economic role shifted; no longer exclusively a supplier of raw materials, it also became a producer of consumer goods. One of the principal contributing factors to the Western economy's maturation has been the supportive role played by the federal government in land distribution, resource utilization, and provision of capital. Thus, while the West has become largely independent of Eastern capitalists, its dependence on the federal government has increased. However, in spite of competition from twentieth-century industrial diversification, the West's old established industries—mining, agriculture, stockraising, and lumbering—have remained the mainstays of the regional economy.

The Mineral Industries

The mining frontier, which in the nineteenth century populated and developed much of the West, continued to exploit the region's established mineral districts and to prospect for new fields. Gold and silver mining declined to a marginal recovery type of operation that included use of dredges in rivers. Precious metal mining was overshadowed by development of base metal resources that were required in ever greater tonnages by the Eastern industrial establishment and by the West's own emerging industrial community. Thus copper, iron ore, lead, and zinc mining became the principal extractive industries of the contiguous Western states and Alaska. Mineral production ranks among the leading industries in Texas, Oklahoma, Colorado, New Mexico, Arizona, Utah, Wyoming, Nevada, Montana, Idaho, and Alaska. In addition, Western mines yield an increasing supply of exotic minerals—tungsten, manganese, molybdenum, antimony, beryllium, lithium, and uranium.

The energy needs of the region and of the nation have largely been met by Western fossil fuel resources. Coal from vast deposits widely dispersed over the trans-Missouri region was used extensively for transportation, industry, and domestic purposes until the 1920s. At that time, it was displaced by another fossil fuel—petroleum and its associate, natural gas. However, great quantities of Western coal continue to be used in electrical generation plants and, since 1970, Western coal in liquified and gassified form has increasingly been used as an alternative energy source to petroleum.

Since 1900 Western oil resources have provided the nation with natural gas and petroleum products in escalating volume. Beginning in southern Kansas and northern Indian Territory before the turn of the century, oil prospectors—wildcatters—explored the entire West, including Alaska and the tidelands. One of the West's most dramatic oil discoveries occurred in 1901 near Beaumont, Texas, when the fabulous Spindletop gusher blew in.

There followed the discovery of the incomparable Glenn Pool near Tulsa, Oklahoma, and successive strikes northward into Kansas set the environs of the rich Mid-Continent Field. Extension of petroleum prospecting from Oklahoma and Texas across the Great Plains, Rocky Mountains, and Great Basin to California has yielded new oil fields in each region.

The seemingly insatiable demand of American industry and the consuming public for more natural gas and petroleum led to the discovery of oil in the tidelands off the Gulf of Mexico and the Pacific Coast. Drillers have opened oil wells 120 miles offshore in the Gulf of Mexico. Pipeline grids carry the natural gas and petroleum to shore refineries. The most recent bonanza oil region is situated on the barren North Slope of Alaska near Prudhoe Bay. A forty-eight inch pipeline, 800 miles long, with an ultimate daily capacity of 2 million barrels, will transport petroleum from North Slope wells to the icefree port of Valdez for shipment by tankers to refineries. In addition, improved petroleum technology has made possible more complete extraction from each well: waterflooding permits oil to be recovered from abandoned wells, and deeper drilling brings up formerly inaccessible supplies. Oil and natural gas wells in the Pecos County, Texas field are over 25,000 feet deep.

Agriculture and Stockraising

The dominant themes in Western agriculture and stockraising during the twentieth century have been continuing and expanding federal support, increase in acres under irrigation, and regional specialization. Associated developments include growth in the size of holdings, concomitant mechanization and reduction in the number of persons engaged in agriculture, and rise of corporate farming. In many cases this growth has resulted in food and fiber production by agribusiness—integrated operations that extend from fertilizer, seed, and machinery supply to land control through production, processing, and marketing.

Initially, aid to Western agriculture consisted of laws providing for generous dispensing of the public domain to farmers and ranchmen. The myth that the agrarian frontier closed in 1890 is denied by the fact that after that date over 600 million acres were still available for homesteading, although much of it required irrigation for successful farming. More land was filed upon under federal land statues between 1898 and 1919 than between 1865 and 1897. Several land laws amendatory to the basic Homestead Act of 1862 were passed by Congress specifically to promote Western agricultural settlement. These included the Kinkaid Act of 1904, which increased to 640 acres the maximum amount of land that could be filed on in western Nebraska. The Enlarged Homestead Act of 1909, in order to encourage dry farming, increased the homestead unit to 320 acres. The last of the homestead laws, the Stock-Raising Homestead Act of 1916, permitted entry on 640 acres. Thus homesteading continued in the West after 1890. In fact, in Montana alone between 1910 and 1922, farmers and stockmen filed on 93 million acres. By 1929, fewer than 200 million acres remained available for homesteading, and most of it required irrigation for successful farming. During 1934–1935, federal officials withdrew from homesteading the remaining unreserved and unappropriated public land in the contiguous United States.

During the latter part of the nineteenth century, many Western farmers and stockraisers situated in areas requiring irrigation found that development of water resources for their lands was beyond their ability. They organized the National Irrigation Congress, which became the principal pressure group promoting assistance to Western agriculture through federally funded irrigation projects. Their appeals led to passage by Congress in 1894 of the Carey Act, which donated large tracts of public land to each of the arid states to enable them to subsidize irrigation projects. The results of projects developed under the Carey Act were not, however, adequate to meet the needs of arid-land occupants. Moreover, the problem of the interstate character of rivers regularly surfaced as individual states sought to develop irrigation projects.

This predicament was remedied in 1902 by the Newlands Reclamation Act, which set aside revenue from sale of public lands to finance irrigation projects constructed under direction of the new Reclamation Service of the Department of the Interior. The costs of constructing irrigation facilities were ultimately to be paid for by water users. By 1920, Reclamation Service projects had brought water to over 20 million acres. Great storage reservoirs were subsequently constructed on the Colorado, Columbia, Snake, Missouri, and Rio Grande rivers and their tributaries to store and disburse water to the parched but fertile peripheral croplands. The Colorado River reclamation brought the rich Imperial Valley of southern California into production. By 1970, of the nearly 200 million acres of Western cropland, about 40 million acres were irrigated. Approximately one-fourth of the water used for irrigation on Western ranches and farms comes from Reclamation Service storage reservoirs. Deep wells provide the remainder.

Other forms of federal aid to Western agriculture and stockraising include annual grants under the Morrill Act for agricultural research to colleges and universities and local service from agricultural experiment stations maintained by the Department of Agriculture. Agronomists carry out research in dry-farming methods, irrigation, and development of drought-resistant grains, fibers, and other crops. At the turn of the century, the Office of Foreign Seeds and Plants of the Department of Agriculture sent teams of scientists to arid countries to study local plants and to select strains of wheat, cotton, alfalfa, date palms, sorghums, and other plants that might be adapted to the western United States. In 1901 the Department of Agriculture established the Division of Animal Husbandry to help ranchmen control stock diseases and improve herds and flocks. And in 1934, Congress passed the Taylor Act, which legalized and regulated grazing on public lands.

World War I was a bonanza time for Western farmers and stockraisers. Supported by federal subsidies, they doubled the region's food production to strengthen the war effort. Additional land was opened, particularly for the production of wheat and cotton. But by 1920, the resumption of European food production and high American tariffs caused European nations to drastically reduce their imports of grain, meat, and fibers. This reduction created an agricultural depression in the West; throughout the 1920s, farm groups sought federal assistance to relieve agrarian distress. Their pressure on Congress crystallized in a plan to establish a federally managed two-price system for farm commodities—one for the domestic market, the other for the world market. A national board would set the domestic prices, while agricultural surpluses would be sold abroad at world prices. The legislation to activate the federal farm-pricing plan was twice vetoed by President Calvin Coolidge. In 1929, the federal government assumed responsibility for farm-commodity prices when President Herbert Hoover signed the Agricultural Marketing Act.

The ensuing Great Depression, however, made it impossible to effectuate the statute, and Western agriculture continued to languish. Recurring natural disasters during the 1930s, including devastating droughts and the wind erosion-induced Dust Bowl on the Great Plains, added to the region's agrarian misery. Western farmers joined with Midwest and Southern agriculturalists to press the federal government for relief. During the early 1930s, Congress adopted several agricultural relief and rehabilitation measures as a part of President Franklin D. Roosevelt's New Deal program. The measures were nullified by the United States Supreme Court. Finally, beginning in 1936, federal laws providing for federal cash support to farmers for participating in conservation programs and reducing production of surplus crops were permitted to stand. The pattern of federal production controls through acreage allotments for grain, cotton, and certain other surplus agricultural commodities, federal price supports, and cash payments to farmers continued through the 1950s and 1960s in various forms. One of these was the Soil Bank program, which provided cash payments for withdrawal of land from production.

In recent years, agricultural support through federal payments to Western farmers has been substantial, particularly for cotton, wheat, and feed-grain acreage reduction. In 1968, Texas led the nation; half a billion dollars in federal funds were paid to its farmers. Kansas was second with $212 million, and California farmers received $111 million.

In the new Western economy, agriculture is specialized, and local production is generally determined by soil and water conditions and markets. The producers are concerned less with family and local use than in keying in on national and world markets. The West produces well over half of the nation's food. Utah, Idaho, Colorado, and California are the leading sugar-beet producers. Wheat, barley, and corn predominate on the northern Plains, and wheat, cotton, and feed grains on the southern Plains. The Pacific Coast is the nation's leading producer of fruits and vegetables, and irrigated cotton is an important crop in Arizona and California. Vegetables, fruit, and grain production predominate in the Northwest. The ultimate in diversity and specialization is found in the California agricultural establishment. In the nation's leading agricultural state, income from farm products exceeded $4 billion in 1970. Less than 10 percent of California's land is in farms, and 70 percent of it is irrigated. Irrigation in the Central and Imperial valleys permit food production all year round.

Throughout the West, farm size has consistently increased. The 160-acre homestead is a tradition of the past; in the 1970s the average farm is 1,500 acres. Concentration of holdings and increased mechanization have produced corporate farming, particularly in California where the mechanized "factories in the fields" yield great quantities of irrigated crops, each operation requiring, in spite of mechanization, large numbers of migratory workers. Even so, the rise of corporate farming, concentration of holdings, and mechanization of Western agriculture have reduced the number of persons engaged in agriculture to the point that farm workers now comprise only 5 percent of the total labor community of the West. This reduction in farm population has produced a substantial rural exodus to the growing Western cities.

Lumbering

The softwood and hardwood forests of eastern Indian Territory—Oklahoma after 1907—and eastern Texas were extensively exploited in the early years of the twentieth century to supply Mississippi Valley and Eastern markets. However, by 1915 the Pacific Northwest, which contains at least half of the standing timber in the contiguous United States, had become the focus of Western lumbering. The region's expanding railroad grid provided export facilities, and large companies began systematic exploitation of the primal forests. At first, the Northwest lumbering industry supplied only the growing West Coast market, but after 1915, due to the opening of the Panama Canal, it began to export to Eastern markets.

As the twentieth-century West increased in population, particularly in the new cities, a wide regional market developed; lumbermen exploited the forests of the Rocky Mountains and everywhere that profitable tree stands existed. Increasingly, Western lumbering has become a scientific industry, with replanting and silvaculture practiced on both private lumber-company lands and in the national forests. Application of new technology and processes to lumbering has also expanded the industry to include a wide range of wood products of which construction lumber is only one. The new wood-derivatives include plywood, chemicals, fiberboard, and pulp. Virtually every part of each tree, including the sawdust, is utilized. The great softwood forests of Alaska augur to become the timber reserves for future national needs.

Fishing

Virtually every port on the Pacific and Gulf Coast of Texas supports a fishing fleet. With refrigeration units on railroad cars, ships, trucks and aircraft, the oceanic harvest provides fresh fish and shellfish for local, Midwest, and Eastern markets. Annually, the Pacific fishing fleet gathers great cargoes of tuna and salmon for delivery to canneries along the coast from California to Alaska. Saturation harvesting has depleted this important food resource and has led to at least the beginning of controls and management, all in the context of conservation.

Transportation

Between 1900 and 1920, there was a sustained expansion of the West's railroad grid, so that at its peak in 1920, the trans-Missouri railroad system contained 120,000 miles of track. By then, alternative, competing transportation systems—the automobile, bus, and motor truck, and expanding Western highways—forced a leveling off in rail expansion. During the 1940s, many rail lines began eliminating passenger service, abandoning sections of roadbed, and concentrating on freight carriage. A revival of interest in moving passengers by rail in the 1960s led the federal government to provide funds to certain Western lines to restore passenger service. The resultant Amtrak System has rehabilitated rail passenger service in the West, as in the East and Midwest, on a limited basis.

A second revolution in Western travel occurred in the twentieth century with the development of the automobile and a system of public roads to accommodate it. Road improvement and construction were pioneered in California; by 1909, the legislature had authorized the construction of a system of paved roads for the state. Three years later, leaders from California and other Western states organized the Lincoln Highway Association to promote construction of a graveled highway from New York to San Francisco. By 1915, the project had progressed to the point that limited automobile travel was possible. The Lincoln Highway generally followed the old Overland Trail route.

Highway engineers have been able to construct routes over sections of the West that railroads had found impossible to negotiate. The Federal Highway Acts of 1916 and 1921 stimulated Western highway development, and between 1919 and 1929, the Western states constructed over a million miles of roads, using federal matching grants. Substantial improvement in the Western highway system came as a result of the Federal Highway Act of 1956, which provided for 41,000 miles of multi-lane highways. The National System of Interstate and Defense Highways, with the federal government supplying up to 90 percent of construction costs, enabled every Western state to achieve paved, highspeed arteries that are integrated into the national interstate system.

The Texas Gulf Coast, Pacific Coast, much of Alaska, and all of Hawaii are part of the American maritime complex. With federal aid, the maritime states have improved harbors and enhanced ocean-traffic facilities. Honolulu and Pearl Harbor in Hawaii received early attention by the federal government, under the aegis of developing naval defenses and anchorages. Around

1900, work began on harbor improvement at San Pedro, California, the port for Los Angeles, with a $3 million expenditure. Later the federal government provided $11 million and the city of Los Angeles $30 million for additional harbor work. By 1933, San Pedro exceeded all American ports except New York in tonnage. San Diego and San Francisco are important naval and commercial maritime centers, and Seattle is the great port of the Northwest, shipping cargoes of lumber, canned salmon, and grain to the Orient and to Atlantic ports. During World War I, federal and local funds financed the deepening of the Columbia River channel; jetties constructed in the estuary and new docking facilities made Portland an ocean port. Houston became the principal port on the Texas Gulf Coast, when, beginning around 1900, federal funds provided the means to open a fifty-mile long ship channel into the Gulf to accommodate sea-going vessels.

Completion of the Panama Canal in 1914 had an immense effect on Western maritime and inland transportation. Within ten years, about half of the West's oil, grain, foodstuffs, and lumber were moving by ship from West coast ports through the canal to Eastern markets. Water-freight rates became substantially lower than land transportation charges, and forced railroads to reduce their discriminatory, often economically stultifying rates in the West.

World War I seeded the aircraft industry in southern California. During the 1920s, commercial aviation plants were established in southern California and Seattle and, during the 1930s, at Wichita, Kansas. These aviation clusters became the aircraft production centers for the nation. By 1925, four transcontinental lines operated from the Pacific Coast. The great air-travel exchanges of the nation are in the West—the new Dallas complex, Houston Intercontinental, Phoenix Sky Harbor, and Los Angeles International. Feeder lines serve most Western communities. Advances in air travel have integrated Hawaii and Alaska into the national life. Technological advances in air travel have miraculously reduced the time required for the Western passage. The Oregon-bound immigrant's six months' crossing in the 1840s—from Independence, Missouri to the Pacific—had been reduced to five days by the railroad by 1900 and, by 1930, to three days by automobile. Jet aircraft has further reduced the time in travel to less than three hours.

THE WESTERN ECONOMY IN 1970

Until World War I, the West was largely a supportive, colonial region dominated by Eastern capital and management and providing raw materials for the growing Eastern industrial establishment and food for the expanding Eastern urban centers. The nation placed even greater demands on the West for food, fibers, lumber and minerals during World War I. Under the stimulus of federal production subsidies, Western farmers and stockgrowers doubled food production between 1916 and 1920.

The industrial surge associated with World War I was largely concentrated in the eastern United States, but some limited dispersal of industry to the West occurred during the war, particularly shipbuilding and aircraft production. Several Eastern manufacturers also established regional and West Coast branches during the war; many of these continued after the war and provided a nucleus for future industry and manufacturing expansion. Government sponsorship of certain war-related industries also had its effect. Shipbuilding became an important enterprise in harbors from Seattle to San Diego, and military aircraft production was introduced into southern California.

The Western Economy and the Great Depression

While the period of the Great Depression, 1929–1941, was a time of general economic malaise in the West and the nation, even then there were signs of Western economic advance and change. New oil field discoveries in Texas, Oklahoma, Kansas, and California produced pockets of boom-type development and assuaged some of the economic suffering by employing large numbers of workers. Heavy production from the new fields soon glutted the market, and $3-a-barrel oil plunged to ten cents a barrel. Action by the governors of Oklahoma, Texas, and Kansas—particularly Governor Ernest W. Marland of Oklahoma—led to state-imposed controls on production and a regional conservation and production control organization called the Interstate Oil Compact Commission.

One of the most significant developments for the Western economy in the period of the Great Depression was the shift in capital sources. Until 1929, most of the trans-Missouri enterprises had been funded with Eastern capital. The collapse of many private fortunes made it more difficult for the customary sources to furnish the capital required in the West, even on the basis of the low-level economic activity induced by the national economic disaster. Therefore, the West looked more and more to the federal government for capital; the government responded, and during the Great Depression, Western dependence for capital funding shifted from private to public sources. Between 1933 and 1939, on a per-capita basis, the federal government spent 60 percent more in the West than in the other regions of the nation in relief and on New Deal programs such as the RFC, FERA, CWA, PWA, CCC, WPA, and REA. Western per-capita expenditures by the federal government amounted to $306, as compared to $224 expended in the Midwest, the next highest region. Thus the West began to move from private to public colonialism.

During the Great Depression, the federal government spent huge sums on public works in the West, increasing vastly the region's industrial-diversification potential. Projects included highway construction and improvement and damming of Western rivers for reclamation. The huge dams increased food-producing areas through extension of irrigation and greatly expanded power resources for future industrial use.

The New West Economy, 1941–1970

The latent economic power of the nation progressed in quantum leaps with the outbreak of World War II. No part of the nation was affected as greatly as the West. Between 1940 and 1945, the federal government spent over $60 billion in the Western states, most of it for defense. The federal policy of dispersing industry particularly favored the West, where aircraft, shipbuilding, munitions, and textile enterprises were established. These new industries became the basis for a continuing economic diversification and sprawl after the end of the war.

Sustained international tensions after 1948, with the federal government supporting for the first time in its history a large peacetime military establishment, favored the West. Research, development, and production staffs composed of scientists, engineers, and technicians collected at defense installations in Texas, New Mexico, Arizona, California, Utah; and virtually every Western state continued work in federally supported military, space, and civilian industries. Federal expenditures for national defense in the West from 1945 to 1960 amounted to $150 billion. In the period from 1961 to 1965, the Department of Defense spent about 20 percent of the total national defense budget in California. During the same period, NASA allocated $5 billion—41 percent of its budget—to California projects.

Since 1946, many Western states have received more funds from Washington than their citizens paid in taxes. The United States government during 1972 spent in Oklahoma for all public purposes $2.8 billion. For the same period, Oklahoma taxpayers paid $1.6 billion in federal taxes. Politically conservative Texas in 1970 accepted in excess of $10 billion in federal funds—twice the value of its mineral production, including oil, for that year. Ultraconservative Dallas County alone accepted in excess of $1 billion.

Thus, federal direction and funding must receive major credit for the industrial miracle that has occurred in the Western economy since 1941. Federal projects and funds, most of them defense and space-related, fed the local economies, supported the rise of new industries, and strongly affected the total regional economy. In reverberating rings of influence, federal direction and funding spread into supporting services and into residential construction industries. The West's growing industrial complex has created abundant employment opportunities, which have attracted additional population, which, in turn, has escalated all aspects of the Western economy.

Character of Western Industry

James Michener has commented on the phenomenal industrial rise of the West in the postwar era, that while Eastern "business leaders still clung to traditional industries that were on the decline; coal, steel, railroads, [the

West] shifted to electronics, the so-called brain factories, and aviation, whose horizons seemed unlimited." [1] Some heavy industry did, of course, develop in the West. As early as 1881, Colorado businessmen collected local and Utah iron ore, coal, and limestone, and established a steel plant at Pueblo. This was the only steel plant in the West for sixty years, for Western industrialization was discouraged by Eastern capitalists through selective investment and discriminatory railroad rates; the control was aimed at checking Western competition with established Eastern industries.

The wide dispersal of war industries with federal support beginning in 1941 led to the rise of steel plants at Dangerfield and Houston, Texas; Tulsa, Oklahoma; Provo and Geneva, Utah; and Fontana, California. These plants, created to produce steel plate for military tanks and for Pacific Coast shipbuilding, continued to function after the war. Other metal-producing facilities in the West, besides copper, lead, and zinc refining, included the production of aluminum and magnesium—light metals required for aircraft and space equipment and for many consumer goods. These industries were concentrated in Washington, Oregon, California, Texas, and Montana.

Most Western industry, however, is the product of new technology. Manufacturing plants producing defense and space equipment and consumer goods are dependent upon Western research centers. The new technology—besides being largely research-related—is almost portable; that is, it is light industry, and the plants are easily moved and maintained. New technology has also materially affected availability of the West's water and power resources. Improved electrical-transmission facilities have reduced line loss in transit, thus enabling, for example, the Bonneville Power Administration in the Pacific Northwest to market electrical power to industries and domestic subscribers in California and Arizona. Since much of the West is arid, lack of water has been a limiting factor in urban and industrial growth and development. The new Western industrial complex and the burgeoning cities require vast quantities of water. Canal and aqueduct construction for long-range transmission of water is possible with new engineering techniques, excavation equipment, materials, and power for pumping to overcome elevation problems. It is common to move water over a thousand-mile course from areas of plenty to areas of need.

The new technology has also produced a host of resource-related industries, further dispersing Western manufacturing to remote regions close to the basic material source. The rich oil fields of the Texas Panhandle support a cluster of petrochemical industrial towns centering on Amarillo. There gasoline and motor oil are refined; but in addition, workmen apply new processes to each barrel of crude oil to derive carbon black, printer's ink, synthetic rubber, solvents, hydrocarbons, asphalt, butane, propane,

[1] Neil Morgan, *Westward Tilt: The American West Today* (New York, 1961), p. viii.

sulphur and sulphuric acid, ammonia and ammonium nitrate, and fertilizer, plus sophisticated fuels for space vehicles.

Besides the generous federal funding of the Western economy, considerable local capital sources have developed. Although most of the funding for Western enterprises in the nineteenth-century exploitive age came from the East, even then some capital was provided by California capitalists and the Bank of California. After 1900, local capital resources began to grow as wealthy immigrants moved West, increasing the strength of banks, particularly those on the Pacific Coast, especially San Francisco. The Federal Reserve System, established in 1913, had the effect of removing the Eastern stranglehold on Western banking, dispersing some capital, and thus making resources more flexible in the West. The new Western economy has produced many local private fortunes, which have added to the region's rapid economic growth. The Bank of America in San Francisco, the largest private bank in the world, has resources of over $12 billion.

Virtually every Western state government maintains two agencies in response to the new economic order: a department of commerce and industry and a division of tourism. The mission of the department of commerce and industry is to recruit industry to the state by offering Eastern industrialists rent-free plant facilities and tax-exempt privileges. Many Western states chart their progress and growth on the basis of new industries and the number of manufacturing jobs created each year. Thus in most Western states since 1941, in part as a result of the industrial-recruitment drive, the number of persons engaged in manufacturing has substantially increased. California, the industrial goliath of the West and the nation, has more of its people engaged in manufacturing than any state in the Union.

State tourist bureaus promote an increasingly important regional industry. Tourism is a leading enterprise in virtually all the Western states, ranking first in Nevada, and near second in importance in California, Arizona, New Mexico, and Hawaii. Through national advertising and other forms of promotion, Western state tourist agencies exploit local natural beauty, historic sites, entertainment—as in Reno and Las Vegas, Nevada—and state and national parks for camping and recreational facilities. Until recently, Western tourism has been a seasonal enterprise, but with the growing popularity of winter sports, many states now maintain a year-round tourist industry.

Maturation of the Western economy since 1941 has produced substantive change in the region's society, culture, and politics. Abundant employment opportunities provided by the new economic order have attracted great numbers of people to the West. In no phase of Western life has this enormous population increase impacted more than on the region's politics. The changes in outlook and leadership produced extend far beyond local and state levels into the national political scene.

SELECTED SOURCES

The most comprehensive survey of the West's economic maturation is *Gerald D. Nash, *The American West in the Twentieth Century: A Short History of an Urban Oasis* (Englewood Cliffs, 1973). Other useful general studies include W. Eugene Hollon, *The Southwest: Old and New* (New York, 1961); Wendell Berge, *Economic Freedom for the West* (Lincoln, Neb., 1946); Neil Morgan, *Westward Tilt: The American West Today* (New York, 1961); Marshall Sprague, *The Mountain States: Arizona, California, Idaho, Montana, Nevada, New Mexico, Utah, and Wyoming* (New York, 1967); Neal R. Pierce, *The Great Plains States of America: People, Politics, and Power in the Nine Great Plains States* (New York, 1973); and *Earl S. Pomeroy, *The Pacific Slope* (New York, 1965).

Studies concerned with specific phases of the modern Western economy include Carl C. Rister, *Oil! Titan of the Southwest* (Norman, 1949); *Carey McWilliams, *Factories in the Field* (New York, 1969); Leonard J. Arrington, *The Changing Economic Structure of the Mountain West, 1850–1950* (Logan, 1963); Ladd Haystead and Gilbert C. Fite, *The Agricultural Regions of the United States* (Norman, 1955); Mary W. Hargreaves, *Dry Farming in the Northern Plains, 1900–1925* (Cambridge, 1957); Vernon W. Ruttan, *The Economic Demand for Irrigated Acreage: New Methodology and Some Preliminary Projections, 1954–1980* (Baltimore, 1965); and Charles M. Gates and Dorothy O. Johansen, *Empire on the Columbia: A History of the Pacific Northwest* (New York, 1967).

Recently published state histories yield fresh information on unit development in Western economic maturation. Some of these studies are Warren A. Beck, *New Mexico: A History of Four Centuries* (Norman, 1962); *James C. Olson, *History of Nebraska* (Lincoln, 1955); William F. Zornow, *Kansas: A History of the Jayhawk State* (Norman, 1957); Andrew F. Rolle, *California: A History* (New York, 1969); and Arrell M. Gibson, *Oklahoma: A History of Five Centuries* (Norman, 1965).

* Available in paperback.

Sharecropper Family Stalled in the Desert near India, California, 1937.

32

Western American Society in the Twentieth Century

CONTEMPORARY Western American society is a conglomerate of ethnic and cultural diversities. Its culture is a composite of frontier residuals clung to by the descendants of Anglo settlers, variant life ways of important Indian, Mexican-American, Oriental, and European elements, and the twentieth-century input of a massive new immigration from the eastern United States. These heterogeneous components are in a state of dynamic flux moving inevitably toward a new regional synthesis. In addition, Western culture is strongly influenced by technology, federal law, administrative rulings, and Supreme Court decisions, all combining to metamorphose the region's economy, reduce its isolation, and erase local differences in viewpoint and practice, style and accent—in effect, replacing regional culture with national culture.

WESTERN ETHNIC MÉLANGE

One of the spectacular developments of the twentieth-century West has been its phenomenal demographic surge. Since 1900 it has received a nearly fourfold population increase. While the Anglo-American component of the Western population has remained predominant through immigration and natural increase, the region's variant ethnic communities have also undergone substantial growth. During the twentieth century, large numbers of Spanish-Americans from Mexico have immigrated to the United States, most of them settling in the old, established Mexican-American communities of the Southwest. The Japanese, already present in Hawaii, were imported to the mainland as agricultural laborers in the early twentieth century. Blacks from the Southern states also relocated in the West, most of them settling in the Pacific Coast states of California, Oregon, and

Washington. And the Indian segment of the New West population, through natural increase, has more than doubled since 1900; by 1975 its population approached the million mark.

Rising consciousness and escalating expectations among Mexican-Americans, Blacks, and Indians inject a fermentive force in Western society. Through demonstrations and occasional overt actions, ethnic leaders strive to achieve for their people a multiracial society that will accord them recognition and acceptance and an equitable share in the West's new economic, social, and political order.

The Mexican-American Community

Mexican-Americans resided in the Southwest before the Anglo-American advent. Nonetheless, until very recently, they, like the Orientals, Blacks, and Indians, have been an exploited, submerged component of Western society. In 1970, there were over 6 million Mexican-Americans in the United States, 90 percent of them concentrated in the Southwestern states of Texas, New Mexico, Arizona, and California. Almost 2 million reside in California; 1.5 million in Texas. The great increase in the Mexican-American population occurred after 1900, when heavy migrations of farm laborers, *braceros*, came from Mexico. The railroad companies also employed large numbers of Mexican-Americans as section hands and dispersed them all across the West. However, even in the 1970s, 80 percent of the nation's Mexican-American population resides in segregated sections of Southwestern towns and cities, in "barrios" or neighborhoods. The Los Angeles Mexican-American population numbers nearly 1 million people; that of San Antonio, 300,000.

Social authorities state that conditions of life for most Mexican-Americans "are at a par or worse than the worst poverty conditions of Blacks." [1] In the Southwest, more than a third live in the most depressing poverty. Their unemployment rate is twice that of Anglo-Americans, and of the employed, 80 percent are engaged in low-skilled, low-paying jobs. The average educational level for Mexican-Americans is eight years of schooling, lower than for Blacks, and considerably below the Anglo-American average of twelve years. Only the Indians have a lower educational level; in south Texas the educational average for Mexican-American children is less than three years.

In the post–World War II era of ethnic consciousness, leaders for the Mexican-Americans emerged, many of them using the "Politics of Confrontation" tactics—boycotts, picketing, voter registration, and demonstrations—to wrest concessions from the Anglo-American establishment. Their struggle for socio-economic improvement has produced a new identity, the Chicano (derived from Mexicano). Chicano activist and socio-economic uplift groups include La Raza Unida and the Mexican-American Youth Organization (MAYO) in Texas, the Alianza—Federation Alliance of Land

[1] Norman (Oklahoma) *Transcript*, January 12, 1970, p. 5.

Grants—in New Mexico, the Crusade for Justice in Denver, and in California the Brown Berets for urban Chicanos and the United Farm Workers Organizing Committee for rural Chicanos.

Chicano leaders in Texas have made appreciable gains for the community by their stress on voter registration, which has resulted in the election of Mexican-Americans to local-government leadership positions including mayor, town council, and school board, and state positions in the legislature. Grants from Eastern foundations have provided funds for legal defense and leadership training. Under Chicano pressure, the Texas State Board of Education has abolished rules that banned the use of Spanish in classrooms and that permitted punishment of Mexican-American children for speaking their native tongue. New curriculum rules include bilingual teaching and courses in the Mexican-American cultural heritage. Chicano power has also forced south Texas communities to alter segregation policies in towns and cemeteries.

In New Mexico, early Chicano activism centered on Reies Lopez Tijerina, founder of Alianza, the Federation Alliance of Land Grants. Tijerina urged Mexican-American unity in the drive for equal treatment, and he developed a plan to recover lands in New Mexico that, he alleged, had been granted to Mexican-Americans by the Spanish and Mexican governments and were subsequently illegally appropriated by the United States and its citizens. During 1966, with a party of fifty followers, he occupied a portion of the Carson National Forest, proclaimed the Pueblo Republic of San Joaquin del Rio de Chama, and filed eviction notices on federal rangers, whom he designated as trespassers. The following year Tijerina and his followers placed the Tierra Amarilla courthouse in northern New Mexico under siege to demonstrate the seriousness of their demand that the allegedly sequestered land be restored to Mexican-Americans. The New Mexico governor mustered a force of 550 national guardsmen and state police with tanks to capture Tijerina and his band. Subsequently a federal court sentenced Tijerina to two years for conspiracy and assaulting a forest ranger; but he was acquitted of a state kidnapping charge growing out of the Tierra Amarillo courthouse siege.

During 1969 Chicano activism in Colorado, organized by the Crusade for Justice, led to boycotts, picketing, and demonstrations to protest treatment of Mexican-American children in the Denver public schools. California Chicano activism has had both urban and rural manifestations. During August 1970, in the course of a Mexican-American antiwar parade and rally in east Los Angeles, involving perhaps 10,000 persons, a small party of militants separated from the parade and set fire to a twelve-block area.

Rural Mexican-American activism in California centers on the United Farm Workers Organizing Committee, AFL-CIO; the union has an estimated 5,000 members and is headed by Cesar Estrada Chavez. This group has concentrated on organizing and improving the lot of workers in the San Joaquin Valley, particularly those employed on grape farms. To accomplish its goal, the United Farm Workers Organizing Committee initiated strikes in the vineyards beginning in 1965. These demonstrations have been followed by national boycotts of table grapes, raisins, and wines produced by area growers. The committee has attempted to organize workers in other California districts, particularly the south. There employers have thwarted unionization through wide use of strikebreakers from Mexico; the latter are transported to the United States each day to labor on the Coachella Valley farms.

The Oriental Community

Japanese, who were established in Hawaii by about 1890, after 1900 were imported in large numbers to labor on the corporate farms of California. They performed the required "squat labor" and field work. Nearly 100,000 Japanese arrived in California before World War I, as well as 10,000 Filipinos and 10,000 workers from India. They suffered the same repression and social rejection earlier accorded the Chinese. California school boards attempted to segregate Oriental children in the public schools, and several Western states, including California and Oregon, adopted alien land laws restricting land ownership by foreigners.

California leaders feared that "by peacefully overrunning the land they would . . . Orientalize" American culture. Woodrow Wilson countered, in his *History of the American People* that in truth it was the Oriental workers' "skill, their intelligence, their hardy power of labor, their knack at succeeding and driving duller rivals out, rather than their alien habits, that made them feared and hated." [2] During the nativist reaction of post–World War I, Congress in 1921 and 1924 adopted legislation excluding all immigrants from Asia. The most extreme, repressive action against Japanese residing in the West occurred during World War II, when joint federal and state action resulted in the relocation of 112,000 Japanese residents on the Pacific Coast, in Hawaii, and in Arizona, and their internment in detention camps in remote areas as far east as Arkansas. During December 1944, the exiles were permitted to return to their Western homes.

As a war measure, Congress in 1943 repealed the Chinese Exclusion Act. Then, in 1952, by passage of the McCarran-Walter National Origins Act, Congress permitted limited resumption of Oriental immigration. By 1970, slightly over 1 million Chinese and Japanese resided in the United States, most of them in Hawaii, California, and Washington.

The Black Community

In the early years of the twentieth century, Western Blacks endured segregation and social repression equal to that inflicted by the dominant Anglo-American community on other unlike peoples. Leaders in Texas and, after 1907, in the new state of Oklahoma, applied the Southern practice of

[2] Woodrow Wilson, *History of the American People* (New York, 1918), Vol. 10, pp. 99–100.

segregating Blacks in towns and schools. Jim Crow laws required Blacks to use separate facilities in parks and public buildings and to ride in segregated railroad cars.

Blacks began to move out of the South and into the West in large numbers during World War I. The flow continued, particularly to California, during the Great Depression. With the expansion of irrigated agriculture in West Texas, New Mexico, and Arizona, large numbers of Blacks also collected there. The largest westward migration of Blacks began during World War II. Between 1945 and 1960, more than 600,000 Blacks moved from the South to the West.

The rising ethnic consciousness of the post–World War II period, focusing on the civil rights movement, began in the eastern and southern United States, spread to the West, and began to bring about improvement of the economic, educational, and social status of Blacks. The nationalizing effect of the Supreme Court decisions contributed materially to this ethnic uplift. In *Guinn v. Oklahoma* in 1916, the court struck down the Grandfather Clause of the Oklahoma constitution and of other state constitutions that excluded Blacks from voting. So began the gradual extension of the suffrage.

Higher education, closed to Blacks except on a segregated basis in Texas and Oklahoma, was opened by the Sipuel and McLaurin federal court decisions during the late 1940s. Then all segregated public schools in the West and the nation were banned by the *Brown v.* Board of Education of Topeka, Kansas decision in 1954.

Activism by Black leaders to obtain employment and educational opportunities for their people has provided an action pattern for the leaders of other submerged ethnic groups in the West. The largest Western concentration of Black population is in California, where 1.5 million reside. Over 300,000 Blacks reside in the Los Angeles suburb of Watts, scene of the devastating riot in 1965. Other Western states with substantial Black concentrations are Arizona, 55,000; Washington, 72,000; Texas, 1.4 million; Oklahoma, 172,000; Kansas, 67,000; and Colorado, 67,000.

The Indian Community

The Western Indian community numbers nearly 1 million people and consists of over 100 tribes speaking nearly 100 different languages. Over 200,000 Indians have settled in cities; the remainder reside on allotments and on 290 reservations. Some reservations are no more than tiny *rancherias* of a few acres in California, while the giant 14 million-acre Navajo Reservation sprawls over portions of Arizona, New Mexico, and Utah. The Western states with the largest Indian population are Oklahoma—the old Indian Territory—with 99,000; Arizona, 96,000; New Mexico, 73,000; Washington, 34,000; and South Dakota, 33,000. California's Indian population numbers 91,000. Most of them are urban Indians who have moved from other Western states in recent times.

After the conquest period of the 1870s, most Indians were concentrated on reservations to become an invisible force in Western society until the 1920s. At that time some public interest in their status and welfare began to develop. In 1924, out of gratitude for Indian military service during World War I, Congress extended citizenship to all Indians. Two years later, federal officials requested the Institute for Government Research, funded by a Rockefeller Foundation grant, to investigate the state of tribal progress under existing Indian policy. Lewis Meriam and a team of specialists traveled over the West during 1927 conducting an exhaustive field survey of conditions among the Indian tribes. The Meriam Report, submitted in 1928, castigated the government's management of the Indian, declaring that its reservation policy had failed to "legislate Indians into white Americans"; it recommended a program to prepare the Indian to live in the dominant society "without being obliterated by it."

In 1933, President Franklin D. Roosevelt appointed John Collier, a social scientist who had served as an officer of the American Indian Defense Association for ten years, as Commissioner of Indian Affairs. Collier seriously applied the recommendations of the Meriam survey. During 1934, Congress adopted the Indian Reorganization Act (Wheeler-Howard Act), which has been called the Magna Charta for the American Indian. This statute repealed the allotment acts, and provided for federal purchase of over 1 million acres of land to be restored for Indian use. It created a revolving fund from which Indians could receive loans to fund tribal agricultural and business projects. Tribes were encouraged to draft and adopt tribal constitutions and to create tribal business corporations to manage the Indian estate. The act substantially expanded the resources appropriated for the education of Indian youth, and it permitted a new policy that encouraged native religion, tribal ceremonies, and crafts. In effect it halted the detribalization process and raised Indian morale by removing the stigma so long associated with tribal culture.

After momentary advances under the Wheeler-Howard Act, the cause of Indian emergence regressed during the 1950s. President Dwight D. Eisenhower's administration was committed to a policy of diminishing the role of the national government in all segments of American society. In a twisted, politically expedient way, the Indian became the prime casualty of this commitment. Presidential aides "speedily learned that in practice it was difficult to find an area where withdrawal of federal services did not evoke anguished outcries from potent pressure groups." [3] Therefore, the relatively inarticulate Indian became the focus of much governmental attention, as bureaucrats and Congressmen sought areas of federal activity that could be reduced and thereby enable the Eisenhower administration to fulfill its commitment.

Senator Arthur V. Watkins of Utah, Chairman of the Senate Com-

[3] William T. Hagan, *American Indians* (Chicago, 1961), p. 161.

mittee on Indian Affairs, was the principal figure in the Congress responsible for altering Indian policy during this period. He was determined to bring Indians into the mainstream of American life, and he regarded the Wheeler-Howard Act of 1934 as coddling of Indians. He advocated repeal of many of its provisions through adoption of the policy of Termination, whereby federal responsibility for the Indian would be ended. Laws Watkins supported during 1953 began the process of Termination by extending state jurisdiction to Indian reservations and directing the Secretary of the Interior to review treaties and laws to find ways for the United States to release itself from responsibility to the Indian. Termination laws also transferred many tracts of tribal land containing timber, mineral, and oil resources to private interests. Opponents of the new policy charged that such private transfers were, in fact, the overriding motivation for the Termination laws.

In 1961, the Kennedy administration began the restoration of many of the principles of the Wheeler-Howard Act. Federal officials stressed self-determination for the Indian and experimented with Relocation, a program providing vocational training for Indians and resettlement with employment in major cities. Over 20,000 Indians participated in Relocation.

Indian activism and militancy have increased in proportion to rising aboriginal consciousness and expectations. During 1944, representatives of over forty tribes organized the National Congress of American Indians. Studies by this group, by the Indian Rights Association, and by other tribal organizations and federal agencies reveal that in 1969 the average annual income for an Indian family was $1,500, as compared to $3,161 for a nonwhite family, and $5,893 for a white family. Indian life expectancy was found to be forty-four, the Indian employment rate was 40 percent, and school dropout rate for Indian children was 50 percent. Over 63,000 Indian families occupied substandard housing, and the Indian infant mortality, tuberculosis, and alcoholism rates were the highest in the nation. The incidence of suicide for Indians was found to be more than six times greater than for any other population group in American society.

Since 1960, Indian reaction to their plight has taken on a militant tone. At the University of Chicago Conference held in 1961 and attended by 500 Indians representing seventy tribes, delegates drafted a Declaration of Indian Purpose, which articulated Indian goals and expectations. Young Indian delegates formed the National Indian Youth Council, which became an activist agency committed to the mobilization of Red Power. Its members joined the poverty march on Washington in 1963. Other activist groups formed by tribal youth include AIM, the American Indian Movement. Indian militants led the Broken Treaties Caravan to Washington in 1972 and demonstrated for six days; their actions included an extended occupation of the Bureau of Indian Affairs Building. The most daring and provocative action by Indian militants occurred during 1973 in South Dakota, where armed Indians performed a symbolic occupation of the village of Wounded Knee and defied an extended siege of federal and state forces. Their principal purpose was to dramatize the maladministration and mistreatment of the American Indian.

WESTERN CULTURAL PROFILE

The rate of cultural change across the West is uneven; some Western states move more rapidly than others from relative frontier colonialism toward regional synthesis and accommodation to the national modes. However, even in the more advanced Western states of California, Washington, Oregon, and Texas there are surviving pockets of frontier style and viewpoint, and a determination to resist change and to retain cherished frontier values. Except in the advanced states, there is a direct correlation between rate of economic change, the concomitant shift from rural to urban preeminence, and at least the modest beginnings of cultural change.

Western Urbanization

While most of the nation had become overwhelmingly urban by 1920, the West continued to be predominantly rural. The dispersal of industry during World War II, which favored the West and abetted its emergence as a modern industrial region, was largely responsible for its change from rural to urban milieu.The maturing Western economy caused the expansion of most existing Western cities, created new cities, and proliferated residential clusters tributary to these cities, in many cases forming megalopolis-type urban complexes.

Thus by 1970, most of the West's population was distributed on an 80 percent urban to 20 percent rural ratio, with California, Hawaii, Texas, Utah, and Arizona the most highly urbanized states. North Dakota, South Dakota, Idaho, and Alaska lag in the regional urbanization thrust; their ratio of urban to rural is approximately 40 to 60 percent. Several Western cities have passed the 1 million mark in population. Los Angeles is the largest Western city with a metropolitan population of about 3 million, while Houston, Dallas, Phoenix, Seattle, San Francisco, and Denver are among the largest Western urban centers.

Technological advances in water-resource expansion, and in transmission facilities for water and electrical energy, as well as the automobile, highway improvements, and air conditioning, have contributed materially to Western urbanization. Vast empty spaces adjacent to Western cities have encouraged a flare in settlement patterns and produced suburban clusters. Dispersed residential settlements, coupled with the technology of travel, particularly the automobile, have enabled the West to avoid some of the faults of Eastern urbanization and industrializaton, including compressed tenement districts for workers and their families. However, critics associated with the ecology and quality of life movements point to tract housing. Such housing, created by what they call the "buffalo hunter mentality" of Western designers, is abominable sacrifice of aesthetics and, in many respects, simply worker's tenements spread wide.

Western Cultural Anomaly

In the midst of the phenomenon of Western economic maturation and urbanization there is the paradox of strong frontier and rural survivals. Nativism, continuing religious orthodoxy and Fundamentalism, intense political conservatism, and compulsive anti-intellectualism flourish in these urban sprawls. The cultural characterization of the Old West pioneer during the 1820s fits many Westerners in the 1970s: on the one hand intensely independent, self-reliant and individualistic; on the other, dependent, cooperative, and group-oriented; religious and irreligious; nationalistic and particularistic; compulsively devoted to self-interest, obsessively materialistic yet, on occasion, public spirited; and anti-intellectual, contemptuous of humanistic enterprises, but supportive of education as long as it is practical.

Western culture is strongly influenced by the region's long period of dependence on the East for political, social, and intellectual guidance. Inevitably, resentment developed among Westerners over their prolonged secondary status in national life. Many reacted with defensiveness, paranoia, puerile braggadocio, and a calculated determination to preserve Western values. This rigidification of Western attitude has colored regional political and social action, and is a prime source of Western conservatism, the stream of which is fed by several contributing sources. One is state legislatures that, in response to wide public demand, have adopted speaker-ban statutes and other preventive laws in an attempt to exclude from the community those with threatening viewpoints. Internally, the colleges and universities have been important agents of change in Western society; and in several cases state legislatures have politicized them, drastically reducing the self-government of higher education and bringing the campuses under closer state surveillance.

Certainly one of the prime sources of recalcitrant Western political conservatism is the presumed threat posed to the Anglo-American establishment by activist leaders of the ethnic groups who seek to achieve for their people a multiracial society. The presumptive elitists feel threatened by demands for recognition and acceptance of Blacks, Mexican-Americans, and Indians, and their desires for an equitable share in the West's new riches and power.

All over the West, citizen advisory committees contribute to the expurgation of threatening ideas from the Western milieu and comprise an important part of the conservative community. These often include advisory committees for state textbook-selection boards. During 1972, in Oklahoma a citizens' group called Parents for God, Home and Country surveyed textbooks used in the public schools for "vulgarity and gruesome passages." A year later in Drake, North Dakota, school officials, pressured by a local parent group, publicly burned Kurt Vonnegut's novel, *Slaughter-house Five*, stating that "the normal way to get rid of trash is to burn it." [4] The school board also directed destruction of works in the high school library by James Dickey, Ernest Hemingway, William Faulkner, John Stein-beck, and James Joyce. Fundamentalist preachers and citizens groups have pressured public school textbook-selection boards in Texas, California, and other Western states in an effort to purge science books of Darwinism and to require textbook writers to include the Creationism viewpoint. Throughout the West during the 1960s, school boards were under pressure from citizens' groups to ban the teaching of information about sex. Several Western state boards of education require "Americanism" courses, and in the Arizona public schools all seniors are required to enroll in a course called "The Free Enterprise System."

Additional sources of the stream of conservatism in Western culture include the John Birch Society and the American Minutemen. Moreover, since 1941, several Western Fundamentalist religious bodies have estab-lished colleges and universities in the West; the curricula of these schools mix religion with economic and social doctrine. Their graduates, some of whom are religious radio and television personalities, have wide constitu-encies. Another force for conservatism in the Western social milieu is the geriatric community. Great numbers of retired persons have settled in the West, many of them in the special retirement cities constructed since 1950. Their influence on local, state, and national elections is considerable.

However, there are countervailing forces in the Western social milieu that contribute toward a more mature cultural synthesis. The West, a colonial dependency of the eastern United States for most of its existence in the national life, received its economic and political direction from Wall Street and Capitol Hill. And in the nineteenth and early twentieth century it was a primitive social region. However, in the mid-twentieth century, as an extension of its economic and political emergence, the West has begun increasingly to contribute to and form the national culture. Its expanding influence in lifestyles, residential patterns, dress, art and architecture, societal forms, science and technology, and political ideology has been nothing short of remarkable.

SELECTED SOURCES

*Gerald D. Nash's *The American West in the Twentieth Century: A Short History of an Urban Oasis* (Englewood Cliffs, 1973) contains the most com-prehensive analysis of Western society since 1900. Supporting works include Neil Morgan, *Westward Tilt: The American West Today* (New York, 1961);

* Available in paperback.

4 *Arizona Republic*, November 15, 1973.

Neal R. Pierce, *The Great Plains States of America: People, Politics, and Power in the Nine Great Plains States* (New York, 1972); *Henry Nash Smith, *Virgin Land: The American West as Symbol and Myth* (Cambridge, 1950; *Ernesto Galarza, *Merchants of Labor: The Mexican Bracero Story* (San Jose, Calif., 1966); Shien Woo Kung, *Chinese in American Life* (Seattle, 1962); Lawrence Lipton, *The Holy Barbarians* (New York, 1959); *Stan Steiner, *La Raza* (New York, 1968); and *The New Indians* (New York, 1968); and *W. Eugene Hollon, *The Southwest: Old and New* (New York, 1961).

33

Politics in the Twentieth Century West

In 1974, four Westerners occupied prime leadership positions in the national government: the president, the speaker of the House of Representatives, the minority leader of the House, and the Senate majority leader. It was compelling evidence that, finally, the West had achieved a position of equality in national political affairs with the other regions of the United States. The political emergence of the West is a recent development and is a concomitant of its economic maturation. For just as the Western economy has undergone a comprehensive metamorphosis in the twentieth century, so has Western politics. Economic change has been the principal force producing the political change and, in charting the Western advance, there is a persuasive correlation between rate of economic maturation and political emergence. Expanding Western economic activity and diversification through industry—particularly since 1941—have greatly increased employment opportunities and attracted large numbers of people to the West. The post–World War II population leap provided the base for increasing the region's political power.

POLITICAL COLONIALISM

The lag in Western political development and its consequently minor voice in the nation's councils was for many years disproportionate to its food and raw-material contribution to the national life. Just as Eastern capitalists exploited the West's rich resources and limited the range of its economic activity to a supportive, colonial role throughout the nineteenth century and for nearly four decades in the twentieth century, so Eastern politicians during the same period exploited the West for partisan purpose, repeatedly crushed the hopes and expectations of Westerners, and held the region in a state of colonial abeyance.

Lag in State-Making

We have discussed earlier how, throughout the nineteenth century, there was a sustained reluctance to accept the New West into the national life as an equal of the East and Old West. In the thirty-year period from 1790, much of the Old West was quickly integrated into the American Union. The New West, however, did not receive the same prompt state-making attention, and—calculating from the first entry of the American nation into the New West in 1803 to the admission of Hawaii and Alaska in 1959—it required 150 years to complete the region's political format. Not until the middle of the twentieth century was the West able to challenge its Eastern masters, assert a determinative force in national politics, and make a substantive contribution to the national life.

The Alaska Territory

Congress adopted the Alaska Organic Act in 1884; the act provided for the essentials of territorial government, but designated this northland province a district rather than a territory. Finally, in 1912 Congress changed Alaska's designation from district to territory and authorized a territorial legislature. Alaska's first territorial assembly enfranchised women. With a functioning territorial government and a voice in Congress, Alaska received increasing attention from the federal government.

One of the territory's most pressing needs was for inland transportation, and in 1914, Congress approved a plan to construct a federally funded railroad from the southern coast to the interior. The Alaskan Engineering Commission, appointed by President Woodrow Wilson, selected Seward on Resurrection Bay as the ocean terminal. The rail line, called the Alaskan Central Railroad, was to cross the Kenai Peninsula to Nenana on the Tanana River, 407 miles inland. Congress appropriated $35 million to fund the project, which was completed in 1923. The Alaskan Central generated the rise of Anchorage and several other towns. Congress also provided financial support for the construction of roads into the Alaskan interior. Beginning in 1901, the War Department opened several pack trails into the Yukon Basin; and in 1917 a graveled road was constructed between Valdez, Fairbanks, and Circle City on the Yukon River.

Alaska's Indian, Aleut, and Eskimo population, estimated in 1900 at about 30,000, also received attention from the national government. Federal Indian policy applied to tribes in the contiguous United States was extended to the aboriginal peoples of Alaska. The measures applied included protection of tribal lands and operation of seventeen government schools for native children. Native Alaskans also received attention from missionary groups. By 1903, Presbyterian, Russian Orthodox, Episcopal, Roman Catholic, Methodist, Moravian, Baptist, Quaker, and Lutheran missionary societies had established eighty-two missions and twenty-four schools in Alaska. The Presbyterian and Russian Orthodox groups were the most active with sixteen missions each. Sheldon Jackson, a Presbyterian leader, was the most active champion of the Alaskan natives. He worked extensively in the United States, before the Congress and the public, promoting Alaska and its aboriginal peoples. Through missionary influence, reindeer were introduced into Alaska to sustain Arctic peoples who faced starvation because of the commercial hunters' slaughter of the whale, walrus, and caribou. By 1903, the Alaskan reindeer herd numbered over 10,000.

The American agricultural frontier approached Alaska with great hesitancy. The principal deterrent was the interior's Arctic climate, which limited the growing season and choice of crops. An act of 1898 restricted homesteads to eighty acres, which, given the climatic limitations, was inadequate. Later Congress increased the Alaskan homestead entry to 320 acres. Some agricultural settlement in the interior occurred after completion of the Alaskan Central Railroad. The most extensive Alaskan homesteading effort occurred during the 1930s in the Matanuska Valley. For a New Deal project to assist 200 economically distressed families from the states, resettlement officials selected the Matanuska Valley. The settlement area was in south-central Alaska, forty-five miles northeast of Anchorage. The federal government assigned each family a homestead with a modern house and provided loans, payable over thirty years, to pay for transportation expenses and purchase tools and equipment. The Alaska Relief Rehabilitation Corporation administered the Matanuska project. The colony prospered after 1940, when the War Department constructed Fort Richardson near Anchorage. The base became a market for the colony's garden produce and meat products.

As in Hawaii, Alaska's remoteness was broken by technological advances in aviation; beginning in 1920, military planes regularly flew to Alaska. Its strategic location on the Great Circle itinerary established its importance as an international air-travel center. Local commercial aviation began in 1924, and thereafter, even Alaska's most isolated sections were served by small private craft. In the twentieth century, Alaska, like Hawaii, became an extension of the American military frontier. Military installations and expenditures, particularly after 1941, fed the economy and produced the substantial population growth that eventually made statehood feasible.

During World War II, the federal government developed a vast naval, army, and air establishment in Alaska to support American military operations against Japan. For a time, Japanese forces occupied Attu and other islands in the Aleutian group. American air power forced enemy evacuation of these strategic stations, which, while occupied by the Japanese, had comprised a serious threat to Alaskan security. During the war, Alaska's internal and external communication and transportation facilities were improved. The federal government built the Alcan Highway, a monumental under-

Politicos from the Outback

The West, long a colonial region dominated by the Eastern Establishment, since mid-century has turned on its creator and increasingly exerts a determinative influence in national affairs. Western political leadership is predominantly conservative, but is

Former California Governor Ronald Reagan (R)
Fred Kaplan

Senator Barry Goldwater
of Arizona (R)
Harry Redl

President Lyndon B. Johnson
of Texas (D)
Fred Ward

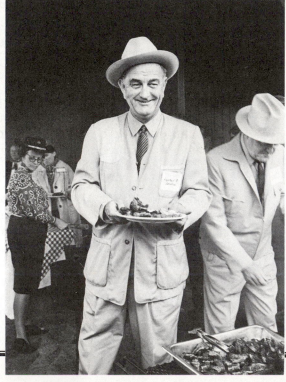

Senator Mark Hatfield of Oregon (D)
Dennis Brack

flavored by a perplexing, simplistic liberalism that augurs neo-Populism. Western politicians feel the new strength and power and confidently assert themselves in the councils of the nation.

(Photos from Black Star)

Senator John Tower of Texas (R)
Fred Ward

Speaker of the U.S. House
of Representatives
Carl Albert of Oklahoma (D)
Bob Fitch

taking that extended from the American border on the Pacific shore across British Columbia to Alaska. Stimulated by increasing military activity, mining, fishing, lumbering, and some agriculture, Alaska's population had increased to nearly 130,000 in 1950; on the eve of statehood it stood slightly over 200,000.

Alaskan Statehood

The Alaskan statehood movement developed during the 1920s. Momentum increased during World War II, and after 1950 both Democratic and Republican parties supported statehood. Leaders in Alaska and Hawaii worked together during the 1950s to pressure Congress into granting statehood. An Alaskan convention drafted a constitution in 1956; and Congress reacted by adopting the Alaskan Organic Act in 1958 and directing a territory-wide referendum. Alaskan voters approved the statehood proposition on a five-to-one ratio, and the forty-ninth state was admitted to the Union on January 3, 1959.

Territory of Hawaii

In 1900, Congress created the Hawaiian territorial government as an essential first step for absorption into the community of American states. Actual statehood for the former island kingdom, however, was delayed nearly sixty years. In the meantime, Hawaii became an important agricultural outpost, with the principal commercial emphasis on sugar and rice production and, after 1910, pineapple culture. With only 300,000 arable acres in a land area of nearly 6,500 square miles, Hawaiian agriculture was of necessity intensive. The three staple crops required a large labor force, which was supplied by the continuing importation of Chinese and Japanese, as well as Filipinos, Koreans, and a sprinkling of Puerto Ricans. Anglos continued to dominate the island's commercial elitist group, but Japanese were the most numerous at the time of annexation; they comprised nearly 40 percent of a population of slightly more than 200,000 people. The native Hawaiians, like the American Indians on the mainland, continued to decline and numbered fewer than 60,000 at annexation. Many of these were of mixed parentage.

Hawaii became an extension of the American military frontier in the twentieth century; the expanding martial presence and the expenditures necessary to support it dominated Hawaiian society and economy. The primary American Pacific defenses were at Pearl Harbor on the island of Oahu. Both the Navy and War Departments each year spent great sums of federal money on Hawaiian defenses. Navy engineers deepened the harbor channel to accommodate larger warships in 1911. The principal army stations in Hawaii were Fort Shafter and Schofield Barracks. Collateral installations included a maritime-communications center, with wireless stations at Oahu providing contact with naval and merchant-marine vessels all over the Pacific. During the 1920s, improvements in aviation and communication technology linked Hawaii to the mainland. The first flight from Oakland, California, to Oahu occurred in 1927. During the 1930s, increasing aviation contact included military flights and civil passenger and mail service maintained by the Pacific flying clipper fleet.

Hawaii became the center of American attention on December 7, 1941, when a covertly placed Japanese fleet loosed a surprise air and submarine attack on Oahu; 2,325 persons were killed—most of them military personnel —188 planes were destroyed, and eighteen naval vessels were sunk or damaged. Before that epochal day closed, President Franklin D. Roosevelt, at the recommendation of military officials in Hawaii, declared martial law for the islands. The blackout and curfew remained in effect until July 1945.

As military officials in Hawaii rehabilitated their battered resources and prepared for counteraction against the marauding enemy fleet, they regarded the presence of 160,000 resident Japanese as an internal threat. Island commanders favored shipping them to the mainland for internment, but local business leaders insisted that Japanese laborers were required to maintain the islands' agriculture and other enterprises. There followed an intensive suppression program. Military authorities banned Japanese-language radio programs and newspapers, closed Buddhist temples and Shinto shrines, and forbade Japanese to possess arms, cameras, binoculars, and shortwave radios. No more than ten Japanese could gather in a single place, and Nisei (second-generation Japanese) who were members of the Hawaiian national guard were disarmed and relieved of duty. Hawaiian military commanders shipped several Japanese leaders to the mainland, where they were placed in camps in New Mexico. Preparations by the Navy and War Departments to carry the war initiative to Japan led to a phenomenal military development in Hawaii. Thousands of war workers from the mainland, most of them Caucasians, migrated to Hawaii. Belated recruitment of Nisei men into the armed forces and their sustained commitment to the American cause and gallantry in action did much to restore the image of the Japanese community in Hawaii.

Hawaiian Statehood

Hawaii's substantive role in the nation's military effort during World War II assured its ultimate absorption into the community of American states. A statehood movement had existed in Hawaii from earliest territorial days, but the former island kingdom faced several obstacles. Foremost among them was the continuing Anglo racial prejudice. To many Americans, Hawaii was a "potpourri of alien blood," a community of unlike cultures; the monistic view that had excluded the southwestern territories from the American Union for so long applied to Hawaii as well. In addition there was the geographic problem of the islands' non-contiguous location. Tradition-bound Americans regarded contiguity an elementary *sine qua non* for statehood.

The Republican party had dominated territorial politics since annexation, but after World War II, the Democratic party became pre-eminent in local and legislative elections. An impasse was created in territorial administration during the 1950s: the Democrats dominated the legislative branch, and the Republicans controlled the executive branch. Samuel Wilder King, the territorial governor appointed by President Dwight D. Eisenhower, vetoed seventy-three acts of the Hawaiian legislature during 1955. Statehood agitation continued to mount. American prejudice was fading, in part because of technological advances in aviation. Expanding air-transport service to Hawaii after World War II produced a dramatic growth in tourism and popularized Hawaii in the American mind.

Hawaiian statehood advocates joined with Alaskan statehood leaders in a combined effort for admission. Their efforts bore fruit in 1958 when Congress passed the Alaskan Statehood Bill. The following March, Congress approved the Hawaiian Statehood Bill. Following a territory-wide referendum that overwhelmingly endorsed statehood, President Eisenhower, on August 21, 1959, signed the statehood proclamation admitting Hawaii as the nation's fiftieth state.

Retention of the Federal Estate in the West

The most dramatic evidence of the West's long status as a colonial region whose lands and resources were managed to serve the national interest is provided by the presence of huge tracts of federal land in the Western states. The United States government owns half of all the land in eleven Western states. In Nevada 80 percent and in Utah 65 percent are under federal proprietorship. In 1970, federally owned and administered lands comprised 770 million acres, or about a third of the landed area of the United States, including Alaska. Federal lands in the West include national forests and parks, military reservations, game preserves, historic monuments, and certain other reserves. In addition, great blocks of land in several Western states are taken up by Indian reservations. The political implications of the presence of huge tracts of federal land in a state are immense. It is a matter that generates intense state-federal tensions and is a source of continuing hostility on the part of Westerners toward the federal government. In addition, it raises serious questions of exploitation and management, taxation, and general jurisdiction.

Much of the federal Western estate grew out of the conservation movement, which has been and continues to be a strong force in Western and national politics. The movement evolved in the latter part of the nineteenth century out of a widening public concern, mostly in the eastern United States and only limitedly in the West, over the wanton waste of the region's land and resources by the exploitive frontier between 1866 and 1900. The conflict between protagonists of the infinite versus finite positions on the scope and future of the Western natural resources had great impact on Western state governments and politics. Many years before the fur men had set the pattern for merciless exploitation of the West's natural bounty.

In less than fifty years they had plundered the New West wilderness of its pelt riches. Their example was followed by miners, lumbermen, stockgrowers, and nesters.

Concerned conservationists urged that the federal government halt this reckless waste of natural resources and apply intelligent control and management to the West's surviving timber, land, water, and minerals. Westerners generally opposed the conservation movement, holding that it slowed the region's economic growth, kept state tax-income low, and created complex, difficult jurisdictional problems.

The two principal types of public reservations comprising the federal estate in the West consist of national parks and national forests. In response to conservationists' pleas, federal officials began withdrawing and reserving certain unique Western natural areas as national parks in 1872, with the creation of Yellowstone National Park. Additional national park reservations include Yosemite (1890), Rocky Mountain (1915), and Grand Teton (1929). Most of the rest of the Western estate consists of public lands classed as national forests. In 1891, Congress passed the Forest Reserve Act, which authorized the president to withdraw from settlement public lands wholly or in part covered by timber. Presidents Benjamin Harrison, Grover Cleveland, and William McKinley withdrew several million acres of Western land under this statute. President Theodore Roosevelt withdrew nearly 150 million acres.

The bureaucracy that manages most of the Western federal estate is the National Park Service in the Department of the Interior and the National Forest Service in the Department of Agriculture. The Forest Service has applied to its assigned territories multiple-use management, assigning to each forest region a use or variety of uses best adapted to that area, including sustained yield for timber, water, and watershed management, recreation use, and preservation of wilderness areas. The Taylor Grazing Act (1934) provided guidance for controlling grazing use of Western public lands. The statute created grazing districts on over nearly 180 million acres and instituted a system of permits to protect the grassland resources of public lands.

Federal agencies have obtained control of certain unique biotic regions, including a cactus area in southern Arizona and a grasslands on the southern Plains. The Panhandle National Grasslands is dispersed over eastern New Mexico, northern Texas, and western Oklahoma. During the searing drouths of the 1930s, this region was a part of the Dust Bowl. In 1938, under authority of the Bankhead-Jones Farm Tenant Act, officials of the Soil Conservation Service purchased 300,000 eroded acres in this southern Plains region, took it out of cultivation, restored the land through revegetation, and created a protective watershed to prevent silting of downstream reservoirs and to aid on-site use of rainfall. Eventually the rehabilitated area was divided into five districts: Kiowa National Grassland in eastern New Mexico; Rita Blanca National Grassland in Texas and Oklahoma;

Black Kettle National Grassland in western Oklahoma; and Cross Timbers National Grassland and Caddo National Grassland in northern Texas— the units comprising the Panhandle National Grasslands. In 1953 the Forest Service took over management of the Panhandle National Grasslands, applying its multiple-use and sustained-yield management practices to include outdoor recreation, rangeland, and watershed and wildlife protection.

Although application of conservation-movement policy to the West has been constructive from the standpoint of the national interest and for long-range resource-management considerations, it has been in direct conflict with the regional Western interests that are generally short-range and exploitive. Conservation action has taken from most Western states vast tracts of land, removed them from private exploitation, and created serious questions of jurisdiction. The drastic increase in Western population in the mid-twentieth century has placed great pressure on the Western states for widening access to land, water, timber, and other essential resources that are present on federal lands but restricted or closed by federal conservation policy. Thus the federal-state conflict over the presence of a vast national estate in the Western states has intensified.

VICISSITUDES OF WESTERN POLITICS, 1900–1941

During the first half of the nineteenth century, Western politics alternated between strong commitment to the Progressive cause—with wide citizen interest and participation in public affairs—and general disillusionment and withdrawal at the failure of the reforms to achieve a new political order. Mobilization of the West into the national war effort during World War I and the military-induced Western economic development and prosperity effectively deflected public attention from local political concerns. The 1920s and the period of the Great Depression were times of extended malaise in Western politics, tinctured with radicalism from the right and the left. In the late 1930s, some local excitement and action were generated by several maverick Western governors who resisted the nationalizing trends of the New Deal. They set the tone for the West's strong conservative tradition, which became an influential force in national politics after 1950.

Progressivism in the West

In the early twentieth century, the Progressive Movement was strong throughout the nation. Westerners widely applied the new reform doctrine in an attempt to break the hold of vested economic interests, purge corruption from local and state governments, and restore government to the people. Western state governments had become almost extensions of the local business community, and the state legislatures and courts often guarded commercial interests at the sacrifice of the public weal. Progressivism provided Westerners the promise and the apparent means to create a new social and political order. Reform currents stimulated by the Progressive Movement included direct legislation through initiative and referendum, recall, and many Populist-inspired changes such as the secret ballot, popular election of senators, the long ballot, and the direct primary. Reform activity in Oregon, California, and Oklahoma illustrate the serious application of Progressive doctrine to state politics.

In Oregon, attention was focused on Governor William S. U'Ren, a Progressive Democrat. He organized the nonpartisan People's Power League, which formulated a program of state political reforms that became known as the Oregon System. Legislative inertia to reform, because of that body's role as protective agent for monopolistic corporations, led U'Ren to resort to direct legislation through the use of the initiative and referendum. He also developed an effective system for controling corporations and setting railroad rates. In California, Governor Hiram Johnson, a Progressive Republican, formulated a reform system that brought the all-powerful Southern Pacific Railroad and other great business combinations under state control. His success in breaking the stranglehold of monopoly on California politics made Johnson a national figure and led to his selection as vice-presidential nominee for the Progressive Party in 1912.

Oklahoma statehood in 1907 came at the peak of the Progressive Movement. Constitutional convention delegates were infected with the reform virus of Progressivism, and they articulated nearly the total spectrum of Progressive doctrine in the constitution. William H. "Alfalfa Bill" Murray was president of the constitutional convention; he and other convention leaders regarded their mission as not simply to create a new state, but to create "a new kind of state." [1] Thus, the Oklahoma constitution stipulated that the long ballot be used and made twelve state executive offices elective. According to the delegates, these measures reduced the appointive power of the governor and deterred executive tyranny. The judiciary was also elective and thus responsive to the people. The text of the constitution was inordinately long as the delegates were determined to spell out their intentions in order to reduce opportunities for broad judicial interpretation. Gubernatorial elections were to be held in off-years, making it impossible for a candidate to ride to office on the popularity of a presidential candidate. The term of office for the governor was set at four years, with the restriction that no governor could succeed himself; the intent was to reduce the opportunity for a governor to build personal power through long tenure. The most powerful branch of the state government was the legislature, for the delegates considered its members closest to the people. The electorate also shared in the legislative function through the initiative and referendum, reserve powers that could be exercised if legislators failed to respond to the popular will.

[1] Quoted in Arrell M. Gibson, *Oklahoma: A History of Five Centuries* (Norman, 1965), p. 332.

Additional political reforms embedded in the Oklahoma constitution included an eight-hour day on public-works projects and in the mines and the banning of child and convict labor. The primary was adopted as the method for nominating candidates for public office, thus reducing the power of party conventions and machines and providing the people a voice in the selection of candidates. Machinery for controlling railroads, monopolies, and trusts was established in the elective corporation commission. The constitutional convention also adopted statewide prohibition of alcohol as a social reform.

The naiveté of Western reformers was reflected in their faith that, having once purged state and local governments of corruption, the Progressive constitutional safeguards would serve as eternal deterrents to recurrence. They failed to consider that, because of the inherent dynamism of politics, particularly in a free society, the reforms of today will more than likely become the subject of future reforms. In fact, undue reliance on the continuing efficacy of their reforms to control the enemies of the people and popular government in itself lowered the level of vigilance. The reformers also failed to reckon with the propensity of power groups to reassert their will and to protect their enterprises from regulation and taxation, to artfully and legally find ways to defeat the system. Such has been the case in most of the Western states that applied Progressive reforms. Shrewd corporation attorneys and business leaders rather quickly found ways to work within the reform milieu and eventually to capture control of the new regulatory machinery and to recapture control of courts and legislatures. Thus the failure of Progressive reforms to protect the public from predatory business combinations and special-interest groups created disillusionment among the people. The intrusion of World War I also absorbed the people, deflecting their attention from local and state political concerns to national and international matters.

Western Political Stagnation

The close of World War I terminated the brief era of prosperity for many Western industries, particularly agriculture. The war-induced expansion of production facilities yielded a glut of food and fibers, while the increasingly restricted markets registered depression-level prices. The depression that engulfed the nation after 1929 was at work a decade earlier in the West, and depressed economic conditions soon had their effect on regional politics. The period from 1920 to 1941 was a time of general malaise in Western politics, disturbed now and then by outbursts of radicalism both from the left and the right. The Socialist party had made great strides in the West during World War I, especially in Oklahoma, where rural Socialism flourished among Farm Tenant Union cells and other distressed groups excluded from the war-time prosperity. Their activity in Oklahoma peaked during 1917 in the Green Corn Rebellion, a Socialist-directed militant resistance movement to the draft.

After 1920, Socialist ferment continued in Oklahoma and throughout the West, taking various forms. The most successful Western Socialist activity during this period occurred in North Dakota under the aegis of the Non-Partisan League. This organization was formed in 1915 by Arthur N. Townley, a bankrupted wheat farmer. The Non-Partisan League program called for public measures to favor depressed farmers: state ownership of grain elevators and food-processing plants—including flour mills and meat-packing plants—and state-owned banks and insurance companies to serve the agricultural industry. Through political action, the North Dakota Non-Partisan League elected a governor and a majority in the state legislature and succeeded in activating its state-bank plan and certain other agricultural reforms. The movement spread to South Dakota, Oregon, Idaho, Colorado, Montana, Washington, and Oklahoma, where the league's program of Socialist action met with varying degrees of success. In Oklahoma, the Non-Partisan League program was adopted by a coalition of labor and farm groups that formed the Farm-Labor Reconstruction League. In 1922 the group elected a governor.

Militant unionism was another product of the Western socio-economic disorientation of the postwar period. After 1900, the Western labor movement embraced railroad and craft unions—most of the latter under the American Federation of Labor—and certain nonskilled labor affiliates, including the Lumber Workers Union, which was concentrated in the Pacific Northwest. Militant unionism came to the West through the Industrial Workers of the World (I.W.W.), an organization formed at Chicago in 1905 and headed by William E. Haywood. The I.W.W. stressed class warfare and revolution, resorted to wide use of strikes and sabotage, and had some anarchist members. I.W.W. agents organized Western dockworkers, miners, lumbermen, and migratory agricultural workers. Its most active affiliate in the West was the Agricultural Workers Organization. During World War I, Western legislatures and municipal governments adopted laws to suppress the I.W.W.; every city from San Diego to Seattle restricted I.W.W. demonstrations and rallies.

During the 1920s, the I.W.W., along with the Socialist-based Non-Partisan League and other leftist groups, provided a countervailing force to intense Western rightist radicalism. The rightist groups grew out of the vigilante action of the Liberty League and other superpatriotic organizations that flourished during World War I. Their self-appointed task was to watch for local signs of sedition, treason, and enemy activity. After the war these radical rightist groups coalesced into the Ku Klux Klan, which had substantial memberships in most of the Western states from 1920 to about 1930. The Klan was particularly active in the new oil-field camps of Texas, Oklahoma, and Kansas, where boomtown violence and minimum law enforcement prevailed. Klan posses were latter-day vigilante committees, enforcing their own brand of private law in the absence of public law. Their misguided attempts to bring order to the oil boomtowns caused unnecessary and unjustified torment for oil workers in search of amusement and recreation. In several Western states during the 1920s, the Klan was a power in local and state politics; its endorsement was often tantamount to election all the way from mayor to governor.

The period between the wars was a time of bitter factionalism among the political parties of the Western states, each reacting defensively or supportively to the local minority leftist and rightist radical groups. Partisan discord within states often led to battles between the executive and legislative branches, sometimes ending in the impeachment of public officials. During the 1920s, two Oklahoma governors were impeached and removed from office, casualties of the disordered state of Western politics.

An important political phenomenon in the 1920s, which became a normal Western reaction by the 1950s, was partisan insurgency. During the twenties, there were several attempts by political parties at the national level to venture change. The conservative West's reaction—when the national party adopted a platform and nominated a presidential candidate incompatible with Western political values—was to openly support the opposition party candidate. This occurred in the 1928 election when the national Democratic party adopted a platform and nominated a candidate unacceptable to certain Western branches of the Democratic party. Several Western Democratic state party organizations supported the Republican candidate Herbert Hoover over the Democratic party candidate Al Smith— a Roman Catholic and an advocate of repeal of the Prohibition Amendment.

Western Politics and the Great Depression

The decade of the 1930s was a time of punishing economic hardship in the West. Depressed markets for the region's primary products—grain, cattle, fibers, minerals, oil, and lumber—created widespread unemployment and social distress. Economic stagnation colored state and local politics. Insurgency among Western Democrats continued, particularly during the late thirties, when the national party offered the region's voters candidates and issues unpalatable to the region. In the prewar period the Democratic party made a strong move to nationalize the economy through its New Deal programs. To gain congressional support for the legislation, Democratic leaders moved to establish a national party coalition, from which the West felt excluded.

Many Western Democratic governors behaved like mavericks in their attempts to check the nationalizing trend and embarrass President Franklin D. Roosevelt and his aides in their management of federal relief and recovery programs. For years Western leaders of both parties had played the antagonist role in the contest over state versus national control of land and resources; early in the century they had sought to gain control over the vast federal estate in the West reserved in the name of conservation. During the 1930s this role escalated into a fierce rivalry between national officials and many Western governors for local control of federal relief and recovery funds. The West received a greater per-capita share of federal funds under New Deal programs than other regions, and state leaders willingly accepted this largesse. But they also consistently attempted to thwart the accompanying federal management of these funds. The already-large resident bureaucracy assigned to manage federal land and resources in the West increased under the New Deal. Under scornful excoriation by particularistic governors, these officials became the local enemy.

Moreover, there was strong reluctance in many Western states to accept public responsibility for social welfare on the large scale required by federal relief programs. Western states were generally slow to adopt New Deal social-welfare programs and labor-reform statutes such as the Fair Labor Standards Act. Conservative governors became local heroes by their defiance of the federal bureaucracy and their attempts to halt construction on dams and other federal projects by resorting to injunctions and use of state and national guard troops. Democratic governors openly supported Republican candidates for the House and Senate in an attempt to reduce New Deal majorities. This practice began to blur the outlines of Democratic and Republican identity and set the pattern and tradition for modern Western conservatism.

WESTERN POLITICS SINCE 1941

Concomitant with the West's economic maturation has been its emergence as a region of influence in national political affairs. Substantive changes in the New West's economy since 1941—including a phenomenal growth in industrialization and vastly increased employment opportunities—produced population increases that have been principally responsible for the region's political emergence. Population increases produced extensive urbanization, which in turn, changed the predominantly rural West into a region of teeming cities. Western politics in the new order are therefore characterized by urban domination, the anomaly of rigidifying conservatism, and major influence in national politics.

Local and State Politics

During 1971, the Citizens' Conference on Legislatures published a performance analysis of the fifty state legislatures. The criteria for judging and rating the legislatures were mostly quantitative, and included judgments about the functional characteristics and degree of accountability of the lawmaking bodies. Most Western legislatures ranked in the upper half, with California rated number one. Hawaii, placing seventh, was the next highest Western state. Texas ranked thirty-eighth, Montana forty-first, Arizona forty-third, and Wyoming forty-ninth. The analysis did not explore qualitative considerations such as the intimate and direct influence of Western politics on state legislatures. Western state governments are, in fact, very nearly extensions of the dominant local economic groups, which control legislatures, regulatory agencies, and courts in order to guard their interests.

Western state politics are usually highly personalized, directed by elitist groups vaguely referred to as the establishment. Recently the Texas establishment was examined and found to consist of a conservative coterie of major-corporation executives, oil and cattle men, newspaper publishers, radio- and television-station owners, and bankers—"an indefinite group that runs the show." Methods of establishment control included use of money, personal leadership, and an "intangible called influence," the members clustering around "mutual interests" for the purpose of preserving "their own power and wealth." One source described the Texas establishment as a "group of people in Dallas and Houston who customarily make their strength known by financing the political campaigns" of their candidates for governor and the legislature and, once elected, "finding ways to bring them from poor boys to rich boys." [2]

The conservative tone of Western politics is reflected in the strong resistance to redrafting state constitutions. Many Western state constitutions are inordinately long, containing specific directives that are actually statutory in character. In the 1970s attempts by citizen-reform groups to obtain conventions to rewrite constitutions were soundly defeated in Utah, Nebraska, North Dakota, and Oklahoma. State leaders were unwilling to risk an open convention where, they seem to fear, new, threatening thoughts might intrude. Thus constitutional change is piecemeal, made by amendment under safe legislative direction and, occasionally, by federal court decisions.

One of the most significant changes in Western politics since World War II has been the shift of power from agrarian, stockraising, and mining interests to manufacturing and service-oriented industries. Legislative reapportionment has moved the power base from rural to urban, but there has been no accompanying liberalization of state politics. The conservative stream continues to run strong. The John Birch Society, although born in New England, is strongest in the West, particularly in Texas and California. Fundamentalist Protestant preachers, including popular radio and television evangelists, mix religion with economic and social doctrine. Organized, militant conservatives inveigh against teaching sex in public schools, octopus rule from Washington, Supreme Court decisions on the death penalty and abortion, public-welfare programs, and high taxes. They promote speaker-ban statutes, anti–evolution laws, and "right to work" laws.

The political response has included legislative attempts to restrict public-welfare participation and more stringent control of public-school curricula. State-supported colleges and universities, which are often regarded as leaders of change and threats to the established social order, have been politicized by legislative action that has reduced their self-rule and brought

[2] *The Gainesville (Texas) Register,* May 1, 1969.

them under closer legislative control. California and several other Western states have seriously considered several unusual proposals. These include: limiting state and federal income-tax levies to 25 percent; restricting local property taxes to 1 percent of market value; limiting use of property-tax revenue to "property-related" public services such as street construction and maintenance; and shifting completely to the state and federal governments responsibility for schools and public welfare.

A reform considered by several Western states is the ombudsman system, in which a public official has the responsibility to receive and act upon citizen grievances against state government. Hawaii and Oregon—acknowledging that the state bureaucracy differs from the federal bureaucracy only in degree of insensitivity—have adopted the ombudsman system, hoping to make state government more responsive to the people. Cynical bureaucratic hardshells often call this official the "state chaplain."

A very important problem for Western state governments is the escalating demands by growing cities, expanding industries, and agricultural and stockraising interests for water. Equitable methods of dividing this precious resource between competing urban and rural users remain to be established. Moreover, the search for new water resources is complicated by the interstate character of Western rivers, which creates competition among the states and with the federal government. California has been a leader in expanding its water resources, particularly for urban needs. As early as 1900, the rapidly growing city of Los Angeles found that local wells and the Los Angeles River were inadequate to the rising water requirements. City leaders conceived a plan to transport water to the coast from the Owens Valley by a 250-mile aqueduct. The continuing growth of California cities has led to additional water-import enterprises, including the Feather River project, which carries water from the moisture-rich northern part of the state to the parched southland over a 600-mile-long system. Texas leaders plan to tap the Mississippi River below New Orleans and to transport water through a 1,000-mile-long system of canals and pipelines to the Panhandle Plains between Lubbock and Amarillo and west to El Paso. Oklahoma City and other Western urban centers are drawing water from even more remote regions.

Operational interstate projects began with the Colorado River project. In 1915, federal officials conceived a plan to impound the Colorado River to prevent such floods as the 1906 inundation, which filled the Salton Sea and threatened the entire Imperial Valley. The project would also provide more water for irrigation and urban use in the Southwest, and for electrical generation. Competition among several Western states for allocation of the Colorado's water and power led Secretary of Commerce Herbert Hoover in 1922 to convene a conference at Santa Fe; delegates came from the Colorado Basin states of California, Colorado, Wyoming, Utah, New Mexico, Arizona, and Nevada. A compact for common development of the Colorado River was ratified by all the participating states except Arizona.

Plans proceeded and, in 1928, Congress authorized construction of an impoundment project on the Colorado near Las Vegas, Nevada; the multiple-purpose project was to provide water for urban and rural areas, generation of electricity, flood control, and recreation. Construction began on the Hoover (Boulder) Dam in 1930, and the project was completed five years later. It provided the pattern for other Western projects requiring interstate and federal cooperation.

Additional Western municipal, state, and federal projects to develop water resources, usually funded with federal support, include desalination projects for irrigation and industrial use and reclamation of water from sewage. In addition, there has been wide resort to what is called weather-modification systems—rainmaking projects—also mostly federally financed with some state and local funds added. Several irrigation and water districts have been formed in the Southwest by civic leaders, farmers, and ranchers, in cooperation with the federal Bureau of Reclamation, to apply new meteorology technology in an attempt to increase rainfall. The usual technique is the seeding of clouds with silver-iodide particles. In California, public utilities have seeded clouds over the western slope of the Sierras for fifteen years. Company officials report that their rainmaking efforts have increased precipitation 10 to 20 percent in the rivers that serve their electrical-generation plants.

Western Politics and the Nation

Since 1941, the West's impact on national political affairs has been twofold: it has both contributed ideology and example to the nation's enlarging conservative community and provided a significant number of national leaders. At the same time, the West has continued to play the antagonist role toward the federal government. As the nation becomes increasingly nationalized in economic policy, management of resources, social welfare, and race relations, Western governors and legislative leaders continue to invent ways to contravene federal laws, regulations, and court decisions, reluctantly submitting only under threat of the withholding of federal funds. And the West continues its contest with the federal government for control of Western land held as part of the vast federal estate. State and local governments generally oppose the conservation policy that regulates use of these lands and thwarts local designs.

Because most of the federal estate is located in the West, it has been subject to extended federal regulation and management. And because of this begrudgingly shared jurisdiction, the Western states have long had to contend with the conservation movement. From the turn of the century, when the federal estate was first established, portions of most Western states have been subjected to federal management programs. During the 1930s, federal intrusion accelerated through application of the Civilian Conservation Corps and Soil Conservation programs to federal lands in the West. Then, during the 1960s, a widening public consciousness and concern for the quality of the environment produced the ecosystem concept and ecology programs. Private conservation organizations focused on the West and the federal estate in the West as never before. These included the Wilderness Society, National Parks Association, Sierra Club, Environmental Defense Fund, Natural Resource Defense Council, and Friends of the Earth. During 1964, conservation advocates were able to obtain passage by Congress of several laws to further protect and restrict access to certain Western areas. The most important was the National Wilderness Preservation Act, by which nearly 50 million acres of Western wilderness in national forests have been withdrawn from general-public access; 10 million acres carry a special designation that bans development of any sort, including roads.

Westerners are gaining some commercial access to federal lands to serve tourism, one of the region's principal industries. By adopting the rhetoric of recreationism and by lobbying federal officials to permit private commercial development of outdoor recreation facilities, developers are gaining access to wilderness areas in national forests previously closed to them. Of the 200 commercial ski areas located in national forests, 46 are in California. Injunctions obtained by vigilant Sierra Club members and other conservation representatives may momentarily check this alteration of long-established policy, but recreationists, proceeding on the maxim that "progress always beats protectionism," eventually triumph.

Because of its growing population, the West's electoral impact has substantially increased in recent years. In earlier times, only in close elections could the region have a dramatic influence on presidential elections. An example was Woodrow Wilson's re-election in 1916. While he lost key concentrations of electoral votes in the East, he carried all of the West, except South Dakota and Oregon. Particularly since 1941, presidential candidates have come to have regard for the West's electoral support.

Also since 1941, the West has increased its share of national political leadership. Only rarely did a national leader emerge from the region before that time. William Jennings Bryan was the first prominent Western political figure. Hiram Johnson, a California reformer, was vice-presidential nominee for the Progressive party in 1912. President Herbert Hoover was a Westerner, as was his vice-president, Charles Curtis. Alfred M. Landon of Kansas was a Republican leader of national prominence during the 1930s, and Jack Garner, a Texas Democrat, served as vice-president during the second term of Franklin D. Roosevelt.

There was a noticeable increase in political influence and power from the West after 1950. For years, Robert S. Kerr of Oklahoma was the acknowledged "uncrowned king of the United States Senate," and the late Sam Rayburn, a Texas Democrat, served as Speaker of the House of Representatives. Dwight D. Eisenhower, a World War II hero and president during the 1950s, was a Kansan, and his vice-president, Richard M. Nixon, was from California. Both major presidential candidates in

1964 were from the Southwest: Lyndon B. Johnson of Texas was the Democratic nominee, and Barry Goldwater of Arizona, the Republican nominee. Californian Richard M. Nixon won the presidency in 1968. Carl Albert, present Speaker of the House, is a Democrat from Oklahoma; John Rhodes of Arizona is House minority leader; and Mike Mansfield of Montana serves as Senate majority leader.

Democratic and Republican labels are confusing in the West because of the region's conservative essence. Westerners may be more realistically identified as associated with partisan galaxies of dominant conservative and minority liberal groups within both parties. "Tory" Democrats, uniting with consistently conservative Republicans, produce a regional coalition that usually supports the Republican presidential candidate. Democrats maintain their identity for tradition's sake, for state and local elections, and, when the national party wins the presidency, to share in patronage and other partisan favors. George Wallace's American Independent Party has not shown much strength in the West, perhaps because the region's own Republican party provides the predominantly conservative voters with palatable candidates and issues. Most Westerners still "hunger for a simpler and more manageable world in which Righteousness is enforced by the Big Stick, the Three R's are taught in Neighborhood Schools, and Punishment inexorably follows crime." [3]

SELECTED SOURCES

The theme of Western political emergence is traced in *Gerald D. Nash, The American West in the Twentieth Century: A Short History of an Urban Oasis (Englewood Cliffs, 1973); Neil Morgan, Westward Tilt: The American West Today (New York, 1961); Neal R. Peirce, The Great Plains States of America: People, Politics, and Power in the Nine Great Plains States (New York, 1973); *W. Eugene Hollon, The Southwest: Old and New (New York, 1961); *Earl S. Pomeroy, The Pacific Slope (New York, 1965); *Robert G. Athearn, High Country Empire: The High Plains and the Rockies (Lincoln, 1965); and Walter P. Webb, Divided We Stand: The Crisis of a Frontierless Democracy (New York, 1937).

*Available in paperback.

[3] The New York Times, Sept. 1, 1968.

Index

Abilene, cattle depot, 478
Absaroka. *See* Crow Indians
Abolitionists, 318, 400, 406
Adams, John Quincy, 160, 179, 218, 318, 326
Adams-Oñís Treaty, 153, 171, 173, 178, 214, 309, 324, 512
Agrarian frontier, 343, 346, 372, 491, 538, 545, 550, 563, 573, 599
Agrarian society, 550–51
Agriculture, 46, 193, 308, 361, 371, 447, 490, 537, 575, 578
Aircraft industry, 578
Alabama, 104, 149, 152, 155, 159, 161, 162, 163, 165
Alabama Enabling Act, 153
Alamo, 316
Alarcón, Hernando de, 38
Alarcón, Martin de, 48
Alaska, 6, 10, 11, 13, 19, 25, 78, 83, 217, 225, 267, 271–72, 275–76, 519, 528, 533–34, 572, 598
Alaska Commercial Company, 533
Alaska Organic Act, 534, 598
Alaskan Central Railroad, 598
Alaskan Government Act, 533
Alaskan statehood movement, 602
Alaskan telegraph, 532
Albert, Speaker Carl, 616
Albuquerque, N.M., 37, 282, 355, 378, 381, 460, 462
Aleutian Islands, 4, 42, 83, 272
Aleuts, 26, 31, 272, 275, 529, 598
Algonquin Indians, 40, 53
Alianza – Federation Alliance of Land Grants, 586–87

Allegheny River, 20, 57, 59, 87, 92
Allotments in severalty, 304
American Board of Commissioners for Foreign Missions, 297, 329, 522
American Federation of Labor, 609
American Fur Company, 185, 245, 255, 257, 260–61, 267, 324
American Indian Movement (AIM), 591
American Revolution, 69, 92, 97, 115, 190
American River, 344, 353, 362, 363
American System (Clay's), 219
American Zion, 347
Americanization process, 513, 519, 556, 565
Ames, Oakes, 466
Ames, Oliver, 457, 466
Amherst, Gen. Jeffrey, 65
Anadarko Indians, 303, 433
Anahuac incident, 314
Anglo-American culture, 5, 10, 553
Annian, Strait of, 40, 229
Apache Indians, 47, 48, 51, 56, 227, 389, 409, 418–19, 427, 432, 435, 446
Appalachian Mountains, 3, 5, 13, 19, 21, 29, 45, 56, 60, 68, 149, 190, 211
Arapaho Indians, 28, 226, 389–90, 428, 432, 435, 538
Arbuckle, Mathew, 291, 294
Arctic Circle, 19, 25
Argonauts, 364
Arikara Indians, 226, 252, 255
Arizona, 4, 24, 43, 49, 76, 77, 225, 227, 263, 362–63, 371, 408, 415,

418–19, 427, 460, 490, 498, 508, 514–15, 572, 580

Arkansas, 6, 20, 21, 36, 155, 164, 166, 169, 171, 175, 177, 180–81, 184, 201, 278, 408, 411, 463

Arkansas Land & Cattle Company, 497

Arkansas Post, 51, 77, 78, 195, 244, 249, 277, 370

Arkansas River, 10, 20, 37, 41, 42, 50, 52, 77, 154, 171–74, 195–96, 199, 226, 235–38, 244, 263, 266, 270, 278–79, 289, 292, 298, 389, 464, 482

Army of the West, 355, 387

Arteaga, Juan, 80

Arthur, Gabriel, 57

Articles of Confederation, 8, 98

Asbury, Francis, 205

Ashley, William, 258

Asinai Indians, 48

Aspinwall, William H., 376

Astor, John Jacob, 255, 260

Astoria, 255–57, 324, 375

Atchison, David, 400

Atlantic & Pacific Railroad, 460, 463

Atchison, Topeka & Santa Fe Railway, 462

Augusta council (1763), 67

Austin, Modes, 120, 194, 310

Austin, Stephen F., 315–17

Bad Axe, Battle of, 138

Baja California, 76, 79

Ball, M. D., 534

Banditti of the Plains, 480

Bank of America, 582

Bankhead-Jones Farm Tenant Act, 605

Banking, 197, 582

Bannock Indians, 421, 427

Baptists, 204, 206

Baranov, Alexander, 529

Barbed wire, 12, 480

Barbour, Henry, 251

Bartleson, John, 333, 345

Base metals, 488, 572

Basin and Range Country, 24

Baton Rouge, La., 90, 121

Baylor, John R., 415

Beale, Lt. Edward F., 378

"Bear Flag Revolt," 356

Beaver, 252, 253, 258, 266, 267, 361

Becknell, William, 195, 226, 277–78

Beecher's Island, Battle of, 439

The Beef Bonanza: or How to Get Rich on the Plains, 479

Bell, John R., 237, 238

Belle Point, Arkansas, 174, 236

Bent, Gov. Charles, 387

Benton, Thomas H., 14, 216, 258, 280, 540

Bent's Fort, 266, 267, 278, 361, 389

Bering Straits, 26, 530

Bering, Vitus, 78, 275, 528

Beveridge, Albert J., 509, 515

Big Foot, 450

Biddle, Nicolas, 231, 326

Bidwell-Bartleson party, 344–45

Bidwell, John, 345, 373

Biloxi, Miss., 42, 49, 165

Bingham, Hiram, 523

Black Hawk War, 138, 185, 290

Black Hills, S.D., 23, 439, 487

Black Kettle, 429, 432, 437

Blackfeet Indians, 52, 226, 231, 245, 253, 254, 258, 261, 390

Blacks, 77, 180, 182, 184, 201, 553, 588–89

Blainville, Celeron de, 59

Blair, Francis P., 387

Blanchet, François, 330

Bloody Fellow, 89

Blount, James H., 527

Blount, William, 109, 119

Blunt, James G., 413

Board of Indian Commissioners, 435

Boatbuilding, 198, 199, 251

Bodega Bay, 275

Boggy Depot, 363, 477

Bogy, Joseph, 251

Bonneville, Benjamin L. E., 262

Book of Mormon, 346, 523

Boomer raids, 511

Boone, Daniel, 74, 75, 87

Boonesborough, Ky., 86, 87

Bosque Redondo Reservation, 418, 427

Boudinot, Elias, 156, 157

Boudinot, Elias C., 510

Boulder Dam. *See* Hoover Dam

Bouquet, Henry, 66

Bozeman Road, 430, 434, 443
Bradburn, John, 314
Braddock, Edward, 60, 73
Braddock's Road, 121
Bradstreet, John, 66
Brant, Joseph, 105
Brazito, battle of, 355
Bridger, Jim, 257, 258, 260, 261
Brisbin, James S., 479
British, 39, 53, 67–68, 88, 92, 151,
    185, 237, 252, 274, 351
British maritime traders, 342
British traders in Old West, 58
Brock, Issac, 127
Broken Treaties Caravan, 591
Brown Berets, 587
Brown, John, 400
Bryan, William Jennings, 567, 615
Bryce, Lord James, 557
Buchanan, James, 353, 400
Buena Vista, Mexico, 355
Buffalo, 28, 38, 195, 226, 236, 249,
    264, 267, 361, 431, 459, 474
Buffalo extermination, 476
Buffalo-hide industry, 475
Buffalo-hunter mentality, 592, 593
Bureau of Reclamation, 614
Burnet, David G., 317
Burr Conspiracy, 110, 308
Bushy Run, Battle of, 66
Businessmen, frontier, 196
Butler, Elizar, 156
Butterfield, John, 381
Butterfield Overland Mail, 381, 455
Byington, Cyrus, 329

Cabeza de Vaca, Alver Nuñez de, 36
Cabin Creek Raid, 414
Caddo Indians, 226, 236, 288, 292,
    303, 408, 433
Cahokia, Ill., 49, 67, 87, 97, 144
Cajan Pass, 261, 282
Caldwell, Kansas, 478, 482
Calhoun, John C., 126, 176, 216, 320,
    397
California, 4, 10–11, 24, 39–43, 76–
    77, 225–27, 261, 263, 266, 324–
    25, 330, 335, 341, 342, 343–46,
    350–51, 355–56, 361, 364, 371,

388–89, 407, 539, 552, 567, 574,
    577, 580
California cattle industry, 370
California Column, 416, 419, 498
California Farmers' Union, 566
California gold fields, 366, 374
California gold rush, 362, 364–65, 373
California Road, 299, 364, 389, 407,
    427
California statehood, 396
California trade, 341–42
Camel Experiment, 378–79
Camp Radziminski, 299, 302
Camp School, 545, 546
Camp Washita, 293, 294
Canadian River, 21, 50, 52, 238, 263,
    265, 279, 294, 419
Canals, 142
Canby, Edward R. S., 415, 444
Cane Ridge, Ky., Great Revival at,
    205–06, 547
Canton, China, 272, 273–74
Capital sources, 579, 582
Carey Act (1894), 574
Carleton, James H., 416, 418, 427
Carpenter, Charles C., 510–11
Carrington, Henry B., 430
Carson, Christopher (Kit), 266, 355,
    418
Cascade range, 25, 324, 353
Cass, Lewis, 137, 141, 258, 298, 335,
    562
Cass frontier defense plan, 299, 562
Catlin, George, 293–94
Cattle, 193, 276, 330, 370, 476–77,
    510
Cattleman's frontier, 480
Cattlemen, 545, 554
Cattle trails, 477–78
Cavalier, Robert. See La Salle, Sieur de
Cavendish, Thomas, 39
Cayuga Indians, 29, 41, 84
Cayuse Indians, 336, 392, 421
Central Pacific Railway Company,
    456–59, 466, 552, 566
Central Plains, 21, 52, 428
Century of Dishonor (Helen Hunt
    Jackson), 451
Charles III of Spain, 75
Charleston, S.C., 57, 164

Chattahoochee River, 20, 40

Chautauqua, 548

Chavez, Cesar Estrada, 587

Cherokee Advocate, 297

Cherokee Commission, 512

Cherokee constitution, 395

Cherokee Indians, 10, 27, 48, 53, 56, 67, 70–74, 84–85, 90, 97, 104, 107, 125, 129, 150–51, 153–56, 158, 174–77, 184, 201, 226, 235, 289, 293–96, 299, 308, 316–17, 364, 395, 406, 411, 422, 424, 462–63, 481, 538

Cherokee Mounted Rifles, 412

Cherokee Phoenix, 156, 157, 158

Cherokee Outlet, 434, 436, 446, 482, 511, 544

Cherokee Strip Live Stock Association, 480, 482

Cherokee syllabary, 297

Cheyenne-Arapaho Reservation, 482, 511

Cheyenne-Arapaho Stock Growers Association, 482

Cheyenne Indians, 28, 52, 226, 389–90, 420, 428–29, 432, 435–36, 442, 538

Cheyenne Transporter, 482

Chicago, Ill., 144, 377, 463

Chicago, Burlington and Quincy Railway, 377, 463

Chicago, Milwaukee and St. Paul Railway, 463

Chicago and Northwestern Railroad, 377, 458

Chicago, Rock Island and Pacific Railway, 377, 463

Chicano. *See* Mexican-Americans

Chickamaugas, 89, 107

Chickasaw Bluffs, 54, 60, 103, 107, 244

Chickasaw Indians, 10, 27, 53, 54–59, 67, 71, 84, 89, 97, 104, 107, 122, 125, 129, 150–53, 158, 162–63, 201, 213, 226, 289, 295–96, 302, 364, 395, 400, 411, 424, 433, 481, 511, 513

Chief Joseph, 227, 446

Chihuahua, Mexico, 10, 77, 195, 236, 277, 282, 340, 355

Chillicothe, Ohio, 105, 111, 116, 198

China trade, 229, 255, 271, 273, 277

Chinese, 458, 524, 552–53, 588

Chinese Exclusion Act, 553, 588

Chippewa Indians, 104, 105, 106, 137, 185–86

Chisholm, Jesse, 264, 478

Chisholm Trail, 478

Chivington, John M., 416, 420

Choctaw and Gulf Railway, 463–64

Choctaw Indians, 10, 53, 57, 67, 71, 84, 97, 104, 107, 125, 129, 154, 159–60, 163, 174–77, 181, 184, 201, 213, 226, 235, 289, 293–96, 329, 364, 395, 406, 411, 424, 433, 477, 513, 538

Church of Jesus Christ of Latter Day Saints. *See* Mormons

Chloera, 160, 163, 192, 296⁻

Chorpenning, George, 381

Chouteau, Auguste, 135, 136, 251, 253, 258, 263

Chusto Talasah, 412

Cincinnati, Ohio, 103, 111, 116, 139, 144, 198, 200

Civil War, 299, 302, 303, 405–06, 410, 428, 434, 477, 542

Civilized Indian frontier, 563

Claiborne, William C. C., 120, 171–72, 178

Claim associations, 185

Clark, George Rogers, 87, 97, 99, 109, 190, 214–15, 229

Clark, William, 134, 135, 137, 172–73, 228–29, 253, 258

Clay, Henry, 14, 126, 184, 216, 218, 398

Cleveland, Grover, 502, 527, 605

Cleveland, Ohio, 139, 144

Clipper ships, 376

Coal mining, 363, 464, 488, 572

Coast Range, 25, 374

Coeur d'Alene Indians, 324, 330, 393

Coffee, Charley, 480

Colbert's Ferry, 477

Collier, John, 590

Colorado, 23, 24, 266, 362, 406, 410, 415–16, 420, 427, 446, 462, 464, 480, 488, 498–99, 503, 553, 564, 572, 587, 609

Colorado Plateau, 24

Colorado River, 24, 37, 76, 77, 79, 80, 227, 261, 340, 375, 389, 397, 409, 460, 488, 613

Colter, John, 230, 252–54
Columbia Fur Company, 261
Columbian Plateau, 24, 227
Columbia River, 24, 79, 229, 231, 255, 262, 324, 328, 330, 335, 365, 398, 578
Colville Reservation (Nez Perces), 446
Colyer, Vincent, 446
Comanche Indians, 28, 47, 48, 51, 56, 226, 249, 252, 264, 279, 288, 290, 293–94, 300, 302, 307, 318, 389, 408, 419, 423, 428, 431–32, 435–38, 448, 482, 538
Commerce, Ill. *See* Nauvoo
Commerce of the Prairies, 281
Company of Explorers of the Missouri, 229
Company of the Indies, 50
Compromise of 1850, 398
Comstock, Henry T., 368
Comstock Lode, 368, 484
Conestoga wagon, 198, 279
Confederate States of America, 401, 405–08, 411, 427
Connor, P. E., 421
Conservation movement, 579, 604, 606, 612, 615
Continental Congress, 75, 84
Cook, Capt. James, 272, 324, 520
Cooke, Jay, 462
Copper mining, 363, 369, 488
Copper Queen Mine, 488
Corn production, 193
Cornwall Academy, 329, 522
Coronado, Francisco Vásquez de, 37
Cos, Martin, 316
Cotton culture, 166, 182, 200–04, 297
Council Bluffs, Iowa, 237, 348, 365, 458
Crawford, William, 92
Crazy Horse, 443–44
Crédit Mobilier of America, 466
Creek Indians, 10, 48, 53, 56, 57, 67, 71, 84, 97, 104, 105, 107, 125, 129, 150–54, 158, 160, 162, 201, 213, 226, 235, 289, 294–96, 395, 406, 411–12, 424, 434, 463, 481, 513
Cresap, Thomas, 73
Cripple Creek, Colo., 485
Crockett, Davy, 216, 316

Croghan, George, 57, 67, 73
Crook, George, 443, 446–47
Cross Timbers, 21, 264
Crow Indians, 226, 253, 390
Crusade for Justice, 587
Cumberland Gap, 20, 73, 74, 75, 98, 122
Curtis Act, 513
Curtis, Charles, 615
Custer, George Armstrong, 437, 439, 443, 487
Cutler, Manasseh, 102

Dade, Francis, 164
Dakota Territory, 402, 443, 490, 498, 500, 505
Dale, Edward Everett, 550
Dalyell, James, 66
Dana, Richard Henry, 343
Dancing Rabbit Creek, 159
Davis, Jefferson, 378
Davis, William Heath, 276
Dawes Act. *See* General Allotment Act
Dawes Commission, 513
De Bourgmoud, Etienne, 52
Declaration of Indian Purpose, 591
D'Eglise, Jacques, 228
Delaware Indians, 10, 27, 58, 66, 78, 85, 86, 92, 97, 103, 104, 105, 106, 123, 174, 226, 236, 289, 308, 394, 433
Demers, Modeste, 330
Democratic-Republican Party, 218
Democratic Party, 218, 409, 499, 502–03, 513, 528
Denver, 368, 410, 458, 463, 478, 485, 587
Denver and Pacific Railway, 463
Denver and Rio Grande Railway, 464–65
Department of the Interior, established, 288
Deseret, 350, 397
Desert Land Act, 491
De Smet, Father Pierre Jean, 330
De Soto, Hernando, 36
Detribalization process, 447–48
Detroit, 49, 53, 66, 83, 84, 87, 88, 91, 93, 97, 105, 115, 127, 141, 215
Dewey, Cmdr. George, 528

De Witt's Corner, Treaty of (1777), 86
Dickson, Joseph, 252
Distilleries, 193
District of Louisiana, 172
Dixon, Billy, 475
Doaksville, Choctaw Nation, 297, 304, 363
Doaksville, Treaty of (1837), 163
Dodge City, Kansas, 478
Dodge, Grenville, 429, 457–58
Dodge, Henry, 290
Dole, Sanford, 527
Domínguez, Francisco, 80
Dominicans, 46, 76
Doña Ana Road, 364, 389
Donelson, John, 70, 98
Doniphan, Alexander, 355
Donner party, 345
Doolittle, John R., 428, 431–32, 435
Douglas, Chief, 446
Douglas, Stephen A., 15, 377, 397, 399, 456, 541
Dragging Canoe, Chief, 85, 89, 90
Dragoons, 293–94, 355
Drake, Sir Francis, 39
Drake's Bay, 39
Dry-farming methods, 468, 492
Dubuque, Iowa, 194, 199
Duer, William, 102
Dunbar, William, 232
Durant, Thomas C., 457
Dust Bowl, 493, 575, 605
Dutch, 4, 41

East Shawnee (cattle) Trail, 477
Eastern Cherokees, 155
Ecology programs, 615
Edmunds Act, 507
Education on the frontier, 203, 213, 545
Edwards, Hayden, 313
Edwards, Ninian, 118, 135, 140
Edwardsville, Treaty of (1819), 136
Ehrenburg, Ariz., 369, 375
Eisenhower, Dwight D., 590, 615
Election of 1844, 320
Electrical-transmission facilities, 581
Ellis, Richard, 316
El Paso, Texas, 46–47, 195–96, 226, 249, 340, 355, 381, 409, 415, 460

Elskwatawa, 123–24
Emathla, 164
Emigrant Aid Societies, 400
Emory, William H., 300, 408
Empresarios, 310, 312–13, 316, 319, 539
Empress of China, 271–72
Enlarged Homestead Act, 573
Episcopal Church, 204, 523
Erie Canal, 137, 141–42
Eskimos, 27, 31, 598
Espejo, Antonio de, 39
Estevanico, 37
Ethnic activism, 589, 591
European immigrants, 373
Evans, John, 229, 420
Ewell, Richard, 392
Exploitive frontier, 474, 489, 493
Extralegal governmental associations, 401, 409, 480

Factories, 149, 160
Fairbanks gold field, 534
Fallen Timbers, Battle of, 106
Fannin, J. W., 317
Far Eastern markets, 272
Farm-Labor Reconstruction League, 609
Farm Tenant Union, 608
Farming, 47, 297, 308, 369, 373, 387, 406
Feather River project, 613
Federal factory (fur) system, 257
Federal Highway Act (1916), 577
Federal Highway Act (1956), 577
Federal lands, 604, 605
Federal land grants, 378
Federal subsidies, 379, 460, 462
Federal roads, 150
Federal spending in the West, 580–81
Federal Western estate, 604, 614
Federalist party, 218
Ferdinandina, 51, 77
Fetterman Massacre, 430
Fetterman, William J., 430
Filibusterers, 308–09
Fillmore, Pres. Millard, 397
Finley, John, 73–74
First California Volunteer Regiment, 416

First Colorado Volunteers, 420
First Dragoon Regiment, 293
Fish, Hamilton, 526
Fishing industry, 576
Fitzpatrick, Thomas, 258, 260, 345, 390
Five Civilized Tribes, 451, 482, 513–14
Flatboats, 116, 142, 190, 199
Flathead Indians, 227, 253, 323, 328, 330
Fletcher *v.* Peck, 102, 151
Flint, Timothy, 203
Florida, 20, 38, 68, 150, 155, 163
Floyd, Charles, 230, 325
Floyd, John, 302, 325
Fontainebleau, Treaty of (1762), 60
Forbes, Gen. John, 60
Forbes' Road, 73, 121
"Force policy," 435
Forest Reserve Act (1891), 605
Forks of the Ohio River, 71
Fort Arbuckle, 299, 389, 407
Fort Bellefontaine, 171
Fort Boise, 329, 333
Fort Bragg, 389
Fort Breckenridge, 389, 409
Fort Bridger, 333, 348, 389, 421
Fort Buchanan, 389, 409
Fort Celeste, 171
Fort Clatsop, 231
Fort Cobb, 300, 303, 406–07, 437
Fort Coffee, 298
Fort Colville, 369, 390
Fort Craig, 389, 408–09, 415
Fort Crawford, 134, 138
Fort Cumberland, 60, 73
Fort Dearborn, 127, 134
Fort de Chartres, 49, 67, 194
Fort Defiance, 379, 389
Fort Duncan, 445
Fort Duquesne, 59, 60. *See also* Fort Pitt
Fort Fetterman, 443
Fort Fillmore, 389, 408, 415
Fort Finney, 104
Fort George, 256
Fort Gibson, 199, 264, 290, 291, 293, 294, 298, 376, 406, 412–14, 445
Fort Gibson, Treaty of (1833), 164

Fort Hall, 267, 327, 333, 344, 345, 389
Fort Harmar, 99, 103, 104
Fort Harrison 127, 134
Fort Henry (Wheeling, W. Va.), 87
Fort Howard, 134
Fortifications, community, 86
Fort Jackson, 171
Fort Jackson, Treaty of (1814), 129, 152, 153
Fort Jefferson, 89, 134, 190
Fort Jesup, 171
Fort Kearny, 336, 379, 389, 420
Fort King Massacre, 164
Fort Kittanning, 87
Fort Laramie, 267, 389, 390, 430, 434
Fort Laramie, Treaty of (1851), 390; (1868), 439
Fort Leavenworth, 280, 298, 299, 355, 389, 419
Fort Livingstone, 171
Fort Lyon, 420, 436
Fort Madison, 172
Fort Manuel, 252–54
Fort McIntosh, 91, 116
Fort McKenzie, 261
Fort Miami, 49
Fort Michilimackinac, 66
Fort Moultrie, 164
Fort Necessity, 59
Fort Nelson, 88
Fort Osage, 171, 236
Fort Phil Kearny, 430
Fort Pickens, 447
Fort Pitt, 59–60, 66, 84, 86–87, 91–92
Fort Quiatanon, 67
Fort Randolph, 87
Fort Reno, 430
Fort Russ, Calif., 275, 529, 531
Fort San Carlos, 171
Fort Scott, 299, 414
Fort Scott–Fort Gibson Military Road, 414
Fort Seldon, 171
Fort Sill, 437–38, 447
Fort Smith, 171, 174–75, 179, 194–99, 200, 236, 238, 263–64, 278–79, 295, 298, 304, 344, 364, 378, 381, 389, 406–07, 411–12

Fort Smith and Western Railway, 463

Fort Snelling, 172, 186, 199, 237, 299

Fort Stanwix, 70, 104

Fort Stanwix, Treaty of (1764), 70, 73, 99

Fort St. Joseph, 66

Fort Sumner, 418

Fort Supply, 436, 476

Fort Toulouse, 50

Fort Towson, 199, 298–99, 376

Fort Union, 261, 389, 408, 415–16

Fort Vancouver, 257, 262, 324, 334, 351, 372, 374

Fort Wallace, 439

Fort Washington, 116

Fort Washita, 299, 376, 389, 407

Fort Wayne, 123, 127, 134, 144

Fort William, 327, 334

Fort Wise, Treaty of (1861), 420

Fort Worth, Texas, 21, 389, 460

Fort Yuma, 375, 381, 389, 409, 417

Fossil fuel resources, 572

Fourth Cavalry, 438, 445

Fowler, Jacob, 264

Fox Indians, 41, 53, 78, 137

France, 4, 11, 13, 39, 42, 45, 56–57, 77–78, 88, 97, 109, 171–82, 185, 215, 274, 339

Franciscan missionaries, 46, 79, 341

Franklin, Benjamin, 92

Franklin, Mo., 195, 199, 278

Franklin, state of, 110

Fraser, Simon, 324

Fredonian Rebellion, 313

Free companies, 413

Free Soil Issue, 395

Freeman, Thomas, 232

Freight caravans, 379, 422

Frémont, John C., 332, 353, 356, 364, 378, 388

French and Indian War, 56, 59, 65, 75

French settlers, 50, 103, 201, 373

French traders, 49, 55–56

Frenchmen, 230, 249, 257, 307

Frisco Railroad. See St. Louis and San Francisco Railway

Frontier democracy, 116

Frontier family, 202

Frontier society, 201–08, 537, 543–58

Fulton, Gov. William S., 184

Fundamentalism, 206, 593

Fur brigades, 258

Fur markets, 245, 267

Fur trade, 8–9, 42, 57, 77, 83, 126, 141, 185, 243, 245, 250, 258, 372

Fur-trade frontier, 144, 187, 195, 228, 263, 563

Gadsden Purchase, 393

Gage, Gen. Thomas, 67

Gallatin, Albert, 122, 178

Galveston Bay, Texas, 36, 313, 464

Gálvez, Bernardo de, 90

Gálvez, Jose de, 76, 79

Garces, Father Francisco, 79

"Garden of the World," 539–41

Gardoqui, Don Diego de, 107

Garner, Vice-Pres. Jack, 615

Gass, Patrick, 230, 231

General Allotment Act, 451, 469, 482, 512, 538, 555

General Land Office, 143

Gênet, Edmond Charles, 108, 215

Georgia Compact, 101

Geronimo, 447

Ghent, Treaty of (1814), 130, 215

Ghost Dance, 450

Gibbon, John, 443, 446

Gila River, 79, 227, 266, 282, 344, 364, 369, 409, 446, 488

Gila River mining district, 369

Gila River route to Calif., 364

Gillespie, Archibald, 356

Gilpin, William, 402

Gist, Christopher, 58, 73

Glenn, Hugh, 251, 264, 277

Glorieta Pass, 416

Gnadenhutten, 92

Gold, 363, 364, 373, 392, 484–88, 533–34

Goldwater, Barry, 616

Goodnight, Charles, 478, 480

Goodnight-Loving Trail, 478

Gonzales, Battle of, 315

Goshute Indians, 421

Gould, Jay, 460

Grain production, 200, 298

Gran Quivira, 36–37, 40

Grand Army of the Republic, 502

Grand Canyon, 24, 37, 266
Grand Ohio Company, 71
Grand River, 251, 290–91, 298, 414
Grand Tetons, 253, 605
Grandfather Clause, 589
Granger lines, 463
Grant, Ulysses S., 435, 503
Grattan, Lt. John, 391
Gray-Kendrick Expedition, 273
Gray, Robert, 228, 273, 324
Great American Desert, 12, 238–39, 283, 350, 479, 490, 538, 540, 562, 563
Great Basin, 46, 227, 249, 261, 262, 265, 266, 282, 339, 345, 346, 350, 353, 361, 371, 372, 397, 400, 422, 490, 505
Great Britain, 4, 45, 56, 80, 83, 93, 103, 126, 177, 179, 214–15, 225, 324–25, 335, 339
Great Circle Route, 282, 344
Great Depression, 575, 579, 589, 606
Great Lakes, 41–42, 49–50, 53, 57, 134, 137
Great Mahele, 525
Great Meadows, battle at, 59
Great Migration, 141, 144–45, 150, 165, 169, 180, 365
Great Northern Railroad, 463
Great Plains, 10, 21, 23, 28, 252, 340, 361, 390, 428, 435, 474, 479–80, 491–92, 542, 554, 575
Great Revival, 205, 208, 547, 556
Great Salt Lake, 261, 344, 349
Great Salt Lake Carrying Company, 379
Great Valley Road, 122
Great Western Cattle Trail, 478
Greeley, Horace, 541
Green Bay, Wis., 41, 65, 97, 126, 137
Green Corn Rebellion, 608
Green River, 252, 260, 262
Greenback movement, 566
Greenville, Treaty of (1795), 106
Gregg, Josiah, 281, 540
Gros Ventres Indians, 390
Grundy, Felix, 126
Guadalupe-Hidalgo, Treaty of (1848), 357, 386
Guggenheim, Simon, 534

Gulf Coastal Plains, 19–20
Gulf of California, 25, 38, 266
Gulf of Mexico, 36, 41–42, 48, 53, 77, 149, 152, 169, 190, 460, 463
Guinn v. Oklahoma, 589
Gunpandama, 293–94
Gwin, William H., 378, 381, 396, 409

Haida Indians, 32, 530
Hamilton, Henry, 84, 88
Hand, Gen. Edward, 86
Hancock, Forrest, 252
Hancock, Gen. Winfield Scott, 431
Hannegan, Edward, 323, 335
Hannibal and St. Joseph Railway, 456
Haoles, 521–22, 525
Harbor improvement, 577–78
Hard-rock mining, 368–69, 484
Harlow, Samuel B., 377
Harmar, Gen. Joseph, 104
Harney, William S., 391, 429, 432
Harrison, Pres. Benjamin, 508, 527, 605
Harrison, Pres. William Henry, 14, 111, 116, 118, 123, 125, 127, 135, 139, 172, 216, 218
Harrod, James, 74, 87
Harrodsburg, Ky., 74, 86–87
Hawaii, 6, 13, 19, 26, 29, 31, 211, 271–73, 276, 329, 519–28, 535, 539, 613
Hawaiian statehood, 603–04.
Hawaiian territorial government, 602
Hayden, Ferdinand, 541
Hayes, Pres. Rutherford B., 503, 564
Haywood, William E., 609
Heceta, Bruno de, 80
Henderson, John B., 432
Henderson, Richard, 71, 75, 98
Henry, Andrew, 254, 258
Henry, Gov. Patrick, 87
Hidalgo, Padre Miguel, 309
Hide and tallow trade, 195, 276, 370
Hill, James J., 463
Hindman, Gen. T. M., 413
Hitchcock, Ethan Allen, 301
Hitchcock Report, 301–02
Holladay, Ben, 455
Holliday, Cyrus K., 462
Holston River, 20, 73, 90

Holston, Stephen, 73
Homestead Act (1862), 479–80, 491, 511, 543–44
Honey Springs, Battle of, 413
Honolulu, 521, 526–27
Hoover (Boulder) Dam, 613–14
Hoover, Herbert, 613, 615
Hopewell, Treaty of (1785), 104
Horses, 38, 195, 308–09, 330, 371, 476
Horseshoe Bend, 129, 153
Houston, Sam, 316–19
Houston, Texas, 578
Howard, Gen. Benjamin, 128
Howard, O. O., 446
Hudson Bay Company, 250, 257, 261–62, 324, 327, 336, 351, 369, 372
Hull, Gen. William, 127
Humana, Gutierrez de, 40
Humboldt River, 262, 344, 345
Hunter, Gen. David, 411
Hunter, George, 232
Hunter, Sherod, 415
Hutchins, Thomas, 101
Hydraulic mining, 484

Idaho, 23–24, 254–55, 362, 389, 421, 439, 445, 484, 487–88, 498, 505, 567, 572, 609
Ide, William, 356
Illinois, 21, 41, 49, 118, 137, 140–41, 146
Illinois Central Railroad, 377, 378
Illinois-Wabash Company, 99
Immigrant guides, 467–68
Immigration fund, Mormon, 349
Impeachment, of Oklahoma governors, 610
Imperial Valley, 574
Independence, Mo., 195, 199, 278–79, 344, 347, 364, 379, 381
Indian activism, 591
Indian Cavalry Brigade (Confederate), 414
Indian Colonization Zone, 155, 177
Indian community, present-day, 589
Indian Country, 177, 288
Indian Expedition (1862), 413
Indian Intercourse Act, 336

Indian irrigation system, 371
Indian policy, 104, 304, 319, 336, 389–94, 417–24, 427–51, 555, 590–92
Indian Reorganization Act, 590
Indian reservations, 447–51, 538
Indian Rights Association, 591
Indian slaveholders, 408
Indian Springs, Treaty of (1825), 160
Indian Territory, 177, 180, 283, 288–89, 291, 293, 295, 297–99, 301–03, 316, 319, 336, 361, 363–64, 370, 373, 381, 389, 393, 406, 408, 412, 417, 423, 438, 444–45, 447, 450–51, 463–64, 471–74, 481, 488, 490, 508, 511, 513–14, 553, 565
Indiana, 21, 118, 127, 134–35, 139–41
Indiana Company, 71
Indians, 199, 411, 551, 555, 589–92, 598
Industrial Workers of the World (I.W.W.), 609
Influence of Sea Power on History, 527
Initiative, the, 607
Interior Plains, 19, 21
Intermontane Basins, 19, 24
Intermontane Plateaus, 19, 24
Interstate Commerce Act (1887), 566
Interstate Oil Compact Commission, (Okla.), 579
Ioni Indians, 303, 433
Iowa, 169, 180, 181, 185, 391, 434
Iowa Indians, 52, 72–73, 83, 174, 185
Irish immigrants, 458, 485
Iroquois Confederacy, 29, 84, 93, 97, 99, 104
Iroquois Wars, 41
Irrigation, 28, 372, 490, 574, 576
Irving, Washington, 291

Jack Rabbit plow, 492
Jacksboro raid, 438
Jackson, Andrew, 14, 129, 151, 155, 157, 204, 216, 218, 289, 316, 332
Jackson, Claiborne F., 411
Jackson, Helen Hunt, 451
Jackson, Sheldon, 599

Jacksonian democracy, 14, 220
James, Edwin, 238
James, Thomas, 264, 277
Japanese, 524, 588, 603
Jarvis, James J., 525
Jay-Gardoqui Treaty (1786), 107, 108, 213
Jay, John, 92, 107
Jay Treaty (1794), 106, 115, 126
Jefferson Barracks, 280
Jefferson Territory, 402, 499
Jefferson, Thomas, 120, 172, 216–18, 229, 244
Jeffersonian democracy, 14, 220
Jerome Commission, 512
Jesuits, 40, 46, 49, 50, 76
Jesup, Gen. Thomas, 164
Jim Crow laws, 589
John Birch Society, 594, 612
John Cleves Symmes Company, 102–03
Johnson, Pres. Andrew, 499, 532, 564
Johnson, Gov. Hiram, 607
Johnson, John, 84
Johnson, Pres. Lyndon B., 615
Johnson, Sen. Robert W., 304
Johnson, William, 68, 84
Johnstone, George, 71
Joliet, Louis, 41
Jones, Anson, 319
Jones, Comdr. Thomas A. C., 352
Jonesboro Road, 122
Judah, Theodore P., 457
Judd, Gerrit, 525
Julesburg, Colo., 429

Kaahumanu, 522–23
Kahunas, 31, 522
Kamehameha, 520, 522
Kansas, 21, 37, 40, 51, 177, 236, 399, 401, 406, 422, 434, 436, 439, 490, 497, 567
Kansas City, Mo., 195, 456, 463–64, 478
Kansas City Southern Railway, 464
Kansas cow towns, 478
Kansas-Nebraska Act (1854), 303, 399
Kansas Pacific Railroad, 431, 463, 475, 478

Kaskaskia, Ill., 49, 52, 67, 69, 87, 88, 97, 144, 196, 251
Kauai, 26, 519
Kaw (Kansa) Indians, 226, 280, 288, 434
Kearny, Dennis, 552
Kearny, Stephen, 348, 355, 387, 391
Keechi Indians, 303, 433
Keelboats, 142, 199, 230, 263, 277
Kelley, Hall, 325, 326
Kendrick, Benjamin, 273
Kennecott Copper Company, 534
Kennekuk, 136–37
Kentucky, 4, 20–21, 73–74, 84, 87, 89, 92, 100, 104, 107, 111, 116, 119, 122, 152, 190, 200, 205, 218
Kerr, Sen. Robert S., 615
Kiamichi Mountains, 50, 237, 363
Kiamichi River, 237, 292, 298
Kickapoo Indians, 10, 41, 67, 78, 97, 103, 105, 106, 123, 125, 136, 140, 201, 226, 289, 303, 308, 319, 394, 422, 444–45, 512
King, Samuel Wilder, 604
Kingsbury, Cyrus, 329
King's Mountain, Battle of, 90
Kinkaid Act of 1904, 573
Kinkhead, Gov. J. H., 535
Kino, Father Eusebio, 49
Kiowa-Apache Indians, 428
Kiowa-Comanche Reservation, 437, 447, 450, 482
Kiowa Indians, 28, 226, 249, 252, 279, 288, 290, 292–93, 300, 302, 389, 391, 419, 428, 431, 435–36

La Bruyère, Fabry de, 52
La Harpe, Bernard de, 50–51
Lake Erie, 49, 58, 66, 99, 128, 139
Lake Huron, 49, 140
Lake Michigan, 89, 137, 140
Lake Superior, 23, 137
Lamar, Mirabeau B., 319, 422
Lanai, 26, 519
Lancaster, Treaty of (1744), 58
"Land clubs," 185
Land grants, 467
Land Laws (1796, 1800, 1804, 1817), 111, 121, 143

Landon, Alfred M., 615
Lara, Bernardo Gutiérrez de, 309
La Raza Unida, 586
Larkin, Thomas, 343, 351, 363, 539
La Salle, Robert Cavalier, Sieur de, 41, 42, 48
Las Vegas, Nev., 277, 278
Latrobe, Charles, 291
La Verendrye, Pierre de, 52
Law, John, 50
Lead mining, 77, 141, 181, 185, 194, 199, 362, 406, 488
Leadville, Colo., 485
Leased District, 300, 302, 391, 408, 433, 437, 478
Leavenworth, Gen. Henry, 293
Lecompton Constitution, 400
Ledyard, John, 272
Lee, Jason, 327, 328, 330
Lewis, Meriwether, 228, 229, 253, 254
Lewis and Clark Expedition, 228, 252
Lexington, Ky., 165, 198
Liberty League, 609
Liliuokalani, Queen, 526–27
Lincoln, Abraham, 498
Lincoln Highway, 577
Linn, Sen. Lewis F., 331–32
Lisa, Manuel, 251–52, 258
Little Arkansas, Treaty of the (1865), 429, 431
Little Big Horn, Battle of the, 443
Little Crow, 422
Little Rock, Ark., 36, 171
Livingston, Robert, 120
Llano Estacado, 21
Logan's Station, Ky., 86–87
Logstown, Treaty of (1748), 58
Long ballot, 607
Long Island, Treaty of (1777), 86
Long, Dr. James, 309
Long, Stephen H., 236–39
Lord Dunmore's War (1774), 74
Los Angeles, Calif., 79, 266, 282, 343, 356, 364, 378, 578
Louisville, Ky., 98, 122, 165, 200
Louisiana, 6, 36, 41, 42, 48, 50, 55, 58, 60, 76–77, 93, 107, 109–10, 120, 150–51, 154, 166, 169, 172, 175, 180, 182, 185, 200, 214–16, 218, 236, 251, 308, 411, 463
Louisiana Purchase, 120, 155, 169, 178, 179, 225, 287

Love, Hugh, 293
Loving, Oliver, 478
Loyal Land Company, 71, 73
Lumbering, 185, 373, 463, 489–90, 576
Lyon, Gen. Nathaniel, 411

Mackenzie, Ranald, 423, 435, 438, 445
Madison, Pres. James, 218
Mahan, Adm. Alfred Thayer, 527
Mail stages, 381, 422
Mallet, Pierre, 52
Mandan Indians, 226, 229, 230, 237, 252, 390
Manifest Destiny, 340, 341, 351, 357, 539
Mansfield, Mike, 616
Manufacturing, 145, 200, 374, 582
Many, Col. James B., 292
Manypenny, George W., 394
Marcy, Randolph B., 364
Marias River, 231, 254, 261
Maritime traders, 271–77, 361, 521
Maritime trader's frontier, 11, 228, 563
Marland, Gov. Ernest W., 579
Marquette, Jacques, 41
Marsh, John, 333, 343, 345
Marshall, James W., 363
Marshall, Chief Justice John, 156
Mason, Col. R. B., 294, 364
Matagorda Bay, 42, 48
Matanuska Valley, Ak., 599
Matrilineal descent, 27, 31
Maui, 26, 519
McCarran-Walter National Origins Act (1952), 588
McCoy, Joseph, 478
McCulloch, Gen. Ben, 411
McGee, Augustus, 309
McGready, James, 205
McIntosh, Lachlan, 91
McIntosh, Chief William, 160
McKay, James, 229
McKenzie, Alexander, 324
McKenzie, Kenneth, 261
McKinley, William, 527, 605
McKnight, William, 277
McLaughlin, John, 257, 325, 327, 372, 374

McLeod, Hugh, 319
McNair, Alexander, 173, 184
Meacham, Albert B., 444
Mecina, Kickapoo leader, 136
Medicine Lodge Council, 432, 434, 436
Medicine Lodge, Treaty of (1867), 433
Medicine show, 549
Meeker, Nathan, 446
Memphis, Tenn., 36, 103, 165, 214, 244
Mendota, Minn., 185
Mendoza, Antonio de, 37
Menominee Indians, 135, 137
Mercer, Asa S., 480
Meriam Report, 590
Mesilla, N. M., 409, 415, 417
Methodists, 204, 206, 328–29
Mexican-Americans, 551, 554, 586–88
Mexican-American Youth Organization, 586
Mexican California, 342
Mexican War, 14, 346, 348
Mexico, 4, 19, 75, 225, 263, 276, 318, 319, 356, 553
Miami Indians, 41, 58, 65, 97, 103, 105, 106, 123, 174, 201, 394, 434
Michaux, André, 109
Michigan, 21, 118, 134, 137, 140–41, 173, 184, 185–86
Mid-Continent [Oil] Field, 573
Middle border country, 308
Mier y Terán, Manuel de, 313
Miles, John D., 482
Miles, Nelson A., 438
Militant unionism, 609
Military bounties, 143
Military frontier, 9, 133, 141, 144, 179, 189, 194, 236, 302, 387, 390, 563, 580, 602
Minersville, Mo. (Oronogo), 195
Mining, 47, 361–62, 387, 463, 551
Mining companies, 367, 369
Mining frontier, 9, 145, 189, 194, 365–66, 370–74, 401, 420, 439, 445, 480, 483–84, 533–34, 563, 572
Minnesota, 6, 21, 140–41, 172, 174, 180–81, 185–86, 201, 226, 391, 402, 422

Minnesota River, 185, 237
Miró, Esteban, 109
Mission Indians, 228
Missionaries, 8, 9, 156–57, 325, 448, 450, 522
Missionary frontier, 76–79, 343, 346, 523, 539, 563
Mississippi, 104, 119, 149, 152, 155, 159, 162, 165, 189, 194
Mississippi Bubble, 50
Mississippi Company of Virginia, 71
Mississippi River, 20, 23, 36, 41, 45, 49, 50, 56, 60, 75, 77, 87, 88, 93, 106, 134, 140, 149–52, 165, 174, 177, 180, 185, 189–90, 199, 211, 213–14, 235, 237, 260, 324, 377
Mississippi Valley, 4, 6, 20, 39, 41, 42, 53, 55, 59, 66, 77, 80, 89, 93, 115, 119, 133, 166, 169, 171–79, 213, 236, 244, 282, 299, 307, 316, 341–42, 377, 455, 459, 465
Missouri, 166, 169, 171, 175, 177, 180, 183–84, 189, 194, 196, 201, 219, 223, 236–37, 256, 258, 278, 297, 310, 330, 340, 343, 463, 540
Missouri Compromise, 219, 320, 395, 397, 406
Missouri constitutional convention, 184
Missouri Enabling Act, 183
Missouri Organic Act, 173, 183
Missouri Fur Company, 245, 253, 255, 258
Missouri Indians, 6, 20, 21, 50, 52, 174, 288, 394, 434
Missouri, Kansas and Texas Railway, 464
Missouri Pacific Railroad, 456
Missouri River, 77, 141, 171, 172, 173, 174, 180, 181, 195, 226, 229, 249, 252, 255, 261, 280, 291, 376, 443, 458, 464
Mobile, Ala., 67, 83, 90, 93, 104, 129, 150, 165
Mobile River, 20, 42, 199
Modoc Indians, 228, 392, 444, 538
Mohave Desert, 261, 282
Mohave Indians, 261
Mohawk Indians, 29, 41, 84
Molokai, 26, 519
Monongahela Valley, 59, 60
Monroe Doctrine, 14, 526

Monroe, Pres. James, 120, 176, 216

Montana, 23, 421, 443–45, 484, 487–
88, 498, 504–05, 552, 572, 609

Monterey, Calif., 39, 40, 79, 273,
341–44, 351, 356, 363, 396

Montoyo, Pablo, 387

Moravians, 92, 156

Morgan, Col. George, 85

Morgan, J. P., 534

Mormon Battalion, the, 348, 356

Mormons, 346, 347, 349–50, 356,
371–72, 374, 379, 395, 397, 410,
421, 505, 523

Morrill Land Grant Act (1863), 491,
574

Morris, Robert, 99, 133, 271

Moscoso, Luis de, 36

Mount Davidson, 367, 484

Mountain Meadows Massacre, 401

Mountain Men, 256, 259, 267, 340,
345, 372

Mounted Rangers, 290, 292

Mowry, Sylvester, 409

Mules, 195–96, 330, 371, 476

Munn v. Illinois (1876), 566

Murphy, Thomas, 429

Murray, William H. "Alfalfa Bill,"
514, 607

Muskingum River, 66, 99

Nacogdoches, Texas, 77, 226, 234,
307, 313

Nana, Apache leader, 447

Narváez, Pánfilo de, 36

Nashborough Compact, 98, 108

Nashville, 98, 119, 122, 150, 165

Natchez Indians, 27, 53, 67, 71, 83,
89, 90, 107, 122

Natchez, Miss., 151, 165, 194, 199,
201, 232, 309

Natchez Trace, 150, 158

Natchitoches, Louisiana, 48, 50, 51,
55, 77, 78, 171, 178, 195, 232,
236, 277, 307, 309, 375

"National Completeness," 219, 239,
298, 307, 332, 336

National Congress of American Indians, 591

National Forest Service, 605

National Irrigation Congress, 574

National Park Service, 605

National Road, the, 122, 139, 142

National System of Interstate and
Defense Highways, 577

Nationalizing currents, 11, 118, 138,
145, 149, 216, 526

Native American Church, 450

Natural gas, 572

Nauvoo, Ill., 347, 348

Navajo Indian, 47, 227, 370, 389, 392,
418, 427

Nebraska, 40, 236, 389, 399, 434,
436, 490, 542, 564

Nebraska plow, 492

Needham, James, 57

Needles, Calif., 460, 462

Neighbors, Robert S., 303

Neosho Statehood Plan, 304

Neutral Ground, 179

Nevada, 24, 262, 266, 282, 362, 367,
401, 406, 410, 421, 427, 484, 490,
495, 564, 567, 572

New Deal programs, 579, 611

New Echota, Treaty of (1835), 157

New Harmonie, Ind., 207

New Helvetia, Calif., 344, 363

New Hope, Calif., 349

New Mexico, 4, 23, 24, 37, 39, 46, 47,
76, 77, 195, 225, 227, 238, 263,
273, 277, 279, 282, 302, 341, 350,
362–63, 371, 389, 392, 397, 406–
09, 418, 427, 460, 487, 490, 497–
98, 505, 508, 514–15, 565, 572,
580

New Orleans, Battle of, 130

New Orleans, La., 50, 51, 67, 68, 77,
78, 87, 88, 89, 90, 104, 106, 109,
118, 120, 129, 150, 153–54, 193–
94, 190–99, 201, 204, 278, 309,
363, 370, 377, 460, 464

New Spain, 39, 45, 76, 307–08

New West, 6, 9, 115, 169, 181, 189,
195, 225, 245, 256, 258, 260, 267,
299, 303, 304, 307, 323, 361, 362,
367, 371, 374, 377, 385, 402, 405–
10, 417, 456, 483–84, 537, 561

New York, Treaty of (1790), 105

Newlands Reclamation Act (1902),
574

Nez Perces Indians, 227, 323, 445,
538

Nixon, Pres. Richard M., 615
Nolan, Philip, 308–09
Nolichucky Settlements, 73, 86
No-Man's Land, 501, 512
Nome, Ak., 534
Non-Partisan League, 609
North Dakota, 390, 505, 567, 609
North Slope of Alaska, 573
North West Company, 251, 250, 257
Northern Pacific Railroad, 439, 462, 475, 504
Northern Plains, 428, 443–44
Northwest tribes, 28
Northwest Ordinance (1784), 99; (1785), 100, 102; (1787), 8, 100, 111, 116, 145, 211, 324
Northwest Territory, 100, 105, 111
Nye, James W., 401

Oahu, 26, 519
Ogden, Peter Skene, 257, 260, 262, 325
Ohio, 8, 20, 21, 92, 101, 104, 116, 122, 134, 139–40, 144, 189, 218
Ohio Company of Associates, 102
Ohio Company of Virginia, 58–59
Ohio River, 20, 41, 42, 49, 56, 58, 67, 68, 70, 73, 84, 87, 88, 91, 97, 101, 104, 111, 115, 118, 125, 129, 134, 142, 144, 149, 150, 181, 199, 200
Ohio Valley, 3, 6, 56, 58, 65, 67, 74, 92, 93, 106
Oil fields, 572–73, 581
Oklahoma, 21, 23, 37, 40, 51, 236, 252, 444, 501, 508, 512, 514, 572, 609, 610
Oklahoma Enabling Act, 514
Oklahoma Organic Act, 512
Old Northwest, 6, 115, 119, 123, 133, 135, 137, 139–40, 142, 144–45, 150, 169, 174, 182, 201, 230, 289, 303, 489
Old Southwest, 6, 115, 119, 123, 133, 142, 149, 150, 151, 152, 153, 154, 164, 169, 174, 181, 182, 200, 489
Old Spanish Trail, 266, 282, 344, 364, 371
Old West, 6, 115, 119, 142, 149, 166, 169, 171, 173, 180, 184, 189, 192,
   194, 199, 201, 203, 211, 219, 245, 287, 346, 538, 561
Omaha Indians, 226, 246, 288, 394
Omaha, Neb., 456, 459
Ombudsman system, 613
Omnibus Statehood Bill (1889), 515
Onate, Juan de, 40
Oneida Indians, 29, 41, 84
Onís, Luis de, 179
Onondaga Indians, 29, 41, 84
Opothleyaholo, 160, 161, 411, 412
Oregon, 25, 256, 262, 273, 276, 320, 323–28, 330–32, 335–36, 339, 343, 361, 369, 389, 398, 421, 490, 497, 519, 539, 607, 609, 613
"Oregon Fever," 323
Oregon immigration societies, 333
Oregon missions, 328
Oregon System, 607
Oregon Trail, 256, 333, 334, 336, 344, 365, 427
O'Reilly, Alexandro, 78
Oriental community, 551, 588
Osage Indians, 52, 71, 174, 234–36, 251, 263, 280, 288, 290, 292, 299, 300, 414, 434
Osceola, 163, 164
Otoe Indians, 52, 174, 288, 394, 434
Ottawa Indians, 40, 65, 97, 103, 104, 105, 106, 123, 434
Overland traders' frontier, 195–96, 277–84, 563
Owen, Robert, 207
Oxen, 195, 371
Ozark Mountains, 23, 194

Pacific Basin, 3, 8, 13, 19, 26, 225, 229, 267, 283, 341, 363, 374, 519–20, 528
Pacific Basin trading frontier, 342
Pacific coast, 24, 75, 169, 181, 267, 409, 416
Pacific Fur Company, 255, 256
Pacific Northwest, 10, 27, 216, 228–29, 275, 324, 332, 335, 374, 489
Pacific Ocean, 5, 6, 8, 13, 38, 39, 45, 78, 178, 215
Pacific Railway Act, 456
Pakenham, Sir Edward, 129
Palo Alto, battle of, 355

Pan-Indian movements, 450, 591–92
Panama Canal, 578
Panhandle National Grasslands, 605
Panic of 1819, 198, 311
Panic of 1837, 333
Paris, Treaty of (1763), 60, 93; (1783), 177, 211, 214
Park Hill, 297
Parker, Quanah, 437–38
Parker, Samuel, 329
Pathkiller, Chief, 156
Patterson, Thomas M., 542
Pattie, James Ohio, 266, 282, 344
Pattie, Sylvester, 266, 344
Pawnee Indians, 27, 52, 226, 234, 249, 280, 288, 434
Payne, David L., 510
Payne's Landing, Treaty of (1832), 163
Payne's Oklahoma Colony, 511
Pea Ridge, Ark., Battle of, 412
"Peace policy," 435, 444
Pearl Harbor, Hawaii, 526, 577
Pearl River, 154, 182
Pecos River, 227, 418
Pensacola, Fla., 4, 42, 48, 67, 71, 83, 90, 93, 104, 153, 201, 447
Peoria Indians, 135, 394
Perry, Oliver Hazard, 128
Petrochemical industry, 488, 572, 581
Peyote. See Native American Church
Piankeshaw Indians, 123, 394
Pierre's Hole, 260, 262
Pike, Albert, 408, 411
Pike, Zebulon M., 177, 178, 234–35, 277
Pike's Peak Gold Rush, 368, 401
Pimeria Alta, 49, 76
Pinckney, Thomas, 108, 214
Piomingo, Chickasaw leaders, 107–08
Pioneer-farmer frontier, 189, 194
Pioneers, 9, 10, 180, 189–92, 196, 204, 543
Pittsburgh, Pennsylvania, 73–74, 86, 89, 97, 106, 116, 144–45, 181, 198, 200, 278
Placer mining, 365, 368, 483–84
Placerville, Calif., 365, 381
Plantation-slave economy, 181, 189
Plantation system, 166, 297, 301, 406
Platte Purchase, 184

Platte River, 52, 177, 226, 252, 267, 270, 442
Platte Trail, 260
Political conservatism, 593
Polk, Pres. James K., 335, 339, 350, 364, 395
Pollock, Oliver, 87
Polygamy, 347, 410, 507–08, 565
Polygyny, 31
Polynesians, 27, 29, 519
Ponca Indians, 226, 249, 288, 434
Pontiac, 66, 67, 73
Pontotoc Creek treaty, 162
Pony Express, 381
"Poor man's camp," 365, 368
Populism, 514, 566–67
Portales, Albert de, 291
Portland, Ore., 375, 578
Portsmouth, Ohio, 139, 144
Potawatomi Indians, 41, 97, 105, 106, 123, 135, 137, 174, 201, 226, 303, 434
Poteau River, 174, 235
Potlatch, 28, 228
Potosi, Mo., 194, 199
Potts, John, 253
Powder River War, 430
Powell, J. N., 430
Powell, John W., 542
Power resources, 581
Preemption Act (1841), 143, 491
Presbyterians, 204, 329
Presidential campaign of 1844, 335
Presidios, 46, 56, 77, 79
Price, Gen. Sterling, 387, 411
Proclamation of 1763, 68, 69, 73
Progressive Movement, 606–07
Promontory Point, Utah, 459
Promyshlenniki, 529, 531
Prophet, the. See Elskwatawa
Prophetstown, 123, 125
Prospectors, 8, 367, 484, 534
Protestant-missionary frontier, 330
Protestantism, 547, 556
Provincias Internas, 76, 78
Pryor, Nathaniel, 251, 264
Public domain, 121, 134, 151, 213, 480, 538
Public roads, 121–22. See also Road-building

Pueblo Indians, 47, 227, 581
Purgatory River, 267, 278
Pushmataha, 158
Putnam, Rufus, 102, 103

Quakers. *See* Society of Friends
Quantrill, Col. Charles C., 413
Quapaw Indians, 71, 201, 226, 288,
    292, 434, 444
Quartz mining. *See* Hard-rock mining
Quebec Act (1774), 69
"Quids," 102

Railhead construction towns, 466–67
Railroad building, 455–64
Railroad promotion of settlement,
    467
Railroad technology, 377, 464-65
Railroads, 422, 428, 456–57, 459,
    463–65, 468, 474, 491, 509
Rainmaking, 614
Ranching, 297, 406, 476, 479–83,
    573, 574
Ranchman's last frontier (Indian Ter-
    ritory), 481
Range-cattle industry, 477–83, 538
Rappites, 207
Raton Pass, 277, 278, 416, 462, 464
Rayburn, Sam, 615
Reclamation Service, 574, 579
Reconstruction, 423, 424, 502
Red Cloud, 429, 434, 443
Red River, 20, 50, 55, 56, 77, 154,
    171, 177, 195, 199, 226, 232, 237,
    249, 251, 295, 298–99, 304, 319,
    375, 427, 437, 460
Red River Wars, 438
Referendum, 607
Religion, 204, 205–08, 450, 547, 556
Relocation, Indian, 591
Removal plan of 1830, 289
Removal program, 287–88, 296, 300
Rendezvous, fur trade, 259, 263
*Report on the Condition of the Indian
    Tribes*, 431
Republican Party, 409, 499, 501, 504,
    513, 528
Resaca de la Palma, battle of, 355
Reservation system, 436, 447–51

"Revolutionary Legion of the Mis-
    sissippi," 109
Rhodes, John, 616
Ridge, Major, 157
Ridge Party, 157
Riley, Bennett, 280, 396
Rio Grande River, 10, 20, 38, 40, 46,
    47, 50, 52, 55, 77, 80, 195–96,
    265, 277, 280, 302, 354, 375, 389,
    408, 415, 419, 445
Rio Grande settlements, 40, 46–47,
    235–36, 239, 249, 277–79, 281–
    82, 363
River steamers, 263, 298
Roadbuilding, 121–22, 150, 197, 213,
    577
Robertson, James, 73, 85, 98, 108, 109
Robidoux, Antoine, 266, 345
Rocky Mountains, 19, 21, 23, 45, 47,
    173, 178, 181, 215, 226, 228, 234,
    235, 237, 252, 258, 263, 266, 324,
    325, 340, 348, 361, 390, 401, 481,
    493, 500, 605
Rocky Mountain Fur Company, 245,
    257, 258, 260, 261, 327
Rogers, Robert, 65
Roman Catholics, 204, 330, 556
Roosevelt, Pres. Franklin D., 575, 590,
    603, 610, 615
Roosevelt, Pres. Theodore, 514, 605
Ross, Chief John, 157
Round Mountain, Battle of, 412
Rowland-Workman party, 345
Rubi, Marquis de, 76
Rundle Station, Ky., massacre, 92
Russell, Majors and Waddell Com-
    pany, 379, 382, 455
Russia, 4, 45, 83, 225, 324
Russian America, 39, 42, 78, 80, 214,
    216, 274, 524, 530
Russian American Company, 275,
    520–21, 529–32
Russian Orthodox Church, 530–31,
    556

Sabine River, 20, 154, 171, 178, 214,
    309, 422
Sac Indians, 41, 53, 78, 137, 434
Sac and Fox Indians, 138, 172, 174,
    185, 394

Sac and Fox Reservation, 445, 511
Sacajawea, 226, 230, 231
Sacramento, Calif., 25, 362, 365, 373, 456–57
Sacramento, Battle of, 355
Salish Indians, 228, 324
Salmon fishing, 228, 533
Salt, 362, 406
Salt Fork River, 236, 434, 446
Salt Lake City, Utah, 349, 350, 372, 378, 379, 381, 401, 458
Salt Plains, 236
San Antonio, Texas, 77, 226, 236, 309, 316, 319, 364, 415, 460
San Carlos Reservation (Apache), 446
San Diego Bay, 39, 79
San Diego, Calif., 79, 226, 266, 273, 275, 341, 344, 356, 381, 460, 552, 578
San Felipe, Texas, 314
San Francisco Bay, 4, 25, 79, 341, 351, 353
San Francisco, Calif., 26, 39, 79, 226, 266, 273, 275, 356, 381, 409, 460, 530, 552, 578
San Gabriel Mission, 261
San Ildefonso, Treaty of (1800), 120, 215
San Joaquin Valley, 262, 266
San Jose, Calif., 79, 262
San Lorenzo, Treaty of (1795), 108
San Luis de Amarillas, 56, 307
San Luis Valley, 235, 420
San Pedro Harbor, 578
San Saba mission, 49, 56
San Xavier del Bac Mission, 49, 79
Sanborn, John B., 429, 432
Sand Creek Massacre, 420, 429, 500
Sand Creek Reservation (Cheyenne-Arapaho), 420
Sandalwood, 274, 521
Sandwich Islands (Hawaii), 11, 229, 272, 273, 274, 520–22
Sangre de Cristo Mountains, 77, 235, 249, 278
Santa Ana, Antonio Lopez, 314, 316, 317, 355
Santa Clara Valley, 79
Santa Cruz River, 361, 409, 415, 487
Santa Fe, N. M., 40, 46, 47, 52, 55, 77, 80, 195–96, 226, 234, 263,
265–66, 278, 280, 282–83, 340, 355–56, 361, 370, 387, 408, 415, 419, 462
Santa Fe Railway Company, 462, 464, 475, 478
Santa Fe Trade, 195, 282, 283, 363
Santa Fe Trail, 195, 278, 283, 319, 364, 379, 389
Santa Rita, N. M., 267, 282, 344, 369, 488
Satank, 432, 438
Satanta, 429, 432, 438
Schermerhorn, John F., 157, 290
Scioto Company, 102
Scott, Winfield, 138, 356
Sea Island cotton, 200
Sea otter, 11, 78, 228, 272, 273, 274, 275, 276
Sears, T. C., 510
Seattle, Wash., 462, 578
Secession Ordinances, 408
Second U. S. Bank, 198
Sectionalism, 368, 405
Segregation, racial, 588, 589
Seminole Indians, 10, 151, 153, 163, 201, 226, 289, 295–96, 395, 406, 411, 424, 481, 513
Seminole War, 164–65
Seneca Indians, 29, 41, 66, 84, 92, 97, 226, 291, 434
Sequoyah's syllabary, 156, 297, 329
Settlement promotion, 467
Seven Cities of Cibola, 36, 37
Seven Years' War, 56, 59, 65, 75
Seventh Cavalry, 436, 439–43, 450
Sevier, John, 85, 90, 109, 110, 126
Seward, William H., 526, 532
Shaler, Robert, 343
Shawnee Indians, 10, 56, 57, 58, 66, 73, 74, 78, 85, 87, 92, 97, 103, 105, 106, 174, 236, 291, 308, 319, 394, 434
Sheepraising, 370, 483
Shelby, Evan, 90
Shelikov, Gregory, 529
Sherman, William T., 435
Shipbuilding, 181, 274, 376, 530
Short-staple cotton, 200
Shoshoni Indians, 226, 231, 421, 427
Shreve, Capt. Henry, 375
Shreveport, La., 370, 460

Sibley, George, 236
Sibley, Henry H., 185, 415
Sibley, John, 232
Sierra Nevadas, 25, 80, 227, 258, 261, 345, 363, 374
Sigel, Franz Gen., 411
Silver City, N. M., mining district, 487
Silver, 46, 283, 406, 483, 485, 487
Sinophobia, 552
Sioux Indians, 52, 137, 174, 185–86, 226, 230, 237, 250, 252, 391, 428–29, 435, 443, 450, 458
Sitka, Ak., 529, 532
Sitting Bull, 443–44, 450
Slacum, William A., 332
Slave labor, 166, 180, 181, 184, 201, 219
Slavery, 296, 311, 320, 386, 553
Slavery extension, 183–84, 218
Slidell, John, 353–54
Slough, Col. John P., 416
Smith, Jedediah, 258, 261, 279, 325, 344
Smith, Joseph, 346–48
Snake Indians, 52, 393, 421
Snake River, 24, 231, 254, 257, 267, 327, 369
Socialism, Western, 608, 609
Society of Friends (Quakers), 435
Sod house construction, 543
Sod plow, 492
Soil conservation, 605, 614
Sonora, Mexico, 76, 365
South Dakota, 23, 390, 450, 484, 487, 505, 567, 609
South Pass, 24, 256, 348, 378, 379, 429, 500
South Platte River, 55, 237
Southern Pacific Railway Company, 460, 462, 607
Southern Plains, 21, 419, 428, 431, 438, 444
Southwestern Territory, 111, 119, 151
Spain, 4, 45, 56, 78, 80, 83, 93, 150–51, 171, 177, 179, 180–82, 201, 214–15, 225, 251–52, 324, 326
Spanish, 36, 39, 57, 77, 88, 103, 106, 118, 232, 256, 263, 275, 341
Spanish-American settlements, 52, 103, 309, 341, 361, 371
Spanish-American War, 528

Spanish California, 42, 79, 341
Spanish-French Wars, 55
Spanish Louisiana, 194, 232
Spanish mercantilism, 341
Spanish mining, 363
Spanish traders, 56
Spanish trappers, 276
Sparks, Richard, 232–34
Spindletop (oil well), 572
Spokane Indians, 228, 393, 421
Spring Place Mission, Ga., 157
Squatters' rights, 143, 185
St. Augustine, Fla., 4, 40
St. Charles, La., 77, 120
St. Clair, Arthur, 105, 116, 118
St. Joseph, Mo., 89, 381
St. Louis, Mo., 77–78, 87–88, 120, 134, 178, 180, 181, 184, 194–95, 199, 229, 245, 251, 255–56, 258, 260, 263, 277–79, 328, 370, 381, 456
St. Louis and San Francisco Railway Company, 463
St. Louis (Indian) Superintendency, 289
St. Paul, Minn., 185, 186
St. Paul and Pacific Railroad, 463
Stage lines, 379
Stanford, Leland, 457, 458
Stanislaus River, 261, 349
Stanley, Henry M., 432
State-making, 498, 564
Steamboats, 142, 195, 199, 278, 375–76
Steel plants, 581
Steptoe, Col. E. J. 393
Stockman's frontier, 189, 480
Stockraising, 8, 9, 46, 47, 310, 361, 369, 370, 371, 387, 447, 476–79, 551, 573
Stock-Raising Homestead Act of 1916, 573
Stockton, Robert, 353, 356, 388
Stoddard, Amos, 172
Stoeckl, Edouard de, 532
Stokes Commission, 290, 291, 292, 294
Stokes, Montfort, 290, 294
Stuart, John, 68, 70, 84
Stuart, Robert, 256
Sublette, William, 327

Sugarcane culture, 200, 524, 526
Sully, Gen. Alfred, 436
Surveying Western lands, 101
Sutro tunnel, 485
Sutter, John, 344, 363
Swan Land and Cattle Company, 480
Swanton, John R., 301

Tahlequah, Cherokee nation, 297,
    304, 363, 395
Taliferro, Lawrence, 186
Tallmadge amendment, 183
Taos Lightning, 265, 340
Taos, N. M., 46–47, 226, 265, 282,
    340, 361, 388
Taovayas, 51, 55
Tatum, Laurie, 435
Taylor Grazing Act (1934), 574, 605
Taylor, John, 508
Taylor, Pres. Zachary, 353–54, 386,
    396, 508
Technology, 12, 189, 200–01, 491–92
Tecumseh, 123, 125, 128, 134–35
Telegraph, 382, 421, 429
Ten Bears, 429, 432
Tennessee, 4, 20–21, 73, 89, 98, 100,
    104, 107, 109, 111–12, 116, 119,
    149, 151, 155, 162, 165, 174,
    190, 200, 205, 218
Tennessee River, 57, 70, 90
Termination, policy of, 591
Territory of Orleans, 172, 173, 182
Terry, Alfred, 432, 443
Texas, 4, 10, 24, 36–37, 39, 43, 47–
    48, 50–51, 55, 76–77, 154, 171,
    178, 214, 225, 236, 263, 297, 304,
    310–12, 323, 336, 339, 346, 348,
    364, 370–71, 406, 408, 411, 417,
    423, 436, 438, 463, 477, 480, 490,
    539, 553, 572, 580
Texas annexation, 318, 320
Texas independence, 319
Texas and Pacific Railroad, 460
Texas Panhandle, 21, 419, 480, 581
Texas Rangers, 302, 319, 391
Texas Republic, 317, 319, 354
Thames, Battle of the, 128
Thayer, Eli, 400
Thomas amendment, 183–84

Thompson, Wiley, 164
Three Forks of the Arkansas, 251,
    263, 277–78
Three Forks of the Missouri, 251, 253,
    258, 261
Thurston, Asa, 523
Tijerina, Reies Lopez, 587
Tilden, Samuel J., 503
Timber Culture Act (1873), 491
Timber and Stone Act (1878), 490
Tippecanoe Creek, 123, 125
Tlingit Indians, 32, 529–30
Toledo, Ohio, 139, 144
Toll roads, 142
Tomasito, Tao leader, 387
Tombigbee River, 54, 150, 199
Tombstone, Ariz., gold field, 488
Tonkawa Indians, 48, 303, 434
Tonty, Henry de, 42
Tories, 93, 94, 215
Tory-Indian forces, 89–92
Totem poles, 32, 228
Tourism, 582, 615
Traders' frontier, 46, 308, 340, 343
Trail of Tears, 158, 162, 165, 289,
    296, 300
Trans-Appalachian region, 3–5, 8, 58,
    67, 85
Transcontinental railroad, 377–78
Transylvania colony, 4, 71, 75
Travis, Col. W. B., 316
Tri-State (mining) district, 195, 488
Trist, Nicholas, 357
Trollope, Frances, 202
Tubac, Ariz., 369, 409
Tucson, Ariz., 226, 361, 409, 415
Tulsa, Okla., 463, 573
Tunkahotohye, 293
Turtle Bayou Resolution (1832), 314
Twin Villages, 51, 56, 77, 234, 249
Twin Villages, battle at, 56
Tyler, John, 320, 335, 526

Ulloa, Sp. Gov. Antonio de, 78
Ulloa, Francisco de, 38
Umpqua Indians, 228, 262, 324
Unassigned Lands, 510, 511, 512
Union Indian Brigade, 412

Union Pacific Railroad, 458–59, 500
Union Pacific Railway Company, 466, 456
United Farm Workers Organizing Committee, AFL-CIO, 587
University of Chicago (Indian) Conference, 591
Unzaga y Amezaga, Luis de, 78
Urban frontier, 145, 165, 196, 198–200, 334, 372, 392
Urbanization, 144, 195, 300, 334, 372, 466, 592
U'Ren, Gov. William S., 607
Urrea, Jose, 317
Utah, 23–24, 257, 266, 282, 401, 406, 410, 421, 427, 446, 484, 487, 497, 505, 507, 565, 572, 580
Utah Commission, 507
Utah Enabling Act, 508
Ute Indians, 47, 226, 389, 391, 419–20, 427, 446
Utopian communities, 206–07

Valverde, N. M., battle of, 415
Van Buren, Pres. Martin, 318
Vancouver, George, 228, 324, 520
Van Dorn, Earl, 299, 302, 391, 412
Velasco, Treaty of (1836), 317, 354
Vera Cruz, Mexico, 47, 246
Verdigris River, 236, 251
Victorio, Apache leader, 447
Villard, Henry, 462
Villazur, Pedro de, 55
Vincennes, Battle of, 91
Vincennes, Ind., 49, 69, 88, 91, 97, 118, 134, 139, 144, 194
Vinita, Okla., 462–63
Virginia City, Mont., 430, 487
Virginia Military Reserve, 99

Wabash decision (1886), 566
Wabash River, 49, 58, 88, 97, 134, 136, 139
Waco Indians, 303, 433
Wagon Box Fight, 430
Wagon Roads, 379, 387
Waiilatpu (Oregon) Presbyterian Mission, 329, 336, 392
Walker, James, 344

Walker, Joseph R., 262
Walker, Thomas, 20, 73
"War Hawks," 126
War of 1812, 14, 127, 130, 133–35, 141, 144, 149–50, 153–54, 178, 199, 218, 251, 256
Washington, 25, 324, 362, 369, 389, 398, 421, 490, 498, 504–05, 609
Washington, George, 59, 74, 86, 215
Washington, Treaty of (1826), 161
Washita Massacre, 437
Washoe District, 367, 484
Watauga Association, 73, 75, 108
Water-powered mills, 193, 199
Water resources, 581, 613
Watie, Stand, 157, 412, 414, 423
Watkins, Arthur V., 590
Wayne, Gen. Anthony, 106
Wea Indians, 123, 394
Weatherford, War chief Billy, 129
Weaver, James B., Populist candidate, 566
Webb, Walter P., 566
Webster, Daniel, 397
West Florida, 71, 90, 93, 119, 120, 152, 154
West Shawnee (cattle) Trail, 478
Western culture, 592, 593
Western economy, 572, 575, 580, 582, 593
Western labor movement, 609
Western politics, 612
Western rightist radicalism, 609
Western society, 551, 585
Western state governments, 606
Western state-making, 385
Westport, Mo., 10, 195, 199
Whaling, 524, 533
Wheat production, 373, 545
Wheeler-Howard Act (1934), 590, 591
White, Elijah, 332
White, James, 109
"White man's road," 439, 447
White River Reservation (Ute), 446
Whitman, Marcus, 329, 335, 336
Whitman Massacre, 336, 392
Whitney, Asa, 377, 456, 540
Wichita Agency, 303, 408
Wichita Indians, 226, 236, 251, 288, 294, 408, 433
Wichita, Kansas, 478, 578

Wichita Mountains, 23, 226, 252, 263, 288, 292, 299, 302
Wilderness Road, 73, 90, 122
Wilkes, Capt. Charles, 332
Wilkinson, James, 109, 120, 129, 172, 177–79, 214, 234
Willamette Valley, 25, 256, 326, 334, 372
Williams, Bill, 266
Willing, James, 89
Wilmot Proviso, 386
Wilson, Jack. *See* Wovoka
Wilson, Pres. Woodrow, 588, 598, 615
Wilson's Creek, Battle of, 411
Winnebago Indians, 137–38
Wisconsin, 21, 137–38, 140–41, 173, 185–86
Wolfskill, William, 266, 282
Woodson, Samuel H., 379
Worcester, Samuel A., 156, 297, 329
Worcester *v.* Georgia, 156
World War I, economic effects of, 578–79
World War II, economic effects of, 581
Wounded Knee, Battle of, 450
Wounded Knee, occupation of, 592
Wovoka, 450

Wright, George, 393
Wyandot Indians, 58, 97, 104–06, 226, 303, 434
Wyeth, Nathaniel, 325, 327
Wyoming, 23, 52, 389, 443, 480, 484, 487, 500, 505, 572
Wyoming Basin, 23, 458
Wyoming Stock Growers' Association, 480

XIT Ranch, 480

Yakima Indians, 228, 323, 393
Yazoo Land Company, 101, 119, 151
Yellowstone Expedition, 237
Yellowstone River, 231, 237, 443
Young, Brigham, 348, 372, 397, 400, 421, 506, 508
Young, Ewing, 266, 326, 344, 372
Yount, George, 266, 282
Yukon River, 528, 530

Zinc mining, 488
Zion Plan, 347, 349
Zuni Indians, 37, 227